A Century of Protests

A Century of Protests

Peasant Politics in Assam Since 1900

Arupjyoti Saikia

Routledge
Taylor & Francis Group
LONDON NEW YORK NEW DELHI

First published 2014 in India
by Routledge
912 Tolstoy House, 15–17 Tolstoy Marg, Connaught Place,
New Delhi 110 001

Simultaneously published in the UK
by Routledge
4 Park Square, Milton Park, Abingdon, Oxon OX14 4RN

Routledge is an imprint of the Taylor & Francis Group, an informa business

Typeset by
Solution Graphics
A–14, Indira Puri, Loni Road
Ghaziabad, Uttar Pradesh 201 102

British Library Cataloguing-in-Publication Data
A catalogue record of this book is available from the British Library

ISBN 978-0-415-81194-1 (hbk)

Contents

List of Tables, Plates and Maps

Tables

Plates

Maps

List of Abbreviations

ASP	*Assam Secretariat Proceedings*
ASA	Assam State Archives
OIOC	Oriental and India Office Collection
NAI	National Archives of India
NDRR	Nowgaon District Record Room
ALCP	*Assam Legislative Council Proceedings*
APBECR	*Assam Provincial Banking Enquiry Committee Report*
APIRR	Assam Police Intelligence Record Room
APWR	*Abstract of the Assam Police Intelligence Weekly Report*
PHA	*Political History of Assam*
NMML	Nehru Memorial Museum and Library

Glossary

adhi bhagi	tenancy arrangement between landowner and tenant or sharecropper wherein landowner's share amounts to half of the produce.
adhiar	sharecropper
agdhan	credit given against the security of produce of peasants
amlah	revenue agent, officials
anna	unit of currency, equivalent to one-sixteenth of a rupee (no longer in use)
atmarakha bahini	self-defence militia
bandha	bonded labour
bar saheb	popular term for district magistrate
barga	sharecropping in Bengal
basti	homestead land
bharga/bhag	share
bhakat	a devotee or a tenant-peasant attached to the lands owned by a *satra* (Vaishnava monastery)
beel	marshy land
bepari	petty merchant-cum-moneylenders
bhog	offering of food and flowers made to a deity in a temple
bigha	a traditional unit of measurement of an area of land, equivalent to 0.33 acres
bhagania	migrant
bhatia	migrant
bhumihin	landless
bidhi babystha	rules and rituals of social customs
brahmottar	grant of rent-free land to Brahmins
chamua	exempted from manual labour, in practice during the Ahom rule
chapori	fertile riverine island tract along Brahmaputra.

chari bhag	sharing out of rent into four parts
chars	sand banks or river islands of Brahmaputra, often sizable, formed by newly deposited silt in the river, appearing and disappearing seasonally, and typically found in Bangladesh and eastern India.
chor	thief
chukani adhi	tenancy arrangement and produce sharing on the basis of cash after crop is sold.
chukti adhi	share-tenancy arrangement wherein a fixed quantity of grain was offered to the landlord by the tenant.
dagies	criminals
dadan	advance loan against crops
dangori	bundles of paddy
debottar	grant of rent-free lands for the maintenance of temples
devalaya	temple
dewania	middleman amongst the East Bengali immigrant peasants who helped them settle in Assam.
dhanir bharal	granaries of rich peasants
dharmottar	grant of rent-free lands for religious and charitable purposes
duars	gateways to the frontier hilly areas
diwani	revenue office
doloi	priest of a temple and also owner of both rent-free and half rent-paying estates attached to the temple.
don/dun	appliance used for measuring threshed paddy and mustard, equivalent to five *sers* or 4.67 kg.
ekchania patta	land settled with peasants for a year, or possession of annual title deed on land.
faria	mobile petty traders
faringati	high land suitable for cultivation of crops other than paddy
gadhan	poll tax
ganj	mart
gola	shops owned by Marwari traders-cum-moneylenders

gossain	chief priest of Vaishnava monastery in Assam
gaon-majur	agricultural labour
garib khetaiak	poor farmer
guti adhi	rent on the basis of equal division of the threshed grain
guchi adhi	equal division of the standing crop
hartal	strike
haat	weekly market
hati	cluster of guild at Barpeta in Kamrup which provided credit
maund	local unit of weights and measures; one maund being equivalent to 40 sers or 37 kg
Idd-gaah	an open field where mass prayers are performed by the Muslims
*jalah-pitani*s	marshy water bodies
jati	equivalent of caste in Assamese society
johala	a caste group from northern India engaged in petty trade
jotedar	a small landlord, mostly found in the districts of western Assam.
kabuli/kabuliwala	Pathan moneylender from Kabul
kabuliyat	title deed
kamla	agricultural labour
mahaldari	lease through auction
*kaya*s	Marwari traders or merchants from the Marwar region of Rajasthan
khadi	traditional coarse wheel-spun cloth popularized by Mahatma Gandhi as a key to rural self-reliance.
khat	hereditary landed estates of the Ahom aristocracy and spiritual leaders
khel	guilds that since the colonial times began to be identified as village units based on
khiraj	land revenue
la-khiraj	perpetually rent-free estates, i.e., estates exempt from government revenue
killa	small huts erected by immigrant Muslim peasants in the professional grazing reserves to mark the occupation of land by them

lathi	bamboo rod
la-khirajdar	owner of *la-khiraj* estate
mandal	revenue official at the lowest level of official hierarchy, responsible for land measurement and keeping of records.
matabar	local leader
matigiri	landloard
mauzadar	revenue official of a *mauza*
mahajan	moneylender cum trader
mauza	revenue circle, ranging in area from a few square miles to 200 square miles
mel	village assembly/council
mohori	a clerk who writes petitions in the court
mukchowani	interest charged by Brahmin moneylenders from the first-time borrowers
myadi patta	land settled with peasants for a long period of time, usually 10–30 years.
nal	land measuring rod
pacca	concrete
nisf-khiraj	inheritable and transferable estates assessed at half rates
pam	land for temporary cultivation in riverine tracts
nisf-khirajdar	owner of *nisf-khiraj* estates
pamua	temporary settlers on the riverine islands
panchayat	village assembly
panda	priest of Brahman caste attached to a temple
pathar	paddy field
patta	deed of title to land
pattadar	landowner or lease holder
piada	agent of moneylender
puja	worship
pranami	a kind of tax paid to the landlord
paikan	artisans or skilled tenants
pirpal	rent-free grants made for the support of mosques
pujabhar	offerings for god during worship
paik	a pre-colonial system of land distribution wherein four individual free peasants were

	grouped into a unit which received land for cultivation from the king, and provided physical service and paid rent in return.
pura	unit of land no longer in use, 1 pura being equivalent to 1.33 acres
raij	collected body of people
raiyati	peasant tenure
raiyat	cultivator
raiyatwari	land revenue settlement directly with individual land holder.
rupit	fertile lands under permanent cultivation
sabha	a formal body or assembly
sadar	district headquarters
sadhu	ascetic/monk
salami	gratuitous offerings
sanyasi	monk/religious mendicant/ascetic
sardar	village headman
sarkari	belonging to the government
satra	a Vaishnava monastery in Assam
satyagraha	strike; non-violent civil disobedience
seva	service
satradhikar	chief priest of a *satra*
sradha	rituals in memory of ancestors
swaraj	self-rule
teli	artisan caste of oil pressers and sellers
tini bhag	sharing out of produce of rented land into three divisions
utuli or *wala*	agricultural labourer of East Bengali origin in Assam
zilla saheb	district collector
zoolum	harassment

Acknowledgements

I have been fortunate enough to receive help from many in writing this book over the course of several years. Late Prof. Suhash Chakravarty at the University of Delhi was generous enough to oversee the progress of my PhD dissertation, which has substantially shaped this book. I owe an intellectual debt to him and my other teachers at Jamia Milia Islamia, Jawaharlal Nehru University and the University of Delhi, from whom I learnt the craft of historical writing.

I have also been inspired by the writings of other historians of Assam: late Heramba Kanta Barpujari, Amalendu Guha, Hiren Gohain, and Rajen Saikia. Further, I have gained immensely from the ideas and the researches of another distinguished group of Assamese scholars: Dambarudhar Nath, Kishore Bhattacharjee, Ranjit Kumar Dev Goswami, and Prodip Khataniar. A few other scholars too have remained a source of constant inspiration: Gautam Bhadra, Mahesh Rangarajan and Ramachandra Guha.

During the winter of 1999 and then again in 2006, I received a research grant and a fellowship from the Charles Wallace Trust, which enabled me to access the invaluable resources of the British Library. Upon completing the book in 2010, I received the Yale University's Agrarian Studies post-doctoral fellowship (2011–12) to research on the environmental history of Brahmaputra river valley and Assam. This brief spell of research helped me give the final shape to the book. At Yale, both K. Sivaramakrishanan (Shivi) and James C. Scott (Jim) were excellent mentors to me.

Numerous friends from across the world have also helped me in different ways in writing this book. The list would be rather long. So, I have decided to omit their names altogether for the fear of forgetting to mention some. All of them, when flipping through the pages of this book, will surely see the stamp of their influence imprinted in many places. Over the years, I have presented parts of this book at different academic gatherings and have learnt enormously from those discussions. I am grateful to all the discussants who provided valuable feedback and inputs.

My Delhi days were made comfortable by two extremely adorable families. The houses of Nandita and Binod Khadria, and Trishna and Sarat Barkakati were an extended home for me. My several spells of work at the British Library became smoother due to the warmth and support of David Southey who kindly shared his house with me. David, an avid reader of books on British social history, fondly listened to the pronouncements of my archival 'discoveries' every evening. My life was made comfortable by these conversations with him.

I am grateful to the staff at the Assam State Archive (ASA), Guwahati, for being extremely generous in catering to my research needs. Dharmeswar Sonowal, Director, ASA, and Tarun Deka and Nupur Barpatragohain, both archivists, were kind enough to help me in my research. Haren Baisya, along with other staff members of ASA, never failed to guide me through the maze of archival records. Special mention must be made of District Record Rooms of Nagaon, Jorhat, Sonitpur, Darrang, and Kamrup, which would remain a treasure trove of resources for future historical research.

Research for this book was done in different libraries. I am immensely grateful to the staff of the S. K. Bhuyan Library, Cotton College, Guwahati; Nehru Memorial Museum and Library, New Delhi; National Archives of India, New Delhi; National Library, Kolkata; K. K. Handique Library, Gauhati University; Nanda Talukdar Foundation, Guwahati; Indian Council of Historical Research Library, New Delhi and Guwahati; District Library, Guwahati; Department of Historical and Antiquarian Studies, Guwahati; British Library, London; Central Library and P.C. Joshi Archives, Jawaharlal Nehru University; Central Library, University of Delhi; Yale University Library, New Haven, Connecticut; Central Secretariat Library, New Delhi; Sahitya Akademi, New Delhi; Central Reference Library, Guwahati; Dibrugarh University Library, Dibrugarh.

I have acknowledged all the individuals whom I have met at different times and places, and who have shared their experiences and knowledge with me, in the bibliography. Several scholars, including Indibar Deuri, Devabrata Sarma and Anil Roychoudhury, kindly shared their private collections of archival material with me during the course of research. Laxmi Nath Tamuly, now a retired bureaucrat and historian on Assam, introduced me to late

Bipul Kalita, the Inspector General of Police (Special Branch). The latter kindly granted me permission to consult records in the record room of the Special Branch of Assam Police at Kahilipara. Baneswar Saikia, a leading communist leader guided me through his experience of Assam's communist movement. I am grateful to all of them.

The Indian Institute of Technology Guwahati, my current workplace, continues to be a source of great support for me. Over the years, I have also taught at different institutions. Students and colleagues from all these institutions have helped me in many aspects of this research. The support of my research students was timely. They will see that their ideas have also been incorporated in this book.

In the last few years I have been a keen observer of rural mobilization by Krishak Mukti Sangram Samiti of Assam. This renewed mobilization of the Assamese rural peasantry often re-stages some of the historical anecdotes that have found place in this book. I can admit that it is only from these recent observations that I have understood the historical agrarian landscape of Assam that, in turn, I have tried to engage with in this book better.

The anonymous editors at Routledge India rescued the manuscript from clumsy arguments and weak narrative. I am grateful to the entire editorial team at Routledge for ably guiding me through the process of publication. Maps in this book were the result of meticulous work of Jayanta Nath. The art work for the cover page was done by Manjit Rajkhowa. I owe thanks to both.

This book has in it much of my first-hand exposure to Assam's everyday rural politics. I owe heart-felt gratitude to my father who, through the hard economic circumstances that he faced and his eventful life as a communist, helped me understand the intricacies of Assamese rural life. It is my regret that he passed away just before this book was finished. My debt to my family is not easy to express in words. Banani and our son Nizan will be only happy to see this book published.

Map 1: The Present State of Assam

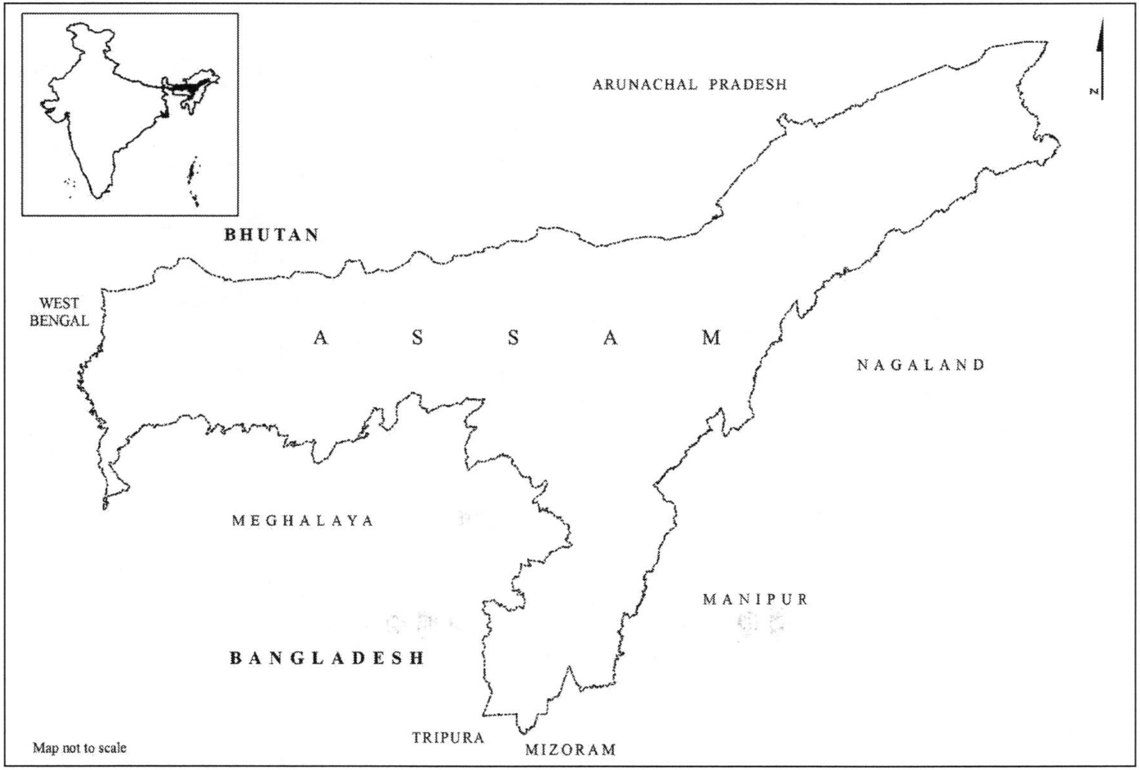

Source: All maps provided by the author.

Map 2: Brahmaputra Valley (At India's Independence)

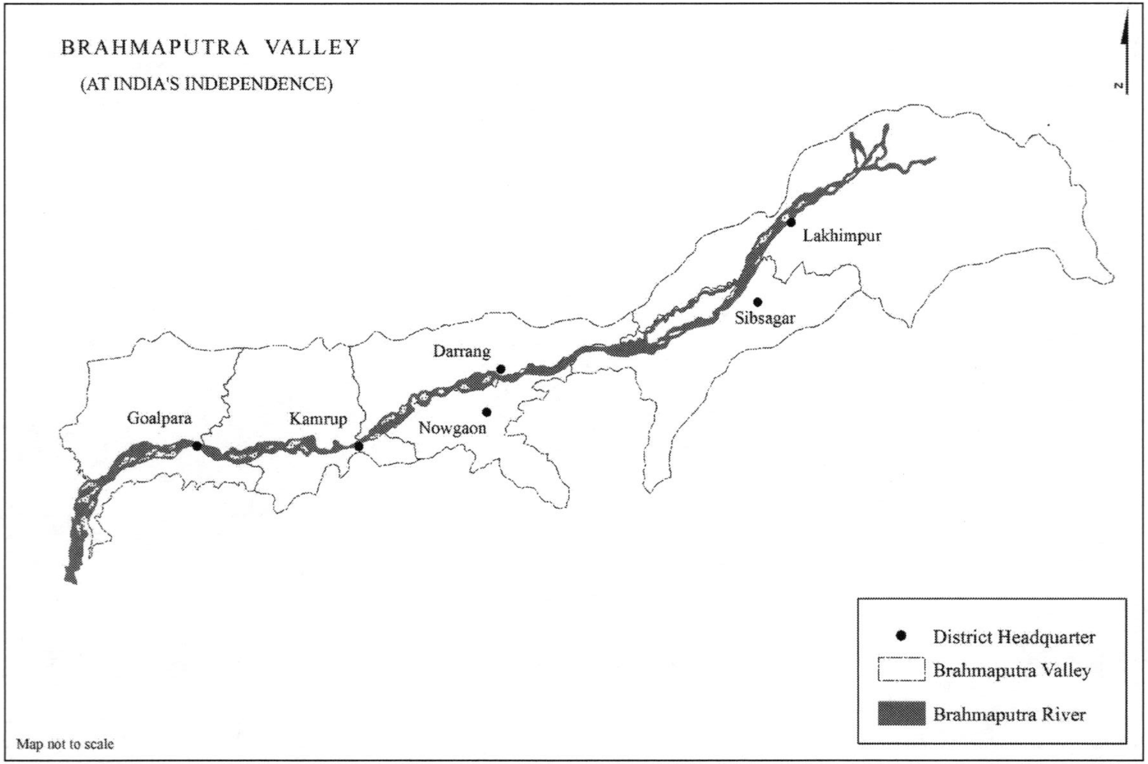

Map 3: Eastern Bengal and the Plains of Brahmaputra Valley

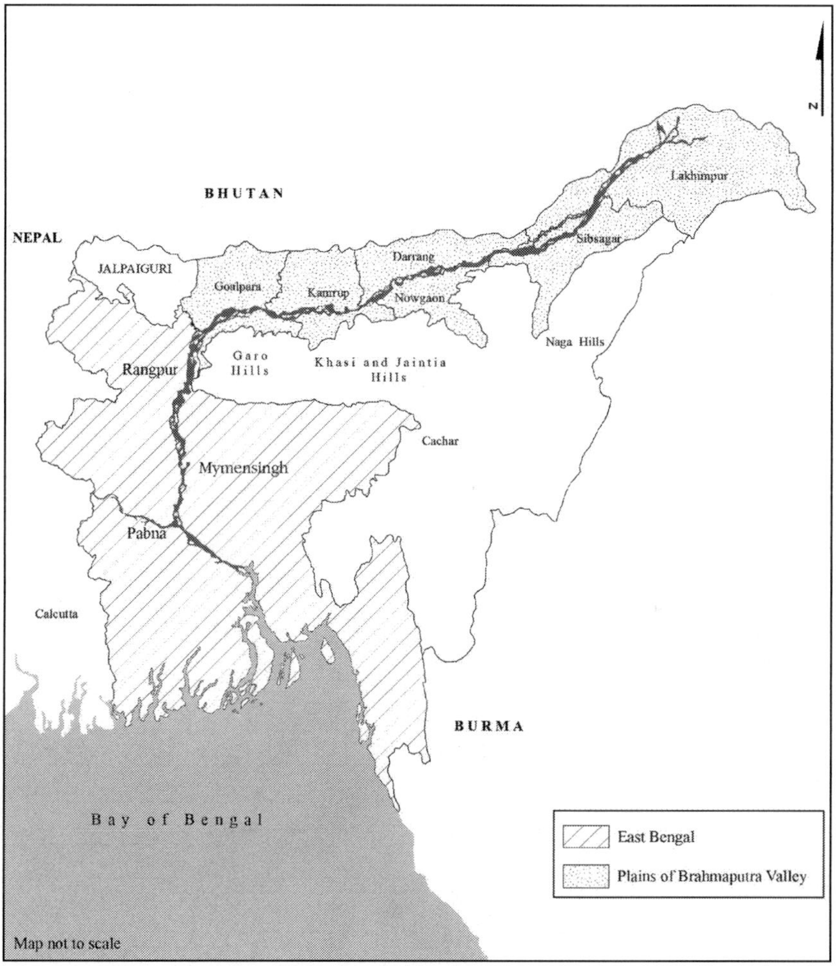

Introduction

> The communist activities . . . have taken a shape of exciting the more ignorant section of the people of this province (and they are many) into acts of violence against the constituted authority, under some plea or other and in a few places they have been successful. But all of them have been put down. The evil however does not seem to vanish so long as the agents are there to work from underground. But what makes the task of Government difficult is that although the intelligence reports reveal that these underground law breakers are doing this thing in this place and that thing in another, few if ever any action is found to be taken either for preventing their mischief as is being committed or in apprehending these underground culprits.
>
> — Gopinath Bordoloi, Chief Minister of Assam, to Jawaharlal Nehru, Prime Minister of India, July 1949.[1]

The unease with which one reads the letter reproduced above, written by Gopinath Bordoloi, the Chief Minister of Assam, was the manifestation of a larger problem of rural unrest that had just swept across many parts of the state.[2] Bordoloi's letter, written after 23 months of India's Independence, decisively tones down an otherwise massive rural unrest into a mere problem of law and order. The circumstances which led Bordoloi to write to the then Prime Minister Nehru are still unknown and a matter for speculation. The standard historical literature on Assam has for long overlooked these widespread events which engulfed rural Assam in the mid-twentieth century. This book departs from the earlier narratives and tells the untold stories which played a significant role in defining the trajectory of modern Assam. The book, by traversing the complex terrain of rural Assam, also narrates the life and times of struggling peasants. On reading these accounts, the readers might agree that Bordoloi and his government underestimated a powerful wave of agrarian unrest that made the peasants prisoners of hope for decades.

Various historical studies on Assam, on the other hand, have no difficulty in portraying an impression of how the contemporary politics of Assam housed complex layers of ethnicity, regionalism and insurgency under a single roof. These works, mostly by political scientists or sociologists, have exclusively displayed how regional economic disparity was successfully metamorphosed into a series of ethnic or other insurgent imbroglios.[3] Attention has been drawn to those 'big and important' events which came to play a crucial role in the making of Assamese middle-class politics. The result is that we get a picture of the continued unhappiness of the Assamese middle class in the new Indian federal structure. What disappears from this account is the narrative of peasant mobilization and unrest which had engulfed rural Assam immediately after Independence and in the following decades. This whole experience of peasant mobilization was a witness to phases of massive ups and downs, but it continued to display its strength in the larger political landscape of Assam. This untold experience of the rural world of Assam was strikingly different from what had been told in this wide range of writings on Assam.

All was not well for the peasants in the first half of the twentieth century. The agrarian crisis got channelized in different ways, though relief did come from the government. But in the 1940s, the situation acquired a dramatic new turn. The crisis in the rural world of Assam in 1947 began to unfold when the Assamese sharecroppers (*adhiar*s) and landless peasants did something unconventional. While Independence was being celebrated on 15th August, challenging the enthusiasm and euphoria of the event, a few — probably less than a hundred — adhiars and landless peasants, making a symbolic protest, took out street demonstrations in the town of Guwahati. As they went in a procession, they shouted slogans stating that they would give only one-fourth of their produce to the landlords. In the previous harvesting season, many of the peasants had even paid much less rent to their landlords. The following sowing season, however, witnessed more trouble: a few landlords evicted their adhiars, though in most places the adhiars successfully resisted such actions.

The next couple of harvesting seasons would witness a repetition of a similar situation. There was virtually an undeclared war in the countryside against Assamese landowners or landlords.[4] Violence erupted occasionally and there were confirmed reports of violent clashes in the countryside. The rural unrest was not confined only to the conflict between the sharecroppers and the landlords.

As the clashes between adhiars and landlords expanded to new areas, giving new fillip to insurgency by the struggling sharecroppers, the landless, Assamese and tribal peasants also infiltrated the government-owned forested lands and tea gardens.[5] They reclaimed patches of land for cultivation, and invited no effective resistance from the government. The European tea planters — the Indian capitalists were yet to take over the ownership of these tea estates — offered only feeble protests. Despite early setbacks, the Assam government, worried about the growing capacity of the peasants to strike back, openly declared its intention to counter these challenges: it forged an alliance with the landlords. Peasant activists were arrested and harsh physical punishment was meted out to some of them.

The leaders of the struggling peasants were usually members of the communist peasant organizations. However, this was not the case everywhere. Often, peasants resisted their landlords on their own, without instigation by the communist leaders. Nevertheless, in the spirit of the then Indian politics, i.e., in the early 1940s, taking advantage of the widespread rural disaffection, the mobilization of peasants by communists had made headway in the countryside. However, unlike the overarching domination of the Congress politics — which, in the heyday of the anti-imperial nationalist movement, was bound to be oriented towards mass mobilization — the communist mobilization in Assam was confined to small pockets. It was difficult to speak against the Congress model of rural mobilization. Communist mobilization of peasants in the countryside in Assam was of recent origin. It was a similar story in the neighbouring north Bengal. The role of the communist mobilization in Assam in the 1940s was clearly in the hands of two ideologically divided communist parties, viz., the Revolutionary Communist Party of India (RCPI) and the Communist Party of India (CPI). A fraction within the Congress, now identified as Socialists, also appreciated the need for defending the cause of the lower strata of peasant society. The communist mobilization gained new ground and was to acquire the shape of a peasant movement by the time India won Independence, when in 1945, one of the communist parties, the RCPI, adopted two slogans: *tin bhag* — one third share — and *nangal jar mati tar* — land belongs to the tiller. These slogans soon became extremely popular amongst sharecroppers and landless peasants. Not only did the slogans crafted in the 1940s help the communist parties expand their rural bases but they also slowly began to challenge the invincible supremacy of the Congress in Assam.

As the peasant unrest grew and peasant protests gained momentum in rural Assam, the Assamese press worriedly portrayed the severity of the situation. Reports that the Assamese and tribal sharecroppers had either stopped paying rent completely or had paid an absolutely decreased amount of rent to the landlords acquired front-page space. The Assamese landlords, in most cases, in order to bail themselves out of this impasse, opted to evict the sharecroppers from their land. The adhiars resisted eviction but such resistance led to police cases or lawsuits. The courts saw more landlords and poor peasants loitering in the veranda, as there were increasing number of cases of land litigation. The Assamese press and the Assam Provincial Congress described the situation as 'social disorder'. The Assam government responded to the peasants' demands and unrest through either legislations or aggressive police repression.

Police aggression continued for the next couple of years (1950–51). The movement came to a temporary halt in 1952, on the eve of the first general election, when communist parties decided in favour of a crucial change in the strategy of rural mobilization. In the general elections, the communist parties registered some decisive electoral gains. A few communist leaders also became members of the Assam Legislative Assembly. Communist victories in the electoral politics, however, meant little for the peasants. The next couple of decades, i.e., 1950s and 1960s, witnessed further unfolding of rural politics, and, by the end of the 1970s, the peasant mobilization came to assert itself decisively in the political landscape of Assam. In 1979, there began a popular nationalist mobilization, and for the next few years, it virtually put Assam and its rural world in a fix. Thousands of peasants, along with their nationalist leaders, came back to the streets to stage demonstrations repeatedly till 1985. However, by that time their demands and their leaders were different.

I

The Assamese peasants of the twentieth century have been remarkably understudied. They found no mention in a wide-ranging scholarship on the making of modern Assam. Notwithstanding this grim picture, a small number of works on Assam have drawn attention to those salient features that shaped the way the Assamese peasant society appears today. A few amongst them have meticulously narrated the key role played by the peasants in the making of the pre-colonial society, economy and polity of Assam.[6] The histories of the Assamese peasant society in the pre-colonial era are essentially narratives of exploitation, economic stratification, limited technological innovation, their ability to overcome the environmental challenges, and finally a history of slow transition from a feudal economy.[7]

The introduction of colonial rule in the early nineteenth century infused a rapid transformation.[8] Historical works on the colonial period are in general agreement over the abrupt but perceptive changes that had crept into the agrarian structure and economy of Assam. By telling the history of the making of colonial agrarian regime, these works perceptively bring out the changes in property regime and land usage pattern, as well as in the emergence of a new and oppressive regime of rent extraction.[9] These issues resurface when one looks into the history of European tea plantation in Assam.[10] The colonial narratives on the Assamese peasantry, however, disagree with these arguments[11] and rather point out a history of indolence of the Assamese peasantry, low population and plentiful resources as factors behind the emergence of tenancy in Assam.

The peasantry in modern Assam convincingly surface twice in the historical works when one reads either the history of the making of the Assamese middle class[12] or of the incidents of peasant resistance against the colonial rule.[13] Such insurgent acts of peasants, as these works readily acknowledge, took place either independently or with the support of the Congress nationalists.[14] Peasants' hard-fought participation in the nationalist movement was thus admired: 'These people constituted authority were indicative of what the mass people could do to shake the foundations of the imperial power'.[15] However, such overt attempts to see peasants as anti-imperialists undermine the complexities of peasant politics.[16] A few other scholars were more convinced of class-consciousness being an indispensable factor of the nineteenth-century Assamese peasant uprisings. For instance, the leading Marxist economic historian Amalendu Guha thus argued, 'Wide spread peasant struggle [was] based on unity of the entire peasantry and a section of the non-cultivating landowners ... it was the poor peasantry and other sections of the rural poor, including the artisans, who actually lent it a militant colour'.[17]

Everyday peasant politics was seen as acquiring prominence only when the anti-imperial nationalist struggle gained momentum. The history of rural politics thus became a history of communalism[18] and migration,[19] a history of Assamese chauvinism,[20] or a history of land conflicts.[21] The image of the 'rebel' Assamese peasant[22] or the romanticized peasants,[23] living in a self-sufficient village system, also frequently surfaces in the modern Assamese literary works.[24] Few passionately crafted Assamese literary works portray how the peasants could even strike a deal with the pre-colonial rulers for securing economic and social privileges.[25] A few have also crafted a saga of a few centuries of journey of the Assamese peasant families.[26] These works have successfully elevated the Assamese peasantry to the position of main protagonists in the making of modern Assam. Peasant families, in these works, tell their stories of struggle, their successes against natural challenges and their consistent tenacity to survive against all odds. These narratives are full of jealousy, rivalries and conflicts over land among peasant families. Folklore, with the overt help of the modern nation-state, plays a key role in keeping some of these memories from the peasant society alive.[27] All these works, however, stop short of crossing the boundary of the nineteenth century leaving the next century completely understudied. And for that matter, in contrast to the eloquent narratives on the fate of the Assamese peasants in the twentieth century, the second half of the century in particular, is largely unknown.[28]

The histories of the Assamese peasant society of colonial and post- Independence period, to put briefly, are carefully submerged under the histories of nations and nationalism. This is unlike their counterparts in many other parts of South Asia.[29] After staging a great comeback, the peasants have, in effect, retreated from the forefront despite some brave attempts to keep them at the forefront of historical scholarship.[30] Fortunately, the new peasant movements[31] and their multifaceted wars against the unfriendly modern times, for example, their ecological battles,[32] have found place in a few recent works.

This book has chosen to address the experiences of the peasantry in the twentieth-century Assam. By the first decade of the twenty-first century, peasant politics had again emerged as a key feature of Assam's political landscape. A careful examination of the history of Assamese rural politics during 1920s and 1980s can lead us towards a meaningful engagement with the dynamics of contemporary Assam; this book is an attempt at such an engagement. But before doing so, we take a short detour of the previous century to understand the shaping of the trajectory of Assam's agrarian economy. For this, we begin by retelling the early days of the engagement of colonial rulers with the peasants in Assam.

II

The political fallout of the first Anglo-Burmese war was the extension of the rule of British East India Company into the Brahmaputra valley of Assam. Once the Company gained control of the territory in 1826, the need for the transformation of land and other natural resources into a capitalist commodity came to occupy the centre stage of colonial administration. The British rulers frequently described a picture of sparse and low-density population in the valley as against abundant reclaimable tracts of arable land. At the same time, the colonial correspondences continued to refer to the region as a territory endowed with abundant and uncultivated land.[33] The Company also understood that it had inherited an effective system of rent collection — known as *paik* system in the eastern and central Assam from the Ahom rulers — from a sizeable population.[34] This system of rent collection would, however, have been highly cumbersome in the age of modern capitalism. In an effort to bring these vast patches of uncultivated land under cultivation and transform the nature of rent collection, the colonial administration, in the next couple of decades, made a couple of experiments on regularizing and documenting land and property ownership. Already, the colonial government had persuasively argued for and encouraged investment to justify such a dramatic transformation of land. While such experiments persisted till the middle of the nineteenth century, the land resources of the province had already become attractive for British tea planters. The planters began to invest enormous amounts of capital to integrate a comparatively less attractive terrain to the colonial economy.[35]

By the 1860s, a *raiyatwari* system of land tenure was firmly in place.[36] However, despite the avowed intention of the colonial government to allow maximum freedom to the peasants as cultivators, landlordism subsequently grew at a faster pace. This, in turn, directly encouraged tenancy cultivation. Moreover, the pre-colonial practices of landed interests were not done away with. Many of these practices, in fact, came to acquire legitimacy through official sanction of the colonial state. After years of experience of the colonial government in managing land relations, both peasant proprietorship and encouragement of landlordism came to be identified with the land tenure system in Assam. This helped in the growth of tenant cultivation, and, by the end of the nineteenth century, widespread practice of sharecropping was noticed by few commentators on the affairs of Assam.

Since 1838, the colonial administration had introduced lease rules known as 'wasteland grant rules' that allowed planters to reclaim vast plots of land for tea plantation. Such rules, however, failed to improve a poor peasant economy; rather it turned out to be an obstacle for further expansion of peasant cultivation. This necessitated a serious look into the issue of land ownership in Assam in the second half of the nineteenth century. In the subsequent period, several policies played an important role in changing the nature of landed property. The government, as has been already mentioned, had decided to introduce raiyatwari settlement in the entire Brahmaputra valley except in Goalpara, the district adjacent to Bengal where *zamindari* system was already in place. The administration also retained many pre-colonial features of land ownership which also created a distinct class of landlords. One of the primary objectives of raiyatwari settlement was to minimize the presence of middlemen between the cultivator and the state. This, the advocates of the settlement thought, would encourage the cultivators to increase production. The contemporary Assamese thinkers also supported the view. Anandaram Dhekial Phukan – an English-educated Assamese scholar inspired by European enlightenment – for instance, while describing the effects of raiyatwari settlement, categorically claimed that 'the recognition of the ryots' rights to proprietorship of their respective holdings is the greatest boon which in our humble judgement, the British Government has conferred on the country'.[37]

By 1870s, the cultivable lands came to be divided into two administrative categories, viz., those under ordinary cultivation and those under special cultivation. As tea plantations predominantly held the lands classified as being under special cultivation, peasant cultivation was mostly confined to those meant for ordinary cultivation.[38] The area settled for ordinary cultivation was held by individual peasants and, in some cases, in compact blocks by religious institutions. Depending on the form of rent, land under the ordinary settlement was further classified into three categories known as *khiraj* (full-revenue), *nisf-khiraj* (half-revenue) and *la-khiraj* (revenue-free). The khiraj land was predominantly owned by individual peasants. In the districts where raiyatwari system came to be implemented, land was given to these peasants on an annual lease.[39] The rate of revenue was adjusted at the time of the renewal of lease. In an annually leased land, the practice was that unless a peasant relinquished the land held in his name the lease was annually renewed. Nonetheless, they resorted to widespread relinquishment, a practice they adopted either in search of more fertile plots of land, or to avoid unnecessary taxation.[40]

Relinquishment soon emerged as a serious problem to the colonial state's desire to see a stable peasant economy yielding substantial revenue. To overcome this difficulty, the government, in 1883, decided to lease out land for a period of 10 years. Such an attempt to stop relinquishment, however, did not stop peasants from seeking only annual *patta* land. The khiraj area was divided into annual patta (*ekchania*) lands settled only for a year, and periodic *patta* (*myadi*) lands settled for a long period of time, usually 10–30 years. While the customary practice in the case of the annual patta land was that the peasant could continue to enjoy the land unless he decided to relinquish his holding in the next year, in the case of the periodic patta, the lease had to be renewed once the term for settlement came to an end.[41] Changes in the form of tenure also brought about changes in the forms of rights enjoyed by the peasants.

The colonial administration also had to take a decision on the pre-colonial rent-free landed estates. After long-drawn debates and a series of investigations into the nature of these privileges, the colonial government decided to retain them and categorized them as la-khiraj estates.[42] Gradually, another hierarchy was created for those estates which failed to prove their pre-colonial credentials. They were then entitled to half-revenue-paying estates and, since 1871, came to be known as nisf-khiraj estates. Initially, such estates were rented out on non-transferable 10-year leases. The number of such estates was higher than the la-khiraj estates. Both these estates, owned by religious institutions and individual landlords, were bestowed with features of landlordism that was characteristic of Bengali zamindars, though their Assamese counterparts had fewer legal and economic powers. The British official B.H. Baden-Powell even went to the extent of terming their privileges as equivalent to the 'temporarily settled estates of upper India'.[43] The owners of nisf-khiraj and la-khiraj estates had to depend on the tenants for their cultivation. There was no tenancy law to regulate the relationship between the landlords and their tenants. At times, the ideological legitimacy of share-tenancy was drawn from cultural and religious customs of the peasant society. The tenants enjoyed the rights of inheritance, and normally were not evicted frequently. Nonetheless, over the years, Assam came to have a raiyatwari system flexible in terms of its authority and application. Peasant proprietorship, along with high rates of concentration of land ownership in the hands of rich landowners, emerged as its dominant feature. A majority of peasant proprietors held land between 20–30 *bighas* and only a few owned larger estates. We will see that the general nature of sharecropping had also varied in correspondence to the nature of peasant proprietorship.

The colonial claim of 'land abundance' was often accepted by the Assamese intelligentsia. The idea of land abundance had come to be closely linked to the notion of wasteland since the early period of colonial rule. According to the Census of 1911, the population density in the cultivated areas of Assam per square mile was higher than the all-India average.[44] Another set of statistics indicates that during 1894–1919, the proportion of the uncultivated area to the net area was higher than the all-India average.[45] What the early East India Company officials noticed was a general decline and the fallow character of agricultural land and forested patches. A high mortality rate due to factors such as a series of civil disturbances (1792–94) and the Anglo-Burmese war (1800–24) led to a decline in agricultural activity which did not change till the end of the century. With a general decline in mortality in the first quarter of the twentieth century, rapid expansion in land reclamation took place. In fact, even by the last decade of the nineteenth century, British officials wondered about the actual availability of agricultural land in certain patches; many insisted on Reserved Forests being declared as open for peasant cultivation.[46] They also noticed an increase in the population density in many villages leading to land fragmentation. Crucial to this discussion was the pattern of agricultural settlement, which was based on rice production in the raiyatwari areas which was so closely linked to the river bodies. This created a disproportionate concentration of agrarian population which partly explains the phenomenon of fallow land in certain locations.

By the second half of the nineteenth century, large areas of forested tracts were leased out for tea plantation. These tracts required clearance by heavy tools, and peasants hardly could afford to execute such reclamation. It is difficult to speculate on whether the area enclosed by the tea planters would have been used by the Assamese peasants in the future. Would such dearth of resources have led to the increasing incidence of sharecropping? Historical evidence does not indicate any large-scale migration of landless peasants from the tea-plantation-dominated districts to Kamrup or Darrang. Thus, the establishment of tea gardens did not necessarily contribute to the increased incidence of share-tenancy in these districts. Such a claim seems to have been raised neither by the Assamese intelligentsia nor by the sharecroppers in the first half of the twentieth century. A weak manifestation of the claim began to appear only after Independence.[47] However, as the tea planters rented out their lands for sharecropping, this, no doubt, significantly contributed to the making of a class of share-tenants. These tenants' history of economic exploitation was different from that of the other Assamese share-tenants.

The remaining uncultivated tracts, mainly the flood plains of Brahmaputra river — known as *chapori* — were exposed to many layers of hazards before they could be converted into cultivable lands. First, these tracts were devoid of any permanence of habitation and thus hardly offered any scope for permanent agricultural activity. Second, these tracts were suitable only for commercial crops, jute in particular. Assamese peasants were yet to become familiar with the agricultural practices associated with jute cultivation, and there was no market to sell this produce. Third, lack of access to various everyday needs in these tracts failed to attract the majority of Assamese peasants to these tracts and eventually these tracts remained unreclaimed. Thus, it emerges that while land abundance was a reality during the early decades of the nineteenth century, it was not so during the subsequent decades.

Events occurred fast in the next few decades. By the mid-twentieth century, the Indian census records viewed the Assamese peasant society as primarily constituted of four categories — often interrelated and overlapping — of landlord, peasant proprietor, sharecropper, and agricultural labourer.[48] While we have already indicated that all-India censuses (for example, the Census of 1951) tended to overestimate the numerical strength of peasant proprietors, a comparison of the figures for 1931 and 1951 evidently illustrates a marked increase in the numbers of sharecroppers in the raiyatwari districts of Assam.[49] Except Nowgaon and Lakhimpur, the other three districts had, by 1951, a fair share of the total agricultural population who had found a means to live as sharecroppers. From the onset of the global Great Depression, the percentage of sharecroppers to the total agricultural population changed at a rapid speed. This also meant that the Depression, which was the first of its kind in the region, left behind a deep impact on the regional economy.

Most probably, the picture presented in the Census of 1951 was not correct. It is important to note that in the absence of a large distinct class of landlords in the khiraj area, the owners of la-khiraj and nisf-khiraj estates came to be identified as the typical landlords. This exclusive class of landlords came to be recognized by virtue of their pre-colonial social privileges as well as the newly required economic privileges. Despite their numerically smaller size, compared to the whole of the population, they were also privileged with a bigger share of the total landholding. According to the Census of 1951, there were 134 la-khiraj estates that comprised a total of 93,059 acres of land. Out of this, Kamrup alone had 34,060 acres distributed amongst 38 estates each of which had an average area of 895 acres, a figure relatively higher than the average estate area of 603 acres in other districts. The district of Sibsagar had 40,894 acres of la-khiraj estates.[50] Nisf-khiraj estates were also concentrated in Kamrup and Darrang.[51] While in 1950 Kamrup alone had 85 per cent of all nisf-khiraj and 40 per cent of all la-khiraj estates in Assam, the distribution of such estates was disproportionate. Most of the estates were concentrated on the southern bank of Brahmaputra, and out of such estates, one-fourth alone was located in the Guwahati subdivision. These estates were mostly owned by the Brahmin or upper-caste families, though in Sibsagar and Lakhimpur they were owned by either the Vaishnava *satras* or Ahom families.

Amongst the absentee landlords in Kamrup and Darrang, women from the higher castes occupied a significant proportion.[52] This can be explained in terms of marriage systems prevalent amongst the upper-caste Hindu families. Caste-Hindu peasantry followed stricter Hindu religious practices. Early marriage of Brahmin girls was widely prevalent. High male mortality resulted in the growth of a large number of widows. Thus, what resulted in Kamrup, Darrang and Sibsagar was a significant orientation of the agrarian economy towards a pattern of landlord–tenant relation.

Apart from these la-khiraj and nisf-khiraj landlords, there was also a significant number of absentee landowners owning khiraj lands. Along with the la-khiraj and nisf-khiraj estates, a substantial number of absentee landowners became a feature of the valley. In Kamrup, a majority of these absentee landowners was from places like Barama, Boko, Palashbari, Sorbhog, or areas adjacent to the town of Guwahati.[53] A small number of absentee landlords, who otherwise owned no land of their own, hired lands from big landlords and subsequently rented them out to peasants on sharecropping basis. Thus, they turned out to be intermediaries between big landlords and tenant-peasants.[54] Probably, a section of peasantry hired land from the nisf-khiraj holders, and it was further let out to sub-tenants. The big landlords owning khiraj land also practised this system. The absentee landowners had mostly small holdings and the majority did not own more than 30 acres.[55]

As the peasant cultivation came to be based on khiraj holding, its increase by way of land reclamation became a key tool through which the peasant society fulfilled its basic need, i.e., land. Over the years, and at least till the end of the first half of the twentieth century, the khiraj area under cultivation increased manifold, mainly through the process of reclamation of wastelands and forests. Table 1 gives us an idea of the distribution of different

Table 1: Categories of Land in Acres (1951)

District	*Nisf-khiraj*	*Lakhiraj*	*Khiraj/annual*	*Khiraj/periodic*
Kamrup	146,332	34,060	470,399	615,325
Darrang	29,068	5,027	325,704	369,799
Nowgaon	6,118	1,537	333,660	342,476
Sibsagar	4,962	40,849	221,349	588,267
Lakhimpur	1,204	1,586	300,954	334,337

Source: 'Note on the Land System of Assam', in *Report on the Census of India*, Assam, vol. 12, 1951, Shillong: Government Press, Table A, p. 427.

categories of land in the middle of the twentieth century, a picture which had been true for the previous 50 years.

Tenancy right in the khiraj land came to attract crucial attention in the Assam administration from 1880s. The Assam Land Revenue Regulation of 1886 empowered the Assamese peasants with substantial rights compared to their previous history of limited legal rights. Such an assurance was important to drive home the point that Assamese peasants could secure stability and thus provide the colonial administration with a steady and uniform supply of revenue. Once both the tea industry and forestry had reached its peak in productivity, the administration began to shift its attention towards bringing more areas under peasant cultivation. In pursuing this policy, in the next decade, the administration made a few attempts to expand the acreage even at the cost of forest conservation programme, so aggressively pushed forward by the Assam Forest Department. Acrimonious debates took place between the managers of forestry and agricultural operations competing for claims over forested land. Contradicting its raiyatwari principles, the colonial administration began to encourage sharecropping as an essential mechanism to bring wasteland under acreage.

III

It was not only the changing patterns of agrarian economy that contributed to the increasing crisis in the agrarian economy, but also the colonial capital and governance which had aggravated the crisis. The ecological features of the valley only compounded the increasing worries of the peasants. The rivers, running across the valley, continuously caused soil erosion and also helped in the formation of new land. The newly formed land was, however, not suitable for permanent cultivation. Recurrent natural calamities added to growing scarcity of land for cultivation to a considerable extent. For instance, earthquakes often forced the rivers to move laterally and change their courses, thus forcing villagers to relocate to new places. The devastating 1897 earthquake had a major impact on the peasant society and continued till the early twentieth century. For instance, in Darrang, the Nanoi river changed its course because of this earthquake.[56] Such events thus forced many peasants to become landless. Another earthquake in 1950 further destabilized the agrarian economy.

By 1838 the colonial government had made an arrangement to parcel out good highlands of the province among the highly productive tea plantations — an arrangement which was to be reinforced in 1859. In 1900, the total area under the tea plantations, though not entirely taken up for tea cultivation, was estimated at 437,636 acres, which was approximately one-third of the total area under peasant cultivation in the entire valley.[57] This area was mostly concentrated in the three districts of Darrang, Sibsagar and Lakhimpur. By the end of the nineteenth century, the tea planters used to let out portions of land from their garden to the garden workers on a sharecropping arrangement. Whether such practices acquired any serious proportion is only a matter of speculation. Questions were also raised by the administration regarding the quest to find out whether these tracts could be brought under peasant cultivation by the Assamese peasants? Did enclosure of land lead to an increasing incidence of land scarcity and consequent increase in sharecropping? However, as mentioned earlier, there is no concrete evidence to suggest that the peasants constrained by the emerging land scarcity in the tea-plantation-dominated districts migrated to Kamrup or Darrang, seeking cultivable land, and thereby increased the incidence of sharecropping in those districts. But what is more crucial is the fact that tea plantation emerged as a powerful agent of land reclamation and landlordism in Assam.

The colonial forest governance became an additional burden and the peasants' traditional dependence on forest land and forest produce was derecognized by the government. The colonial forestry programme had made a start from the second half of the nineteenth century.[58] The creation of an independent forest department in 1874 brought about more strict rules and regulations regarding the forest areas. These rules eventually forbade the peasants from collecting firewood or reclaiming land for cultivation from the forests. Although it began on a small scale, the enormity of the problem grew as the area under forest conservation expanded in the years to come. From a mere 270 square miles in 1874, Reserved Forests increased its area to approximately 4,000 square miles prior to Independence. Creation of Unclassed State Forest as another category of state-owned forests, with an area of 14,844 square miles in 1947, was in direct conflict with future peasantization, since sizeable portions of forest area that came under the Unclassed State Forests, could have been brought under the plough in the near future.

The Assam Forest Regulation of 1891 brought more problems to the lives of the peasants. The regulation discontinued the practice of shifting cultivation. The unauthorized felling of trees in the Reserved or Unclassed State Forests was made punishable. Earlier, the Assam Land Revenue Regulation had allowed the peasants to clear any wasteland for which settlement could be claimed. In spite of these hurdles, the peasants continued to practise shifting cultivation, either ignoring the rules or escaping the supervision of the forest department. This forced the forest department to re-examine the matter. Many within the department, however, realized that it would be difficult to continue with such strict prohibition.

The most important intervention came in 1915 when the Indian Inspector General of Forest protested against this practice of shifting cultivation on land reclaimed from forests insisting that harmony be maintained between the Assam Forest Rules and Assam Land Revenue Regulation manual. He cited instances of how peasants, without any claim on the newly declared Reserved Forests, would cut down trees for expansion of cultivation and would claim a patta for the reclaimed land later on.[59] The Assam Forest Department thus had no other choice but to ban the felling of trees for shifting cultivation in 1915. Moreover, once a forest area was declared a reserve, villages inside the forest were shifted to other places, and in most cases, the villagers were asked to vacate in a short period of time. Rehabilitation did not figure at all in the official scheme of things. Neighbouring villages were also debarred from the rights of access to forest land and use of forest produce they had been enjoying from the earlier times. The village roads were closed. Most of the time, the forest department opened up some parts of the Reserved Forest for grazing purposes, but sometimes closed a few areas to the entry of animals.[60] This restricted the free movement of herds. Often, the village cattle were found in the custody of the pounds, and the peasant families owning the cattle had to pay some amount for retrieving them. This led to three simultaneous developments. First, there was a gradual erosion of the erstwhile customary forest rights of the Assamese peasantry; those who were primarily affected began to settle in the outskirts of the forested tracts. Second, the area meant for grazing got reduced. Third, the practice of shifting cultivation, not essentially slash-and-burn cultivation, was adversely affected.

IV

This book begins by examining the economic and social processes that helped in creating the afore-discussed agrarian landscape of Assam in the first half of the twentieth century. The first chapter examines the importance of sharecropping as a central element in the peasant economy. Usury became an integral part of the peasant economy and played a crucial role in leading to an increasing incidence of sharecropping. The peasant economy felt the force of abrupt change with the attempted move for commercialization of agriculture. A few hundred thousand peasants from the neighbouring East Bengal (now Bangladesh) villages began to move into the lowlands along Brahmaputra river, especially as jute cultivators. Thus, by the middle of the twentieth century, the Brahmaputra valley had been firmly integrated with the subcontinental colonial economy.

As the peasant economy underwent rapid transition, it was increasingly becoming difficult to withstand economic misfortunes. The rural society responded to these difficulties in many ways. Chapter 2 surveys the rural responses till India's Independence. The period was marked by three broad types of rural unrest: (*a*) simmering tension between those who had and who did not have land, (*b*) increasing competition over arable land, and (*c*) increasing conflict between indigenous and migrant peasants. Both Indian National Congress and Muslim League leaders could tactfully mobilize the disgruntled rural population. The pinnacle of such developments was the events of 1946 when the migrant Muslim peasants confidently asserted their claim for a homeland.

Chapter 3 discusses how the communist parties began to articulate the agrarian question differently when the rural crisis deepened further. In this new situation, the sharecroppers and landless peasants came into the forefront of rural politics. The left-wing peasant organizations categorically demanded a decrease in the *adhi*. They also demanded that land be owned by the tiller. Coinciding with this demand was RCPI's agitation with the popular slogan of 'independent Assam'. While the latter demand did not find many followers, it resulted in a new offensive against communist organizations by the Assam government. But it was equally becoming difficult to ignore the rural unrest, and the legislators came together to support and protect the interest of the adhiars. In March 1948, the Assam government passed the Assam Adhiars' Protection and Rights Act which conceded a crucial concession to the adhiars' demand, eventually leading to further consolidation of the peasant movement.

The twentieth-century experiment in legislative debates crystallized and foregrounded the peasant question more aggressively. Factoring in this development, the next chapter examines how both Assam Legislative Council and Assam Legislative Assembly were caught up with the peasant question. The legislators could hardly ignore the rural forces and the peasant question made forceful and recurrent appearances in the legislative debates. Despite limited electoral compulsions, the legislators made frantic attempts to save their respective constituencies from any eventual fallout of the rural discontent. Whether it was usury, land alienation, migration, or increased rural unrest, the peasant question remained one of a central concern in the legislative history of Assam, an examination of which is the thrust of Chapter 4.

The peasant mobilization became more intensified and expanded to newer areas after the harvesting season of 1948. The events occurred fast and it appeared as if the peasants were going to win their case. The state-owned forestlands, other wastelands or tea gardens were forcefully occupied by them. Despite the enactment of Assam Adhiars' Protection and Rights Act, the adhiars were facing increasing threats of eviction, and in many places, they even forced the landlords to accept their demands. The provincial government viewed peasant mobilization as a distinct collapse of the law-and-order situation. Landlords regarded it as an unlawful denial of their privileges and also an erosion of their social prominence. However, the retreat of peasants from radical agitational politics in the face of a combined offensive of the government and landlords soon became visible by 1952. Chapter 5 surveys this apparently radical stage of the peasant movement.

The apparent success of the peasant movement till that time was accomplished through a careful strategy of peasant mobilization as well as the ability of the communist peasant organizations to respond to the immediate crisis in the rural society. The best example was the inclusion of the issue of acute food scarcity that hit many parts of western Assam, into the programmes of peasant mobilization. These peasant organizations understood the urgency of carefully mobilizing rural women in order to make the movement more impactful. As the movement progressed, other dimensions of the Assamese rural society — for instance, the caste question — came to manifest their crucial relevance. The sixth chapter discusses these issues.

With the first Indian general election in 1952 around the corner and the communist parties deciding to seek some gains by participating in electoral politics, the peasant movement temporarily weakened. The period was also marked by changing ideological moorings of the Indian communist parties. The period thus was a temporary relief to the landlords. The peasant leaders, who had developed the strategy of confrontational politics and had taught it to the peasantry, were destined to take the beatings and lapsed into a short lull. The movement and its implications, however, continued to haunt the memories of the landowning families in the years to come. The peasants continued to suffer, but organized movement resurfaced in the next couple of decades — decades that were often overshadowed by politics of ethnicity or regionalism. The landlords tried to retain their control over land.

Chapter 7 discusses, in detail, how during the 1960s and the 1980s, the Assamese nationalist landed gentry managed to resume their pivotal role. The concluding chapter seeks to explain the continued relevance of the peasant question in the larger political and social landscape of contemporary Assam in the light of the overall thrust of the book.

1

An Agrarian Setting: 1900–50

In the winter of 1893–94, the peasants of Assam — cutting across caste and class distinctions — protested against the increasing land revenue imposed by the colonial government in the *raiyatwari*-settled districts of the Brahmaputra valley.[1] Such protests only marked the beginning of a widespread resistance against the colonial state. However, valiant defiance of the government in the 1890s hardly helped the peasants improve their own lot. Rather, their resistance to the imposition of a relatively inflexible revenue demand in cash would meet with more trouble in the following decades.

By the last decade of the nineteenth century, the agrarian economy in the Brahmaputra valley had undergone dramatic transformations. A combination of factors, both external and internal to the rural agrarian life, shaped the course of these transformations. Introduction of new land ownership rights for ryots, a new land revenue system, increasing land revenue, immigration of land-seeking population from East Bengal and cattle breeders and pastoralists from Nepal into the Brahmaputra valley, and settlement of tea plantation workers in agricultural lands — all directly influenced the agrarian scenario. Additionally, the introduction of a state forestry programme and, to some extent, the introduction of tea plantations reduced the land available for an ever-increasing rural peasant population. Unlike the case in other parts of the British India, however, depeasantization did not set in and agricultural acreage continued to increase in Assam. This largely helped in the expansion of small peasant holdings. In that era of new possibilities, the prospect of a better future for the Assamese landed gentry, however, was still gloomy. Between 1870 and 1950, an estimated 700,000 hectares of dense forests and woodlands were put under cultivation. Not all of these were converted for small peasant production though the Bengali immigrant peasants came to own a sizeable portion.[2]

By the mid-twentieth century, the peasants in Assam had been subjected to more misfortunes than in the previous century. Along with the widespread practice of sharecropping, rural indebtedness was on the rise.[3] Furthermore, areas available for cultivation shrank in size, as either more cultivable land became part of the Forest Department or it was parcelled out into tea plantation estates.[4] Pressure on arable land increased with the reclamation of riverine areas by peasants from East Bengal, now Bangladesh. The land reclaimed by the immigrant peasants was used by the local peasants in a limited manner. Much later, these reclamations of land would become a burden on the Assamese peasants. Meanwhile, introduction of jute cultivation in the first few decades of the twentieth century further exposed the valley's peasant economy to market forces. The results of these were soon visible. Sandwiched between colonial laws on transactions in land and revenue burden on the one hand, and demographic pressures on the other, the Assamese peasants were subjected to a life of uncertainty and limited economic opportunities. In the 1930s, as the Great Depression set in the Western world, the valley's agrarian economy began to show signs of fissures. As the peasant society tried to withstand these economic pressures despite expansion of area under peasant holding, both sharecropping and landlessness became dominant features of agrarian economy and relations. This chapter explains the changes that took place in the rural economy of the valley during the first half of the twentieth century.

Sharecropping and Agrarian Economy

The extent of sharecropping in the raiyatwari areas of Assam can be ascertained from the official enquiries made during the two rounds of land resettlement operations in the first half of the twentieth century. This is indicated by Table 1.1.

Table 1.1 clearly shows that the incidence of sharecropping was very high in the two districts of Kamrup and Darrang. Taking into account the *nisf-khiraj* and *la-khiraj* estates, Kamrup, with one-fourth of its total agricultural land under sharecropping, was the

Table 1.1: Area under Sharecropping (1900–30)[a]

	Khiraj area		*Nisf-khiraj estates*		*La-khiraj estates*	
Districts	*1st resettlement*	*2nd settlement*	*1st settlement*	*2nd settlement*	*1st resettlement*	*2nd resettlement*
Kamrup	13.78	5.15	51.78	NA[b]	46.36	NA
Darrang	8.79	6.34	36.36	42.09	56.23	68.91
Nowgaon	2.32	NA	52.55	NA	68.91	NA
Sibsagar	6.6	2.76	NA	NA	NA	NA
Lakhimpur	5.19	2.76	NA	NA	NA	NA

Notes: [a] Percentage of area under sharecropping out of total land area.
[b] NA: Data not available.

Source: Calculated from land revenue settlement reports of respective years.[5]

best example of the widespread nature of sharecropping. Further, intra-district or intra-locality variation of the incidence of sharecropping was often noticed. It was in the highly populated tracts where 'practically all the available land ha[d] long been taken up' that 'khiraj land was sublet to any appreciable extent',[6] but revenue records suggest that the area under sharecropping did not exceed one-tenth of the total cultivated area. The Barbhag *mauza* in Kamrup had, on an average, one-tenth of the total *khiraj* area under sharecropping. Unlike the Barbhag mauza, the Panbari mauza had more than one-third of area under sharecropping. The high incidence of sharecropping was due to the presence of landed interest among the urban absentee landowners in these areas. A majority of Guwahati-based absentee landowners had landed interest in Panbari and also in similar other mauzas, and they engaged tribal peasants as their sharecroppers. In fact, by the second round of land resettlement in the 1920s, the landholding of urban landowners had increased exponentially. If one took into account other areas, one could see that approximately one-fifth of the cultivable land on the south bank of Brahmaputra in Kamrup district was under sharecropping. The rate of incidence also varied depending on the geographical location of the arable land. In places close to the Brahmaputra river, the incidence of sharecropping was low. For example, in places like Barpeta or Bajali, located in the north-western bank of Kamrup district, approximately only 1 per cent of land was under sharecropping. This low incidence of sharecropping can be explained by the fact that these riverine areas were reclaimed only in the early twentieth century. Also, a sizeable section of the population in these areas was engaged in trade. This minimized the pressure on land. Further, peasants who wanted to increase their landholdings could do so by clearing and bringing new areas under cultivation in places not far away from their villages. These places would be close to grasslands or riverine forested areas. Such practices came to be largely known as *pam* cultivation, a term otherwise reserved for temporary cultivation of winter crops.[7]

It was a similar situation in the district of Darrang. Except in a few scattered patches, sharecropping was fairly widespread across the district.[8] The two rounds of land revenue resettlement in the first half of the twentieth century put the figures of the incidence of sharecropping at 8.94 per cent and 6.34 per cent, respectively.[9]

Compared to this picture of decreasing incidence of sharecropping in proportion to the total cultivable land, there was a 72 per cent increase in the total area held under sharecropping.[10] Increase of acreage under sharecropping needs to be particularly explained with reference to the growth of absentee landownership. Debendra nath Mukherjee, the resettlement officer of the district, explained the phenomenon in terms of the increasing number of tea garden labourers renting in land from a growing number of absentee landowners.[11] Mukherjee noticed that in the eastern parts of the district, which had large belts of tea plantation, former tea garden labourers became the central feature of sharecropping.

Other raiyatwari districts reported relatively lower incidence of sharecropping than Kamrup and Darrang. For instance, in Sibsagar, the first round of resettlement (1902–6) estimated an approximate 6.6 per cent of the total khiraj-settled area under sharecropping. The next round, however, registered a sharp fall. Similarly, during the first round of resettlement, the incidence of share tenancy in Lakhimpur was reported to be 5.19 per cent of the total khiraj-settled area. In certain localities, the rate of decrease was above average: for example, Dibrugarh had a 7.6 per cent decrease followed by Subansiri at 5.5 per cent.

These figures, however, hardly give the true picture of sharecropping in the valley. A better picture emerges if we take into consideration a proportionate share of the total population engaged in sharecropping. The number of *adhiar*s in the raiyatwari districts is shown in Table 1.2. As can be inferred from the table, compared to the low incidence of sharecropping and low area under sharecropping, the percentage of peasant population engaged in sharecropping was higher.

All the raiyatwari districts uniformly shared a high rate of increase in the total number of adhiars after 1931. The percentage of adhiars in relation to the total population dependent on agriculture also continued to increase. Sharecropping continued to dominate as the foremost form of agricultural practice in the days after Independence, despite its overall portrayal as an insignificant 'smaller class' by the Census of 1951.[13] Though uniform statistics were not available after independence, an independent survey taken in 1951 for Darrang and Sibsagar largely confirms this trend. While Sibsagar had more than 8 per cent of its land under sharecropping, Darrang had more than one-tenth of

Table 1.2: Number of Adhiars in Raiyatwari districts

Districts	*1901*	*1911*	*1931*	*1951*	*Percentage of increase between 1901 and1951*	*Percentage of adhiars out of the total no. of peasant families*	
						1931	*1951*
Kamrup	52,667	152,677	151,749	226,389	330	7	18
Darrang	6,385	131,538	9,653	206,216	3,130	6	32
Nowgaon	3,961	135,565	5,685	100,832	2,445	4	13
Sibsagar	14,033	228,075	8,988	174,090	1,140	3	22
Lakhimpur	4,141	69,777	4,321	55,727	1,245	3	9

Source: Prepared from census tables of the respective years.[12]

its land under it.[14] Darrang had one-fifth of its khiraj land under sharecropping and Sibsagar, approximately 11 per cent.

The practice of sharecropping in the first half of the nineteenth century was highly localized and varied from district to district. Higher incidence of sharecropping was confined to areas adjacent to towns. The remarkable growth of a class of absentee landowners — the result of land speculation from the last decade of the nineteenth century — became a key factor in helping consolidate incidence of sharecropping. The very high incidence of tenancy in nisf-khiraj and la-khiraj estates prevalent in the nineteenth century continued to prevail in the subsequent period as well. The tenancy in these estates differed from sharecropping in the khiraj area in terms of both the rights and privileges enjoyed by the adhiars and the form of rent. This particular aspect will be discussed separately.

Are these official accounts about the spread of the practice of sharecropping reliable? Probably not, if we take into account the possible discrepancies in the way the prevalence of sharecropping was reported. The extent of sharecropping turned out to be low as landlords often concealed the existence of sub-tenancy. This was so, mostly because of their belief that recording might have troublesome legal consequences for their occupancy rights. The revenue officials had no doubt that, in reality, there was a marked difference between what was actually happening and what was officially reported on sharecropping. Following is a representative explanation by a revenue official who perceptively reminded that

> where khiraj lands are only temporarily sublet, the land-holders often tried to suppress the existence of sub-tenancies, apprehending that the entry in the records might affect their title adversely and the tenants also in such cases where not at all interested in having their names entered in the records. Besides there might have been cases where both the landlord and tenant were absent at the time of record-writing and the villagers present could not supply any correct information about the tenancies.[15]

What led to such concealment of facts? There was a growing awareness among the landlords about a probable move on the part of the tenants to demand occupancy rights. From the last decades of the nineteenth century, the revenue officials in Assam highlighted the need to accord occupancy rights to the adhiars in the

Brahmaputra valley. This anticipation was further strengthened by the legislative action – the passing of Goalpara Tenancy Act in 1922. In the wake of legislative debates, the question of tenancy rights in Goalpara became a matter of serious worry for the landlords in Goalpara, and subsequently concealment of facts became a regular practice among them. Though a public debate on the rights of the adhiars in the raiyatwari areas was yet to begin, the prolonged legislative debates on the Goalpara tenancy question was enough to produce an uncertainty among the absentee landowners in the raiyatwari districts with regard to the security of their landed interests. For the landowners, the best way to escape from these uncertainties was to conceal facts about sharecropping. The impact of these developments was felt in other parts of the valley too; hence, understandably one comes across a low figure of area under sharecropping that was far from being authentic.[16]

Similarly, figures on sharecropping would seem to be low if one does not take into account the relative expansion of acreage. For instance, in Darrang, though the percentage of subletting was shown as decreasing, there was also an approximate 218 per cent increase in the total khiraj land between 1900 and 1931.[17] As the total acreage had increased along with the relative increase of population, a relative decrease of 2.45 per cent in areas under sharecropping does not necessarily indicate a steep fall in the incidence of sharecropping. This explanation also holds true for Kamrup. The district witnessed an increase of 180 per cent in the khiraj area during this period, while it registered only an 8.6 per cent decline in sharecropping. The relative expansion of the khiraj area also needs to be seen in the context of the reclamation of khiraj land by migrant peasants. Revenue officials admitted that

> the main reason why in spite of increase in the total area sublet . . . the percentage shows a decrease . . . is that the large area newly opened out . . . was mostly cultivated by the owners themselves and contained a comparatively small proportion of area occupied by tenants.[18]

There was also an increase in the demand for wastelands. Such a demand came mostly from the Assamese absentee landowners. At the same time, an increase in pam cultivation in the vicinity of the villages was also noticed by revenue officials.[19] The newly reclaimed land was cultivated with the help of wage labourers. This marked the beginning of a process whereby the Assamese absentee landowners began to hire outside labour in addition to the work they put in themselves. From the 1940s, a sizeable number of Assamese absentee landowners began to employ wage labourers to replace adhiars. An increase in the employment of wage labour also led to a proportionate decline in sub-tenancy.

The districts of Darrang, Nowgaon, Sibsagar, and Kamrup also witnessed an increase of population since the Census of 1891. This demographic rise has been explained primarily as an effect of a decline in the mortality rate as also the rate of migration of rural population from the districts of East Bengal. The rate of increase in the number of absentee landowners and tenants was higher than that of the increase in population. For instance, there was a marked increase in the total percentage of sharecroppers in Kamrup and Sibsagar between the Censuses of 1891 and 1901.[20]

The changing parameters of estimating occupational categories as used in the census also merit consideration in order to understand the questionable estimates of sharecropping. These figures, quoted in Table 1.2, however, will not provide us with an insightful perspective about the official figures of sharecropping if we do not take into account the operational aspects of the occupational categories used in the Census of 1951. The Census of 1951, unlike the previous censuses, narrowed down the scope of people depending on agriculture. Apparently, the Census of 1951 emphasized that 'the preponderance of "owner–cultivators" is the most important and characteristic feature of our agricultural class-structure'.[21] These figures have been challenged and called 'agrarian revolution by census redefinition' by D. Thorner who has recommended 'great caution' in reading them.[22] Thorner has also pointed out the several layers of complexities involved in the way agrarian categories were defined in the Census of 1951, leading to a strikingly low number of sharecroppers as compared to owner–cultivators.

Sharecropping and Rent

Apart from the growing strength of sharecropping, the burden of high rent rates imposed on the adhiars was also increasing. If there was a high variation in the incidence of sharecropping, the nature and volume of rent also varied. The practice of having different forms of rent is indicated by a range of Assamese terms , viz., *adhi*, *guti adhi, chukti adhi, guchi adhi,* and *chukani adhi.* The implications of these different forms of rent varied from region to region; however, essentially, the overall rent burden remained the same. Though it is difficult to give an accurate idea of the rent levied, it is true that harsh practices of rent extraction continued from the nineteenth century and became worse in the next century.[23] Revenue officials were unanimous in alleging that landlords often provided incorrect information about the rent charged and received which was rarely contradicted, even by the tenants.[24] In the late nineteenth century, officials believed that no extra payments were generally demanded over and above the stipulated share in the produce, which was either in kind or cash. They also thought that while the landlords demanded the government revenue as their rent from the adhiars, in most cases this practice varied according to circumstances such as soil fertility, respective contribution of the two parties and also the market prices of the produce.

The landowners would choose to take rent either in cash or kind depending on their requirement, the prevailing market rates and also their ability to negotiate with the adhiars. By the early twentieth century, more adhiars were paying their rent in cash than those in the late nineteenth century. The practice of taking rent in either cash or kind, and sometimes both, was also widespread in all raiyatwari districts.[25] A significant change occurred in the post-Depression period: with the prices of paddy increasing, cash rent became more attractive for landlords.[26] One of the reasons why cash was preferred was often the lack of space to store the paddy in a granary. Falling prices, along with cash scarcity, compelled the landowners to find every possible opportunity to extract cash rents. But wherever it was difficult to receive cash, they took in kind. The situation became worse in Kamrup and Darrang where the demand for land became more acute, enabling the landlords to bargain with their adhiars more effectively.

Rent burden in different forms of sharecropping worked out to be of a similar nature. Rent was extracted through various manipulations. Often, the landowners would charge extra rent for their expenses on seeds or transplantation costs, or both. Some forms of rent agreement became highly taxing. For instance, under the chukti adhi system, rent was fixed speculatively. This often pushed the adhiars more or less to the verge of subsistence-level existence. With the Brahmaputra valley being more prone to crop failures, this form seemed to be particularly taxing for the sharecroppers. The adhiars were further required to provide the landlords with various customary services like ploughing, reaping, pressing sugarcane, thatching houses, etc., which further depleted their physical strength and economical resources.[27] The landowners also imaginatively employed other means of extracting more from their adhiars. The most prevalent practice was the wrongful use of the land measurement stick known as *nal*. The length of this measuring rod varied according to the length of landowners' hands. Thus, an enhanced share could be obtained by using a nal shorter by one or more cubits than the government-specified nal of 8 cubits. For example, a seven-and-a-half cubit pole led to an enhancement of about 15 per cent and a seven-cubit pole, a 30 per cent increase.[28]

Several other factors helped landlords impose high rents. For instance, in Kamrup, both the scarcity of land and also the higher numbers of adhiars fetched landlords high rents. High rents also depended on the density of population in the villages. The adhiars in village Panbari paid rent rates equal to those prevalent in 'first-class' villages though the village was classified as third-class.[29] High intensity of sharecropping also meant that landowners were extracting more from the adhiars. In such cases, for instance, an adhiar would be asked by a landowner to thresh paddy or help in harvesting. While fertile lands would always attract more adhiars, the inferior ones were also usually rented out at rates, usually at a par with the government-approved rate. Renting such lands could even involve adhiars' liability to render services in addition to paying cash rent.[30] Some landowners increased their profits by charging a higher local rate in addition to their share. Sometimes, the adhiars had to pay an *anna* (one-sixteenth of a rupee) or two on each revenue receipt that the landlords gave.

Usually, the government-approved rate was charged only for those lands that were rented out for a short span of time and at a short notice. In such cases, even under a chukti adhi arrangement, the rent paid was double the government-approved rate. Such practices were more prevalent where adhi was in high demand such as the areas close to towns.[31] If the landowner lived in the town, the adhiar had to make sure that the crop was delivered at his house.[32] It was rare for the adhiar to retrieve the transport cost he incurred. Sometimes, he would be given lunch at the landowner's house and a few other things, for example, garden produce, to be taken back home. In the event of land being of poor quality, which did not attract the adhiar, the landowner was forced to rent it out without bargaining on the rates much. In some places, lands were sublet on half-share terms, in which case the landowner got half the produce and paid the land revenue as well as the cost of reaping and removal.[33] In most cases, like the Assamese adhiars in the densely settled villages, former tea garden labourers renting lands close to tea gardens paid high rent.[34] The tea planters who rented out their lands also charged rates higher than the government-approved rate, in either kind or cash, or both.[35] The Assamese landowners who rented out land to the former tea garden labourers had better bargaining power vis-à-vis the latter. As the latter had either retired from their work in the gardens or wanted to add to their meagre income from the garden job, they were forced to work under harsh conditions.[36] Lack of resources or less familiarity with an area's culture and geography worked as constraints because of which the labourers were either unwilling or unable to migrate to other distant places to reclaim land for cultivation.

If the adhiars were exposed to high rent demand, their fellow tenants in the nisf-khiraj and la-khiraj estates were not better-off either. Often, due to a range of complex extra-economic coercions, the rent collected by these estates turned out to be much higher than the government-approved rate. As early as the first decade of the twentieth century, all official accounts continued to concur on the fact that these tenants paid higher rent besides rendering some customary services.[37] Traditionally, big estate owners like the Kamakhya temple or Parbatia Gossain (an important nisf-khiraj owner from Kamrup) not only used to sublet their lands entirely on cash rent, but also compelled their tenants to provide seeds, manure and other requirements.[38] Extra-economic coercion on the tenants was common. New tenants had to pay a form of first-time negotiation rent known as *salami* or *mukhchowani*.[39] They were charged other types of payments such as *seva*, *puja*, higher local rates, cost of rent receipts, or a grazing fee. The levies thus appeared unending. From the early twentieth century, Parbatia Gossain began to impose the kind of levies that the zamindars of Goalpara had been imposing before. There were various such customary duties. For instance, in *bhogdani* land, the adhiar paid *bhog* in kind instead of cash rent, apart from rendering other customary services demanded by the temples or *satra*. In *dharmottar*, *paikan* and *pirpal* lands, the adhiars, if they did not pay their customary dues, had to pay half of the government revenue as rent to the funds of the temple, satra or mosque. The *brahmottar* landlords, in their attempt to extract as much out of the tenants as possible, fixed exorbitant rents, quite often 'leaving nothing for them'.[40] Such was the situation that by the 1920s it was a common practice of these satras and temples to realize even full government revenue from their tenants though they had to pay no (or only half of the) government-approved rate. In Darrang, the Darrang-Raj estate charged rent at the government-approved rate but collected an extra 3 annas as the local rate. Its tenants also paid a *pujabhar* consisting of rice, goat and pigeon.[41] The estate further charged

> a pujabhar consisting of rice, goat or pigeon has [*sic*] to be supplied by the tenants according to the means. Those who cannot pay the full quota of the pujabhar have [*sic*] to render personal service for about a week.[42]

Rendering services like making the roof of thatched houses was not uncommon for tenants.[43] As in other estates, in Darrang-Raj estate too, the new tenants paid salami or mukhchowni to retain the land at least for the next cultivating season. In the 1880s, Extra Assistant Commissioner Fatik Chandra Baruah, investigating the working of these estates, noticed the woeful life of the tenants which compelled him to think that 'whatever may be law of land a *la-* or *nisf-khirajdar* is a little lord over his own holding'.[44]

The appropriation of economic surplus by landlords was not the only contributor to the tenants' pitiable condition of being under continuous burden of exactions. The social hegemony of landlords was another addition to their woes. In Sibsagar and Lakhimpur districts, the majority of tenants in the nisf-khiraj and la-khiraj estates were of tribal origin who did not subscribe to caste rituals. The Vaishnava satras from amongst the la- or nisf-khiraj estates played a crucial role in the 'Hinduization' of their tribal tenants.[45] Hinduization led to the assertion of socio-cultural superiority by the Hindu la- or nisf-khirajdars over the latter as well as to the latter's compulsion to render various unpaid services. Such practices, often involving both consent and resistance, were widely reported in the Assamese press.[46]

Sharecropping in Raiyatwari

What led to the widespread prevalence and intensification of sharecropping in the raiyatwari areas of Assam? And how did this practice of sharecropping, within a short period of time, become an integral element of the valley's agrarian economy? To understand these developments better, we need to go back to the nineteenth century when the absentee landownership was rapidly developing in the raiyatwari districts.[47] A careful examination of the practice of raiyatwari principles in Assam will partially answer some of these questions. First, the new property relationship in land, as manifest in the creation of the raiyatwari system, created space for the growth of sharecropping. Secondly, the rush for land-reclamation by growing numbers of Assamese absentee landlords contributed to the growth of a class of sharecroppers.

By the last decade of the nineteenth century, the Assam revenue department had been desperately trying to expand the acreage.[48] The only way to achieve this was to rely on a class of landlords who would be motivated to gain from the expansion of cultivation. This meant that the Assam administration needed to encourage the proliferation of absentee landlordism within a raiyatwari framework. The absence of a class of agricultural labourers had become a stumbling block to fulfil this desire of the revenue managers. An alternative could, then, be the promotion of sharecropping. Official encouragement of sharecropping was solicited by a section of the growing Assamese middle class. This also ensured a major departure from the initial advocacy of strict adherence to the principles of raiyatwari system, as was echoed by many such as Anandaram Dhekial Phukan (1829–59), the foremost amongst the nineteenth-century Assamese intelligentsia. For instance, in 1898, the powerful Jorhat Sarvajanik Sabha (JSS) — a leading proponent of the cause of the Assamese, middle class formed in line with similar pan-Indian bodies — while advocating the practice of sharecropping in khiraj land, claimed that the 'middleman is not only politically important, but also necessary for the extension of cultivation'.[49] The Sabha was not alone in making this claim. Various other bodies representing the interests of Assamese middle class strongly argued for the official encouragement of sharecropping.[50] An emerging Assamese middle class, mostly consisting of bureaucrats, pleaders, traders, and other professionals, began to accumulate wasteland grants from the last decade of the nineteenth century.[51] The Famine Enquiry Commission of 1888 reported how the *mauzadars* found tenancy as a convenient way of getting their newly acquired lands cultivated.[52] This emerging phenomenon of absentee landownership and sharecropping went hand in hand and acquired bigger dimensions in the early twentieth century.[53] These absentee landowners defended the practice of sharecropping as a means of augmenting their income. For instance, Nabin Chandra Bordoloi, a prominent Congress leader and also an upcoming tea planter, while discussing the condition of the Assamese clerks in tea gardens in an influential debate in the Assam Legislative Council, argued that 'the terrible question before everybody is [was] how to eke out one's existence and how to earn a decent living . . . A job in a tea garden or [the job of] a clerk in a government office would not satisfy everyone now while higher posts were not plentiful either'.[54] And, by the early twentieth century, the Assam administration came to accept the practice of sharecropping as an inevitable phenomenon. Though the twentieth century inherited the various forms of tenancy from the nineteenth century, the new century witnessed the development of many new features in the system as well as inclusion of new areas under sharecropping. As mentioned earlier, from the first decade of the twentieth century, the practices of adhi came to be noticed in several new places. These practices were more complex than they appeared to be.

It was against this background that the need for silent official encouragement to sharecropping as a crucial means for expanding the acreage began to be increasingly felt. Protracted official debates granted official legitimacy to sharecropping as an important means of transforming the agrarian situation of Assam. Officials in the Assam revenue administration was convinced about the need to encourage the practice of sharecropping as a means of urgently addressing the problem of a stagnant peasant economy. Asserting this position, Henry Cotton, Chief Commissioner of Assam, claimed in 1898 that

> in discussing any scheme of colonisation, the raiyatwari tenure, which obtains in all the temporarily-settled portions of Assam, should be

adhered to, and the colonists settled as cultivators immediately under Government without the intrusion of a middlemen, and I have no hesitation in expressing my opinion that a raiyatwari settlement is impossible.[55]

Sharecropping as Choice

An increase in rural population invariably did not lead to rapid land fragmentation in Assam. Also, compared to the population growth in the first half of the twentieth century, increase in the acreage remained low. The previous century also witnessed some of the worst mortality rates. The worst affected areas were the districts of Nowgaon, Darrang and Sibsagar; population in Darrang alone decreased by one-fifth between 1891 and 1901. The sudden fall in mortality rate, mainly due to the disappearance of epidemics from the second decade of the twentieth century, played a considerable role in increasing a population dependent on agriculture.[56] Between 1901 and 1941, the raiyatwari-settled districts of Assam registered an approximate increase of 46 per cent in the total population.[57] This rise was not merely a proof of healthy birth rate, but also the effect of immigration of peasants to the western districts of Assam and of labour force into the tea gardens. Compared to this, the expansion of acreage in the khiraj land was estimated to be only 41 per cent between 1901 and 1941.[58] This mismatch between population growth and expansion of acreage increased the possibilities of land fragmentation, mutation of landholdings and growth in the population density of villages. Fragmentation of landholdings became a matter of concern for the peasant families. Peasants' petitions repeatedly cited extensive mutation in their holdings. These petitions claimed that it was common for the peasant families to be left with only 2–3 *bighas* of land in their possession as against their original share of 8–9 bighas.[59] Exercising the easiest option of escaping from this misfortune, many became sharecroppers through negotiation with the rich peasants of the village or worked as agricultural labourers.

The colonial officials frequently alleged that in the caste-Hindu-dominated Assamese villages, the peasants would rather prefer holding on to highly mutated paternal lands to reclaiming land in distant areas. Typically, officials lamented that an Assamese peasant 'would probably get government wasteland if he went a little further but to save himself trouble, he preferred land in the village'.[60] But is this what really happened? Contrary to such claims, there is evidence of peasants reclaiming land in distant places. Popularly known as pam cultivation, mostly in *char* or *chapari* areas with large holdings, such reclamation and cultivation of distant lands had a crucial significance in the agrarian economy of Assam. Not widely practised, such agrarian activity was also often limited to the cultivation of winter crops.[61] The rich peasants undertook such farming mostly to augment their surplus income. The poor peasants, however, could not afford to do so.

To a great extent, the religious ties between the landlord (i.e., temples and satras) and the tenants restricted the latter's mobility. This patron–client relationship between land-owning religious establishments and their tenants often gave a feeling of social and cultural security to the latter against all odds. Some tenants preferred security in bondage to freedom with insecurity. For example, the tenant-peasants or *bhakats* staying in the close vicinity of Barpeta satra did not move out of the satra-owned lands despite the presence of fallow land in the neighbourhood.[62] Similarly crucial were the characteristics of a caste-Hindu Assamese peasant village.[63] The religious and kinship ties and the caste-centric hierarchical social organization forced the Assamese peasants to continue staying and working in their densely populated villages. The prevalence of the saying, *bheti erile man jai* ('one loses one's social identity if one moves away from the traditional home'), is indicative of this phenomenon of sentimental attachment of peasants to their villages.

If some hard-hit peasant did not move out, it was also due to certain other factors that were mostly beyond his physical or financial ability to cope with. One such crucial factor was ecological, viz., the topography of uncultivated tracts. These tracts were densely overgrown with shrubs, tall grasses and trees and even traversed by wild animals. The Assamese peasants did not have the tools to clear this dense overgrowth. Fire played only a marginal role in clearing it and preparing the tracts for shifting cultivation. Apart from technological constraints, in the early twentieth century, Assamese peasants had to face the combined onslaught of recurring floods, and depredations of wild animals and pests. Attacks of locusts were widespread throughout the nineteenth century and in the early decades of the twentieth century.[64] An earthquake of 1897, measuring 8.7 on Richter scale, followed by another one in 1950, substantially redefined the course of Brahmaputra, particularly in eastern Assam, and thereby submerged large patches of cultivated land[65] which were thus rendered inaccessible to peasants and hence unusable for cultivation. Similarly, all the districts were faced with the threats of ravages by wild animals which hampered the healthy growth of crops by damaging them. Not only that, their presence also impeded the process of land reclamation. One report describes how in Sibsagar district, newly reclaimed fields were always surrounded by jungles inhabited by rhinoceroses and tigers which preyed on crops and cattle respectively.[66] Another report recounts how wild elephants attacked the paddy fields close to the forests of Darrang for more than 5,000 times within a period of four months![67] The peasants did not have any means to counter all these threats.

One of the most puzzling questions that haunted the colonial revenue officials was: why in spite of 'land abundance', sharecropping or tenancy was so widely practised in Assam? As discussed earlier, this argument of land abundance was not true. In fact, there was not much land available for cultivation. The colonial government's emphatic argument that the Assamese landowner often rented out land not because of any economic compulsion but as a means to extract more earning, might be closer to the truth. Often, sudden unavailability of wage labour forced medium landowners to rent out lands, mostly on a temporary and informal basis. This was done with the hope that when labour became available for hire again, the landowner would do away with sharecropping. However in some cases, like that of a widow being a landowner, sharecropping would acquire a permanent form. The Brahmin landowners, socially prohibited from holding the plough, also rented out land on a more or less permanent basis.[68]

Migrant Labourers Become Sharecroppers

Two interrelated but distinct phenomena not only contributed to the quantitative growth of sharecropping, but also significantly, and quickly, transformed the nature of agrarian relations. An immediate factor, and a welcome relief for the Assamese landlords, was the availability of former tea garden labourers, whose contracts with the tea planters had just been over, for farm work.[69] When their contracts came to an end, the majority did not return to their ancestral villages. Further, they did not possess enough resources to sustain themselves and had to seek alternative avenues of livelihood such as sharecropping, since they already had some experience of renting some portions of garden land to produce food crops for sustenance. The tea planters also used to encourage this practice of sharecropping so as to overcome occasional food grain crises.

By the end of the nineteenth century, the practice acquired greater currency. Both tea planters and Assamese landowners began to rent out their lands to these labourers whose contracts for work in tea gardens had expired.[70] Consequently, not only could the landowner ensure that his newly acquired land was cultivated, but he also found that the profits were considerable, as the rent rate was sometimes as much as three times higher than the government-approved rate. For example, this practice was typically prevalent in the Kathiatali and Sahari mauzas of Nowgaon district where tea garden clerks, contractors and petty government officials, or absentee landlords rented out land to derive an additional income.[71] This system of leasing land was quite commonplace in certain other places in eastern Assam such as Dibrugarh which was surrounded by a number of tea gardens with a heavy presence of labourers. It was in these places that 'the well-to-do inhabitants had made it a practice of taking up *rupit* land and sublet to labourers'.[72] Similarly, the districts of Darrang, Sibsagar and Lakhimpur with a predominance of tea gardens had a considerable number of sharecroppers. Table 1.3 gives a broad idea of the numbers of tea garden labourers working as sharecroppers.

The second crucial factor for the growth of sharecropping was the migration of Muslim peasants from East Bengal. A couple of decades after their arrival and their subsequent occupation of land in Assam, they began to accumulate more land. Often, they would buy land from their Assamese land-owning neighbours, both caste-Hindu and tribal.[73] Years of good harvest would fetch them profits which they would use to buy more land. Though they bought only small pieces of land, often, there were instances of their buying more than 500 bighas of land. In one case, a Hindu migrant peasant bought an entire village in Nowgaon. Obviously, it

Table 1.3: Number of Former Tea Garden Labour Tenants

District	*1925–26*	*1930–31*	*1935–36*	*1939–40*	*1942–43*	*1945–46*
Kamrup	811	909	513	371	370	370
Darrang	7,432	7,379	13,200	13,379	10,296	5,609
Nowgaon	508	318	71	276	276	286
Sibsagar	6,940	6,185	5,130	5,839	4,431	5,038
Lakhimpur	3,933	4,143	6,943	6,818	7,462	7,901

Source: Prepared from *Annual Report on the Land Revenue Administration of Assam* of the respective years.

was difficult to bring these lands under cultivation without engaging labourers. As only a few amongst the migrant peasants could buy a lot of land, this led rapidly to some stratification among the migrant peasants. These nouveau riche peasants known as *matabar*s not only exercised hegemonic authority over their fellow poor peasants, but also employed seasonal labourers to cultivate their lands. The seasonal agricultural labourers known as *kamla*s came from East Bengal during the sowing and harvesting period.[74] While most returned to their ancestral villages in East Bengal after the sowing or harvesting season was over,[75] some stayed back permanently. With limited resources such as a pair of bullocks and a plough, they could afford to rent in land from the matabars.[76] Over the years, their number began to swell and this numerical strength brought them a new social identity. New words, viz., *wala* in Nowgaon or *utuli* in Kamrup, were coined to signify their class status.[77] A conservative estimate in 1931 suggests that at least one-third of the migrant peasant population could be identified as labourers or sharecroppers.[78] The practice of sharecropping acquired a new dimension when a new stratum within the peasant society, without any significant tenurial rights, became sharecroppers within the raiyatwari system. This was more or less the case in places like Nowgaon, Tezpur, Mangaldai, and Barpeta.

In the second quarter of the twentieth century, renting out to the migrant peasants had become a preferred practice of the Assamese landlords, mostly in Kamrup, Darrang and Nowgaon districts.[79] The migrant Muslim East Bengali adhiars were ready to pay more rent than what an Assamese adhiar would be willing to pay.[80] A typical case was that of Nowgaon where sharecropping was practised mostly on an annual lease, on land that was less than 3 per cent of the total khiraj land. The migration of East

Bengali peasants changed the entire situation. In the first two decades of the twentieth century, it was not difficult to find repeated claims suggesting that 'there is tendency in the Assamese living in or near the immigrant area to sublet the surplus land to the immigrants on adhi term ... the more prevalent practice is both for the well-to-do Assamese and immigrants to employ servants on their lands'.[81] In the next few decades, it became customary for the rich Assamese peasant to engage either wage labourers or adhiars from East Bengal.[82] The practice became so commonplace that the Line Inquiry Committee thought that the migrant peasant was as 'welcome as serfs to Assamese middle class but was to be debarred from acquiring independent status'.[83] The entry of migrant peasants into such a relationship with Assamese landlords signalled a crucial departure in the regional agrarian economy.

The reclamation of land by East Bengali peasants' had put an effective end to rapid fluctuations in the total area under cultivation in the central and western parts of the valley.[84] These fluctuations in acreage, termed by the revenue officials as 'relinquishment', was a matter of serious worry for the British revenue officials as they considered it a threat to revenue collection.[85] Moreover, the landowners' expectation of high rents from the migrant adhiars would lead to increasing conflicts between the migrant and Assamese adhiars.

The combined presence of former tea garden labourers and migrant peasants thus helped create a moderate hope for the Assamese landlords to augment their income from land. However, given the landowners' previous experience with purchases of land at speculative prices, it was not likely that their hopes of making profit would be easily fulfilled. Land speculation was not entirely new to the valley.[86] At the same time, more land came under sharecropping. This happened mostly when the Assamese absentee landlords in their eagerness to rent out land to this new class of migrant peasants accumulated surplus lands.[87] They not only acquired wasteland leases but often manipulated existing legal provisions to buttress their claims to more land. The entry of migrant peasants further expanded the scope for land speculation. The migrants would estimate the price of land on the basis of the gross value of crops in an agrarian cycle, and be ready to pay rent rates higher than what their Assamese counterparts would.[88] The phenomenon acquired such massive proportions that a worried revenue official even demanded imposition of legal restrictions on land purchase and transfer to counter such malpractices.[89] Alongside land speculation, the incidents of tribal peasants selling their annual *patta* lands were widely reported.[90] Once they were sold, the tribal peasant would reclaim another piece of wasteland and claim tenurial and legal security of its possession. However, he would then sell it to land-seeking migrant peasants, and the process of transfer of lands from one person to another would go on.[91] From the second quarter of the twentieth century, the colonial government initiated land resettlement schemes which turned out to be a boon for land speculators. They easily manipulated the legal category of landless peasants to acquire more land leases.[92] This partly explains the growth of a class of Assamese absentee landlords.[93] For an early-twentieth-century Assamese absentee landlord, profit from sharecropping arrangement was lucrative, as it required a nominal investment of capital and was also devoid of various other kinds of investment needed for agricultural production.

Tenancy in Rent-free Estates

The rent-free estate owners known as nisf-khirajdars and la-khirajdars, free from the raiyatwari revenue obligations, weilded more social and economic influence than did the rich peasants. When these estates were constituted or retained with their pre-colonial features, tenancy practices were found to be widely prevalent.[94] Large bodies of tenants were found mostly in compact blocks in these estates. For example, in 1883, two landed estates in Kamrup, one held by a Brahman preceptor and another by a temple, accounted between them for no less than a thousand tenants. By 1880, almost all such tenants were found to be paying cash rent supplemented by token service and payments in kind or rent in kind (i.e., agricultural produce) only to a marginal extent, and that too only in the case of rupit lands in densely located tracts where such lands were available. The landlords, as religious heads, exercised enormous social authority over their tenants. Attention has already been drawn to the existence of a patron–client relationship between the two.[95] These estates were under a natural obligation to take recourse to tenancy. The tenants were generally known as *paiks* or bhakats, symbolizing an enduring socio-economic relationship with the landlords. The estate owners' choice for employing wage labour to cultivate their lands had limitations. This was mainly because of the unavailability of wage labour and the presence of a large number of tenants who had strong religious ties with the landlords. Thus, these estates had no other choice but to fully resort to sharecropping, a situation similar to that in the khiraj lands.

Of the total number of such estates in the raiyatwari-settled areas, the three districts of Kamrup, Darrang and Sibsagar had the largest share. In 1951, there were 134 la-khiraj estates, with an average of 895 acres per estate, of which the district of Kamrup alone had 38 estates accounting for 34,060 acres. The average size of an estate in Kamrup, which was 603 acres, was higher than that in other districts.[96] Also, both Kamrup and Darrang had a high concentration of nisf-khiraj lands totalling 146,332 and 29,068 acres respectively. For instance, in a classic example of landlordism, the Darrang-Raj family had 19 nisf-khiraj estates amounting to 53,836 bighas. In Kamrup, 'subletting was common among the bigger estates. La-khiraj, nisf-khiraj and special estates are almost entirely cultivated by tenants'.[97] The percentage of subletting in these two kinds of estates was quite high in Kamrup, i.e., 59 and 68 per cent for nisf-khiraj and la-khiraj estates respectively during the resettlement of 1928. Another official account claimed that in Darrang the 'larger *nisf-khirajdar*[s] sublet their land to tenants. Most of these tenants have been in occupation of their holdings for generations and are seldom disturbed in their possession … subletting was practised by the holders of khiraj lands'.[98] Though the other districts' share of nisf-khiraj land was marginal, the practice of tenancy there did not differ from that in Kamrup and Darrang.[99] For instance, in Nowgaon, out of the 8,074 and 4,853 bighas of nisf-khiraj and la-khiraj lands respectively, 52.55 and 68.91 per cent of land were rented out.[100]

In most cases, la-khiraj and nisf-khiraj estates were composed of good cultivable lands, usually identified as rupit or *basti.*[101] A nisf-khirajdar or la-khirajdar was generally a manager of a temple, a *doloi* or a g*ossain* or might even be a paik performing special duties in the temple. Being forbidden by religious and cultural customs, they never took to actual cultivation. Tenancy thus became an integral feature of these estates. Tenants even occupied lands for several generations.[102] Only in a few cases did the tenants assert their occupancy claims. The maximum incidences of tenancy were found in such estates. The accumulation of wealth was also relatively higher in these estates, as they did not have to pay any revenue or paid only half of the rent that was collected.

In the first few decades of the twentieth century, a complex situation emerged in the rent-free estates. As the nisf-khiraj and la-khiraj estates frequently failed to pay revenue to the government, they were auctioned out. Such auctions were reported from the last quarter of the nineteenth century,[103] but as they became more frequent, they were widely advertised both in *The Assam Gazette* and the Assamese-language newspapers from 1935.[104] These auctioned estates normally comprised large areas. An instance of such a case was reported in 1935 when an estate of 887 bighas in Kamrup was sold out to Marwari traders.[105] In another instance, a nisf-khiraj estate with an area of 831 bighas belonging to a locally influential Ratnewsar Deva Adhikari Mahanta in Nowgaon was auctioned off.[106] Owned earlier by a single landlord, the auctioned estate was sold to a number of absentee landowners leading to its fragmentation.[107] The estate, once auctioned to more than one absentee landlord, was further parcelled out to several absentee landlords, such third-party transfers leading to increasing fragmentation.[108] To get immediate returns from their new investments, these landlords demanded high rent from their tenants. Failure to pay the rent usually resulted in the eviction of the existing tenants although this had been uncommon previously. As the situation deteriorated, in 1928, a settlement officer, admitting the tendency of these new nisf-khirajdars to acquire new tenants, made a scathing attack on such practices. He suggested that negotiations between the new landlords and tenants were rather vaguely based 'on the absence of law disregarding all consideration of custom, equity and good conscience'.[109] The tenants in nisf-khiraj estates who had been in occupation of the land for generations enjoyed the rights of occupancy tenants.[110] The government also believed that they might be regarded as occupants as far as their interest in the cultivation of the land was concerned. Some of the new landlords, however, rented out land to the immigrant peasants.[111] This first began in the char areas of Barpeta, but the other districts soon followed the example. The nisf-khiraj estates of Darrang-Raj family were rented out to Hindu immigrant tenants. These tenants paid full rent and rendered all kinds of other extra-economic services.[112]

The earlier discussion highlights how the raiyatwari system, as it came to be implemented in Assam, fuelled the growth of sharecropping. The retention of landed estates in the form of la-khiraj and nisf-khiraj not only thwarted the successful implementation of the raiyatwari system, but also actively encouraged tenancy. Similarly, after years of experience, the government realized that raiyatwari had failed to invest enough capital that would change the scenario of agrarian production in the province. This compelled the government to rethink the entire regime of natural resource management of the province.

The proliferation of sharecropping as a means of changing the prospects of agrarian production received official encouragement. This was similar to the creation of a landed class of the zamindars in the neighbouring province of Bengal. Yet, the hardest hit were the peasants of Kamrup and Darrang. A high population density had already lowered the land–people ratio to a point of no return. The peasants from East Bengal had settled down in these districts, restricting the local peasants' access to wastelands and other resources. The population growth in Assam between 1901 and 1951, most noticeably in the western districts of the valley and largely due to the influx of both migrant peasants and former tea garden labourers, has been estimated at 138 percent.[113] An official estimate in 1921 put the figure of peasants who migrated to the valley at roughly one million.[114] In the aftermath of this new demographic boom, soon, sharecropping and usury emerged as serious threats to the agrarian economy. Sharecropping was portrayed as an instrument of development at the hands of the absentee landowner, but it turned into a mechanism of socio-economic exploitation. A political movement in the middle of the twentieth century tried to address these issues, though with limited success.

Migrations, Land Reclamation and Production of Jute

In the early twentieth century, the riverine areas of western Assam were exposed to a phase of rapid land reclamation. This, in turn, had effects on jute cultivation and factory production of jute

Map 1.1: Raiyatwari Districts of Brahmaputra Valley

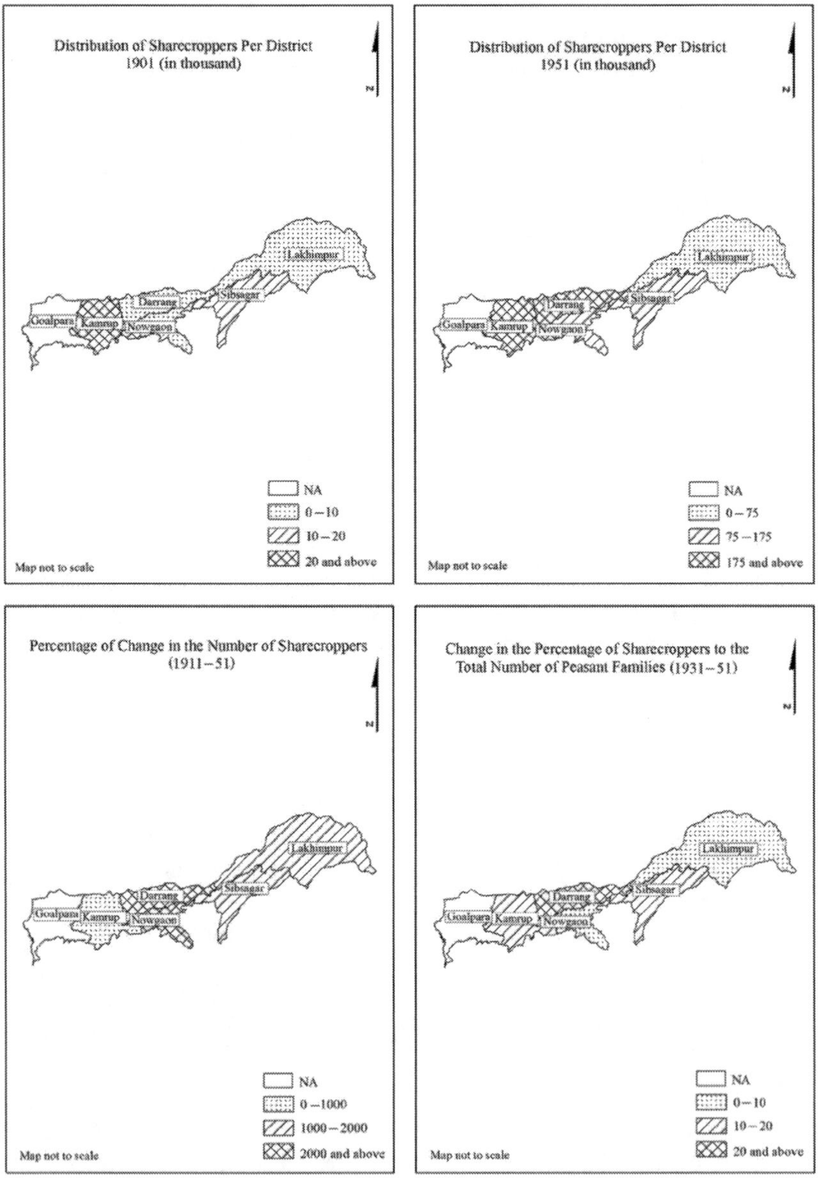

(Map 1.1 *contd.*)

Raiyatwari Districts of Brahmaputra Valley

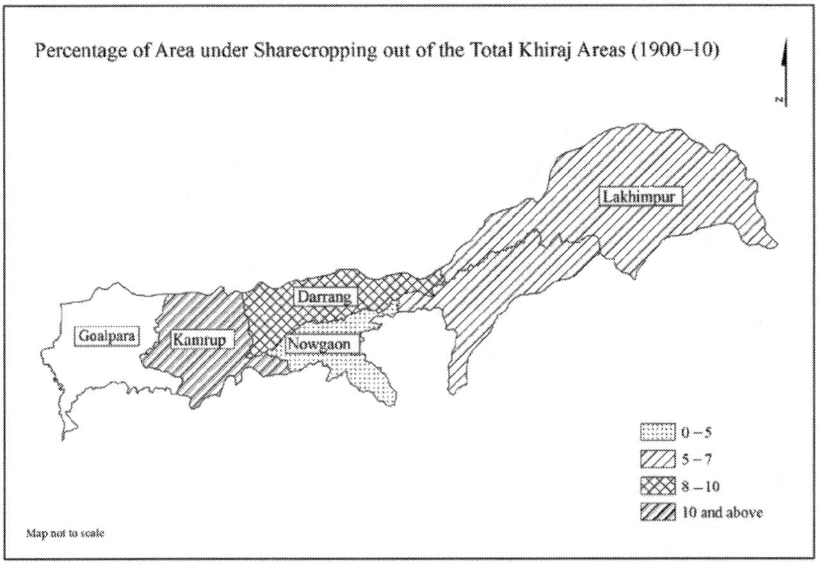

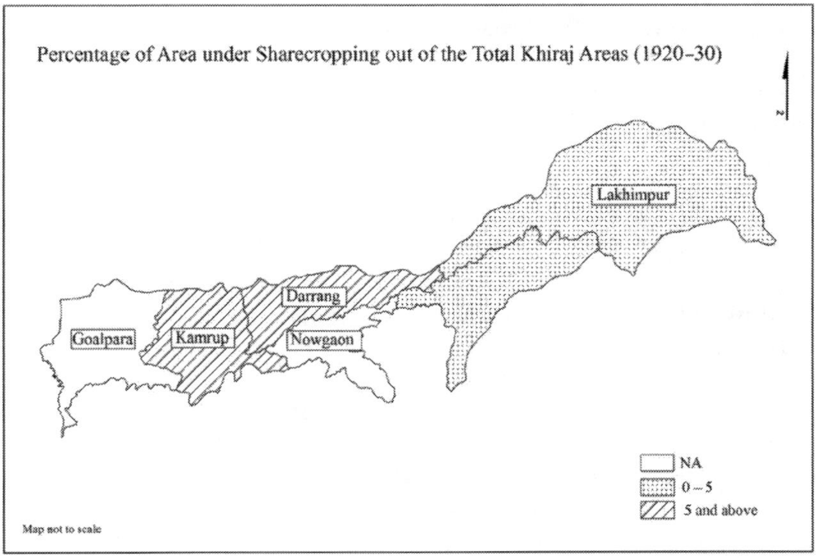

products in Bengal.[115] Between 1897–98 and 1919–20, export of raw jute increased by more than three times from that part of the country.[116] Arguably, jute turned out to be the highest export revenue earner for India in the early twentieth century. This had a crucial role in ensuring the British government's favourable balance of trade vis-à-vis the US or Germany.[117] Jute cultivation was, by the 1870s, deep rooted in Bengal. Demand for raw jute was increasing regularly as Bengal then had a highly organized jute industry. The British jute industrialists in Bengal were encouraged to look for more land to grow the golden fibre, as land in Bengal was exhausting its potential to support more jute cultivation by that time.[118] They looked to the riverine areas of western Assam as new areas of jute production. Many became convinced that the riverine tracts in the valley, mostly consisting of savannah, similar to those in Bengal, would be best suited for jute cultivation. The texture of soil, rainfall pattern and availability of clear water in the alluvial tracts of the valley made them perfectly conducive to jute cultivation.

The actual transition towards large-scale cultivation of jute was preceded by a long governmental enquiry and some localized experiments in jute cultivation. By the end of the nineteenth century, the Assam administration became confident that the riverine and char areas of Brahmaputra were suitable for jute cultivation. Such areas were located in Nowgaon, Lakhimpur, the eastern part of Darrang, the eastern *duars* of Goalpara, and the Barpeta subdivision of Kamrup.[119] Prior to this, jute had been grown in a limited acreage in Goalpara, and on a very limited scale in other districts and that too mostly for domestic consumption. In 1898, F.J. Monahan, Assistant Director of the Assam Land Records and Agriculture Department, in an exhaustive report on the possibility of jute production in Assam, agreed that as Assamese peasants would not expand their jute acreage, the peasants from the neighbouring East Bengal could be encouraged to reclaim some land from the western part of the valley.[120] He was supported by Henry Cotton, the newly appointed Chief Commissioner of Assam. Pressure was mounting from the Bengal Chamber of Commerce and jute industrialists to open up low-lying tracts in the western and central parts of the valley to jute cultivation.[121] By that time, not only 'intensive margins' of land use had been exhausted in East Bengal, but famines in the Bengal's countryside during 1896–97 had also forced people to emigrate from the densely populated tracts of East Bengal. The Government of India had already advocated that the valley needed 'the stout and fanatical Mohamedan of Eastern Bengal'[122] as the best choice to convert these areas into jute-producing fields. The importance of Bengali farmers as the future settlers in the valley continued to get official support. These farmers were 'hardy and prolific cultivators ... gradually working their way northwards. These people are accustomed to the risk arising from diluvion and devastating floods, which other cultivators are unwilling to face'.[123] Revenue officials in Assam had already noticed with concern the apathy of Assamese peasants towards jute cultivation. Decades before, in 1873, J. Sherer, Deputy Commissioner of Nowgaon, had also noticed this aversion.[124] Sherer had noted that whatever limited jute cultivation was carried out in the district, it was not at the expense of paddy cultivation. The officials, however, did not mention any lack of capital and trade incentives for the expansion of jute cultivation in these districts.

Then, how does one explain a lack of interest for jute cultivation in Assam in the nineteenth century? This can be explained if we look at how jute cultivation and fibre production required, apart from the land, a certain kind of labour, which was not very easy to get. Jute was a labour- and capital-intensive crop. The production of fibre also required access to clear water bodies. While labour was scarce, the Assamese peasants did not learn the delicate methods which were essential for removing the fibre from the dead woods. The alternative way was to bring peasants from the delta of East Bengal. These farmers had already accumulated several decades of experience in jute cultivation. A long history of intense clashes between the Muslim tenants and their Hindu landlords in East Bengal would also make the former open to the new possibility of migrating to uplands in search of arable land.[125] Also, the valley largely shared a similar ecology with its contiguous neighbour — north-east Bengal — from where most future migration would take place. Linguistic–ethnic similarities, the idea of the Brahmaputra as an ecological common, ecological crisis in the East Bengal villages, and a shared history of economic exchanges across this micro-region also became crucial in inducing migration. Riverine and railway routes made travel comparatively easier. Unlike the immigration of workers into the tea plantations, this immigration did not require creation of any massive state infrastructure. At the most, it would require a few days of walk upland across rivers and wetlands to reach the western districts of Assam. To boost their earning, the zamindars in Goalpara had already inducted some of these peasants as tenants to begin jute cultivation in the chars. This early and limited venture did not demoralize anybody.

And, during the 1910s and 1920s, large patches of lands, including uncultivated low-lying riverine areas, un-classed state forests[126] and later grazing reserves were reclaimed by the migrant peasants[127] who quickly brought these areas under jute cultivation. The magnitude of this expansion can be understood from the fact that acreage under jute cultivation quickly increased in Assam – from 38,568 acres in 1904 to 137,337 acres in 1920.[128] Area under jute cultivation increased mostly in Nowgaon and Kamrup districts but not in Goalpara. In 1933, the area under jute cultivation reached an all-time high of approximately 303,000 acres. This was almost a 45 per cent increase from 1920. The jute prices had begun to fall since then, and it continued to decline under the adverse impact of the Great Depression on the jute market.[129] After the Great Depression, the expansion became slow and achieved a marginal growth only to reach the figure of 382,917 acres in 1950. Rapid expansion of acreage was also associated with increasing incidence of usury and land speculation. The pace of rice production did not match that of population growth. The area under rice cultivation remained almost static,[130] thereby substantially contri-buting to the increase in food prices after 1930, which has already been discussed in another section.[131] Assam's agrarian economy took a decisive turn and came to have an enduring impact on the regional polity.

Through this rapid land reclamation through massive state inducement, not only was Assam's agrarian economy quickly commercialized and firmly integrated with the colonial economy, but this also reduced resources available to Assamese peasants. Land reclamation and subsequent expansion of area under jute cultivation resulted in localized clashes between migrant and Assamese peasants. Political negotiation ensued and in 1928, the government not only re-affirmed its faith in further reclamation of riverine areas, but also provided more institutional support. A railway network along the north bank of Brahmaputra was put in place to connect the jute-producing areas with Bengal.[132] A new scheme of land settlement, officially described as the Colonization

Programme was adopted in 1928 to boost further migration. The scheme was initially introduced in Nowgaon.[133] In 1929, it was further extended to the professional grazing reserves, i.e., areas of Barpeta and Mangaldai districts, reserved initially for cattle breeding. The government sanctioned a scheme of land settlement, whereby the new settlers would pay the same revenue as the pre-existing peasants did, on payment of a premium of Rs 25 per bigha in three instalments. Most of the migrant peasant families were given land ranging in area from a minimum of 6 bighas up to a maximum of 20 bighas. Various welfare mechanisms were instituted to induce the peasants from East Bengal to settle without any hindrance. Muslim officers were appointed to the post of Colonization Officer who was responsible for opening up new reserves for settlement.[134] With the introduction of the land settlement scheme, a large number of petitions seeking land grants virtually 'poured in' from the East Bengali peasants.[135] A total of 47,636 acres of land were settled by the colonists (both Muslim and Hindu) in Nowgaon during the period 1928–31.[136] Amongst the migrants, Muslim peasants formed the majority. The pace of the arrival of peasants was so fast that even various local boards failed to keep pace with the demands of infrastructural development.[137] But the situation took a different turn as the Great Depression set in. Jute prices fell drastically, and consequently the pace of the arrival of East Bengali peasants began to slow down. The migrant peasants too began to shift to paddy cultivation as jute prices fell. This also meant that they had to look for newer areas suitable for paddy cultivation unlike their customary preference for low-lying lands suitable for jute cultivation. This immediately resulted in their clashes with paddy-producing Assamese peasants. Also, those who had already immigrated to Assam were not better either. Many failed to pay their revenue, and the government adopted coercive measures to realize it. But when crop failure and bad market ensured no profit to the jute producers, often the government was forced to suspend the collection of revenue.[138] The Assam Revenue Department earned an amount of Rs 443,717 as the premium received from the sale of land during the period 1928–35.[139] Migrant peasants needed initial investable capital for the cultivation of uncultivable land. Credit market, therefore, expanded. Credit required for jute cultivation was supplied by

Calcutta-based managing agencies through networks of Marwari and Assamese traders. Among the creditors, Marwari merchants, who would soon control the supply of raw jute to industries in Bengal, loaned money more readily than the Assamese traders-cum-moneylenders.[140] But it would be incorrect, however, to infer that the Marwari traders were the only source of credit as will be seen from the following discussion. These traders also diverted their investment from mustard seed cultivation to jute production in the districts of eastern Assam.

Rural Credit and Peasant Pauperization

In the first half of the twentieth century, as in the contemporary peasant economy of the rest of the country,[141] indebtedness was not only integral to the peasant economy of Assam, but also, not surprisingly, had worsened since the previous century.[142] The peasants treated moneylenders with bitterness and distaste. The latter were known as *mahajans* and often peasants called them *petua mahajan*, meaning an awfully bad-looking and distasteful man.[143] The importance of usury never became marginal even after independence though a credit market operating within the banking sector became a good alternative. The moneylenders lacked organized networks to operate in the countryside. They derived social legitimacy for their profession through various social customs.

Statistically, usury, practised on a smaller scale, became manifest in course of population census conducted in the late nineteenth century.[144] The Census of 1881 registered the number of people earning their livelihood from usury as 2,414, while the next round of Census in 1891 registered a lower figure of 1,791. The Census of 1901 enumerated a total of 2,935 moneylenders from various social backgrounds. The actual number could have been more, since as many as 164 peasant families practising usury were shown as practising the same only as a secondary profession.[145] Besides, there were 4,472 shopkeepers who also lent money. The highest concentration of moneylenders was in the district of Kamrup with 76 families being professional moneylenders.[146] One single woman earned her livelihood as a professional moneylender, as the Census of 1901 noted. The professional moneylenders kept servants or agents (*piadas*) to help recover the loan. In the Census of 1911, the total number of moneylenders was estimated at 2,151, which again increased to 4,722 in the Census of 1921. This increase was because of the arrival of Muslim moneylenders from East Bengal who mainly operated amongst the migrant East Bengali peasants. We do not have statistical data about moneylenders after 1931, as subsequent censuses ceased to take note of usury and usurers. Interestingly, as we will discuss in Chapter 4, 1920s and 1930s was the time when the subject of usury was widely discussed in the Assam Legislative Assembly.

There is no doubt that the actual figures would have been more than what was estimated, as 'there [were] disguised moneylenders in the villages'.[147] Transactions were made on 'good faith' and mostly without any documentation. Official records like debt litigation records, in fact, indicate that rich peasants often lent money whenever a fellow villager, ordinarily a poor peasant, asked for some in times of need. The transactions were one-sided: the terms and conditions were mostly dictated by the rich peasants-cum-moneylenders. It was often the case that an illiterate peasant was asked to put his fingerprint on a blank paper as evidence of the transaction. The blank paper with a fingerprint, retained by the moneylender, would be used by him as a 'document' in the civil court to defend his case, when the peasant failed to return his loan within the stipulated period. The moneylender, with the help of his servant, often manipulated the blank 'document', fixing the interest without the consent of the borrower.

Despite the apparently low figures of the incidence of moneylending in official census reports, its understandable severity became apparent in the 1920s, when the Assam government came out with a detailed and elaborate report on the practices of moneylenders in the province.[148] The Provincial Banking Enquiry Committee Report (hereafter, Banking Report), as it was known, in the third decade of the twentieth century, drew a graphic picture of the problem of peasant indebtedness in Assam. The impact of moneylending on the peasant economy is further affirmed by the fact that The Assam Moneylenders Act, forbidding moneylenders from imposing a higher interest rate, was tabled and passed in the Assam Legislative Assembly in 1934 without any rigorous opposition.[149]

The Banking Report estimated the debt burden of the entire province at Rs 220 million, a figure 20 times higher than the annual land revenue earnings of the province. To cite an example of the acuteness of indebtedness, an estimated 81.5 and 78 per cent of all peasant families had a debt burden of an average of Rs 229 and Rs 235 in the two districts of Darrang and Nowgaon respectively.[150] There is no dearth of cases of an entire population of a village being in debt.[151] According to the Census of 1911, there were 685 moneylenders per 10,000 landowners and 153 moneylenders per 10,000 cultivators in Assam.[152] The interest rate varied from place to place and it was not unusual to find moneylenders charging very high interest rates, sometimes amounting to even 500 per cent of the principal. Most of the moneylenders who deposed before the Banking Enquiry Committee admitted to charging approximately 37 per cent of the principal amount as interest annually.[153] To compound the problem, there were other exactions as well. For example, in Kamrup peasants paid a sum known as *mukhchowani* apart from the interest. These moneylenders, mostly upper-caste men, would deduct a sum from the principal amount as a customary charge. Such charges were legitimized by religious sanction.[154] Assamese landowners also lent money to the immigrant peasants at a high rate of interest.[155] The interest rate charged was also highly variable, but in most cases the repayment of the principal was due after six months, i.e., after each crop season came to an end. The high rate of interest from which the moneylenders heavily profited reduced the immigrant peasants to extreme poverty. They charged interest at the rate of 37.5 per cent per month. The Bengali traders charged a monthly interest rate of two annas per rupee. The Marwari traders also advanced money to the East Bengali peasants at high rates of interest and made them hypothecate the crops.[156] Both in Darrang and Nowgaon districts, the East Bengali peasants borrowed money from Assamese mahajans or *farias* against a mortgage of either some personal security like ornaments or their crops.[157] They were charged a rate of interest depending on the market prices of agricultural produce.

Owing to the non-existence of a distinct professional moneylending class in the nineteenth century, the peasants mostly depended on rural traders-cum-rich peasants known as mahajans whose position were well entrenched by the legitimacy derived from various village customs.[158] A mahajan could either be a Brahmin priest, a well-to-do fellow villager, a Marwari merchant, or a local trader–moneylender who normally bought the agricultural produce of peasants. This custom is still prevalent in most districts of the valley. The trader-cum-moneylender provided *agdhan* — credit given against the security of produce of peasants. The role of the trader–moneylender, also known as *bepari*, was confined to select areas, where mostly mustard seed was grown. But in the twentieth century there were more people than in the nineteenth century who lent money and charged high rates of interest. Apart from the Marwari traders, a moneylender in the twentieth century could be even a well-to-do former tea-garden labourer, a villager vendor, a pleader clerk, or a *kabuli*[159] of Kamrup and Nowgaon.[160] It is, however, doubtful if there was any large-scale credit flow from the kabuli moneylenders to the Assamese agrarian economy. The kabulis simply supplemented the village mahajans or trader-cum-moneylenders in the peasant economy. Some kabulis even borrowed from Marwari traders and then lent it out at a higher rate of interest. The shopkeeper also sold his goods on credit in return for peasant produce at a low rate.[161] Others, mainly well-to-do cultivators, saved money and lent it out to needy peasants. In places like Barpeta, rich peasants and petty traders loaned money to the immigrant peasants who had settled in the char areas.[162]

The presence of Marwari mahajans was all pervading. In the first decade of the twentieth century, at least two Marwari shops were commonly found in almost all the mauzas of Nowgaon.[163] Describing a characteristic moneylender, the Famine Enquiry Commission noted in 1945 that the village moneylender was usually a Marwari trader who 'fills up blank in the rural economic system and cannot be easily challenged' in Assam. The Commission also admitted that he had too much say in what crop the cultivator would grow, and was the primary channel for the marketing of agricultural produce of the peasants. This invariably helped him retain his control over the peasant economy. His control was so deep rooted that 'he [could] retard the flow[of credit] to suit his benefit rather than that of the cultivators'.[164]

Moneylending was confined mostly to the informal sector. The absence of a distinct professional moneylending class in these districts, as pointed out before, facilitated the operation of informal credit market in a much safer way, as it was not necessary to prepare any legal document. Peasants thus could borrow either in cash or in kind, on 'good faith' or through a petty trader. Absence of any legal document became a boon for the moneylender but a bane for the peasant. But who were these moneylenders? The Banking Report claims:

> The main source from which the agriculturist derives his loans are the village mahajans, the buyer of the produce, co-operative societies and other creditors. Under the village mahajans we include the professional village moneylender other than a buyer of the purchase. In the Assam valley they would include occasional Assamese and Barpeta moneylenders, those village marwari[s] and telis who don't stipulated for the well to do ex-teagarden labour who lends out his savings. This class also includes the shopkeeper who sells goods on credit.[165]

In some cases, the creditor was often a fellow villager, but it was not clear whether he was charged a nominal rate of interest or higher rate. To quote the Famine Inquiry Commission again, in Assam 'the village moneylenders is [*sic*] usually a Marwari combining money lending with trade'.[166]

The presence of kabulis who did not have any source of livelihood other than moneylending in lesser number in Kamrup and Nowgaon, however, did not have any significant bearing on the peasant economy.[167] It is not clear whom these kabuli moneylenders usually dealt with, but many of them operated in towns like Rangia or Nowgaon. Probably, their operation was restricted to a limited population and never served to torment the peasants.

In Barpeta subdivision, it was found that the rich peasants and petty traders lent money to the immigrant peasants who were settling down in the char areas of the subdivision.[168] There were community funds known as the *hatis* for the peasants to borrow money from.[169] The total number of such hatis was found to be 22. Customary donations by petty traders were pooled to form the hatis. But, in most cases, these funds were meant for petty traders. It is not clear whether the peasants borrowed from these funds. When anyone borrowed from a hati, an interest of 12 per cent was charged by the hati.

Well-to-do peasants from all the raiyatwari districts of Assam saved money and lent it out to the fellow needy peasants.

Sometimes, villagers working as vendors, pleaders and clerks also lent money. There were moneylenders who might have been either traders or well-to-do cultivators, and who borrowed money from the Marwari and non-Marwari traders having interest in the peasant production and then lent it out at a higher rate of interest. Sometimes, a peasant would rent out his lands to another one who would take half of the total crop as his share and pay the land revenue.[170] The Assamese traders, due to their lack of larger trading and mercantile networks, remained a lesser player than their Marwari or Bengali counterparts. This also left them with limited resources at hand. Assamese traders who bought agricultural crops were mainly from places like Sualkuchi and Barpeta in the Kamrup district. They bought these crops mostly from the immigrant East Bengali peasants, former tea garden workers and Miri (a tribe) peasants from the districts of eastern Assam. These traders advanced credit to these producers and in turn pre-fixed the prices of crops. After harvesting, little profit was left for the producers, forcing them to fall back on their creditors to secure credit for the next sowing season as well. Thus this vicious cycle of indebtedness went on.

Why did the peasants borrow money? The colonial administrators held a unanimous view in this regard. Most of the officials were quick to suggest that the socio-cultural practices of the peasant society were more than responsible for the peasants' indebtedness. Kanaklal Barua, an Assamese official and also a prominent historian, in his testimony before the Royal Commission on Agriculture in India, brought out some of the principle factors behind the peasants' borrowing. These included: investment in various agricultural operations, viz., purchase of plough, cattle and agricultural implements; expenses on various social occasions like marriages and funeral ceremonies; purchase and improvement of land and dwelling houses; and clearance of family debts, land revenue or rent.[171] The Banking Report suggested that these causes were in addition to other causes such as crop failures due to seasonal floods and attacks by insects, pests and wild animals; cattle mortality; want of good seeds;[172] accumulation of old debts; agricultural unviability of land owing to the division and fragmentation of holdings; and litigation expenses on property disputes.[173] They were further convinced that consumption of opium, *ganja* (cannabis) and country liquor was also an important cause for borrowing, but were also quick to add that the opium-eaters found it difficult to borrow, as a 'confirmed opium eater who does little work would not receive much credit from the moneylender'.[174] The poor peasants pledged to have their dues paid off by their family members put in the service of moneylenders, thereby giving rise to an arrangement called *bandha* or bonded labour.[175] Colonial officials indicted the social practices of the tribal and tea garden labourers, which were instrumental for their being more prone to borrowing than the Assamese peasants.[176] Immigrant peasants also spent a good deal of borrowed money on wage labour during jute cultivation. They even borrowed money to buy land.[177]

But it was not always the poorest who were indebted. Wealthier peasants also borrowed money for the purpose of securing for themselves certain material conveniences. Those who were relatively better-off borrowed money on their personal security or against their property as collateral. It was rare that in the first case the peasant could return the money that he borrowed without causing much damage to his economic standing. Yet another significant cause of borrowing was the need for money to purchase manure, pay land revenue and hire wage labour. Peasants even borrowed from the mauzadar to pay off their revenue. There is also evidence of rich and enterprising landowners borrowing high sums of money for agricultural needs. However, there is no doubt that the consequences of their borrowing were less damaging. A typical example is that of Debeswar Deva Goswami borrowing money from Marwari moneylenders to cultivate sugarcane in more than 100 acres of land.[178] Gradually, with the establishment of various co-operative credit societies in the province, wealthy landowners came to replace the Marwari traders. In particular, the rich landlords reaped benefits from the establishment of such societies.[179]

However, these colonial narratives of peasant indebtedness ignore the intricacies of moneylending within the peasant economy. Though, in most cases, borrowing was done for unproductive non-agricultural purposes, it was also the peasant's poverty and his continuous failure to mitigate his sorry financial plight that naturally took him to the moneylender. While he did not profit from agriculture, he continued to reel under the heavy demand of cash revenue and rent. It was not that the peasants liked to borrow. In spite of the repeated portrayal of improving economic condition of a peasant family by the colonial officials, the reality was that agriculture on his small holding was never economically viable. The Assam government, in a 1921 survey of the budget of peasant families, admitted that peasant families having less than 20 bighas of cultivable land were in debt unless they were supported by non-farm income.[180] While the average productivity of soil also diminished, the cost of most of the basic necessities of life doubled and the value of land also went up four times compared to what it was 20 years before.[181] In the mid-twentieth century, the average holding per peasant family was less than 15 bighas and it was very likely that the average peasant family was prone to indebtedness.[182] In many instances, it was also extremely difficult for the peasant to get a loan against his annual patta land. The moneylenders refused to accept it as security and demanded exorbitant rates of interest. The peasants had no other way but to agree to such rates.[183]

It is important to understand the market mechanism that forced peasants into indebtedness in order to know the relationship between debt and peasant economy. Peasants were integrated within the market in a complicated way. Except in big towns like Guwahati or Dibrugarh where there were a few big trading houses, the trade in agricultural produce was mostly confined to brisk transactions in the weekly rural *haat*s, Marwari *gola*s and sometimes in the village shops. Ordinarily, the buyers were the village Marwari traders, telis and *johalas*.[184] The Marwari merchants established their shops even in remote corners of villages.[185] Official accounts narrate how in various parts of rural Assam, the Marwari petty traders procured agrarian produce from the village markets and exported it to certain key trading centres, mostly in and around Guwahati. Guwahati-based merchants, on the other hand, exported the collected produce either to eastern Assam or, in a limited quantity, to Shillong. Traders from Bengal, using riverine transport networks, collected peasant produce from Kamrup and Goalpara. Farias further reinforced these trade networks. Trading practices amongst the erstwhile tribal communities like the Garos, who would exchange various forest products such as lac, pan and other vegetables for formal agrarian products, also strengthened. Assamese traders who came from western Assam traded primarily in mustard.[186] They mostly bought mustard and paddy from the former tea garden labourers and Miri peasants of eastern Assam, and jute from the immigrant peasants. On the other hand, the Marwari traders and moneylenders too did their best to take every scrap of crop against their loan.[187] Most often, the Marwari traders entered into the peasant household economy by supplying yarn to women for use in their household weaving. The women used to purchase yarn on credit on the understanding that they would repay the loan after the harvesting season. Essentially, the numerous haats that afforded the peasants an easy means of disposing of their surplus produce, however, never gave them a high profit.[188]

The distance from the main trading centres, along with poor roads, which limited the mobility of peasants, ensured the continued presence of intermediaries between the peasants and the traders. Usually, the markets in Guwahati regulated their crop prices periodically. A distance of 10–12 miles meant a difference in price of 2–3 annas per *maund*.[189] However, the opening of the Eastern Bengal Railways in 1910 increased the importance of some of the existing trade centres on the north bank of Brahmaputra away from Guwahati. This brought relief to the peasants. Because of a close connection between feeder roads and railways, the prices in Calcutta had an impact on their trade. By the second decade of the twentieth century, nearly every railway station came to have a market. Rice and mustard oil mills were established in the new trading centres of the districts of western and central Assam. Such centres became the new markets for collection and export of peasant produce. This reoriented the economic forces operating in the rural areas of western and central Assam. As the seasonal and irregular waterways were regularized, by a faster and dependable railway service[190] these areas became closely tied to the outside market forces. Probably, this could have helped eliminate some of the middlemen to some extent.

Though improved communications reduced the gap between the peasant and the merchant, the former knew little about the market mechanism. Traders came to the villages in bullock carts and purchased the peasants' produce at prices much lower than those in the market.[191] The peasants had to sell their produce either to procure for themselves some basic necessities like salt or to pay off debts or land revenue. Constraints of monetary debt, distance and trader/moneylender-controlled haats always rendered the peasants' profit marginal.

In the remote villages, the merchants exploited the tribal peasants through other forms of expropriation. Early in the nineteenth century, Francis Buchanan noted how the traders cheated the tribal peasants in the district of Goalpara.[192] The trader would establish a gola with the intention of monopolizing the trade — the salt trade in particular. When the price of salt, adulterated with dust, was Rs 5.50 per maund in the Goalpara town, these traders sold it to the Garo peasants at the rate of Rs 8 per maund.[193] Providing a glaring example of such exploitative nature of the market, Buchanan reported how they exchanged this salt per maund for 3 maunds of unprocessed cotton.

More than a century later — after Buchanan had noticed the beginning of market mechanism in the 1820s — the practice of usury became acute wherever there was a market. Revenue officials suggested that these markets had, through time, become more indispensable for meeting the everyday necessities of the peasants. By the twentieth century, a large number of former tea garden labourers were in the clutches of Marwari traders. A settlement officer in Nowgaon remarked that indebtedness was high in the villages where there were regular bazaars and Marwari shopkeepers. However, he was not right, he wrongly believed that often temptation rather than need was the main cause for local peasant to buy goods.

While we have explained the nature of market mechanisms, we may note that the agrarian economy also played a vital role in the flow of credit through these mechanisms. This became crucial and proved to be more far-reaching with the settlement of immigrant peasants from East Bengal. Before many of them settled down and began a new peasant life, they had fallen prey to the market fluctuations. The only advantage that they had was their familiarity with the agro-ecological setting. Upon their arrival from Bengal, they did not have enough capital to begin farming. They had no other way but to borrow money from the mahajans at exorbitant rates of interest. These peasants, soon after settling down, began to cultivate cash crops, jute in particular. This was a remarkable phenomenon in the agrarian economy of the region. Till the arrival of immigrant peasants the most widely cultivated cash crops in the Brahmaputra valley had been mustard seeds followed by sugarcane. The role of trader-cum-moneylenders had been very negligible in such cash crop production. Such production system was mostly dependent on household labour. The trade in these crops had been limited to the local Assamese traders from places like Sualkuchi or Barpeta.

The beginning of large-scale production of jute, however, changed the agrarian situation.[194] It so happened that by 1936, on the eve of the Second World War, Assam came to occupy the third position amongst the Indian states producing jute.[195] The unavoidable necessity of capital, mostly in small amounts, for investment in the cultivation and production of jute compelled the East Bengali peasants to look for credit.[196] Unlike their Assamese counterparts, they had no social network to sustain the inflow of capital within their peasant society. In most of the cases, they had to fall back on the credit market operated by the *dewania* or the mahajan. These moneylenders provided them with the required loan, but they retained the right to market the produce. They remained the vital link between the various jute-trading agencies and jute cultivators. The general impression in the official circles was that these creditors knew that immigrant peasants did their best to clear off the loans if they could and they would not overtly resist paying high rates of interest.[197] They made every effort to ensure that the mahajan got the jute crop as was agreed. The immigrant peasant had no other way but to come back to the same money-lender for his next year's needs and pay back the loan. Soon, since he had to take a loan next year as well, he never recovered from the vicious cycle of indebtedness. The jute-growing Muslim peasants' smallholding structure simply failed to sustain itself without mercantile capital and usury.

The Great Depression of the 1930s had a severe impact on the agrarian economy of Assam. The resettlements of the 1920s had already increased the revenue demand by an average of 20 per cent.[198] However, there was a series of protests against this revenue hike in Kamrup. At the same time, moneylending too increased during this period. Scarcity of cash, demand for revenue in cash and higher prices of essential commodities forced the peasant families to borrow from the moneylenders. The high prices of paddy, jute and mustard began to come down from 1929–30.[199] Yet, there was no reprieve for the peasants throughout the decade of 1930s. A revenue official describing the condition in 1935 admitted that

> [the] material condition of the people remains must the same [*sic*] as in the last year and the immediate outlook as not hopeful than it was. There is scarcity of money everywhere and the people find it very difficult to pay their land revenue and to repay agricultural loans. Distress warrants do not bring more than rupee or two and village lands when put up to auction for areas of revenue either fail to elicit a bid or sail for totally inadequate prices.

The situation worsened to such an extent that even hoarded wealth and secret private savings had to be brought out to pay off either revenue or interest on loan.[200] Even officials admitted that in order to meet their revenue demands and interests in loan, 'peasants sold their cattle and the ornaments of their womenfolk found their way to the Marwari shops'.[201] During these years, money deposited by the mauzadar in the treasury was full of old and soiled rupee notes.[202] For the revenue officials, it was very difficult to recover the revenue and this situation continued till the post-independence period.[203] By 1935, the debt burden had become so high that W.L. Scott, Finance Member in the Assam Legislative Council, thought that the 'amount involved in rural indebtedness was so "great" that the resources of this province would not be able to meet them'.[204] The failure to pay land revenue resulted in the confiscation of the peasants' properties. Table 1.4 illustrates such cases wherein peasant property was sold at auctions.[205]

The districts most severely affected by confiscation and auctioning of peasants' landed property during this period were Kamrup, Darrang and Sibsagar.[206] Many of the peasants failed to repay their old debts because of the hardships caused by the Great Depression. The worst sufferers were the immigrant peasants. The rapid pace at which these peasants had migrated and settled in the districts of western Assam suddenly slowed down.[207] This was mostly due to a sharp fall in the jute prices during this period — according

Table 1.4: Numbers of Property Sold at Auction (1925–46)

	1925–26		*1930–31*		*1935–36*		*1940–1941*		*1945–46*	
District	*I*	*II*	*I*	*II*	*I*	*II*	*I*	*II*	*I*	*II*
Kamrup	23	36	211	106	784	556	1,129	657	417	258
Darrang	0	6	17	9	128	1,093	34	197	3	11
Nowgaon	0	29	39	8	223	328	92	214	0	11
Sibsagar	66	53	215	155	303	1,056	291	1,116	152	123
Lakhimpur	56	28	96	37	211	195	113	94	10	11

Note: I – movable property
II – estates

Source: Prepared from *Annual Report on the Land Revenue Administration of Assam* of the respective year.

to an estimate, by approximately 57 per cent between 1929 and 1934.[208] The peasants fell more into the grip of the moneylenders as the prices of jute and mustard further decreased in the 1930s. The fall in the prices of rice and jute was first noticed in 1929 and continued till 1939. It came to an all time low in 1933.[209] The situation was noted by the Assam administration in a captivating way:

> The immigrant population who mostly reside in the riverine areas suffered the most as in addition to the failure of the ordinary crops the jute on the sale of which they depend though generally more abundant than usual fetched such poor prices as often to be not worth cutting.[210]

The situation deteriorated to such an extent that even moneylenders were unwilling to provide money on credit. Such a situation hampered the immigrant peasants from getting credit from the moneylenders as freely as before. Moreover, they had no adequate system of storing their produce and this compelled them to sell jute at an abnormally low price. The only respite was for the old settlers who, compared to the newcomers — as many in the revenue department believed — were in a better financial position and even had houses to store the produce without having to borrow any money. It was during this time that many of them began to cultivate paddy, thus bringing about a change in the immigrant peasants' crop preferences. The crisis immediately compelled these peasants to organize a series of meetings to pressurize the Marwari traders to advance credit.[211] In places like Darrang, even the district administration had to negotiate with the Marwari trader–moneylenders on behalf of the immigrant peasants for advancing loans.[212] But their general refusal to provide credit also caused further dissatisfaction amongst the immigrant peasants which even led to a rumour that they were going to loot Marwari shops. The anxiety and severe hardships caused by this crisis was deeply felt by the immigrant peasants. A small book called *Pater-Kabita-Huyal Goni*, written by a literate immigrant peasant, graphically described the situation.[213]

Dictated by the exigencies of the Second World War, the prices for jute began to rise significantly. The break came after 1942 when the prices began to rise and continued till 1950, except in 1946.[214] In 1942, the prices went up quite high.[215] The rich peasants benefited from the profiteering during the short spell of higher prices of jute. Significantly, the profit thus earned was invested in buying more agricultural land. The immigrant Muslim peasants bought more agricultural land under cultivation during this period leading to high speculation in land prices in places like Nowgaon.[216] After a long gap of a decade, the Assam administration asserted in 1943 that peasants 'materially improved their condition by trade and sale of agricultural produce'.[217] However, the real beneficiaries were the rich peasants along with the middlemen in trade and commerce. The benefits of the increased prices never went to the actual producers. In fact, the higher prices of other essential products like cloth and household commodities took away even the minimum profits the poor peasant could make. On the eve of the Second World War, even as the jute prices were high, the immigrant peasants could not enjoy the benefit of price rise, as, by the time prices rose, the 'commodity already had passed from the hands of the grower to the middlemen'.[218] On the other hand, high prices affected the immigrant peasants severely as it did the other poor peasants. They had to buy most of their food items from the market and had to share the increased price burden when buying the household commodities. The rich peasants who produced enough crops for the market reaped the benefit of high prices during this period.[219] The only possible choice before the poor peasants was to enter into credit relations with the moneylenders only to subsequently lose their land to them. The burden of loan repayment became more unbearable. It also became difficult to get new loans. The poor peasants could not get the benefit of price rise, as they had to buy other consumer items at an equally high price.[220] The prices, however, subsequently fell in the international market. Years later, in 1946, a severe flood caused extensive damage to the crops. The peasants in Assam suffered in two ways: they had to sell more paddy and jute to get cash in the wake of the low prices of their produce, while they also produced less in that year. But the prices increased sharply in the prices in the subsequent year, and kept rising till 1950. Faced with an odd weather, the peasants were exposed to an unstable market with no protection against these contingencies.

Often, the creditors allowed the debt to fall into arrears. This happened especially when they were not sure of getting good prices for the crops. But when the time to return the loaned money in the form of crops came, the peasant had no escape from falling prey to low market prices for his crops. Further, the time for the repayment of loan coincided with the harvesting period, depriving him of a good profit. In most cases, peasants sold their crops to their creditors. The price they used to get was much lower than what they could have got in a competitive market, if they had waited for a few more months.[221] In 1906, a rupee for 12 *dons* was found to be the rate frequently agreed on, but interest was to be paid in advance. In some cases, the produce of a bigha of paddy land was to be given as interest on an advance of Rs 20.[222] In the 1920s, the mahajans usually demanded repayment of the interest in crop. With the increased prices of crops, the moneylenders were more anxious to get repayment in kind.[223] If the peasant was unable to pay from the proceeds of crop sales, the moneylenders would confiscate the land. Land mortgage, as it ensured the security of the credit, was most commonly sought for if the moneylender happened to live in the villages.[224]

With gradual commercialization of agriculture, coinciding with the opening of vast patches of land by the immigrant peasants from East Bengal and the subsequent expansion of jute cultivation, usury acquired a larger scale and a more complex dimension. Not only did the social composition of moneylenders gradually widen, but their penetration into the peasant economy also increased. While Marwari traders became an important instrument in the flow of money into the credit network, others with limited access to credit capital also came to play a vital role in the sustenance of the credit market. For example, rich Assamese peasants or absentee

Assamese landowners invested in the credit market with loans from Marwari traders. Their sole interest was to gain access to land, whereas the Marwari traders wanted the production of crops to continue. As these traders did not have any means to practise cultivation on their own, they wanted a more safe and comfortable relationship with their debtors. However, this did not mean that they wanted to put their capital at stake. Thus, they advanced money to the debtors depending on market conditions or the kind of crop that would be produced by the debtors. It is also significant that the market prices of various cash crops were always dependent on the markets in Calcutta, and this also ensured that the integration of the local economy with the larger colonial economy was achieved.

Was There Landlessness?

Did indebtedness speed up a process of transfer of peasants' land to their creditors? That land transfer was slowly acquiring a serious dimension came to be widely discussed for long amongst the revenue officials in Assam. It so happened that in July 1919 the Assam administration passed a notification preventing the sale and transfer of the annually leased land to absentee landowners without the approval of the District Commissioner. In September 1919, the restriction was further extended to the periodic patta land.[225] The intention was to check the transfer of ownership to the absentee owners, which would allow the latter to play a key role in agrarian production. In all probability, this restriction, however, failed to prevent the intended transfer. In 1928, S.P. Desai, the settlement officer of Kamrup district, could still notice the incidence of such transfers.[226] A couple of years later, the Banking Committee also expressed its complete displeasure at the total failure of its plan. It also reminded the government of 'the facts that the land in the Assam valley was passing it [*sic*] to hands of Marwari'.[227] During their investigation, the Banking Committee also noticed that the moneylenders who gave advances to the peasants were unable to realize the loaned amount and the debtors' lands were transferred to them by private negotiation. In most of the cases, the Marwari moneylender retained his possession over such land without any legal transfer. This he did by continuing to pay the revenue in the name of the former owner, but most of the time he would also sublet the land to the same peasant.[228] Occasionally, Marwari or Bengali shopkeepers got such land cultivated by hired labour and used their own cattle and seed to avoid falling under this restriction.[229] As early as the Census of 1911, lands thus acquired by an emerging Marwari trader-cum-landlord were found to have been leased to former tea garden labourers on a sharecropping basis.[230] But it is difficult to presume that such phenomenon was widespread during that time. Such land was sublet to new adhiars at rates much in excess of those assessed by the government as land revenue. There was no security of tenure and the adhiars were entirely at the mercy of these moneylenders-cum-landowners.[231] Thus, though the Marwari traders rarely transferred the title of the land lease to their own name, they became the de facto owners. This would only lead to a misconception about the transfer of land from peasants to traders within the official circles. Thus, the Famine Enquiry Commission of 1943 felt that transfer of land to non-cultivating landowners had not yet reached overwhelming proportions.[232]

In the absence of any legal prohibition, borrowing was much easier. Peasants could borrow either in cash or in kind, on good faith or through a mediator. As mentioned earlier, the non-existence of any valid legal document was very convenient for the moneylenders but proved to be harmful for the peasants. In fact, it did not deter the Marwari traders from offering advances to the peasants. A settlement officer in Darrang noticed that Marwari traders did not even hesitate to make advances even if the land was only on annual leases.[233] They charged higher interest for such land and were careful not to advance more than what they could reasonably expect to realize from the crops.

A settlement officer of Nowgaon who deposed before the Banking Committee spoke on the intricacies of usury in the villages in 1929. He said that, in the villages, moneylenders gave loans in order to acquire lands.[234] In these cases, moneylenders were the rich peasants who would borrow money from the Marwari traders and lend out to the poor peasants at a higher rate. The borrower peasants were forced to write off their rights over their land once they failed to return their loan. The rich peasants-cum-moneylenders accumulated land in this process. By 1929, it was found that almost each mauzadar owned a large area of land, which he would have acquired by lending money to cultivators. Often, they would convert the revenue arrears into a loan and make the peasant sign a bond. And soon, he would acquire the land of the defaulter for himself as agreed upon in the bond. In the 1930s, the moneylenders and others who had interest in land occupied more and more land, as is illustrated in the following table:

Table 1.5: Khiraj Land Held by the Marwari Traders

(*In acres*)

District	*1920–21*	*1925–26*	*1930–31*	*1935–36*	*1939–40*	*1942–43*	*1945–46*
Kamrup	3,157	3,348	3,908	5,698	6,398	6,049	5,773
Darrang	3,618	4,982	4,360	6,492	8,791	10,909	13,544
Nowgaon	1,514	1,252	2,254	3,050	3,015	2,739	2,533
Sibsagar	4,392	4,738	6,290	7,740	8,043	9,446	8,479
Lakhimpur	3,700	3,434	5,304	7,859	9,269	9,348	9,290

Source: Prepared from the *Annual Report on the Land Revenue Administration of Assam* of the respective years.

A revenue official in Dibrugarh noted that the figures were probably larger than what is officially presented (see Table 1.5). He described how the public discussion on the possibility of introducing tenancy legislation in the raiyatwari areas of Assam had often created panic among the absentee landowners leading to massive underreporting. That the Marwari traders openly endeavoured to prevent the names of their tenants being recorded was repeatedly mentioned by the revenue officials.[235] In certain areas, such as that inhabited by the former tea garden labourers in Naduar,[236] peasants were forced to be adhiars in their own land mainly because they failed to repay the credit to Marwari creditors. [237] Given this patchy legal safeguard, the peasants continued to lose their lands to their creditors. Such incidents of land transfer became frequent in the post-Depression period. Peasants could not recover from the debt burden for a long time. By 1940, land transfer to the non-agriculturist was an everyday phenomenon. This subsequently helped in the growth of both the numbers of landless peasantry and sharecroppers. Broadly speaking, the trader–moneylender nexus remained in the forefront of this credit market. The moneylenders in Assam, despite their access to the land, continued to allow the land to be cultivated by former peasant-owners. On the other hand, the combined effects of a greater involvement in the market economy and a permanent cycle of indebtedness resulted in a process of proletarianization of the peasantry in the raiyatwari districts of Assam through rapid land alienation.

The Peasant Economy and Agrarian Relation

Did sharecropping as a system emerge as structurally distinct from that of the peasant smallholdings which were vested with *raiyati* rights? Apparently not; sharecropping and peasant smallholding overlapped. To understand it better, we need to refer to our discussion, in the introductory chapter, on the agrarian typology of the valley. The broad picture of the agrarian typology outlined by the Census of 1951 was one of a raiyatwari-settled Assam predominantly characterized by smallholding peasant cultivators constituting 65–78 per cent of the total population dependent on agriculture. A majority of these peasant cultivators owned land less than 30 bighas.[238] A small number of peasants, mostly from Kamrup, Darrang and Sibsagar, owned land above 30 bighas. Constituting 9–32 per cent of the total number of peasant families, the sharecroppers followed these small peasants. In Darrang, approximately one-third of the population was registered as sharecroppers.[239] Compared to the smallholdings of the peasant proprietors, the condition of the sharecroppers was no better.[240] The average size of their holdings was also smaller and the majority of them — approximately 74 per cent — rented land less than a bigha. Only 3 per cent of the sharecroppers rented land above 31 bighas. Such incidence of smallholding in sharecropping was clearly determined by an urge for maintaining the subsistence levels of small peasant families rather than a drive for profit for the landowners. Smallholdings were economically not viable either and not meant for cash crop production. With such smallholdings, it was also difficult for sharecropper families to uplift their economic status. A budget prepared for an ordinary peasant household in 1921, referred to earlier, bears testimony to this fact.[241] The budget estimated that a peasant family having 20 bighas of land could not be regarded as more than a subsistence-level family. This estimate also suggested that six acres of landholding could only allow a peasant family to live just above the subsistence level. From the data, it would not be difficult to conclude that most of the sharecroppers were just below that level. The situation would have been worse in the remote villages where peasants were likely to get a lower price for their produce. It was thus rare for these sharecroppers to improve their economic conditions.

The peasant society also had a small presence of agricultural labourers, i.e., an approximately 2 per cent of the total agricultural population according to the Census of 1951. This number could be more in reality as there were a number of sharecroppers who supplemented their income by occasionally resorting to agricultural labour.[242] The abolition of slavery might, apart from other historical factors, have led to the creation of such a workforce in the nineteenth century.[243] In the nineteenth century, there were three types of agricultural labourers in the Brahmaputra valley: bonded labour, wage labour and labour based on mutual co-operation. The new form of labour relationship in the rural society was also very different from the practices of the next century. In the twentieth century, the agricultural labour force chiefly came to be comprised of the migrant labourers (kamlas) and the recently pauperized landless peasants. In three districts of Kamrup, Darrang and Nowgaon, the presence of an increasing number of agricultural labourers was because of the arrival of migrant Muslim landless peasants who could not afford to acquire new land for cultivation. Some migrant peasants also brought with them agricultural labourers to work in their land. Both Assamese and migrant landowners began to engage these labourers for catering to their agricultural needs. The kamlas, along with the increasing numbers of Assamese landless peasants, constituted a significant group of agricultural labourers.[244]

But it was the significant growth of absentee landlords that became a crucial factor in the growth of sharecropping. They were distinctly different from la-khiraj and nisf-khiraj estate owners. A majority of these absentee landlords were owners of small-holdings having not more than 30 acres of the land rented out. The best and typical example of absentee landlords playing a crucial role in the agrarian relationship was that of mauza Beltola in Kamrup. With an overwhelming presence of absentee landlords, mostly based in the town of Guwahati, the mauza consisted of as many as 20 villages.[245] Prominent Assamese Congress political leaders had landed interests there. The peasant society in Beltola consisted of small peasant-proprietors, sharecroppers or agricultural labourers, and a small number of absentee landowners.[246] In some areas, the number of sharecroppers far exceeded the number of peasant proprietors.[247] The example of the village Saokuchi was more striking where all the resident 447 families were entered in the census records as share-tenants. Similar was the situation in most villages adjacent to Guwahati where sharecropping was the chief characteristic of the agrarian relations.[248] Such examples were not rare in the other districts too. On the other side of this high concentration of sharecropping were those villages where there were only landlords.[249] Nevertheless, this picture of preponderance of sharecroppers was true for the majority of the areas of rural Assam.

The portrayal of the agrarian economy of the Assam in this chapter indicates that by the mid-twentieth century, amidst shrinking agrarian resources, the peasants in the raiyatwari districts of Assam became highly stratified and impoverished. They were burdened with more misfortunes than in the previous century. Sharecropping and usury emerged as serious impediments to the well-being of the peasants. While the peasants' prospects of finding an alternative source of avenue was rare, beginning with the economic depression of the 1930s, the pressure on the agrarian peasant economy increased manifold. Peasants lost their land. This led to an increasing number of people being listed in the contemporary records as landless peasants. This complex re-alignment of the agrarian economy — predominantly characterized by sharecropping — including rural credit and small peasant holdings as well as landlessness also redefined the agrarian relation and nature of rural politics, as will be seen from our discussion in the following chapters.

2

Rural Society, Rural Politics and Nationalist Peasants

The central theme of this chapter is how the Assamese peasants acted and reacted politically as the agrarian economy began to witness a transition. This chapter — against the backdrop of the discussion in the previous chapter — assumes that with the increasing pressure on land and the growing stratification within Assamese peasantry, the nature of rural politics underwent several layers of transformation. Rapid changes in agrarian relations led to a transition in rural politics, and the Assamese peasantry was soon to become highly politicized. The first few decades of the twentieth century was marked by intense rural political dissent staged both away from and within the spectacular nationalist political programme. Yet, the discontent of peasants rarely acquired the shape of a formal political dissent against the colonial state. Apparently, such protests appeared, as represented in the official accounts, more as individual initiatives of a few 'discontented peasants' than as acts of 'formal' resistance against the state policies. An important, but rather neglected, aspect that can give us insights into the making of Assamese rural politics is the petitions of peasants to the ruling elite.[1] While petitioning emerged as a widely popular form of rural politics, the nationalist political programme tried to integrate these politicized rural masses into its own domain. This chapter begins with a discussion on this complex transition of rural politics.

Humble Petitions and Brave Demands

After putting up several brave fights with the colonial rulers in the nineteenth century, Assamese peasants silently disappeared from the world of 'political action' for a long period of half-a-century. They would again resurface only in the middle of the next century. Did they remain silent spectators to their world of misery during this interim period? If one reads the volumes of petitions submitted to their rulers, contrary to the official accounts, one would come across histories of peasants' continuous engagement with their rulers, articulation of their grievances, protests against arbitrary land policies, and demands for the redressal of their grievances. Submitting petitions was a new form of protest to them. They had spoken to their rulers or hurled foul words at them in the previous centuries, too. The nineteenth-century experience was, however, different. A single petition would be submitted on behalf of an entire village or a community seeking remedy to their grievances. Often, such petitions would be written by the most revered and educated men of the village or the community. An illustrative example is that of a petition submitted by Anandaram Dhekial Phukan, the young English-educated liberal Assamese youth, who was to become a junior bureaucrat in the East India Company administration soon. His much-talked-about petition to A.J. Moffat Mills, the touring Sadar judge of the Company, supposedly captured the collective aspirations of Assamese peasantry and aristocracy.[2] Such petitions were mostly a collective and highly formal affair, and yet less popular. On behalf of the peasants, petitions were deftly prepared mostly by Assamese educated liberals for whom the modern legal language embodied an enormous hope for justice. The form and tone of the petitions were modelled on the languages of the erstwhile aristocracy and the emerging Assamese nationalists. Similarly, a small group of Assamese nationalist landed gentry defended their landed interests by a careful use of a very formal, legal and constitutional language. However, beyond this world of formal petitioning, peasants met the touring imperial officials in groups and voiced their concerns and grievances. Unfortunately, such encounters came to be officially recorded only when the rulers and the peasants were in disagreement over crucial government policies, enhancement of revenue being one amongst them.

Decades later, early in the twentieth century, the Assamese peasants, either individually or collectively, began to submit petitions to their rulers more frequently. Meanwhile, their distresses also increased. In marked contrast to a few representational bodies who could speak to the colonial rulers on behalf of the middle class or the ruling elite, there was no such organization – except a few *sabhas* – that could defend the interests of these aggrieved peasants. Therefore, these peasants had no alternative except to send an endless number of petitions with the hope of getting justice. Petitions became a key instrument through which peasants articulated their grievances and sought remedy. The peasants' world of politics came to be expressed through these petitions.[3] These petitions, as also their content, increasingly pointed to the changing nature and form of negotiation between the Assamese peasants and the government. Further, the language of the petitions embodied an increasing political awareness of the Assamese peasants and their willingness to rely on this means to negotiate with the rulers. These petitions were often addressed to a district magistrate or his deputies. In the last century, these officials, over a period of time, had come to occupy, by replacing the erstwhile Assamese king or his officials, the most important place in the peasants' world of social justice.

Moreover, these petitions, in marked contrast to the nineteenth-century petitions written in English by the elite patrons of the peasants, now came to be written mostly in Assamese or Bengali. This was also the time when peasants' voices came to be heard more directly. Use of Assamese or Bengali in the petitions of East Bengali immigrant peasants altered the nature of engagement of the peasants with their rulers, thereby adding a new dimension to the tone and form of the petitions. To put it simply, this entire process added a new meaning to the everyday village discourse. These petitions were rarely written by the peasants themselves and mostly by professional petition writers popularly known as *mohori* in lieu of a small remuneration, a practice that continued till the present times.[4] Often, a mohori would be a resident of the village that the petitioners belonged to, or from a neighbouring village. This ensured that the petitions were structured in the formal court language and yet retained the unrefined nature of the peasants' language. The writers would habitually put the oral submissions of peasants into the templates of petitions that evolved from the colonial court culture over a period of time. Petitions in formal court language helped to camouflage the peasants' aggressive 'rustic' tone with a language of deference. If it was a case of collective bargain, the village headman mobilized his co-villagers in putting their signatures on the petition and his signature would appear first among those of his fellow signatories. Reading a selection from a wide range of petitions would surely help one make sense of the rural polity of Assam during this period. This section aims to make sense of the overall polity of Assam rather than index peasant grievances.

The Assamese peasants' petitions, some of which have fortunately found their way to the archives, graphically portray their desperation and miseries, and effuse their hope of getting justice. The twentieth-century petitions not only were forceful requests for reduction of land revenue, but also demonstrated an engagement with the modern ideas of enlightenment and progress as promised by their colonial rulers. An illustrative example is that of a petition submitted by a few Assamese peasant families in 1935 complaining to the Deputy Commissioner of Nowgaon about the miseries effected by the local railway line.[5] Peasants in several parts of India had already begun to discuss how the railway tracks had come to intensify local floods, but the theme of the petition was something unusual. It was an era of great confidence among the Assamese as well, as the Assamese liberal intelligentsia was sure of the good fortune brought about by the railways. Peasants claimed that in spite of their protest a railway line had been constructed by taking over their permanently owned agricultural land. They argued that the railway line had become an additional burden for them as they had to pay taxes for grazing their cattle near the railway line, at a time when they could not even pay their land revenue. If they failed to pay this grazing tax, the railway authorities would take the cattle into a pound which caused them more trouble.[6] The petition urged the authorities to withdraw the local tax imposed by the railways. The Deputy Commissioner of Nowgaon, while expressing his 'anxiety because of considerable hardship of the peasants',[7] asked the Divisional Engineer of Assam–Bengal Railway Company to put an end to the practice of leasing out lands for grazing cattle. The Divisional Engineer, however, categorically refused to accept the proposal of the Deputy Commissioner, thus leaving the peasants to continue paying taxes.

The Assam–Bengal Railway Company used to lease out its land to peasants in order to collect exorbitant grazing tax. The railway tracks in western and central districts of Assam, many of which were laid in the first few decades of the twentieth century, traversed through fertile agricultural areas.[8] As sizeable areas of agricultural land came under the occupation of the railways, the peasants' access to these areas including their traditional grazing *pathar*s were prohibited. Not only did the railways impose local taxes causing hardships to peasants, but the latter also knew that these railway tracks, which crisscrossed the countryside, were instrumental in causing frequent floods. This realization was strangely missing from the enlightenment discourse of the Assamese elite even though it was often reflected upon by a section of colonial technocrats. In the 1920s, an increasing number of Assamese peasants complained to the administration about the havoc created by the sudden damage to railway tracks during annual inundation. An instance of such critical engagement with the state is a 1927 petition of peasants from Raha in Nowgaon describing how the Kalong river had damaged the railway tracks and inundated vast areas under cultivation.[9] Not only were the houses of many peasants who lived along the tracks submerged, but those who had raised winter crops were also hard-hit by the damage to crops. The petitioners thus urged the administration to urgently restore the broken parts of the tracks to avert more floods in the recent future.[10]

The petitions contained not only criticism of the government's development works, but also frequently protests against the curtailment of the peasants' customary rights, whether that of access to forests or traditional fishing areas. An illustrative example is the petition of the peasants of Barapujia and Charaibahi in Nowgaon submitted to the Deputy Commissioner in 1941.[11] The peasants complained that the village fishery was the only place from where the villagers used to collect their daily supplies of fish. The fishery was sold in an open auction organized by the administration, restricting their traditional rights of access to it, leading to a loss of occupation for the local fishermen and forcing the peasants to buy their daily supply of fish from the local market at a higher price. In their petition, the peasants also pleaded for settlement of the ownership of the fishery 'with some chosen persons on behalf of the villagers at a reasonable price' instead of the present owner. The petition was signed not only by the fishermen, but also by others from the non-fishing caste.

In another similar example from 1941, peasants from Panidihing mauza in the district of Sibsagar petitioned before the district administration claiming fishing rights inside a neighbouring Reserved Forest. The administration conceded the demand with a rider that such access would be for domestic needs only.[12] But this did not necessarily improve the situation. Fishing was central to the livelihood of fishing communities like Kaibarta, while other rural men of non-fishing caste too were dependent on it as a secondary means of livelihood. Peasants used to collect their daily quota of fish from numerous village ponds, *beel* and small rivers. Since the second half of the nineteenth century, the colonial government had auctioned out the rights of fishing in natural water bodies to the highest bidders. In this process, the traditional fishing rights were bestowed only on the highest bidders. Often, such bidder-cum-fish-traders did not belong to the fishing community. This meant that not only were the members of the fishing community deprived of their traditional fishing rights and sources of livelihood, but often the bidders also employed the traditional fishermen as wage labourers.

The peasants in several places also opposed the creation of grazing reserves, as they resisted the denial of traditional fishing rights. These special grazing reserves were created in various parts of the valley to boost the production of milk. The Assam administration, in order to convert 'non-productive' tracts within Reserved and Un-classed State Forests into arable land and thereby maximize revenue, began advocating the demarcation and reservation of specific tracts as professional grazing reserves in 1912.[13] The revenue department believed that these grasslands would rarely come under peasantization or be part of the forestry programme, and hence they could be reserved as professional grazing reserves. The other factor which hastened such a decision was the increasing immigration of Nepalese grazers into Assam. Though insignificant in terms of number and geographical distribution,[14] their migration came to be seen as destructive of the forest wealth.[15] Residing mostly in the riverine areas of Brahmaputra and along the low-lying jute-growing areas, Nepalese grazers became the central element inside the grazing reserves. A substantial portion of these grazing reserves was in the three districts of Kamrup, Darrang and Nowgaon.[16] By 1946, the total area meant for professional grazing reserves stood at 864,944 *bighas* constituting a small share of the total geographical area of the valley.[17] Apart from these reserves, there were village grazing grounds to provide fodder for the village domestic animals. The Deputy Commissioner was authorized to create these grazing grounds depending on the village needs. Quite often, the reserves were formed by requisitioning land from the peasants' *patta* land. In 1935, there were approximately 201,029 acres of land reserved as village grazing grounds in the *raiyatwari*-settled districts. Villagers had access to these grazing grounds without restrictions, though these reserves were situated in the distant outskirts of villages.

Wild animals used to frequent these grazing grounds and the peasants could hardly take their herds to these reserves to graze. Villagers often protested against the creation of these reserves. A representative example is that of the villagers of Birah-Bebejia of Nowgaon, who complained that these lands, their best cultivable *rupit* lands, in 'which they bore the heat and burden of the day to reclaim and cultivated for years'[18] were forcibly taken away from them and made into a village grazing reserve. As a result, as they claimed in their petition, they had been driven to utter ruin and destitution and their material condition had changed from bad to worse. The Commissioner of the Assam Valley Division B.C. Allen agreed to exclude these portions of land from the grazing reserves.[19] This concession led to the submission of more petitions demanding similar concessions.[20] Influential and well-off peasants who had access to officials in the revenue department could make delimitation of grazing reserves an effective means of land distribution policy. Thus, benefits often went to those who, even though they had land, claimed they were landless peasants. Those who did not gain from such concessions and were truly landless could only protest against such illegality through another round of petitions. What then was the content of these petitions?

Petitioners did not shy away from referring to social and cultural clashes within their villages. These petitions tell us that land conflicts frequently and overtly became a part of the *khel* system within the Assamese village structure. Khel is a rural social organizational division based on caste and religious affiliations.[21] The system remained the most vibrant unit wherein village politics repeatedly surfaced. It also became the rallying point for economic competition. The situation in the Birah-Bebejia village also conformed to this pattern of economic competition over grazing areas and a number of petitions cleverly hinted at this.

Thus, another petition would claim that the previous petition was nothing but a conspiracy from the peasants from another khel to claim land in the disputed grazing reserves in Bangthai, Mahekhosa and Manepowa. The petitions draw attention to the fact that a few socially powerful peasants had already transferred land from these reserves into their names.

Till the outbreak of the Quit India movement in 1942, the discontent of Assamese peasants and their political actions remained mostly channelized into submitting petitions and memorials, and making representation before the administrative authorities. The political force unleashed by the Quit India movement, however, gravely affected the social equilibrium of agrarian relations. Peasants temporarily channelized their resistance to various social institutions by joining the pan-Indian anti-imperial nationalist struggle. The resulting political 'chaos' was further legitimized by an appeal made by Mahatma Gandhi and the Indian National Congress to the peasants, asking them to take up local issues and not pay revenue to the government.[22]

What led the peasants to resort to such mass petitioning? The impact of the Great Depression continued throughout the 1930s. The peasants, however, continued to pay revenue till the end of the decade. The break came during the Gandhian Civil Disobedience movement during which the peasants refused to pay revenue to the government. There was continuous pressure from the *mauzadar* to pay the revenue. The peasants protested against a move by the mauzadar to attach their property in case of non-payment of revenue. These forms of protest were widely covered in the Assamese press.[23] The issue surfaced in the Assam Legislative Assembly too. In 1941, the government asked all the mauzadars in Nowgaon district to pay the revenue by 30 November.[24] Majority of peasants had not yet paid their revenue. The mauzadars attached the properties of several poor peasants. Also, large-scale land transfers from peasants to their creditors began. Poor peasants were the worst victims of these land transfers. Land disputes became an everyday phenomenon. Such disputes resulted in murder, litigation and an increasing number of other crimes in Kamrup, Darrang and Nowgaon. There were cases of riots arising out of land disputes.[25] The largest number of thefts, reported from Kamrup in 1945, resulted from a poor rural economy,[26] as increasing number of people from rural areas were arrested on charges of theft, burglary and house breaking. The immigrant East Bengali peasants constituted an important section of those jailed for such crimes.

The agrarian relations in the 1930s and 1940s were characterized by such widespread unrest. There was despair all around. The primary disputes were articulated in the form of land problems though peasants had other problems as well. For instance, they had to cope with devastating floods and extreme crop price fluctuations, as well as land speculation. All sections of the peasantry found themselves caught up in these unprecedented economic uncertainties. The immigrant East Bengali peasants were further caught between the turmoil of economic depression and the emergence of nationalist politics. Peasants found a ray of hope in the revenue officials, preferably the Deputy Commissioner, popularly known as *zilla saheb* or *bar-saheb* who, they thought, could possibly redress their grievances. While making representations before the zilla saheb, it is beyond doubt that both the poor and the rich thought in different ways about their respective gains though both showed their solidarity of belonging to the same village. The village elite guided the poor and often the village headmen became their spokesman.

Peasants and Nationalist: The Ryot Sabha Movement, 1933–39

The widespread peasant discontent of the 1920s and 1930s became a fertile field for the Assam Congress leaders to implement the party's political programme.[27] From the mid-1930s, Assam Congress initiated a concerted attempt at peasant mobilization, which eventually came to be known as the *ryot sabha* movement. It mobilized peasants, organized annual conferences where Congress nationalists delivered lectures and sought government intervention as a remedy for the peasant's hardships. This movement became an important platform for the mobilization of Assamese peasantry vis-à-vis the colonial state. Began as an instrument of the Congress to enter village politics, ryot sabhas articulated the peasant question in a clear political language. They became an important mechanism through which the Assam Congress succeeded in creating a support base for their political demands.

Ryot sabhas had been in existence in the valley since the late nineteenth century. Many of them even survived the Civil Disobedience movement during 1919–22. But a stronger and renewed attempt to revive the idea of a ryot sabha movement began when the Assam Provincial Congress Committee attempted to come closer to the Assamese peasantry in the 1920s. An increasing number of Assamese Congress legislators, such as Rohini Kanta Hati Barua and Padmanath Gohain Barua, spoke of their concern about the sufferings of peasants in the Assam Legislative Council. The second-generation Assamese Congress leaders still retained a close link with their native villages. In the 1930s, when the All India Congress Committee also began to reorient its programmes to accommodate the interests of peasantry and also expand its mass base, the Assam Ryot Sabha movement popularized the Congress programmes. Like the ryot sabhas in Assam, the All India Kisan Sabha movement (AIKS), with a strong socialist and left orientation had already made its way in making a strong case for peasant politics in northern Indian provinces.

These scattered ryot sabhas acquired a coherent shape in 1933 with the formation of the Assam Ryot Sabha. Its first conference was held in Tilikiam near Jorhat, a stronghold of Assam Congress. Veteran Congress leaders and influential speakers like Nilamoni Phukan, Nabin Chandra Bordoloi and Krishna Sarma attended the conference.[28] The Sabha, with Nabin Chandra Bordoloi, and Krishna Sarma as the President and Secretary respectively, brought under its umbrella more than 200 such ryot sabhas spread over mostly eastern Assam districts. A yearly membership fee of one anna gave a more organized character to the peasant mobilization and movement. Peasants' concerns and grievances were given a clear political tone through these sabhas. The sabhas also managed to gain concessions from the government. Soon, the annual conferences began to attract more and more peasants. The Assamese newspapers widely reported the activities of these sabhas. The Congress leaders from Assam thought that the Congress had really succeeded in attracting Assamese peasants into its fold.[29] In retrospect, Krishna Sarma, an active leader of Assam Ryot Sabha, thought that these sabhas helped the Assamese peasants become more politically organized. He described how the inspired Assamese peasantry took to certain activities like repairing of roads, digging of river channels, etc., in the 1930s.

Two years later, in April 1936, the second annual conference of the Sabha was held at Dergaon, also near Jorhat.[30] Presided over by the prominent Assamese Congress leader, Harekrishna Das, a surgeon by training, the conference was attended by more than 2000 people including both Congress leaders and peasants. This conference adopted as many as 36 resolutions out of which 20 were directly related to the peasant question. The most important demand was 50 percent reduction in land revenue which immediately caught the imagination of the peasants. Another resolution, defending the interests of the rich peasants, demanded a change of law for non-auction of minimum five *puras* of land in case of failure to pay revenue. The presidential address deliberated not only upon the peasant question but also upon the wider areas of nation, *swaraj* or the larger responsibility of the Congress. The president assured the peasants that swaraj would help them get rid of their problems. He clearly suggested that Assamese peasants were the basis of the Assamese nationality. He used the words, the Assamese *jati* and the Assamese peasant, synonymously. He was also categorical in saying that though everybody had their share in the Congress party, it was the peasants and labourers who had more claim. The presidential speech also turned out to be a platform for contesting the East Bengali peasants' immigration to Assam. Harekrishna Das blamed the East Bengali peasants for their 'false superiority complex'.[31] He reiterated that the immigrants in Assam did not take any interest either in the development of the province or in its political life. They lived an isolated life and were not interested in the happiness and sorrow of the country. Having come to Assam, they had seen a better lifestyle than in their home country and, as a consequence, maintained a somewhat dreamy sense of superiority. Other speakers expressed that they were extremely hurt by the facts that even Congress members had been working against the interests of Assamese nationality. The Assamese nationality question thus dominated the political tone of ryot sabhas.

The ryot sabhas continued to hold their conference and pressurize the Assam government till 1939. A few representative examples will help us understand the functioning and activities of these sabhas. The conference of Khetri-Dharampur ryot sabha, held on 24 February 1936, was attended by leading Congress leaders, including Gopinath Bordoloi and Hemchandra Barua.

The president of the organizing committee of the conference was Padmanath Goswami, a local mauzadar. The *Sadiniya Assamiya* reported that the conference asserted the fact that Congress was the only platform through which the condition of poor peasants of Assam could be ameliorated. Hence, the betterment of poor peasants could be achieved by strengthening the Congress. Out of the seven resolutions adopted in the conference, one resolution demanded revenue remission, as the recent flood had destroyed the paddy crop raised by the local peasantry. Another resolution pleaded for a grant of Rs 200 for repairing a local pond, establishing a local school with vernacular medium of instruction, provision of government financial support to the local primary school, and improvement of the local road. In another resolution, the Congress members were asked to concentrate more on the local constructive works. For instance, Raha ryot sabha urged the government to build a canal to drain out the rivers Kapili and Kolong by linking it with the Brahmaputra.[32] This was rather an ambitious demand and new to the Assamese political imagination. Quite a few ryot sabhas expressed their grievances against the railway authorities. For instance, Langpata ryot sabha urged the railway department to remit the newly imposed tax on peasants for grazing and fishing near the railway lines. Cherakapar ryot sabha, apart from raising the demand of revenue reduction, also passed resolutions urging the local board's intervention in the improvement of the local school as also in the resolution to the problems created by the proximity of the railway line to the grazing and fishing areas.[33] The ryot sabhas were also organized in the satras as well. One such ryot sabha existed in Dihing satra in north Guwahati.[34] There, the sabha focused more on religious questions. Garpara satra in the Rahjari mauza also organized a ryot sabha with *Satradhikar* Keshavananda Deva Goswami as its president.[35] Similarly, in his presidential address to the All Assam Ryot Sabha, held in 1936, Nilamoni Phukan, a leading Congress leader, elaborated on such issues as better civic condition for peasants, decrease in land revenue, more schools in rural areas, etc. The second annual All Assam Ryot Sabha adopted 20 resolutions, but did not take into consideration the problems of sharecroppers or landless peasants.[36]

The tribal peasantry had a limited influence on the functioning of ryot sabhas. Mostly hinduized tribal peasants came under its fold. In programmes and actions, their ryot sabhas did not differ from other ryot sabhas. For instance, as late as 1939, Miri tribal peasants formed ryot sabhas and subsequently appealed to their landlords of the nisf-khiraj and la-khiraj estates to grant revenue concessions, as was committed by the colonial state. One such ryot sabha, viz., Sadaou Dakhin Anchal Miri Ryot Sanmilan adopted a resolution which 'appealed to the satradhikar of the Auniati satra to grant a revenue remission of 8 *anna* in the Debottar lands of the *satra*'.[37]

Parallel to the Congress-led ryot sabha movement, the Congress Socialist Party also began to address the peasant question. It organized peasants under the banner of Krishak Sanmilan. It did not have much presence but even its small efforts could make a significant impact on the existing peasant question. For instance, Uttar Kamrup Krishak Sanmilan, in its conference held on 3 March 1936 and presided over by Pandit Pratap Chandra Goswami, a local schoolteacher influential in provincial politics,[38] adopted eight resolutions, out of which two resolutions paid homage to the death of Emperor George V and Nabin Chandra Bordoloi, the provincial Congress leader. It also demanded that Nalbari be made a subdivision of Kamrup district before the reforms of 1935 Act was implemented. In another resolution, it was demanded that, considering the low productivity and poor condition of peasantry, the government should decrease the revenue. Teok Krishak Sanmilan made a similar demand like those of the ryot sabhas.[39] The Sanmilan demanded that the government should establish a separate university in Assam. It also resented the government's move to establish government-aided Bengali-medium schools in Assam. The ryot sabhas also took up the issues of large-scale transfer of lands from the indigenous peasants to East Bengali immigrant peasants. Naduar ryot sabha, for instance, in its tenth annual session, conveyed its concern to the Assam Governor that the continuous increase in revenue demand had compelled local peasants to sell land to East Bengali peasants. It thus demanded a decrease in revenue demand to check this process of land transfer.[40] There were also complaints from ryot sabhas that many colonization schemes included land for firewood collection and cattle grazing. Though the ultimate beneficiaries were the colonial state in such deforestation programmes, the visible agents of the breach of Assamese peasants' rights to the access and use of forests and grasslands were the East Bengali squatters. This led the local peasants to complain against such squatting and demanded that the squatter be evicted.[41]

The ryot sabha movement, however, kept a safe distance from the peasant question in Goalpara. There, the lead role in the peasant mobilization was played by Nikhil Goalpara Krishak Sanmilan. This platform chiefly emerged out of the conflicts between zamindars and tenants. Most members of the Sanmilan were communist leanings, though interestingly, its first annual conference held on 1 and 2 March 1936 was presided over by none other than the leading Congress leader Omeo Kumar Das. There was participation of peasants and tenants in large numbers.[42] The conference highlighted the lacunae of the Goalpara Tenancy Act (1922). The grievances of tenants and landless peasants of the Bijni and Mechapara estates also came into the centrestage of discussion.[43] In the following few years, Sanmilan's programmes came closer to those of the provincial Congress and demanded that the Assam Ryot Sabha recognize it as its integral part.[44] Munsi Abauddin Khan, a leading man of the Sanmilan, had no hesitation in addressing Nabin Chandra Bordoloi as a 'real friend' of the peasants of Assam. Such negotiations worked and the second conference of the Assam Ryot Sabha expressed its sympathy for the demands of the Sanmilan.

The emergence of Ryot Sabha movement in Assam was concurrent with the mass contact programme of All India Congress Committee. The ryot sabhas' primary agenda was the demand for revenue remission, which assumed urgency after the Great Depression of 1930s. Eventually, the Assam provincial government conceded the demand by allowing a 33 percent revenue remission. Other programmes came mostly out of the plan and programme of the Congress party.[45] The ryot sabhas also incorporated the question of ban on opium consumption and *khadi*-spinning, in line with the larger framework of the Indian nationalist movement and the idea of swaraj. It must be also mentioned that local influential persons headed the ryot sabhas. The middle peasants and the village elite having a close link with the Congress formed the core of ryot sabhas, which left little space for the lowest strata of the agrarian society to articulate their grievances. Almost every mauza by 1940 had a ryot sabha.[46] The ryot sabha movement created a new tradition of peasant politics, though limited in scope, for articulating the peasant grievances. It created a space for the identification and articulation of local problems as well. Consciousness of exploitation found a place in everyday discussion. Localized political mobilization became widespread through small meetings. Petitioning became an important aspect of peasant politics. It allowed for the limited participation of poor peasants. But, in spite of their demand for the reduction of revenue demand by 50 per cent, the ryot sabhas did not attempt to address the problems faced by landless peasants and sharecroppers. While the large network of ryot sabhas created their own space amongst a large mass of peasants, the political tradition created by them failed to accommodate the Assamese poor peasants in their political programmes.

Migrant East Bengali Peasants: 'The Trouble Maker?'

Not long after their arrival in Assam, as discussed in the previous chapter, the East Bengali immigrant peasants brought on to themselves the wrath of Assamese press, Assamese politicians and Assamese peasants. This resulted in stereotyping these immigrant peasants and did not take long to sow distrust between the Assamese and the immigrant peasants. This stereotyping, along with a history of dispute over resource-sharing, continued to polarize the Assamese rural society for a long time. In order to understand this history of rural polarization, one needs to understand the divided attitude of the Assamese elites to the issue of land reclamation in Assam. This ambiguity can be traced back to the last quarter of the nineteenth century when the issue of wastelands in Assam drew the attention of different cross-sections of the society. There was a general agreement in the late nineteenth century amongst the Assamese elites that rapid reclamation is to be welcomed. Gunabhiram Barua (1837–94), for instance, welcomed immigration.[47] In the subsequent decades, the Assamese rich peasants, traders and absentee landlords, as explained earlier, profited immensely from the settlement of immigrant peasants. But this situation did not persist for long. Jnananath Bora (1890–1968) wrote an influential piece on the question of the presence of 'foreigners' in Assam, but was silent on land reclamation by the East Bengali peasants.[48] Bora was, however, critical of the ubiquitous penetration of non-Assamese merchant capital in rural areas, which, he averred, would be against the interests of Assamese bourgeoisie, as they could hardly compete with alien merchant capital. In contrast to Bora's silence on immigration of peasants from East Bengal and their land reclamation, Assamese nationalists began to express their apprehension about the continuous immigration in the 1930s.[49] Kamalakanta Bhattacharya (1855–1936), an Assamese nationalist, saw no reason why the question of Assam's underdevelopment should not be seen in the context of land reclamation by East Bengali peasants.[50] Rapid land reclamation, he argued, would bring peril to the future generations of Assamese peasantry. Bhattacharya was not the lone voice — such concerns continued to be voiced by other nationalists as well. The Assamese politicians agreed with Bhattacharya. Three leading members of the Line Enquiry Committee,[51] about which we will discuss subsequently, wrote a dissenting note:

> We look upon the Assam Valley as of home of the Assamese people ... If they had the sovereign power today they would have still resisted occupation of the lands here by outsiders against their will by armed force if necessary ... Development of the province should not be the only consideration-nay not even the main consideration. The settlement of wastelands in the province is a very important duty of the Government no doubt ... But in this matter too the interest and well-being of the children of the soil should be the primary concern of the state.[52]

The Assamese press expressed its disapproval of the immigration of East Bengali peasants and rapid land reclamation by them. Be it in literary journals or newspapers, suspicion and distrust of immigrant peasants were widely articulated. The press indicted the East Bengali peasants for their alleged involvement in petty village robberies and theft, a view which has largely persisted till contemporary times. The lead was taken by *Assamiya*, a popular Assamese weekly. *Bilasoni*, a literary journal published from Majuli, the stronghold of Assamese Vaishnavism, claimed that the *Mymensinghia jati* (immigrant peasants from Mymensingh district of Bengal) were like dacoits, they did not heed anybody; the mauzadars,[53] as a result, were unable to collect revenue. It further argued that the English rulers had done great injustice by giving a place to this jati in the middle of the peaceful Assamese country.[54] *Chetana*, another literary journal and a mouthpiece of the nationalist Assamiya Samrakshini Sabha, supported *Assamiya* and complained that peasants from East Bengal were usurping immovable property of the local peasants and even tried to elope with the local women. 'It is becoming impossible [for Assamese women] *to move around* [freely]', the journal reported.[55] The idea of disruption of social norms allegedly caused by the immigrant peasants repeatedly appeared in the Assamese press during this period.

The Assamese legislators did not lag behind the press in vilifying the immigrant peasants either and termed the new comers as nuisance too. They alleged that the East Bengali peasants quite often stole cattle or paddy. The legislators branded the East Bengali peasants as trouble-makers and defended the cause of local peasants. They made speeches in the Legislative Assembly retelling the woes of local peasants and accused the East Bengali peasants as the sole factor behind the rising crimes in the countryside. In 1945, the legislator from Barpeta, Kameswar Das, spoke at length about a robbery which had taken place at Baghbar in Barpeta. It was an Assamese village surrounded by East Bengali peasants. A robbery in the house of a prominent villager Nareswar Gaonbura redefined the relationship between the villagers and the East Bengali peasants. Villagers testified before to the police that a few neighbouring East Bengali peasants had committed the crime, thereby leading to further rivalries between the East Bengali peasants and the villagers. The villagers further complained that molestation of their women, encroachment upon their patta lands, stealing of their mustard and other crops, and recourse to verbal threats and physical violence by the East Bengali peasants were becoming an everyday experience. Das also claimed that many of the villagers had stopped going to the fields and had asked local officials for protection.[56] In the 1940s, more legislators, including Karka Dalay Miri, Rabi Chandra Kachari, Dhirsing Deuri, Lakhswar Borooah, Beliram Das, and Ghanashyam Das joined him in recounting similar stories.[57] In 1941, even a moderate Congress legislator like Lakhswar Borooah mentioned the aggressive attitude of East Bengali peasants. For him, this aggressiveness was manifest in their wanton trespassing into the lands of Assamese peasants and pilferage of their crops as also offences against woman. He strongly asserted that various such crimes had 'disturbed the peaceful atmosphere of the local rural people[*sic*]'.[58]

Legislators of tribal origin like Dhirsing Deuri also reported about the miserable times, during which tribal peasants lost their land to the East Bengali peasants.[59] Giving an example from the Mikir hills, he claimed that about a hundred tribal peasants had been living and cultivating land for more than two years in an area known as Pamila Ali in the Jarabari mauza. But the East Bengali peasants approached the Deputy Commissioner to include the village in the land colonization programme. Conceding to their demand, the Deputy Commissioner evicted the tribal peasants and asked the Muslim East Bengali peasants to settle there. There were more such claims of acts of aggression committed by the immigrant peasants. Reference was made to another such incident in the Laharighat mauza. Land speculators from amongst the East Bengali peasants managed to get the periodic patta renewed in their names though it was reserved for the tribal peasants. This resulted in the forcible seizure of paddy from the fields and granaries of local peasants. Several other members reaffirmed the growing clashes between the East Bengali and Assamese peasants.

The Assamese peasants' attitude to the East Bengali peasants did not differ either. A typical example of their attitude can be understood from a petition submitted by some peasants in Nowgaon. The petitioners from the village Gotonga narrated their woes and lodged a complaint against the settlement of East Bengali peasants. The petitioners complained that the settlement of immigrant peasants had obstructed their access to the nearby beel, ponds and streams to fetch water, or to fish. They complained that their presence in the villages was a threat to the Assamese women and gave an example of how a young Kachari girl was ill-treated by some immigrant peasants.[60] The immigrant peasants on their part strongly opposed these allegations. Another petition from a neighbouring village reaffirmed the allegation of their neighbours and complained to the police that 'the East Bengal peasant had often committed theft in their paddy fields on the onset of the harvesting season'.[61] They lamented how this growing fear led a majority of Assamese peasants to leave their villages only to allow immigrant peasants to be the predominant inhabitants.

How does one explain such allegations and counter-allegations? Some answers can be found in the pattern of economic and social relations between the immigrants and the Assamese. The Assamese peasants remained aloof from the everyday life of the neighbouring immigrant peasants. Limited interaction took place when it came to the question of land transaction between the two, or in cases like that of an Assamese landowner hiring an East Bengali peasant as his or her sharecropper. Also, the immigrants remained dependent on the Assamese landlords and traders for credit. Despite this economic interdependency, the cultural isolation of the two communities was somewhat visible. The social interaction was confined to limited exchanges, barring some exceptions. The immigrant Muslim peasants came to be considered outcastes by the Assamese caste Hindu households. This isolation resulted in distrust and antagonism, and while this was largely due to religious differences the latter was not always the reason. Government officials also did not ascribe this antagonism to communal divide. The Deputy Commissioner of Darrang wrote to the Commissioner of Assam valley Division that he was not sure how far the Assamese peasants were antagonistic to the East Bengali peasants on religious grounds.[62] An officer at Dolgaon, the place that witnessed a major drive for eviction of immigrants in 1946, mentioned an incident that had occurred two years earlier in 1924: when a few Mymmensingia Hindu peasants had approached him and asked for *sarkari* land far away from a village of Assamese Hindus, he had asked some of the Assamese peasants if they had any objection, pointing out that the claimants were all Hindus, '[b]ut they shook their heads and said they were all the same — Hindus and Muslim — as they were all same as they came from Mymmensing'.[63] The officer did not forget to mention that Kachari peasants had no objection to this settlement either. He explained that the Kachari peasants might have looked at the matter partly considering the prospect of earning a profit by offering their help to clear the land for the East Bengali peasants who would pay 'an excellent price'.[64] Despite this economic transaction happening amongst some of the peasants, isolation and religious differences were further reinforced through the rapid circulation of stories — sometimes real and sometimes fictitious — that the Assamese heard about thefts and robberies committed by their Muslim immigrant neighbours. In fact, there was no means to validate these stories. The Assamese peasants had 'heard all about' the East Bengali peasants and believed that 'they are all *dagies*, thieves, dacoits, murderers, and ravishers'.[65] The Assamese peasants thus considered the Muslim East Bengali peasants as a social nuisance and the root of all sorts of social evils.

Official discourses further helped in portraying the immigrant peasants as trouble-makers. The Assam administration clearly identified the East Bengali peasants as 'a troublesome neighbour'. While the revenue officials were more careful in underlining the larger picture, the police expressed strong views about the immigrants. In a note to the Line System Committee, the Inspector General of Police of Assam mentioned that no less than 11 police stations were established between 1923 and 1937 to regulate the settlement of immigrant peasants.[66] He also reported that since the onset of the Great Depression, incidents of 'petty crimes' allegedly committed by immigrant peasants in areas like Kamrup, Darrang, Nowgaon, and Goalpara had increased manifold.[67] With the impact of Depression becoming real, most of the districts reported increasing incidences of theft and robbery. In 1931, the Inspector General of Police commented on the gloomy picture of Nowgaon because of the increase in serious crimes committed by the *Mymmensingia* as the migrant East Muslim peasants were known. He noted that the crimes might have been due to poverty caused by a fall in jute prices. He, however, could hardly restrain himself from suggesting that immigrant peasants from East Bengal were also accompanied by a 'large number of dangerous characters'. For him, the remedy seemed to lie in an increase in the number of police stations and magistrates to deal with criminal cases. In 1931, the Deputy Commissioner of Kamrup attributed robberies to East Bengali Muslim peasants and Kachari peasants, but at the same time agreed that this was due to their difficult economic conditions.[68] In the same year, the police in Dalgaon in Darrang district reported that 95 per cent of the Mymmensingia peasants were without proper food and had come in batches to the police station asking for relief. The District Deputy Commissioner proposed to even give these settlers loans for subsistence. Special police guards were posted to guard Marwari shops in the area, as there were rampant rumours that the needy East Bengali immigrants might loot them.[69] The impression of the East Bengali peasant as more prone to committing crimes only continued to gain popularity in various circles. Beginning with 1943, and for the next couple of years, frequent references to the increase in criminal activities among the immigrant East Bengali peasants were made in official reports.[70] Such views were held by senior and junior officials. In 1943, the Deputy Commissioner of Nowgaon reported how the East Bengali peasants took every possible piece of land for cultivation and even encroached upon the state-owned lands.[71] Years later, in 1945, the Chief Secretary of Assam attributed the increasing incidence of robbery in Nowgaon and Darrang to the East Bengali peasants.[72] Such views only persisted and East Bengali peasants were increasingly seen as potentially criminal elements. Gradually, petty crimes were overshadowed by narratives of clashes over land between the Assamese and the immigrant peasants. Describing the origin of a riot in April 1945 at Raha in Nowgaon district, the Chief Secretary reported how land disputes could lead to severe communal clashes. In this particular incident, the Assamese peasants relinquished a few plots of land under annual lease to the government which, in turn, leased them out to the East Bengali peasants. This led the Assamese peasants to reassert their traditional rights over land, resulting in a riot.[73] Narratives of such clashes occupied an important place in the everyday Assamese rural discourse in the 1940s. Increasingly, there were reports of murders,[74] thefts of cattle,[75] robberies, attacks on police stations,[76] and offences attributed to the immigrant East Bengali peasants.[77] Officials also expressed their fear about possible food riots.[78] Often, such claims were exaggerated. At least, one such a case of 'theft of grazing revenue amounting Rs 2,900 from Kamrup district by the migrant peasants' was 'found to be false' upon investigation.[79]

The stereotyping of East Bengali peasants as prone to committing crimes was part of the larger official discourse on the poorer classes. Examples were not rare to find to vindicate this stand. Thus, between 1934 and 1950, on an average, out of the total persons jailed, an estimated 70 per cent were agriculturists.[80] For the officials in East Bengal, burglary (by far the most common crime), rioting, abduction, and murder were common in Mymmensing district in the early twentieth century.[81] A great majority of the petty crimes had their origin in land disputes although they often appeared under the guise of rescuing cattle from the pounds or petty assaults.[82] Many of these cases resulted from the uncertainty surrounding the security of tenants' rights to land use and the boundaries of their holdings. At the same time, the immigration of East Bengali peasants' — already highly taxed and exploited by zamindars, and subject to other untold sufferings and miseries — to Assam was a result of their pursuit for the betterment of their economic and social position. As they settled down in Assam, their hope of a good life was shattered to pieces. In the early twentieth century (1905–28), jute prices were high and yet they became victims of indebtedness and continued poverty. Far from having economic security, many East Bengali peasants immediately after their resettlement in Assam fell prey to the machinations of moneylenders, petty leaders and corrupt revenue officials. Also, to add to their woes, immigrant peasants got unwittingly embroiled in land disputes that figured quite prominently in the second quarter of the twentieth century. These disputes had occurred earlier also but the community leaders invested a new political meaning into these disputes — they perceived them as a way to further the political mobilization of immigrant peasants along communal lines — in the wake of the new electoral politics and the formation of Assam Legislative Assembly.

Meanwhile, immigration of peasants from the northern districts of East Bengal continued unabated. As mentioned earlier, cultivation in several districts of northern East Bengal had already reached a point of saturation.[83] Emigration from these areas could hardly restore stability to the agrarian economy of East Bengal. The anxieties of these peasants immigrating to Assam were perceptively captured by their compatriot peasant-poets. In 1930 (1337 in Bengali Era), an East Bengali peasant, Kari Muhmmad Abdul Hamid, who had migrated to Nowgaon a couple of years earlier, wrote a long poem entitled *Hual Goni: Pater Kabita*.[84] The anxiety and severe hardships resulting from the economic and social crisis faced by the immigrant peasants came to be critically reflected in the poem. Hamid began by admitting that jute cultivation had led to all their miseries and added that it would not be wrong to suggest that they were living in hell. They had to live in a state of starvation. They had to clear jungles, import high-quality bullocks to undertake cultivation. He, however, did admit that jute production had once brought them wealth and prosperity: they could build good houses, and some amongst them even bought horses. Nevertheless, tragedy entered their livelihood once they fell into the trap of creditors who charged them a high interest rate and their entanglement in the cycle of indebtedness formed a key theme of the book. The East Bengali peasants had to virtually beg before the creditors for credit. It would be wrong to believe that the creditors did not like to advance credit. Rather, they created a situation whereby they misled the debtors into believing that they had bestowed a favour on them out of pity for their condition, by advancing them credit. The immigrant peasants thus lived in a state of perpetual indebtedness. Describing how the creditors manipulated the borrowing process, Hamid wrote that if a creditor entered an amount of Rs 1000 as credit in his ledger, he would actually give Rs 700–800 only. He further emphasized:

> *Koto hal mare mare, kosto kare pater karone*
> *Kayanar gudame seche bhare bina dhane*
>
> (How much ploughing had been done, how much hard labour for jute cultivation, but finally one hands over the entire crop to the store house of Marwari creditor without any value.)

Hamid believed that immigrant peasants had also fallen into the trap of a luxurious lifestyle. They spent a lot by borrowing from Marwari creditors without knowing the consequences. Hamid had no doubt that no peasant could ever free himself from the clutches of his creditor/s. It was in the poem that he indicated an important phenomenon: the intricate relationship between usury and commercialization of agricultural production. Declaring the arrival of a pan-South Asian trend in agriculture, i.e., commercialization, Hamid notified that unlike their Assamese counterparts, East Bengali peasants had to continue with jute farming, as only that could help them have access to cash and repay their credit, but they, in fact, could never recover from the debt burden. The creditors bought their produce at a pre-agreed rate which was terribly lower than the market rate, and hence the potential profit from each cycle of crop remained very low for the peasants. While cultivating jute, they could hardly spare any land for paddy cultivation, and thus were forced to buy rice at a higher price, this further adding to their miseries. The picture of the peasant society that the poem portrayed was a unique one, a picture that is needed in order to understand the agrarian situation of Assam from the perspective of immigrant peasants.

As if the troubles caused by complex working of market forces were not enough, the immigrant peasants fell prey to intense competition over access to *sarkari* land. This happened as and when riverine tracts were fully reclaimed. Newly arrived immigrants had to search for lands in other areas. Often, such localized competition was fanned by village leaders variously known as the *mattabar*s, *sardar*s, etc. Intrigue, conspiracy, forgery, and litigation became part of their new life.[85] The trouble which visited the countryside on the eve of the Great Depression of 1930s, by abruptly bringing down jute prices, continued to play havoc till the outbreak of the Second World War. In the period of the War, there was a scarcity of food items and consequent increase in food prices. The Bengal famine of 1943 brought further mayhem in Assam's countryside.[86] Thousands of starving East Bengali families migrated to the valley to escape from hunger and starvation.[87] The East Bengali peasants already settled in the valley too suffered the worst as the prices of rice increased drastically.[88] The social support system of the East Bengali peasantry in Assam was very fragile; there was little to sustain them during those days of extreme poverty. There were widespread reports of land disputes amongst the East Bengali peasants. Incidents of violence occurred when fellow villagers were attacked by immigrant peasants demanding money and other property. The situation became so grave that even an influential Muslim League member's house in Barpeta was robbed and the leader was murdered.[89] The worried Assam government distributed a meagre one bigha of land per family during this period among the East Bengali peasants.[90] Such land was suitable for growing jute but low prices of jute did not convince the peasants to undertake such cultivation. The immigrant peasants were headed towards difficult times.

Contested Frontiers and Restricting Reclamation

That the East Bengali peasants came to face opposition from a wide cross-section of Assamese peasantry is clear from the earlier discussion. Equally vocal in their criticism of the influx of immigrant peasants were bureaucrats in the revenue and forest departments, European tea planters, Nepali grazers, and Assamese politicians.[91] The newly reclaimed lands wherein the immigrant peasants were settled had been either a common resource for Assamese peasants or grazing grounds for Nepali grazers. Most often, Assamese landlords directly financed the Nepali grazers. Any decrease in the area available for cattle grazing thus impacted the economic interests of Assamese landlords. Similar pressure to keep intact the grazing reserves was mounted by Assamese peasants.[92] The forest department officials too contested the settlement as disruption of their conservation programme. With the demand for forest produce in the European market increasing in the wake of the First World War,[93] the department demanded a regime of more effective preservation of better-yielding forested lands.[94] European planters also suggested that good cultivable lands be preserved for the future expansion of tea plantations.[95]

The continuous pressure from tea planters' lobby succeeded in disallowing the conversion of floodplains of eastern Assam into a jute-producing area. This, along with the differences in the nature of soil between the western and eastern parts of the valley, finally confined the settlement of East Bengali peasants only to the western and central districts of Assam. Their settlement was not a smooth process and resulted in a fierce contest over wastelands. The Assamese peasants, with their population slowly recovering from an era of dreadful mortality, demanded that they be first settled in these wastelands. Already, even before the land colonization scheme began in 1928, revenue officials had noted the increasing pressure of East Bengali peasants for gaining land in the high-lying areas, compared to their initial preference for low-lying areas.

Faced with increasing pressure to restrict migration of different interest groups, the Assam administration was forced to redefine its land settlement policy. In 1919, the Assam administration, as a measure to contain this resentment among the Assamese peasantry, decided to restrict the settlement of East Bengali peasants in lands previously held by the Assamese peasants or those in the highlands. To make such restriction a law, the administration began to issue, both to Assamese and immigrant peasants, land under annual leases only.[96] The administration felt that land given to the Assamese peasants, if not kept under annual lease, would mean transfer to East Bengali settlers for perpetuity. Such annual patta lands could not be sold and did not entail any right of transfer either. Assamese landlords did not support this administrative move and organized meetings protesting against this new rule.[97] But such legal restriction did not help in containing peasant resentment against immigration. To resolve this tricky situation, the Assam administration, strongly backed by provincial politics, evolved a mechanism to regulate the settlement of immigrants in 1920.[98]

This mechanism, known as Line System, was aimed at ensuring a spatial separation of Assamese peasants from East Bengal migrant peasants. A village road or natural boundary would be a dividing line between the settlements of the two groups. In many places, these lines, even in the late twentieth century, acted as boundary between the settlements of Assamese and the erstwhile immigrant peasant populations. The East Bengali immigrants were not supposed to cross over the line in search of land. Though the Line System was introduced to restrict the movement of East Bengali peasants into Assamese villages and their fields, such restrictions could be hardly implemented. In fact, these lines led to petty disputes and turned out to be a bone of contention. For instance, the Assamese peasants protested against the settlement of East Bengali peasants inside the Assamese line,[99] while the East Bengali peasants repeatedly demanded that an Assamese line be converted into a mixed line which would ensure their equal right of settlement.

The settlement of East Bengali peasants in the Assamese line, many Assamese peasants believed, meant infringement of the social norms. Some felt that it was an attempt of powerful, land-hungry immigrant peasants, who were socially and culturally alien to Assam, to snatch away their lands, thus adding to their insecurity. This insecurity was the result of both the speculative land market and the cultivation of jute by the East Bengali peasants that afforded them better access to the much-needed agricultural capital. For instance, their encroachment upon a grazing reserve at Samoria satra in Kamrup was seen as an assault on the religious sentiments of Assamese Hindus.[100] Several instances of encroachment by the East Bengali peasants or the 'mass raid', a term used by the legislators, created panic among the Assamese peasants, resulting in their petitioning or sending telegrams to the government for redressal. These petitions expressed the panic among the distressed Assamese peasants. A representative example of such widespread panic is a petition signed by 'more than 200 signatories'.[101] The peasants named in the petition were poor Kachari peasants of the Kaoribaha village of Howli mauza, who had settled there before the settlement of 1924–25 and got tenurial rights. The petition claimed that the East Bengali peasants had forcibly occupied their pam houses, erected their own houses and damaged their crops by letting out cattle into the fields. This had caused great panic among the petitioning peasants.[102] The petitioners demanded the eviction of encroachers as the latter were disrupting their economy.[103] Such claims and counter-claims were reported across western and central districts of Assam.

The Assam government realized that in the wake of a general fall in revenue collection, a further expansion of acreage would only help it recover from this crisis.[104] This quickly paved the way for repeated rounds of land settlement in the 1920s. However, addressing the concerns of Assamese peasants, many in the administration agreed that peasant cultivation and grazing were not complementary activities and could not be carried on simultaneously. They therefore suggested that the areas reserved for professional grazing reserves were probably too large for the requirements of the Assamese peasants or grazers and could be thrown open to cultivation by the East Bengali peasants. To effectively control any kind of mounting pressure from the Assamese peasants, the government took care to keep a limited number of these reserves beyond the scope of settlement, but there was more trouble to come.

Political Dynamics of Land Distribution

'Land to the landless peasants' was the most frequently used slogan since the formation of the Assam Legislative Assembly. In the first session of the Assembly in 1937, there was a discussion on the practicability of the Line System and thenceforth the government continued to receive reports and rumours of a belief growing stronger in popular minds that the Line System was about to be abolished and encroachments upon the government land would become more common.[105] In the latter part of 1939, the Congress ministry in Assam led by Gopinath Bordoloi adopted a resolution on the question of land settlement which continued to have long-term implications for the regional polity. The government decided to deny permission for settlement in grazing reserves and declared that it would regulate the settlement of landless peasants of the province including immigrant peasants on the available wastelands. The land to be given to each peasant family would be a maximum of 10 acres. It also decided to evict all immigrant settlers from areas declared as 'protected tribal blocks' in the submontane areas.[106] However, the resignation of the Gopinath Bordoloi-led Congress ministry in November 1938 meant that the policy could not be executed. In 1940, the new Assam government adopted a series of measures to distribute land among the landless peasant families. Accordingly, in December, the government gave wide publicity to its intention to settle all landless Assamese and East Bengali peasants. The government made it clear that it would consider only those East Bengali peasants who had arrived in Assam before 1938 and whose lands had been eroded by the Brahmaputra river. A landless peasant was required to submit an application with a court fee of eight annas.[107] In the case of tribal peasants, the evidence of occupation and reclamation of land was itself considered a formal application for settlement.[108] Subsequently, though landless peasants were settled, there were instances of even rich peasants accumulating land in this process. Years later, in December 1943, revising its earlier policy, the government directed that, in the case of new settlements, not more than 10 acres should be settled with one person.[109]

Meanwhile, the Assam Provincial Muslim League demanded a complete rejection of the Line System. In its first annual conference held in November 1939, the League formally rejected this system. Chief Minister Muhammad Saadulla who led the Muslim League government in Assam held an all-party meeting in May and June 1940 to deliberate on this system and finally adopted a scheme for further distribution of land. Accordingly, the Assam government adopted a resolution in June 1940 restricting the settlement of wastelands with any immigrant peasants entering Assam after 1 January 1938. It decided to go ahead with a scheme for providing land to the Assamese peasants and other eligible immigrants, favouring the former in the order of priorities. It further decided that priority be given to flood- and soil-erosion-affected population and those who had settled inside the Assamese lines. Eligible applicants were to be settled in wastelands in specified development areas, on payment of a stipulated premium, in blocks segregated for different communities as before. A special officer was appointed to examine the extent of land which could be thrown open for settlement without affecting the local demands for grazing areas and the need for forest conservation. As the land settlement dynamics began to unfold, in July 1942 the Bengal Legislative Council demanded that the Indian government bring an end to all the hurdles that had stood in the way of immigration to Assam. Consequent to this, in August 1943, the Muslim League government in Assam adopted another policy of distribution of land among the landless peasants under a scheme known as 'Grow More Food'. Envisaged as part of a larger national programme, this scheme made room for de-reserving grazing reserves in districts of western Assam so as to distribute lands among different communities. Further, it was also decided that surplus reserves be opened in all the submontane areas as also in districts of eastern Assam for settlement of landless Assamese peasants.[110]

Revenue officials in Assam, however, maintained that there was no surplus land available for new settlements.[111] In spite of the opposition of revenue officials, the Muslim League ministry threw open grazing reserves for immigrant peasants. From September 1943 to August 1944, an estimated 34,000 acres of grazing reserves were distributed among the East Bengali as well as the Assamese landless peasants.[112] Patches of land falling beyond the purview of grazing reserves, estimated at 62,000 acres, were settled with the East Bengali peasants in the two districts of Nowgaon and Kamrup.[113]

These programmes of land settlement, which came in quick succession, re-aligned the equation between the political parties in Assam. Both Muslim League and Congress were clearly divided on this issue. Muslim League maintained that there had been no discrimination against the Assamese peasants as regards land settlement. Abdur Rouf, Revenue Minister in the coalition government led by Premier Sir Syed Muhammad Saadulla, admitted that, of the total land distributed in the years 1941 and 1942, only 13 per cent were settled with the East Bengali peasants.[114] Maulana Abdul Hamid Khan (1880–1976), the Muslim League member of the Assam Legislative Assembly from western Assam, defended the immigrant peasants' rights over agricultural lands in Assam. He hoped that Assamese people would welcome these newcomers for the progress of the economy of Assam.[115]

In 1945, the Muslim League government adopted two land settlement resolutions after a three-party conference arrived at a consensus. The resolutions formulated a policy of distributing land among the landless peasants. It undertook to settle wastelands in Goalpara, Kamrup, Darrang, and Nowgaon with the landless peasants of all categories including the pre-1938 immigrant peasants. The settlement would be subject to the availability of wasteland, and land was to be allotted to different communities in separate community-wise blocks according to their requirements. This will be discussed in detail in Chapter 4.

The Congress came to power after the interim election in February 1946.[116] The government spelled out the need for a re-examination of the *Assam Land Revenue Manual* so that the interests of the local peasants as also the pre-1938 immigrants could be protected.[117] The government began the preliminary work towards this and the Assam Land Revenue Regulation Manual (Amendment) Bill was placed in the immediate post-election session of the Legislative Assembly.[118] In May 1947, with the country's independence approaching, Bishnuram Medhi, the then Revenue Minister in the Congress interim ministry, made a distinction between the migrant question and the problems of Assamese landless peasantry.[119] He asserted that the migrant question of Bengal should not be a burden on the Assamese landless population. He pointed out that there were more than 75 lakh bighas of wasteland lying vacant in Bengal and it was the duty of the Bengal government to distribute land among the Bengal peasantry. He further accused the Muslim League of intensifying a Pakistan movement in the name of giving land to the East Bengali peasants. Surendranath Buragohain, representative of the powerful Ahom community, opposed the Muslim League government's policy of giving land to the immigrant peasants. He admitted: 'when this government embarked on this policy of land settlement to outsiders in 1943 August my Association was the first in the province to raise its voice of protest'.[120]

Repeated changes in the land distribution policy brought uneasiness in different circles. Even the revenue officials expressed their displeasure. A junior revenue officer in Mangaldai opined that a different interpretation of the new land settlement policy would give free scope to land speculators. He commented that this stand of the government would deprive the poorer people, both East Bengalis and indigenes, of their legitimate share of land and force them to sell their annual pattas.[121] He also noted that those who had extensively encroached on the government land or purchased annual patta lands were mostly well-to-do East Bengali peasants. They had extensive land already settled with them or acquired by way of purchasing the periodic patta. He cited an example from Dalgaon where the land settled on an annual basis with the tribal people comprised an area of 2,432 bighas out of which the East Bengali peasants had purchased 441 bighas. He did not forget to mention that the tribal peasants had left the village.

Claiming Land: Unfolding Social Dynamics

The process of land reclamation — an offshoot of various land settlement policies — was more complex than it appeared. Various peasant communities took advantage of such land settlement policies. Land distribution led to a thriving market in land speculation. Legal stipulations against such land speculation could hardly be effective. A few peasants wanted to gain profit from a temporary rush for land. One plot of land would be sold to two customers at the same time; the tribal peasants did not remain far behind in this speculation: they sold their annual patta lands bypassing legal restrictions. Like moneylenders and absentee landowners, petty officials or clerks in the revenue department also profited from these deals, helped by laxity of rules and frequent changes in government policy on land settlement. Anecdotes of people from the revenue department, *mandals* in particular, helping the East Bengali peasants to settle in grazing reserves or inside the Assamese lines were in wide circulation.

Often, the East Bengali peasants came to possess the arable lands, cleared and vacated by the tribal peasants, which led to their frequent clashes with the latter. Both groups, however, had their respective share of responsibilities leading to the dispossession of tribals. How intricate the process of dispossession was can be understood from a very interesting instance. A few Hindu East Bengali peasants in Nowgaon came to the Deputy Commissioner to complain how they were cheated by a few Assamese tribal peasants.[122] These Hindu immigrant peasants in their complaint described how some tribal peasants sublet land to them. Subsequently, the Kachari peasants sold their annual lease lands to their Hindu immigrant sharecroppers. As per rule, this was illegal land transfer as the land was within the Assamese line. The Commissioner of Assam Valley Division, who was the higher revenue appellate authority, cancelled this land transaction. While the Kachari peasants got back their land, they did not return the money they received from the migrant sharecroppers.

This incident further tells us how such disputes arose and how they were intertwined with intricate layers of rural and nationalist politics. Land disputes and assertion of proprietary rights over small plots of land became matters of intense rural politicking. In this instance, we further learn how due to sparse population, as well as the weak nature of land tenure based on collective ownership by tribal peasants and the advent of the East Bengali peasants in districts of western and central Assam, the Assamese line was converted to a mixed village. The East Bengali peasants were allowed to settle within that village. Encouraged by this stand of the government, the East Bengalis settled in these lands, also inhabited by the tribal peasants. The East Bengali peasants took possession of the government lands which lay within the lands of tribal peasants. The settlement of the East Bengalis also blocked the free passage of tribal peasants to the nearby beel. The tribal peasants protested and petitioned before the revenue officials that the East Bengali peasants had encroached upon their land. The East Bengalis, on their part, argued that their 'removal from these lands would bring economic hardship to them'.[123] The revenue officials argued that 'when the East Bengalis initially came and occupied the land in question there was no protest or resistance on the part of the tribal peasants'.[124]

An Assamese pleader Mahichandra Bora and Muhammad Amiruddin represented the suit of the Kachari peasants and the East Bengali peasants respectively. Both of them were Legislative Assembly members and took active part in the assembly debates on land settlement policy. Meanwhile, the Line System Enquiry Committee report and simultaneous debates in the Legislative Assembly had unleashed a lot of discussion in the rural society. It is difficult to trace the possibility of petitioners taking the initiative of filing a legal suit. At some stage, the political leaders took the initiative to articulate the grievances of the Assamese rural society. Some Muslim peasants tried their best, and often succeeded, to retain ownership of their landholdings, by falling back on the strength of the Muslim Personal Law. Once a suit was filed in the court against a Muslim peasant by his lender claiming to recover the mortgaged property, the Muslim peasant would cleverly declare that the property was already gifted to his wife and hence he did not own it any more.[125] Such clever use of the provisions of Muslim personal law often prevented the money-lenders from filing and wining land mortgage suits.

Despite such localized resistance of Assamese peasants to the immigrants occupying more land, the Assamese landed class nevertheless gained from the expansion of acreage at the hands of immigrant peasants. The expansion of jute cultivation was also hugely remunerative to both the Assamese and Marwari money-lenders. And they had gained from a speculative land market as well. Many of them entered into deals with the immigrant peasants.[126] Paltry gains were made by a few former tea-garden workers by selling land at higher prices to the immigrant peasants. Allegations of illegal land transfer inside the Assamese line to the immigrant peasants were widespread in the 1940s. The Congress-led ryot sabhas also took up the issue of large-scale transfer of lands from the Assamese peasants to the immigrant peasants. The situation got aggravated after the formation of the Muslim League ministry in 1937, and demand for the abolition of Line System became popular amongst the East Bengali peasants.

Grazing Reserves: Space for Political Peasants (1943–46)

Contest over grazing reserves had the widest possible impact on the peasantry and the politics of Assam in the mid-twentieth century. Such conflicts over land were not confined only to East Bengali and Assamese peasants. Contest over common lands between the tribal peasants and the Nepali grazers could be also noticed since the 1920s, but became more visible in the 1930s. Karka Dalay Miri, a member of the Tribal League in the Assam Legislative Assembly, argued that the creation of professional grazing reserves had restricted lands normally taken up for shifting cultivation by Assamese tribal peasants. He gave the example of how the government's decision to create grazing reserves, to be settled with the Nepali grazers in Golaghat and Dibrugarh, had displaced the Miri peasants from their habitat.[127] As the Miri peasants resisted the formation of grazing reserves, the government reduced the total area of the grazing reserve. Such voices of protest against land settlement were directed not only against Nepali grazers but also against the East Bengali immigrants. Several Tribal League members also demanded, during Assembly debates, that the immigrant peasants should not be given any further land to settle in. Against these demands, the Nepali grazers found support to their claim for expansion or creation of new grazing reserves. Sarveswar Barua, another member of the Assembly, claimed that, as grazing reserves had been thrown open for settlement, the grazers had to shift from one district to another in search of pastures.[128]

Notwithstanding such opposition to land settlement, political consensus veered towards the settlement of grazing reserves with the landless peasants. A few assembly members even thought that peasants from northern India could be settled there in order to counter the pressure of East Bengali peasants. Such views were held by none other than the senior Congress leader Rajendra Prasad. Prasad, in 1926, thought that if Bihari immigrant labourers who came to Assam for seasonal work settled down by taking land from the government, that would decongest districts like Chapra in Bihar.[129] His brother, along with a few others, tried out this idea but were never successful, though a few Bihari labourers were soon to begin their life as either sharecroppers or small peasants. Meanwhile, the Assam government decided to settle all the available wastelands in the valley with the landless peasants.[130] While land was to be allotted to the peasants of different communities, up to a maximum of 10 acres per peasant, the settlers who had reclaimed land before January 1938 were to be evicted. By another subsequent order, the government anounced its intention to protect the tribal peasants.[131]

Amidst such subtle moves, in 1943, the Saadulla ministry, as mentioned before, authorized the deputy commissioners 'to open portions of professional grazing reserves found by them according to the standard laid down by government as surplus to requirement'.[132] In the first phase, i.e., the winter of 1943, six grazing reserves were thrown open in Nowgaon.[133] A few other reserves were also opened up for settlement in Kamrup and Darrang.[134] And the opening of the grazing reserves for cultivation by landless East Bengali peasants expanded the scope of conflict between different groups. Yet, such de-reservation of grazing reserves could not contain the land in other grazing reserves from being brought under cultivation by the East Bengali peasants. The League members still believed that there were enough wastelands in every district which could be made available for settlement with any Assamese who was in need of it.[135] The settlers, on the other hand, came to believe that the government would be inclined to bringing in laws which could legalize their squatting on government land. The presence of Muslim League ministers in public meetings and the representation of East Bengali members to the Assam Legislative Assembly reinforced this idea.

Land revenue official S.P. Desai, who had several years of experience in the revenue administration in Assam and had pursued the issue of settlement of the East Bengali peasants in the grazing reserves, noted the gravity of the situation. Desai admitted that, insofar as the East Bengali peasants were concerned, the legal enforcement of Assam Land and Revenue Regulation of 1886 that spelled out the rules for clearing of government land was virtually non-existent. Drawing attention to a new development, i.e., intra-valley movement of East Bengali peasants in search of land, Desai noted how since the publication of the government resolution on the land settlement policy in August 1944, *dewanias* brought peasants from various places of Kamrup and Goalpara to reclaim lands in Nowgaon. Desai noted that new bamboo sheds and temporary huts were springing up every day inside the grazing reserves. He also cited evidence of East Bengali peasants meticulously evading the revenue officials to lay claim to land in the grazing reserves. He also found that East Bengali peasants absolutely ignored the revenue officers 'so much so that they even refuse[d] to answer questions put to them'.[136] Following is a graphic description of the situation inside a grazing reserve, given by Desai:

> The few Nepali grazers and Assamese *pamua* finding no protection from anywhere gave *dohai* in the name of king Emperor. To this, some East Bengalis were said to have replied that the East Bengalis themselves were the king. They felt that the law was meant for them and not for East Bengal. All section[s] of local population was [*sic*] greatly perturbed and their talk exhibits deep-seated bitterness against the East Bengalis, who did not listen to protests. The only alternative for the grazers was to migrate.[137]

For the East Bengali migrant peasants, it was the ecological features of the grazing reserves which drew them closer to these areas. Because of their grassland and alluvial character, such grazing reserves were not only easy to reclaim by way of burning during winter but could also be easily made ploughable. These areas were also as suitable for paddy production as for jute cultivation. In fact, due to rapid increase in paddy prices as well as a serious shortage of paddy, the immigrant peasants were more interested in the production of paddy than jute in the low-lying areas such as the grazing reserves. As the winter of 1944 approached, the East Bengali peasants began to cultivate land inside various grazing reserves in the central and western districts of Assam.[138] By then, they had completed the encroachment upon various grazing reserves, mainly in three districts, viz., Darrang, Nowgaon and Kamrup. Beliram Das, a Congress member in the Assam Legislative Assembly, lamented that 'in several places the grazing reserves all had been encroached upon with little exception'.[139] These encroachments resulted in clashes between Nepali grazers, Assamese peasants and East Bengali peasants. In places like Mangaldai, the grazers complained that they could not graze their cattle as the East Bengali peasants either maimed their animals or impounded them. Committees were formed to protest against the opening of grazing reserves for cultivation.[140] Grazers argued that since some of the grazing reserves which had been thrown open for cultivation were situated on highlands and worked as shelter during floods, their opening up to peasants would pose further danger to their cattle and buffaloes.

There was official evidence of disputed claims over land in the grazing reserves and of events leading to clashes in the reserves. An illustrative example is that of Alisinga grazing reserve in Darrang. Clashes occurred between Nepali grazers and East Bengali peasants there in February 1945. There were also reports of arson and rioting.[141] The reserve was mostly used by the Nepali grazers though the Assamese peasants also grazed their cattle there. In June 1944, portions of this grazing reserve were thrown open to East Bengali peasants. The grazers did not protest immediately, but in March 1945 they submitted a petition to the Deputy Commissioner protesting against this settlement. They also complained that the new settlers had since then created troubles for them in the reserve and neighbourhood repeatedly. However, the East Bengali peasants had another story to tell. They claimed that while they were clearing off the jungles and making preparations for building their houses, Nepali grazers came armed with deadly weapons, forcibly drove them out of the area and demolished their houses. In some cases, the grazers could get direct support from their neighbours, from other Assamese peasant groups, such as Tiwa tribal peasants in Kamrup in February 1943.[142] At the same time, some Assamese peasants also followed the route of immigrant peasants and reclaimed land from the grazing reserves.

In another instance, Pukhuripar professional grazing reserve in Kamrup had been occupied by Kachari, caste-Hindu and Assamese Muslim peasants since 1938. The district administration evicted these peasants, but subsequently the immigrant peasants occupied it.[143] The official documents are abundant with representations of Assamese landlords and peasants' critical participation in the land reclamation process. The Line System Enquiry Committee mentioned several instances of Assamese land speculators operating in Nowgaon, especially in the earlier days, making profits from selling lands that they had either taken up especially for that purpose or had not taken up at all.[144] The Committee also admitted the non-availability of much evidence of any considerable body of landless people among the Assamese who would be able to colonize the undoubtedly large areas of wastelands in some of the districts.[145] Yet, there were instances of encroachment despite local protests.

Nonetheless, grazing reserves became an important political space where various peasant groups asserted their rights. The initial confrontationist stand was that of the Nepali grazers, who protested against the opening of professional grazing reserves to the East Bengali settlers, arguing that their right to graze cattle in the reserves had been curtailed.[146] Clearly, this was a conflict between two economic activities — agrarian expansion by the East Bengali peasants, viewed by colonial officials as highly profitable, and another non-agricultural economic activity of grazing projected by the grazers as their natural privilege.[147]

As early as 1928, the Nepali grazers of Barpeta[148] requested the provincial finance minister for eviction and cancellation of pattas issued to the East Bengali settlers.[149] They complained that the East Bengali peasants in connivance with the local revenue officials had cultivated land inside the grazing area. Simultaneously, the East Bengali peasants also claimed their right over these lands on humanitarian grounds. They demanded conversion of various grazing reserves into arable lands on the ground that they were too large for grazing which caused immense harm to cultivation.[150]

In the subsequent years, their pressure to open grazing reserves increased. Meanwhile, a government proposal for eviction had quickly changed the pre-independence political scenario in Assam. Encroachment upon the grazing reserves being a matter of serious concern for the Congress-led Assam government, it was unable to regard such heavy encroachment, which had taken place in some areas, with equanimity.[151] The climatic period was 1946–47, during which the impending Partition of the country increased the political mobilization of East Bengali peasants by the Muslim League in Assam. Also, during this period, while the tribal peasants lost out to the immigrant peasants in the land settlement process, the Assamese identity centred on caste system and indigenous origin became more crystallized.

East Bengali Peasants, Muslim League and the Idea of Pakistan

Till 1945, clashes between the East Bengali immigrant peasants and the Assamese peasants had remained localized. Control over grazing reserves and access to sarkari wastelands remained the central issue. The Assamese peasants and their nationalist leaders asserted their natural right over grazing reserves while the new settlers argued that their claim over these lands was justified on humanitarian grounds. Years of institutional support could be another major factor for intensifying clamour for such rights. As the Second World War came to an end, there was a tumult in the political life of the valley. As the Pakistan movement gained momentum in East Bengal and its Muslim-dominated areas, unoccupied wastelands in different parts of western and central Assam became the key focus of a renewed phase of politics.[152] Years of anti-Line-System agitation assumed new dimensions and became integrated with the pro-Pakistan movement. Also, the site of confrontation shifted from the areas demarcated by the Line System to the unoccupied wastelands. The unoccupied and unploughed wastelands had different meanings for different people: the Assamese peasants thought of these lands as places rife with possible conflicts and anti-social activities, while for the immigrant peasants they were a future heaven. This new wave of politics ensured that the immigrant peasants, for the time being, would be a central element in the political landscape of Assam.

Both real-life political mobilization and public rhetoric became the hallmark of a short period of political upheaval. The bond between political rhetoric and popular mobilization was reinforced swiftly when the enigmatic Maulana Abdul Hamid Khan, popularly known as Bhasani, emerged as the popular face of Muslim League in Assam.[153] Bhasani gave a new twist to the politics of Assam Provincial Muslim League. He emerged as the uncontested leader amongst the immigrant East Bengali peasants, particularly the poor ones. Apparent conflicts between Bhasani and Muhammad Saadulla became visible. Bhasani accused Saadulla as being the representative of Muslim elites and it worked. Saadulla was soon to be replaced as the popular face of Muslim League in Assam. Already, Bhasani, under the banner of Asom Chasi Majdur Samitee, had been leading a popular movement against the existing Line System, both inside and outside of the Assam Legislative Assembly. His political career in Assam began on the footing of anti-zamindari movement which gave him high popularity amongst the poor migrant peasants. According to Bhasani's biographer, his communist political leanings were well known, but soon his political trajectory became entangled with sectarian politics. To defend the cause of immigrant peasants, he had to counter the demands and criticism of Assamese peasants. It was for this that the majority of Assamese peasants and nationalists — the latter were yet to recover from the grouping imbroglio — came to consider Bhasani as a practitioner of extremely communal politics.[154] As he aggressively spoke for a merger of Assam with Pakistan, his version of politics was condemned, and rightfully so, by the Assamese nationalists.[155]

By 1940, the Assam administration became increasingly concerned about its inability to generate revenue from the professional grazing reserves. Urgent steps were thus required. The best option before it was to protect the reserves against further settlement and simultaneously ensure increased milk production. The district revenue officials began to suggest the necessity of a comprehensive law for the reserves so as to deal with the menace of massive settlements. They even proposed that wooden posts be erected at reasonable distances to mark out the boundaries of the reserves in order to protect them from the 'invasion of the

East Bengali peasants'.[156] Both Congress and Muslim League governments were under pressure to evict the encroachers from the state-owned forests or grazing reserves, but their course of actions followed different trajectories. In 1942, the Assam government directed that in the 'interest of the grow-more-food scheme encroachers growing food crops will not be evicted and their crops not destroyed'.[157] As the Assam government began to face various obstacles in carrying out its eviction programme, the subsequent land settlement policy adopted by the Muslim League was a somewhat more flexible stand.

Another phase of eviction was effectively initiated in November 1944 when the East Bengali peasants, who had reclaimed land in grazing reserves of Bhangbari and Fulung near Guwahati, were ousted. Immediately after this eviction on 11 November 1944, Bhasani brought an adjournment motion against the action.[158] Faced with a strong pressure from the Muslim League, the government had no other option but to stop the eviction programme. However, in spite of the pressure, the government was gearing up its administrative machinery to complete the programme by September 1945.[159] It also passed a resolution on 15 January in 1945 to give political legitimacy to this imminent eviction programme.[160] The resolution conveyed the government's decision to settle land in the four western districts of the valley with landless people of all classes in the province but with certain conditions. As mentioned earlier, it further asserted that all encroachers who had encroached upon the professional grazing reserves after 1 January 1938 would be evicted.[161] At the same time, the ongoing policy of de-reservation of grazing reserves was discontinued. The deputy commissioners were instructed to see that the grazing reserves were kept free of encroachment through eviction of trespassers. The government, through this resolution, wanted to ensure that all recent encroachers were evicted. But those encroachers who could prove that they previously held lands which had been eroded or lost on account of military requisition would be allowed a time limit of six months to move to other lands which the government would provide for them under the scheme.

This new eviction programme was to give a fresh impetus to the internal dynamics of the East Bengali peasants in Assam. The eviction first began in Darrang. By May 1946, the government had completed eviction in nine grazing reserves and the total number of encroachers was 2,886 including 2,214 East Bengali Muslim peasants, along with 293 tribal and caste-Hindu peasant families. The Assam Provincial Muslim League (APML), with its considerable strength in the provincial legislature, declared the government's eviction policy as against the interests of East Bengali peasants and decided to put up a strong resistance.[162] More specifically, it decided to instigate the Muslim peasants to encroach upon the reserves and other wastelands in Assam. Between 12 and 14 March 1946, there were meetings, processions and *hartal*s by the Muslim League to protest against the eviction of Muslim settlers.[163] The APML further intensified its pressure against eviction and decided to observe 31 May 1946 as a day of protest against alleged inhuman atrocities on East Bengali peasants. Public meetings adopted resolutions condemning the Congress government. These public meetings also expressed their determination to resist eviction by all means.[164]

This determined eviction drive would force the immigrant peasants to stand behind the Muslim League more strongly than before. Previously, the East Bengali peasants who had settled inside the grazing reserves were not largely bothered by this eviction drive. They had been made to understand that their crops were immune from such state-led offensives. Unlike the Assamese peasants, the East Bengali peasants had some crop or the other being raised throughout the year. Many believed that the government would not damage their crops in the time of famine in Bengal. In fact, standing crops in the field indeed made it difficult for the government to carry out eviction and rendered any proposed eviction totally ineffective.[165] The East Bengali peasants' cultivation practices thus turned out to be a good political mechanism to make eviction ineffective. Moreover, the typical way in which an East Bengali peasant encroached upon the grazing reserves was as follows: huge areas of grassland were surrounded and enclosed by thin lines of houses and crops. Shortly thereafter, the grazers, for whom the professional grazing reserves were earmarked, would be denied access while more areas would be reclaimed by the East Bengali peasants.[166] The administration usually sent notices to the settlers to produce evidence that there were not encroachers. The settlers were under the impression that any evidence of their loss of land due to soil erosion caused by rivers would save them from eviction. The deputy commissioners too would often report about their receiving a number of petitions from the East Bengali peasants claiming loss of land due to flood and erosion. Many submitted written documents of landholdings to prove their point. Many also claimed that their occupation inside state-owned forests or grazing reserves was due to these losses.[167] They further claimed that their agricultural lands in *chapari* were subjected to frequent soil erosion.

When the Assam government declared its intention to evict the immigrant settlers from the grazing reserves in 1946, this only helped in creating a strong communal solidarity among the immigrant peasants across several areas. Their eviction, in fact, consolidated their religio-communal identity, eventually leading to the communalization of peasant politics. The demand for inclusion of Assam in Pakistan gained ground from April 1946 and soon this became a rallying point for Muslim immigrant peasants.[168] The Pakistan movement, as it reached its peak, further reinforced this solidarity and, in several places, united immigrant peasants in direct confrontation with the Assamese peasants. Popular literature, written both in East Bengal and Assam, articulated their hopes of immigration and its aftermath.[169] The common memories and traditions of East Bengali peasants played a functional role in the articulation of their protests against the government's eviction drive.

The Bhasani-led APML decided to mark a 'Direct Action Day' on 16 August 1946.[170] Marking this day was aimed at holding protests against the recent eviction drive. Their refusal to be evicted was seen by the East Bengali peasants as synonymous with their demand for Assam's merger with Pakistan. Bhasani asserted that inclusion of Assam in Pakistan was the only way to rescue the immigrant peasants from the oppressive regime of the Congress government.[171] Indeed, as days passed on, the East Bengali peasants came out in large numbers to participate in APML-arranged meetings and strongly resisted the eviction programme. A mass frenzy was created by small roadside public meetings. In a most significant public meeting in Mangaldai, attended by 'thousands of East Bengalis', 'armed with *lathi*[s]',[172] Bhasani challenged the Gopinath Bordoloi-led Congress government in Assam and claimed that Pakistan was the only way out of this conflict-ridden situation. Confidential police notes mentioned that before the meeting thousands of East Bengali peasants marched on the streets of Mangaldai, led by Bhasani riding on an elephant.

Official communication further noted that the East Bengali peasants were armed with *lathi*s and that the traffic was closed for several hours. The treasury and the deputy commissioner's office were surrounded and the League flag was hoisted. Bhasani asked the East Bengali peasants 'to resist government measures to the last drop of [their] blood'.[173] He told his highly charged audience that they should not vacate a single inch of their land. He also urged them to cultivate or erect houses whenever there was a wasteland and not to pay revenue. He assured them that they could travel in trains without ticket if necessary.[174] The police soon informed the government of the APML's instructions to all its district committees to organize a Majahad army of about 1,00,000 men in the province. The League suggested that the members of the army sign a pledge in the name of Allah to abide by its directions.[175]

As Bhasani emerged as the legitimate leader of immigrant Muslim peasants in Assam, Muslim League's anti-eviction programme was metamorphosed into a powerful Pakistan movement and caught the imagination of the Muslim peasantry. In the next few months, Bhasani travelled widely in different parts of western Assam, met the local Muslim League activists and asked them to resist eviction. The police reported that he undertook a tour of Chayagaon in Kamrup where eviction was about to start.[176] He met the Muslim League members in Bongaigaon and 'gave then *instructions* to organize Muslim League National Guards in every village urging them to sacrifice all for the name of Pakistan and to be ready for direct action'.[177] In the subsequent days, the Muslim League workers organized agitations by the immigrant peasants who had settled on the government land.[178] There were meetings in mosques and private houses where discussions were held on offering resistance to eviction.

The East Bengali peasants fully supported the Muslim League's agitational politics. They knew the dependence of local markets on their produce and their political resistance was aimed at paralyzing this system. In several places of western Assam, as the police reported, they stopped selling milk or vegetables to the Hindus. '*Bhatia*s at Bhasanichar, from originally where Bhasani came, were obstructing boats coming towards Dhubri and the boats other than those which carried goods for Muslims, were not allowed to come towards Dhubri'.[179] This boycott spread to other adjoining areas as well. In Goalpara, as the East Bengali peasants boycotted the Dhubri and Gauripur bazaars, severe scarcity of vegetables, milk, eggs and other such produces of daily use was reported.[180] In some places, Nepali milkmen refused to supply milk to their Muslim customers and Muslim peasants also refused to supply the Nepali milkmen food grains.[181] In December 1946, Saadulla, otherwise a soft-spoken politician, strongly condemned the government's eviction policy as 'mendacious in parts, misleading in general and malicious as a whole'.[182]

Early in January 1947, the APML decided to re-launch their civil disobedience movement against the eviction policy.[183] In an important meeting of the Bengal and Assam Muslim National Guard Conference, held on 2 March 1947, a resolution was adopted to give a new direction to the Civil Disobedience Movement to be launched by the APML. The leaders who came to the meeting from different parts of Bengal and Assam declared that if necessary they would send the Muslim National Guards (a loosely organized armed militia raised from among the followers of Muslim League) to Assam to resist the eviction policy. They urged for the immediate enlistment of 10,000 Muslim National Guards from all classes of Muslims, especially youth, 'to fight British imperialism, the Congress and Line System of the Assam government'.[184] In another meeting, held in the same evening in a nearby *Idd-gaah*, Bhasani argued that their movement was against the caste-Hindu Congress and the government's eviction policy. He threatened resistance through force against the eviction policy if the order was not withdrawn in 15 days. An ultimatum was sent to the Assam government informing that the order would be resisted by a Civil Disobedience Movement of Muslims from all over India. The meeting also demanded that those already evicted be resettled in the lands from which they had been dispossessed.

And, in the next couple of days, hundreds of public meetings, along with impressive processions of immigrant peasants in Kamrup, Darrang and Goalpara, including Guwahati, helped to create a sense of communal solidarity mainly around the slogan of Pakistan.[185] This was also accompanied by encroachment upon the grazing reserves.[186] The activities of APML coordinated by its top leadership immediately spread to various parts of the valley. Ajmal Ali Chaudhury, the National Council member of Muslim

League, addressed a well-attended meeting at Sonaibali in Nowgaon where he appealed to the East Bengali peasants to grab all the wasteland, sacrificing their life, if necessary.

Between September 1946 and March 1947, the League succeeded in mobilizing a large number of Muslim East Bengali peasants to resist eviction and claim new government lands. Places like Barpeta, Mangaldai and Nowgaon witnessed sporadic conflicts. In some places, the East Bengali peasants resorted to petty thefts in the neighbouring paddy fields of the Assamese peasants.[187] Their resistance to the eviction programme and support for the Pakistan movement received additional momentum with the construction of *killa*s or small huts in the grazing reserves. For instance, a number of killas were constructed in Barpeta. Meetings and processions were held regularly, followed by reclamation of lands in the nearby grazing reserves.[188] A large crowd of East Bengali peasants led by their dewanias cleared land in the Mandia grazing reserve on 21 March 1947.[189] The Leaguers had decided to encroach upon this grazing reserve in a meeting held two days earlier. Policemen from the Railway Armed Force challenged this action which resulted in the death of 12 peasants. State offensive only convinced the immigrant peasants of the need to be more forceful and tactful in their actions. Reclamation of one grazing reserve would result in a spiralling impact, as the forceful occupation of Kumolia grazing reserve in Tezpur did. Hearing the success of Kumolia action, the Leaguers encouraged land reclamation in the Mandia, Fulora and Theka-bari grazing reserves in Barpeta.[190] The settlers would usually erect bamboo huts with raised earthen floors as the mark of their occupation. Thereafter, some 'hide-and-seek' would be played between the settlers and the police: for instance, at Fulora and Theka, the settlers abandoned their huts upon hearing about the approach of the police party, but returned as soon as the police left. However, months later, on 11 June 1947, as the chances of Assam being included in Pakistan faded away, the Muslim League called off their anti-eviction movement.[191]

In the backdrop of pro-Pakistan mobilization of immigrant peasants and localized clashes between them and the state as well as the Assamese peasants, the Assamese peasants were actively mobilized by the Asom Jatiya Mahasabha.[192] The Mahasabha articulated its fear of the imminent danger of Assam being included in Pakistan and asked the Assamese peasants to counter this threat. In some places, the Assamese peasants responded to the Mahasabha appeal by organizing meetings or seeking state help. There were reports of the formation of *atmarakha bahinis* (self-defence forces). Public meetings were organized in a concerted effort to enlist the support of Assamese peasants against the immigrant Muslim peasants. The centre of such meetings was western Assam, where fiery speeches were given by none other than Ambikagiri Raichaudhuri, President of the Mahasabha. In one such meeting held on 28 March 1947 at Howli and attended by people from more than 50 villages, it was decided to form atmarakha bahinis in every village to protect the Assamese peasants from 'the attack of East Bengali peasants'.[193] *Dainik Assamiya* reported that, Roichaudhuri had also called for Nehru's advice in the event of Muslim League's attack on Assam.[194] The impact of this fear was felt in the districts of eastern Assam too, even if there were no East Bengali settlements there. The Sibsagar District Congress Committee, in an emergency meeting, expressed its concern on the recent political programme of the Muslim League. It urged the Assamese people of all communities 'meticulously to defend the country from the impending attack of the East Bengali peasants'.[195] These measures of 'defending the country' would include self-defence and support from the government.

Clashes took place between the East Bengali and the Assamese peasants or Nepali grazers near various grazing reserves. They had also taken place before the actual League mobilization began. In March 1945, *Dainik Assamiya* extensively reported such a clash in the Koimari grazing reserve, where the Assamese peasants had also recently reclaimed land. The newspaper further reported that the attack was allegedly by the East Bengali settlers on the *khat pam* of the Assamese peasants.[196] The Assamese peasants urged the government to provide them with police support. Instigation by the Muslim League further intensified these clashes. A clash in the Latoria grazing reserve in Barpeta in November 1946 resulted in the alleged killing of Nepali grazers.[197] Elders from villages in the neighbourhood of Latoria appealed to the Commissioner of Kamrup to provide them security against any attack by the East Bengali peasants.[198] They claimed that the *char*s in western Assam were witnesses to regular meetings of immigrant Muslim peasants which were presided over by none other than Bhasani. News of these meetings being attended by more 'dreadful' and 'physically stronger' Pathan Muslims was also in circulation. The East Bengali peasants, according to the Assamese villagers, had reportedly asserted that the military would not be there for long and that 'there would be a repetition of the Noakhali'.[199] Noakhali, a district in East Bengal, had seen horrific communal violence in November 1946, the news of which had already reached the valley.[200] Fear gripped other distant villages too, and the Deputy Commissioner of Kamrup received another petition signed by 41 Assamese peasants and traders from the close-by Dakonia grazing reserve claiming that the fear of violence arising out of the news of Latoria incident and the meetings at the Dakonia reserve loomed large on their minds. These peasants admitted that for the previous two days they had neither been able to eat nor been able to sleep. They thus urged the district administration to provide armed police protection in the area.[201]

The Kurua reserve in Mangaldai also became a site of tension between the two communities.[202] A large number of Assamese peasants from this area, including the village headman, mauzadar and others, submitted a petition to the Deputy Commissioner narrating their perceptions of the danger of violence. Threats of violence emanating from various Muslim villages spread fear in the Assamese villages. On the other hand, communitarian solidarity of the Assamese caste-Hindu peasants quickly reinforced the East Bengali Muslim peasants' solidarity. For instance, in Bhabanipur, Kamrup, news of religious chanting during a festival in a Hindu village immediately led to an assembly of Muslims in a neighbouring Muslim village in apprehension of an attack by the Hindus. On their part, as the Hindu villagers learned about the Muslim congregation, the former assumed that the attack would be made by the East Bengalis, which in turn put them in a state of alert.[203]

However, the pro-Pakistan mobilization had a very limited appeal for the Assamese Muslim peasants. The presence of Assamese Muslims — those who came to Assam during the Mughal-Ahom wars and thereafter and had adopted Assamese cultural practices — in the pro-Pakistan meetings was thus minimal. In fact, there was apprehension on the part of Assamese Muslims about the political goals of the Muslim League. A public meeting of the Assamese Muslim peasants in Jorhat in April 1947, presided over by Pitambar Deva Goswami, the Satradhikar of the Garmur satra as well as a powerful leader of the Assamese

Hindu peasants and a sympathizer of the Hindu Mahasabha,[204] lamented the fact that the Assam government had not distributed land amongst the Assamese Muslim landless peasants. Another resolution adopted in the same meeting described how the East Bengali Muslim peasants who had recently immigrated and settled in Assam had been a social nuisance to both Assamese Hindus and Muslims. The government often received telegraphic messages from the Assamese Muslims opposing the settlement of East Bengali peasants.[205]

Despite occurrences of localized clashes, the highly politicized East Bengali peasants neither came into widespread and direct clashes with the Assamese peasants nor threatened to claim the latter's lands. The continuous efforts of Muslim League leaders to popularize the demand for Assam's merger with Pakistan by mobilizing the East Bengali peasants remained confined to professional grazing reserves or Reserved Forests. By early May in 1947, though the intensity of pro-Pakistan movement had diminished and the possibility of inclusion of valley districts in Pakistan did not seem to be a reality any more, the APML, as the police admitted, held about 450 meetings, 180 processions drawing a total participation of about 400,000 Muslims in Assam. On three occasions, communal violence was met with shooting by the police resulting in the death of 14 peasants and injury of 20 others.[206] Most of the meetings were held in Goalpara, Barpeta and Darrang where the East Bengali immigrant peasants had recently settled in the professional grazing reserves. These areas were thus witnesses to violence by peasants driven by their hopes and fears. The idea of merger with Pakistan had taken deep roots in the minds of East Bengali peasants. They thought they would get land in Pakistan, while the Assamese peasants feared an imminent danger of loss of their lives and lands in the new Muslim-dominated nation. The threat of another wave of peasant immigration from East Pakistan — the new name of East Bengal after Partition — did not disappear entirely. Illustrative of such lingering fear was a 1962 letter by Pitambor Deva Goswami, who had defended the cause of Assamese Muslims in 1947, to Prime Minister Jawaharlal Nehru, reminding him of the imminent threat of Assam being invaded by East Pakistani immigrants.[207]

The Muslim League was abolished in Assam in March 1948.[208] Meanwhile, a large number of Muslim immigrant peasants from western Assam, along with Bhasani, went back to East Pakistan.[209] There was no estimate of those people who crossed over to the new nation. The Assamese peasants quickly reoccupied the land vacated by the East Bengali peasants; in some places, the Assamese sharecroppers replaced the East Bengali sharecroppers. As worries of Partition began to disappear, fresh immigration from East Pakistan into the valley began. In 1950, the Indian parliamentarians largely agreed that half-a-million people had entered Assam from East Pakistan.[210] These included many Hindus too and not all of them were peasants in search of land. A sympathetic Indian government initially decided to settle some of the refugees in Assam. The Assam government, supported by Asom Jatiya Mahasabha, bitterly opposed such proposal.[211] Officially, the newcomers were considered not immigrants in search of land but infiltrators from a hostile East Pakistan. However, as India strengthened its anti-Pakistan stand, in February 1950 the Indian Parliament passed an act, which, it was agreed, would help expel the infiltrators. A couple of years later, the Assam government admitted that several thousand bighas of land had been already 'encroached by the Muslims East Pakistani peasants'.[212] The government also agreed that the East Bengali peasants who had come earlier continued 'to encroach into government land'.[213] The Congress ministry directed that 'no East Bengali should, under any circumstance, be offered settlement'.[214] At the same time, public meetings attended by the Assamese peasants passed resolutions asking the government to allow them to settle in government lands and Reserved Forests. Often, they told the government that such reclaimed land would be used for community farming only.[215] In the meantime, another story had begun to unfold in the countryside, more of which will be discussed in the next chapter.

3

Tenants, Sharecroppers and Communists

In the 1940s, when the popular peasant politics was at its peak, the Assamese sharecroppers could hardly find any political mentor for them. The previous chapter discussed how nationalist and religious politics, and more or less independent peasant actions continued to hold sway over rural politics in Assam. While the Muslim League brought hope for better socio-economic conditions to the East Bengali peasants, the Congress nationalists reached out to the Assamese peasants, mostly rich and well-to-do ones. Their *ryot sabhas*, strategically defending the interests of the Assamese rich peasants–traders–moneylender network, continued to consolidate the Assamese peasants' interests. On the other hand, the East Bengali poor peasants, supported by their rich brethren, eagerly looked forward to effective political mobilization by the Muslim League. In the meantime, the plight of sharecroppers and landless peasants in the valley hardly found a voice in the political programmes of both the Assam Congress and the Muslim League. Occasionally, both would come to the rescue of these peasants in the legislative space but did not effectively advocate the protection of their interests. Despite this gloomy picture in the 1940s, some amongst the Assamese tenants in the rent-free estates and the sharecroppers took the risk of inviting the wrath of their arrogant and powerful landowners. This was a little odd in the high days of nationalist politics. A small section of the Assamese youth, only recently christened in the communist doctrine of politics, tried to carve out a space within the nationalist political programme. They thought that the nationalist political perspective on the Assamese peasant question would not be able to help rescue the downtrodden amongst the Assamese peasants from decades of exploitation. Did they succeed? To know this, we must begin our discussion with an enquiry into the early days of politics surrounding tenancy.

Landlords Faced the Wrath of Tenants

It was not all well for the Assamese landlords, the custodians of *nisf-khiraj* and *la-khiraj* estates, in the twentieth century. Like them, zamindars in the neighbouring Goalpara had a troubled time too. Their tenants had given them tough resistance earlier in the Mughal times.[1] In the nineteenth century, they had either refused to pay rent or learned the usefulness of British colonial laws in challenging their powerful landlords. The zamindars had filed suits against the tenants, seeking recovery of rent. The number of litigations multiplied and one estimate put the figure at 5,782 during 1907–17 in Goalpara and Dhubri courts. The tenants went to the appellate authorities and a few even reached the Calcutta High court. And when they failed to get any safeguard against the zamindars' exploitation, they had taken recourse to physical force against the zamindars.[2] The la-khiraj and nisf-khiraj estates had not fared well either in terms of tenant–landlords relationship, and conflicts between the two were frequent.

The perceptive Assamese thinker and historian Gunabhiram Barua (1834–94) did not fail to bring to the forefront this crucial aspect of the strained relationship between *Satradhikar*s — as owners of la- and nisf-khiraj estates — and their *bhakat*s in his social satire *Ram Nabami*, now considered a classic.[3] Many others agreed with him in condemning the exploitation of tenants by their landlords. By the end of the nineteenth century, managing these landed estates had turned out to be essentially a cumbersome process. In the 1880s, with the promulgation of the Assam Land Revenue Regulation of 1886 and enquiries being made into the affairs of these estates, tenants acquired a veneer of legal protection. Eventually, a number of nisf-khiraj and la-khiraj estates witnessed protracted legal battles between tenants and landlords over issues of ejection, occupancy rights, etc. Tenants scored some decisive victories.[4] Indeed the 1886 regulation paved the way for the beginning of a new era of peasant consciousness. The latter would be based on a notion of individual ownership of land rights advocated by this regulation. This freedom would also be a hallmark of peasant protests in the next century as we will see in this book.

There is no concrete evidence to know whether the history of tenants' resistance in Goalpara inspired their fellow-tenants in Kamrup — which is in close physical proximity and has had a shared cultural ecology with Goalpara — but by the early twentieth century, rumblings of discontent against the landlords could be heard. An incident dating back to 1917 throws some light and helps us understand this discontent in such estates.[5] The strained landlord–tenant relations came to light when the tenants of the nisf-khiraj estates of Parbatia Goswami,[6] a leading owner of la-khiraj and nisf-khiraj estates in Kamrup and whose forefathers were invited to Ahom kingdom to preach Hinduism, submitted a petition before the Chief Commissioner of Assam.[7] The tenants reported the harassment meted out to them by their landlord and demanded immediate enquiry into their grievances and their urgent redressal. Despite having tilled the land for several generations, they claimed that they were treated as temporary tenants. Condemning such discrimination, they demanded tenancy rights which would give them the right to sell, inherit, and own the lands they had been cultivating and thereby ensure protection against eviction. They also demanded that the landlord only collect rent at the government-approved rate. The Assam government instituted an enquiry into the matter and several layers of tension between the landlord and his tenants came to light. The landlord, represented by his clerk Ram Charan Talukdar, could not deny any of the tenants' allegations.[8] The enquiry officer of the government found that unless cesses were paid a tenant was not only denied a rent receipt but was also threatened with eviction by the landlord. He also found that the landlords did not recognize the inheritance rights of tenants unless cesses were paid. This amount due from a tenant went up to Rs 100.[9] It is not clear whether the tenants had thought of hiring someone to represent their case before the government, but they did come themselves before the revenue officer to argue for their case.

A.H.W. Bentinck, Deputy Commissioner of Kamrup, opined that the levy of unofficial taxes like *pranami* and *salami* by landlords was illegal. The Assam government admitted the illegal nature of such cesses.[10] While agreeing with the government's position on such illegal cesses, Bentinck doubted whether the Assamese nisf-khiraj estate holders would ever refrain from levying such taxes. He was rather convinced that even if the administration wanted to prosecute the landlords, the tenants, in view of the insecurity of their tenure, would never come forward to oppose the landlords.[11] Expressing a sympathetic concern for the tenants, Bentinck tried to understand the reason why they only rarely articulated their grievances against their landlords. He claimed that they knew that the landlords regarded them as temporary occupants and, due to absence of any legal safeguards, continued to thrust upon them various undue and illegal taxes. He categorically told his government that if the tenants approached the court, they knew well that they would face further threat of eviction from their landlords and would even be evicted. Also, according to him, they were not even sure whether the court's verdict would be in their favour or not. However, he emphasized that it would not be desirable to compel the nisf-khiraj holders to give up the right of seizure of their tenants' properties. He might thus have been right in suggesting the reason why in most cases tenants refrained from entering into a legal suit against their landlords. The incident involving Parbatia Goswami, nevertheless, showed that the relationship between landlords and their tenants became worse. The tenants, with a substantial presence in the district,[12] had a chance of gaining a temporary but key moral victory over their landlords and this convinced them to continue a prolonged legal fight. The higher appellate court in Calcutta heard a number of appeal suits filed by both sides on matters of eviction or claims to occupancy rights.[13]

The relationship between landlords and their tenants further worsened in the 1930s. The Great Depression of 1929 and the general economic decline equally impacted these estates as the landlords demanded rent in cash and refused to grant any concession. The tenants were no better off than their brethren in the raiyatwari areas, where even the mauzadars' payment to the government treasury had 'become a thing of the past'.[14] They drew their ideological inspiration from the social imagination of a no-rent campaign. Years before, Assamese ryots had resisted the demands for rent payment and, as a response to the nationalist programme, had staged a series of no-rent agitations.[15] Now forced by a general economic collapse as well as recent memories of no-rent agitation, the tenants became hopeful of seeking justice against their landlords. Things began to take shape when, in 1933, the governor of Assam received a petition signed by approximately 2,000 tenants from Kamrup and seeking government intervention for halting the harassment meted out by their landlords. Unfortunately, no details are available now for us to know what led to the tenants being organized in huge numbers. The incident eventually turned out to be one of the largest mobilizations of tenants in the valley. They argued that absence of a legislation to safeguard their interests had made their relationship with the landlords very insecure.

The tenants drew attention to the fact that for generations they had been occupying and cultivating the estate lands, and yet, it did not ensure them any occupancy right and they 'could be turned out at the sweet will of their landlords'.[16] They also claimed that there was nothing to protect them from the consequences of wrong measurements of land by their landlords. They further claimed that the landlords recorded on paper more area of land rented out to the tenants than what the latter actually held. This meant that they had to pay more rent. They argued that a review of the documents would even reveal that they possessed more land than the total area of the landlords. Absence of a clear occupancy rights was central to all these problems, according to them. Nor were they protected against the illegal cesses imposed by the landlords. In many cases, they claimed, local taxes, other than land revenue, payable by the landlords to the government were collected from the tenants. They poignantly described how their 'landed property fetches but little value'[17] and pointed out the problems faced by the landlords in recovering rent in cases when the tenants did not have enough movable property.

The tenants' protests were not confined to petitioning only. They secured crucial support from people like Rohini Kumar Chaudhuri (1889–1955), a lawyer and Congressman. Chaudhuri spoke at length on the floor of the Assam Legislative Council, defending their rights.[18] The petition against Parbatia Goswami was undoubtedly an outcome of a carefully articulated collective opinion of the tenants of Kamrup. Tenants from other areas were not far behind. Officials admitted that the example of Kamrup was immediately echoed in other parts of the valley. The Assam administration admitted that 'after the application was made from Kamrup there have been frequent references to the subject in various parts of the districts'. Reports on meetings demanding a legislation on the tenancy question poured in from other raiyatwari districts of Assam.

The tenancy question had acquired a larger dimension by the mid-1930s. Though the spirit of the Civil Disobedience movement receded, the political ambience surrounding a short visit of Mahatma Gandhi to Goalpara in 1934 and the making of the Assam Tenancy Act 1935 kept the spirit of the tenants high. Neither did the agrarian economy show any signs of improvement. Recurrent floods during 1934 and 1936 further worsened the rural economy.[19] Tenant protests could be frequently noticed in the second half of the 1930s. In 1938, the Deputy Commissioner of Nowgaon took note of how the tenants in nisf-khiraj and la-khiraj estates of the district had begun to challenge the undue privileges of their landlords. Writing to the Commissioner of Assam Valley Division, the Deputy Commissioner not only informed him about the new collective consciousness of the tenants gained under the Congress leadership but also noted that there had been a tendency among the tenants to

> revolt against the *la-khirajdars* and *nisf-khirajdars* due to encouragement they get from certain irrespective persons who prefer to make drastic reformation and turn the world into a utopia by the stroke of a pen ... received several complaints to that some irresponsible Congressmen are spoiling the tenants of la-khirajdars and nisf-khirajdars and *adhiars* ... not to pay rent to their landlords.[20]

The Deputy Commissioner further acknowledged that it was becoming increasingly hard for the *nisf-khirajdar*s to collect rent from their tenants. He explained that, as the landlords had no power to attach the moveable property of the tenants, they invariably had to go to the civil courts to file suits against them for realization of their dues. The courts did not have any means to ensure speedy collection of rent. In the meantime, the Assam Tenancy Act — the circumstances leading to its enactment is discussed in the next chapter — came into force in 1936. The Assamese press gave wide publicity to the provisions and the scope of the Act.[21] The landlords began to feel the brunt of the Act from their tenants and realized that their tenants would be susceptible to more politicization. Landlords in the raiyatwari areas were also taken aback by the new development. To circumvent such an adverse situation, they resorted to manupulating the provisions of the Act so that they could still deny their tenants the occupancy rights. Very often, they would change their tenants or adhiars. However, such attempts of eviction did not go unnoticed. In 1938, the Deputy Commissioner of Nowgaon noted how 'the adhiar does not always continue as adhiar of a patta-holder [read landlord]. Different persons take up adhi cultivation according to the conveniences and therefore they cannot be termed as permanent *raiyat* and no tenancy right accorded'.[22] To avoid such mischievous tactics adopted by the landlords, the tenants also demanded an amendment to the Act. Such demands, however, were ignored by the district administration did not favour granting occupancy rights to the tenants.

On the other hand, the adhiars also sought occupancy rights in the annual *patta* land which they had been cultivating as sharecroppers for years. The landlords, on their part, thought that it would be best to convert such annually leased lands into *myadi patta*, land leased for a longer period of time. The growing anxiety of the landlords about the impending loss of their privileges is best captured in the words of Haladhar Bhuyan, a leading Congress leader in Nowgaon. Reacting to a government proposal for the conversion of special annual patta land into a periodic one, Bhuyan categorically wrote:

> [T]here is a system in our country, probably all over the country, to get land cultivated on adhi and similar other *chukti* terms by the patta-holders. The wrong impression that the cultivation of annual patta lands by a person on any pretext gives him the right of ownership is largely responsible for such misapprehension and the growing tendency for conversion of such lands into periodic patta.[23]

As the situation deteriorated, the Assam government, after initial hesitation, in 1940, initiated measures to prepare the records-of-rights of the tenants in nisf-khiraj and la-khiraj estates of Kamrup as per the provisions of the Assam Tenancy Act.[24] The record-of-rights were prepared in several *mauza*s of Kamrup, but this did not actually lead to the grant of any occupancy rights. Along with nisf-khiraj and la-khiraj estates, *khat*, *chamua* and khiraj lands, included in the religious grants, were covered by the record-of-rights. However, only the privileged tenants with occupancy rights were considered for the preparation of the record-of-rights.[25] While preparing the record-of-rights, the tenants were asked to specify the land which they were occupying and their usual method of rent payment. The process of inclusion of lands in the record-of-rights was uneven. In the valley, this was the first-of-its-kind process wherein the tenants were given the hope of protection against the uncertainty of tenancy. However, sharecroppers in khiraj estates still remained outside the purview of any such arrangments for tenurial security. The tenant protest, noticed by the Deputy Commissioner of Nowgaon, was nothing but an outcome of the notification for the preparation of record-of-rights.[26] Tenants from other parts of Assam also made similar demands but failed to gain any concession similar to those in Kamrup. The tenants from a landed estate, i.e., Karanga *satra* in Auniati, Sibsagar, too expressed their dissatisfaction, in a petition with the fact that the estate-owner had not granted them any remission of rent. Their demand for remission of revenue came in the wake of the Assam government granting remission of revenue to the ryots in 1932–33.[27] The tenants, mostly belonging to the Miri tribe, demanded that the Satradhikar — landlord or estate-owner — should grant them remission as had the Assam government. They also complained that instead of giving a *pacca* receipt (printed receipt), the landlord or his agents wrote the word 'received' with pencil in the patta without specifying the amount. They protested against the extra charge levied on them if they failed to pay the rent in time. They further complained about not getting occupancy rights. This petition clearly indicates the collective political consciousness of the tenants.

The 1930s saw some re-alignment in tenancy politics. The role of the catalyst was played by the Assam Tenancy Act of 1935. Though the Act brought only the tenants of la- and nisf-khiraj estates under its purview, it added a new dimension to the demands of the sharecroppers. On several occasions earlier, they had pressed the government for the implementation of the Act in their favour, as they also did years later in Nowgaon: in 1938, the Deputy Commissioner of Nowgaon, in an official correspondence, noted how 'there has been a persistent demand for granting occupancy right lands under *adhi*, *bharga* and *bhag* system in the temporarily settled areas also'.[28] He also noted that the sharecroppers claimed that this could be affected by amending the Act.[29]

In the late 1930s, relations between the landlords and the adhiars further worsened. Even the intense Congress mobilization of Assamese peasants, through networks of ryot sabhas, failed to check such deterioration. Often, these ryot sabhas turned out to be breeding grounds for peasant discontentment. On one occasion, Chatia Garekagaon ryot sabha organized a conference called Assam Praja Sanmeelan in Chatia village of Darrang district on 28 March 1936.[30] The Sanmeelan indicated a radical departure from the conventional mobililization techniques of and the kind of issues addressed by the ryot sabhas on several accounts. The conference was amongst those held parallel to the ryot sabha movement as they were engineered by an increasingly influential socialist wing within Assam Congress. The conference also drew the attention of the Governor-in-Council to the various problems arising out of the landowner–sharecropper conflict such as the exorbitant rent charged by the landowners. Like tenants seeking immediate remedy to these grievances, but short of demanding the abolition of the adhiar system, the conference attendees demanded only a minimum fixed rent. A resolution adopted in the conference also condemned the use of physical coercion resorted to by landowners against their adhiars for recovering rent,[31] citing the incident of one landowner breaking into the granary of his adhiar, Malladev Hazarika, in his absence and taking away his paddy. The participants also protested against the fact that landowners often demanded to know on which day the adhiars would pay the rent. Another resolution blamed the Assam government for not bringing the Assam Tenancy Act into force, as the landlords continued to charge exorbitant rents with impunity in spite of the Assam government's policy of revenue remission, and the Act could only prohibit them from doing so. The conference attendees fully endorsed the idea of extending the government policy of rent remission in khiraj estates to la- and nisf-khiraj estates. They even proposed in another resolution that the Governor-in-Council take steps to prevent the estate-owners from extracting any additional taxes and personal services from the tenants.

It was further argued in the conference that as crop prices had decreased and the ryots were unable to pay the rent, the government should fix the rate of rent at not higher than Rs 4 per *pura*. It was agreed that the sharecroppers were still exposed to exploitation due to non-application of the Assam Tenancy Act and urged the government to implement the Act.[32] In yet another significant resolution, they also brought forth the apparent feeling of disdain and neglect of the Assamese society at large — a society largely dominated by the high-caste and the rich — towards the sharecroppers. The Asamiya Samraksini Sabha, a leading Assamese nationalist forum, also took notice of these resolutions and brought the matter to the notice of the Assam Ryot Sabha.

To sum up, the conference highlighted two issues very clearly: first, the tenants were in no mood to pay high rent to the landlords and second, they wanted the government to bring the Assam Tenancy Act into force. In fact, the Act did come into force the very next year, i.e., 1937. But, in reality, little was done to execute it. Rapid fall in crop prices and the resultant severe cash scarcity put various sections of the rural peasantry, including tenants and adhiars, under acute distress. Rent remission was the best possible remedy that the tenants and the adhiars could hope for. However, there was little sign of the duo joining force against the landlords. It was only in 1947, that the Assam government received several representations from the sharecroppers demanding amendments to the Act.[33] But, this new awareness about their rights and their growing politicization was not without any background.

Assamese Youth Learned Communism

In the 1920s, a few from amongst the Assamese literati sought alternative answers to the range of questions that the nationalist propaganda had brought forward. The ideas of colonial modernity and its offshoots shaped the tastes and sensibilities of the Assamese literati in late nineteenth and early twentieth century. On the conditions of rural population, they upheld mostly a romantic view of an ideal society unperturbed by discontent. However, the later years of the 1920s witnessed some sharp departure from this view. Sympathetic accounts of the lives and activities of peasantry slowly found way into the Assamese literary space. Later literary critics of post-independence period identified this tradition as 'progressive' and 'Marxist'.[34] These new 'progressive' writings expressed displeasure at the simplistic nationalist representation of Assamese society and dared to portray a complex and painful picture of the society. Space had been already created for the onset of a progressive trend within this powerful yet liberal Assamese nationalist tradition, as reflected in the Assamese literary practices, when they introduced its readers to the major upheavals in the early-twentieth-century Russia, especially the 1917 revolution. This new liberal tradition gained momentum in the 1930s with the publication of two literary journals *Jayanti* and *Abahan*, along with others.[35] Both these journals encouraged an exchange of socialist and communist political ideas on the Assamese society from a Marxian perspective. For the next few decades, this literary perspective was to remain a key and dominant trend in the Assamese literary culture.[36] Those who participated in this literary tradition came from diverse backgrounds but essentially agreed on the need for an alternative political culture to bring about change in the Assamese society. A few amongst them — for instance, Bhabananda Datta (1918–69) and Jyotiprasad Agarwala (1903–51) — with their intimate experience of the European Socialism tried to appeal to the political sensibilities of both liberal and conservative elements among the Assamese nationalists and elites. Their literary works, along with those of others with similar persuasions, could, however, moderately resist the conservative elements in the political and literary landscape of Assam.

With the growing dissatisfaction amongst the Assamese tenants and sections of literati in the valley, the ideology of the Indian communist parties began to draw attention of a few Assamese youths. Many of them came from a rural background and would have a short stint of education in Guwahati, which was fast emerging as the cultural and educational capital of the valley, and carve out a significant career in Assamese student politics. A good example is that of Uma Sarma who later became a prominent communist leader. He came from a poor family of Goalpara and had to struggle for his livelihood while studying.[37] Almost all the students from rural background came to study in the Cotton College, which was established in 1900 with a view to paving the way for modern British educational establishments in the valley. The college was the only hope for Assamese students aspiring for higher studies. Many of them went on to play an important role in the politics of the region in the mid-twentieth century. With the establishment of the college, the migration of Assamese students to Calcutta for higher education declined. A residential campus further helped to build a good network for students from different parts of Assam. Several experiments in encouraging social intercourse among students, such as eating and living together in hostels, often helped them rethink about and interrogate their conservative social values, borne out of their poor living conditions and their exposure to socio-cultural barriers between people in the rural setting. It was in the 1930s that the college became one of the platforms for the popularization of political ideas among the students. Some of them had already been introduced to the nationalist political discourse propagated by the Congress. In the public grounds adjoining the campus, popularly known as the 'Judges Field', the Assam Congress used to hold regular political meetings. Students' participation in these meetings was generally impressive, and many of them either took active interest in understanding the complexities of nationalist politics, or would at least be familiar with the anti-imperialist slogans. That the college had already become an important place of student polities became a matter of concern for the government. Government officials began to note with serious concern that students were becoming more keen on listening to the political speeches of Congress leaders. The hostel wardens were asked to keep a strict watch on students who had socialist leanings.

Meanwhile, the attention of a section of Assamese youth was drawn to the popular communist literature, already circulating in Guwahati. A few young men, inspired and motivated by such literature, would get together and form study circles, a concept not unfamiliar in India at that time. A handwritten news magazine called *Ahuti*, which was to be the first political magazine in Assam, had a wide readership among students. There were also a few physical training camps in the 1930s in Guwahati, which the students were encouraged to join. These camps and study circles were the channels through which Marxist ideas were disseminated among students. Even some of the Assamese nationalists, for instance, firebrand leaders like Chandranath Sarma or Ambikagiri Raichaudhuri, could speak with considerable authority on the aspirations of the Assamese society. Yet, there was no communist organization and the Congress remained the most dominant and powerful one in the region. A beginning was nevertheless made with a section of youth forming a branch of the Bengal-based Communist League, which soon came to be known as the Revolutionary Communist Party of India (RCPI). It gathered some following amongst the Assamese students in Guwahati.

In Bengal, the Communist League was formed by breaking away from the Communist Party of India (CPI). It was headed by Saumendranath Tagore (1901–74),[38] a grand-nephew of Rabindranath Tagore and a Trotskyite in political orientation but never a member of the Fourth International.[39] Saumendranath's early political career began within the larger umbrella of the Peasant and Workers Party in Bengal, but soon he went to Europe for studies. He ended up being in British and German prisons for his anti-colonial political activities. When he came back to Bengal, dissatisfied with the role and practices of the CPI, he broke away to form a small splinter group called Ganabahini Group, soon to be known as the Communist League and later rechristened as RCPI in 1938.[40] He criticized the Indian National Congress as well for its 'bourgeoisie character' and stressed the necessity of forming a party with the support of peasants and workers. Thus, there was some ambiguity in the League's understanding of the class character of the Congress. The League, however, declared Congress as 'a multi class organization' whose 'social base is wide enough to enfold vast masses of the middle class, peasantry and workers'.[41] Shortly after this, in 1938, he visited Assam with the intention of expanding his organizational network. During this visit, he addressed the students of Cotton College. The visit was coordinated by Debendranath Sarma (1902–89), a Congressman who also had an exposure to the socialist and communist activities in Bengal. Tagore's visit to the college was a widely publicized affair.[42] He could influence a few students who had some exposure to communist literature and political methods. The Russian revolution and the establishment of a socialist regime had a forceful impact on these young Assamese students who were actively looking for an alternative political programme. A branch of the Communist League or RCPI was thus formed in October 1939,[43] and several students from Cotton College joined it.[44] The next move for these youths, through the RCPI's student wing Assam Provincial Student Federation (APSF), was to contest the annual election of the college student union, which they eventually won on the strength of their ideological influence. For several years thereafter, the APSF retained its hold over the union.

On the eve of independence, the RCPI voiced its opposition to the British Cabinet Mission's grouping proposal of 1946 — which would have placed Assam in a Muslim-dominated group — thereby signalling its commitment to the nationalist agenda.[45] The movement against the grouping proposal, led by the Congress, had already garnered mass support in Assam.[46] The APSF, in its eight annual provincial conferences held at Goalpara, too opposed this proposal as a 'national problem'.[47] By addressing the question of Grouping, the RCPI carved out a niche for itself in the mainstream politics of Assam. Tagore, while addressing a meeting in 1946, called the grouping question an 'echo of the Pakistan movement'. He asserted that accepting the grouping would not only cause the destruction of Assam but would also go against the sovereignty of India. Hence, he appealed, 'All Indians should reject this demand'.[48] In early 1947, the APSF, in another conference, discussed the question of the future of Constituent Assembly formed for drafting the Constitution of India. Rejecting the idea of Constituent Assembly on the ground that after Independence power went into the hands of Indian bourgeoise only, it passed a resolution 'to build up a movement of the peasants, labours and middle class to reject the constituent assembly'.[49]

In Bengal, Tagore and his RCPI began to organize the peasants and workers in panchayats, a close parallel to embryonic 'Soviets'. He thought that these panchayats would compete with the new Congress-led government for a share in the power and would ultimately lead to the establishment of Workers and Peasants Constituent Assembly in a future socialist India. He also visited the valley, spending a long time there. His visit and the public deliberations drew the attention of the Assamese pro-Congress press too. Throughout his tour along with Assamese RCPI leaders, he continued to articulate their opposition to the Constituent Assembly. He appealed for the establishment of village panchayats to thwart the British imperialism. In a meeting in Dibrugarh, presided over by Bishnu Prasad Rabha, Tagore appealed to the Assamese members in the Constituent Assembly 'to reject the grouping'.[50] He also asked the 'younger generation to form panchayat[s] in the villages and to get freedom from the British imperialism'.[51] In another meeting in Digboi, Tagore spoke to coalmine workers.[52]

Given the popularity and the towering image of Assam Congress leaders, it was an uphill task for the RCPI to gain any ground as an alternative political formation. However, it still took up the gauntlet. The RCPI, in the typical style of communist mobilization, initially concentrated on organizing the labouring class in Guwahati.

In the absence of a distinct industrial labouring class in Assam, apart from the plantation workers, and with the Congress having a strong and powerful presence amongst the tea garden workers, the natural choice for the Communist League was to make an attempt to mobilize rice mill workers, drivers of horse-driven carts, or workers of steamboats.[53] The young League members tried to indoctrinate a few hundred workers into the communist ideology through regular meetings, but such mobilization programmes were bound to be ineffective in a largely agrarian society. Their language and slogans barely attracted the workers. In Bengal, the RCPI leadership had already begun to counter the CPI and the Congress socialists.[54] The RCPI, unlike the CPI, extended its support to the Quit India movement. Participation in the movement not only gave a critical opportunity to the communist youth to learn the tactics of mass mobilization but also helped them avoid getting alienated from the masses at this critical phase of political transition. In the next couple of years, a two-way process began which resulted in limited popularity of the RCPI, and some attempts by it to mobilize the Assamese peasants.[55] Despite an increase in demand for raw materials, the war-time opportunities did not bring an end to the hardships of the Assamese peasants. Some benefits of this rising demand went to the East Bengali peasants who cultivated jute. It was a critical juncture to rethink the Assamese agrarian question.

The Assamese ryots had a brief stint in the political programme of the Congress. The Congress-led ryot sabhas, approximately 200 in number, gave a new perspective to their local problems: their problems began to be seen in more broadly in terms of the nationwide impact of colonial rule on the agrarian societies rather than as localized landowner–peasant/tenant conflict of interests. Whatever peasant mobilization took in the valley in the 1930s, it was primarily under the auspices of Congress, which, as a multiclass organization, provided opportunity to the *jotedar*s in Goalpara, rich Assamese peasants, and the middle class to participate in its programmes. The hardships of sharecroppers, landless peasants and agricultural labourers, however, did not find any place in the discussions of ryot sabhas.[56] The Congress leaders saw Gandhi as speaking on behalf of the peasants. Nehru lectured Indian peasants on the importance of India as a nation.[57] The Assamese Congress leaders, too, toured villages and lectured the ryots on the evils of opium addiction, benefits of *khadi* and *swaraj*. A few even expressed their dislike of the immigration of East Bengali peasants.

This brief engagement of Assamese ryots with the nationalist politics might have created some euphoria. However, Congress nationalists were not the only ones to mobilize the peasants in Assam. The RCPI too formed the Krishak Banua Panchayat (KBP) as its peasant wing in May 1940.[58] Hierarchies of organizational units were formed, a feature typical of a communist organization. The lowest unit of the KBP was called Gaon Krishak Panchayat.[59] The KBP enrolled peasants as its members on an annual membership fee of three annas.[60] Kedarnath Goswami (1901–64), the first president of the KBP, had a rich experience of working with the workers and peasants in eastern Assam. Previously, he had also mobilized the tea garden labourers of Assam Railways and Trading Company, as also the ferry workers in Dibrugarh. Editor of the English daily *Times of Assam* and trained in nationalist Congress politics, he left Congress to join the KBP.[61] The RCPI, articulating agrarian issues, gave a class dimension to the nature of peasant unrest. A conference, held in 1945 and presided over by Goswami, articulated the KBP's stand on the issue of Assamese sharecroppers and landless peasants and emphasized the need to mobilize them. The conference ruled out any broad alliance with any trade union organization, but adopted a resolution to work amongst the sharecroppers and tea plantation labourers. With an eye on the vast labouring population in the tea gardens, it endorsed the need for the opening of two separate Assamese and Hindustani propagation fronts for popularizing the slogans of the RCPI.

The RCPI was not alone in challenging the nationalist understanding of the peasant question, held by the Congress. A few Congressmen, disillusioned with the party's moderate political programmes, were ideologically attracted to the socialist ideas. Alongside the ryot sabha movement, leading dissident Congressmen with socialist leanings formed separate peasant organizations. In 1936, some amongst these socialists such as Dhiren Datta, Khargeswar Tamuly and Jadu Saikia formed one such peasant organization called Haloa Sangha in Golaghat. The Sangha raised the slogan 'land to the tiller' and essentially spoke on behalf of the poor peasants. A couple of years later, in the 1930s, in the backdrop of the Congress-led mass mobilization programme and ryot sabha movement, these socialist groups gained more visibility.

This dissent against the Congress was further reinforced in 1940 when the Assam Provincial Congress Socialist Party (APCSP) was formed in Golaghat, with Sriman Prafulla Goswami elected as the first Secretary.[62] As it was essentially an organization of the socialist members of Assam Congress, the choice of Golaghat as the venue of its first meeting was to avoid any direct condemnation from senior Congress leaders. The sympathizers of the CPI, being a banned group during this period, also became members of the APCSP. Attended by the students and peasants from the neighbouring villages, the meeting was widely publicized by the Assamese press.[63] The Assamese press continued to support this new political move as several 'letter[s] to the editor' were published in support of this development.[64]

A year later, more units of the APCSP were formed in Dibrugarh and Goalpara, but this did not result in any significant organizational expansion and it managed to resurface on the political landscape only during 1946–47.[65] One of the reasons for the APCSP's failure to expand its reach in the early 1940s was its inability to keep the communist friends of CPI and RCPI on its side. At the national level, towards the end of 1940, the ideological rift between the CSP and the CPI began to widen and soon they parted ways,[66] which also meant the CSP's failure to keep the communist members within its fold. As a majority of the leading members of the APCSP were ideologically more inclined towards the CPI, their relationship with the CSP could not be sustained. This strategic separation only helped the independent growth of the CPI in Assam. The communists ousted from the CSP — and the latter itself was virtually defunct — formed the Assam Provincial Communist Party (APCP) in January 1943. These young communist founder-members had a brief career in student politics; many of them had interacted with leading Indian communist leaders and had travelled widely in various parts of Assam.[67] Communist-orientated student politics began to expand from 1939 when the All India Students Federation (AISF) attempted to mobilize students in the valley.[68] Between 1939 and 1943, the young AISF members were in regular interaction with the CPI leaders from Bengal and Surma valley in southern Assam. They were also successful in building links with the scattered working-class population across the valley.

Primarily, orientated towards working amongst the labouring class, the CPI had not, till 1947, been able to successfully organize the Assamese ryots. Neither did it have any visible presence amongst the approximately 3,90,000 tea garden workers. The communists could thus wield only limited influence on the series of labour strikes that occurred in the Digboi refinery in eastern Assam.[69] In 1936, an Assamese youth named Jaganath Bhattacharya of Sibsagar, then studying in Benaras, joined the CSP and participated in the Indian National Congress conference at Lucknow, where the All India Kisan Sabha (AIKS) was formed.[70] The AIKS, whose leadership 'was comprised of motley crowd of Marxists, Fabians, Gandhains and orthodox Hindus'[71] was yet to place itself on a distinct political trajectory. In the subsequent years, as the AIKS was distinctly becoming a CPI-led peasant organization, initiatives were taken by the AIKS leadership, which included Mansur Habib of Bengal and Lala Sardendu Dey with years of experience in the AIKS, to form a provincial unit of the AIKS in Assam.[72] By 1943, there was only one member in the AIKS from Assam while the primary members of its provincial units had increased to 1,008 in the Brahmaputra valley.[73] Politically positioning on the anti-zamindari plank and a slow increase in membership could not give the AIKS any room for significant expansion in the valley. At the same time, the CPI also gradually began to mobilize the disgruntled peasants under the banner of Haloa Sangha, rechristened as Krishak Sabha.[74] Some efforts were also made to mobilize the Assamese tenants under its banner. Throughout the 1940s, and till the communists became successful in mobilizing the ryots in 1947, the Assamese Congressmen either remained skeptical about the ability of communists to mobilize the peasants, or tried to ignore their activities.

The Peasants and the Peasant Question in Assam: Not an Implausible Outlook

> Every ryot in Assam is the absolute master of his lands, from which he is never liable to be ousted until he relinquishes it out of his own free will.[75]

In 1853, Anandaram Dhekial Phukan might have been right about the tenurial rights of Assamese ryots. However, he did not live long to see the rapid transition that had engulfed the Assamese peasant society. Decades later, Gunabhiram Barua, who was a cousin of Phukan and a junior officer in the Assam administration, and who had reminded the government as early as 1893 that it would be disastrous to try to extract more revenue from the ryots, also thought that '[a]s a nation the Assamese are neither too rich nor too poor'.[76] Such views came to be contested by the Assamese literati towards the second quarter of the twentieth century when they voiced competing views on the condition of Assamese ryots. However, not all these perceptions were motivated by a desire to see some radical changes in the Assamese peasant society.

In the 1940s, the presence of communist organizations also meant a reorientation in the political consciousness of the Assamese peasant society. A desire to see an improvement in the conditions of ryots forced a new perspective to develop on the agrarian question in Assam. In other parts of India, the policies and practices of the Congress emphasized the romantic notion of a united peasant society and the benevolence of landlords. However, in the wake of a new wave of anti-landlord peasant mobilization in northern and some other parts of British India, Congress started expressing some fresh perspectives on the Indian peasant question.[77] Slowly, an anti-landlord stand was gaining ground within the Congress. In Assam, the majority of the Assamese Congress leaders came from an urban social milieu, but it would be wrong to suggest that they cut all their associations with the peasant society. Many of them, being absentee landowners, were still dependent on the agricultural production. Despite their sensitivity to the peasant question, they rarely could rescue them from the clutches of the trader–moneylender–landlord nexus. Also, the Assam Congress largely remained silent on the peasant question and continued to uphold a romantic view of a peaceful and conflict-free Assamese countryside.

In contrast, the Assamese communist leaders had different views on the peasant question. Such views were reflected in their works — mostly literary pieces, booklets or pamphlets — published in the 1940s. Although never written eloquently, they were primarily meant for the indoctrination of new party workers. Whether such writings had mass appeal, or whether the Assamese peasants agreed with this portrayal of their lives at all, is difficult to know. For instance, the RCPI leader Kedarnath Goswami articulated a broad communist approach to the peasant question in 1942 beyond the influential framework of nationalist discourse.[78] Like many other contemporary Indian Marxist views, Goswami's was a broad outline of the trajectory of the Assamese peasantry's prospective transition to socialism. He claimed that only a socialist intervention could lead to the emancipation of Assamese peasants, but he fell short of highlighting what would be the nature of this emancipation. He even castigated the Assamese peasants for their ready submissiveness to their rulers and their attachment to traditional values, which worked as a hindrance to their upliftment and was a cause for their failure to be a part of the larger socialist movement. However, he left no impression on sharecroppers and landless peasants, and the RCPI had to wait for another couple of years to publicize more concrete views on the peasant question. This seemed to be accomplished with the publication of *Biplabi Khetiak* (*The Rebellious Peasant*). Written in the name of Bhupen Mahanta (1919–2006) — a young RCPI leader who later became a successful entrepreneur — and published by Guwahati-based Radical Institute, a popular name for the office of the Communist League, this work contained the RCPI's political discourse on the 'peasant question'.[79] This book, priced at one anna, was intended for wider circulation as it was written at a time when the movement of sharecroppers and landless peasants was gaining popularity. The Government of Assam perceived this work as 'a Marxist view of the exploitation of Indian peasantry under the British rule, criticizing the Congress and advocating a peasant movement on communist line',[80] and readily proscribed it.

Amongst the issues that *Biplabi Khetiak* highlighted was the dependence of Indian middle class on agriculture, the widespread indebtedness of peasants, the pitfalls of the zamindari settlement, and the high revenue demand in the raiyatwari areas. The tea planters, with their extensive land grants, were called big landlords by *Biplabi Khetiak*, and in doing so, it marked a departure from the nationalist understanding of landlords as benevolent. The book also accused the government of allowing the tea gardens to continue enjoying these land grants and of allowing concessions to them in matters related to tax and revenue. It further claimed that three-fourths of the tea estates never paid any taxes.[81] As similar concessions were extended to the Goalpara zamindars and rich Assamese peasants, the entire revenue burden had to be borne by the poor peasants. This forced the peasants to pay one-eighth of their total income as revenue to the government.

But who would defend the interests of the poor peasants, as the Congress, having close ties with the tea planters, zamindars and moneylenders, could hardly afford to protect them? This meant that a communist peasant organization could only remedy the situation. That the Assamese peasant society was a stratified one, unlike how the nationalists viewed it, was further highlighted in some other works.[82] The RCPI also conducted investigations in the villages to understand the social composition of the peasant society.[83] It also reminded the government that it was the Guwahati-based absentee landowners who had significant landed interests in the Beltola mauza, which was to emerge as a prime area of communist mobilization.[84] The absentee landowners took

> half of the total produce from the adhiars, i.e., almost 3 *maunds* per *bigha* and they gave half to 1½ annas of revenue to the government. In this process, the landowners earned more than one lakh from the poor peasants alone in the Beltola mauza.[85]

The Congress socialists had a slightly liberal view. A work with a liberal title *Khetiak*, published in 1948 by the Barpeta branch of CSP, put forth the socialist perspective on the Assamese peasant question.[86] Coinciding with this, the Congress socialists also published its manifesto on agrarian policy.[87] For the CSP, the key issue haunting the Assamese peasant society was price rise.[88] Like their communist friends, the socialists also wanted the sharecroppers to be given occupancy rights, the sharecropping and zamindari systems to be abolished, and the Assamese landless peasants to be given land. They argued that the complicated land system must be replaced by a simple relationship between the tiller and the welfare state of independent India. On the issue of awarding compensation to the zamindars for the loss of their lands which would be redistributed, they thought it was neither desirable nor possible to pay compensation, but the land acquired from them must be redistributed among the landless peasant families.[89] Before a complete abolition of sharecropping could be accomplished, the Assamese sharecroppers, they argued, should be entitled to occupancy rights and a fair share of the produce. They did not seek a radical change in the crop-sharing arrangement and only demanded that the landowners do not get more than double the government land revenue. The CSP emphasized that all land settlements be made and all land disputes be adjudicated by village panchayats only. The CSP reiterated that the land crisis could be handled by creating groups of volunteers, known as the 'land army' (cadres drawn from the CSP to lead a land-occupation movement) without bringing large tracts of unploughed wastelands under cultivation. Moving away from the land question, the CSP, the Congress and ryot sabhas, also sought to have embankments built to prevent floods, peasants provided high-breed cattle and canals constructed for irrigation which would lead to higher crop yields.

Articulating a similar stand, the CPI in Assam argued its case on behalf of the poor and middle peasants, and agricultural labourers.[90] Explaining the reasons for a rapid stratification in the Assamese peasant society, the CPI agreed that moneylending had led to large-scale land alienation — an estimated 30 per cent of the total agrarian population had become landless after the Second World War, and another 25 per cent had small landholdings, compelling them to work as agricultural labours. The CPI also criticized the Assam government for its failure to redistribute land amongst the landless Assamese peasants.[91] Most importantly, the CPI agreed that immigration of East Bengali Muslim peasants to Assam had acquired a larger political dimension: it was unabated due to the continued oppression of Muslim peasants by Bengali Hindu zamindars and the availability of unploughed and arable wasteland and absence of zamindari oppression in the Brahmaputra valley.[92] The CPI also asserted that the landlords of Bengal were directly or indirectly encouraging migration 'to divert the rising peasant movement against their own oppressive system'.[93] It further pointed out that vested interests both among the Assamese and the Bengalis had never desired, or at least at that point of time did not sincerely desire an equitable solution to this vexed problem. The emerging Bengali landlords and big jotedars in Assam, the latter being mostly rich Muslim immigrants, did not want any permanent solution to this land settlement problem. This was so because once the land settlement question was solved, their avenues of exploiting poor landless immigrants by engaging them as cheap labour in their big landholdings or by taking money from them through the allurement of giving them land, would be over for ever.[94]

Months before independence, the CPI in Assam articulated its position clearly on the land settlement programme of the Assam provincial government. In 1946, as already discussed, the immigrant, Assamese and tribal peasants were mobilized along communal lines. The immigrant peasants developed great communal solidarity. Perhaps, the CPI tried to avoid another round of communal violence and thus focused on the issue of immigrant peasants. On the other hand, the Tebhaga movement raging in the neighbouring Bengal province compelled the Assam Provincial Organizing Committee (APOC) of the CPI to highlight the problems of adhiars and landless peasants in Assam. The CPI General Secretary P.C. Joshi asked his Assamese comrades to show solidarity with the Tebhaga movement.[95] However, a distinct form of CPI-led anti-landlord peasant mobilization, known as Nankar movement, began to be noticed in different parts of the Barak valley in southern Assam. There is no evidence of the APOC taking a definite stand on the sharecroppers' issue till 1947. It appears there was a delayed intrusion of the CPI into the question of landless peasants or sharecroppers. The official CPI history does not have an explanation of this delay either. However, the proceedings of the first provincial conference of the CPI and other sources might give us clues to understanding this problem.

Gaurishankar Bhattacharjya, the forerunner in the APOC, while discussing the problem of sharecropper–landlord conflict, explained that most of the landlords in Assam were primarily middle-class government employees who, struggling to run their families with their limited income from salaries, were left with no other choice but to buy a little piece of land and rent it out. He reiterated this explanation in the 1952 budget session of the Assam Legislative Assembly, adding that the sheer scale of sharecropping in Assam was due to the Assam government's inattention to the problem of inadequate pay of its middle-class employees. He again raised the issue in the APOC conference in Guwahati in 1948, stating that that as the government employees did not get adequate pay, they were compelled to take up other businesses or buy some land and get it cultivated through the adhi system in order to get the requisite supply of the staple foodcrop, i.e., rice. They, in fact, lived a miserable life till death: they worked 8–10 hours a day and, sometimes, carried their files back to their homes to finish the work, yet they did not get adequate pay to fulfil their basic needs. For this reason, they were compelled to realize 16–20 puras of paddy for every pura of land. When peasants made an agitation to reduce this rate, the leaders of the APOC claimed that they had instigated the peasants against the government.[96] The first annual conference of APOC adopted resolutions, which gave directions to the party cadre 'to make propaganda for abolition of zamindari, for giving land to the landless, for payment of revenue in cash in lieu of produce, for abolition of eviction'.[97] However, the conference avoided the 'land to tiller' slogan and also did not demand a stop to the sharecropping system.

The sharecropper's Tebhaga movement, along with the 'land to tiller' slogan, had reached its height of popularity in the districts of Bengal.[98] The Bengal government passed an ordinance conceding the demands of the Tebhaga movement. The success of Tebhaga was reason enough for rejoicing for the communist peasant organizations elsewhere. All these developments helped the conference decide to recruit Red Guards only from the peasants. The Red Guards would propagate the party programme on different fronts, assist in keeping party discipline, stand up against police repression, and combat the enemies of peasants and labourers.[99] Accordingly, a few units of the CPI were formed in Pandu, Guwahati, Khetri, Lumding, Tinsukia, Naharkatia, Dibrugarh, and Digboi to 'work amongst the peasants'.[100] Immediately after independence, the CPI adopted a few more resolutions on the peasant question. It demanded that landlordism in all forms be abolished and all landholdings of over 50 acres in the Brahmaputra valley be redistributed among the landless and poor peasants with a minimum of 10–15 acres of land. It also demanded that interim relief be given to tenants and sharecroppers by reducing rent in cash or kind, granting occupancy rights to sharecroppers and all tenants-at-will.[101] The CPI further demanded that no land be given to new immigrants to Assam.

Bishnu Prasad Rabha, a gifted dancer, singer and orator who had joined the KBP in 1945 and soon became a charismatic communist leader, gave a new dimension to the Assamese peasant question through several of his literary works in Assamese.[102] He, like many of his communist friends, was influenced by the political developments in communist China. His literary works outline the RCPI's early understanding of the peasant question. The exact relation between Rabha and the RCPI in the early stage of the peasant movement remains unclear. Rabha, in his statement in 1952 before the magistrate who was presiding over his trial on the charge of being a member of the banned CPI, admitted that though he knew the party members closely, he was not a full-time RCPI member till 1949.[103] However, he authored several works under the directions of the party. His works capture the sorrowful conditions of Assamese peasantry, portray the poor as capable of resisting the landowners and prophecize the imminent collapse of the exploitative social institutions. In his imagination, the Assamese village was clearly divided into two worlds, one of the exploited and the other of the exploiters. He drew his ideas from Marxism but had clear sympathies for Chinese communism. He also translated popular literary works portraying Chinese rural life or Russian experiments in communism into Assamese.[104] Rabha's creative works could thus explain the complex agrarian relations of Assam from a Marxist perspective and in simple and comprehensible language.

If Rabha explained the agrarian relations in a language understood by peasantry, the RCPI further elaborated the nature of the participation of working class and peasantry in the Indian freedom movement. It claimed that both working class and peasantry, through their economic organizations, could not indeed participate as a class in the political struggle for national independence. It was through the political party of the proletariat that the working class and the peasantry, fashioned into a distinct political force in the process of active political struggle, would participate and guide the national revolution. The RCPI decided to form an independent communist organization of working class, peasantry and Assamese middle class, and to set up local united front action committees including the organizations of workers, peasants and students in order to wage a struggle on appropriate and concrete anti-imperialist issues. The RCPI also attempted to appropriate the platform created by the Congress and even hinted about the possibility of forging a tactical alliance with the Congress. This strategic position provided ample opportunity to the RCPI to become an important political force in Assam later on. The peasant organizations were expected to be led by the 'revolutionary labourers'. This stand on peasant mobilization was similar to the line adopted by the communist parties elsewhere in India and the world. Thus, like the communist parties elsewhere, those in India denied independent revolutionary agency to the peasants. However, some space was given to the development and articulation of the peasants' collective mentality, the benefits of which could be taken by the labourers, and this joining of forces by the duo would ultimately lead to the independence of the country. However, the practical difficulties faced in mobilizing the peasants and the opposition from the Congress mass mobilization forced the RCPI to redefine this thesis. The phase of RCPI's isolationist attitude towards the Congress was over during the Quit India movement. Local issues came to determine the peasant question in the RCPI discourse. In particular, the problem of landlessness and the adhiars' question clearly dominated its agrarian programme.

Krishak Banua Panchayat Mobilized Adhiars: Exploring Rural Networks

The Marxist view of the peasant question alone could not be a practical roadmap for the successful mobilization of the Assamese peasants. Peasants' hardships were not limited to economic exploitation by moneylenders, bazaars, or landlords but marked by layers of complex social relations including caste hierarchies, rivalries and negotiations, or restrictions imposed by the *khel* system. Apart from different forms of economic exchanges, there were socio-cultural barriers between a tribal and a caste-Hindu peasant. Instances of a caste-Hindu peasant looking down upon a tribal peasant were not few, although there was no uniform pattern in such discrimination. In some cases, the unequal relations between caste-Hindu and tribal peasants replicated the landowner–tenant relationship. Castes hierarchies were noticeable and often came to be reflected in various areas and at several levels. The Congressled ryot sabhas operated through these intricate social hierarchies. Could a communist organization, generally dismissive of caste inequalities, have overcome this intricate system of hierarchical social relations in its attempt to mobilize the sharecroppers and landless peasants?

Some of these complex issues were addressed during the Quit India movement. The movement, by virtue of its extraordinary growth and spread as a popular upheaval, mounted the largest ever challenge to the colonial government since 1857. Rural politics got a fresh lease of life during this period. More importantly, once again the government 'disappeared' from the villages. The movement left an enduring impact on rural social relations.

Alliances were formed between peasants across caste barriers. A few years later, this erosion of caste barriers in social interactions in the wake of the solidarity created by the Quit India movement would significantly help the communist organizations to mobilize peasants. Ideologically, the RCPI believed that the popular movement in Assam resulting from the Quit India movement had the fundamental potential of transforming itself into a larger political movement to be led by peasants and workers. On their own, some members of the RCPI, under the banner of the Radical Institute, even helped the masses use locally made weapons to attack government officials and properties.[105]

While the political training of Assamese peasants by the RCPI cadre became a reality during this period, leaders of the KBP learned their first-hand experience of speaking to and organizing the Assamese peasants on the southern bank of Brahmaputra in Kamrup. The KBP could make some inroads in Palashbari, located a few miles west of Guwahati. The locality, close to Brahmaputra, was densely populated, mostly by Assamese caste-Hindu peasants. The Marwari firms used to purchase peasant produce from there and market it in Guwahati and Calcutta, thus making this locality an important trading base. Of the total rural population, approximately 17 per cent were either adhiars or landless labourers. The majority of adhiars had landholdings of less than 6 acres. Similar was the situation of the ryots the majority of whom had less than 5 acres.[106] The KBP leaders came in contact with the landless peasants and sharecroppers of Palashbari — another example of communists providing non-local leadership to the rural populace in their struggle for their demands. Such instances of the entry of urban leaders into the rural landscape were not new as the Congress leaders too used to visit villages. The man who facilitated this programme of direct contact with the villages was Govinda Kalita, a popular Congress leader from Palashbari. The place had a brief history of peasant mobilization under the leadership of Kalita. Between 1942 and 1945, he had mobilized the landless peasants and sharecroppers against their landowners.[107] The KBP roped in Kalita which turned out to be quite advantageous for the organization. He himself did not see much of a difference between the work of the KBP and that of the Congress which he left, since as a Congress leader he had already mobilized the Assamese landless peasants seeking land from the government.

In 1941, a 'thousand ryots', 'carrying red flags'[108] from Palashbari, along with those from neighbouring Boko and Chayagaon mauzas — with a strong presence of Bodo, Rava and caste-Hindu Assamese sharecroppers and landless peasants — came in a procession to the deputy commissioner's office demanding land from the neighbouring Reserved Forest.[109] Many of these ryots had recently lost their lands to soil erosion caused by floods. As a consequence of this agitation, the revenue administration distributed land among the landless peasants in the neighbouring Reserved Forest.[110] Seeing the popularity of Kalita as a leading voice of the peasants, the KBP elected him as the General Secretary of Kamrup unit.[111] This was no doubt a reasonable move and added strength to the weak and nebulous organizational network of KBP.[112] In the next couple of years, the KBP came forward to organize peasants against landowners in Kamrup and later established itself as a successful mobilizer of peasants.

Another illustrative example of a similar peasant movement is that of Dusuti Mukhur Andolon — a local movement over the repairing of a broken bridge on a river in Barbhag on the northern bank of Brahmaputra in Kamrup district. When a bamboo bridge that used to connect villages on both sides of Baraliya river and facilitate the movement of goods and people broke down, the district administration, unwilling to repair it, engaged a boatman on contract to ferry the villagers on the payment of a charge. The villagers did not like this new arrangement and appealed to the administration through a petition to repair the bridge. As the administration refused to do away with the ferrying system, a series of protests led by the KBP leaders were staged. Villagers from the neighbouring areas too joined the movement. As the movement grew, the administration agreed to repair the bridge. With this success, the villagers began to appreciate the KBP's role and the KBP became a 'legitimate' representative/spokesperson of the peasants' grievances.[113] It continued to rely on the strategy of securing the help of local charismatic figures like Kalita. Similar was the case in Beltola where the KBP leaders accepted an invitation of a *sanyasi* to mobilize the tribal sharecroppers and landless peasants. The sanyasi, known by the name of Ramdas Babaji, played a key role in helping Haridas Deka, a KBP leader, familiarize himself with the agrarian relations in Beltola. A meeting between the KBP leaders and the sharecroppers led to an understanding that the latter would give one-fourth of their produce to the landowners as rent and pay half the earlier interest rate to the moneylenders on the loans taken by them, but only in return for a receipt.[114] A few landowners hesitantly agreed to the new arrangement. Despite this limited success of the KBP in helping strike a deal between the sharecroppers on the one hand and the moneylenders and landowners on the other, more sharecroppers were encouraged to enrol as members of the KBP. With the increasing membership, the KBP's anti-landowner propaganda flared up in the locality.

Charged by these successes, the spirited RCPI leaders, more convinced that the Quit India movement was instrumental in fomenting this extraordinary popular movement, travelled far and wide and engaged with local issues and grievances. With a large number of landless peasants and sharecroppers, southern Kamrup became an obvious choice as a site of peasant mobilization by the KBP. The majority of landless peasants and sharecroppers were Ravas and Bodos, besides being caste-Hindu Assamese. Soon, a large area of southern Kamrup came under the KBP influence.[115] One young RCPI activist later recounted how they explained the nature of British rule in India and the nature of Congress to the peasants: 'We explained to them about the political situation after the Second World War and the need for the formation of a socialist labour–peasant party with its aims and objectives.[116] The KBP cadres would visit the villages in a group of 3–4 with political literature on communism. The villagers were convinced by the cadres, of the government's failure, and unwillingness, to deliver justice. The local youths were given the responsibility to explain the aims and objectives of KBP to fellow villagers. The latter were told that their landowners who lived in the nearby towns were their enemies and had no reason to taking away their crops. An official reported how these cadres 'worked among the peasants and labourers and take their food with the villagers. So they are not required to spend money from their own pocket'.[117]

By 1945, the KBP gained some success in mobilizing the sharecroppers and landless peasants. That these gains were quickly used by the RCPI to strengthen its role in the larger political landscape of Assam can be illustrated by one example. In Guwahati on 25 July 1945, there was a demonstration of approximately 200 sharecroppers and landless peasants from Palashbari, Bangara and Bhanguripara in south Kamrup. The demonstrators, led by

RCPI leaders Haridas Deka and Tarunsen Deka, walked down the main streets of the town, assembled in the Jubilee Garden and submitted a memorandum to the Deputy Commissioner.[118] Their demands included: (*a*) adequate supply of foodstuffs, clothes and yam; (*b*) removal of taxes on tobacco and betel nuts; (*c*) distribution of land for cultivation amongst the landless Assamese peasants; (*d*) maintenance of the Line System 'for the interests of the people of the province';[119] and (*e*) immediate release of political prisoners. More such meetings were organized, thereby effectively expanding the outreach of RCPI.

These meetings, in most cases, also turned out to be a platform for resisting government programmes affecting the everyday life of poor tribal peasants. What came in for harsh criticism was the *beggar* system — a system wherein villagers living in the vicinity of Reserved Forests were compelled to provide free labour to the Forest Department — in the forest villages of southern Kamrup. One such meeting in Boko mauza, attended in large numbers by the inhabitants of different villages adjoining the Reserved Forests spread across Bakeli, Luki, Pachim-Chamaria and Boko mauzas, protested against the beggar system.[120] The attendees also demanded that the government more effectively handle the problem of hoarding of foodcrops and clothes by rich peasants and mercantile houses. In the wake of the Bengal Famine of 1943, food shortage had already engulfed Assam, along with Orissa and Bengal. The eastern borders of Assam were already marked by tension and increasingly being converted into an active war zone. The sale of the hoarded foodcrops by rich peasants and mercantile houses to traders in Bengal at higher prices depleted the stock of paddy in Assam. Such instances of black-marketing and smuggling of paddy was regularly reported.[121] Coupled with this, perennial bad weather and floods caused extreme hardships to the peasants.[122] There was a phenomenal rise in prices, while famine or quasi-famine like situation was reported from different localities.[123] The communist leaders, capitalizing on the deteriorating situation, stepped up their anti-government propaganda. The Assam government, in order to remedy the situation, initiated paddy procurement programme and engaged Steel Brothers Company to procure paddy from the villages for supply to the urban areas. Compulsory paddy procurement aggravated the discontent amongst a wide cross-section of Assamese rural population.

The RCPI asked the villagers not to sell paddy to traders and asked the traders not to purchase for the purpose of export.[124] 'Store paddy' and 'villagers shouldn't sell it to the military or any government agents' became highly popular slogans amongst the villagers.[125] The RCPI cadres either seized carts and boats carrying procured paddy or, in some places, enforced a prohibition on the sale or purchase of paddy. In some other places, they forcibly seized the surplus stocks of paddy from rich villagers and sold them at low prices to the poor villagers. The meagre profits earned from such sales were distributed among the families of rich peasants whom the stocks had been seized from.[126] These acts were received well by the Assamese poor peasants. The government too admitted that the communist influence had expanded to other districts, for example, Lakhimpur and Cachar, the two districts mostly inhabited by tea garden labourers. An official report, for instance, recognized the increasing 'influence of the communists ... due to their endeavour for voicing the popular feeling over general economic grievances'.[127]

Birth of a Movement: Communists and Countryside

The inroads gradually made into the rural politics, prompted both the RCPI and the CPI to showcase their popularity and give a common ideological orientation to these scattered political agitations in the countryside. The RCPI organized several conferences in 1945 in the valley. Attended in large numbers by poor Assamese peasants, these conferences played a leading role in providing a common platform for the articulation of multiple reshaping their local discontents. Subsequently, the sharecroppers and landless peasants became the key focus of the KBP which had acquired a limited and localized but significant experience in mobilizing peasants though it did not have any concrete programme on the sharecroppers' and landless peasants' issues. One of the first conferences that the RCPI organized under the banner of KBP was held in November 1945 near Bhanguripara in Palashbari.[128] The leading communist leader Shaukat Usmani (1901–78) also attended the conference. This well-attended conference — a police intelligence report claimed that there were 4,000 attendees — deliberated on the condition of Assamese sharecroppers and landless peasants. Marking a radical departure from the earlier strategy of mediating negotiation between sharecroppers and landowners (as happened in Beltola), the conference adopted resolutions signalling a confrontation between sharecroppers and landowners as the only way to overcome the crisis. Four crucial resolutions adopted at the conference decided that (*a*) sharecroppers would give only one-fourth of their produce to the landowners; (*b*) there would be a decrease in the interest demanded by the moneylenders; (*c*) sharecroppers would resist any eviction from their land by the landowners; and (*d*) government-owned wastelands should be distributed among the Assamese landless peasants. Another resolution reportedly called for 'the liberation of the peasants and labour from exploitation'[129] and simultaneously extended support to the Congress-led freedom movement. Confronting landowners ideologically was not too difficult a proposition in the 1940s. The All India Congress Committee under the guidance of Jawaharlal Nehru had already signalled its political willingness to abolish the zamindari system.[130]

The first crucial test of land reform, as a prelude to the zamindari abolition bills to be passed after independence, began when Congress ministries came into power in Assam in 1938–39. The various tenancy acts passed during the tenure of Congress ministries laid the foundation for the future land reform programme in the country. Enacting the legislation was the first experience of exercising substantial legislative power for the Indian nationalists. The widespread Kisan Sabha movement, particularly in Uttar Pradesh and Bihar, had already popularized the demand for the abolition of zamindari system. The Krishak Praja Party in Bengal too had directed its agrarian programme against the zamindars. All these crucially helped to reorientate the Congress agrarian programme towards land reform. Against this backdrop, the KBP's demand for the abolition of absentee landlordism, zamindari and moneylender-trader nexus, and for the redistribution of land among landless peasants thus did not seem to be impractical. The Bhanguripara resolutions were certain to become attractive to the Assamese sharecroppers. Buoyed by the success of Bhanguripara conference, the KBP organized another meeting in Bangara in southern Kamrup which was attended by its members from other districts.[131] This conference took the Bhanguripara resolutions to a more radical level. The meeting adopted a resolution asking adhiars to give a decreased share of their produce to the landowners and also pegging this share at 8 puras for *faringati* land and 12 puras for *rupit* land. It passed another resolution asking adhiars to resist any attempt made by the landowners to evict them from the lands they had been cultivating. The two conferences in Bhanguripara and Bangara, by refocusing the nationalist political approach on the Assamese peasant question and also challenging the existing agrarian relations, sought to mobilize the Assamese peasants on the following issues: (*a*) decrease in the share of produce demanded by the landowners as rent; (*b*) decrease in the rate of interest charged by the moneylenders; (*c*) demand for a receipt of the acceptance of adhi arrangement from the landowners; (*d*) occupation of wastelands and distribution of plots therein among the landless and those who had less land; and (*e*) stoppage of eviction of the sharecroppers and grant of land to the tiller.[132]

The RCPI rightly gauged the militant mood of the sharecroppers. Its radical slogans thus became quickly popular. And during the harvesting season of 1946–47, sharecroppers told their landowners that they would pay the rent in kind only at a new rate. Meanwhile, the KBP leaders travelled through villages and interacted with the sharecroppers whom they told inspirational stories of misbehaviour with and humiliation of the landowners by the rebellious peasants. The sharecroppers became convinced that they could bargain effectively with their landowners. In the wake of growing popularity of the KBP, more branches of KBP were formed in villages.[133] But in the absence of enough evidence, we cannot gauge the exact responses of the sharecroppers to KBP's mobilization programme. The fear of eviction by landowners loomed large and it was not unlikely for the sharecroppers to hesitate taking a strong and non-negotiable stand vis-à-vis the former. Nevertheless, local units of the KBP and a strong presence of the sharecroppers helped the latter to withstand any pressure, as was the case in Palashbari. With the sharecroppers becoming active as KBP members from 1945 under the pragmatic and popular leadership of Govinda Kalita and with a majority of villagers being sharecroppers, Palashbari turned out to be one of the earliest strongholds of the sharecroppers' movement.[134] Such gains achieved by the sharecroppers and landless peasants as the grant of wastelands for cultivation by the government, were a reason enough for sharecroppers in the neighbouring Chayagaon and Boko mauzas to join the movement soon. They also demanded redistribution of land from the *chapori* areas and the Reserved Forests among the landless peasants. Several meetings were also organized by the KBP units to better articulate the local grievances.

The RCPI was not alone in mobilizing the peasants. In 1946, the CPI also adopted a similar programme on the sharecroppers' and landless peasants' question in Assam. Till then, the activities of CPI had been mostly confined to the mobilization of tenants in Goalpara and Cachar districts around the anti-zamindari and Tebhaga slogan.[135] Already, the Tebhaga movement in the neighbouring north Bengal had influenced the Rava and Hajang tribal peasants in Goalpara to give one-third of their produce to their landowners. Conflicts between landowners and tenants had already surfaced as well. The Bodo and Kachari tribal tenants in western Assam had already come under the influence of a socio-religious reform movement called Brahma movement which raised the level of their political awareness. The CPI under the banner of Krishak Sabha (KS) in Goalpara stepped up its efforts in mobilizing the tenants against their zamindars and expanding its organizational outreach. It organized meetings attended in large numbers by Muslim, Hindu and Bodo peasants.[136] The CPI had some early and crucial gains in terms of mobilizing tenants and landless peasants and of voicing their demands when, in December 1946, Goalpara Zillah Krishak Sabha, an infant branch of the AIKS, in a meeting chaired by Pranesh Biswas, a CPI leader, passed several resolutions which tried to coherently articulate the existing peasant discontent. The resolutions not only made a strong demand for the abolition of zamindari system, but also sought to fix higher prices for paddy, jute and mustard.[137] The meeting also demanded an immediate end to the payment of illegal customary payments charged by the zamindars.[138] A month later, in January 1947, Parbotjowar Krishak Sabha, while reiterating these demands, further demanded a decrease in land revenue and free access of villagers to timber and firewood from the nearby Reserved Forests.[139] A later account (by P.C. Biswas) agreed that the CPI's modus operandi was to form a local committee of the KS whenever rumblings of discontent among tenants was noticeable, but essentially a centralized movement led by the CPI was missing from the zamindari areas.[140]

Away from the zamindari areas, the CPI-led KS made a concerted attempt to strengthen its base amongst the sharecroppers in raiyatwari areas after 1946. In the meantime, in eastern Assam, the CPI had some success in making the Haloa Sangha an integral part of the KS. The rich experience of Dhiren Datta, a socialist Congress leader with an intimate knowledge of Assam's countryside, became crucial for the expansion of the KS' organizational work. Making a modest beginning in 1945, the CPI organized the sharecroppers in Sapekhati mauza, Golaghat. But it was in Guwahati where the CPI meetings drew larger audiences of poor Assamese peasants, and workers from railway, shipping, postal service, press, electricity, and banking sectors. The CPI could also manage to mobilize the tribal sharecroppers in Beltola.[141] These early gains were further consolidated in 1946 with the Assam Provincial Krishak Sabha (APKS) holding its first provincial conference in Thekeraguri, Nowgaon. Despite opposition from the Congress cadres, the conference was attended by Assamese poor peasants, as also by the KS representatives. The conference brought out the CPI's uneasiness about taking on the Assamese absentee landowners head on. In an attempt to overcome the growing conflicts between landowners and sharecroppers, the conference emphasized the need for unity of the different strata of Assamese peasantry.[142] Unrestrained immigration from East Bengal was viewed as a move to turn Assam into a Muslim majority province, so that it could qualify for inclusion into East Pakistan. What led the CPI from refusing to take the sharecroppers' localized agitation to the level of an organized political movement? The answer can be partly found in the draft resolution of the Assam CPI in early 1947. In this little known but rather long resolution, the Assam CPI, emphasizing its anti-grouping stand, appealed for the right of the 'Assamiya' people to self-determination, which essentially meant 'a *collective and united fight of the Assamese people*' (emphasis added) against the 'British imperialist rulers'.[143]

Meanwhile, the ground reality had changed rapidly. A series of peasant movements swept across the country and captured the imagination of communist leaders. In January 1947, P.C. Joshi, General Secretary of the CPI, urged the provincial committees to embark 'on immediate solidarity campaign with the Tebhaga struggle'[144] in other parts of India. While the Government of India agreed that the Tebhaga 'agitation and activity in pursuing this movement has reached a crescendo', Joshi thought that 'what is possible in Bengal's villages is possible anywhere'.[145] He exhorted the committees 'to work up solidarity among sections of the people by taking Tebhaga as an inspiring example'[146] and appealed to the KS to launch the broadest possible campaign by popularizing the demands and the heroism of the peasants. For the CPI, the struggle in northern Bengal was the 'response of the awakened peasants' and it urged that the KS use this struggle to mobilize the Assamese peasants. As the All India Kisan Sabha (AIKS) started campaigning for increasing its membership in the valley — its membership in the valley rose from 1,500 in 1944 to 7,900 in 1945 — small meetings, many of which took place in Goalpara, were reported from across the province. As the mobilization of peasants intensified, despite the opposition of the zamindars, the tenants came forward to take a lead in mobilizing their fellow villagers.[147]

After independence, the CSP, which was till then moderately active amongst the Assamese sharecroppers under the name of Krishak Sabha, was rechristened as Socialist Party of India (SPI). It also formed a peasant organization, Talatiya Ryot Sangha. In several meetings, mostly held in the districts of eastern Assam, the SPI urged the sharecroppers not to give more than the government-approved revenue as rent to the landowners.[148] In April 1948, the SPI, in its Titabor conference, passed resolutions proposing a new rate of rent which was differentially based on the quality and area of land.[149] Although the SPI asked for a reduced rate of rent payable by the sharecroppers, it argued that until the total abolition of the zamindari system, the existing practice of sharecropping should be pursued. Given that in many parts of southern Kamrup, the sharecroppers had stopped paying rent to the landowners, such a liberal position would not appeal to the sharecroppers or, at the most, may bring some temporary relief to the panic-stricken landowners. As this position on the rental agreement was not going to work, the SPI tried to bring the landless peasants on to its side and reiterated that 'the landless peasants must get the land.'[150]

As mobilization of the rural populace by communists intensified, by the early months of 1947, the Assam government began to consider the communist mobilization as a serious threat to its authority. The Chief Secretary of Assam warned his junior officers about the 'manifestations of an objectionable' mobilization in Assam which 'had not hitherto been so serious'.[151] He, however, agreed that the province was ideal for such activities with 'large centres of labouring population'.[152] The government also admitted the strong presence of communists throughout the state.[153] It also circulated internal notes about how the communists were 'planning to renew the Tebhaga campaign',[154] and how they had stepped up their campaign against the landowners and renewed a call for 'right to forest produces'. The administration believed that 'their aim was nakedly to use mass meetings in order to awaken what was called the struggle sentiment'.[155] The Government of India too concurred with this assessment of the communists' role and warned the Assam government about the possibility of Tebhaga agitation in Cachar influencing the discontented tea garden workers to make a more radical political move. It further cautioned the Assam government about the need to 'firmly handle' the situation before the 'mischief-makers acting in the guise of communist propagandist' took the situation beyond control.[156] The government, in an attempt to 'firmly' assert its hold, pointedly attributed the primary responsibility for such mischief to the KPB. It noted with apprehension that the RCPI was the 'only vocal section' amongst the peasant organizations encouraging the landless peasants to fight against the landowners. The government also admitted that their propaganda had worked well, that they had made advances in different localities, and that the tribal peasants were being 'subjected to [their] agrarian propaganda'.[157] Instances were cited from Palashbari where the peasants 'in support of their demand were occasionally staging ready demonstrations'.[158] The extreme anxiety of the government was also a reflection of the ground reality. Amidst intense pro-Pakistan movement, the communist peasant organizations had virtually captured the rural political landscape. Though this shift in the political alignment was no proof of electoral popularity of the communist blocks, the Congress-led government had reasons to be worried, as we will shortly discuss.

As the country was preparing for independence, the tenants and sharecroppers, already handicapped by the government's food procurement policy and increasing scarcity of clothes, were asked by the communist organizations to stop paying rent to their landowners.[159] Between January and June 1947, the communists also succeeded in organizing workers of match factory in Dhubri,[160] tea garden workers, landless peasants who were asked to occupy unoccupied government lands,[161] and manual workers like cleaners engaged by municipal bodies.[162] While the zamindars or landlords threatened the tenants or sharecroppers with eviction, the communist leaders encouraged the latter to physically challenge any such move.[163] This open resistance was not unexpected given the heightened polarization in the agrarian relation, whereby battle lines were drawn between landowners and sharecroppers over the issues of rent and occupancy rights.

Conflicts Surfaced in the Winter of 1947–48

Independence in 1947 was perceived by the CPI and the RCPI as false since both believed that this independence meant freedom for the Indian bourgeoisie only. Their slogan, *yeh azadi juthi hai* ('this freedom is a false one'), did dampen the popular excitement at the attainment of freedom, but both soon agreed to work within the limits of Indian Constitution and law.[164] The Assamese press, however, did not take notice of this dismissal of the much-awaited freedom by the CPI and RCPI. While at the national level, the communist leadership was yet to grapple with the political meaning of independence, the ground reality was fast changing.[165] Rooted in much localized political programmes, the CPI and the RCPI both began to intensify their activities. Towards the end of 1947, as the harvesting season approached, the KBP and the KS, separately but not collectively taking full advantage of the prevailing chaos and exhilaration surrounding the country's independence, intensified their programme of mobilization, especially and visibly amongst the sharecroppers in southern Kamrup. Other large parts of the district, mostly on the northern bank of Brahmaputra, had not been able to overcome the anxiety surrounding the growing pro-Pakistan movement among the East Bengali immigrants. The localized rural tensions, centred on disputes over grazing reserves between Assamese peasants and East Bengali immigrants, had not subsided either. Though there were reports of anti-Bengali propaganda in Guwahati, the rural southern Kamrup was comparatively free from this development. These areas also did not see any Congress mobilization and it was not difficult for the left organizations to make inroads there.

Sharecroppers and landless peasants across the southern bank of Brahmaputra in Kamrup were now determined to challenge the landowners. For instance, Beltola, Rani, Chayagaon, Boko, and

Palashbari turned out to be strongholds of these defiant sharecroppers. Village meetings deliberating on the plight of sharecroppers became an everyday phenomenon.[166] In an attempt to unify the interests of a wide cross-section of peasantry, these meetings accommodated the political programme of the erstwhile ryot sabha movement or, sometimes, the AIKS demands. For instance, various resolutions pressed for abolition of the zamindari system, payment of land revenue at a differentiated rate according to the quality of land, grant of patta to the peasants occupying the government land, and reservation of lands for tribal peasants.[167] A consensus on the rate of rent to be paid by the sharecroppers and on a specific set of demands in the interest of the agrarian labourers was still missing from these resolutions. Occasionally, the sharecroppers compelled the landowners to accept one-third of the produce.[168] On its own, the KBP influenced the sharecroppers not to pay the rent as fixed by the landlords, but did make them pay the actual land revenue as fixed by the government.

The actual proof of the KBP influence on the sharecroppers came in for trial in January 1948, when harvesting was over and the landowners began to collect their share of the produce. The sharecroppers reiterated their wish not to pay rent to the landowners and were ready for a final assault on them. Illustrative of such open defiance was a meeting, held in Beltola on 7 January 1948, fairly attended by both tribal and caste-Hindu sharecroppers and chaired by Aniram Basumatari, a popular leader among the tribals. In the meeting, the sharecroppers reiterated their categorical refusal to give adhi.[169] And that was what really happened. In some localities, the sharecroppers completely stopped paying rent or paid it at a reduced rate, asked the landowners to give them a written receipt of the rent paid, and told them that they would not work for them for free. Some sharecroppers, either variously related to or dependent on the landowners, were, however, reluctant to agree to this arrangement fixed by the KBP, and the KBP threatened these recalcitrant peasants that their crops would be forcibly reaped by the KBP cadres.[170] Refusal to pay rent also prompted the landowners to evict their sharecroppers. In most cases, the latter resisted the move.[171]

Gains made in southern Kamrup encouraged the sharecroppers in other areas not to part with their crops for paying rent to the landowners. Conflicts between the two were reported from villages in Dibrugarh and Sibsagar. In the entire Sibsagar district, the sharecroppers either stopped paying adhi to their landlords or agreed to give only one-fourth of the produce. In Madhupur, Amguri, landowner–sharecropper conflicts acquired a critical turn as the sharecroppers of 'six mauzas have[*sic*] stopped giving paddy to landowners. They agreed to give one fourth of the produce to them or, in lieu of it, land revenue in coins'.[172] Consequent to this agitation, some landowners like Mahendra Saikia of Titabor, accepted one-fourth of the produce from their sharecroppers.[173] In Furkating, Sapekhati and Janji, which were strongholds of the CPI, while the sharecroppers insisted on paying rent only in cash, some small landowners aligned with them and thus gave strength to the movement.[174] Like the sharecroppers of Jhanji, the Ahom sharecroppers, a majority of whom were still under the influence of All Assam Ahom Sabha and were suspicious of the Congress' attitude to their community's interests, refused to pay rent as well.

In many places, adhiars realized that unless they were members of the communist peasant organizations they would not be able to resist eviction alone. In Nowgaon, in the densely populated and flood-prone areas like Jagi, Dharamtul, or places like Hojai and Lanka with a large concentration of landless peasants, the KS mobilized the peasants. While 'no rent' slogan attracted the sharecroppers, the slogans of 'no eviction, proper distribution of land and forcible occupation of land' also drew a wide cross-section of peasants to the fold of KS.[175] Demand for the abolition of various revenue-free estates, viz., *debottar*, *brahmottar*, fee-simple grants (lands leased to tea planters at low rates), nisf-khiraj and la-khiraj grants, also surfaced.[176] The KBP and KS organizational spheres hardly overlapped, but both worked in close proximity. The exact influence of KS is difficult to gauge, but by early 1948 the CPI had also mobilized the adhiars in southern Kamrup, and the influence of KS was concentrated in a few villages of Khetri and Beltola.[177]

In eastern Assam, the CPI began to lead more coordinated organizational activities among the sharecroppers and landless peasantry from March 1948.[178] However, a centralized peasant organization of the CPI was lacking till November 1948. Whatever may be the case, once the CPI-affiliated peasant organizations were formed, conflicts between landowners and sharecroppers became noticeable. While the KBP refused to give any concession to the landowners, the KS apparently demanded that, in an attempt to defuse further conflicts, the government distribute unploughed government land among the landless peasants. Land occupation was also reported from Kaki in Nowgaon with active support from the KS.[179]

Government Taken Aback, Landlords Recuperated

> The fight of the landless peasants in Assam is gradually in rapid advance under [the slogan,] 'land to landless, no payment of unjust interest, pay revenue in coins in lieu of paddy' ... [A]t this the landlords are hatching various sorts of plots against the innocent peasants or for their imprisonment. Simultaneously the RCPI is launching a move against the capitalist at Beltola Rani Palashbari Bangra and Chayagaon etc ... [T]he activity of this party on land affairs is in throughout the province.[180]

The government had no doubt that the sharecroppers succeeded in gaining control over their crops. In January 1948, it was informed by its intelligence wing about how the adhiars were refusing to pay rent to their landowners. Over the next few weeks, official intelligence reported how

> adhiars had refused to part with their produce with the landlords mostly in the southern bank of the Kamrup district. Almost everywhere in the south bank of the Brahmaputra ... some agitation has been going on between the landlords and the ryots are [*sic*] refusing to give their landlords the paddy on adhi system'.[181]

In the next two months, the helplessness of the government became apparent as the police continued to report how 'due to the present activity of the communist all the cultivators have [*sic*] gone against their landlords'.[182]

The Assamese press also worriedly took notice of the 'serious turn of the situation due to these conflicts as more news of such nature were coming in'.[183] Warning the government of the deteriorating situation, it recounted how 'from the reports, which are coming from the villages, it is feared that the problems of landless peasants would turn out to be a huge problem'.[184] It admitted that '[a] lot of news is coming telling the stories of conflict between the landless peasants and the rich landlords'.[185] The press further reported about the increasing reclamation of land by the landless Assamese peasants in the tea gardens at a time when Assamese businessmen were trying to own such wastelands.[186] Despite this defence of landowners, the Assamese press also published experiences of rural Assam written by lesser-known or anonymous writers.[187] Illustrative of such portrayals was a report on the condition of sharecroppers in Bihali, Darrang:

> The ninety[-]five percent population of the Bihali cannot have a meal for the whole year due to their small land holding. They have to rent in the land from the rich peasants of the area, as they do not have any other alternative. Those who have more than 900 to 1000 *pura* of land rent out on condition of 25 to 30 *dun* of paddy per bigha. If the sharecropper failed to give the share to the landlords, the latter create lot of problem. They also take rent for a higher amount of land compared to the actual holding of the sharecropper ... how long the peasants have to suffer at this condition?[188]

The government, in order to pre-empt a further deterioration of the situation, conducted a census of the Assamese landless peasants in January 1948. However, this exercise was never conducted with any serious intention to alleviate their conditions and was mostly confined to a few mauzas of Sibsagar.[189] This census, nevertheless, brought both hope and worries to the sharecroppers and landless peasants, as well as to the landowners. Mounting pressure exerted by the landless peasants forced the government to initiate the reclamation of lands. The reclaimed wastelands, fully exempted from revenue, were given to the co-operative societies.

The landowners found themselves in an unprecedented and precarious situation. Some of them agreed to receive a decreased rent, and this harsh reality became a matter of concern for the landowners. In the recent past, they had never experienced a similar opposition from their sharecroppers. This forced them to seriously find out a mechanism to keep intact their rights and privileges. In public meetings largely attended by landowners, they tried to gain support of adhiars for their privileges. They also began negotiations with the members of political parties seeking their immediate intervention. In Kamrup, the landowners formed Kamrup Pattadar Sangha as early as December 1947.[190] The Assamese press described the collective efforts of landowners as crucial to bringing ‘peace’ to the conflict-torn countryside. The majority of Congress leaders too extended their support to the landowners’ demands.[191]

In the meantime, talks were in air about a possible framing of a law to defend the interests of the sharecroppers. The absentee landowners of Guwahati came forward to mitigate this eventuality and prompted their other fellow landowners to resist a further blow to their interest. A public meeting held at Curzon Hall in Guwahati on 9 January 1948, attended by about 200 absentee landowners and presided over by Kamakhya Prasad Barua, a retired judge, made it clear that the absentee landowners were in no mood to be let down by the sharecroppers’ agitations.[192] They urged the government to frame a law on the subject of tenancy immediately and to protect the present system of adhi and *chukani* till the framing of a new law on sharecropping. They also demanded that a law to protect the interests of the sharecroppers be framed in consultation with the landowners. Closed-door negotiations and public meetings of the landowners led to the formation of a committee to negotiate with the sharecroppers. Soon, there appeared fractures in the collective unity of the landlords, and the *dolois* (owners of religious estates in southern Kamrup) formed a separate body called Kamrup Doloi Sanmilani, to press for their demands, as they nurtured different grievances against their tenants. They feared that the proposed bill on zamindari abolition would also lead to the seizure of estates attached to religious institutions, and thus tried to influence the government against this bill.[193]

In some places, individual landowners tried to negotiate directly with their adhiars. Many of them were small landowners and did not have ways to seek new sharecroppers. In 1948, Harinarayan Barua, a leading socialist Congressman from Sibsagar, referring to similar attempts at negotiation made by the landowners, admitted that ‘for the past two years they (landlords) were trying their best to reach an amicable settlement between the landlords and adhiars, as the latter had stopped paying rent for the year’.[194] At the same time, the landowners also perceived the non-payment of rent as a breach of social norms. Several landowners from southern Kamrup complained to the Kamrup administration about ‘illegal acts’ or ‘misbehaviour’ by their tenants and sharecroppers. They further complained of receiving threats from their sharecroppers when they attempted to collect rent. Even if they could collect their rent from some of the sharecroppers, there would be others waiting to snatch away the rent. This also resulted in the imposition of fines on, threats of assault on and social boycott of those who agreed to pay or paid rent to the landowners. The helpless landowners could only claim that 'mischief mongers were spreading various slogans . . . to incite people to break law'.[195]

More surprises were lying in wait in the Assam Legislative Assembly. The success of communist peasant organizations in mobilizing sharecroppers, landless peasants and a section of landowners who agreed to the sharecroppers' demands became a matter of grave concern to the Assam Congress. The Assamese press had already drawn a worrisome picture of rural Assam, and from March 1948, the Assam Legislative Assembly began an intense debate on the issue. Several members across the spectrum of political ideologies expressed concerns about the 'communist mentality of the adhiars' and the 'growing hostility between the adhiars and the landlords', 'the result of which might be a revolution'.[196] They also complained about the 'loss of social honour because of abuses, slander inflicted by the adhiars' and 'enormous economic hardship' to the landlords.[197] The man who came forward at their hour of crisis was Muhammad Saadulla, a Muslim League leader and ex-premier of the province. The absentee landowners had already urged Saadulla to defend their cause. Describing the plight of landowners, mostly from Guwahati and including the *pandas* of the Kamakhya temple, Saadulla reminded the government that the communists 'had set up vigorous propaganda in Kamrup against landlords by mobilising the tenants who were willing to pay their rent'[198] and lamented about the fact that the landowners had been deprived of their 'usual rent'.[199] Others were not short of condemning the sharecroppers either. Beliram Das, another Congress legislator, also agreed that

> [t]he cultivators of south Kamrup have suddenly refused to pay *chukani* paddy to the landowners for the year 1947-48, according to the persistent preaching of the communist agitators. Numerous meetings have been held in different mauzas on the south bank of Kamrup where inflammatory speeches were made by some persons inciting the tenants not to give any paddy to the landholder disowning legal obligations.[200]

The intelligence officials continued to warn the Assam government about the seriousness of communist activity among the sharecroppers in Kamrup. Typical of such warning were statements like: 'The communists have not failed to foster agrarian discontent in the Kamrup district. They have achieved some results after the independence at Bongra';[201] or 'organizations like the RCPI are working up certain anti-government feelings among ryots especially in Kamrup district'.[202] That such mobilization of sharecroppers had acquired a serious dimension was admitted by the Assam administration as early as 1947. Describing the condition of rural Assam, Harold Dennehy, Chief Secretary to Assam government, anxiously reported that

> the communists have shown that they have at least a widespread organisation and that by applying shamelessly political motives to the approach to labour they are capable of stirring up a great deal of trouble; the technique appears to be to look for any signs of discontent or gullibility in respect of labourers['] needs and then make a facile promises [*sic*] of obtaining various, and often quite impossible, ends.[203]

Despite such warnings, the government failed to visualize the enormity of unrest in rural Assam. It thought that though the 'communist have[*sic*] been busy everywhere' they were 'practically in Cachar and Goalpara' only.[204] The government, nevertheless, admitted that

> [t]hey plan[*sic*] to renew the Tebhaga campaign and to make play with all local grievances about customary exactions of landowners, right to forest produce and the like. Their aim is[*sic*] to use mass meetings in order to awaken what is called the struggle sentiment.[205]

Yet the government continued to believe that, unlike the communist movement in the other parts of the country, in Assam, the intensity of the movement would remain confined to the tea gardens only. However, Dennehy perceptively wrote to a junior officer:

> [T]he manifestations of an objectionable character haven't [*sic*] hitherto been serious in Assam as in provisions containing large centres of labouring population or inflammable material, but they [intelligence officers] feel[*sic*] that there have been indications [of unrest in rural areas] ... particularly in respect of the population on tea gardens.[206]

Dennehy instructed the deputy commissioners to arrest all communist-minded people and file criminal lawsuits against them under the Assam Maintenance of Public Order Ordinance, which had already come into effect since 1946. The government eventually made it an act in 1947. The district administration directed the village headmen to force the adhiars to pay rent. However, such notices could hardly force the adhiars to do so. Dejected by such utter refusal to pay rent, Beliram Das, the chief spokesman of the landowners, admitted that 'the gaonburas [village elders] and *raiyats* [were] not giving' any attention to the 'notices sent by the deputy commissioner to pay *chukani* paddy'.[207] The situation hardly improved over the next few months.

A Movement Widened: Seeking New Friends

With the apparent success of adhiars in refusing to pay rent and asserting control over their crops, the communist organizations sought new friends to build up a larger movement. Desertion of workers and violent confrontations between workers and planters almost became part of everyday life in tea plantations in the 1920s and 1930s. Such sporadic but relentless protests in the tea gardens had already threatened the stability of the industry. The workers had been only recently mobilized by the Congress-affiliated Indian National Trade Union Congress. The communists too had expressed their solidarity with the labour unrest in tea gardens, and communist mobilization amongst tea garden workers made some headway as well.[208] But there was little to suggest that the Assamese peasants and disgruntled tea garden labourers became united under any common banner. Even if there were brief spells of mutual sympathy, those could never metamorphose into joint political actions. Why did the lower classes from different communities and work experiences not come together to press their demands and give a new shape to their actions? While the communist parties perceived the needs of sharecroppers, landless peasants, or tea garden workers from a class perspective, it was the Assamese peasants' caste and cultural consciousness which prevented them from joining forces with the plantation labourers. The latter remained outside the socio-cultural milieu of Assamese peasants' and their nationalist leaders' social imagination. The Assamese peasants hardly interacted, economically and socially, with the tea garden labourers. They knew little about the latter's hardships. The Assamese nationalist landed gentry only considered the tea garden workers as a source of cheap labour. In contrast, however, the immigrant Muslim peasants who regularly mingled with their Assamese peasant neighbours in bazaars, grazing fields, *beels* or, occasionally, at local fairs, became their political allies. But this alliance would stay only for a short while. A new spate of immigration from East Pakistan after 1947 would rapidly destabilize this short-lived political alliance.

This new phase of Assamese peasant politics was marked by new slogans, different from those popularized earlier by Assam Congress or All Assam Tribal League. The decade-long ryot-sabha-directed Assamese peasant politics had temporarily taken a back seat. Further, communist peasant organizations entered into the space of agitational politics vacated by the All Assam Tribal League which had already joined the Congress-led government in Assam in 1945.[209] In the 1940s, the League was successful in raising the political consciousness of and articulating the grievances of tribal peasants on the issue of land settlement.[210] Charismatic but disenchanted Tribal League leaders like Aniram Basumatari and Daben Khaklari joined the RCPI and their influence over the tribal peasants came in handy for the RCPI to mobilize the tribal adhiars.[211] Their appeals to these adhiars for pay revenue in cash rather than in kind became highly popular.[212]

After 1947, the intensity of the mobilization of immigrant East Bengali Muslim peasants reduced. Their charismatic leaders had already left for East Pakistan and they were to be guided by few elite leaders. The Congress government in Assam faced the enormous task of handling the flow of refugees from East Pakistan. The government also slowed down the eviction programme which the communist organizations began to oppose on humanitarian grounds. Though the CPI urged the government to stop further migration from East Bengal, it was in the forefront of mobilizing the already settled immigrants against the government's eviction policy. It extended support to anti-eviction meetings, organized by the erstwhile Muslim League leaders in Nowgaon and attended by thousands of peasants.[213] These meetings urged the government to distribute land amongst the landless peasants. Similar meetings took place amongst the immigrant peasants in Darrang where the CPI-led KS units were formed to extend support.[214] Meanwhile, the

Congress government in Assam, hard-pressed by the rural unrest, was compelled to concede some of their demands in the form of the Assam Adhiar Rights and Protection Act of 1948. On the other hand, the Indian communist parties, giving a new twist to their agrarian programme, perceived this rural unrest as a ground for challenging the Congress-led new national government. [215]

4

Peasants, Nationalists and Political Possibilities (1920–48)

Before explaining the further deterioration of rural agrarian relations, let us examine how rural politics and the agrarian question shaped the Assamese legislative and electoral politics. The agrarian question, in fact, dominated the legislative debates; it was in these debates that a wide cross-section of landed interests defended their rights and the government rolled out limited legal concessions. As the rural interests came onto the surface on the floor of legislative bodies, the colonial government kept itself at a safe distance.

The questions that present themselves to us in our inquiry are many. What forced the legislators to engage with the peasant question? How did the legislative debates turn into an institutional mechanism of controlling rural discontent? Could the interests of Assamese sharecroppers, as well as those of indebted and landless peasantry be protected? The legislators in Assam Legislative Council (hereafter Council) and Assam Legislative Assembly (hereafter Assembly) mostly belonged to the middle-class and landed gentry with economic interests in the agrarian economy. Between the 1920s (from when Council began to function a little more effectively) and 1948 (when the Assam government of independent India introduced a bill ostensibly to protect the interests of Assamese sharecroppers), these legislative houses passionately debated to bring some legal protection to four enduring problems, viz., land alienation, usury, tenancy, and sharecropping — all of which had transformed the agrarian economy since the nineteenth century. However, it was only in the 1930s that the agrarian question began to acquire a distinct shape when the ruling elite in Assam, i.e., the colonial government and the landed gentry, was forced to address the problems arising out of three key areas of the agrarian economy — usury, land settlement and tenancy. Thus, the agrarian question continued to occupy the centre stage in the political discourse in the years to come, as we will see in this chapter.

Protecting Tenants: Friends and Foes

Despite rumblings of dissent from the tenants in the valley, often surfacing in public discourse, the Assam Land Revenue Regulation of 1886 could not ameliorate their grievances. The Regulation ensured tenurial security to sharecroppers in the *raiyatwari* districts, but provided for no mechanism to give them occupancy rights. Moreover, it did not protect the rights of the tenants on *khiraj*, *la-khiraj* or *nisf-khiraj* lands. But the tenants were increasingly aware of their rights and their legal status omitted from the Regulation.[1]

As we look into the history of tenancy legislation, we can see that the first proposal for tenancy legislation was mooted in 1882 when a draft tenancy regulation was prepared. At that time, the Bengal Landlord and Tenant Procedure Act of 1869 was in force, not legally but in spirit, in the raiyatwari areas of Assam as a means of arbitration in tenant–landlord disputes.[2] In the 1880s, as the promulgation of a land regulation was being discussed, Charles Elliot, the Chief Commissioner of Assam, advocated for extending the Bengal Tenancy Act to the province. The move, however, failed to garner enough support from the Assamese landlords who feared loss of their crucial privileges vis-à-vis their tenants. Further, an impression prevailed within the administration that there seemed to be 'no urgent demand for it'[3] as the total area sublet to tenants was comparatively small. Many in the administration agreed that the 1869 Act was sufficient to regulate the landlord–tenant relation in Assam. Years later, in 1896, William Ward, Chief Commissioner of the province, reiterated the urgency of a special tenancy act.[4] This led to a renewed attempt to regulate the landlord–tenant relationship in 1897 in the newly reclaimed wastelands of the valley.[5] This move only invited the strongest ever protest from the Assamese landlords, forcing the proposal to be shelved.

The Assamese landowners never refrained from defending the practice of sharecropping. Signs of their protests against the government's attempts to regulate sharecropping became visible in the last few years of the nineteenth century. In 1896, the Assam government proposed to bring amendments to the prevailing land settlement rules in the province, which, it thought, had allowed the growth of absentee landlordism. Aimed at restricting the growth of absentee landlordism and stopping the practice of sharecropping in the newly settled wastelands, the amendment proposed that the wastelands be granted to ryots only for cultivation. Lobbies of landlords strongly opposed this proposal. Jaganath Barua (1851–1907), a leading planter and nationalist, submitted a petition to the government in his capacity as the president of Jorhat Sarbajanik Sabha, an organization of educated Assamese nationalists.[6] Barua pointed out that since the total area of cultivated land in the raiyatwari-settled districts of Assam was less than one-fifth of the cultivable wasteland thereof, any attempt at dismantling the practice of sharecropping would adversely affect the prospects of cultivating the bulk of the land and 'would seriously impede the future development and progress of the province'.[7] The effect would be that, as Barua thought, the right to engage sharecroppers appertaining to landowners — for whom sharecropping was the most important means of bringing these lands under cultivation — would be denied to them. Transfer of land would be difficult, with the result that no capital could be invested in agriculture and no one would come forward to acquire landed property in Assam.

A similar protest was registered by the Upper Assam Ryots' Association and the Committee of Assam Association, both representing the combined interests of Assamese landlords and traders.[8] The Upper Assam Ryots' Association believed that the principal aim of the proposed rules was 'to prevent the growth of a class of middlemen or landlords and to secure in future a direct settlement between the government and the actual cultivator in respect of all lands taken up for ordinary cultivation'.[9] The Association pointed out several reasons why these principles would prove disastrous. First, the Assamese cultivators, being mostly poor, could never cultivate more land than was absolutely necessary for fulfilling their basic needs. Second, the Assamese middle-class had not yet learnt the ways and advantages of farming on a big scale as in the more advanced countries of the West. Third, the direct and immediate effect of the amended rules would be to altogether check the reclamation of wastelands for the purpose of peasant cultivation. Babu Gunjanan Barua, a pleader from Sibsagar, claimed on behalf of the Committee of Assam Association that the Assamese landlords generally did not take up lands only with the intention of renting them out but 'had to engage sharecroppers when they failed for any reason to cultivate by them'.[10] Barua further pleaded that 'those who could afford to keep more land, take them and cultivate as much as they could, hired out the rest and got something for their investment or labour which was rightly due.'[11] The Committee was of the opinion that depriving the Assamese landlords of profits from their investments in land or from the labour of their sharecroppers, was against the principles of political economy. These voices were joined by none other than the powerful lobbies of tea planters, who used to rent out their surplus land to the tea garden labourers. J. Buckinghum, the chairman of the Assam branch of Indian Tea Association, submitted a memorandum opposing such amendment.[12] In the face of such protests, the government could not proceed with the proposed amendment.

There is evidence of growing unrest among the tenants in the next few decades. They made several appeals to the government seeking protection of their interests and reduction in the exorbitant rate of interest charged by the landlords. The districts of Goalpara and Sylhet under permanent settlement had their own tenancy acts in the 1920s. For the raiyatwari areas also, J.E. Webster — who had vast experience in dealing with the tenancy problem of Bengal and Cachar — drafted a bill in 1922 to address the tenancy problems.[13] The government published it with slight modifications on 30 May 1922. The draft bill accepted, in principle, that though serious abuses had not occurred in the relations between the landlords and tenants 'there was every likelihood of their occurring in the future and that the opportunity should be taken of providing in advance against them by framing simple legislation suited to the comparatively simple landlord and tenant relation.'[14] The bill also highlighted two points: the landlord had no right to enhance rent and there was no protection for the tenants against eviction. The bill was strongly supported by the official members of the Council but there was vehement opposition from the non-official members, among whom the landlords were dominant. The bill was dropped eventually.

In the 1930s, the question of landlord–tenant relationship resurfaced with the success of the Civil Disobedience movement in the valley. A no-rent campaign severely threatened the already fragile landlord–tenant relations, particularly putting the landlords of nisf-khiraj estates under a lot of stress. In 1933, the Assam government received a petition signed by 2,000 tenants of Kamrup, seeking redressal of their grievances.[15] This was one of the largest mobilizations of tenants in the nisf-khiraj estates before independence. There is no record, however, of the circumstances that led to submission of the petition.[16] The tenants, in the petition, complained that the absence of legislation had made their position very insecure. Some of them had been, for generations, occupying particular plots of land for cultivation as well as staying in the homesteads they had built in those plots. But they had no occupancy rights and could be turned out at the sweet will of their landlords, who were not bound to give any justification for taking such action. Undoubtedly, the petition was an outcome of a carefully articulated public opinion in the entire district and had an impact on the tenants of other areas too. Thus, Rohini Kumar Chaudhury, a vocal member in the Council, worriedly admitted that 'after the application was made from Kamrup there have been frequent references to the subject in various parts of the districts'.[17] In some parts of eastern Assam, meetings demanding a legislation on the tenancy question were held. Most of them were organized by comparatively rich tenants and often gained significant support from poor tenants. The leading Assamese nationalist paper, *Tinidiniya Assamiya*, published a series of editorials in support of such a legislation. The government also admitted that there was growing reluctance on the part of tenants to pay rent.[18] The landlords, unable to extract rent from their tenants and facing severe hostility, reluctantly agreed to support the passage of an act to clearly define their relationship with the tenants.

In 1933, a six-member team of the Council recommended the necessity of such a piece of legislation to the government.[19] In March of the same year, Rohini Kumar Chaudhury, himself a landlord and more than willing to defend the interests of landlords, moved a resolution urging the government to introduce a bill to regulate the relations between tenants and landlords in the raiyatwari or temporarily settled areas of Brahmaputra valley.[20] The government thus had two options before it — either to enact a special tenancy act, or extend some provisions of the Goalpara Tenancy Act to the raiyatwari districts.[21] A.J. Laine, the finance member in the Council, expressed his doubts about the second option on the ground that the tenancy conditions in Goalpara differed, due to historic and other factors, from those of the raiyatwari districts. But as demands for the grant of occupancy rights to tenants in the raiyatwari districts increased, the Council recommended a tenancy legislation for all temporarily settled areas on 21 March 1933.[22]

The Government of Assam introduced the Assam Tenancy Bill in 1934. The bill was initially published in *The Assam Gazette* on 12 September 1934, but hardly sparked any public debate. Before introducing it in the Council, Laine admitted that for the 'tens of thousands of agricultural tenants in various temporarily settled districts, a tenancy legislation is urgently required'.[23] He emphasized that the bill was aimed to regulate the relations between landlords and tenants in the temporarily settled areas of Assam. He added that protection to the tenants would be given without seriously encroaching on the just rights of the landlords. The government admitted that as 'there is no rent law in force … tenants in this province are mere tenants-at-will and enjoy no special protection or right'.[24] The bill invited strong protests from the landlords. As it was sent to the landlord-dominated select committee, the latter demanded that only Kamrup be brought under the purview of this bill. The committee voted 6 to 5 to exclude all districts except Kamrup from the scope of the bill. The government refused to proceed with the truncated bill and the issue came to a standstill temporarily.

As the discontent among tenants spread from Kamrup to more areas, in March 1935, restoring the original scope of the bill, the Council, by an overwhelming majority, decided to reintroduce it. Accordingly, on 7 June 1935, Laine introduced a motion for a recommitment of the bill. After its recommitment, the select committee's report was again presented before the house, and the discussion formally began. Members, cutting across varied ideological moorings, participated in the debates. Most non-official members, primarily representing the interests of Assamese landowners, agreed that the bill must not harm the rights of Assamese landowners. Brindaban Goswami, a select committee member and a landlord, thus told the house, 'At the time when I asked the government for legislation ... I thought of such legislation for lands which are known as *nisf-khiraj*, *debottar* and *brahmottar* ... [W]hen I understood that the bill would also include even the khiraj lands I was surprised.'[25] The majority of non-official members became vocal in support of khiraj landowners. As the debate on various provisions of the bill progressed, it appeared that only the tenants belonging to nisf-khiraj estates were to get security of tenure and occupancy rights. There was also a demand from planters' lobby in the Council to keep the tea garden owners out of purview of the bill. The idea of defending the landowners' interests eventually prevailed in the debates. For instance, several motions and amendments were put forward, the majority of which tried to safeguard the khiraj landholders' interests.

The house witnessed the longest debate on four similar proposed amendments which tried to exclude various categories of sharecroppers from the definition of tenant.[26] One of these proposed amendments argued that 'a person who holds land immediately under government or who cultivates land as *adhiar, bhagidar* or *bargadar* or *holi-bargadar* is not a tenant within the meaning ... of the tenant'.[27] The select committee decided to include a different clause covering the ryots with occupancy rights and, at the end, it was decided that the sharecroppers would not be included in the definition of tenant. No one in the Council realized that this exclusion would help in further deteriorating the relationship between landowners and sharecroppers. This eventually led the government to bring a bill for discussion in 1948, which came to be known as the Adhiars Protection and Rights Act.

The Assam Tenancy Act was passed in the Council in June 1935 but came into effect only in 1937.[28] Officially, the Act extended all the rights accorded to tenants under the Goalpara Tenancy Act and the Sylhet Tenancy Act to all tenants.[29] It categorized the tenants as ryots and under-ryots. It further divided the former into three different categories: privileged ryots, occupancy ryots, and non-occupancy ryots. The privileged ryots were entitled to hold land paying rates of rent not exceeding the revenue rates. The nature of the right of occupancy defined the other two categories of tenants. Prior to this, tenants had no legal rights in matters of occupancy and transfer of lands they cultivated, a situation that made them merely tenants-at-will. They benefitted partially from the existing social customs and the landlords' complete dependence on them. The Act only promised inequitable rights and failed to bring any significant relief to the tenants. It partially benefitted the privileged and occupancy tenants, but could neither protect the non-occupancy tenants nor fix the rate of rent to be paid by the non-occupancy tenants. More importantly, given the nature of agrarian relations in the raiyatwari districts, the scope of the Act remained limited to a small area as it did not include the sharecroppers within the definition of tenant.

Why did the rights of sharecroppers not become part of this Act? The Assam Provincial Congress Party hardly showed any interest in their problems. The Great Depression of 1930s and the Civil Disobedience movement channelled the peasants' and sharecroppers' discontent towards a new direction. Local peasant organizations were either newly formed or re-activated during this period and made such demands as reduction and remission of land revenue, distribution of agricultural loans, abolition of cart tax, etc. As discussed in Chapter 2, in order to bring these local movements under one banner, the All Assam Ryot Sabha was formed in 1933 with mauza-level units. Local Congress leaders and rural landed gentry formed the majority of members of the organization, and participation of the peasants was also much higher. However, it did not address the problems of adhiars; it rather worked closely with the Congress to refrain from defending their rights. Thus, the tribal peasants and adhiars were also left out of the fold of the Ryot Sabha. In the Legislative Council, the Congress was primarily concerned with the resettlement operation in the temporarily settled areas and the demand for reduction in land revenue rates. The issues of increasing conflicts between landowners and tenants over their respective rights and privileges, and usurious moneylending hardly featured in the discussions. Such avoidance of the tenants' problems was bound to create repercussions in the rural life. To protect itself from any rural protests, the Congress defensively claiming that it had been instrumental in passing several new acts in the Legislative Council which were aimed at redressing the discontent of peasants only.

The Assam Tenancy Act faced the strongest opposition from the *satras* and other religious institutions on the ground that it granted occupancy rights to their tenants, which meant gradual erosion of their coercive power over their tenants. The Congress leaders, whose ideological and social affinity with these institutions was well known, could not choose to ignore resentment of these landowners.[30] The Congress-led Assam assembly thus eventually conceded their demands, and in 1940 the Act was further amended. The amended Act did away with the status of 'privileged and occupancy ryots' granted to the tenants of estates owned by religious establishments and reduced them to the status of mere tenants. The government admitted that, as a result of the amendments, the tenants of religious establishments stopped paying rent. It was reported that 'great difficulty is experienced in realizing rents from tenants and in paying government revenue by managers of land to temples or other religious institutions'.[31] Significantly, the amendment also made way for preparing the record-of-rights for all such tenants. Decades later, in 1970s, the Act would be further radically amended but under the pressure of newer social circumstances, as will be discussed in Chapter 7.

Containing an Agrarian Crisis: Usury and Legislature

By the early twentieth century, as discussed in Chapter 1, rural credit had become a matter of concern for the colonial officials in Assam, as it did for their counterparts in rest of British India. The officials viewed rural credit as immensely harmful to the well-being of rural economy in general. Such a view influenced the government to take steps in 1919 to prohibit the transfer of land from debtors to creditors, a measure which, however, turned out to be ineffective.[32] Like the officials, the legislators in Assam could not evade the question of growing indebtedness of the peasantry. The most vocal members in the Council were from Surma valley in southern Assam. Concerns about the issue were first expressed in 1923 in the Council by Munawwar Ali, a lawyer and a popular leader of the Muslim tenants in the Surma valley.[33] Ali moved a motion demanding an enquiry into the extent of indebtedness and moneylending practices in Assam. He emphatically argued, 'We know indebtedness, usury and high interest are eating into the very vitals and marrow of the teeming millions of this province'.[34] However, Ali could hardly muster enough support for his motion. His counterparts from the Brahmaputra valley were either silent or could not see why such an enquiry was needed. For instance, another member, Abdul Majid (1867–1924), a barrister and retired judge, tried to dissuade Ali by suggesting that the Usurious Loans Act of 1918 was more than enough to regulate usury-related disputes between moneylenders and peasants. The government also rejected his suggestion for instituting an enquiry by arguing that such a move would not resolve the usury-related problems and neither was it was feasible. Between 1921 and 1928, the Council hardly witnessed any further debate in this matter. But that did not stop Ali from reiterating his demand for government intervention to address the ills of usury in 1928. A staunch opposition to this proposal came from none other than Muhammad Saadulla, Minister in the Council and knighted in 1928, who reminded Ali that 'enquiries of this nature are useless'. Saadulla disagreed with Ali by claiming that indebtedness was not of real significance in Assam. Ali's proposal met with the same fate as in 1921, but the government did promise an enquiry in the future. Despite this unfortunate fate of his motion, the official concerns about the problem did not die out. Finally, in 1929, the government formed a five-member committee to enquire into the practice of usury in the province.[35] The committee's exhaustive report virtually portrayed a worrisome picture of rural indebtedness in Brahmaputra and Surma valleys.

What had led the legislators from Brahmaputra valley to avoid pressurizing the government for instituting an enquiry into the usury? In the Brahmaputra valley, usury was fast emerging as an integral element of the rural landscape. The direct beneficiaries of the practice were Assamese rich peasants, landlords and officials, as well as Assamese and Marwari traders. Till 1930, the rural credit primarily impacted the East Bengali immigrant jute cultivators. Those who did not cultivate jute suffered little. It is the influential lobby of Assamese and Marwari creditors who dissuaded the legislative members from Brahmaputra valley from taking against any measure against the practice, which would directly harm them. Unlike the legislators from Brahmaputra valley, the Muslim legislators from Surma valley could hardly ignore the rural discontent arising out of usury, since the bulk of creditors in the valley, as in Bengal, were predominantly Hindus and the tenants-cum-debtors, Muslims.[36] Thus, such complexities underlying the practice could not unite the Council.

Indebtedness rapidly aggravated in the 1930s and the ground reality changed in the Brahmaputra valley. The Great Depression, as discussed in Chapter 1, eqaully impacted the tribal, Assamese and East Bengali peasants. Acute cash scarcity enabled the moneylenders to charge exorbitant rates of interest. Though the Usurious Loans Act of 1918 was in effect in the province, it did not stipulate the maximum rate of interest that could be charged by the moneylenders. But this did not yet prompt the legislators from Brahmaputra valley to relook into the issue of usury; rather they publicly opposed any move to regulate usury. However, in 1933, Maulavi Khalique Chaudhury, a legislator from Surma valley, armed with a convincing official report on the seriousness of usury in Assam, brought back the issue into the Council.[37] He demanded urgent legislative measures to control the high rate of interest charged by the moneylenders. He also demanded that the maximum rate of interest be fixed at 12.5 per cent. Most members from the Brahmaputra valley rose up against any such move. For instance, an Assamese member from Brahmaputra valley, Sarveswar Barua (1891–1975), a lawyer and *mauzadar*, claimed that 'the necessity of the borrower is higher than the necessity of the lender'.[38] Chaudhury's motion of amendment in defence of usury was withdrawn on the assurance from the government that in a short time-span an official bill would be brought in the Council.

In the meantime, most provincial governments in India began to regulate usury.[39] Official condemnation of usury too increased. A couple of years later, in 1936, the Imperial Legislative Assembly agreed to carry out an all-India survey of indebtedness.[40] The provincial government introduced the Assam Moneylenders Bill in 1934.[41] The bill was sent to the landlord-dominated select committee[42] which took only four days to return the bill after accepting amendments. The legislators from Surma valley submitted a lone note of dissent. The bill, though, was finally passed. The Assam Moneylenders Act forbade the charging of compound interest, and fixed the maximum rate of simple interest at 12.5 per cent on secured loans and 18.75 per cent on unsecured loans.[43] It also prohibited moneylenders from entering a larger sum in their ledgers (than they actually loaned) in the bonds signed by peasant-debtors.

The Assam Moneylenders Act came into effect in the Brahmaputra valley from April 1937. In the same year, the Assam Debt Conciliation Act was passed.[44] Approaching Debt Conciliation Boards, formed as result of the Act, was supposed to be a comparatively easier for the poorer peasantry seeking relief from their creditors. The Boards could settle disputes related to amounts up to Rs 5,000, while their jurisdiction remained within the area where the peasants lived. But both these pieces of legislations effectively legalized usury and strengthened the creditors' stranglehold over debtors. Moneylenders brought suits against the defaulting peasants in the Boards. Between 1938 and 1939, beginning with the creation of the first Board in southern Kamrup in 1938, more boards were established in places like Chayagaon, Guwahati, Nowgaon, Tezpur, Mangaldai, Nalbari, and Barpeta, where trader–usurer nexus had already made deep inroads.[45] Most of the Boards came to be dominated by landlords and moneylenders. Moneylenders secured the transfer of mortgaged land into their names from their debtors. Though the moneylenders could recover their earlier loans, they detested these Boards as the legal limits on the quantum of capital they could loan to the debtors discouraged them from keeping more capital in the credit market. By 1946, however, all these Boards were closed down under the combined pressure of traders and moneylenders.[46] The issue of providing legislative relief to the indebted peasants came to haunt Assamese politicians again in the 1970s, forcing the Assam Legislative Assembly to pass another legislation in 1975 to regulate the practices of rural moneylenders.[47] These legislative exercises, however, never brought any significant relief to the indebted peasants.

The Sharecroppers at the Forefront

The landlord–sharecropper conflicts occupied the centre stage of rural politics in Assam by the winter of 1947, forcing a re-alignment of political equations in Assam. More worrying for the Congress government was that the sharecroppers could garner support from the leading Assamese nationalists who were closely aligned with the Congress party. One illustrative example is that of Ambikagiri Raichaudhuri (1885–1967), the founder of Assamiya Samrakshini Sabha and a vocal defender of Assamese linguistic and cultural identity, who in a well-attended meeting of Karbi sharecroppers in Sonapur, eastern Kamrup, demanded the abolition of sharecropping system.[48] Known for his fiery speeches, Roy Chaudhury agreed with the peasants that giving land to the tiller was a just and rationale demand. Not all Congressmen, however, agreed with Ambikagiri. The Assam government too had only recently received volumes of memoranda from a wide cross-section of sharecroppers demanding amendments to the Assam Tenancy Act of 1935 and grant of occupancy rights to them in the raiyatwari areas. Groups of sharecroppers suggested that this could be achieved by amending provisions of the Assam Tenancy Act of 1935.[49] Landlords, on their part, strongly opposed any move for granting occupancy rights and defended the need for continuing with the practice of sharecropping. The Nowgaon Bar Association, largely representing the landlords' interests, made a representation before the Assam government, opposing the grant of occupancy rights to sharecroppers. Concurring with the Nowgaon Bar Association, the Deputy Commissioner argued that a sharecropper did not always rent in the same plot of land or from the same landlord and thus was not entitled for occupancy rights. He admitted that landlords frequently changed their sharecroppers, but wrongly believed that they did not take advantage of the latter's lack of occupancy rights. He, therefore, maintained that the sharecroppers could not be called permanent ryots and no tenancy rights should be accorded.[50]

The sharecropping question came back to haunt the Assamese politicians and middle class again in the 1930s. The practice of sharecropping was best defended during an enquiry into the Line System in 1937. While sharecropping emerged as an agreeable means of bringing wastelands under plough, public debate flared up asking whether immigrant East Bengali peasants should be engaged as sharecroppers or not. Speaking before the Line System Enquiry Committee, Dhaniram Talukdar, an influential landlord and also the chairman of the Local Board in Barpeta, favoured engaging immigrant East Bengali small peasants as sharecroppers. Talukdar argued that there could not be any objection to the Assamese landlords engaging immigrants as sharecroppers, provided they did not claim occupancy rights over the lands they tilled and the landlords did not transfer the same to them under any condition.[51] Jadav Chandra Das, Secretary of the Barpeta Bar

Association and supported by a majority of landlords from Barpeta and Nalbari, did not disagree with Talukdar. [52] He testified before the Committee, 'They may be engaged as *adhiars* and not as sub tenants provided they are not allowed to reside within the Assamese line, otherwise the indigenous landholders be made punishable with fine and confiscation of land'.[53] Given their landed interests, it was not difficult to understand such a stand taken by the landlords. But it was the Assamese Muslim peasants from Kamrup who opposed immigrants being engaged as sharecroppers within the Assamese-dominated areas.[54] Many of them argued that given the gap between the demand for and supply of agricultural labourers, the immigrant sharecroppers, 'if they were able somehow to settle anywhere even temporarily',[55] would claim permanent occupancy rights. As one of them deposed before the Committee, 'Rather they would try at the best of their capacity, even at the cost of their lives to retain it permanently.'[56] Many also foresaw increasing clashes over land between a growing indigenous population and immigrant peasants and thus appealed to the government to take 'strict steps to put a stop to this evil and selfish practice of the Assamese landholders'.[57] In contrast to the strong advocacy by the Hindu landlords of Barpeta and Nalbari of the employment of immigrants as sharecroppers, Hindu landlords in Nowgaon had a slightly different viewpoint. Though many favoured such an arrangement, they thought that it was better that the immigrant sharecroppers remained outside the Assamese line. Purna Chandra Sarmah, a pleader and a leading Congressman, argued that there should be no sharecropping within the Assamese line on annually settled lands. The sharecropping could be allowed in case of permanently settled lands only if under no circumstances could such lands be sold or transferred to them when the Assamese peasants did not exercise the right of preemption. These testimonies point to a clear agreement amongst the Assamese landlords on renting out land to East Bengali immigrants as well as a clear unwillingness to give them occupancy rights.

A decade later, the Assamese landlords had to seek support of their political leaders to defend their interests from an increasing number of hostile sharecroppers who were unwilling to accept the terms and conditions set by them. Under such pressures from the landlords and in the face of sharecroppers' stubborn refusal to pay rent, Bishnuram Medhi, Revenue Minister in the Assam government, in 1948, introduced the hurriedly drafted Assam Adhiars Protection and Rights Bill in the Legislative Assembly. Medhi admitted, 'As a matter of fact we have received a large number of complaints from the *adhiars* ... exorbitant rent is realized from the tenant'[58] He also admitted that the sharecroppers' movement had forced the government to introduce the bill in a hurried manner.[59] The government claimed that the main

> 'aim [of the bill was] to protect the interests of the tenants and to reduce the rent in kind ... giving some relief to the *adhiars* so that they cannot be unreasonably evicted by the landlords at their whim, to give them security of tenancy and also leave a sufficient quota earned by their labour and capital'.[60]

The government further acknowledged that, despite agricultural prices rising precipitously, it was only the landlords who could derive the benefits instead of the sharecroppers.[61] The government was worried about the fact that the sharecroppers' movement could go out of control and seriously dislocate the rural support base of the Congress party.

The government did not expect any trouble in getting support for the bill from any quarter though the Muslim League — then left with only limited popular support, as a majority of its charismatic leaders including Bhasani had migrated to East Pakistan — demanded that the bill should be publicized in the press for eliciting public opinion.[62] Congress members, however, disagreed with the league's suggestion and argued that any further delay in the passage of the bill would worsen the situation. Members across the political spectrum graphically portrayed the enormity of landlord–sharecropper conflicts and did not deny that it was the key issue in the then political arena of Assam. Saadulla, the then leader of opposition and a Muslim League member, reminded the house that 'the communists ... have stepped up vigorous propaganda in the district of Kamrup against delivering their rent in kind'.[63] Harinarayan Barua, an influential Congress member and a landowner from Sibsagar, said:

> We are not ignorant of the powerful *adhiars* movement which is now going in Sibsagar ... the movement has reached such a situation that at many places the matigiris could not think of visiting their *adhiars*

> for fear of losing their social status [due to possible humiliation at their hands] ... at Borhola and Titabor there are large *adhiars* ... where the movement is gaining momentum.'[64]

At the same time, pro-landowner voices too became louder. Dharanidhar Basumatry, a Congress leader from Bodo community, claimed that 'deputations were received which suggested that the adhiars should be protected from the exploitation of the landlords'.[65] The government had already received representations from the Assamese landowners too, seeking measures to avoid any further loss in their control over their resources. This meant that the government could not afford to delay seeking a middle path, and therefore, it refused to send the bill to a select committee of the house. However, to avoid any embarrassment for bypassing the legislative procedures, the Congress had already tried to take the landlords into confidence.[66] An enquiry committee, mostly consisting of landlords, was instituted in Jorhat in January 1948 to seek opinions of both landlords and sharecroppers about the bill.[67] There is no way of knowing whether the warring sharecroppers found any interest in this negotiation or not, but some sharecroppers, mostly under the influence of the CSP-led Assam Talatiya Ryot Sangha, deposed before the committee. The Congress Socialist Party (CSP) also expressed apprehension about this enquiry and demanded an intensive investigation to find out how much land an average sharecropper's family needed for a comfortable living. While the majority of small or medium landlords saw the bill as a threat to their rights and refused to give consent to any new rent arrangement, the rich landlords instantly understood, in the penultimate hour, that the bill would be in their favour.[68] A landlord, who owned 15 *puras* of land of which he rented out 12 puras, while deposing before the committee, made it clear that if the government went ahead with any new rent arrangement he would rather let his land remain fallow rather than rent it out to the sharecroppers.[69] However, another landlord, having 1500 puras of land and involved in various forms of sharecropping arrangements, expressed his willingness to any new negotiation.[70] Thus, the landlords had mixed opinions about any possible new rent arrangement arising out of the bill.

The anxiety of Assamese politicians about the bill was also clearly visible. They did not want to lose any opportunity to defend the landowners. Legislators across the political spectrum quickly agreed to pass a bill. Most realized that eventually the interests of landlords would be taken care of indirectly by protecting the interests of sharecroppers. The government, backed by their support and also apparently driven by the desire to win over the agitating sharecroppers, conveyed its willingness to protect their interests.[71] Meanwhile, before the bill was presented in the Assembly in 1948, the communist organizations kept pressurizing the government to pass the bill.[72] At the same time, demonstrations and public meetings organized by them continued to pressurize the government against making the bill a pro-landlord one, but these could hardly influence the political alliances forged inside the Assembly.[73]

Finally, as the bill came up for discussion, it unfolded a complex maze of conflicting social interests. Soon, it became clear that the Assembly was more sympathetic to the landlords than to the sharecroppers. Also, the members of the Assembly were not sharply divided along political lines. After independence, the Assembly was left with predominantly Assamese nationalists whose alliance with the landlords was well known. Partition had made the Muslim League, consisting of only those leaders who had decided not to migrate to East Pakistan, politically insignificant, and ideologically they came closer to the Congress. The All Assam Tribal (plains) League (hereafter Tribal League) and representatives of tea garden labourers were the only possible hope for the sharecroppers. The Congress, which had already sought support from all its members to support the bill, expressed an urgent need for framing a law to defend the interests of landlords. The Muslim League challenged whatever limited concessions that were granted by the bill to the sharecroppers and criticized the government for giving 'enough leniency [*sic*] to the *adhiars*'.[74] Accusing the government of not being sensitive to 'the plight of these landlords' and for 'biting more than what they chew',[75] the League demanded that till the 'price of agricultural produce [continued to be] high',[76] the rent in kind may be fixed at one-third of the produce. The League's most prominent spokesman, Saadulla, himself having landed interests in various places of Kamrup and backed by Guwahati-based Assamese landlords, even warned the government that

> if [they] go on without looking in to the interests of the landlord, the landlord [would] be forced to go the civil courts and cultivate their

land through their own tenants or by hiring labourers and poor people who may be quite willing to work on wages'.[77]

Admitting that the '*adhiars* had stopped giving rent to Guwahati-based Hindu and Muslim'[78] landowners, Saadulla tried another trick by defending the landed interests of the *panda*s of the Kamakhya temple. The non-Congress members in the opposition criticized the government 'for weakening the position of the landlords'.[79] The Muslim League members argued that in giving relief to the tenants, the bill 'ignored those who possess small plots of land and who cannot be called zamindars in the accepted sense of the term. There are thousands of people who own only 4 to 5 *pura* of land each'.[80] Two members representing the tea garden labour community extended their support to the bill.[81] A worried Binode Kumar J. Sarwan, a tea garden representative in the Assembly from Darrang, reminded the government that 'if this house [did] not proceed with the necessity of the bill and pass it very quickly . . . the poor people who are deprived of the means of living might decide that necessity knows no law',[82] and that, '[t]he present plight of *adhiars* has been deplorable as the landlords are continuously encroaching more and more on the rights to subsistence conditions of the *adhiars* whose families are suffering untold miseries'.[83] The members agreed on the sharp deterioration in the relations between adhiars and landlords. Most argued that crop-sharing on an equitable basis was more popular than payment of rent in cash. But very few denied that adhiars, apart from giving a share of produce, also had to render customary services. The members frequently referred to the 'communist mentality of the *adhiars*',[84] 'growing hostility between the *adhiars* and the landlords', the result of which might be a 'revolution',[85] 'loss of social honour because of abuses [and] slander inflicted by the *adhiars*'[86] and 'enormous economic hardship[for the landlords]'.[87]

Finally, the Congress made its intention clear by stating, '[W]e the Congress party stands for . . . to[*sic*] bring amicable settlement between all parties and groups so that one section . . . does not suffer due to exploitation by the other'.[88] Implicit in this statement was the fact that the Congress party, whose political foundation lay on the support of landlords, could not ignore them as their political ally. The party made it clear that the 'government is not going to harm the landowner's interest, rather it is an effective safeguard [for it]'[89] and assured that the absentee landowners would be allowed by the provisions of the bill to get their lands cultivated by hired labourers.[90]

The government accepted several amendments which finally shaped the bill in favour of the landlords.[91] The original bill did not have any clause which allowed the landlords to evict their adhiars for any petty reason. One instance of a clearly circumvention of the original radical promises of the bill was an amendment moved by Beliram Das, a Congressman and also a landlord. Das, backed by the landlords, wanted, by way of the proposed amendment, to allow them to retain their land for 'residential or horticultural or piscicultural or poultry farming or dairy farming or similar other purposes'.[92] Das argued that the bill in the present form did not allow them to evict their sharecroppers unless the land was needed for paddy cultivation. As the government accepted the amendment, given the fact that the Assamese landlords were hardly into such agrarian activities, it essentially foiled the promises made by the bill. Though feeble attempts were made to keep rich landlords beyond the scope of this provision, for instance the amendment moved by Maulavi Muhammad Abdul Kashem from predominantly East Bengali-settled Dhubri constituency, the government did not allow such changes to be made.[93] The landlords' interests further stood protected when another amendment, moved by P.M. Sarwan seeking a provision that landlords should not be allowed to evict the sharecroppers in order to get their land cultivated by 'hired labourers or dependants',[94] was rejected by the government. These pro-landlord amendments allowed the landlord to evict an adhiar on the slightest pretext, for example, if the latter failed to deliver the share within the prescribed time. The Act also stipulated that a sharecropper should not keep a plot of land fallow or sublet it to others. All these essentially allowed the landlords to retain their superior authority over the sharecroppers.[95]

Lakshmidhar Borah (1903–83), a Congressman with socialist leanings, moved the only pro-sharecropper amendment to be accepted by the government.[96] Almost all other members explicitly defended the cause of the absentee landowners.[97] They admitted that this group of people comprising the absentee and medium landowners would suffer the most if the adhiars refused to pay. The expansion of Congress mass base also depended on their crucial support. Meanwhile, arguing that some variations be allowed to the bill's application as the practice of sharecropping differed from locality to locality, the government also reserved its right to extend the bill to a particular area of the state.[98] In fact, as we will explain later, the implementation of the Act in an area would come to be determined by local political compulsions, arising out of the growing conflicts between landlords and sharecroppers.

Was it a Radical Act?

A pro-landlord bill was finally passed without any hassle on 3 April 1948 with the support of Muslim League. The bill received the consent of the Assam governor on 3 June and a gazette notification was published on 16 June.[99] The Assam Adhiars Protection and Regulation Act of 1948 (the Assam Act 12 of 1948) defined adhiar as one who, under the system commonly known as *adhi*, *barga*, *chukti-bhag*, or *chukani*, cultivates the land of a landowner on the condition of delivering a share or quantity of the produce of such land to the latter. It further defined landlord as a person under whom the adhiar holds the land. This vague definition of landlords and adhiars left out the tea estates and religious institutions, which comprised an important part of the landholding class with a predominance of tenancy relationships. The Act allowed the sharecropper to continue cultivating the adhi land 'until he voluntarily relinquishes the land or is ordered [to do so] by a revenue officer'.[100]

Elaborate provisions were made to describe all circumstances under which a landowner could demand the eviction of the adhiar. A revenue officer was authorized to order an adhiar to stop cultivating an adhi land and evict him in case he received a complaint from his landlord. The Act justified the superior rights of landowners over the sharecroppers' right to occupy and cultivate the land. Section 9 incorporated the provision of appeal by adhiars to a higher authority. Another provision of the bill upheld the supremacy of the revenue officer and thus restricted the jurisdiction of civil courts in these matters. The Act also provided that the landlord would retain one-third of the produce in case he supplied plough and cattle and the adhiar only helped in the cultivation; and one-fourth of the produce in case he did not supply plough and cattle. The provision allowing the adhiar to retain two-third or three-fourths of the produce marked an important departure from the customary practice of landlord claiming adhi (half of the produce) under the adhiar system. A Muslim League member even quoted a vernacular lexicon to justify the adhi system of sharecropping as the most equitable one.[101] The official position, however, was that the landlords had drawn enough benefits from the high prices of agricultural produce, since the difference between the revenue paid to the government and the amount retained by the landlord was very high. In the districts of eastern Assam, the landlords rented out one pura of land for 40–50 puras of paddy as rent, while the market price of paddy was Rs 8 per maund and the revenue payable to the government was Rs 8–10 per pura.[102]

Ideologically, though the government professed an anti-landlord position, the Act itself turned out to be strongly pro-landlord. It only gave legitimacy to sharecropping and none to the slogan of 'land to the tiller' that the peasants' movement had popularized. It contained sufficient provisions to allow the landlord to evict his adhiars for any flimsy reason. Although the main demand of adhiars for giving one-third or one-fourth of the produce to the landlords was conceded, they were not given any protection against eviction. By withdrawing the space for judicial intervention and giving supremacy to revenue officers and civil courts in case of disputes between landlords and adhiars, the latter's position was necessarily strengthened. Further, the Act was to be enforced in a particular locality or area only after proposals came to the government from the concerned revenue officers whose social relationship with the landlords was beyond doubt.[103] If the landlords could variously influence the actual implementation of the Act, it understandably did not give any occupancy or transference rights to their tenants who were reduced to the insecure position of tenants-at-will.

It was during the 1930s that the demand for such rights was raised by various categories of tenants; it was further echoed by peasant organizations in the 1940s in all raiyatwari districts. The Assam Tenancy Act of 1935 granted occupancy rights only to those tenants who had been cultivating land for more than 30 years continuously. This had a spillover impact on khiraj landholdings too. As the landowners were aware of this provision, they did not allow their adhiars to cultivate their lands for a long duration. Neither the provisions of the Act nor the debate in the Assembly put an end to the payment of rent in kind. In fact, the Act did not make any difference between rent in cash and kind. It, on the other hand, allowed the payment of rent in kind or cash.[104] The government admitted that the landlords were enjoying the benefits of high prices of agricultural produce by collecting it from their adhiars and selling it in the market. But all the same, it refused to interfere with the practice. After the Second World War, high prices of food crops and extreme cash scarcity created a situation wherein the landlords began to prefer rent in kind. In the previous chapter, we have discussed how during the initial stage of adhiar agitation, the adhiars demanded that the practice of collecting rent in kind be stopped, since it proved more exploitative and detrimental for them. The adhiars who had land under chukani system suffered the most, as during the period 1943–47, when the production of both cash and food crops was low.

In the volatile political landscape of pre-Partition legislative politics, the Muslim League's support to the cause of poor Muslim peasants was well known.[105] The League extended its crucial support to the 'grow-more-food' scheme and land settlement policy, and opposed the Congress government's eviction programme. The League's pro-peasant position was due to the necessity of safeguarding the interests of peasants who had recently migrated from East Bengal to Assam. This stand, however, took an abrupt turn after independence: the Muslim League members who remained in Assam legislative politics took a strong pro-landlord position. Saadulla strongly defended the position of Guwahati-based landowners. The Congress party, on the other hand, did not articulate any clear policy towards small peasants, sharecroppers and other lower strata in the agrarian structure during the period between 1937 and 1947. But the expansion of Congress' rural mass base was made possible through the network of ryot sabhas, in which the Assamese rich and middle peasants played a leading part.[106] Tribal peasants remained outside these political networks; a small section of rich landowners and educated elite among different tribal peasant communities formed the Tribal League, which would work closely with the Congress nationalists thenceforth.[107]

The Ground Reality

The Assam government quickly enforced the Assam Adhiars Protection and Regulation Act in southern Kamrup, the most conflict-torn region of the valley where both landlords and sharecroppers

Plate 4.1: *Panchayat*, mouthpiece of the RCPI in 1950 commenting on Zamindari Abolition Bill

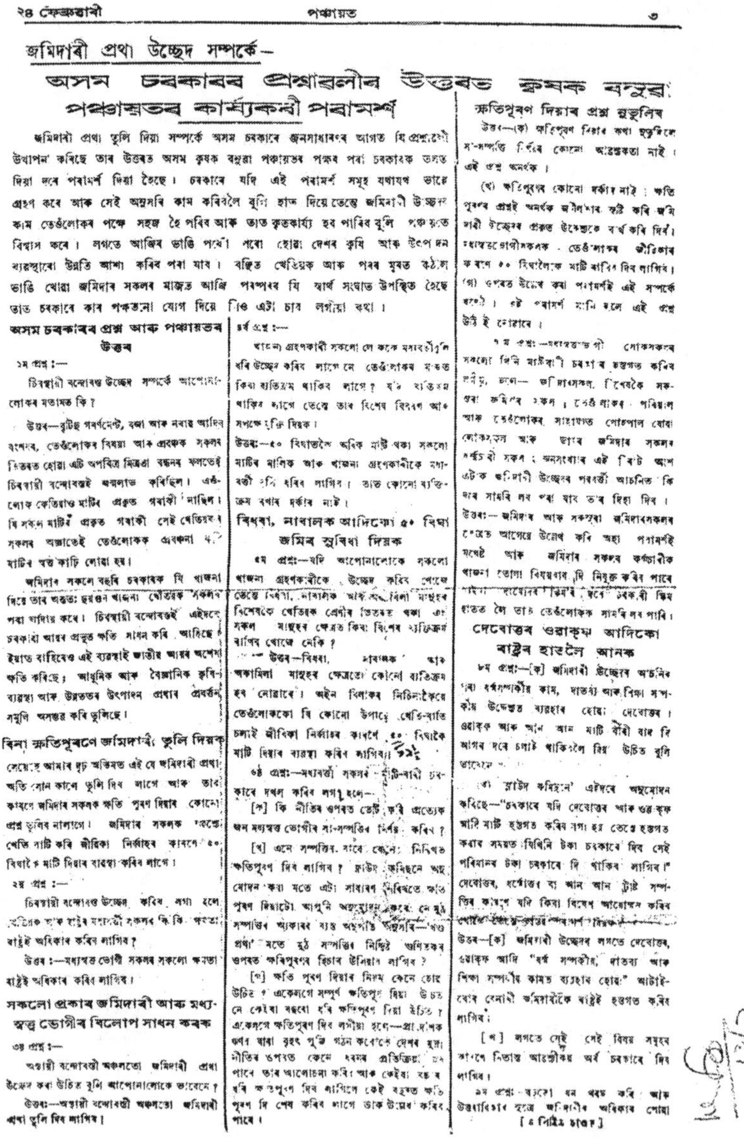

Source: Assam Police Intelligence Record Room (APIRR), Guwahati, 1950.

tried to establish their might. In 1948–50, the Act was extended to other parts of the valley. However, it did not mean an end to the no-rent campaign of communist peasant organizations. Rather, it consolidated the sharecroppers' struggle in more areas. The communist peasant organizations immediately criticized the Act as pro-landlord, but did not stop from claiming it as a victory of the sharecroppers' struggle. For instance, the Krishak Sabha (KS) termed the effects of the Act as illusory and criticized the government for empowering the landlords to evict their sharecroppers.[108] They argued that the Act was a mere mechanism to defuse the intensity of the ongoing sharecroppers' movement.[109] Its parent party, the CPI, however, outlined the possible benefits that the Act could deliver to the sharecroppers. It translated the Act into Assamese language and distributed it widely in the villages.[110] The Krishak Banua Panchayat (KBP) came down heavily on the Act in its mouthpiece *Panchayat* but, like the CPI, did not refrain from calling it a victory of the sharecroppers' movement.[111] While it criticized the government for allowing the landlords to evict their sharecroppers, it also demanded that land be given to the tiller.[112] It claimed the Act had 'enough legal provisions in favour of the landowners and the rights of the *adhiars* [were] still insecure ... [T]he adhiar [had] to go to the court to demand his reinstatement in the earlier land'.[113]

At the same time, the KBP, feeling cornered by the government's concession to a new rate of rent (i.e., one-fourth of produce), as demanded by it earlier, appealed to it that the sharecroppers be given only one-sixth of the produce. The Revolutionary Communist Party of India (RCPI), meanwhile, continued with its opposition to the Act, holding processions and demonstrations, mostly in the localities adjoining Guwahati. In these demonstrations, poor Assamese and tribal peasants also joined with the sharecroppers.[114] They demanded replacement of rent in kind with rent in cash.[115] This opposition to the Act was not uniform everywhere and district committees of the RCPI were divided over the issue of whether to support or oppose it. Open support to the Act came from Nowgaon unit of the RCPI, since adhiar mobilization was not as powerful there as in Kamrup and Darrang. The sharecroppers' movement did not find any strong appeal in the district due to their insignificant numbers, and numerically weak sharecroppers there could not afford to lose the minimum benefits accorded by the Act, while in Kamrup, owing to the greater numerical strength of sharecroppers, there was scope for a better bargain. On its part, the CSP mildly criticized the Act, expecting that it would protect the interests of adhiars, but such protection depended on its effective implementation.[116] It thus wanted the Act to be implemented in different parts of the valley.[117]

The Assamese press was all in praise of the efforts made by the government. The *Dainik Assamiya* admitted in an editorial that 'the problems of *adhiars* were known and such an Act was long pending'.[118] It expected that 'now the condition of the *adhiars* would be ameliorated and the communist would not be able to hijack the tribal people'.[119] The *Assam Tribune* believed that the sharecroppers would be saved from the clutches of the communists and congratulated the government and the Congress for 'keeping its generous eyes on the landowners'.[120] The *Natun Assamiya* commented that 'the country would be saved now from the destruction of the communist who incited people to create social disorder'.[121] The landlords were more forthcoming in their praise for the Act. Local meetings — like the one held at village Hokartup in Barpeta[122] — were held across the valley defending the Act. The Guwahati-based Pattadar Sangha, a platform for sections of landlords, agreed that the Act was necessary, but it also criticized the government for allowing them to get only one-third or one-fourth of the produce.[123] Nevertheless, it also appreciated the fact that enough provisions had been made in the Act to allow them to retain their land, and quickly resolved to organize the landlords from other parts of the valley to counter the sharecroppers. As the ryot sabhas had lost their political importance which had acted as the primary platform for the landlords, a more cohesive organization was needed as a suitable bulwark against the political mobilization of sharecroppers.

That the peasant question became an important agenda in the political landscape of Assam in the post-independence period became clear from the way it came to the centre stage of legislative politics. To a large extent, the peasant politics determined the political alignment in both the Legislative Council and the Legislative Assembly. There were a few problems which kept surfacing in both houses for a long time. They were the questions of tenancy, rural indebtedness and land settlement among various groups of peasantry. These questions continued to dominate the discussions in the Assembly in the post-independence period.

Promise of Land Settlement (1940–50)

As the sharecroppers began to challenge the landlords' dominance in the agrarian economy, the best way for the latter to deal with an uncertain political future was to allow a section of landless peasants to occupy and cultivate unploughed government land. This meant that the government had to deal with two sets of contending interests: first, the Bengal jute industries' unremitting pressure to expand jute cultivation in the valley combined with the promise of the Muslim League to give land to Muslim tenants, and secondly, the Assamese landlords' attempt to defuse any further deterioration in their control over the agrarian economy combined with the tribal leaders' relentless push for distribution of land amongst the landless tribal peasants. In the 1940s, land to the landless tribal peasants turned out to be a key political slogan in the arena of legislative politics.

Who were these landless tribal peasants? By the second quarter of the twentieth century, those tribal communities that were living in and dependent on the forested tracts, or were yet to become a 'modern ryot' by subscribing to the colonial legal system, fast emerged as those that did not have enough access to land or other resources. Their practice of shifting cultivation and mobility across ecological zones stood in contrast to the modern notion of a ryot as a peasant practising sedentary agriculture and paying regular revenue to the government. Some survived by being a tenant of an Assamese landlord. Some failed to retain their parcels of land in the wake of rapid monetization and cash crop production. All these combined to consolidate a class of tribal landless peasants. But, if there was a class of landless peasants waiting to reclaim unploughed land for cultivation, where were these tracts of lands available? Generally described and categorized as wasteland, these government lands comprised mostly Un-classed State Forests came to occupied by the landless tribal peasants.

A brief overview of a decade (1940–50) of land settlement policies pursued by successive governments in Assam will help us understand the shifting alliances of all categories of peasants and the ruling elites. Towards the end of 1939, the Assam Congress government adopted a crucial policy statement on future land settlements in the province. The government, according to a new policy, would not settle landless peasants inside villages and professional grazing reserves and declared that it would regulate settlement of the landless peasants of the province, including immigrants. The land would be given to a maximum holding of 30 bighas per family. It also decided to evict all migrant settlers from areas declared 'protected tribal blocks' in the submontane region.[124] But the resignation of the Gopinath Bordoloi-led Congress government could not bring about the implementation of this policy. On the other hand, the Assam Provincial Muslim League, in the first annual conference held in November 1939, rejected the idea of the Line System and demanded its total abolition.

The new Chief Minister Saadulla of the Muslim League held an all-party meeting on 31 May and 1 June 1940 to deliberate on the continuance of the Line System.[125] As a follow-up to the meeting, a scheme was adopted on 21 June, putting a ban on the settlement of wastelands with any immigrant who entered Assam after 1 January 1938 and settling land with Assamese and tribal peasants except immigrants who came before 1938. The government, in order to withstand popular opposition to any settlement with the migrant population, also made it clear that all such settlements would be in the order of priority, and the Assamese and tribal peasants would be favoured. This scheme was eventually published in *The Assam Gazette* on 4 December 1940. A special officer was appointed to examine whether the proposed areas in a district could be opened for land settlement without any detriment to the districts' normal requirement for grazing and forest reserves. He also had to ensure that the settlement would be confined to indigenous landless people and the pre-1938 immigrants. Besides, the flood- and erosion-affected people, illegally squatting in some villages and grazing reserves within the Assamese line, were also to be accommodated. Eligible applicants were to be settled in wastelands in specified development areas, on payment of a stipulated premium, in blocks segregated for different communities, as before.

On 16 July 1942, the Bengal Legislative Council asked the central government to bring to an end all the hurdles that had stood in the way of land settlement with immigrant peasants in

Assam.[126] Consequent to this demand, the Assam government, on 24 August 1943, adopted the 'grow-more-food' scheme of distributing land among the landless peasantry. Under this scheme, the government decided to de-reserve select professional grazing reserves in Nowgaon, Darrang and Kamrup districts and distribute the land in these reserves to different communities. It also decided to open surplus reserves in all submontane areas as also in Sibsagar and Lakhimpur for settlement of land with landless indigenous peasants.[127] The colonial revenue officials, however, maintained that there was no surplus land available for carrying out this new settlement.[128] In spite of their opposition, the Muslim League ministry threw open a few professional grazing reserves for immigrant peasants to settle in. Under the 'grow-more-food' scheme, a large number of reserved lands in Lakhimpur, Sibsagar and Nowgaon too were thrown open to them. From September 1943 to August 1944, an estimated 85,000, 12,000 and 5,000 bighas were opened in the districts of Nowgaon, Lakhimpur and Sibsagar, respectively, for immigrants as well as indigenous landless peasants.[129] During this period, 52,496 and 134,050 bighas of government lands were settled with migrant peasants in Nowgaon and Kamrup, respectively.[130]

In 1945, the government adopted two land settlement resolutions after a three-party conference of Congress, Muslim League and Tribal League arrived at a consensus. It undertook to settle wastelands in Goalpara, Kamrup, Darrang, and Nowgaon with landless peasants of all categories, including the pre-1938 immigrant peasants. The settlement would be subject to the availability of wasteland and land was to be allotted to different communities in separate community-wise blocks, according to their requirements. The Congress government that came to power after the interim election on 11 February 1946,[131] spelt out the need for a re-examination of *Assam Land Revenue Manual* so as to protect the interests of local peasants as well as the pre-1938 immigrants.[132] The government began the preliminary work, and in the session immediately after the Assembly elections, the Assam Land Revenue Regulation Manual (Amendment) Bill was placed in the Assembly for discussion.[133]

The land settlement question had brought about different alignments in the relations between political parties represented in the Assembly during the tenures of both ML and Congress governments. There was, for instance, a distinct polarization between the Muslim League and the Congress. The former maintained that it had never discriminated against local/indigenous peasants in its land settlement policy. For instance, the Revenue Minister in Saadulla government, Abdur Rouf, argued that in 1941–42, a total of 4,003,266 acres of land were distributed and out of this only 515,486 acres, i.e., 13 per cent were settled with the immigrants.[134] The remaining portion had been settled with the local peasants. The communal representation in the provincial legislature from 1937 crystallized the growing conflict between immigrants and tribal peasants. Abdul Hamid Khan, the Muslim League representative from western Assam, defended the immigrant peasants' rights over wastelands in Assam. He hoped that the Assamese people would welcome these newcomers for the progress of the economy of Assam.[135]

There was a sharp Muslim–Hindu polarization, both within and outside the Assembly, in matters of land settlement. This trend continued till the eve of independence. On 17 May 1947, as independence was approaching, the Revenue Minister in the interim Congress-led government, Bishnuram Medhi, made the distinction between the immigrant question and the problems of landless peasantry.[136] He asserted that the immigrant question in Assam was not the same as the problems of landless peasants. He pointed out that there were more than 7,500,000 bighas of uncultivated wasteland in Bengal. It was the duty of the Bengal government to distribute land among the Bengali peasantry. He further accused the Muslim League of intensifying a pro-Pakistan movement in the name of distributing land among the immigrant landless peasants. At one point of time, Surendranath Buragohain, the Ahom spokesman in the Assembly, and a future ally of the League, criticized the Muslim-League-led government's policy of land settlement as biased towards the immigrant peasants.[137] He claimed that 'when this government embarked on this policy of land settlement to outsiders in 1943 August my Association [All Assam Ahom Sabha] was the first in the province to raise its voice of protest'.[138] Buragohain might have been talking only on behalf of the Ahom peasantry. But others did not fall behind. Land settlement policies advocated by different governments encouraged various communities to lay claim over government land. The Kaibarta peasantry, for instance, demanded that, as most of them did not possess any agricultural land, they should be given land.[139]

A few amongst the Assamese peasants also believed that there was a systematic official policy under the Muslim League government to deny the indigenous peasants any land. In a letter written by 'an old peasant' from Sibsagar appeared in *Dainik Assamiya*, he accused the government that the wastelands were in the register of the *mandals* only. Many of the wastelands were mainly *beels*, hillocks, rivers, and *jalah-pitanis*. The problems of landless peasants remained a pertinent question in Assam.[140] *Sadiniya Assamiya*, in an editorial, commented that settlement of land was an urgency and that numerous landless indigenous peasants in the province needed land though there were not enough wastelands in Assam. It further demanded that indigenous peasants be preferred first while distributing land. It pointed out that the loss of arable land to soil erosion caused by annual floods also added to the problems of landless peasantry. This had led to the emergence of peasant movements for land in parts of Mangaldai and Golaghat, the editorial admitted.[141]

After independence, the growing demand for land and mobilization of sharecroppers compelled the Congress to reorient its policy towards the poor peasantry. The Assam Provincial Congress Party adopted a resolution in early 1950 to organize the adhiars, landless peasantry and agricultural labourers. A committee was formed to organize them under the broad umbrella of the Congress, as they were being 'sought to be owned over by interested parties with various slogans'.[142] The committee took up the initial organizational work for 'forming unions in line with trade unions'.[143] This resulted in the reorganization of ryot sabhas. The reorganized ryot sabhas, despite limited appeal and spread, tried to address the peasant question in a form different from that of the 1930s. For instance, they emphasized the need for the government's attention to the issues of food scarcity and establishment of food stocks. They asked the peasants to raise three crops a year in order to overcome the food crisis. They advised the government to rehabilitate the flood-displaced peasants as well. Often, the government quickly agreed to such pieces of advice. For instance, in 1950, the peasants in the northern belt of Kamrup, who were displaced due to flood in Brahmaputra and resultant soil erosion, were expeditiously rehabilitated in the Malaibari area of Kamrup district.[144] However, on 19 January 1951, in Silchar in the Surma valley, the Congress admitted that the government, in reality, had failed to distribute land among landless peasants.[145] It argued that landlessness was still acute, and the land question was the most troubled chapter in the political life of Assam. Hence, distribution of sufficient land to the landless peasants should be the upmost task of the government, as the Congress asserted.

Meanwhile, the Assam government also passed two important legislations, viz., the Assam Land (Requisition and Acquisition) Act of 1948 and the Assam State Acquisition of Zamindari Act of 1951. Both these legislations, as will be discussed in Chapter 7, aimed at tenancy reform and land settlement and had a far-reaching impact on the peasantry. The first Act allowed the government to take away extra land from tea gardens and distribute the same among landless peasants. The tea planters and zamindars in Goalpara could initially offer only a weak resistance to the second Act but were emboldened to resist both Acts by similar acts of resistance from the other parts of India.[146]

Beyond the Nationalist Paradigm: Tribes and Land Question

The Assamese nationalist politics had a critical influence on the tribal communities in the first half of the twentieth century resulting in the growth of independent tribal political bodies. These political bodies, primarily formed to shape and articulate the ethnic aspirations, however, soon began to address the agrarian question. The estranged relationship between the caste-Hindu Assamese and the tribal communities often came to the surface. Several communities, the Bodo and Ahom being the main ones, had already articulated their opposition against the cultural hegemony of Assamese caste-Hindu nationalists. In the first few decades of the twentieth century, a section of Bodo-speaking tribals had already shifted its allegiance to a more liberal religious practice known as Brahma.[147]

The nationalist mobilization helped to form several political platforms based on ethnic markers, which often successfully negotiated with the Assamese nationalists and also the British government to gain limited benefits.[148] Protest against social discrimination, or parity with the Assamese middle class in privileges, were the hallmarks of these early negotiations, but soon the Assamese nationalists also raised the question of 'large scale land transfer' from the tribal peasants to the East Bengali immigrants. The subject was clearly articulated by Bodo, Rabha, Tiwa, and Karbi-speaking tribal leaders as well. In the wake of Muslim League's demand for the cancellation of Line System in the 1930s, the tribal organizations extended their determined support to its retention as a crucial mechanism to check further alienation of tribal peasants from land. These bodies essentially believed that the Line System was a correct protective institutional measure to check tribal land alienation and also give recognition to the distinct ethnic identities of tribal peasants.[149] The Tribal League, formed in 1933, emerged as a key common platform of various ethnic bodies and vociferously asked for the continuation of the Line System.[150] In 1939, the Tribal League took a resolution asking the government to make laws that would check the large-scale transfer of land from the tribal peasants to the absentee landowners and immigrants.[151] Bhimbar Deuri (1903–47), a pleader and General Secretary of the Tribal League, distanced himself from both the Assamese Congress nationalists and the Muslim League and demanded the faithful implementation of the Line System.[152]

Meanwhile, the Tribal League aligned itself with the Congress government in Assam and became a crucial partner in the government. But this did not deter it from demanding a specific programme aimed at checking tribal land alienation. It exerted repeated pressure upon the government in both the Legislative Council and the Legislative Assembly to conduct an enquiry into the number of tribal landless peasants and distribute land among these peasants.[153] Years later, the Tribal League also garnered the support of tribal leaders from the hills, and this led to the formation of The Central Organization of Assam Tribes in 1945. A convention of a wide cross-section of tribal leadership in Shillong in 1945 asked the Assam government to safeguard the interests of tribal population and demanded that no more immigration be encouraged from East Bengal; it also asked for the eviction of East Bengali settlers from Reserved Forests and from other areas. The convention asserted that unless such steps for preventing further immigration were taken, the 'peace loving children of the soil'[154] could not be saved from economic and political ruin.

In eastern Assam, rather than aggressively pushing for exclusive land settlement with the tribal peasants, the emerging All Assam Ahom Sabha not only addressed the land question from a different platform but also failed to become a distinct political formation. In the political discourse of the Ahom Sabha, the land question surfaced rarely but differently during its most crucial phase of political mobilization (1935–48).[155] An illustrative example of the new ways of thinking of the Sabha was the public appeal of Radha Nath Handique (1847–1952), an Ahom entrepreneur and tea planter, who, in 1935, urged that the Ahom peasants, rather than holding on to small patches of land near their house, could otherwise improve their lives by reclaiming land in the distant jungles. Handique referred to recent successes in land reclamation made in eastern India like that of Daniel Hamilton, a Scottish entrepreneur who had established farms in Bengal where the youths from the Bengali middle-class families were encouraged to take up land for cultivation. If anything like that happened there, he suggested, the Ahom youths should take to cultivation.[156] Inspired by the successful colonization scheme, launched in the 1920s, through which East Bengali peasants were settled in different parts of western and central Assam, Handique urged the government to make room for a similar arrangements for the Ahom peasants.

Given the recent economic improvement of the Ahom community, such a stand of the Ahom Sabha was not unexpected. The contrasting stands of the Tribal League and the Ahom Sabha, the former opposing the colonization scheme and the latter demanding the expansion of the scheme which would pave way for formation of rich or middle peasantry, did not last long. Meanwhile, a land settlement scheme in line with the colonization scheme exclusively for the Ahoms was not realized, and the Ahom Sabha broke its silence on the government's land settlement policy in 1941. It urged the government to distribute land amongst the landless peasantry in Assam and unleashed a scathing attack on the government for allowing migrations to continue. Within a few years, the Ahom Sabha began opposing the land settlement policy of the Assam government too. The Sabha, in 1944, strongly opposed the proposal of the Assam government to distribute land among the East Bengali immigrant peasants. It demanded that the unploughed government-owned lands in Assam be distributed amongst the Assamese peasants, tea garden workers, and immigrant settlers who were residing in Assam.[157] It argued that the remaining land should be preserved for the Assamese peasants though the immigrant peasants who had come earlier also should not be deprived.[158]

The Assamese nationalists were aware of their benefits from immigration and resultant changes in the agrarian economy but were unwilling to forgo their demand for cultural hegemony over Bengali-speaking immigrants. But they argued their case differently. The most illustrative example of their positive towards immigration is that of the Asamiya Samrakshisini Sabha, formed in 1926 as a platform of vocal Assamese nationalists. In one of its first public statements, the Sabha argued that the immigration of peasants from East Bengal was 'to save it [Assam] from existing economic crises'.[159] It strongly argued that if the immigrants were willing to accept Assamese as their language, 'the Assam government and the Assamese people should welcome them'. However, the Samrakshini Sabha argued that if the immigrants refused 'to accept these terms, the government should redefine its land distribution policy'.[160]

Several other nationalists re-affirmed this new nationalist discourse on migration. Nilamoni Phukan (1880–1978), an Assamese nationalist, a gifted orator and a Congressman, argued in 1935 that endless immigration into Assam worried the Assamese people as the immigrants 'could not live peacefully and most of them were Muslim'.[161] While he highlighted the religious and racial inferiority of immigrants, but at the same argued that if the immigrants became 'Assamese it will be better for them and Assamese people would also not have any serious problem'.[162] Meanwhile, a section of Assamese nationalists, Phukan included, also began to share the idea of reframing the land settlement policy 'in such a way that sufficient land was reserved for the future progeny of Assam'. Jnananath Bora, another leading proponent of the Assamese nationalist discourse on immigration, made an effort to differentiate between various groups of immigrants and suggested that they be assimilated into the Assamese society.[163] The European tea planters should be ranked first among those who had been heavily exploiting Assam, he suggested.

Away from the real politicking and widening Assamese public discourse on immigration, the tribal political leaders continued with their relentless campaign to keep tribal habitats from being taken by the immigrants.[164] They regretted the gradual transfer of land from the tribal peasants to the immigrants, and their campaign highlighted the role played by the bureaucracy and the loopholes in the government's land settlement policy in helping this land alienation. Outside legislative politics, the revenue officials again encouraged the settlement of land with immigrant peasants and issued pattas at speculative prices.[165] They had pointed out that the Assamese peasantry had been involved in land speculation and sold these lands at high prices to the immigrant peasants. While there was a growing concern about land speculation and land transfers to immigrants within the intelligentsia, a few amongst the local peasants benefitted from the Line System and from selling land at speculative prices. But there was another angle to this aspect of the land question. As early as 1926, the government had tried to bring an amendment to the *Assam Land Revenue Manual*, banning the transfer of land to the immigrants.[166] Even then, officials had agreed that a large number of pattas had been transferred to the immigrant peasants at a higher price.[167] The landlords were divided in their opinion about the amendment.[168] The government then had realized that the opposition to any such amendment was stronger and withdrew it subsequently.[169]

Securing Space: Land for Tribal Peasants (1947)

The demand for a secured and exclusive habitat for tribal communities began to gain ground years before independence. The Tribal League continued to bargain with the Congress nationalists to achieve this end. In 1946, the Assam government agreed to reserve lands for tribal communities in the form of 'tribal belts and blocks'.[170] A year later, in 1947, the government amended the Assam Land Revenue Regulation of 1886 to institutionalize this executive decision taken in 1945 of reserving land for the tribal population of Assam. The primary principle behind this state intervention to regulate peasant settlement was based on the Line System. Bishnuram Medhi, the then Revenue Minister in the Assam government, introduced a bill on 1 September 1947 seeking an amendment to the Assam Land Revenue Regulation of 1886. This would allow the Assam government to adopt those measures

> 'as it deemed fit for the protection of those tribal and other communities, who on account of their primitive condition and lack of education or material advantages were incapable of looking after their welfare, in so far as such welfare depends upon their having sufficient land for their maintenance'.[171]

This proposed land settlement policy, however, did not involve a sizeable proportion of land. Areas under tea gardens, la- and nisf-khiraj estates came to be excluded. The government tried to allay the fears of other dominant non-tribal communities who might be residing within such excluded areas by reserving its right to define who needed protection.[172] The Congress nationalists and the Tribal League were united against the weak resistance offered by the Muslim League.[173] The Muslim League — the recent history of eviction being fresh in their mind — offered weak resistance on grounds of the explicit religious nature of this policy.[174]

The League's most vocal voice was Maulavi Muhammad Roufique from Nowgaon. Roufique, supported by Saadulla, expressed his apprehension that such state interventions would make many Muslim peasants liable to eviction. The League members thought that if the bill was allowed for public debate it would create a division amongst the Assamese landowners and might finally delay any such state measure. Supported by the Tribal League and the 'backward caste' representatives, the Congress ministry refused any such concession to the demands of the League. This quickly re-aligned the political formations and the polarization along communal line became clear within the Assembly. The League then proposed that the government should allow only the tribal population to get the benefits of tribal belts and blocks, as had been laid down in the 1945 land policy. The Assamese landlords were openly hostile to any such idea, and the government too refused to accept the idea that this exclusion should be only for sociologically defined tribal communities. Bishnuram Medhi suggested that such a specification in favour of the tribal peasants would deprive the other backward communities, such as Scheduled Castes, former tea garden workers and peasants from other tribes, of the benefits from this legal safeguard. But the government did not allow an amendment on the demarcation of the territorial jurisdiction of tribal people. The government, however, allowed an amendment which would enable it to evict anyone who had settled in the tribal belts and blocks without the government's sanction.[175]

As the tribal belts and blocks were formed, approximately one fourth of the total land in the Brahmaputra valley was earmarked for them.[176] This special provision of land settlement — though intended to keep these areas free from non-tribal landlords, among others — could hardly jeopardize the interests of Assamese landlords; further, land was earmarked for tribal settlements in remote and less fertile areas and thus were insignificant from the perspective of the Indian forestry programme, etc. The interests of capitalist enterprises, like tea plantations, remained legally protected. This legal protection balancing the interests of tribal peasants, tea planters and landlords, overlooked two other fundamental causes of tribal land alienation, i.e., predominance of traders and moneylenders in the tribal economy and the lack of tenurial security of tribal sharecroppers. The legal mechanism, thus, did not emerge as a strong deterrent to creating a land market. A powerful forestry programme, bureaucratic and political manipulation of land settlement initiatives, over a period of time, further made these legal protections ineffective. Outside the tribal belts and blocks, the Indian forestry programme, meanwhile, continued to confine the tribal peasants to limited pockets and limited share in land for cultivation. A decade later, not only the Indian forestry programme but also a series of development programmes further weakened the original principle of this policy of land settlement with tribal peasants.[177] Dissent began to be voiced and, decades later, became a critical ideological pillar for a renewed phase of ethnic movements.

5

Rural World Upside Down: The Valley during 1948–52

The Assam government's concession to the sharecroppers' struggle, in the form of regulating the amount of rent demanded by the landlords, however, could hardly contain the rural discontent. The promise of distributing land among the landless also could not be materialized in an effective manner. Further, the Assamese ruling elite made it clear that it could no more promise distribution of cultivable land to the landless peasants. Amidst this increasing rural discontent and desperation as also in the wake of the news of Assam government enacting a law to legitimize the sharecroppers' demands, hope and anger both crept deep into the minds of the Assamese peasantry. Meanwhile, the Congress leaders with their vast networks of cadres were busy in the nitty-gritty of governance of the new nation-state and this helped the communist peasant organizations to step, with a renewed vigour, into the affairs of the rural world. This renewed phase of peasant mobilization by the communists, however, coincided with new strategies and tactics adopted by both the Revolutionary Communist Party of India (RCPI) and the Communist Party of India (CPI). By May 1948, the new political strategies and tactics began to have an impact on the rural world, as manifest in a powerful sharecroppers' movement, reinforced by another movement of the landless peasants which would soon dramatically transform the agrarian relations in several districts of Brahmaputra valley. The movements, for the next couple of years, virtually displaced the landlords' control over land and paralyzed the government. This chapter recounts this momentous period of dramatic events.

Challenging the Nation: Communist Political Programme

The CPI held its Second Party Congress in Calcutta in 1948. As the leading communist party of the country, albeit with a low vote share in the 1946 provincial assembly election,[1] the CPI was in a dilemma whether to pursue a path of constitutional communism or resurrect itself as a true revolutionary party. Puran Chand Joshi, General Secretary of the CPI, was of the opinion that the party must support the Congress-led Indian government, as it represented a wide spectrum of public opinion. Joshi was also of the opinion that the Congress leadership had many progressive leaders. At this party congress, however, a majority of members were not ready to accept Joshi's argument, and his political thesis was rejected in favour of an alternative and more radical strategy proposed by Bhalchandra Trimbak Ranadive. Ranadive proposed an inauguration of a 'developing revolutionary wave' within the country as 'India has never before seen such a sweep'.[2] For Ranadive, the country had 'never seen the armed forces collapsing so easily before popular pressure; never seen the working classes fighting with such abandon and courage'.[3] Ranadive claimed that the Indian Government, manned by leaders of the National Congress, was the 'avowed enemy of the national democratic revolution'.[4] Reacting to the birth of Indian nationhood after independence, he ridiculed the 'transfer of power' as one of the biggest pieces of political and economic appeasement of the Indian bourgeoisie. And, thus, there was no doubt, according to him, that from the standpoint of a future socialist revolution all that freedom meant was thenceforth the bourgeoisie would guard the colonial order. He was quick to claim, 'The leadership of the Indian National Congress, representing the interests of the Indian capitalist class, thus betrayed the revolutionary movement at a time when it was on the point of overthrowing the imperialist order'.[5]

The CPI, through its censure of the entire Indian freedom movement and nationhood, gave wide currency, when India attained freedom, to the slogan: *yeh azadi jutha hai* ('this is a false freedom'). The CPI was mandated by the Ranadive line to lead and organize an armed struggle. The party believed that this would eventually replace the present Indian state with a republic of workers, peasants and oppressed middle classes.[6] This meant taking a confrontational position with the symbolic agents of the government. The CPI's Assam Provincial Organizing Committee (APOC), however, maintained a critical distance from the Ranadive line. It came under fire for daring to defy the Central Politburo and was dissolved by it.[7] Under pressure, eventually, it agreed to the programme of an armed struggle of peasants and labourers against the Indian nation-state.

A similar fate waited the RCPI in the early months of 1948. The party was sharply divided on the issue of the path to be taken after liberation from colonial rule. Saumendranath Tagore argued that the party's task 'lies in preparing the masses for the struggle for power'.[8] The group led by Saumendranath were strongly against the idea, which was doing the rounds within the party at that time, that 'revolutionary offensive of the proletariat consists of a successive number of local insurrections'[9] and suggested that such an idea was 'quixotic and is fundamentally wrong'.[10] Saumendranath's ideas, however, could not convince leaders like Pannalal Dasgupta who, being in broad agreement with the view of Ranadive, thought that the time was ripe for overthrowing the Indian government. Pannalal, with years of experience in organizing extremist activities behind him, was more than convinced about achieving his goal and thought — in line with the recent communist revolution in China — that they could over throw the bourgeoisie-led Indian government by establishing their power bases in smaller regions.[11] Pannalal's disagreement with Saumendranath on the future political strategy of the party grew, and Pannalal was expelled from the party in February.[12] However, large numbers of party cadres were still with him and months later, in May, he organized a conference in Birbhum, West Bengal, to decide the future course of RCPI under his leadership. The Assam unit of RCPI remained loyal to him.

Haren Kalita, the then General Secretary of the RCPI's Assam unit, and Haridas Deka agreed with the strategy proposed by Pannalal and decided to go for an immediate armed revolutionary insurrection.[13] In February 1949, with this aim of 'making free and liberated zone',[14] the RCPI faction led by Pannalal staged an unsuccessful but meticulously planned and daring armed raid at Dumdum airport, Dumdum jail, munitions and arms factory in Kasirpore, and held the town of Basirhat in the outskirts of Calcutta as hostage for 24 hours.[15] Inspired by this daring, yet unsuccessful armed insurrection, the party had also decided to build up a movement for the independence of Assam from India.[16] In doing so, the party was, to a large extent, ideologically influenced by several independent movements in countries on India's eastern border.[17] As an experiment, they decided to liberate certain areas of the valley from the control of the Indian government. Haridas Deka, the energetic and young RCPI leader and the key man behind the organizational efforts of RCPI in the valley, later reflected on how they became convinced that the ongoing sharecroppers' movement would hardly be able to gain anything substantial from the Indian state, and that an armed insurrection of masses aimed at capturing political power was the need of the hour, as the government initiated a policy of severe repression of the sharecroppers' movement.[18] To give a more concrete form to its political position, the RCPI held a conference in Khowang in Dibrugarh. In the conference, it decided to form a few military units from amongst its cadres and the 'Gana-bahini', as party's 'armed mass front'.[19] The slogan of 'liberated zones' raised in the conference was to become popular amongst the RCPI cadres.[20] The Assamese sharecroppers and landless peasantry, however, understood these slogans differently: they thought these would mean their complete control in matters of rent, common property and free access to government-owned forest land.

Arming the Sharecroppers

> [T]he tribal people of the Guwahati subdivision have become communist minded . . . they are refusing to pay one fourth of their produce.[21]

Both the RCPI and the CPI, in the summer of 1948, in tune with their policy of total rejection of the Congress government, began propagating various anti-government slogans. Meanwhile, their peasant wings, the Krishak Banua Panchayat (KBP) and the Krishak Sabha (KS) respectively, which had gained experience in the previous years, were able to mobilize more sharecroppers in other parts of the valley. As the sharecroppers continued to resist the landlords, the Assam government swiftly extended the Assam Adhiar Rights and Protection Act of 1948 to areas on the southern bank of Brahmaputra in Kamrup district in June, keeping other districts beyond its purview.[22] For the other districts, a wait-and-watch policy was to be followed. But the sharecroppers in these

Plate 5.1: Pamphlet on peasant question issued by Krishak Sabha of CPI, 1950

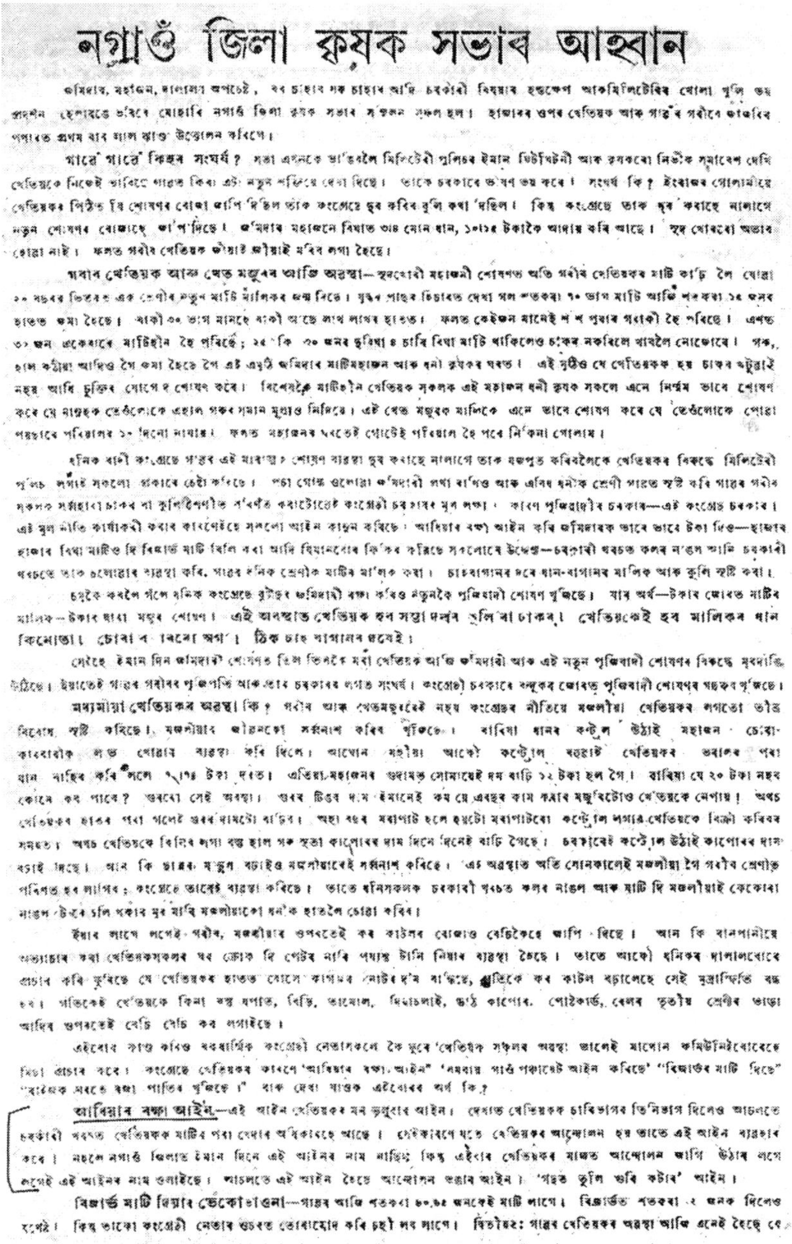

Source: Assam Police Intelligence Record Room (APIRR), Guwahati, 1950.

areas too were hopeful of the Act's implementation and warned the landlords that they would give them the amount of rent as prescribed by the Act. In the next few months, sharecroppers further intensified their movement in Darrang, Sibsagar and Lakhimpur districts. They either declined to pay rent, or paid only one-third of the produce. In southern Kamrup, sharecroppers from Palashbari, Rani, Boko, Beltola, and Chayagaon completely refused to pay rent to their landlords. They had already withheld it in the winter of 1947–48.[23] In Palashbari, the sharecroppers gave one third to one fourth of the produce to the landlords.[24] In some cases, they invited the landlords to their house and gave only one-fourth of the rent.[25] And in other cases, the landlords were asked to send their bullock carts to the villages to collect one-fourth of the rent.[26] In these localities the landlords tried to either negotiate or threaten the sharecroppers if they refused to pay rent. The government too admitted that relations between landlords and sharecroppers in southern Kamrup had deteriorated to a 'serious level'.[27] This sharp polarization in the agrarian relation convinced the KBP that it was more appropriate to demand that the village panchayat be the supreme arbiter of any sharecropping-related dispute and rent agreement.[28] They even went one step ahead and declared that adhi land be taken into possession by the sharecroppers without giving any compensation to the landlords.[29] Also, both KBP and KS tried to popularize the slogan of 'land to the tiller' and decided to take possession of land from the landlords and distribute it among either sharecroppers or landless peasants. This stand of KS and KBP signalled the sharecroppers' unwillingness to get evicted in case landlords decided to be firm and asserted a claim on their land.[30] That both KBP and KS were 'exciting the villagers not to pay any land revenue to landlords in kind' came to be frequently mentioned in police records or the Assamese press.[31]

But, by the summer of the 1948, before the sharecroppers could derive any benefit from the Act, the summer being mostly a sowing season in the valley, the landlords had begun either to negotiate or evict their sharecroppers. For most landlords, forcible occupation of their lands was rather a surprise. They had hardly anticipated that their sharecroppers, whom they considered as their trusted and subservient tenants, could turn so intimidating. The landlords' anxiety did not go unnoticed by Assamese litterateurs. In 1950, Prafulladatta Goswami, a perceptive Assamese writer and, later on, a folklorist, portrayed these anxieties in a leading Assamese literary work.[32] The landlords had two options before them: either challenge their sharecroppers, or negotiate with them. Wherever there was a strong presence of communist peasant organizations, the landlords tried to come to a settlement with the sharecroppers. Mostly small and medium landlords came forward for a negotiation with their sharecroppers.[33] The unswerving refusal of the sharecroppers to pay rent compelled these landlords to agree to their demand of putting place a new rent arrangement as suggested by them, as well as to renew their contracts for the next year. On their part, the landlords continued to pressurize the government to help them collect rent. Police raids were thus conducted to collect rent from the rebellious tribal villages,[34] but sharecroppers also vehemently protested against the seizure of paddy and arrest of their leaders. The police, in the face of their collective solidarity, could rarely succeed in collecting rent.[35] Undeterred by the use of force by the government and landlords, the sharecroppers resorted to various kinds of defensive tactics to protect their paddy. The intelligence officials reported how the tribal peasants would collectively either flee to nearby jungles and hills or hide their crops.[36] Failing to seize paddy from tribal villages, these landlords renewed their parleys with sharecroppers.

In Beltola, the Pattadar Sangha, a loosely organized platform of the Guwahati-based absentee Assamese landlords, tried to reach a settlement with the sharecroppers and agreed to receiving a reduced share of produce as rent.[37] But, the majority of sharecroppers did not agree to this settlement and refused to part with their paddy. Failure to convince them only led the Kamrup district administration to go for another round of negotiation. A joint committee of the representatives of landlords and officials tried to work out a settlement.[38] The committee persuaded the sharecroppers of Beltola to give 10–15 *puras* of paddy to landlords, a deal rejected by the sharecroppers. Persuasion could hardly sway the sharecroppers. Refusing to be daunted by such skilful persuasion of and propaganda among the sharecroppers by the government and landlords, the KBP in Beltola stepped up its anti-landlord propaganda and distributed leaflets asking the sharecroppers 'not to pay any land revenue to the landlords'.[39] On the other hand, failing to reach a settlement, the government decided to arrest the most recalcitrant of sharecroppers and their leaders.

Consequently, many KBP cadres and sharecroppers were arrested at Khetri, Beltola, Saokuchi, Bonosora, and Rani, all in Kamrup.[40] The KBP cadres, on their part, too decided to intensify the agitation and went to the extent of courting arrest.

The rich landlords across the valley, commanding a hegemonic position in the agrarian society and enjoying privileged access to the administrative machinery, had already rejected the Assam Adhiar Rights and Protection Act. They decided not to accept the new rent arrangement stipulated in the Act, took the help of police to collect rent, refused to renew their sharecroppers' contracts, and decided to evict them in case of non-payment of rent.[41] It was at this stage that the organizational networks of KBP played a crucial role in defending the sharecroppers' tenancy rights to land. The KBP meetings exhorted them to continue 'to cultivate the land in spite of the protest of the landlords, because they are the actual tillers of the land and hence the owners of the same at the moment'.[42] It also encouraged them 'to take possession of the land of their landlords with a plea that rent will be paid according to the decision of the panchayat'.[43] More and more Assamese and tribal sharecroppers in Kamrup confronted their landlords' attempts to evict them or transfer land to other sharecroppers. In some cases, the landlords even sold their land to absentee landlords though they were still under the control of the pre-exisitng tenants.

Outside the villages, those who responded positively and quickly to the movement of traditional sharecroppers were the former tea garden workers who had taken to sharecropping on the land set aside for cultivation in tea gardens by the planters in Kamrup and vicinity. Like sharecroppers in the villages, these tea garden labourers cum sharecroppers began to give one-third to one-fourth of their produce, depending upon the quality of the land, as rent to the planters.[44] Meanwhile, sharecroppers from other parts of the valley also followed the path of protest shown by their counterparts in Kamrup. In Golaghat, the Assamese sharecroppers stopped paying rent to their landlords for 1947–48 harvesting seasons.[45] They received the news of the passage of the Act as their legitimate due. They believed that the Act had legitimized their earlier attempt at withholding the payment of rent. Threats of being denied rent by their sharecroppers looming large, the landlords from Golaghat and neighbouring areas, like their counterparts in Kamrup, refused to renew the contracts with their pre-existing sharecroppers in the summer of 1948. In the wake of threats of eviction by landlords, both KBP and KS mobilized the peasants to reclaim land from landlords. In many cases, they even successfully took away the land from the landlords.

In official parlance, confrontation between landlords and sharecroppers was termed as 'breach of the peace'.[46] On the other hand, resistance to eviction helped in building solidarity amongst sharecroppers and often resulted in considerable mass mobilization.[47] In most places, resistance to eviction became successful due to the combined efforts of both sharecroppers and local units of peasant organizations. However, challenged by the sharecroppers, rich landlords went to the civil courts seeking eviction of their sharecroppers. Summary verdicts were given in favour of landlords. Only in a few cases were legal battles protracted. Not many lawyers, given their landed interests, were willing to defend the sharecroppers. In some places, communist leaders with their legal training came forward to help the sharecroppers but they too were outnumbered by those who came forward to help the landlords. Contrary to the government's expectation that the Act would minimize the intensity of sharecroppers' movement, the latter, in fact, entered into a more complex world of legal and political battles.

The Harvesting Season: January–March 1949

In the good harvesting season of 1949, the events of 1948 were successfully restaged in spite of all senior leaders of the KBP being put behind bars, including those who had been arrested in the winter of 1948, and others going underground. It so happened that new leadership emerged from amongst the agitating sharecroppers to replace the earlier crop, and kept the peasant organizations alive and active in the next phase of the movement. The KBP and KS organized numerous village meetings in Kamrup and Darrang. In its rather romantic endeavour to create a 'free-zone' — a liberated space free from all forms of state machinery — the KBP renewed its demand for stoppage of rent payment in kind and issue of receipts of rent to sharecroppers by landlords, and reiterated that the continuance or non-continuance of *adhi-bhagi* system should be decided by the panchayat. The slogan of *tini bhag* (one-third) or *chari bhag* (one-fourth) also began to metamorphose into the slogan of 'land to the tiller'.

Across rural Kamrup, sharecroppers refused to share any part of their produce with the landlords. The government too admitted this development.[48] During this time these areas witnessed a stiff resistance of sharecroppers to the landlords' attempts to forcibly collect rent from them. Large numbers of tribal villages in Kamrup reported clashes between the two. A conservative official estimate put the figure of such clashes at 12 in Beltola in early 1949.[49] There were instances of landlords forcibly trying to seize the sharecroppers' paddy and the latter successfully thwarting their attempts.[50] Even leading Congress leader Harekrishna Das, himself a landlord, could not protect himself from his sharecroppers' assault.[51]

There were also instances of peasants from neighbouring villages showing their solidarity with the ones fighting their landlords, but some villagers still weren't against the landlords. These villagers became crucial allies for landlords in the latter's attempts to establish their control and ownership over their lands. Often, these isolated families were engaged by the landlords to persuade the sharecroppers to part with their produce. In most cases, such families had to bear the brunt of agitating sharecroppers, who even physically assaulted them.[52] The landlords initially persisted in asserting their rights over the produce through persuasion and, later, threats. Many could not withstand the constant threats of landlords and agreed to pay rent. But, the landlords could not proceed further, as other sharecroppers and communist cadres challenged or even assaulted them. Those who began to pay rent were rich sharecroppers, but they instantly invited the antagonism of their poor fellow sharecroppers, often resulting in incidents of violence.[53] The police worriedly admitted how the KBP cadres threatened those sharecroppers who paid rent in Beltola.[54]

Meanwhile, the government came forward to help landlords in securing their rent. For instance, the police searched the granaries of sharecroppers and tried to seize paddy. This resulted in clashes between the two[55] and, consequently, to the arrest of those who refused to pay.[56] They also arrested the leaders and supporters of KBP and KS. Police repression in rural Kamrup compelled the KBP and KS workers to find out new areas to continue their activities in. However, this only helped in the spread of the adhiar movement to new areas. For instance, it began to intensify amongst the

Bodo-Kachari sharecroppers across rural areas of Darrang.[57] The latter initiated a campaign to stop paying not only rent to their landlords but also interest to the moneylenders. Local tribal leaders played a leading role in exhorting the sharecroppers to refuse to pay rent.[58] Sharecroppers in southern Nowgaon, eastern Sibsagar and Dibrugarh[59] too refused to share their produce with their landlords.[60]

In Nowgaon, where some landlords used to engage agricultural labourers to reap their share of produce, the latter joined the sharecroppers' struggle as well: they refused to work for the landlords, demanding enhanced wages and reduced working hours.[61] Their refusal to work for the absentee landlords resulted in damage to standing crops.[62] Sharecroppers in other areas also resisted the landlords from taking away their share of produce as rent.[63] In some places like Farkating and Madhupur, they paid their rent in cash or only one-fourth of produce. Many landlords with medium holdings agreed to accept this share[64] and many of them also joined their struggle, since they were dependent on their labour and thus left with no alternative but to extend crucial support to them. In Sibsagar, both CPI and CSP, with a strong presence in Titabor, Amguri, Khari and Katia, also mobilized the sharecroppers.[65]

Sustained resistance of sharecroppers to their landlords in large parts of the valley achieved fruition through their early assertion of control over both their crops and lands. They were also supported by their womenfolk. In fact, their hold on their land was always consolidated only by their appropriation and deployment of family labour. Frequent village meetings organized at the behest of KBP and KS in Kamrup and Darrang, exhorting sharecroppers not to pay rent to their landlords further reinforced this radical resistance. At places where the sharecroppers succeeded in retaining their control over land and produce, the sharecroppers' struggle entered a stage of heightened conciousness. In Beltola, till 1950 the most successful area of the struggle, as the movement entered a new phase, posters displayed new demands aimed at securing the support of a wide cross-section of poor peasantry. One such poster aimed at roping agricultural labourers in, read: '[W]e will not reap the paddy unless we are given a wage of Rs 4, and 8 hours of work; no to adhi; rent will be in cash not in kind; no to eviction; land to the tiller'.[66] The KBP primarily relied on the headmen in tribal villages, where traditionally they commanded respect and social influence, to secure the support of the entire villages. Moreover, villages adopted radical slogans and steps on their own to challenge any attempt of landlords to evict sharecroppers and claim more rent. For instance, the KBP unit in Khalaighogra mauza of Kamrup district decided to form volunteer corps, not to defy police and revenue officials and forbade the sharecroppers to pay rent to their landlords.[67]

Eviction, Resistance and Control over Adhi: 1949–51

In the summer of 1949, as the sowing season began, tribal sharecroppers again faced the harsh reality: the landlords had opted for either keeping their lands fallow or renting them out to new sharecroppers, mostly caste-Hindu Assamese, immigrant East Bengalis or Nepalis. As the sowing season began, the tribal sharecroppers were hardly aware of the fact that their contracts had been terminated. Thus immediately provoked and determined to repossess their lost lands, they quickly retaliated by seizing land from the new sharecroppers. An illustrative example is that of a lawyer and landlord from Panbazar in Kamrup, Umesh Chandra Sen, who evicted his tribal sharecroppers in Beltola and rented out his lands to some new caste-Hindu Assamese sharecroppers, thereby prompting the evicted sharecroppers to resist the newcomers and refuse to part with the lands they had been tilling.[68] Similar incidents of clashes between the new sharecroppers and the old tribal sharecroppers who eventually managed to retain their control on their lands were reported from Sibsagar, Nowgaon, Lakhimpur, and Darrang.[69] The sharecroppers also resisted their landlords' attempt to sell off their lands to comparatively more powerful and richer landlords who were willing to risk incurring the wrath of sharecroppers.[70] In several places, where trader–moneylender nexus had a crucial role in dispossessing the sharecroppers of their land and produce, sharecroppers also targeted moneylenders. For instance, moneylenders' records were burnt down in Sualkuchi, Palashbari, Tihu, and Rangia. In Sualkuchi, angry sharecroppers, led by their charismatic leader Bishnu Rabha, snatched away these documents from the moneylenders' houses and eventually burnt them.[71] Collective resistance of sharecroppers, finally, paved the way for securing them right to cultivate land for the next season in most places.

During the 1949–50 harvesting season, the KBP and the KS collectively renewed their anti-landlord propaganda and new areas reported adhiar–landlord clashes.[72] However, neither the landlords nor the sharecroppers were willing to part with their rights over land, and clashes between the duo had already spread to a large number of places. There was, however, some signs of rupture in the movement when, for instance, in some rural areas of Darrang, the sharecroppers offered to give one fourth of their produce to the landlords who, though, did not accept it.[73] But as large numbers of sharecroppers reaped the paddy and took it away into their houses, the landlords were prevented from getting their share.[74] In the meantime, the CPI also joined the RCPI in mobilizing the sharecroppers. The Assam CPI Provincial Committee, reprimanded by the National Committee, now directed its cadres not to court police arrest and compromise with the landlords. It further instructed the cadres to ensure that the sharecroppers and landless peasants do not surrender their right of possession of lands and the sharecroppers completely reject the Adhiar Act. It also asked the sharecroppers not to part with their paddy for the landlords.[75]

As the harvesting months approached, landlords in the neighbourhood of Guwahati continued their negotiation with their sharecroppers. At the former's initiative, a number of public negotiations took place. Such conciliatory approaches were mostly rejected by the sharecroppers as they were convinced of their movement's success.[76] Most importantly, Ahom sharecroppers in Sibsagar, who constituted the majority of rural population in eastern Assam, also joined the sharecroppers' struggle at that time.[77] In some instances, the Ahom sharecroppers even demanded the intervention of the administration.

However, the situation took a new turn during the sowing season of 1950, a turn comparatively favourable for the rich landlords as they could get relief from the civil courts which ordered the eviction of sharecroppers who refused to pay rent. Bolstered by the court orders, the landlords took the help of police to forcibly evict their sharecroppers. In most cases, the landlords kept their lands fallow[78] and, in the majority of cases, could get back their land from the control of the combined forces of sharecroppers and peasant organizations. In some cases, sharecroppers still managed to cultivate the land, but during the harvesting season of 1950–51 the landlords successfully forcibly collected their rent with the help of police.[79] The communist peasant organizations, on their part, made a frantic bid to convince the sharecroppers not to pay rent to their landlords and even revenue to the government.[80] The landlords too filed an increasing number of lawsuits in the civil courts seeking eviction of their sharecroppers. As a retaliatory move, the peasant organizations helped the sharecroppers to seek a judicial review of the eviction orders passed by the civil courts. The sharecroppers also resorted to forcible retention of lands for several reasons. First, the fact that there were other peasants ready to replace the pre-existing sharecroppers and till the land gave the landlord confidence to evict the pre-existing sharecroppers at their will.[81] By the 1940s, as discussed in Chapter 1, the issue of land scarcity had come to occupy the centre stage of Assam's political landscape. It was further compounded by the concentration of large landholdings in the hands of a few rich peasants and tea planters, and by the alienation of independent tribal peasants from their lands. Secondly, the process of de-peasantization of the tribal peasants was a recent phenomenon, still alive in the early 1950s in the minds of these peasants. Thus, the non-availability of lands and de-peasantization combined to provoke the sharecroppers to articulate their grievances against the landlords and resort to insurgent acts.

On the other hand, the Tezpur Talatiya Ryot Sangha, an organization formed by the CSP, staged mild protests against the eviction of sharecroppers.[82] It demanded from the government the implementation of Assam Tenancy Act which, in fact, had no provision to safeguard the interests of sharecroppers. It also appealed to the government for debarring the landlords from filing cases of eviction. For instance, in a public meeting held at Titabor in 1951, the CSP criticized the landlords for refusing to comply with the provisions of the Adhiar Act. Bhubanchandra Buragohain, who presided over the meeting, agreed in his speech that the refusal of the landlords to comply with the Act was a matter of grave concern.[83] The meeting resolved that the sharecroppers should give only 15–20 puras of paddy or one-third of their produce to their landlords depending on the quality of the lands they tilled.

This was a new political position taken by the CSP which was then involved completely with the sharecroppers' movement.

By that time, i.e., early 1950s, the tenants of la-khiraj and nisf-khiraj estates had emerged as important partners in the sharecroppers' struggle, giving a new impetus to the movement. They primarily reiterated their old demands dating back to the 1930s. The most prominent example of tenants' defiance of their landlords was in the Kamakhya temple of Kamrup. The *panda*s of Kamakhya temple, who were also small landlords of the estates attached to the temple, had faced the refusal of their tenants to pay rent as early as 1947. A couple of years later, i.e., by 1949, the tenants had begun to search for less agitational methods to assert their claims over the lands they tilled. They had rather begun to seek the government's help to persuade their landlords to accept their demands. In 1952, Kamrup Devalay Ryot Sangha, a loose organization of tenants of the temple estates in Kamrup, finally submitted a petition to the government expressing their grievances.[84] The tenants described how the rent regulations framed by *devalaya*s (temples) were against their interests. They also demanded an amendment of the Assam Tenancy Act 1935, which had empowered the *doloi*s to evict them. But in many cases, they rallied around the peasant organizations and refused to part with their produce.

The tenants of the *satra*s too were not left out of the ongoing peasant mobilization. They were inspired by the growing public opinion in their defence. Even a conservative newspaper like *Dainik Assamiya* widely reported on the condition of tenants in Auniati Satra in Sibsagar, a stronghold of Assamese upper-caste landed gentry, and demanded radical improvements in their condition. Support also came in from Congress; for example, the local Congress committee in Barpeta, western Kamrup, complained to the government about the growing harassment of these tenants. The Congress leaders tried to negotiate with the estate owners, asking them to be more tolerant of their tenants. However, the total disregard of the public opinion by these landlords — who till the early decades of the twentieth century exercised considerable influence on their tenants and disciples — was exemplary. The Assamese liberal nationalist literati had already been penning down their disapproval of the oppressive social hegemony of these landlords, popularly known as *gossains*.[85] The gossains' hegemonic position as supreme arbitrators in the rural disputes had declined as the colonial institutions gradually displaced them; they even unsuccessfully tried to forge alliances with the literati to maintain their traditional authority. The tenants also realized that the gossains' powers over them had crumbled before the might of colonial administration. Their public censure and diminishing authority thus combined to inspire their tenants to join the larger sharecroppers' movement.

For the landlords as a class, a possible way to overcome the crisis of their authority, apart from state support which will be discussed shortly, was to either secure support of their pre-existing poor sharecroppers or engage new ones. Their recourse to both these measures happened mostly after 1951. The first signs of rupture in the collective solidarity of the sharecroppers and thereby gains for the landlords became visible with continuous state repression. Large numbers of poor sharecroppers failed to withstand police repression. Further, in many cases, traditional patron–client relation between the adhiar and his landlord had not completely died out, and was rather restored when in 1950 a devastating earthquake and subsequent food crisis struck Assam. The landlords also began to replace the pre-existing sharecroppers on their estates with their own relatives or peasants from the villages whom they could trust and whose loyalty they could easily command, as a way to escape the onslaught of the sharecroppers' movement.[86] They invoked the provisions of the Adhiar Act which entitled them to do so.

The social relationship between the Assamese landlords and their tribal and Assamese Hindu sharecroppers was principally based on the former's ability to extract rent and other customary services, and impose their social hegemony. As the rebellious sharecroppers began to exercise control over the land and the produce, this relationship began to weaken. But it was the immigrant Muslim sharecroppers who remained out of this struggle and continued to pay their rent and even helped the landlords in pressurizing other Assamese sharecroppers to pay rent. This alliance between immigrant sharecroppers and Assamese caste Hindu landlords was conditioned by two factors. First, on the north bank of Brahmaputra in Kamrup, Darrang and Nowgaon, the Assamese Hindu landlords began to replace their traditional sharecroppers with immigrant Muslim sharecroppers. The latter shifted to both cash crop production as well as multiple crop production. Production of jute had been yielding high profits since 1945.[87] The Calcutta-based jute mills continued to encourage expansion of acreage under jute cultivation. The Partition further forced more peasants from East Pakistan to immigrate to West Bengal and Assam, thereby increasing the number of immigrant landless peasants (both Hindus and Muslims) manifold and allowing the landlords to benefit from engaging them as sharecroppers. In fact, in many places primarily characterized by a numerically dominant presence of Muslim immigrant sharecroppers, the Assamese Hindu landlords succeeded in evicting their pres-existing tribal or Assamese Hindu sharecroppers. Secondly, lack of integration into the Assamese society and increasing scarcity of material resources forced the immigrant Muslim sharecroppers to stay outside the fold of the sharecroppers' struggle. Muslim sharecroppers and small peasants were still dependent on the Assamese landlord–moneylender–trader nexus to sustain their cash crop production. It should be noted that decades of nationalist rhetoric had kept the immigrant Muslim peasants socially isolated. Their lack of social integration, largely conditioned by the absence of religious mobilization, worked to the advantage of the Assamese landlords. Leading Muslim League leaders in Assam allied with the Congress leaders. Partition also deprived the immigrant Muslim peasantry of a leadership which could counter the anti-immigrant nationalist political discourse, leaving them at the mercy of the numerically dominant Assamese landlords.

In some places, both Assamese and tribal sharecroppers remained outside the movement and refused to obey the directives of communist peasant organizations.[88] Many of these sharecroppers continued to pay rent to their landlords as they feared losing the land they tilled. Such cases were reported from places where sharecroppers were fewer than landlords and mostly poor.[89] In Janji, Sibsagar, when a journalist asked a sharecropper why he had paid rent to the landlord according to the earlier norms and reminded him of the Adhiar Act, the sharecropper promptly replied, 'I am getting land from the landlord as I am giving half of the produce, but if I give one-third of rent he would not give land to me in the next year'.[90] In case of sharecroppers defiantly refusing to pay rent, the landlords, as pointed out earlier, had the option to sell off their lands when they lost all hopes of collecting rent and recovering their control over them and were swayed by a growing popular perception of the possible loss of their occupancy rights.[91] Such circumstances thus made them deem it better to sell their landholding which had been rented out to sharecroppers, apart from the ones under their personal control to those who could afford to buy, for instance immigrant rich peasants from different parts of Kamrup, Nowgaon and Darrang, who had profits from the 1940s' jute boon to buy such land.

Unfulfilled Promises

As mentioned earlier, despite its initial promises, by the summer of 1948, the Assam government could implement the Adhiar Act only in southern Kamrup and Golaghat. All other districts had to wait for months and years for the implementation of the Act.[92] This delay was largely due to the opposition of landlords supported from within the government. In most places, the Act came into effect only after it had become toothless when manipulated by the powerful landlord lobby. Yet sharecroppers did not lose heart and continued to pressurize the government to implement it. Between 1949 and 1954, the Act was implemented in a phased manner but only after the sharecroppers forced the government to do so through their intensified agitation.[93]

However, it did not take long for the landlords to shift the weight of law in their favour. Several key amendments were carried out in the Act, limiting its scope in favour of the landlords. Eviction, accompanied by verbal and physical threats and police support, turned out to be the most important and popular method for the landlords to re-assert their control over land. In most cases, they evicted their sharecroppers, citing urgency of selling their land for personal needs.[94] Besides drawing benefits of the law, in some cases, landlords even broke social taboos and tilled their own land. A case in point was Jorhat, a stronghold of Assamese upper-caste absentee landlords who stayed in urban areas, where Brahmin landlords, when denied rent by their sharecroppers, ploughed their plots themselves to prove that they were equal to the task.[95] This was indeed an attempt of the Assamese Brahmin landlords to withstand the agitation of sharecroppers that further got intensified with the popularization of 'land to the tiller' slogan. This slogan, while immensely reinforcing the sharecroppers' hold over the land they tilled, forced the landlords to imaginatively 'liberate' their land by taking to cultivation.

The Assam Adhiar Rights and Protection Act of 1948 also served as a catalyst in breaking all previous records of rent litigations across the valley.[96] In the past, protracted rent litigation was reported mostly from the zamindari areas of Goalpara, and the nisf-khiraj and la-khiraj estates of raiyatwari areas. The Assam Tenancy Act of 1935 could hardly instil confidence in the tenants of nisf-khiraj or la-khiraj estates. The landlords also hardly felt the necessity of securing themselves against any adverse impact of the Act. The situation changed dramatically after 1948 when the worried Assamese landlords took advantage of their easier access into juridical–administrative infrastructure to shield their landed interests. [97] Getting an eviction order became easy for them and they were sure to manipulate the clauses of the Adhiar Act to their favour. The landlords, though, confronted with the refusal of their sharecroppers to give half of the produce, could secure relief from the revenue courts. The Adhiar Act, by keeping judicial jurisdiction out of bounds, empowered a revenue office, an office much more likely to be less neutral and often dependent on the patronage of landlords, to arbiter in disputes between the landlords and their sharecroppers.[98] And as the landlords could effectively use the courts as the best possible means of safeguarding their control over land, they safely began to defy the Act more openly. Even initiatives taken by the Congress party advising them to comply with the provisions of the Adhiar Act could hardly convince them.

Overt bureaucratic bias in favour of the landlords did not deter the sharecroppers from challenging their landlords and continuing to pressurize the government for the full implementation of the Act. For instance, both eviction and demand for full rent were forcibly resisted by the sharecroppers with the help of local communist peasant organizations. As rural agrarian relations quickly deteriorated once the Act came to be implemented, the law also became a crucial marker of the heightened political consciousness of the Assamese peasantry and their increasing understanding of their tenurial rights. Not only did they demand the implementation of the Adhiar Act but they also wanted the government to provide them with benefits under the Assam Tenancy Act of 1935. Implementation of the provision of record-of-rights for the tenants under the Assam Tenancy Act became their most important demand. An illustrative example is that of the tenants from Uttar-Barisal and Nij-Barisal in Paschim Barbhag mauza of Kamrup, who, in 1949, urged the Assam Revenue Minister to enter their names in the record-of-rights.[99] Such instances of tenants seeking relief under Act were also widely reported in the Assamese press.

The Adhiar Act served to act as a catalyst for the reorganization of the already weakened communist peasant organizations whose cadres were mostly behind the bar. It became a new rallying point for many communist leaders to prove their comeback. Despite ideological disagreements between them and their open criticism of the Act, they made all efforts to popularize the Act, even requesting the sharecroppers to pay rent as per the provisions of the Act. Meanwhile, peasant organizations also exhorted the landless peasants to fight the police — and even seize their arms and ammunitions[100] — and to re-occupy the lands they had been evicted from. As peasant organizations had to keep the sharecroppers and the landless peasants together, they tried to built up joint front. Knowing well that payment of rent would ensure their tenancy rights to the landlords' lands, they thus appealed the sharecroppers to pay rent while exhorted the landless ones to claim new land. Before the agitating peasants could accomplish these tasks, the news of the government's decision to extend the implementation of Adhiar Act to new areas fuelled their mobilization in open defiance of their landlords across the valley.

The Act indeed contributed to intensifying the clashes between sharecroppers and landlords everywhere. The former did not limit themselves to the methods of struggle taught by the peasant organizations, but used all available avenues to defend themselves from, as well as defy, their landlords. In village meetings or gatherings, they criticized the landlords for their manipulation of the Act, and the bureaucracy for not implementing the Act in collusion with landlords. They also unilaterally agreed that the Act had essentially failed to deliver the justice promised to them.[101] The landowners made use of all available bureaucratic, legal and social institutions to defend themselves from or get rid of their defiant sharecroppers.[102] However, it was not true that only the landlords first went to the court. In some places like Amguri in Sibsagar, sharecroppers, when evicted by their landlords, went to the courts first, but not all of them won their cases.[103]

Often, such court trials became subjects of larger public interest.[104] As sharecroppers from various places raised the demand that rent be collected according to the terms of the Adhiar Act, or by landlords personally from the fields, clashes between them and their landlords increased, but the government tried to shield the latter from violence.[105]

The government's decision to expand the reach of the Act to new areas was conditioned both by the continuous, but localized, agitation of sharecroppers and by the local Congress units' understanding of the ground reality in their respective areas of operation. The latter faced forceful demands for implementation of the Act from the sharecroppers, making the party realize that only the implementation of the Act could restrain the further spread of the rural discontent and thereby also assure it of its much-needed legitimacy as a ruling party.[106] The Left wing of Congress, i.e., the CSP, also pressurized the government to expand the area covered by the Act.[107] Places like Sibsagar, where landlords had a strong presence, saw increasing mobilization of sharecroppers in support of the Act. Sibsagar District Congress Committee left no stone unturned to pressurize the Assam Congress to seek the extension of the Act from the government.[108] Resolutions vocalizing this demand, too, were passed at the behest of local Congress leadership.[109] However, the landlord-dominated district-level Land Settlement Advisory Committee emerged as an effective obstacle against such move by vetoing a motion for the immediate enforcement of the Act.[110]

Unlike the passage of the Regulation of 1886 and the Assam Tenancy Act of 1935, that of the Adhiar Act generated a good deal of enthusiasm, albeit short-lived, among the Assamese peasantry. The Adhiar Act — then a part of the everyday rural vocabulary — as an instrument of social justice, came to be widely perceived as a pro-poor peasant law. The landlord lobby, with support from Congress nationalists who were at the helm of the government, exercised its influence to minimize all possible positive impact of the Act. The rural discontent, largely directed by the sharecroppers' movement, was further neutralized by reviving the by-then-defunct network of ryot sabhas. The ryot sabhas incorporated the sharecroppers' problem into their programme from 1948. Once again, the ryot sabhas came back into the front pages of the Assamese press. But their activities gradually diminished again after 1950.[111] The Assamese rich landowners tried to regain their social and political control of the agrarian landscape and this showed positive results after 1950. Despite their early worries about the Act, the landlords also increasingly realized that it would not be harmful to them as it essentially centred on the rent-sharing question which would not challenge their ownership of land.

In Search for Land: Struggle for Land?

From 1948, giving a new turn to the sharecroppers' movement, the Assamese and tribal landless peasants became its integral partners when communist peasant organizations not only gave a wide currency to the slogan of 'land to the landless peasants' but also exhorted them to occupy the government-owned lands. They demanded that grazing reserves, wastelands in tea gardens, forested land and unploughed land of rich landlords be distributed amongst the landless peasants. The socialists were more categorical in making these demands than their communist counterparts. A year before, in 1947, the CSP had asked for a census of landless peasants in Assam and demanded that lands be distributed among these peasants. Leading socialist leaders Sankar Chandra Barua and Lakshmi Prasad Goswami had extensively toured the rural areas of eastern Assam, asking landless peasants to reclaim government-owned lands. Resolutions demanding land for the landless peasants were passed in the village meetings organized by socialists.[112] The CPI-led KS also concurred with the demands raised by the CSP. In particular, the Sibsagar district unit of KS repeatedly urged the government to stop eviction of squatting peasants, to compensate the evicted peasants, hold a census of landless peasants, and distribute land from professional grazing reserves and Reserved Forests.[113]

The land occupation movement spread to various places of the valley but followed two different trajectories. In western Assam, unlike the powerful sharecropper movement, the agitation of landless peasants remained confined to a few localities and did not find too many followers. The protest against the eviction of sharecroppers remained the key focus of Assam's rural politics. Upbeat by their limited success in the sharecroppers' movement, the RCPI tried to mobilize the Assamese and tribal landless

Plate 5.2: A 1949 issue of *Swadhinata*, the mouthpiece of RCPI

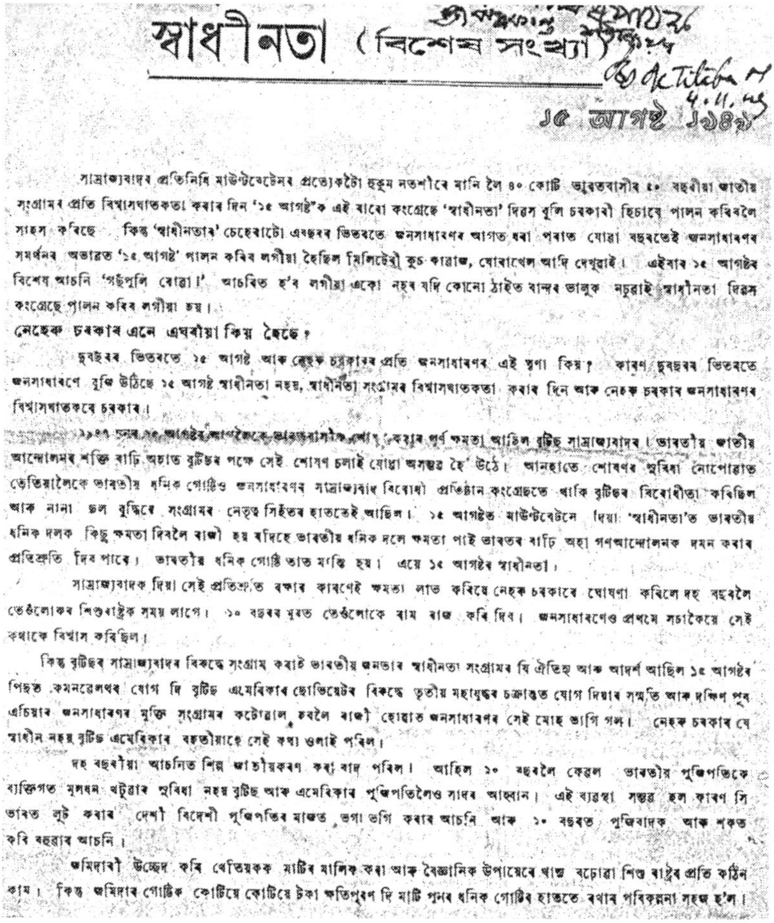

স্বাধীনতা (বিশেষ সংখ্যা)

১৫ আগষ্ট ১৯৪৯

সাম্রাজ্যবাদৰ প্ৰতিনিধি মাউণ্টবেটেনৰ প্ৰত্যেকটো হুকুম নতশীৰে মানি লৈ ৪০ কোটি ভাৰতবাসীৰ ৫০ বছৰীয়া জাতীয় সংগ্ৰামৰ প্ৰতি বিশ্বাসঘাতকতা কৰাৰ দিন '১৫ আগষ্ট'ক এই বাৰো কংগ্ৰেছে 'স্বাধীনতা' দিৱস বুলি চৰকাৰী হিচাপে পালন কৰিবলৈ সাহস কৰিছে। কিন্তু 'স্বাধীনতাৰ' চেহেৰাটো এবছৰৰ ভিতৰতে জনসাধাৰণৰ আগত ধৰা পৰাত যোৱা বছৰতেই জনসাধাৰণৰ সমৰ্থনৰ অভাৱত '১৫ আগষ্ট' পালন কৰিব লগীয়া হৈছিল মিলিটেৰী কুচ কাৱাজ, ঘোৰাখেল আদি দেখুৱাই। এইবাৰ ১৫ আগষ্টৰ বিশেষ আচনি 'গছপুলি ৰোৱা!' আচৰিত হ'ব লগীয়া একো নহব যদি কোনো ঠাইত বান্দৰ ভালুক নচুৱাই স্বাধীনতা দিৱস কংগ্ৰেছে পালন কৰিব লগীয়া হয়।

নেহেৰু চৰকাৰ এনে এঘৰীয়া কিয় হৈছে?

দুবছৰৰ ভিতৰতে ১৫ আগষ্ট আৰু নেহেৰু চৰকাৰৰ প্ৰতি জনসাধাৰণৰ এই ঘৃণা কিয়? কাৰণ দুবছৰৰ ভিতৰতে জনসাধাৰণে বুজি উঠিছে ১৫ আগষ্ট স্বাধীনতা নহয়, স্বাধীনতা সংগ্ৰামৰ বিশ্বাসঘাতকতা কৰাৰ দিন আৰু নেহেৰু চৰকাৰ জনসাধাৰণৰ বিশ্বাসঘাতকৰে চৰকাৰ।

১৯৪৭ চনৰ ১৫ আগষ্টৰ আগলৈকে ভাৰতবাসীক শোষণ কৰাৰ পূৰ্ণ ক্ষমতা আছিল বৃটিছ সাম্রাজ্যবাদৰ। ভাৰতীয় জাতীয় আন্দোলনৰ শক্তি বাঢ়ি অহাত বৃটিছৰ পক্ষে সেই শোষণ চলাই যোৱা অসম্ভৱ হৈ উঠে। আনহাতে শোষণৰ সুবিধা নোপোৱাত তেতিয়ালৈকে ভাৰতীয় ধনিক গোষ্ঠীও জনসাধাৰণৰ সাম্রাজ্যবাদ বিৰোধী প্ৰতিষ্ঠান কংগ্ৰেছতে থাকি বৃটিছৰ বিৰোধীতা কৰিছিল আৰু নানা ছল বুদ্ধিৰে সংগ্ৰামৰ নেতৃত্ব সিহঁতৰ হাততেই আছিল। ১৫ আগষ্টত মাউণ্টবেটেনে দিয়া 'স্বাধীনতা'ত ভাৰতীয় ধনিক দলক কিছু ক্ষমতা দিবলৈ ৰাজী হয় যদিহে ভাৰতীয় ধনিক দলে ক্ষমতা পাই ভাৰতত বাঢ়ি অহা গণআন্দোলনক দমন কৰাৰ প্ৰতিশ্ৰুতি দিব পাৰে। ভাৰতীয় ধনিক গোষ্ঠি তাত মান্তি হয়। এয়ে ১৫ আগষ্টৰ স্বাধীনতা।

সাম্রাজ্যবাদক দিয়া সেই প্ৰতিশ্ৰুতি ৰক্ষাৰ কাৰণেই ক্ষমতা লাভ কৰিয়ে নেহেৰু চৰকাৰে ঘোষণা কৰিলে দহ বছৰলৈ তেওঁলোকৰ শিশুৰাষ্ট্ৰক সময় লাগে। ১০ বছৰৰ মূৰত তেওঁলোকে ৰাম ৰাজ কৰি দিব। জনসাধাৰণেও প্ৰথমে সচাকৈয়ে সেই কথাকে বিশ্বাস কৰিছিল।

কিন্তু বৃটিছৰ সাম্রাজ্যবাদৰ বিৰুদ্ধে সংগ্ৰাম কৰাই ভাৰতীয় জনতাৰ স্বাধীনতা সংগ্ৰামৰ যি ঐতিহ্য আৰু আদৰ্শ আছিল ১৫ আগষ্টৰ পিছত কমনৱেলথৰ যোগ দি বৃটিছ এমেৰিকাৰ ছোভিয়েটৰ বিৰুদ্ধে তৃতীয় মহাযুদ্ধৰ চক্ৰান্তত যোগ দিয়াৰ সম্মতি আৰু দক্ষিণ পূব এচিয়াৰ জনসাধাৰণৰ মুক্তি সংগ্ৰামৰ কটোৱাল হবলৈ ৰাজী হোৱাত জনসাধাৰণৰ সেই মোহ ভাগি গল। নেহেৰু চৰকাৰ যে স্বাধীন নহয় বৃটিছ এমেৰিকাৰ ৰক্তীয়াহে সেই কথা ওলাই পৰিল।

দহ বছৰীয়া আচনিত শিল্প জাতীয়কৰণ কৰা বাদ পৰিল। আছিল ১০ বছৰলৈ কেৱল ভাৰতীয় পুজিপতিক ব্যক্তিগত মুলধন খটুৱাৰ সুবিধা নহয় বৃটিছ আৰু এমেৰিকাৰ পুজিপতিলৈও সাদৰ আহ্বান। এই ব্যৱস্থা সম্ভৱ হল কাৰণ সি ভাৰত লুট কৰাৰ দেশী বিদেশী পুজিপতিৰ মাজত ভগা ভগি কৰাৰ আচনি আৰু ১০ বছৰত পুজিবাদক আৰু শকত কৰি বঢ়োৱাৰ আচনি।

জমিদাৰী উচ্ছেদ কৰি খেতিয়কক মাটিৰ মালিক কৰা আৰু বৈজ্ঞানিক উপায়েৰে খাদ্য বঢ়োৱা শিশু ৰাষ্ট্ৰৰ প্ৰতি কঠিন কাম। কিন্তু জমিদাৰ গোষ্ঠিক কোটিয়ে কোটিয়ে টকা ক্ষতিপুৰণ দি মাটি পুনৰ ধনিক গোষ্ঠিৰ হাততে ৰখাৰ পৰিকল্পনা সহজ হ'ল।

Source: Assam Police Intelligence Record Room (APIRR), Guwahati, 1949.

peasants in Kamrup and Darrang districts. Its peasant wing, the KBP, successfully mobilized the landless peasants of southern Kamrup to reclaim land from Makeli grazing reserve though they were soon evicted by the government.[114] Such cases of eviction soon after land reclamation were, however, few and far between.[115]

Several areas of western Assam witnessed another crucial development. Large numbers of immigrant East Bengali Muslim sharecroppers and peasants emigrated from Assam to East Pakistan after 1948, a process that continued till 1949.[116] This emigration, caused by their vision of a grim future in independent India, largely took place from western Kamrup and Goalpara.[117] The majority of émigré Muslim peasants were sharecroppers of Assamese Hindu landlords and their emigration forced the Assamese landlords to invite the Assamese landless peasants to work for them as sharecroppers.[118] Whether such replacement was communally motivated or not would be difficult to determine, but that many amongst the Assamese sharecroppers would have rejoiced at getting back their land which they had lost a couple of years earlier to these immigrant Muslim East Bengali sharecroppers was beyond doubt.

Compared to a rather low-intensity battle of Assamese landless peasants for occupation of unploughed land in western Assam, in both Sibsagar and Lakhimpur the demand for land emerged as a key issue of intense peasant mobilization. In eastern Assam, agitation for land distribution spread to large areas, had a massive following and remained conspicuous for a long time. In these areas, years of annual flood-induced soil erosion had compounded the problem of land scarcity. The slogan of 'land to the landless peasants' quickly became popular and emerged as a rallying point in intensifying peasant mobilization. The landless peasants demanded that the wastelands be settled with those who had lost land due to their submergence and soil erosion caused by floods.[119] This intense mobilization and absence of a powerful state-led counter-resistance to the mobilization finally paid off and peasants occupied plots inside government-owned lands, professional grazing reserves or tea gardens.[120]

By 1948, the idea that the government would distribute land amongst the landless peasants in the near future had gained popularity in the everyday rural discourse of the valley.[121] By the end of that year, large numbers of Assamese landless peasants, such as those from Silakhati Bokota of Sibsagar district, and not belonging to any peasant organization, could be seen roaming around in the nearby grazing reserves or distant places in search of arable land. Before the next sowing season, many, like the tribal peasants who reclaimed the Majpathar grazing reserve in Sibsagar or the Takalimari grazing reserve in Lakhimpur, were indeed successful in finding land for cultivation. They would clear jungles, and plough their plots.[122] Elsewhere, groups of peasants — as was the case with 200 peasants of Thaora in Sibsagar who also reclaimed land from the Rajmai Tea Company — collectively continued to occupy land inside tea gardens. However, rarely did they occupy individual landlords' lands though there is also evidence of such isolated acts.[123]

As the tea gardens and grazing reserves emerged as the centre of attention of this land-occupation movement, both CSP and CPI began to mobilize landless peasants, whether Assamese, tribal or former tea garden workers (now seen as landless peasants), in the neighbourhood of these areas.[124] For instance, the KS cadres exhorted landless peasants from Chetiagaon and Maliagaon villages neighbouring tea gardens in Sibsagar to occupy the garden lands. The collective agitation of tea garden workers and Assamese landless peasants, with the former having years of experience in waging a relentless struggle against tea planters, the CPI thought, would be able to sustain the agitation.[125]

The government spared no time to counter such activities and promptly evicted the squatters. Defending such eviction, many within the administration thought, would be an easier task as 'the land was occupied without any plan, there was no class consciousness amongst the Kishan and the peasants were under the illusion that the government would not evict them'.[126] But eviction only boomeranged. The anti-eviction agitation led by the sharecroppers had already acquired popularity and further reinforced the anti-eviction agitation of their landless brethren. The success of anti-eviction agitation of the sharecroppers also benefitted the peasants organizations by making them popular and enthusing them to take up the cause of landless peasants. The evicted peasants quickly realized that formation of a unit of a communist or socialist peasant organization would be a more powerful defence mechanism against eviction; many landless peasants thus began to enlist themselves as members of peasant organizations. But in most places, particularly Sibsagar, they reclaimed lands independently, without being part of any peasant organizations.[127]

Despite resistance from the government, the agitation for 'land to the landless peasants' continued to intensify. Towards the end of 1949, the CSP began to form a special unit known as 'land army' in Mangaldai and Golaghat to direct and organize land occupation drives. Public meetings were organized asking landless peasants to be members of a 'land army'.[128] These meetings also announced decisions to occupy wastelands inside tea gardens.[129] The Assam government was also questioned for delaying the process of acquiring wastelands of tea gardens. Processions and demonstrations too were staged.[130]Also, in November, Assam Krishak Sabha declared a six-point charter including the demand for distribution of wastelands of tea gardens, and other lands among the landless peasants on a co-operative basis. To mark the announcement of this momentous charter, 20 November was declared as Kishak Divas.[131]

By early 1950, peasants began to squat in the unploughed patches of tea gardens, professional grazing reserves and Reserved Forests. While the government offered only a weak resistance, street processions and demonstrations before the offices of district collectors became frequent. Often, such demonstrations were preceded by localized agitations demanding land from the government or even squatting in government-owned lands. In most cases, demonstrators came with specific demands and could identify the patches of land from either a neighbouring tea garden or a grazing reserve that they wanted to reclaim. An illustrative instance of such land reclamation happened in Diplonga tea garden in Darrang. In February 1950, a demonstration of several hundred peasants, from the eastern part of the district like Satiya, Jamuguri, and Chariali mauzas, urged the Deputy Commissioner to redistribute wastelands of the tea garden 'within a period of seven days'.[132] The demonstration was preceded by a CSP-led agitation in the tea garden, during which some Hindu and Muslim peasants both had already reclaimed land. Arrest of some agitating peasants did not make the peasants' withdraw their demands.[133] The Deputy Commissioner promised to concede their demands and requisitioned land from the garden, but the actual redistribution could never take place.[134] Following another round of agitation, the peasants finally encroached upon the lands inside the tea garden again in January 1951.[135]

Agitation for reclamation of land from tea gardens spread like wildfire and most areas witnessed a rush for reclamation, similar to that in the Diplonga tea garden. In March 1950, a KS meeting demanded that the owners of tea gardens in Titabor distribute their wastelands among the local landless peasants.[136] Anonymously written letters published in newspapers reported a preliminary estimate of the wastelands in tea gardens. One report pointed out how 'some of 1,000 acres of land were lying waste, useful for cultivation in Tonna tea gardens'.[137] Such reports also pointed out that tribal landless people would be willing to settle there from the nearby places. In some places, landless peasants could reclaim more than 1,000 acres of land. On the other hand, the government and the Congress began to increasingly challenge such reclamation. For instance, in Lakhimpur, local landless peasants occupied 1,000 acres of land from the Tangia tea garden in October 1950 but could not finally assert their control over the land due to police action.[138]

In tandem with strengthening its own organizational structure, the CSP also staged *satyagrahas* to pressurize the government to distribute land among the landless peasants. While CSP-led land agitation found many followers, it was the satyagraha at Giladhari tea estate in Golaghat which marked the resounding success of CSP's method of agitation.[139] The Assamese landless peasants from various parts of Golaghat had already petitioned to the administration, seeking distribution of wastelands from this tea garden, but the government paid no attention. The satyagraha drew support from a wide cross-section of people. Not only did an increasing number of landless peasants join the programme but support also came in from middle-class families and tea garden workers. As the movement showed some signs of success, a co-operative was formed amongst the landless peasants to carry out collective farming in the reclaimed land.

As the satyagraha began, *Sadiniya Assamiya* claimed that '350 landless Assamese peasants forcibly occupied 35 acres of requisitioned land of Giladhari tea estate to protest against the delay in the distribution of the land'.[140] The government declared this land reclamation illegal, evicted the squatters and arrested a few. Resistance to squatting also came from local Congress units. Congress leaders like Dandeswar Hazarika and Rajendranath Barua, both members of the Assam Legislative Assembly, spoke publicly against such underhand tactics of CSP to reclaim land.[141] Determined, the CSP, however, did not give up and decided to replicate the Giladhari satyagraha model in other districts.[142] The Giladhari satyagraha thus became a major success of the CSP in mobilizing local landless peasants.[143] It was inspiring enough for landless peasants in other areas. Soon, similar protests took place in tea gardens of Mangaldai and Jorhat.[144] In November 1950, the

CSP cadres occupied 1,600 acres of land of Sarusarai tea garden in Jorhat.[145] The police arrested the squatters, including the Secretary of the Jorhat unit of CSP. And this story of agitation for land reclamation and state repression continued.[146] The CSP continued to intensify its demand for distribution of fee-simple land of the tea gardens among the landless peasants.[147] The CPI too was not far behind from staging similar protests and, in several places, government-owned lands or lands of tea gardens were occupied.[148] Often, both CPI and CSP also jointly mobilized landless peasants.[149]

The agitation for land haunted the Congress government in early 1949, forcing the Assam Provincial Congress Committee (APCC) to adopt a resolution on this matter. In fact, it was only from 1949 that the Assam Congress's concern over land scarcity began to surface. On different occasions, the Congress leaders appealed to the landless peasants to move into unploughed tracts where there was sufficient land rather than forcibly squat in tea gardens or Reserved Forests.[150] In October 1949, Bishnuram Medhi, the then Revenue Minister, while addressing a public meeting, appealed to the landless people to move to distant places. There were instances when peasants in certain areas actually followed his advice.

And, now under compulsion, in a resolution adopted in Silchar, the Congress party urged the Assam government to de-reserve the Reserved Forests, to requisition the tea garden wastelands and government wastelands and to distribute them among the landless peasants urgently.[151] The Congress leaders, in several well-publicized meetings, advised the peasants not to squat in the tea garden lands and persuaded them to refrain from forceful land occupation. The Congress party's attempt to regulate and channelize the peasant struggle into a legal battle did not, however, find any support from the peasants themselves. For instance, in a public meeting, organized under the Congress banner, landless peasants threatened to forcibly occupy all wastelands of the tea gardens if the government failed to give land to them within 25 days. Amidst intense peasant mobilization to occupy tea garden lands, the Congress could secure crucial support from Tea Labourers Association (TLA), a loose association of tea garden workers with loyalty to Congress-led Indian National Trade Union congress (INTUC). Jogendranath Rajmedhi, office bearer of the Association and General Secretary of the TLA-affiliated Dumduma

Central Chah Majdur Sangha, while presiding over a public meeting, assured the peasants that 'the government would do the needful for distribution of land'.[152] Such open pledge from tea garden workers union helped in restraining tea garden workers from joining the rebel peasants. But Rajmedhi's assurance could stop the landless peasants and agricultural labourers from joining the ongoing sharecropper movement.

The increasing intensification of peasant mobilization compelled the Tea Planters Association to demand urgent government intervention. While some planters sought legal help, the planters' lobby in the Assam Legislative Assembly impressed upon the government the urgency of the matter. The Indian Tea Association even went a step further and argued that 'the trespass was a step indicating lawless communistic tendencies of the people rampant in Assam; [and that] the matter should be taken up with the provincial cabinet'.[153] In January 1951, the Planting and Commerce group in Assam legislature wrote to the Assam government alleging mass land reclamation.[154] Given the pressure being built up by peasant mobilization, the government, however, could not afford to side with the planters and was only forced to defend the rebel peasants. The government decided to enforce the Assam Land (Requisition and Acquisition) Act of 1948, aimed at the acquisition of surplus wastelands from various tea gardens and the distribution of such lands among landless peasants.[155] In an effort to bring the situation under control, this pro-active stand taken by the government was widely publicized. It appealed to the peasants not to forcibly occupy land from the tea gardens and promised that it would undertake the responsibility of providing them with land. And it was not lying.

In February 1951, the Deputy Commissioner of Darrang issued a pamphlet explaining the provisions of the 1948 Act made by the government and appealed to the agitating peasants not to go for forcible occupation of lands.[156] Despite the administration's veiled threat to the agitating peasants that in case they continued with their agitation they might be deprived of the benefits of government's land distribution scheme — 'If peasants encroached in to some land before it was requisitioned than there will be delay in land requisition ... those who go for Satyagraha they will be debarred from the land distribution'[157] — forcible occupation of government lands did continue. The government nonetheless deployed the police to evict the squatting peasants.

Despite increasing police repression of the agitating peasants, the government was eventually forced to requisition the lands of tea gardens and distribute parts thereof among these peasants on annual leases.[158] The government had already signalled its willingness to abdicate its control over the state-owned unploughed lands. It realized that its defunct land settlement policy had only reinforced the landless peasants' movement. Between 1950 and 1952, Assamese legislators extensively debated the subject of land settlement on the floor of the Assembly. Many hoped that a well-orchestrated land settlement programme would be able to defuse the powerful sharecroppers' movement. By the end of 1950, the government began a moderate initiative for distribution of land among the landless peasants. The immediate beneficiaries were villagers residing near Reserved Forests. *Natum Assamiya* reported an instance of the government allowing more than a hundred landless peasant families to settle as forest villagers in the Doiyang Reserved Forest.[159] While local Congress leaders were entrusted with this task of identifying landless families and carrying out land distribution, the non-cultivating landlords capitalized on their access to the political machinery as well as bureaucracy to occupy the lands distributed in this process.[160] However, the fact that landlords took such undue benefits of land distribution did not go unchallenged and widespread discontent surfaced.

Conflicts also surfaced over the issue of who should be preferred in the process of land distribution: a poor landless peasant from a neighbouring village or another poor landless peasant from a distant village. Land distribution in Jokaichuk and Motiyari grazing reserves of Charing mauza in Sibsagar district is illustrative of such growing disgruntlement.[161] Landless peasants from the neighbourhood immediately complained that they, in spite of being landless and residing in the vicinity of the reserves, could not get land while 700 bighas of land were distributed among the peasants from a distant place. The conflict-ridden situation compelled the Assam Provincial Congress to send Bimala Prasad Chaliha, the local member of Assam Legislative Assembly and an influential leader amongst the nationalist Assamese landlords, to intervene in the matter. At the same time, as the peasants' hope of getting land was dashed to ground due to official apathy, the state machinery's preferential treatment to the immigrant East Pakistani peasants was also challenged in the public discourse.[162]

The forcible land reclamation drive at the initiative of the CSP and the CPI continued till 1951, and thereafter they encouraged the agitating peasants to take recourse to law for acquiring land.[163] Various peasant organizations also kept alive their demand for the distribution of government-owned wastelands or lands requisitioned from tea gardens till 1951.[164] The number of landless peasants supporting such mobilization kept increasing. On 22 January 1951, a group of 3,000 peasants, mostly from the eastern part of Nowgaon, led by CSP leader Rupram Sut, staged a demonstration in Nowgaon. The demonstrating peasants put forward several specific demands before the Deputy Commissioner: (*a*) these lands should be given to collective farm societies, not individuals, (*b*) these should be distributed before the beginning of harvesting season, (*c*) the government should do away with the policy of extracting from the peasants the costs incurred in requisitioning land, and (*d*) the mischievous activities (e.g., threatening peasants in the event of their cattle straying into the garden lands) of tea garden owners should be stopped.[165]

Towards the end of 1950, the slogan 'land to the landless peasants' found many followers. The number of landless peasants suddenly swelled after 1950. This was because those who lost lands to an earthquake in 1950, soil erosion caused by annual floods and deposition of silt on their fields joined the ranks of landless peasants. The devastation caused by an earthquake in 1950 was colossal and official accounts readily admitted this. Consequently, a sudden increase in the demand for land also helped in intensifying and unifying the formerly scattered movements. Local politicians campaigned on behalf of such landless peasant families for land grant.[166] More local leaders emerged to take initiatives to intensify such mobilization. Even Congress leaders stepped in and their intervention mostly helped in ensuring that land reclamation remained largely non-violent. Further, this tactful extension of support by Congress to the land reclamation agitation helped it make inroads in those areas, for instance Golaghat,[167] which had been predominantly under the influence of communists or socialists. Also, as the state machinery remained a silent spectator to these developments or posed no resistance, local-level mobilization of landless peasants was further heightened. By the end of 1950, more petitions demanding land had reached the government than ever before. By the end of 1951, a legislator reported that in the Jorhat subdivision alone there were more than 1,00,000 landless peasants who had applied for lands.[168] Poor peasants were joined by non-cultivating families which wanted to own lands to rent them out later. For instance, clerical staff in the tea gardens of eastern Assam had sent numerous such petitions.

Yet, compared to the spiralling number of petitions from landless peasants, the government could manage to distribute land only among a few of the petitioners. For instance, during 1948–49 and 1949–50, only 247 and 334 families respectively were given land in the Sibsagar subdivision.[169] During 1949–50, the government claimed to have settled more than 150,000 bighas of land with a total of 1,800 families. However, these families did not essentially turn out to be landless as the government also considered even peasant families having only bare minimum land as landless peasants and accordingly distributed land among the five-member families, each with a holding of less than 20 bighas and the families of more than five members, each with a holding of 30 bighas.[170]

As the government began to enforce the Assam Land (Requisition and Acquisition) Act of 1948, 70,170 bighas of surplus land in tea gardens were acquired by 1950.[171] Out of this land, 15,408 bighas were settled with 1,703 landless and flood-affected peasant families and the rest with immigrants from East Pakistan. The government also distributed 12,746 bighas of wasteland in tea gardens in 1951.[172] Requisition of land from tea gardens continued and till the middle of 1952, the government collected an estimated 33,000 bighas of land from the various tea gardens of Darrang district. Most of these were distributed among 3,964 families, the majority belonging to former tea garden labourers.[173] Similarly, the government also parcelled out land from grazing reserves or Reserved Forests and, for some time, from Un-classed State Forests.[174] In May 1950, the government instructed superintendents of grazing reserves to open 3,000 acres of land for distribution, of which a maximum of 10 bighas could be allotted to each claimant family. Till the end of the year an estimated 40,000 bighas of land from grazing reserves were settled with the landless peasants. This was apart from another estimated 37,290 bighas of land settled with 6,300 peasants.[175] These figures only tell how ineffective and limited the government's effort was.

Did the landless peasants' struggle for land occupation and the sharecroppers' movement share a common political programme? There was evidence of many sharecroppers, such as those from Namsungi village in Lakhimpur district, joining landless peasants in their agitation for land.[176] Many sharecroppers believed that this was their chance to become independent peasants which would save them from the clutches of landlords. In eastern Assam, even landlords extended their support to the landless peasants' movement.[177] This was so because the landless peasants' agitation had come as a relief to them, as it turned out to be a great opportunity to divert the attention of sharecroppers from the ongoing sharecroppers' movement, thereby reducing pressure on them. Further, they knew that the collective agitation of landless peasants and sharecroppers would be directed against the European or non-Assamese tea planters.

Communists and Government: Repression and Recuperation

Under pressure from the landlords and in the wake of failure to secure the support of sharecroppers and landless peasants across the valley, the beleaguered Assam government finally began to crack down on the communist peasant organizations. In 1948, the government geared up the police administration to suppress the movement; the police arrested agitating sharecroppers on the one hand and gave protection to landlords on the other.

The government had begun to be worried of communist activities by 1947. As early as February 1947, Harold Dennehy, Chief Secretary to the Government of Assam, directed his junior officers to keep a track of 'any individuals' having communist leanings. This perceptible change in the attitude of the government to the communists was caused by the growing peasant mobilization in the wake of the Tebhaga movement in the neighbouring province of Bengal.[178] Many within the government also realized that the mobilization of peasants by communists in eastern India was supported by communist groups in South-East Asian countries. The government's worries were best reflected in a private communications between Chief Minister Gopinath Bordoloi and Prime

Minister Jawaharlal Nehru. Bordoloi worriedly wrote to Nehru how

> [t]he communist menace is scotched for the time being and so far as internal security of the province is concerned there need not be any anxiety. It is true that more important leaders are yet underground. But it is expected that it will not take long before some of them, at any rate will be found out. Some activities among the tribal people and the students are yet there, but they are now being met be propaganda by the Congress people in some places.[179]

Throughout his brief tenure as the head of the government from 1947 to 1950, Bordoloi continued to write to Nehru about the impending danger of communist activities in Assam. His fear was further strengthened with the news of 'communist threat' on the eastern border of the country becoming more real. He informed Nehru that the 'communist menace from the side of Burma is assuming a threatening attitude'.[180] Indeed, the increasing communist mobilization and changing political climate in China remained a matter of concern for the governments both in Assam and in Delhi for years to come.[181]

In 1948, the government enforced the Assam Maintenance of Public Order Act of 1947, which apparently allowed the government to arrest political leaders on suspicion and detain them without trial. Subsequent to the Act coming into force, many communist leaders and cadres were either placed under home detention or were arrested.[182] Though lawyers, sympathetic to the communists, tried to argue their cases in the courts, challenging the validity of the Act, it did not go down well with the judiciary.[183] The Assamese politicians also fully approved the government views on the communists.[184] Arrest of several key leaders like Govinda Kalita who had spearheaded the sharecroppers' movement in southern Kamrup and was arrested in September 1948, or Bishnu Rabha who was arrested on 17 July 1952 along with most others though warrant of arrest had been issued much earlier, was a setback to the movement.[185] Arrest of leaders was followed by the declaration of several districts, part or in whole, as disturbed areas.[186] Police deployment was increased in villages where sharecroppers continued to be unyielding to pressure.[187] Punitive tax was imposed in entire Beltola.[188]

But all these did not deter the communists from continuing with their activities. In 1950, the government finally decided to seal the fate of communist parties. In July of the same year, the RCPI, including its all front and underground organizations, was declared unlawful.[189] Though this did come as a surprise, it forced most leaders who were not arrested or were released recently from prison to go underground. Between 1950 and 1951, the police arrested 1,250 RCPI activists,[190] out of which 115 were convicted. Several of them were kept as détenues. At the same time, the government continued to desperately strengthen its intelligence network. Demand for an increase in police intelligence activities was already being raised since 1948. S.P. Desai, Chief Secretary to Government of Assam, emphasized the necessity for 'much more training and in methods that will succeed against such menaces to the state as the RCPI personnel armed with deadly weapons'.[191] He was not alone in making this demand; even officers in the districts asked for an improved and better intelligence network.[192]

Though there is not enough information on what was done to improve police intelligence, but the network of village defence organizations was evidently reorganized. These organizations came to be controlled by local Congress leaders. The cadres were recruited from the villages. This eventually gave the police crucial access to erstwhile inaccessible villages. Equally worrisome for the government was the communist propaganda through pamphlets and other printed material. The police proscribed the pamphlets issued by peasant organizations.[193] Most of the proscribed pamphlets were propaganda writings or appeals to various sections of peasantry to participate in the communist-led peasant movement. The Assamese press gave wide publicity to police receiving villagers' support against communist leaders.

However, such news was not always true. The days of underground activities of Bishnu Rabha is now part of modern folklore. Many communist leaders, like Rabha, could prolong or evade their arrest as villagers used to conceal them. Autobiographical accounts of communist leaders recount exhilarating memories of how villagers, mostly tribal peasants, outsmarted the police by resorting to lying and trickery and thereby helping their leaders escape from imminent arrest.

The police torture of villagers to extract information about fugitive communists was not approved by public opinion. An adjournment motion brought by Emrain Hussain Chaudhury in the Assam Legislative Assembly reflected this situation. In the motion, Chaudhury, while disapproving the communists, condemned the 'harassment caused to the general public of Sibsagar and Sarbhog areas by the Military in detecting alleged communists.'[194] He alleged that for hunting down a few communists, the entire Sibsagar district had been declared a disturbed area, leading to harassment of all people. Meanwhile, the government succeeded in getting the much needed support for its anti-communist drive from the Assamese urban intelligentsia. As a part of this move, more than 40 influential people took an initiative in mobilizing people in Sibsagar town for a public meeting aimed at discussing the 'law and order situation'. The meeting discussed at length the need to frame policy to curb communist influences.[195] The much needed support for this anti-communist drive came from the local Congress units which became active in eliciting urban support for the government.[196] The leading paper *Assamiya* extended full support to the government. Regular reports on the police success in controlling the communist activities were published. These media campaigns succeeded in disassociating the peasant question from the communist mobilization. The administration hoped that an ideological rift between the CPI and the RCPI would render the communist mobilization ineffective. The ideological conflicts between the communist parties were thus widely reported in the press and this created confusion amongst the educated supporters of the communists. The government's clever manipulation of the internal divisions of communist parties paid off in 1952 when the CPI-affiliated Lakhimpur Krishak Sabha accused the RCPI of terrorizing the public.[197]

By early 1951, the police claimed to have covered an estimated 1,120 square miles of the Brahmaputra valley under its regular patrol.[198] The government continued to include Beltola in the list of disturbed areas and justified doing so by claiming that 'looting of rice and other heinous crimes are still going on there'.[199] More and more prize money was declared on information on underground communist leaders.[200] The police seized arms from the secret camps of RCPI.[201] *Natun Assamiya* told its readers how heroically the police, by capturing these arms from the communist secret camps, had foiled the dreams of the communists to establish a 'red regime'. The government widely circulated pamphlets asking people to co-operate in its anti-communist operation. Anti-communist operation continued to be extended to other areas even after 1951. Such operation began in northern Kamrup from 20 April 1952 and resulted in the arrest of 238 people. Often, the government termed such action as curbing 'dacoity'.[202]

The state repression compelled the communist organizations to adopt a new strategy. From 1950, their leaders concentrated more on their own safety and security than on sustaining the movement or remaining at the forefront of peasant mobilization. The police remained vigilant about all activities of the RCPI and the KBP activists till 1952. Bringing great relief to the worried government, the superintendent of police of Kamrup commented in September 1952 that the RCPI was at a low ebb as most of its leaders had been arrested, but the claim was essentially a misreading of the ground situation.[203] This can be easily grasped from a commentary published in *The Times of India* in 1951: the commentator anxiously noted that 'perhaps nowhere in the country, not even in Telengana, has the communist menace assumed such dangerous proportions as in Assam ... has almost become almost a replica of the Communist-infested'.[204] For once, rightly, the paper reiterated that 'communism ... is a symptom of economic disorder',[205] but as remedy it suggested that 'without exploitation and development of the State's resources an effective check of this ideology'[206] would not be possible, a position the communists vehemently disagreed with.

Reflection and Reorientation: Towards a Parliamentary Agitation

> The CPI committed the blunder of failure to build up the movement from above and RCPI committed the blunder of failure to build up the movement from below.
>
> RCPI, April 1952[207]

The powerful anti-communist operation, launched in different parts of the valley and continued for a long period of time, coincided with internal debates of CPI and RCPI. Ideological debates would lead to a split within the RCPI in 1952.[208] This was preceded

Plate 5.3: Pamphlet issued by the Communist Party of India (CPI) asking the Assam government to withdraw its ban on the CPI

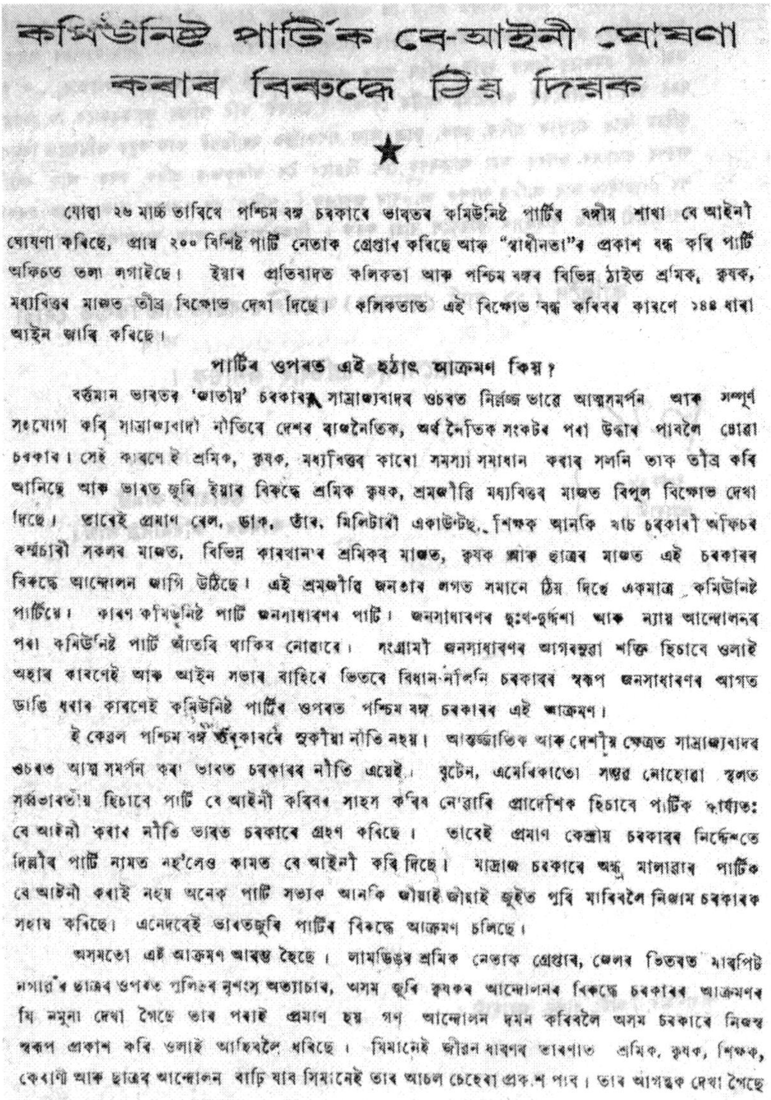

কমিউনিষ্ট পার্টিক বে-আইনী ঘোষণা কৰাৰ বিৰুদ্ধে থিয় দিয়ক

★

যোৱা ২৬ মার্চ তাৰিখে পশ্চিম বঙ্গ চৰকাৰে ভাৰতৰ কমিউনিষ্ট পার্টিৰ বঙ্গীয় শাখা বে আইনী ঘোষণা কৰিছে, প্রায় ২০০ বিশিষ্ট পার্টি নেতাক গ্রেপ্তাৰ কৰিছে আৰু "স্বাধীনতা"ৰ প্রকাশ বন্ধ কৰি পার্টি অফিচত তলা লগাইছে। ইয়াৰ প্রতিবাদত কলিকতা আৰু পশ্চিম বঙ্গৰ বিভিন্ন ঠাইত শ্রমিক, কৃষক, মধ্যবিত্তৰ মাজত তীব্র বিক্ষোভ দেখা দিছে। কলিকতাত এই বিক্ষোভ বন্ধ কৰিবৰ কাৰণে ১৪৪ ধাৰা আইন জাৰি কৰিছে।

পার্টিৰ ওপৰত এই হঠাৎ আক্রমণ কিয়?

বর্ত্তমান ভাৰতৰ 'জাতীয়' চৰকাৰে সাম্রাজ্যবাদৰ ওচৰত নির্লজ্জ ভাৱে আত্মসমর্পন আৰু সম্পূর্ণ সংযোগ কৰি সাম্রাজ্যবাদী নীতিৰে দেশৰ ৰাজনৈতিক, অর্থনৈতিক সংকটৰ পৰা উদ্ধাৰ পাবলৈ যোৱা চৰকাৰ। সেই কাৰণেই শ্রমিক, কৃষক, মধ্যবিত্তৰ কাৰো সমস্যা সমাধান কৰাৰ সলনি তাক তীব্র কৰি আনিছে আৰু ভাৰত জুৰি ইয়াৰ বিৰুদ্ধে শ্রমিক কৃষক, শ্রমজীৱি মধ্যবিত্তৰ মাজত বিপুল বিক্ষোভ দেখা দিছে। তাৰেই প্রমাণ ৰেল, ডাক, তাঁৰ, মিলিটাৰী একাউণ্টছ, শিক্ষক আনকি বহু চৰকাৰী অফিচৰ কর্ম্মচাৰী সকলৰ মাজত, বিভিন্ন কাৰখানাৰ শ্রমিকৰ মাজত, কৃষক আৰু ছাত্রৰ মাজত এই চৰকাৰৰ বিৰুদ্ধে আন্দোলন জাগি উঠিছে। এই শ্রমজীৱি জনতাৰ লগত সমানে থিয় দিছে একমাত্র কমিউনিষ্ট পার্টিয়ে। কাৰণ কমিউনিষ্ট পার্টি জনসাধাৰণৰ পার্টি। জনসাধাৰণৰ দুখ-দুর্দ্দশা আৰু ন্যায় আন্দোলনৰ পৰা কমিউনিষ্ট পার্টি আঁতৰি থাকিব নোৱাৰে। সংগ্রামী জনসাধাৰণৰ আগৰণুৱা শক্তি হিচাবে ওলাই অহাৰ কাৰণেই আৰু আইন সভাৰ বাহিৰে ভিতৰে বিধান-নলিনি চৰকাৰৰ স্বৰূপ জনসাধাৰণৰ আগত ভাঙি ধৰাৰ কাৰণেই কমিউনিষ্ট পার্টিৰ ওপৰত পশ্চিম বঙ্গ চৰকাৰৰ এই আক্রমণ।

ই কেৱল পশ্চিম বঙ্গ চৰকাৰৰে স্বকীয়া নীতি নহয়। আন্তর্জ্জাতিক আৰু দেশীয় ক্ষেত্রত সাম্রাজ্যবাদৰ ওচৰত আত্মসমর্পন কৰা ভাৰত চৰকাৰৰ নীতি এয়েই। বৃটেন, এমেৰিকাতো সন্তুষ্ট নোহোৱা স্বগত সর্ব্বভাৰতীয় হিচাবে পার্টি বে আইনী কৰিবৰ সাহস কৰিব নোৱাৰি প্রাদেশিক হিচাবে পার্টিক কার্য্যতঃ বে আইনী কৰাৰ নীতি ভাৰত চৰকাৰে গ্রহণ কৰিছে। তাৰেই প্রমাণ কেন্দ্রীয় চৰকাৰৰ নির্দ্দেশতে দিল্লীৰ পার্টি ন্যামত নহ'লেও কামত বে আইনী কৰি দিছে। মাদ্রাজ চৰকাৰে অন্ধ্র মালাবাৰ পার্টিক বে আইনী কৰাই নহয় অনেক পার্টি সভ্যক আনকি জীয়াই জীয়াই জুইত পুৰি মাৰিবলৈ নিজাম চৰকাৰক সহায় কৰিছে। এনেদৰেই ভাৰতজুৰি পার্টিৰ বিৰুদ্ধে আক্রমণ চলিছে।

অসমতো এই আক্রমণ আৰম্ভ হৈছে। লামডিঙৰ শ্রমিক নেতাক গ্রেপ্তাৰ, জেলৰ ভিতৰত মাৰপিট নগাৱঁৰ ছাত্রৰ ওপৰত পুলিচৰ নৃশংস অত্যাচাৰ, অসম জুৰি কৃষকৰ আন্দোলনৰ বিৰুদ্ধে চৰকাৰৰ আক্রমণৰ যি নমুনা দেখা গৈছে তাৰ পৰাই প্রমাণ হয় গণ আন্দোলন দমন কৰিবলৈ অসম চৰকাৰে নিজস্ব স্বৰূপ প্রকাশ কৰি ওলাই আহিবলৈ ধৰিছে। যিমানেই জীৱন ধাৰণৰ তাৰণাত শ্রমিক, কৃষক, শিক্ষক, কেৰাণী আৰু ছাত্রৰ আন্দোলন বাঢ়ি যাব সিমানেই তাৰ আচল চেহেৰা প্রকাশ পাব। তাৰ আগন্তুক দেখা গৈছে

Source: Assam Police Intelligence Record Room (APIRR), Guwahati, 1950.

by another split in 1951 when Kedarnath Goswami, a senior KBP leader, decided to form a party along with his supporters.[209] A conference held in Basugaon, Goalpara, formalized this split. The new political position of the RCPI became public as early as April 1952.[210] In self-criticism, the party admitted that the movement had failed to mobilize the peasantry from below. It also realized that it did not stress on the building up of a mass base. It also criticized the CPI for failing to organize the struggle well and for its avowed emphasis on industrial workers. The CPI also gave a new direction to the party programme.[211] It is, however, not clear at what moment did the CPI develop a different thought about the ongoing peasant movement. But it is clear that the party began to have a rethink about the movement by 1952. Many, including Bishnu Rabha disagreed with the romantic adventurism of communist leaders. There was a fresh reappraisal of the nature of agrarian relation in Assam. Later on, Pranesh Biswas, a leading CPI leader, reflected how

> [m]any of the sharecroppers were poor, illiterate, unorganized and were dependent on the landlords in different ways. Moreover, many of the landlords were the petty owners, viz. teachers, clerks, soldiers, widows. If we give only one fifth of the produce how will they survive ... in the raityatwari settled areas of Assam there was no rich landlords, it was the middle class who cultivate their land on adhi.[212]

Most communist leaders realized that in the process of mobilizing the sharecroppers they had also lost critical support of the majority of Assamese small peasants. The CPI leader Gaurishankar Bhattacharjya also echoed a similar sentiment in 1952. During this time, the CPI oriented its policy towards participation in the India's first general election. In its national conference held at Calcutta in 1951, it adopted a new political programme. The party admitted:

> We have to realize that although the masses are getting fast radicalized and moving into action in many parts of the country, the growth of the mass movement has not kept pace with the growth of discontentment against the present government ... [W]e must fight the parliamentary elections and election in every sphere where the broad strata of the people can be mobilized and their interests defended.[213]

The impending general election also temporarily halted the communist mobilization of the peasantry. The CPI decided to participate in the general election in 1951. This ideological shift towards a parliamentary democracy coincided with the CPI's willingness to work with 'all classes, parties, groups and organizations' to defend Indian nationhood.[214] In the first general election to Assam Legislative Assembly, the CPI contested for 18 seats, won one seat and got an impressive 13.75 per cent of the total votes polled in the constituencies they contested from.[215] In October 1952, the government also withdrew the ban on the RCPI which had forced the latter to work underground.[216] But, both CPI and RCPI had already begun to lose critical support from sharecroppers who were alienated by state repression.

By the end of 1952, the rhythm and intensity of organized peasant movement in the Brahmaputra valley, which had triggered hopes and posed many challenges, came to a temporary halt. However, the retreat of communist peasant organizations also created a political vacuum which was soon filled by Congress-led peasant organizations. The distressed peasants, trained to resort to confrontational politics by their communist leaders, were now encouraged to seek favour from their landlords and the government. For some time, the administrative machinery was also encouraged to be responsive to the peasants' grievances. The Assam government formed land settlement advisory committees in different districts. These committees, however, came to be dominated by representatives of rich landowners, traditional landlords and the Assamese nationalist political elite, thereby definitely bringing a short-lived relief to the rich landlords, as also to the tea planters.

The sharecroppers' and the landless peasants' movement had spread to various parts of the valley, bringing both excitement and new challenges to small peasants, sharecroppers and landless peasants. The hopes of the leaders of peasant organizations who were convinced of the complete success of the peasant movement also ran high. They believed that the payment of adhi to the landlords had completely stopped, that the landlords had failed to enter the villages, much less evict their sharecroppers, that the sharecroppers had retained their lands, that the village panchayats had become paramount, that the state administration had disappeared from the villages, and that the contractors of the forest

Plate 5.4: RCPI mouthpiece *Lal Nichan*, April 1952

লাল নিচান

দ্বিতীয় বছৰ প্ৰথম সংখ্যা
২৩ এপ্ৰিল, '৫২ চন। মূল্য এক অনা

বিপ্লৱী কমিউনিষ্টৰ কৰ্ত্তব্য

দলৰ কেন্দ্ৰীয় কমিটিয়ে পাৰ্টিৰ বৰ্ত্তমান নীতি ও কৰ্ত্তব্য নিৰ্দ্ধাৰণ কৰিছে। "আমাৰ বৰ্ত্তমান কৰ্ত্তব্য" (The task of the our) বোলা কিতাপ খনত দলৰ বৰ্ত্তমান নীতি ও কৰ্ত্তব্য লিপিবদ্ধ কৰা হৈছে। ইয়াৰ ওপৰিও দলৰ মধ্যবৰ্ত্তীৰ কালৰ এখনি আচনি আৰু প্ৰাথমিক আন্দোলনৰ আন এখনি আচনি দলৰ কেন্দ্ৰীয় কমিটিয়ে প্ৰস্তুত কৰিছে। এই বিলাকৰ ওপৰত প্ৰত্যেক সভ্যৰে মতামত ও সমালোচনা প্ৰাদেশিক কমিটিৰ ওচৰলৈ পঠাব পাৰে।

বৰ্ত্তমান নীতিৰ সাৰাংশ হ'ল—আৰ, চি পি আই ও চি, পি, আইৰ ভুলৰ কাৰণে ভাৰতৰ মুক্তি সংগ্ৰাম সাময়িক ভাৱে ব্যৰ্থ হয় আৰু বুৰ্জ্জোৱা শ্ৰেণীয়ে প্ৰথম পৰ্য্যায়ত জয়লাভ কৰে। চি, পি, আইৰ ভুল হৈছিল সংগ্ৰামৰ ওপৰৰ প্ৰস্তুতি নকৰাটো আৰু আৰ, চি, পি, আইৰ ভুল হৈছিল গণ-সংগ্ৰামবোৰ তলৰ পৰা প্ৰস্তুত কৰি নিনিয়াটো—গণ-সংগঠন ও গণ ঘাটী প্ৰস্তুত কৰাৰ ওপৰত গুৰুত্ব নিদিয়াটো।

বুৰ্জ্জোৱা শ্ৰেণীয়ে যদিও প্ৰথম পৰ্য্যায়ত জয়লাভ কৰিছে তথাপি বিপ্লৱৰ বাস্তৱ অৱস্থা একবিন্দুও আমাৰ প্ৰতিকূল হোৱা নাই বৰং ধনী শ্ৰেণীৰ গভীৰ ও চিৰস্থন অৰ্থনৈতিক সঙ্কটে বিপ্লৱৰ সম্ভৱনাক আৰু প্ৰখৰ কৰি তুলিছে। ধনী শ্ৰেণীৰ সম্পূৰ্ণ জয়লাভ হ'ল হেঁতেন যদি তেওঁলোকৰ অৰ্থনীতিক পুনৰজ্জীৱিত কৰি তুলিব পাৰিলে হেঁতেন। কিন্তু দেশীয় ও বিদেশী ধনী সকলে অৰ্থনীতিক পুনৰজ্জীৱিত কৰি তোলাৰ কোনো সম্ভাৱনা নাই বৰং সঙ্কটক অতি গভীৰ কৰিহে তুলিছে আৰু এই সঙ্কটৰ পৰা হাত সাৰাৰ কাৰণে এক মহাযুদ্ধৰ আশ্ৰয় বিচাৰিছে। কিন্তু কি শান্তি কি যুদ্ধ উভয় অৱস্থাতেই ধনতন্ত্ৰবাদ মৃত্যুৰ ফালে দ্ৰুত অগ্ৰসৰ হব ধৰিছে। ধনতন্ত্ৰবাদৰ এই সঙ্কটৰ কাৰণেই সংগ্ৰামৰ সম্ভাৱনা আগতকৈও বাঢ়িছে।

গতিকে আজি আমাৰ প্ৰধান কৰ্ত্তব্য হ'ল জনসাধাৰণৰ আন্দোলনক পুনৰজ্জীৱিত কৰি তোলা। জনসাধাৰণৰ দৰিদ্ৰতাৰ লগে লগে চৰকাৰৰ বিৰুদ্ধে যি তীব্ৰ ঘৃণা ও বিদ্বেষৰ সৃষ্টি হৈছে তাৰ ফলতে নতুন গণ-আন্দোলনৰ জন্ম দিবৰ বাধা। এই ক্ৰমবৰ্দ্ধমান অসন্তোষৰ মাজেদি গণ-শক্তি সংহত কৰি প্ৰবল গণ-আন্দোলন গঢ়ি তুলিব লাগিব। আজি আমাৰ আশু কৰ্ত্তব্য হ'ল গণ-শক্তি বৃদ্ধি কৰা ও তাক সংহত কৰা। ইয়াৰ কাৰণেই আজি আৱশ্যক সৰ্ব্বত্ৰ গণ-সংগঠনবোৰ গঢ়ি তোলা। আমি এদিন যেনেকৈ সংগ্ৰামৰ ওপৰৰ প্ৰস্তুতিৰ কাৰণে প্ৰধান গুৰুত্ব দিছিলোঁ আজিও তেনেকৈ প্ৰধান গুৰুত্ব দিব লাগিব গণ-সংগঠনৰ ওপৰত। "সংগঠন কৰা, সংগঠন কৰা" এইয়ে হৈছে আমাৰ বৰ্ত্তমান ধ্বনি। জনসাধাৰণক সংগঠিত কৰাৰ এই প্ৰাথমিক কাজ খিনি নকৰিলে আমি কোনো

✻ মে দিৱস পালন কৰক ✻

অহা ১লা মে তাৰিখে গাৱেঁ, চহৰে চাৰিওফালে মে দিৱস পালন কৰক। এই দিৱসত ৰাজবন্দী মুক্তি ও বিপ্লৱী কমিউনিষ্ট পাৰ্টিৰ পৰা নিষেধাজ্ঞা প্ৰত্যাহাৰৰ দাবীত সভা, শোভাযাত্ৰা, প্ৰদৰ্শন কৰক। চাৰিওফালে প্ৰাচীৰ পত্ৰ লগাওক।

পাৰ্টি তহবিলত ছয় হাজাৰ টকা লাগে

অহা মাহত পাৰ্টি তহবিলৰ কাৰণে ৬০০০৲ টকা সংগ্ৰহ কৰাৰ অৰ্থে সকলো পাৰ্টি সঙ্গঠনে, ও পাৰ্টি সভ্যই চেষ্টা কৰক।

নিম্নলিখিত হাৰে জিলা কমিটিবোৰে টকা তুলি দিব:—
শিৱসাগৰ—১০০০৲ যোৰহাট—৫০০৲ লক্ষীমপুৰ—৫০০৲ উত্তৰ কামৰূপ—১০০০৲ দৰং—৫০০৲ দক্ষিণ কামৰূপ—১০০০৲ দক্ষিণ গোৱাল পাড়া—৫০০৲ নগাওঁ—৫০০৲ উত্তৰ গোৱাল পাড়া ৫০০৲

Source: Assam Police Intelligence Record Room (APIRR), Guwahati, 1952.

department were working in the hill forests after taking permission of the panchayats. They also believed that expectation of the peasants had been met to a certain extent. For instance, Kotora, a boatman and an erstwhile supporter of the CSP who helped in its political activities in the neighbourhood of Guwahati, later reclaimed land in northern Kamrup with the help of CSP workers. In a couple of years, he cultivated it to produce crops, though, of course, this land was without tenurial security.[217] Like many across other districts, he too remembered those tumultuous days of political action described in this chapter, which helped them in their pursuit of freedom from an oppressive social structure.

6

Rural Mobilization, Social Dynamics and Rural Politics

For the peasants of Assam, the experiences of the mid-twentieth century were richer and more complex than was expected by the communist organizations. A reading of the previous chapters would have given the reader a picture of typical communist peasant mobilization. But the rural lives and rural politics did not necessarily follow the wishes of communist leaders. The communist leaders were forced to respond to local crises, manoeuvre their tactics to suit localized conflicts, or give in to social dynamics that were not strictly economic in nature. In fact, these deviations from the standard communist programme of action and recurrent surfacing of intensely localized issues had impacted the peasant mobilization process more forcefully than many communists would have liked to believe. Everyday lives of the Assamese and tribal villages in the 1940s and 1950s were more complex than one would like to imagine. Not only were they suddenly caught in the grip of a severe food crisis but caste, community, religion, and gender dynamics also came to play a crucial role in the rural politics affecting them. These complexities could not be negotiated merely through standard political rhetoric of congress nationalists, communists and socialists. They required paying careful attention to — or sometimes nurturing of — the intricate social dynamics that had deeply impacted the social history of Assam. The rural social dynamics, in fact, began to unfold itself beyond the confines of communist mobilization. Very often, such unfolding of social dynamics overlapped with the communist mobilization. This chapter attempts to explore some of the broader issues that redefined the trajectory of peasant unrest and mobilization in the mid-twentieth-century Assam.

Where is Food? Break the Granaries

Not long after the Bengal famine of 1943, i.e., from 1945, districts of western Assam also came in the grip of a severe food scarcity. The crisis was further aggravated by the Assam government's programme of forceful paddy procurement after independence. It was against this background that villages in western Assam witnessed widespread food riots during 1949–51. These food riots were generally characterized by seizure of paddy from the granaries of rich peasants, landlords, or from the rice-husking mills by poor peasants. The *bhakhuri bhanga*, as these food riots involving forced entry into the granaries came to be popularly known in western Assam, was principally directed by the Krishak Banua Panchayat (KBP).[1] In the traditional Assamese villages, the granary was usually built as a separate structure in front of the house. While granary was a symbol of wealth and social status of a rich peasant during 1949–51, it turned out to be a curse for many landlords or rich peasants during the food riots. The KBP's modus operandi was simple: the cadres would go to the houses of select rich peasants and forcibly collect paddy from their granaries. A decision to collect paddy from the landlords' granaries would be taken collectively in a meeting in villages severely affected by food scarcity. The KBP cadres, after identifying the landlords, rich peasants and *mahajans* who had fully stocked granaries, would send intimidating messages to them asking to distribute the surplus paddy left after retaining what was required to fulfil their minimum needs. If they refused to accept these demands, the KBP cadres, accompanied by other poor peasants, would visit their houses and normally take out the entire stock of paddy from their granaries. After giving back a certain amount to the owner, the KBP cadres would distribute the remaining stock among poor peasants, who came with gunny bags to collect their share of paddy. The stock was distributed among them according to the size of their families. Food riots began to intensify after the kharif crop was harvested in 1949. These widespread attacks on the granaries of landlords immediately drew the government's attention.[2] The bewildered government even likened these activities to those of the legendary Robin Hood.[3]

In most cases, the landlords would remain mere spectators to the forcible seizure of their foodgrains and found no time to inform the police as it used to happen all of a sudden. Often, the landlords would be in a state of shock to see in the morning an assemblage of poor peasants breaking into their granaries.[4] For instance, the police reported that an Assamese landlord in Ranimauza in Kamrup even could not inform them though he saw that his fellow villagers, all carrying small gunny bags, had already taken away the paddy from his granary.[5] However, though he resisted, he was not physically assaulted. At the same time, there were instances of violence erupting in such operations. For instance, a Nepali agricultural labourer and his wife, employed with a landlord, were shot at with a revolver for refusing to help the peasants in removing paddy from their landlord's granary.[6] There are also instances of houses of landlords, rich peasants and moneylenders being set on fire, or the moneylenders being given false promises that their paddy would be returned with interest once the harvesting season was over.[7] For instance, in Sotamatia village near Beltola, peasants looted the granary of Gharasan Rabha, a middle peasant as well as a moneylender but promised that they would return the paddy with an interest amounting to 1 maund of paddy for every 4 maunds of paddy that they had taken away.

It became common for the rich peasants in Beltola to receive letters threatening them with seizure and distribution of their paddy during this period.[8] One such letter received by a landlord in Beltola contained these intimidating words: '[T]he time has come ... the blood suckers of the poor peasants should gave up all their paddy stock because of the peasants had taken up powers with themselves'.[9] The Assamese landlord who received this letter complained to the police that 'he saw the letter lying in front of the house when he woke up in the morning'.[10] Posters were also put up on the walls of the houses of Assamese landlords in Beltola demanding distribution of their stocks of paddy. Another rich Assamese peasant from Beltola reported to the police how he saw a poster pasted on a coconut tree near the gate of his house when he got up in the morning. The poster warned him of severe consequences if he did not part with his paddy the next day.[11]

Granary looting became a popular mode of peasant protest in the villages of southern Kamrup and Darrang in 1950 and 1951.[12] During this period, reports that 'owing to the action of the communists some granaries of the rich people ... were looted and as such paddy is not available in that area' poured in.[13] Food riots became highly successful in places like Beltola and Rani where the KBP cadres incited the poor to take away paddy from the granaries of landlords and others.[14] Many tribal peasants joined the food riots in Darrang as well. In one instance, an estimated 800 tribal peasants led by the KBP cadres assaulted two landlords and took away paddy from their granaries.[15] At the same time, food riots were not widely reported from districts of eastern Assam, except Sibsagar which witnessed only a few such incidents.[16] As food riots spread through the rural western Assam, areas with predominant presence of traders saw an increase in such incidents.[17] For instance, both Tihu and Palashbari, with their widespread network of Marwari *golas*, became vulnerable to such threats throughout 1950. Instances of attacks on rice-husking mills owned by Marwari traders in Palashbari,[18] or golas owned by Marwari traders in Tihu were widely reported in the Assamese press.[19] Peasants seized both cash and rice from these mills and golas.

As the situation worsened, Bishnuram Medhi, the then Chief Minister, in February 1950, admitted that the KBP activists had looted the rice-husking mills in Kamrup and Darrang.[20] Notwithstanding this, the Assam government failed to bring the situation under control and the frequency of such attacks increased. The Marwari traders in Palashbari formed an association called Kamrup Marwari Panchayat and sent a telegram to the Indian Home Minister, requesting for his urgent intervention in the matter. They also sought the help of the Chief Minister of Rajasthan. Their telegram to the latter stated: '[S]ituation growing worse at Palashbari area due to stray slogans and looting against Marwari community'.[21] They demanded that immediate steps be taken to save them from the communist trouble. But nothing could save these traders.

The situation only became worse.[22] The Assamese press also continued to report glaring instances of granary looting. For instance, in July 1950, *Natun Assamiya* gave front-page coverage to an incident of looting in Baridua near Guwahati.[23] The paper reported how an estimated 1,000 peasants, mostly tribal and Nepali, armed with small weapons and led by communist leaders, had looted several granaries. The seized paddy had been distributed among the peasants on the spot. A month earlier, in June 1950, *Sadiniya Assamiya* reported that 'some 500 people under the leadership of few absconding communists'[24] forcibly took away paddy, amounting to approximately 1,000 maunds, from the granaries of several rich peasants in southern Kamrup. In another report, *Sadiniya Assamiya* worriedly admitted that consequent to this incident in particular, panic had spread amongst the local population.[25] Reports of attacks on Marwari golas also continued to pour in. For example, in August 1951, a small crowd near Garal in Palashbari attacked Masaddilal Sarma, a Marwari owner of a trading firm, Bherudhan Chanth Mal Traders, of Goalpara, who was on his way from Guwahati to Goalpara. The crowd looted the stock of grocery items from his vehicle.[26]

The Revolutionary Communist Party of India (RCPI) released a number of leaflets appealing to the peasants to seize paddy from the granaries of rich peasants.[27] These pamphlets also spelt out the ideological legitimacy of their decision to incite the peasants. For example, one such pamphlet argued that 'in the present condition of poverty and starvation, the granary of the rich men is the only alternative. There is no other way that the poor peasants can get their food. Likewise in the good days the rich men also take all kinds of benefits from the poor peasants'.[28] Another leaflet appealed to the rich peasants and landlords to share their paddy with the poor peasants.[29] Yet another one appealed to the Assamese rich peasants to share their paddy stock with 'the starving peasants from southern Kamrup'.[30] The RCPI argued that huge stocks of paddy had been kept 'in *dhanir bharal* (rich man's granary) and the hungry peasants should not hesitate to loot those granaries'.[31] Such appeals did not stop pouring in from the RCPI till the end of 1951.[32] Several other leaflets lauded peasants from the districts of western Assam for achieving success in their 'granary breaking' movement. Alongside, the RCPI also successfully mobilized the Assamese and tribal peasantry against the government's paddy procurement policy in 1951. A number of procurement officers were assaulted by the peasants at the behest of the RCPI.[33]

Food riots was not a novel feature of peasant unrest in the Brahmaputra valley during the 1940s. In Assam, colonial officials had documented the earliest such looting during the peasant disturbances of 1893–94. Such incidents from similar areas were again reported when during the Civil Disobedience movement in 1930–31, tribal peasants from western Assam widely resorted to looting of shops.[34] But in order to explain the popularity of granary looting as a mode of peasant protest during 1949–51, we need to examine the agrarian scenario of Assam from the 1940s onwards.

Though the impact of Bengal famine on the Brahmaputra valley was very limited, the general stock of food-stuffs and clothes diminished fast after the Second World War. This led to a phenomenal hike in the prices of paddy and other food items.[35] The price rise was first noticed in 1940 when the Assam government reported that 'prices have ruled generally higher this year than in 1939'.[36] The price of paddy, in particular, strikingly increased from an approximately Rs 1 to Rs 8 per maund to Rs 18 per maund.[37] Due to this sudden hike, the peasants sold their stocks of paddy for making quick profits, thereby contributing to the depletion of the overall stock of paddy in their villages over the next few years.

The situation was further made difficult by the government's food procurement policy. The Indian government, in order to meet with any eventuality arising out of the Bengal famine of 1943, passed the Hoarding and Profiteering Ordinance to fix the maximum prices of different foodgrains and essential commodities.[38] In fact, since 1942, the Assam government had initiated a procurement policy to meet the eventuality of an impending famine-like situation, which had already engulfed the neighbouring Bengal.[39] As a part of this procurement policy, the Steel Brothers Company Limited was authorized to regulate and monitor the sale and purchase of paddy in Assam. The company was entrusted with the procurement work and was given the monopoly right to buy paddy and rice from various districts.[40] The agents of the Steel Brothers, as also the contractors from various tea gardens, entered the villages to collect paddy.[41] Soon, there was protest against the procurement programme since the peasants felt that the programme would force them to part with their meagre produce, and the government had no other option but to let the procurement work be taken over by the state machinery in July 1946. But even the modest procurement work which was completed failed to meet the demand for food in Assam, and from 1947, the government began importing Burma rice from the central government stocks to cope with the deficit in production. In December 1945, the Assam government had also fixed the maximum price of paddy at Rs 6 per maund. This pricing policy was further reviewed towards the end of 1947.[42] Meanwhile, in order to make the paddy procurement policy attractive to peasants, the government announced its decision to distribute tin sheets among those who would give paddy to the procurement agencies. This policy affected even the majority of rich peasants as they had to give away most of their paddy to the government.

The condition became further complicated in 1946 when there was a steep fall in the paddy prices to as low as Rs 2. This sharp fall in the paddy prices compelled the peasants to sell more paddy to sustain their families. The poor and middle peasants were the worst hit compared to the rich peasants as the latter could survive such short-term market fluctuations. Continual crop failure, since 1943, mostly due to recurrent floods in Kamrup, Nowgaon, Sibsagar, and Lakhimpur had already drawn the rural world into a condition of extreme food scarcity.[43] The food situation of Sualkuci in south Kamrup became so acute that Congress legislator Beliram Das had to draw the attention of the Assembly to it. Das complained that as the state government had restricted the movement of rice and paddy from other districts, local inhabitants of Sualkuci were virtually in the brink of starvation.[44] He cited instances of how they bought rice and paddy from Darrang and other districts of eastern Assam at high prices. In some places, he informed the Assembly, floods had reduced the acreage to three-fourth of the pre-existing acreage and this further aggravated the situation.

In 1945, *Sadiniya Assamiya* reported how 'flood has brought excessive damage to winter crops in the Khata, Bahajani, Uparbarbhag, Pakoa Khetri, Dharnapur, and Barkhetri mauzas' of Kamrup.[45] The weather had been generally unfavourable for the crop throughout the valley since 1944. The crop, especially in low-lying areas of most of the districts was damaged by floods. Pests also damaged the crop to some extent in the districts of Darrang, Nowgaon and Sibsagar.[46] And, in 1947, with a sudden influx of a large number of people in Kamrup and Goalpara due to Partition, demand for rice increased. The local paddy production failed to meet with this growing demand. The selling price of paddy was abnormally low while the buying price was high. In some cases, peasants tried to sell home-husked rice to get a higher price than paddy though it did not fetch them any extra profit as the government had fixed a lower price for the home-husked rice than for the mill-husked rice. A couple of years later, in 1950, paddy prices began to rise and almost reached the double of the controlled rate.[47] In 1951, the peasants in the Garamur and Saraibahi areas bought rice for Rs 50 per maund.[48] In Dibrugarh, rice was sold at an abnormally high price of Rs 80 per maund.[49]

As peasants demanded the curtailment of prices of rice as well as a hike in the paddy prices,[50] the Assam government fixed the price of paddy and rice at a comparatively much lower level.[51] In spite of this, as the government admitted, the peasants were not forthcoming to dispose of their produce in the market. Hoarding, unfavourable weather and continued influx of refugees from East Pakistan, actuated the price rise. The availability of paddy in the open market decreased, as a major portion of the paddy procured by the procurement department was strictly reserved for the tea garden workers. The government showed no interest in temporarily closing the rice mills, but at the same time, the export of paddy from the state was banned till 1951.[52] Peasants resorted to several mechanisms to avoid the government's food procurement policy. Many a time, the government admitted that without the help of the village headmen the procurement policy could not be successful.[53] There was thus collective resistance to the procurement of paddy from the villages. Poor peasants hoped that if they continued to resist the procurement policy of the government, landlords would distribute paddy from their granaries in the time of crisis.[54] This would also minimize the risk factor in the looting of these granaries. The procurement policy, therefore, led to popular resentment in the rural areas.[55]

A moderate rise in the jute prices was noticed after 1950. A section of the Assamese peasantry also began jute cultivation with a hope of making profit. The price rise acted as an incentive for the Assamese peasants to divert their paddy lands to jute cultivation. Consequently, the acreage under jute began to rise. Owing to this shift, the area under paddy cultivation decreased leading to a sudden scarcity of paddy.[56] As jute cultivation was more important in the districts of western Assam, the scarcity of paddy was more acutely felt there.[57] Moreover, in the aftermath of Partition, a large number of Muslim peasants who left for East Pakistan had disposed off their entire stock of paddy at very low prices. Large quantities of foodgrains were completely destroyed in Goalpara and Kamrup. Consequent to this volatile political situation, Muslim peasants kept their land fallow for a couple of years. They returned to the fields only during the harvesting season of 1951–52. The result was a general decline in rice production and consequent price rise. During 1950–51, the total rice yield fell by an estimated 4,41,500 tonnes as compared to that in the previous year.[58] High fluctuation in the crop production was followed by the great earthquake of 15 August 1950. The earthquake resulted in sudden environmental disturbances. Heavy floods causing extensive crop-damage were reported. Natural calamities completely destroyed large quantities of food-grains.[59] The government conservatively pegged the figure of damaged crops at 4,852 tonnes of paddy and, in the course of the communal disturbance, 14,226 tonnes. Large tracts were left uncultivated during the period of sowing and transplantation. Consequent to this, a sudden price rise was reported. This marginally benefitted the rich peasants as they were able to sell the paddy and reap profits.

Between 1948 and 1951, the Assamese press repeatedly claimed the existence of a famine-like situation in western Assam. A letter, published in *Dainik Assamiya* in 1948, described how huge stocks of paddy were transported out of the villages.[60] The letter blamed widespread market speculation, hoarding, export of paddy, and transfer of land as a result of the trader–moneylender nexus. On several occasions, the government was criticized for its failure to regulate prices. Many appealed to the government for the grant of remission of land revenue.[61] Desperate attempts were made to draw the government's attention to the worsening situation: 'ninety-five percent people do not have anything to eat ... if they had money also, they could not eat anything, as the granaries are empty. They were desperately looking for paddy ... the government should utmost care so that people could get paddy at controlled price.'[62] In south Kamrup, crop failure mainly due to pest-attacks was reported during the harvesting season of 1949–50.

There were also complaints of rice being sold to traders at speculative prices across the borders in East Pakistan. Complaints were made against some paddy-husking mills for forcibly collecting paddy from the villages. *Sadiniya Assamiya* gave a moving description of how villagers in the neighbourhood of Guwahati were constantly in search of rice and often remained starved for days.[63] It even claimed that several villagers with additional stocks of paddy had refused to sell their stocks for the fear of not getting extra profits.[64] Public meetings urged the government to undertake urgent remedial measures.[65]

The victims of the situation were primarily poor peasants. They failed to withstand the crisis caused by a couple of years of food scarcity. The traditional and widespread subsistence peasant economy, reflected in a popular saying, *aakalo nai bharalo nai* ('no famine, no surplus'), had literally failed. A majority of the peasant population became vulnerable to this crisis. At the same time, these peasants could not escape the stranglehold of the procurement programme of the government.[66] The crisis left no other option for the poor peasants but to be part of the propaganda of the KBP and loot the granaries of the landlords. The 'granary breaking' movement slowly gained popularity amongst the poor peasants from 1949 and continued till at least the early days of 1952.

The subject of the acute food scarcity came to be extensively debated in the Assam Legislative Assembly.[67] The Assembly, throughout the period of 1944–52, witnessed several adjournment motions on the 'acute shortage of foodstuffs and textile' in Assam.[68] A particularly heated debate took place in 1950. The government came out with a different explanation for the phenomenon and felt that the price rise was caused by the earthquake and flood in 1950 — an explanation that was nevertheless partially true.[69] The government, however, admitted that the economic condition of peasants continued to be deplorable as the prices of essential commodities remained high. It further maintained that peasants either could not produce enough foodgrains to sustain themselves for the whole year or failed to purchase the foodcrops due to abnormal price rise. That the Assamese middle class was also hard hit was readily admitted by the government.[70] Several Congress members in the Assembly argued that a similar condition had prevailed prior to 1950 and to put a check on this deteriorating condition, 'there was no protective measure from the authorities, our government . . . frequently appealing to the good sense of these black marketers, profiteers and hoarders to refrain from these sins against society'.[71] The Assam government admitted that everyday reports were coming from almost all quarters 'complaining to government about abnormal rise of prices, sometimes very much beyond the purchasing power of the average section of people, not to speak of the poorer classes'.[72] Complaints had 'even come from quarters, which are generally regarded as surplus areas of our state'.[73] The government was clearly in despair. A legislator desperately sought the goodwill of the rich to help the poor. A local Congress committee at Teok in Jorhat even appealed to the Assamese rich peasants to sell paddy at the rate of Rs 2 per *dun* to the poor peasants. The Assamese press had to lament that only a negligible number of rich peasants did so. Parallel to the food riot was an increase in petty crimes.[74] The government attributed this increase to the increasing political mobilization arising out of economic insecurity.

To explain the popularity of the granary-breaking movement in western Assam which was greater than that in the districts of eastern Assam, we need to examine the different patterns of paddy storage in western and eastern Assam though it does not solely explain the larger picture. In eastern Assam, paddy was stored as *dangori* — bundles of paddy crops — in the granaries of most peasants. The bundles were threshed only when paddy was needed for either consumption or selling. In western Assam, cattle was used to generally thrash the paddy before it was stored.[75] It was easier to carry grains than bulky paddy from the villages of eastern Assam.

The severe economic crisis after Independence brought more miseries to the peasant households. The crisis was further accentuated by the scarcity of cloth and yarn. In 1948, the state government admitted its anxiety about the increasing cloth scarcity in the province.[76] The transport system of Assam was also thrown out of gear by the Partition. From the end of January 1948, the East Bengal Railway drastically restricted and virtually banned the influx of goods into Assam from Calcutta. This led to a severe scarcity of yarn in Assam. The impact was acutely felt by peasants families and many found the communist peasant mobilization as the best possible way of expressing their discontent. The government was forced to look into this issue. However, a direct rail link between Assam and the rest of India was established only in January 1950.

This crisis was not unique to Assam. The Independence and Partition severely disrupted India's food stock. To overcome this crisis, the Indian government experimented with several food procurement programmes after Independence.[77] Assam was one of the states which were asked by the Indian government to contribute to the central pool of foodgrains.[78] Assam, considered along with Orissa as the two food-surplus states, began exporting rice — 10,000 tonnes in 1950 — to other states of India after Independence.[79] This severely drained the state's stock of rice to the detriment of its increasing population. By the end of 1950, in a memorandum submitted to the central government, the Assam government admitted to a famine-like situation and expressed its inability to export more rice.[80] The memorandum read: '[I]t will not be incorrect to say that in many areas actual famine conditions has obtained and that unless the position was quickly retrieved the consequences are bound to be serious'.[81] The government further admitted 'the absolute non-availability of rice is also reported from many areas'.[82] Subsequently, cheap grain shops were opened in all districts to remedy the situation.[83]

By early 1951, as the food situation further deteriorated, the government tried to implement the procurement policy more effectively. It announced several schemes to make effective the Assam Foodstuffs (Foodgrain) Control Ordinance of 1951.[84] As a precautionary measure, the government, by supplying the cheif-grain shops with less quantities of foodgrains, reduced the supply of rations earmarked for the tea gardens and made them depend on the paddy grown by these gardens. Various checkposts were established to enforce strict control over the movement of paddy. By early 1952, with the gradual withering away of peasant organizations, the food riots also became a story of the past. The food shortage essentially improved the KBP's capacity to bring more peasants into their fold. They had successfully organized the peasants and succeeded in extracting concessions from the government. However, because of a stable crop production and the government's policy, the food situation improved, and the strategy for peasant mobilization did not work out.

Gendering Agrarian Communism

In the 1990s, Assam witnessed a decade of political violence powered by an ideology of resistance to the Indian state. Hundreds of youths, who were members of a banned organization called the United Liberation Front of Assam (ULFA) and demanded secession of Assam from India, were arrested. Most of these arrests resulted in sudden and spontaneous protests by women, mostly from villages. These protests were widely reported in the Assamese press as a significant moment in the history of women in Assam. A parallel can be drawn between the situation in the 1990s and what happened in 1948–52 though they were not similar in origin. How does one explain this continued support of women for political struggles of various kinds, for instance, those of sharecroppers? Did the divergent historical experiences of tribal, low-caste and high-caste, or Muslim women combined to catapult the staging of powerful protests against exploitation by the landlords? Did the women from the middle or rich peasant families play any crucial role in the different phases of peasant movement? If it was so, was it critically different from the previous experiences that the women in Assam gained during the anti-imperialist nationalist mobilization? [85] This section explains these issues by introducing the readers to broad patterns of women's participation in agrarian communism.

Women's entry into the arena of peasant mobilization, particularly the sharecroppers' movement during the 1948–52, occurred at a critical juncture. It began when the landlords tried to assert their control over both rent and land. Entry of women into the movement reinforced — thereby adding new creativity to — the old forms of resistance. For many of them, the recently gained political experiences, the memories of the Quit India movement in particular, came in handy. Sudden demonstrations and processions, mostly by women, became an everyday feature of the period. There were numerous examples of spontaneous mobilization of women peasants to assert their control over their land. Official accounts were full of women's 'bravery' in resisting the landlords' attempts to assert their control over the sharecroppers' produce. A typical example of such accounts was the story of how in 1949 'about 80 tribal women compelled' two landlords who had 'gone to Gaoghuli and Kotahbari under Beltola mauza ... to give an understanding not to visit those villages to collect adhiar revenue before they would let them go'.[86]

A month later, in March 1949, the state police again reported how it faced stiff resistance from the women when it went to Beltola 'in search for the underground communist leaders'. As the police tried to resist the agitated women, they became violent. Not only did they reach out to their neighbouring villagers, but they also forcibly searched police vehicles, took away cycles or paddy which the police had confiscated from them. Police later admitted that not a single male was seen amongst the agitating crowd.[87] In another incident, in January 1949, police went to Beltola to investigate reports of clashes between sharecroppers and landlords; it could arrest only two peasants against whom the landlords had registered cases. As the police took away the arrested, 'a mob of 50/60 women intercepted them on the way ... with broom and *lathis*. They demanded unconditional release of the arrested villagers'. The police stated that they were 'very violent and did not listen to the police' and it was only after some initial jostle that they could forcibly free the arrested from the protection of women.[88]

Such examples of direct confrontation between women and the police were the last means of defence of their land and crop that the sharecropping families could use against their landlords. Women took such radical steps, in absence of their male family members, more spontaneously. Such radicalization was facilitated by several factors. First, many believed that the police would not arrest women and this acted as an important factor for the sustained offensive by the women.[89] Second, the tribal social setting characterized by limited patriarchy, also facilitated the widespread mobilization of women. Third, in most places they knew the local topography well, as they frequently visited the hilly forested, terrains for collecting firewood and food (i.e., roots greens, edible plants, etc.), an experience that gave them a decisive advantage if they chose to retreat in the wake of any adverse eventuality, for instance, a police peration to hunt down any communists hiding among the peasants.

Spontaneous participation of women could be noticed during the most politicized phase of the movement. They confronted the landlords and the police, employed creative defensive use of chilli powder or brooms, tried to protect their crops and offered passive resistance. Their resistance was mostly spontaneous and localized and yet aggressive. This open and confrontational attitude of the woman was mostly apparent in the tribal villages. To protect a hiding communist leader, they would readily give false replies to the police, or even chase away the raiding police parties. On several occasions, women hurled abuses at the landlords when they tried to collect rent from their sharecroppers.[90] There are references to women protecting paddy and household properties when male members escaped to the forests or hills to avoid arrest. Describing such an incident that took place on the night of 23 April 1949, the police noted:

> [T]he houses of Pakhari Kachari and others of Satgaon under Beltola mauza were searched for the underground communist. Then the female inmates of the houses raised an objection for the search and sent information to other women of the same village. After a few minutes about 50/60 women gathered over there and abused the police party for making search in their village.

The police admitted that 'had there been any arrest of those women, it is obvious, [*sic*] would have obstructed the police party, in future if there be any arrest in that village, there may be clash between police party and women'.[91] This prediction of the police came true when 'instances of assault on the police by women'[92] continued to be reported. A worried police administration had no other option but to admit that 'from this it is apparent that the party's technique to set up bands of militant women to form the vanguard of attack on the police is now being increasingly used'.[93] We will shortly come back to the issue of the communist mobilization of women.

Some women also came to the streets to join processions organized by communist parties and shouted slogans against the government. The Assamese press, normally shying away from reporting such activities, often re-ported such processions and demonstrations. For instance, *Natun Assamiya*, in November 1949, reported about a procession in Guwahati of about 300 tribal peasants, with a predominant presence of women, who came from the outskirts of the town.[94] They, with red flags in their hands, shouted slogans demanding land for the tiller.[95] Women members also provided critical logistic support by acting as couriers and providing safe passage to the absconding communist leaders.[96] Even women from the Assamese urban middle-class families gave shelter to the absconding communist members. However, isolated such examples might be — like that of Haren Hajra, a well-known physician and communist leader in Jorhat who was given shelter by women from an urban middleclass family when he went into hiding — they showed the sympathy, however little, that the communist mobilization could gain from women.[97] Some women cadres even went underground but were arrested more easily by the police.[98]

This unprecedented political mobilization of women from peasant families was, however, both due to a structured entry of women into communist parties and due to a crucial dependence of peasant cultivation on women labour. The crucial importance of women labour in the making of Assam's peasant economy has been discussed in Chapter 1. This did not go unnoticed in the perceptive eyes of the young communist leaders (most of whom interestingly were male). This led to the careful nurturing of women units within the communist parties. Unlike the case of late-nineteenth-century peasant uprisings, the Assamese women came to participate in mass movements only during the Gandhian upsurge. Yet, very rarely could women, except a few like Chandraprova Saikia (1901–72), play an effective and decisive role in the policies and programmes of a popular movement led by Congress. However, this too changed, at least temporarily.

Like their counterparts, in other parts of India, both the RCPI and CPI emphasized the necessity of having separate women wings in their organizational structure.[99] The popularity of these wings increased when the peasants' claim over land and crops was at stake. Most of these women's units were loosely organized groups meant for carrying localized anti-landlord activities.[100] The women fronts of the CPI and RCPI were christened as Mahila Atmarakha Samity and Pragati Nari Mukti Sangha. Their cadres were recruited from both caste-Hindu and tribal peasant families.[101] Only a few amongst them had formal education.[102] Elementary training in communist ideology was part of their indoctrination into the organizational fold.[103] It is difficult to understand the enduring impact of this indoctrination. Often, these women cadres succeeded in articulating independent views on matters of organizational activities. Away from their centrality in the organization of family labour, this freedom of expression was also largely derived from the liberal social organization of the peasant society, i.e., the influence of moderate matrilineality accrued from tribal society.

The status of women cadres within the organizational structure of the parties, which was predominantly male-dominated, was flexible. Women cadres from poor peasant families often presided over the proceedings of meetings.[104] Only a few were allowed to lead from the front.[105] The illustrious career of Kamala Majumdar in the RCPI was an example of this recognition. Majumdar, who joined the ranks of the RCPI as a young student in 1947, transformed herself into a charismatic personality in the party.[106] Her clarity of political opinion earned her the charge of editing and publishing the party organs, *Lal Nichan* and *Panchayat*. Several other women leaders like Hena Ganguly were as vocal and articulate in their political articulation. Several of them took a leading part in the organizational activities of the communist parties. For instance, Usha Datta Verma of Indian Peoples Theatre Association organized guerrilla training for KBP cadres in the hills adjoining Beltola.[107] When she came to Assam to train the KBP cadres, she found several woman cadres in those training camps.

Several district committees of the CPI too had a strong and substantial presence of women cadres.[108] For instance, the women front of the CPI in Sibsagar was formed towards the latter part of 1948. The official accounts had no doubt that 'the CPI laid much stress to organize a strong women front in the district to make the democratic revolution a success'.[109] The Assam police even thought that 'there was no dearth of militant women in the district but women leadership to organize and guide them was wanting'.[110] Every comrade was directed to encourage his woman relatives to be enrolled as party members.[111] However, often, there was opposition from male cadres to what they perceived as the increasing expansion and primacy of women fronts.[112] Before the middle of 1949, the CPI did not have any organizational activities carried out by women in Kamrup as also other districts,[113] but from mid-1949 then it came to have an impressive number of women activists and leaders.[114] More women units were formed in the western parts of Kamrup like Khetri and Beltola.[115] These were followed by holding of small village conferences as a show of strength. Units were formed by enlisting women from the poor peasant families.[116]

On different occasions, women fronts reached out to the nationalist constituency of the Assamese society whose liberal views were well known. In 1948, Chandraprava Saikia, the illustrious Congress leader and chairperson of the Provincial Women Conference, presided over a meeting of tribal peasants in Beltola, largely attended by women.[117] Her fiery speech was widely reported in the Assamese press. Saikia impressively spoke against the existing exploitative agrarian relations. She expressed hope for an end to the Zamindari system and had no doubt that 'the tribal peasants should be protected from the rich peasants, if necessary by buying the lands, as it is a tribal dominated area'.[118]

Thus, a couple of years of mobilization yielded some positive results. There was a radical transformation in the political culture of the mobilized women from poor tribal and caste-Hindu peasant families. The activities of the Pragati Nari Mukti Sangha finally invited the wrath of the government. It was banned along with the RCPI and several of its cadres were arrested. The government was increasingly worried of the fact that the women from poor economic backgrounds were proving to be more militant and that this would result in their giving a serious and stiff resistance to the government. Thus, official records stated how 'such situation would mean that more militant women would join from the railway workers and postal and telegraph employees'.[119]

If this was the case of politically mobilized women amongst Assamese and tribal women, the women from amongst immigrant East Bengali families had different stories to tell. The communists did not organize them and the Muslim League had no political programme for them. This meant that they remained outside the purview of the political mobilization that the Assamese and tribal women had experienced. Women from these families, with no organized political voice, silently underwent multiple levels and forms of oppression. They were reduced to the most deplorable strata, faced abusive language and were always physically intimidated. Did they resist all these indignities? We can reasonably assume that they did so very rarely. But given an opportunity, they also articulated their grievances in the hope of getting justice.

An account reproduced here from the Line System Enquiry Committee Report vividly describes the tragedy which befell them.[120] Lalita, a Hindu immigrant woman, narrated her story of humiliation when some Nepali grazers attacked her. She told the Committee that her house was set on fire when she was alone inside, busy preparing a meal. When the house was set afire, her children had not yet eaten their food. She was not even allowed to bring out her belongings. She stood outside as a mute spectator only with a basketful of rice. The grazers claimed that it was not her house but theirs. They abused her in obscene language. They threatened her when she tried to collect a few household articles. Her experience was, however, not unique. Another Muslim immigrant woman peasant in Barpeta described her story of humiliation.[121] She claimed that on the day of the incident she was alone in her house with her children. Many persons came and began abusing her. They set her house on fire leading to burning of a little paddy and a few pieces of cloth. Unable to do anything, she went to her brother's house. But as she walked a little way, one man came and caught hold of her clothes. She and her children started crying loudly. They even assaulted her brother who came to protect her.

These two examples represent the general condition of women from both Hindu and Muslim immigrant families. Social humiliation and economic oppression became part of their everyday lives. The Muslim League hardly accommodated their grievances within their political programme. The political programmes of the RCPI and the CPI, at the height of their anti-landlord mobilization also failed to address these concerns. Despite these organizational shortcomings, the experience of the 1940 in a limited way gave a new political orientation to the Assamese and tribal women from peasant families.

Peasants, Vaishnava Reform and Community Aspirations

As the landlords indignantly reacted to the news of communist mobilization — and also that of the rapid reconfiguration of the Assamese rural politics — a section of them began to face resistance from an unexpected quarter. Unlike those of the communist mobilization, the pattern and forms of this resistance was different. The language of protest was not that of denial of rent to these landlords but was one of reconfiguration of institutions and social practices which were central to popular Assamese Vaishnavism.[122] This section examines the growth of these new practices and their crucial relevance to the making of a peasant movement.

By the early twentieth century, as discussed in Chapter 2, dissent against the orthodoxies of Vaishnava religious institutions, viz., satras had already surfaced. One of the reasons behind the growth of this dissent was their control over landed properties. As discussed earlier, most of them had at their disposal landed properties — constituting a substantial portion of rent-free estates across the raiyatwari areas of Assam.[123] Land ownership, the main source of economic prosperity at the time, gave these satras decisive advantage in defining social practices. Also, the main offices of the majority of the satras were held by Brahmins.[124] Over a period of time, elaborate Brahmanical rituals — under the patronage of the satras and overruling simple Vaishnava rituals — came to dominate social practices at large. By the early twentieth century, these Brahmanical rituals, like observing mourning for more than a month, or payment of extra taxes and rendering of physical labour by tenants of satras, etc., were at odds with the emerging social dynamics in the Assamese society. For instance, in the event of death of a family member, the new mourning rituals for the duration of one month deprived a poor peasant family of the opportunity to work for an entire agricultural season while traditionally only the Brahmins in Assam had observed 10 days of ritual impurity. Not only were these practices becoming economically unbearable for poor peasant families but rich and powerful peasant families from non-Brahmin background, who through their education had found employment in the colonial administration, too increasingly considered these practices at variance with their growing social aspirations. Social conflicts were the inevitable result of this new dynamics and thus a phase of moderate Vaishnava reform began.

The institutionalization of social dissent was facilitated by several interrelated processes. It began with the reconfiguration of a religious institution, i.e., *Namghar*s — the prayer house. Compared to the satras, which were often located in far-off places, the Namghars were not only situated within the villages, but also acted as institutions to arbiter village disputes. They emerged as key institutions of Assamese Vaishnava social organization by the sixteenth century, but it was the satras which continued to enjoy a pivotal role in social arbitration. By the late nineteenth century, these pre-existing Namghars had emerged as an alternative to satras. Their emergence also coincided with the recasting of *khel* — a pre-colonial Assamese social institution based on similar principles as was the guild system.[125] The khel — a religious division within villages which had socio-political functions apart from organizing various professional castes — by the late nineteenth century had been restructured as village units with Namghars as a central rallying point, members of which subscribed to the same caste and religion.[126]

In 1930s, coinciding with the powerful Civil Disobedience movement, a small group of non-Brahmin elite came together to form an organization christened as Sankar Sangha (hereafter, Sangha) which resisted socio-religious practices nurtured by satras. The birth of Sangha, later to be known as Sri Sri Sankardev Sangha, in 1930, was a manifestation of the changing order of the Vaishnava institution and its conflicts with Brahmanical rituals and social norms. [127] The Sangha was to cement the anti-Brahmanical social dissent that had already seen sporadic manifestations. The new movement began as a critical engagement with various Brahmanical rituals which had become an essential part of the Assamese Vaishnava practices. The crucial point of disagreement was whether non-Brahmins could perform death rites in 10 days or not, such a practice being restricted only to the Brahmins.

As a growing number of non-Brahmins began to perform death rites in 10 days, they defended this practice by a critical reading of the Assamese as well as Sanskrit *shastras*.[128]

For an Assamese Vaishnava believer, a shastra or *puthie* meant (primarily) the works of Sankardev (1449–1568) or his chief disciple Madhavdev.[129] Unlike the situation in the first half of the nineteenth century, more numbers of Vaishnava followers could read such shastras on their own as printing press had made these works easily available and accessible in the second half of the century. For instance, *Nam Ghosa*, one of the central scriptures for Assamese Vaishnavas and written by Madhavdev was printed in 1856. More manuscripts came to be printed in the last quarter of the century.[130] Bringing a new life to the reading practices of Vaishnavas, various Assamese works composed by Sankardev and his disciples were read, either privately or collectively, without the help of a Brahmin or other traditional readers from the upper caste. Widespread reading of shastras resulted in a growing awareness of Vaishnava teachings and simple social practices like Sankar's rejection of rigid caste rules. This also resulted in sustained public debates. Closely resembling the traditional Indian *tarka-sabha* — public debates on matters of religion, among other issues — these debates saw intense public engagement which questioned the relevance of various popular Brahmanical rituals in a Vaishnava social milieu. Most of these debates, however, centred on the aspects of *bidhi-babystha* (rules and regulations) for various life-cycle rituals like marriages, death ceremonies, etc. Resistance to orthodox practices and resultant ideological encounters led to acrimonious social rivalries. This critical engagement brought the members of Sankar Sangha in direct conflict with the socially empowered members of the Brahmin class and other upper class caste landed families.

The Sangha owed its origin to spirited public debates and defiance of Brahmanical rituals initiated by a number of Assamese public figures. A few amongst them — Ramakanta Muktiar and Haladhar Bhuyan, for instance — contributed significantly in shaping these early debates into a nascent social movement. Bhuyan, belonging to a landed family of Nowgaon, had already stepped into provincial Congress politics. A studious political activist, Bhuyan also had keen interest in matters of social organization. He was already a familiar figure in the Assamese public life both for his key role as a Congress nationalist as well as for his criticism of a recent attempt to draw similarities between the ideological moorings of Sankardev with Chaitanya, the medieval Bengali Vaishnava preacher. This was a subject of intense nationalist dislike.[131] As a Congressman, he travelled extensively, gaining a vast first-hand experience of the popular religious practices in different parts of the province. Bhuyan owned landed property and one could safely identify him as a middle peasant.[132] As a member of the Assam Legislative Assembly, he too defended the interests of the Assamese landlords.[133] Bhuyan, along with Muktiar, a practising Vaishnava and a known authority on the Vaishnava rituals and texts,[134] publicly espoused the cause of bringing changes into the everyday Brahmanical rituals of Vaishnava peasantry.[135] The first conference of Sankar Sangha was held in 1935 at Nowgaon. Chaired by Gopikavallab Deva Goswami (1876–1948), a well-known scholar from Golaghat, educated in Calcutta and known for his reformative mind, an estimated 3,000 people attended the conference.[136] Such public gatherings crystallized diverse views on social rituals and helped in shaping the trajectory of a non-Brahmanical social movement.

Sangha's defiance of the Brahmanical social rituals was soon to become popular among a wide cross-section of Assamese non-Brahmin — but mostly from lower castes — Vaishanvites.[137] A number of satras with a non-Brahmanical background also supported the Sangha and helped in its expansion. The non-Brahmin Assamese middle and rich peasants who became critical of the Brahmanical orthodoxies of the satras also became part of the Sangha. Soon, armed with growing popularity the Sangha initiated several programmes in order to do away with the elaborate Brahmanical rituals. There was an apparent simplicity in their inexpensive rituals. Thus, the Sangha discarded the satra, disapproved of the Brahmanical priests, formed village-level units, allowed membership to these units on the payment of a token subscription, and elected its own officials who would act as priests. They asserted that religious ceremonies could be practised in a simplified manner. New simplified rituals also meant a very small financial burden on the peasant families. The Sangha began with the public defence of the 10-day death ritual of a leading family from Golaghat. This new ritual for the non-Brahmins benefitted the Assamese Vaishnava poor and middle peasants who had suffered severely during the economic turmoil of the 1930s while the Brahmanical rituals continued to be a profound socio-economic burden.[138]

The Sangha, arguing for a purer and simpler form of Vaishnava rituals, in fact, rescued the poor peasants from the burden of expensive social customs. Between 1930 and the 1950s, these critical engagements took a clear political shape. The response of the Assamese non-Brahmin poor peasants to the egalitarian morals prescribed by Sangha appeared appealing for various reasons. Not only did the new rituals substantially reduce their economic burden of conducting social ceremonies but also released them from the powerful control of satras. As these new rituals also reduced the time taken for the performance of various family ceremonies, they guaranteed a return to 'normal' life within a short period of time. Previously, a mourning family normally completed the entire ritual process in as many as 30 days. Such a long duration often led to a hiatus in agrarian activity. Such sudden breaks in the agrarian cycle forcing even a small peasant to rent out his land to a sharecropper were everyday experiences. Such elaborate Brahmanical rituals also involved an additional burden on the family budgets. Witnesses from Assam deposing before the Royal Commission on Agriculture, as discussed in Chapter 1, reported the widespread observance of such practices leading to perennial indebtedness.

The Vaishnava rituals which were restructured or devised by the Sangha had a direct bearing on the everyday lives of peasants, the poorer ones in particular. These considerably reduced the socio-economic burden of the poor peasants allowing them momentary relief during the hard times of 1930s and 1940s. The Sangha's popularity amongst the non-Brahmin Assamese villages also owed to its new organizational structure. With its large ever-expanding number of branches and all of them firmly being integrated into the village Namghars, a new power equation emerged. The Sangha, because of its new egalitarian ideals and driven by the need for bringing large sections of non-Brahmin population into its fold, encouraged a wider participation of poor peasants in its programmes. The poor Vaishnava peasant families by virtue of being part of a new organizational structure and holding offices also felt empowered. By being members of a social organization which allowed them to perform various socio-religious roles, which had been preserved for the Brahmins, the poor peasants were invested with a new authority. Power came to them through their ability to negotiate various socio-cultural practices and also village resources.

After Independence, the Sangha came to acquire an increasing number of followers from amongst the Assamese non-Brahmin peasant families. In the wake of growing peasant discontent, the relation between the poor peasants and Brahmin or other upper-caste landlords had already reached a low ebb. The Sangha successfully channeled this discontent into an anti-Brahmin and anti-landlord movement. With this, the Sangha unleashed a political programme and declared its opposition to the dominance of satras and their socio-economic privileges. In 1950, it adopted a resolution targeting the landed properties of satras and blamed the Brahmin-dominated satras as exploitative institutions. Further, in 1952, it adopted a resolution, in a conference held in north Lakhimpur, demanding that as 'the *devottar* and *brahmottar* lands have not benefitted the *raij*, the government should abolish these land grants along with zamindari abolition'.[139] A similar resolution urging the government to abolish the devottar and brahmottar lands owned by Brahmin landlords was also adopted by the Tezpur branch of the Sangha.[140]

If non-Brahmin Vaishnava peasantry found an alternative avenue to vent its social and economic grievances, the *kaibartas*, traditionally recognized as a lower caste and largely dependent on fishing and cultivation, looked forward to some decisive assertion after decades of social mobilization.[141] That the kaibartas — kaibartas were previously known as *dom*, *keot* or *kewat* and by the late nineteenth century came to be increasingly known by this name when they represented less than 1 per cent of the Assam population according to the Census of 1881 — came to be known was itself a reflection of a social process involving a transition from the exclusive practice of fishing to peasant cultivation as a source of livelihood.[142] Thus, the Census of 1881 highlighted the distinction between *halwa* (peasantry) and *jalwa* (fishermen) *kewats* living in large numbers in the districts of western Assam, the former being accorded higher status in the social hierarchy. Increasingly, the members of the caste regarded the title *dom* in contempt and chose to be called as *nadiyals* or kaibartas.

In the 1920s, as the kaibartas began to mobilize themselves, they drew their ideological inspiration from a Gandhian campaign for an egalitarian society with equal status for upper and lower castes. It was not an easy task. In places like Guwahati or Barpeta, they often faced resistance from upper-caste associations. For instance, leading Assamese nationalist and Hindu reformer Gaurikant Talukdar's purification movement opposed the social aspirations and mobility of the kaibartas.[143] But, as in other parts of India, the census enumeration — of particular interest was the Census of 1921 — gave a crucial opportunity to the members of lower castes to redefine their social identities whereby we find many beginning to use new surnames.[144] This also led to the reconstruction of a contested history of Assamese caste system. Several genealogies were authored recasting and upholding the traditionally higher ranks of upper-caste families.[145] These new developments also strengthened the communitarian identities of lower castes. The community mobilization of kaibartas received another shot in the arm with a new political development — the arrival of Simon Commission in India — when leaders of this caste sought concession from the Commission as members of the Depressed Classes.[146]

The mobilization of kaibarta community was further reinforced through the public celebration of community festivals and historicizing of community legends from the 1920s.[147] One of the illustrative examples was the festival of Radhika Sati.[148] The resurfacing of this legend from being an obscure narrative embedded within the biographical annals of the Assamese Vaishnava saints to being a public festival indicated the changing dynamics of the kaibarta community. As a legend, this narrative, revolving around the heroic deeds of a kaibarta woman in the time of Sankardev who successfully found ways to help agricultural fields from being inundated by flood water, became crucial to the community as it tried hard to prove its social importance, uplift the kaibarta women from their lowly social status and resist challenges from the upper castes. The public celebration of Radhika Sati legend invested the community with a much-needed solidarity and political legitimacy. It not only re-affirmed the status of kaibartas as an integral part of the Assamese Vaishnava tradition — and thereby the Assamese *jati* (nation) — but also ensured their legitimate position within the Assamese peasantry.

From the early twentieth century, with fishing and water bodies coming under state control as well as commercialization of fishing beginning earlier in the nineteenth century, members of this caste slowly took to cultivation rather than fishing. S.N. Dutta, an official in the Revenue Department in Assam, noted, in 1930, how 'there is a growing disinclination amongst the Nadiyals to sell fish. They now style themselves Kaibarttas and aspire to rise in the social scale by giving up hereditary profession'.[149] Dutta also did not forget to mention that this lucrative business had been slowly taken over by the East Bengali fishermen. But their search for land was mostly futile. This shift from fishing to cultivation — and thus the growth of a class of landless peasants — came to be partially reflected in the agricultural census taken during the Census of 1951. The government responded by de-reserving some grazing reserves and this came to be officially reflected in the 1945 land settlement policy, discussed in Chapter 4.

Such a land settlement policy did not go down well with the upper-caste Assamese peasantry. On several occasions, the latter violently resisted such land settlement. An illustrative example was the public protest by a collective of upper-caste peasant families in Sibsagar against land distribution policies.[150] The clash took place when in 1943, an estimated 122 kaibarta landless families were settled with land in the Jokaichuk Grazing Reserve in Sibsagar. Members from two dominant caste groups — Brahmin and Kalita — strongly protested against this, but this protest fell short of turning into a communal clash, as the government admitted, due to the intervention of local authorities. But the simmering tension did not subside. A couple of years later, in October 1945, a bigger crowd consisting of members of the upper-caste peasantry attacked the kaibarta peasants inside the erstwhile grazing reserve. An official account gives the following details of what happened: '[A] remarkable attack was made by the villagers in Sibsagar ... on men of the depressed class who had been settled on land once reserved, they forcibly reaped the crops and destroyed the house'.[151] The Assam government condemned the incident as 'one of the savage and inhuman attacks'.[152]

Similar incidents continued to surface time and again. And, with a newly gained political solidarity, the members of the kaibarta community sought relief from the Congress political programme looking up to their Congress leadership. For instance, a leading member of the community, Mahendranath Hazarika, a Congress legislator who began his political career on the eve of the advent of Simon commission, gave the guidance and leadership to the community. The All Assam Kaibarta Sanmilan — a collective platform with a strong allegiance to the Congress — tried to counter such opposition from the upper-caste peasantry.[153] The Sanmilan apprised the Assam Provincial Congress Committee (APCC) of its strong disapproval of such social violence.[154] The Sanmilan — in its 11th conference held in May 1947 at Majuli, the stronghold of Assamese upper castes, and presided over by two leading Congress leaders, Banshidhar Dutta and Mahendranath Hazarika, adopted crucial resolutions. This gave a new political orientation to an erstwhile communitarian platform, which, however, could hardly and rarely challenge the Congress political programmes. While one of the resolutions strongly backed the eviction policy of the Assam government, another resolution demanded that zamindari system be abolished in Goalpara and the zamindars' lands be used for settling the low-caste peasant families. The Sanmilan also urged the government to distribute wastelands amongst the kaibarta families. Seeking tenurial security of their occupancy, it further appealed to the government to enact legislative measures so that landlords of the religious estates do not evict their kaibarta tenants. It urged the government to pass another legislation to give occupancy rights to the kaibarta peasants cultivating in such estates. It demanded the fixing of rent, provision of agricultural credit and a reduction in the land revenue. To lower the burden of land revenue on the Assamese peasants, it urged the government to increase the taxes on tea gardens and industries. The Sanmilan finally raised issues of social discrimination prevalent in the satras.

Whatever might have been the outcome of these demands, the Congress government was not willing to concede them, but the Sanmilan succeeded in making the agrarian question the primary concern of the kaibartas. The demand for land reform never disappeared from the political programme of the Kaibarta Sanmilan. In 1949, the Sanmilan — in its next annual conference, held in Golaghat and widely covered in the Assamese press — again demanded that the government begin land reform and distribute land to the landless kaibartas.[155] The Sanmilan, more importantly, by bringing forth the question of the kaibartas' natural rights over resources, sought an abolition of the existing *mahaldari* system in the water bodies and urged the government to settle fisheries only with the community.

As we examine the process through which the Assamese Vaishnava peasantry and the lower-caste peasantry reconfigured their political future, it will be appropriate to briefly refer to the cultural landscape where the tribal and Assamese peasantry interacted with each other in complex ways. The tribal peasants' entry into the peasant mobilization programme of 1940s and 1950s must also been seen in the backdrop of the cultural politics of Assam. Several Assamese literary works, produced during the colonial period, are proof of this social alienation of the tribal peasantry from the larger nationalist discourse of the Assamese caste-Hindus. Many of these works succinctly narrated how this discrimination was variously put into practice. Often, this alienation was reflected in the social relations between an Assamese caste-Hindu landlord and his tribal tenants. A number of cultural practices, viz., restricting interdining or intermarriage, well-entrenched in the Assamese social system, further reinforced these discriminations. The influential *Satradhikar* of Garmur Satra in Majuli admitted that even Vaishnava religious converts were not allowed to come within the precincts of the Assamese temples: Namghar and *Kirtanghar*.[156]

It was in this setting of a widespread cultural and social discrimination that the tribal sharecroppers or tenants articulated their dissent against their Assamese landlords in a more radical language than did their Assamese counterparts. Also, crucial for the radicalization of tribal peasantry was a growing advocacy for a tribal identity in the cultural and political landscape of Assam from the early decades of twentieth century.[157] Social alienation of the tribal peasantry further reinforced the institutionalization of their economic exploitation. The limited opportunities offered by the legislative reforms, however, did not play any role in reducing the existing social inequities. Over the years, they became accustomed to the language of passive resistance which also turned out to be a tradition of political rebellion or protest. This was in sharp contrast to the social setting of an Assamese village and agrarian relations therein. The agrarian relations between an Assamese tenant and his landlord within a Vaishnava village, in particular, were continuously reinforced by the rural traditions and customs. For instance, kinship and caste played a key role in cementing a patron–client relationship between a landlord and his tenants. This was more distinct in those spheres of agrarian setting where Vaishnava religious institutions were predominant. Again, a landlord's decision to rent out his land to a sharecropper was often dependent on the considerations of caste and other socio-cultural dynamics within the village which often came to be institutionalized through the institution of khel.[158] There were instances of clashes within villages as a result of land disputes, but we have little evidence of a tenant or a sharecropper challenging the social hegemony of the landowner within the same khel. The khel supported its economically distressed members either by way of financial aid or favourable social negotiation. Anyone outside this intricate social arrangement would not only remain exposed to uncertainties but the social bonding between a tenant and the landlord would also remain fragile.

Rural Mobilization and Political Violence

Away from this complex social scenario of villages, the communist leaders continuously resorted to political violence in order to both avoid state repression and resist landlords. This relentless political violence became synonymous with the social identity of the RCPI. And years later, legends were born out of this new political culture. The RCPI adopted guerrilla tactics to resist state repression. To familiarize its cadres with the tactics and strategy of guerrilla warfare, the RCPI published a booklet titled *Guerrilla Warfare* in 1949. Cadres were given training in the use of arms. Indeed, a limited number of weapons — mostly those left by the Japanese Army during the Second World War — were collected from the state's eastern frontier. Such training often came in handy to resist police repression and also collect money from various sources. The RCPI termed such acts of collecting money as 'money action'. Official narratives predictably referred to such cases as 'dacoity' or 'robbery'. The banks, *mauzadar*s, rich traders, or landlords were the usual targets.[159] The police, between 1949 and 1950, registered 964 cases of 'dacoity' and 'robbery' committed by communist cadres.[160]

The annihilation — typical of communist mobilization — of the enemy of peasants was another aspect of peasant mobilization.[161] The communist leaders believed that this would help in garnering support for the peasant organizations as well as creating an impact at the local level. Murders were also justified on various counts. In one such instance, the police reported the murder of a 'notorious litigant of village Sibpur of Udalguri police station in Darrang ... by some of his co-villagers to get rid of formers [*sic*] unbearable *zoolum* to the people in general over land dispute'.[162] In another such incident, early in 1950, Ganga Sarma, a Congressman from Pachaniapara in Palashbari, was shot dead while he was speaking in a meeting. The police claimed that those who shot Ganga Sarma belonged to the RCPI.[163] Autobiographical accounts of the RCPI leaders described how such acts were committed as part of their mobilization tactics. The RCPI leader Tarunsen Deka, in his autobiography, admitted how the murder of Ganga Sarma took place though he denied his own involvement.[164] Towards the latter half of 1950, one Guduram Barman, another Congress worker from Belsor in Nalbari, while returning home at night, was waylaid and killed by a group of RCPI activists. In his dying declaration before the police, Guduram accused that RCPI activists had fired at him.[165] In the mid-1950s, one Bhudhar, a mauzadar of Nitaiphukhuri in Sibsagar was killed. Before his murder, he had received several anonymous letters accusing him of anti-communist activities.[166] Most of those who were killed were landowners who refused to co-operate and accept the terms laid down by the communist peasant organizations. The government claimed that there were as many as 12 murders committed by the RCPI activists in 1950.[167]

Such localized political violence against the landlords was combined with direct offensive against the police as well. In 1951, the government noted that 'a peculiar feature of rioting cases during the year was ... (how) in several districts determined attempts were made on the police parties engaged in doing their lawful duties'.[168] Often, the local KBP cadres attacked the raiding police team while the latter was trying to help the landlords in collecting their rent. In January 1949, five — many were never reported —

such cases of rioting, confinement and assault on the police were recorded in Beltola.[169] Numerous examples of such cases can be found from the neighbourhood of Guwahati where the tribal sharecroppers had shown exemplary initiative in resisting any attempt on the part of the landlords to collect rent. As state repression intensified, the RCPI also resorted to symbolic protests to challenge the government. Sporadically, its activists pulled down the India's national flag. Reporting one such incident which took place in Sarupeta, Kamrup, the police mentioned how the RCPI had 'earned notoriety in connection with the pulling down of the national flag' when 'a group of people numbering 250 led by RCPI activists pulled down the national flag and hoisted the red flag in its place'.[170]

The anti-landlord propaganda was carried out in those villages where there was a predominant presence of poor peasants and sharecroppers.[171] This helped in the instant mobilization of the whole village. The physical absence of landlords in such villages was an important factor in the mobilization of tribal peasants. Such mobilization happened in various parts of southern Kamrup, like Beltola which was chiefly characterized by the heavy presence of sharecroppers, as also in tribal-peasant-dominated areas of Darrang. The physical absence of landowners in such villages gave sufficient space to the communist organizations to mobilize the sharecroppers and make them abide by the demands of the communist organizations. Compared to this, those villages with both sharecroppers and landowners showed mixed reactions to communist activities. The presence of small landowners, but not numerically very strong, became favourable for the mobilization of peasants. Haridas Deka mentions the initial favourable response of the small landowners to the KBP's activities and their co-operation with the KBP.[172] The peasant mobilization took an effective form when the KBP or KS cadres helped the peasants in retaining the land for the next year from the landlords despite their refusal to give half of the produce as rent to the latter. Membership of the KBP or the KS also came in handy for the sharecroppers to contest litigations.[173]

The participation of small peasants, agricultural labourers and others from lower classes also helped in the radicalization of the sharecroppers' movement. The shopkeepers, petty moneylenders, and those in the lowest rank of police service often supported the movement. Official accounts are full of such instances. For instance, we are told how in Janji, Sibsagar, Sorukan Gogoi, a shopkeeper of Garmur, allowed the 'communist workers' to 'hold group meetings and carry on propaganda'.[174] Or, in Amguri, Kanthiram Gogoi, a constable posted at the Amguri police station, was 'helping the communist workers against whom warrants of arrest have been issued to absconding by giving them information'.[175] Aniram Basumatari who was a police constable would become an important leader of the KBP.[176] Moreover, a few in the lower ranks of the government service, like Ratneswar Gogoi and Radhika Dutta, the *gaonbura* and *mandal* of Mamun Moran village respectively, also collaborated with the communist organizations. A senior police official reported that

> underground communist workers take shelter generally either in the house of the mauzadar, the Kamrupia utensil shop on the roadside or in the hostel of Namati high school or in the premises of the Namati co-operatives or in the house of the manager of the co-operatives.[177]

But it was Bishnu Rabha who came to the centre stage of peasant mobilization and rapidly acquired a much popular and powerful image of a legendary leader. Rabha had been participating in the activities of RCPI since 1945, but he became a formal member of the party only in July 1948.[178] He travelled extensively — according to his own claim, an estimated 10,000 miles[179] — across the length and breadth of the Brahaputra valley to mobilize the peasants. His numerous writings represented a wide range of intellectual and political interests. His immense popularity amongst the tribal peasantry has been recounted in a number of literary works.[180] He worked both underground and in the open and remained at the various fronts of the party. Often, he travelled to Calcutta to interact with and take instructions from senior party leaders. Villagers too escorted him while he was trying to evade police arrest. Assisted by rural youths, Rabha could successfully penetrate the village networks and mobilize the peasants. All this ensured that the KBP leaders had to rely on him for the mobilization of peasantry.

It was his lifestyle, which was similar to the everyday life of an ordinary peasant in Assam, that considerably worked to his advantage when compared to his comrades or, for that matter, the Congress leaders. He would happily drink rice beer, dance around bonfire and tell stories in the languages of the peasants. Frequently, he would invoke historical anecdotes to explain the causes of the present miseries of the peasants.[181] Rabha could persuade the villagers through his fine musical compositions and narration of the glorious past of a locality. Time and again, he emphazised the contribution of tribal society in the making of Assamese nationality. Such efforts of his also helped in recovering the lost faith of the tribal peasants in the nationalist programme. Before becoming a communist leader, Rabha had participated in various nationalist cultural programmes, written and retold the cultural history of Assam and its people.[182] His visits to a large number of villages across the valley, long periods of stay with villagers, his mastery over a number of local languages and deep insights into the rural society and history made him a hero.[183] Rabha broke with the conventional method of party meetings and would easily mingle with people in village gatherings. In the evenings, as he interacted with and listened to villagers passionately, he could sense their anger, and recast this very anger against the landlords through creative use of language, weaving a rich fabric of political consciousness into their minds. He narrated to the villagers, for instance, even in the paddy fields, the story of how in 'another' village the KBP had succeeded in 'teaching' an appropriate lesson to the village landlord.[184] This helped in breaking the boundaries between other communist leaders and the rural population at large and thereby facilitated the entry of the former into the rural world of Assam.

The entry of communist peasant organizations into the Assamese rural world was facilitated through the careful use of an existing space of protest and resistance, with or without the aid of nationalist mobilization. Often, locally influential *sanyasis*, an influential rich peasant, or school teachers came in handy to bridge the gap between the communist peasant organizations and the peasants.[185] The local leader's participation in the mobilization process helped in wider and sustained participation of the peasants. Many local leaders had associated themselves with the everyday problems of the peasant society either at the collective level or at the individual level for a long time. The appearance of the peasant organizations in the scene only gave a new thrust to the existing understanding and ways for the resolution of those problems. At times, these local leaders crossed their conventional boundaries of activity and mobilized peasants in the adjoining areas. Dambarudhar Injal, Aniram Basumatari, or Bolo Basumatari, who began their organizational activities in the Beltola area, later moved to the remote villages of southern Kamrup. Often, a prominent local leader who was working with party leaders came from a different locality. The best example of this was the charismatic Khagen Barbarua. He was the President of the KBP during 1948–49.[186] Barbarua was also a student leader and General Secretary of the student union of Cotton College.[187] He, along with Haren Kalita and others, worked amongst the peasants in Namtiali, Messagarh, Thetamuria, Cherakapara villages of Sibsagar district. Barbarua was popular among the villagers, and the police believed that none could dare speak against him.[188] The police also claimed that the charisma of Barbarua had immensely helped a large number of RCPI cadres in Kamrup to seek shelter from the villagers. In several villages of eastern Assam, like that of Namtiali School in Sibsagar, Barbarua had large numbers of 'staunch followers'.[189] The 'Robin Hood' image of Barbarua thus occupied a substantial part of official correspondence within the Assam administration.

The emergence of local leadership was more complex, as it was associated with local customs and practices of the villagers. There also emerged a layered form of leadership. The state-level leaders and senior cadres of the peasant organizations travelled in the different areas and gave instructions about the strategy to be adopted by the village-level leaders. Often, outside leadership withdrew from acts of direct mobilization creating space for the local poor peasants to take the lead. However, this happened mostly when the police repression compelled the senior leaders to go underground. Such tactics did not go unnoticed and the government in one such instance reported how, in the wake of police repression in Sibsagar, the KBP decided 'to transfer the leadership of the Kishan movement to poor *jangi kishans* to make it a success'.[190]

As the state oppression increased and penetrated new areas, both the KBP and the KS reoriented their political programmes to achieve collaboration, even if it turned out to be of a temporary nature, between the Assamese middle and poor peasants. Such an urgency to reconfigure their attitude towards the middle peasants was conditioned by a new ground reality. The Assamese landlords had manipulated the state machinery and laws to counter the challenges from poor peasants and sharecroppers. This combined challenge of the government and the landlords to the sharecroppers could be overcome, as both KBP and KS realized, only through an alliance between middle and poor peasants. Also, there were already signs of trouble amongst the sharecroppers as many of them began to pay rent to the landlords indicating rupture in their solidarity. The best opportunity for such an alliance between the Assamese middle and small peasants came in the wake of the government's paddy procurement programme when the Assamese middle and small peasants showed signs of hostility to the government as well as to the landlords. The KBP was never tired of highlighting the necessity of roping the middle peasants in their programme of peasant mobilization though it did not consistently accomodate their concerns. Haridas Deka, when informed that the only opponent in the Kendukuchi area against KBP's political programme was a local *mahajan* who was also a middle peasant owning a small grocery shop, a bullock cart and a few *puras* of land, he readily agreed that 'that such mahajans are found in most of the villages. They are not our class enemy. They should be taught with our ideology and objective. They should be either brought into our fold or make them neutral'.[191]

Deka indeed succeeded in convincing the mahajan and the KBP activists to trust each other. The mahajan admitted that many like him had been living in fear of a communist attack. He also emphasized that he had never been against the communists despite getting warnings from them nor had he been an informer for the police. A temporary friendship was ensured between the mahajan and the communist workers. The former also agreed to help the latter as and when needed.

The communist peasant organizations also worked closely with the wandering *sadhus* (monks) though their social presence was limited in Assam, to mobilize the peasants. Sadhus were found distributing communist leaflets in different parts of western Assam.[192] Police arrested five such sadhus in Guwahati and Darrang in 1949. The *Sadiniya Assamiya* claimed that one sadhu called Hansa Fakir took a leading role in organizing an attack on a landowner in Kamrup.[193]

The cadres of the peasant organizations often attacked those who defied the decision of their leaders. The *Dainik Assamiya* reported how in February 1949 the KBP cadres and other sharecroppers set fire to several houses of one Motiraj, the headman of Udalbakra village in Beltola along with his 2,000 puras of paddy, since he paid rent to his landlord.[194] In another such incident, the KBP cadres burned down a Nepali sharecropper's house as he had paid rent to his landowner. Such sharecroppers had withdrawn from the movement when it became violent.

If such violence was not enough, communist groups openly fought against each other. The RCPI accused the CPI of being an agent of the Russian government and the CPI accused the RCPI of being an enemy of Russia.[195] The acrimony reached a high point by 1952 when the CPI-led KSs began distributing pamphlets against the KBP. The CSP maintained a critical distance from such acrimonious rivalries between the KBP and the KS. But often, it lashed out at the KBP for instigating the peasants to take to arms. Notwithstanding the limited practical difficulties faced by the communist peasant organizations, such inter-party rivalries nonetheless left a deep scar on the political culture of the state. The government was also quick to capitalize on these differences.

Political violence was not limited to rural areas only. In July 1949, a meeting of the Indian Peoples Theatre Association attended by artists, literati and railway workers at Naliapool in Dibrugarh turned violent and led to several deaths.[196] This violence in an urban area immediately provoked a sharp reaction from the nationalist Assamese intelligentsia.[197] The government also intensified the suppression of communists.[198] Not everybody agreed with the nationalist condemnation of Naliapool violence. For instance, Jyotiprasad Agarwala, who was himself a liberal and well-known sympathizer of the communists and who also attended this meeting, thought otherwise. Jyotiprasad denounced political violence but persuasively argued that political violence committed by people was primarily a result of the failure of the Indian nation-state.[199] But such reasoning could hardly convince the Assamese nationalists. Armed with increasing support of the nationalist intelligentsia against political violence, the government even claimed: '[W]e have won the first round in our fight against the communists'.[200]

Nevertheless, years of intense peasant mobilization failed to build up a common platform for the various peasant organizations across caste and community divisions. The support came mostly from the sharecroppers, and poor and landless peasants among the tribals who were at the forefront. The Assamese middle peasants extended their support but, over and over again, they also became targets of the communist cadres. Unlike their counterparts in western Assam, where the peasant mobilization was mostly of the tribal sharecroppers the caste-Hindu Assamese peasants in the districts of eastern Assam fully participated in the movement. The communist mobilization of the 1940s both ignored and manipulated the social complexities of the Assamese peasant society. But such tactics of peasant mobilization was pitifully dismissive of the crucial transition which had taken place in the social world of the Assamese and tribal peasants. The nationalist and ethnic aspirations of the communities — an imperative element in the peasant society — rarely found a place in the communist political programmes. This increasingly alienated them from the cultural politics of rural Assam. The resistance of the communist-inspired poor peasants, sharecroppers and landless peasants to state repression was essentially short-lived. The communist mobilization of the peasantry had played an essential role in crystallizing an agrarian question within the nationalist political programme and had helped open new political possibilities away from the latter. In essence, the communist mobilization of the peasantry successfully integrated this agrarian question into the political landscape of Assam but failed to sustain it in an imaginative fashion. How the Assamese nationalist politics significantly appropriated this space in the subsequent decades is further examined in the next chapter.

Plate 6.1: Letter from Bishnuprasad Rabha to his communist colleagues, 1953 expressing concern about the ideological stand of RCPI

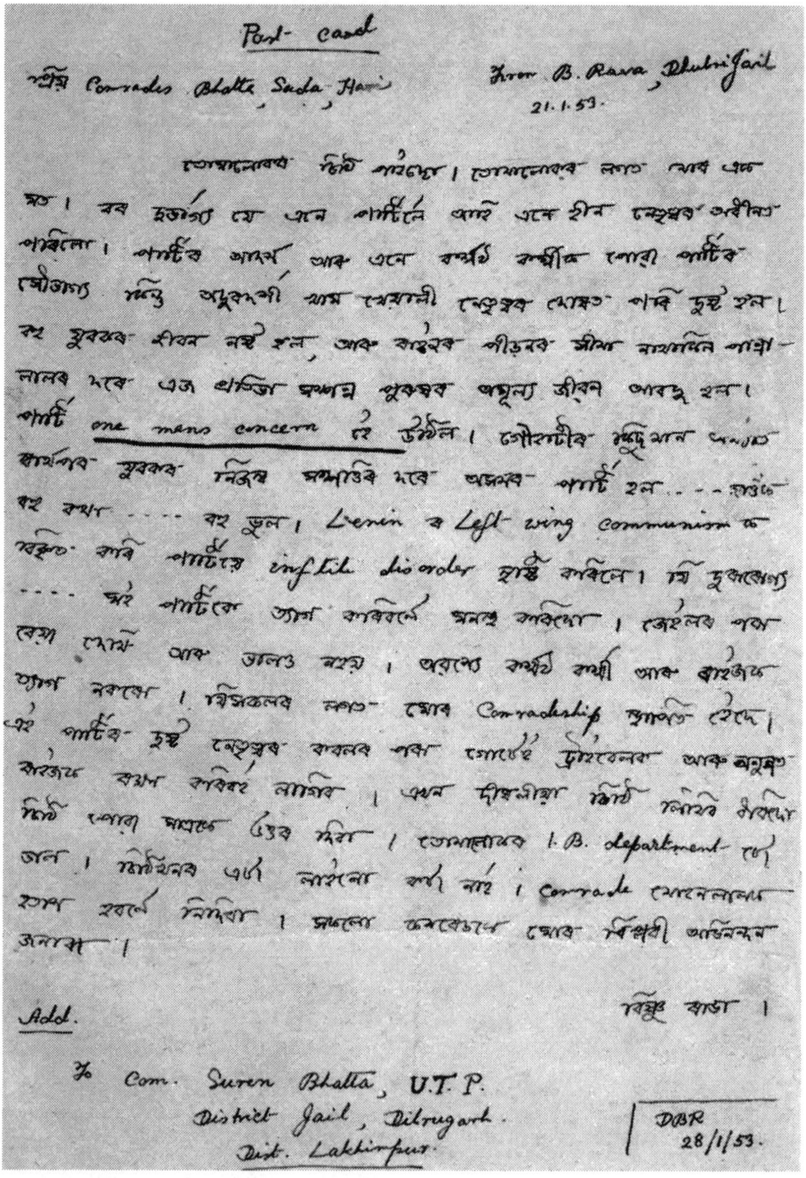
Post card

Comrades Bhatta, Suda, Hari

From B. Rava, Dhubri Jail
21.1.53.

[illegible]

Add.

℅ Com. Suren Bhatta, U.T.P.
District Jail, Dibrugarh.
Dist. Lakhimpur

DBR
28/1/53.

Source: Author's personal collection.

Plate 6.2: News of political violence in Naliapool, Dibrugarh, July 1949

ডিব্ৰুগড়ত কমিউনিষ্টৰ ধ্বংসাত্মক আচানৰ ঘটনা

নলীয়াপুলত পুলিচ কৰ্ম্মচাৰী হত্যা আৰু উন্মত্ত জনতাৰ লগত পুলিচৰ সংঘৰ্ষ

৬ জন পুলিচ আহত দুগৰাকী তিৰোতা নিহত : ৪২৫ জন গ্ৰেপ্তাৰ আৰু ১৪৪ ধাৰা জাৰি

ডিব্ৰুগড়—স্থানীয় নলীয়াপুল ৰেলৱে কলনীত যোৱা দেওবাৰে ঘটা ঘটনাৰ সংশ্ৰৱত ৪২৫ জনক গ্ৰেপ্তাৰ কৰা হৈছে আৰু মঙ্গলবাৰৰ পৰা নগৰত ১৪৪ ধাৰা জাৰি কৰা হৈছে।

প্ৰকাশ যে সেইদিনা এটা জৰুৰী কাৰণে কলনীলৈ যোৱা টাউন হাব ইন্সপেক্টৰ শ্ৰীযুত গোবিন্দ দাস নিৰুদ্দেশ হয় আৰু পিছত ডেপুটী কমিচনাৰ আৰু সশস্ত্ৰ পুলিচ বাহিনীয়ে প্ৰায় পাচঘণ্টা বিচাৰি উক্ত দাসৰ মৰাশটো উলঙ্গ অৱস্থাত এটা কুৱাৰ ভিতৰত পুতি থোৱা অৱস্থাত উদ্ধাৰ কৰে। তেওঁৰ সাজ-পাৰ আৰু বিকলভাৱেটো পোৱা নগল। এই পুলিচ কৰ্মচাৰীজনক নিৰ্দ্দয়ভাৱে হত্যা কৰা হৈছে বুলি আৰু নলীয়াপুল কলনীৰ এই ঘটনাৰ লগত কমিউনিষ্টৰ "চৰকাৰী কৰ্মচাৰী হত্যা আৰু ধ্বংসাত্মক কাৰ্য্যৰ আঁচনিৰ সম্পৰ্কে আছে বুলি ধাৰণা কৰা হৈছে।

কলনীত পুলিচ হাব ইন্সপেক্টৰৰ অনুসন্ধানৰ উদ্দেশ্যে বিচাৰি ফুৰোতে শ শ উত্তেজিত নৰ-তিৰোতাই নানা ধৰণৰ ধ্বনি কৰি এছিড আৰু শিলগুটি মাৰিবে ডেপুটী কমিচনাৰক আক্ৰমণ কৰে। আত্মৰক্ষাৰ কাৰণে পুলিচে প্ৰথমতে লাঠি চালনা কৰে আৰু সাৱধানসূচক গুলী মাৰে। তেতিয়াও উন্মত্ত জনতা ছত্ৰভঙ্গ নোহোৱাত পুলিচে বাধ্য হৈ গুলী চালনা কৰে। তেতিয়াও জনতাই সঙ্কেতসূচক ধ্বনি কৰি পুলিচক বাধা দিবলৈ চেষ্টা কৰি থাকে। উন্মত্ত জনতাৰ এটা দলে কিছুমান তিৰোতাক আগতলৈ পুলিচৰ গাত এছিড মাৰে। ফলত তিনি জন পুলিচৰ মুখ আৰু গা পোৰে।

এই ঘটনাত মুঠতে ছজন চিপাহী আহত হয় আৰু পুলিচৰ গুলী চালনাৰ ফলত এজনী তিৰোতা মৰে আৰু আন এজনী আহত হয়। পিছত হাস্পতালত সেইজনী তিৰোতাৰো মৃত্যু ঘটে। গুলী লাগি আন দুজন মানুহো আহত হয়।

সদিয়া সময়ত পুলিচে কলনীৰ পৰা প্ৰায় ৩০০ মানুহক গ্ৰেপ্তাৰ কৰি আনে। এওঁলোকৰ ভিতৰত ছাত্ৰ, ৰেলৱে কৰ্মচাৰী জড়িত আছে আৰু এজন সাধুবেশী মানুহো ওলাইছে। তেওঁ কোনোবা ডাঙৰ কমিউনিষ্ট নেতা বুলি সন্দেহ হয়।

উন্মত্ত জনতাৰ ভিতৰত পুৰুষ স্ত্ৰী নিৰ্ব্বিশেষে নেপালী, নগা, বঙালী আৰু অসমীয়া মানুহ আছিল।

প্ৰকাশ যে সদৌ অসম শান্তি সভা উপলক্ষে সেই ৰেলৱে কলনীত ১, ৫, ১৬ আৰু ১৭ জুলাই তাৰিখে "গণনাট্য সঙ্ঘৰ" উদ্যোগত অভিনয় চলিছিল। এই অনুষ্ঠানৰ কাৰণে বিভিন্ন ঠাইৰ পৰা তেওঁলোকৰ মনোনীত দৰ্শক আহিছিল। কেইজনমান বাহিৰা মানুহে অনুষ্ঠানত যোগ দিবলৈ চেষ্টা কৰা বাবে ১৬ তাৰিখে ৰাতি ভাও হতাহতি হয়। এই ঘটনা সম্পৰ্কে থানাত ৰিপৰ্ট দিয়া বাবেই পিচদিনা হাবইন্সপেক্টৰ জনে তিনিজন চিপাহী আৰু এজন পুলিচ কৰ্মচাৰীক লৈ কলনীত সেই সম্পৰ্কে তদন্ত কৰিবলৈ গৈছিল।

কলনীত হোৱা এইবোৰ অভিনয়ৰ অনুষ্ঠান আচলতে কমিউনিষ্টসকলৰ ধ্বংসাত্মক কাৰ্য্যৰ আলোচনা সভা বুলিহে সন্দেহ কৰা হৈছে।

ঘটনাৰ পিছত পুলিচে কলনী খানাতালাচ কৰি বহুতো এছিড বাল্ব, এছিডৰ পাত্ৰ ডেগাৰ, হাতবোমা আৰু কিছুমান কমিউনিষ্ট কাগজ-পত্ৰ পায়।

ঘটনাত নিহত হোৱা তিৰোতাগৰাকীৰ গাত পোৱা কাগজ পত্ৰত চৰকাৰী কৰ্মচাৰীক হত্যা কৰা আৰু ধ্বংসাত্মক কাৰ্য্য সম্পৰ্কীয় সম্পূৰ্ণ আঁচনি এখন পোৱা গৈছে বুলি প্ৰকাশ।

Source: Department of Historical and Antiquarian Studies, Guwahati, 1951.

7

Peasants, Law and Nationalist Identity: An Unfulfilled Dream

Years after they began their struggle against the landlords and government, the sharecroppers and landless peasants in Assam were under the impression that they would win. They gained little concession either from the landlords or from the government. The landlords continued to evict the sharecroppers. They ensured their complete control over their landed property. The widespread practice of landlords seeking equal share of the produce continued. But the sharecroppers did have some relief. In many places, landlords could not enforce a regime of exploitation any more. Landless villagers went out in search of land. They went out to far-off places; they reclaimed forested lands and converted these patches into agricultural fields. They undertook this strenuous physical work on their own. The government did not give any legal recognition to their newly reclaimed fields. But lack of tenurial security did not bother them much, as the Assam Forest Department was busy with the task of timber extraction, lacked understanding of its territorial limits and did not have any mechanism to gauge the intensity of forest clearance by them.[1]

As discussed in the previous chapter, the communists, on their part, meanwhile got busy with something else. Months before the first general election in 1951–52, their leaders became sceptical about their own political ideology and strategy. The Communist Party of India (CPI) admitted that the Ranadive line that it had so passionately pursued since 1948 could provide little relief to its political programme. They rejected their resolution of armed struggle in 1951.[2] They also expressed their willingness to participate in the first general election of the country. The Pannalal Dasgupta faction of the Revolutionary Communist Party of India

(RCPI), the dominant group in Assam, also followed a similar line. Pannalal took to the Gandhian political methods.[3] There was growing dissatisfaction within the party about its methods of attaining political goals. Many began to shift loyalties to the CPI. Dissatisfaction amongst the left leaders and activists became apparent. In 1953, Bishnu Rabha, the charismatic and impulsive peasant leader, wrote from prison to another comrade lamenting how leaders' individualistic concerns had led to the peasant politics' downfall.[4] Sudden change in the tone of communist programmes left the peasant movement leaderless. The CPI contested the first Indian election. The RCPI did so in the second election of 1957. In the election to the Assam State Assembly, the communist parties registered an impressive presence and a few of their leaders were elected into the Assembly.[5] They initiated some brilliant debates in the Assembly on the agrarian question. Their concerns were mostly restricted to an effective implementation of tenurial laws, but they did not muster enough numbers to pressurize the Congress nationalists to bring some radical amendments in land laws.

The communists' entry into electoral politics, however, had limited impact on the peasants' struggle. The sharecroppers and landless had to carry on their struggle against the landlords and continue their search for land. Their struggle, however, took different forms and became less violent. The communists, matured with the recently gained experience of being part of the electoral politics and leading years of movement, began to mobilize the disgruntled peasants afresh. They went back to the sharecroppers and landless peasants. This renewed mobilization rapidly gained strength in several pockets. The revival of communist rural mobilization, however, could not restore the communist peasant organizations, the Krishak Banua Panchayat (KBP) in particular, its former height of popularity. They had partially lost their credibility, and had become a fortress behind which the struggling peasants took shelter. The new tenancy laws — and the promises associated with them — increasingly drifted the peasants away from the communist parties. The latter also failed to creatively integrate these legal instruments into their political programmes. Even assuming that they had the will, they failed to visualize the enormity of the problem created by the enactment of new laws.

Tenancy and rent disputes in the civil courts fast emerged as an important form of the sharecroppers' movement. Civil suits, however, could hardly bring relief to the sharecroppers. Further, the bureaucracy was hardly willing to give them any concession. In most cases, the civil suits were decreed in favour of the landlords.[6] One reason behind this dramatic defeat of the sharecroppers was the fact that they did not have a battery of lawyers who could defend their cases in the courts. The Bar in Assam had a long experience in civil or rent suits. One could hardly make any difference between the interest of the Bar and landlords. Before the coming of the Assam Adhiar Rights and Protection Act — the interests of the landlords being well protected under the law — it was easier for the Bar to defend the interests of the tenants. The Bar, though, fought a few cases on the rent and tenancy question, but their impact was mostly localized. The passing of the Adhiar Rights and Protection Act left the sharecroppers alone to decide their own fate. A nationalist bureaucracy which used to patronize the tenants also seemed to withdraw its support. In the 1950s, on several occasions, when sharecroppers sought the help of the Assam Revenue Department to allow them to pay rent in cash, the latter refused such concession by arguing that the existing legal provisions could not compel the landlords to receive rent in cash.

Meanwhile, two other pieces of legislation occupied central attention and had enormous impact on the agrarian relations. Both the Assam State Acquisition of the Zamindari Act of 1951 (hereafter Zamindari Abolition Act) and the Assam Fixation of Ceiling on Land Holdings Act of 1956 (hereafter the Ceiling Act) had a direct bearing on the landed interests of the Assamese nationalists. A bill to abolish zamindari was introduced in the Assam Legislative Assembly in 1949 when the sharecroppers' movement in the *raiyatwari* areas was at its peak. The scope and provisions of the bill were modelled after the United Provinces Zamindari Abolition Bill.[7] Steered by the Nehruvian Congress leadership, the United Provinces model retained provisions of both adequate compensation for the zamindars and adoption of raiyatwari system as a uniform model for the entire country. The zamindars of Goalpara challenged this bill and used various channels to register their protest. In a memorandum submitted to the Assam government, the zamindars cited many reasons which they thought were reasonable enough for the continuance of their rights as landlords. The zamindars reminded the government that they were not 'ordinary zamindars ... They are like the feudal lords ... They exercised great influence in the locality. The Zamindars played a great role in sobering influence on the tenantry'.[8]

The bill despite strong protest from the zamindars — in the form of both legal and political battles — was finally passed in 1951. But this would soon result in a protracted legal battle by the zamindars in defence of their privileges. Trying to sabotage the Act, Raja Bhairebendra Narayan Bhup, zamindar of Bijni, who led the motley group of zamindars and ranks of intermediaries argued before the Supreme Court of India that the Act 'was not enacted according to law and infringed the fundamental rights'[9] of the zamindars as provided under the Indian Constitution. The Supreme Court was, however, not convinced by the zamindars' argument and upheld the Act in 1956. The Act became operative initially in Goalpara from April 1956 and later on in Cachar.[10] The Act abolished the zamindari estates and provided tenurial rights to the tenants along with both occupancy and hereditary rights. The zamindars not only got compensation but they also manipulated the Act through fraudulent transfer of land to someone else's name or large-scale destruction of forest wealth in their estates.[11] The zamindars' other solace was that they also had won the appreciation of the Assamese literati through their patronage of Assamese language and literature. But more importantly, it soon became clear that a mere piece of legislation could not succeed in displacing the vast number of intermediaries between the zamindars and tenants.

The social impact of the Ceiling Act was weaker compared to the Zamindari Abolition Act as it was rarely put into action. Even if it was executed it would have covered only a very small section of the landlords in Assam.[12] Those who faced the sudden volte-face of the government and had to part with their land to the tenants or landless peasants reacted aggressively. The memory of the Ceiling Act has kept haunting many Assamese landowning families till date. But the Act failed to ameliorate the problem of landlessness. These administrative measures or new legal instruments nonetheless began to shape the rural mobilization in Assam. It did not take long to make room for nationalist politics within the broader framework of tenancy politics. The penultimate moment of this transition of tenancy politics to identity politics was the year 1979 in which the Assamese peasants, students and middle class joined ranks to defend a nation's interest — land and resource. The following sections examine how this transition unfolded.

Hopes of Land Settlement

> It seems that our State Government ... declare [*sic*] a clear cut land policy, as a result of which the problem is becoming and more complex day by day and one does not know where it will lead us ultimately.
>
> Assam Pradesh Congress Committee, 1955[13]

By the time the new Indian Constitution was adopted, the growing peasant discontent across the country could not any more be controlled merely through half-hearted measures. Promises of land reforms had to be translated into reality. Beginning with the UP Zamindari Abolition Act, other states also saw a slow beginning of land reform. Soon, however, these reforms faced legal challenges from landlords. Implementation of land reforms thus got delayed and complicated. A part of the task of land reform was left to the Indian Planning Commission to articulate. On the other hand, completion of zamindari abolition, imposition of ceiling on upper limits of landholdings, tenurial security, and consolidation of land holdings became the crucial areas in which state governments were asked to formulate laws.[14] Not all of them were successful and the All India Congress Committee (AICC) was forced to re-look into the question of land reform in the second half of the 1950s.[15]

This general trend was set to define the tone of the Assam government's agrarian reform programme. The experience of 1948–52 was quite worrying for the Assam government. The communist mobilization had given the Congress a tough time in consolidating its rural social bases. As discussed in Chapter 5, the outline was already spelled immediately after Independence. As one such measure, the Bordoloi government, by amending the Assam Land Revenue Regulation of 1886, introduced the institution of 'tribal belt and block' to safeguard land alienation amongst the tribal peasantry. This mechanism, however, was the result of a simplistic understanding of the tribal economy. This understanding ignored the complex growth of legal categories and complexities of the agrarian economy in the valley. In the long run, this institution never became successful in checking land alienation and ensuring tenurial security of the tribal peasantry. Meanwhile, communist rural mobilization urging the government to settle peasants on the land acquired from unploughed government land or even from the wastelands of the tea gardens continued to intensify.[16]

But more was yet to come in the 1950s. However, as mentioned in the previous chapters, the Assam Pradesh Congress Committee (APCC), since 1945, had begun to re-orient its agrarian reform programme.[17] This was a response to the growing popularity of the communists amongst the tribal and others in the countryside.[18] In 1950, the APCC also formed a committee to organize the agricultural labourers, landless peasants and sharecroppers of the province.[19] That this only led to further consolidation of the communist mobilization became more than apparent after the result of the first general election was out. A year later, in 1951, the APCC admitted that despite some attempts, the question of landlessness was yet to be resolved successfully.[20] The result was an endorsement of a policy of land distribution by the APCC amongst the poor or landless Assamese and tribal peasants.

At the same time, bringing modifications into its existing land settlement policy, the Assam government, in 1950, declared that no Muslim peasant from East Pakistan would be entitled to land settlement without its special permission.[21] This strong stand of the Congress helped in wooing the nationalists in Assam but could hardly be an effective mechanism for addressing the tenancy question. At the same time, though hard-pressed by its own peasantry, the Assam government also tried — under pressure from the Indian government, and also Nehru's strong advice to the Assamese Congress leadership to be less sectarian — to seek a way out to accommodate those who had recently migrated from East Pakistan after partition. There was no general consensus among the Assamese political leadership on whether refugees from East Pakistan should be given land to settle on or not. The Assam government led by Bishnuram Medhi carried out a programme of land settlement for these immigrants after 1951.

By the beginning of the Second Five Year Plan period, it became clear that, despite the introduction of legal and administrative measures, the problems of tenancy rights and land settlement had only worsened. It was very rare for land settlement measures to be seriously put into action, even if its implementation meant favouring only the rich. At several places, the Congress had to bear the brunt of peasant discontent. Several Assamese Congress members wanted the APCC to seriously look into the land reform measures and bring some relief as mandated within the AICC land reform programme.[22] A proposal for the formation of a Land Development Advisory Committee was readily agreed upon by the Assam government. Very soon, these committees came to be constituted by those whose allegiance to the Congress was well known and who were hardly in a position to defend the interests of the poor. The committees awarded land settlement to the rich or whom they considered as potential followers of the Congress.

Rural discontent, in the meantime, continued to grow. The bureaucracy readily blamed the sharecroppers and the landless for their failure to reap the benefits of the laws and institutions. They questioned whether the tenants or sharecroppers were at all aware of the provisions of the Acts that had been instituted by the Assam government. Apprising the government of the larger scenario, a senior bureaucrat in the Assam Revenue Department had no hesitation in saying that 'our state seems to be lacking not so much in the legislation as in implementation. Implementation involves organization, training, propaganda, staff, and those in turn involve money'.[23]

Notwithstanding such attempts, flocks of landless villagers continued to move out from their densely populated villages or recently flooded villages in search of land. Was there enough land available at the disposal of the government to pursue a liberal land settlement policy? In 1957, the Assam government could not give a firm answer to a question asked by Khagendranath Barbarua, the firebrand RCPI leader, in the Assam Legislative Assembly. Despite the government's silence on this matter, which was whether sufficient land was available for a massive land reform programme or not, the answer was apparent in several official reports. In the 1960s, the Revenue Department made it clear that the state did have enough land for distribution amongst the landless peasants.[24] Another survey put the figure of landless peasants at 15.6 per cent of the total population of the province; the former was put at 1.2 million. The survey also noted that an estimated 52.3 per cent population did have less than 3 acres of land.[25] Official estimates published as late as 1990s by the Assam government noticeably indicated a smaller landholding pattern — an average of 1 hectare per peasant family — which was a clear indicator of scarcity of agricultural land. The government apparently admitted that a sizeable section — 16 per cent of the total landless population — of the rural population was practically landless in the state after one decade of Independence.[26] The actual number of landless population would have been higher since this figure included only those who had only a bare minimum of land to subsist on. If one considers those who held some additional land but could not sustain themselves, the figure would be more.

The only option before the Assam government, then, was to distribute land in the government-owned forests or the grazing reserves. The APCC — as renamed after Independence — openly articulated its position in this matter. Bimala Prasad Chaliha, the President of APCC, in a letter written to the Assam government seeking land for landless peasants of Sibsagar, wrote that

> the problem of landless agriculturalists is gradually assuming a great magnitude. I have no doubt that if the present states of things are allowed to continue the reactionary forces will take full advantage of the situation and it will go out of control before long. I am one who is against de-reservation of Forests Reserves but so far Sibsagar ... is concerned since no waste lands available I am obliged to suggest that land is provided to the landless people if necessary by de-reservation of one of the Forest Reserves.[27]

This meant that the government needed to pursue its land settlement programme more persuasively. Chaliha had no doubt that the government-owned forest lands should be the new site of land reclamation. This reclamation could be achieved with the tacit support of the Revenue Department. The government was also not against according the Revenue Department priority over the Forest Department — the custodian of the forest lands — in deciding the affairs of the forest lands. Giving further impetus to this growing concern, the government, in 1958, adopted a resolution, to distribute land from forest lands, tea gardens, grazing reserves, or any government land among landless people.[28] Gradually, the Forest Department was asked to virtually withdraw from asserting its absolute right to various government-owned forests in the state. There is no available statistics to know how much land was actually distributed from the forests. The Assam Forest Department was able to regain its control over forested tracts only after 1980 — when the Indian

Forest Conservation Act was passed — leading to an acrimonious struggle between the Revenue and Forest Department.[29]

In 1963, the Standing Committee of the Assam Congress Parliamentary Committee on Forests strongly advised the Forest Department to explore as much as possible the possibility of settling land in the Un-classed State Forests. The party, however, took a cautious position. It suggested that precaution should also be taken to avoid clearance of Sal-containing tracts.[30] It so happened that by 1970, the Revenue Department became the *de-facto* authority in these forest areas and began to distribute lands among the landless peasants. The Revenue Department aggressively pressurized the Forest Department to explore possibilities of deforestation of more forested tracts for peasant cultivation[31] and this encouraged landless peasants to continue to migrate into the forested tracts and reclaim land, a process that went on till the 1980s.[32] Most of this migration happened whenever there was flood-induced erosion or other such natural calamities. Those who became landless after mortgaging their lands to the moneylenders also joined those who went out in search of land.[33] A few amongst them were those who, like those who migrated to Nambor Reserved Forests, also became victims of displacemental works.[34] The peasants who reclaimed land in these forested lands, however, never got any tenurial right over their lands. Their unsecured occupancy soon became a rallying point for their political mobilization.

As the peasants settled down in these forest areas, they began to face hostility from various quarters. The first challenge came from the tea plantation companies in Nambor-Doyang in the latter half of 1960s. They parleyed with the administration to evict peasants who had occupied their land. This led to occasional evictions in the late 1960s and early 1970s. Peasants protested mostly through negotiation with the district administration to retain their occupancy rights. Such evictions were not really supported by the Assam government and hence never acquired a momentum. But soon peasants not only sought government interventions but also went on a path of political struggle. The first-ever peasants' struggle to secure their land rights began in 1968 in Doyang. They were organized by left and socialist organizations. Several hundreds of peasants re-asserted their claim for control over lands which they had occupied in the tea estates.[35] While the tea plantation companies challenged the reclamation of land by the peasants in the 1960s, they succeeded in garnering strong support from the Congress government. They were thus were not evicted from the tea garden lands.

Amidst this increasing mobilization of the landless peasantry in the 1960s, the Assam government tried to implement the Bhoodan programme. The Congress government also expected relief when Vinoba Bhave, a close follower of M.K. Gandhi, 'vowed to collect 50 million acres of land from India's landlords by the simple process of "looting with love"'.[36] During his one-and-a-half years of tour in Assam during 1961–62, he tried to popularize the slogans of the Bhoodan–Gramdan movement. Bhave's initiative for the land gift (Bhoodan) movement began in 1951 when he appealed to individual landlords to grant land to the poor. A year later, he introduced the concept of the Gramdan (village-as-gift), with the villagers voluntarily transferring ownership of their lands to the village Gram Sabha (Assembly).[37] His public lectures in Assam, mixed with a fair sprinkling of knowledge of Assamese Vaishnavism, drew crowds but could deliver little. Nevertheless, drawing upon his popularity, the Congress-led Assam government passed two legislations — the Assam Gramdan Act of 1961 and the Assam Bhoodan Act of 1965 — to legitimize land donation. Till 1967, the movement could gain 23,000 acres — predominantly consisting of inferior land — out of which a mere 500 acres were distributed. In most cases, the landlords either tried to redefine their relationship with their *adhiars* by symbolically donating the land or took back the land that they had donated earlier.[38] In several places, affected landlords tried, often with success, to resist implementation of such land acquisition programmes. Landlords cited their individual right over their lands as the reason for their unwillingness.[39] The Gandhian Bhoodan–Gramdan movement failed to effectively defuse the tense agrarian relations and at the most remained as a symbolic gesture.

Despite some pro-active measures, the APCC was not still convinced of its success in securing control over the sharecroppers and landless villagers as the latter were still vulnerable to communist mobilization. The Congress knew that the challenges of 1948–52 were not yet over. The occasional amendments to legal measures also could not ensure the restoration of amicable relations between the absentee landlords and the sharecroppers.

This uneasiness became manifest in occasional public statements of the Assamese Congress leaders. The worry of the Congress became clearly evident when, in 1967, Mahendra Mohan Chaudhury, Revenue Minister in the Assam government, suggested that sharecroppers should give only one-fifth of their produce.[40] Chaudhury's pro-peasant and anti-absentee-landlord stand came to have a decisive role in challenging the left-led sharecropper movement.[41] Along with the land settlement programme, the government also carried on an eviction programme in the government-owned land. Though such programmes were undertaken sporadically, they resulted in strong protests by the peasants. In western Assam, such protests in 1966 led to the death of three tribal peasants in police firing.[42]

Pressure was put on various religious institutions — legally holding *nisf-khiraj* or *la-khiraj* lands — to be part of the government's land requisitioning programme. These institutions could offer little resistance to the programme and protect their land holdings. The increasing popularity of the Sankar Sangha movement, discussed in Chapter 6, had already weakened these landholding religious institutions. As more tenants withdrew their allegiance, the *satras* were deprived of their material and social gains. Given the changing circumstances, the government also passed the Assam State Acquisition of Lands Belonging to Religious or Charitable Institution of Public Nature Act of 1959 with an intention of acquiring land from these estates.[43] The history of this Act went back to 1958 when the Assam Hindu Religious Endowment Bill was introduced in the Assam Assembly. The bill was intended to acquire land rights for religious estates like satras or temples. Exclusion of individual landlords, who still held religious estates, resulted in protests and the bill had to wait till 1959 when it was passed as the Assam State Acquisition of Lands Belonging to Religious or Charitable Institution of Public Nature Act of 1959. Religious institutions, in the meanwhile, pressurized the Assam government to keep them outside the purview of any such land reform programme. They were able to enlist the support of several leading Congress leaders including President of India Rajendra Prasad who wrote to the Assam Congress leadership to reconsider their position. Armed with several far-reaching provisions and the government only agreeing to pay compensation to these estates, the Act immediately faced the wrath of the satras. A legal battle could not defend their interests but delayed its implementation till 1965. The execution of the Act could hardly result in the acquisition of less than 40,000 hectares of land in the next one decade.[44] Land thus recovered — often consisting of swampy, unreclaimable patches — was hardly redistributed amongst its tenants and years later the land went back to the possession of the landlords. Tenants in these estates could not get any occupancy rights in the meantime. The task of recovering land from the satras was more complex than a simple mandate of a land reform programme. The government swiftly passed the blame onto the tenants — citing their lack of any record-of-rights — for its inability to enforce the Act. Most satras, till them displaying public rivalries and citing differences in social practices and religious rituals, reorganized themselves under an already existing umbrella platform called Assam Satra Mahasabha. The renewed negotiations with the government ensured that they did not have to abdicate their rights on landed property.

Sharecroppers: Who Will Speak for Them?

The communists and socialists together could return 13 members — one-tenth of the total strength of the house — to the second Assam legislative assembly.[45] Though the Congress-led government had more than a comfortable majority, this combined communist–socialist block (there was, however, no electoral alliance between the two) was worrying the Congress a bit. But this re-alignment also helped to bring back the agrarian question into the centre stage of the Assamese polity. Unlike the experience of pre-Independence-era legislative politics, now both tenancy and landlessness became a central concern of the Assamese peasantry. Two leading communist members, Gaurishankar Bhattacharjya of CPI and Khagendranath Barbarua of RCPI, through their intelligent political rhetoric, sharpened the peasant question to attack the government programmes. The Assembly was witness to prolonged debates, which covered topics from the land settlement question to tenancy reform. Political debates inspired disgruntled peasants too. A shift from the nationalist orientation of the Assamese peasant question to tenancy rights and landlessness now forced re-arrangement of the already enacted legal measures. Under pressure, the APCC also decided to mobilize the sharecroppers under the banner of the Assam Adhiar Association, but its efforts failed to elicit any major response from the sharecroppers.[46]

Meanwhile, as mentioned earlier, various legislative enactments and their half-hearted implementation — from the Adhiar Act to the Zamindari Abolition Act — did not go well with the communist parties. State interventions were seen as a mere instrument of consolidation of vested interests of the landlords in the state bureaucracy. Pranesh Biswas, the outspoken leader of the CPI, writing in the *All India Kisan Sabha News Bulletin* in 1952 and commenting on the outcome of the Zamindari Abolition Act strongly opined how 'this Government does not visualize anything of the sort and relies absolutely on the bureaucratic machinery to introduce and implement such reforms which only hoodwink the peasants'.[47] Biswas was echoing the general mood amongst the left parties. Attention was equally drawn to the ineffectiveness of the Adhiar Act of 1948. Peasant organizations and communist leaders had already aired their disenchantment of the actual strength of the Act. That the landlords were using the provisions of the Act to safeguard their interests had already become apparent.

As it became clear, the Adhiar Act brought a number of difficulties rather than ameliorating the conditions of the *adhiars*. Assamese legislators began to demand further modifications to the original Act. The Assamese nationalist leaders also realized that all was not well in the villages. In 1951, during the September session of the Assembly, for instance, Nilamoni Phukan moved a resolution seeking further amendment to the Act. He commented that the Adhiars Act had not improved the lot of adhiars and that there were loopholes, which were not beneficial to the adhiars.[48] The government wanted to allow each peasant family an economic holding mainly on the line recommended by the Agrarian Commission.[49] Phukan again raised the issue in the September session of 1952.[50] He urged the government to amend the Act in such a way as to give the tenants occupancy rights, as well as incentives for cultivators, to improve the landholdings for landlords. Radhikaram Das pressed the issue in the same session in view of the fact that there were various defects in the act leading to constant clashes.[51]

Under pressure from the Congress nationalists, the Adhiar Act was amended in 1952. The amended Act discomfited the adhiars more; the respective rights of tenants and adhiars became distinct. The government made it clear that an adhiar was a temporary occupant and his period of occupancy extended for the period the crop was grown and harvested. Once the crop was harvested and the landlord's share delivered, he had no other right. On the other hand, in the village economy, this system of cultivation had come to stay, many members strongly argued.[52] The adhiars were categorized as temporary occupants and thus occupancy rights had been denied to them. A Congress legislator, Hareswar Das, expressed it in clear terms when he said that the government 'cannot give occupancy right to the *adhiars*'.[53]

Neither the Treasury nor the Opposition bench could ignore the pressure from the small and medium landowners. Many admitted that amongst the Assamese lower middle class, there were people having small areas of lands which they got cultivated by adhiars. 'Notwithstanding all the solitude we have for the adhiars, we cannot ignore the cases of the poor landed middle class'.[54] Gaurishankar Bhattacharjya, departing from his ideological stand taken a couple of years earlier, argued that

> there was some intermediate section in the peasant society which depended not only on their own labourers but also to a certain extent on giving their land in *adhi*. It would be really an ideal condition to see that all land belonging to the tillers only but that could not be done today. Hence in the fitness of things, there should be some provisions for protection of petty landholders like widows, schoolmasters and government clerks.[55]

This pro-small landowner position of the CPI needs a better explanation. The small and middle peasants are important constituents of the Assamese middle class, which played a significant role in the politics of Assam. The failure to get an impressive share of seats in the 1952 Assembly elections compelled the CPI to think anew about their alliance with the social groups.[56]

By 1952, as Congress retained power decisively after the general election, and as the communist mobilization slowed down, the peasant rebels formed their own peasant organizations in their own areas. These organizations, with erstwhile communist leaders amongst them, were styled similar to the KBP or the KS but were mostly locally rooted. Their primary hope was to seek an extension of the Act into their own localities. Despite the gloomy picture, sharecroppers continued to pressurize the government to extend and implement the Adhiar Act. A striking example of such widespread demand for extension of the Act into other areas was a public demonstration that took place in Dhubri, the western most town in the erstwhile zamindari district of Goalpara, where 3,000 sharecroppers, mostly smallholding and landless peasants in small batches from different rural areas under the banner of Jukta Kishan Sabha, joined in a spectacular rally and demanded the implementation of the Act in Goalpara.[57]

Similar was the story from the north bank of Brahmaputra in Kamrup where, despite a sharecropper's agitation, the Act was not extended and the sharecroppers formed the Uttarpar Krishak Sanmilan (UPKS). In a well-attended meeting in November 1953, the UPKS urged the government to make the Act operational and also to bring amendments into the Act.[58] It further stipulated that obligation to deliver one-fourth of the produce to landlords be common to all sharecroppers and that the peasant organizations be consulted by the landlords while making a fresh contract or deciding the rent. Among other demands raised by the UPKS, the most important one was that the women harvesters be legally allowed to retain one-sixth to one-eighth of the produce.[59] Resolutions, which were passed at the village level, concurred on asserting that the sharecroppers continued to be harassed.[60] Thousands of tenants belonging to various nisf-khiraj estates in Kamrup organized protests against their landlords and also highlighted the latter's coercive methods to extract more rent from the tenants.[61]

As members of the communist parties began to strongly push for securing more rights for the sharecroppers, the Assam government, in 1957, introduced several amendments supposedly aimed at lending further effectiveness to the Act so as to make it more pro-sharecropper in orientation. Yet members across party affiliations believed, for instance, that the amendments brought in 1957 to the Act would continue to support the landlords in allowing them to evict sharecroppers even on a small pretext.[62] In fact, an amendment brought in 1957 further ensured that absentee landowners could continue to rent out land with legal support. The Act mandated, supported by the Ceiling Act of 1957, that a sharecropper would be legally entitled to a maximum of three acres of land to cultivate. This ensured that a sharecropper would remain at the edge of economic marginality. Some relief did come from legal quarters. Despite appeals from the landlords, the higher courts refused to give any leniency to them even if they tried to evict their sharecroppers.[63] One observer, who sympathized with the cause of the Act and who travelled to rural areas of Kamrup, claimed that landlords had successfully evicted their sharecroppers in a widespread manner.[64]

Though by 1960, the Act had been extended to most areas of the valley, it hardly became effective as the landlords used their great influence on the bureaucracy. The communists continued to pressurize the government to implement the Adhiar Act. Public meetings also adopted resolutions urging the sharecroppers not to give more than one-fourth of the standing crop to their landlords.[65] Public oaths were taken by the sharecroppers to resist the landowners if they tried to transfer land to any other sharecroppers than the current ones. At the same time, the Congress admitted its utter failure to implement the land reform programme. In 1964, the All India Congress Committee (AICC) instructed the APCC to form a committee to look into the land reform question in the state.[66] Sarat Chandra Sinha, President of the APCC — and later the Chief Minister of the state — as member of the committee admitted that despite some legislative and bureaucratic measures, the condition of tenants had not seriously improved. He clandestinely admitted that neither the Adhiar Act nor the Ceiling Act had been implemented with serious intentions. Land acquired under the Ceiling Act till the middle of 1964 was a mere 18,000 acres affecting only 262 landlord families.[67]

The Deepening of the Agrarian Crisis

The political history of Assam took a new turn after 1960. This was the period of Assamese nationalist mobilization centred on questions of language, infiltration from East Pakistan and severe food crisis in the mid-1960s. Assam also witnessed a number of other political developments like re-organization of the territorial boundaries of the state and emerging political relationship with the hill districts. The Assamese language movement which erupted during 1960–61 successfully polarized the Assamese and Bengali communities in both the Brahmaputra and Barak valleys, as the Surma valley came to be increasingly known after Partition.[68] Political repercussions of a powerful movement demanding a petroleum refinery in the state had not yet died down either.[69] At the same time, a series of natural disasters had already further worsened the land crisis. Devastating floods repeatedly occurring between 1956 and 1967 in the Brahmaputra valley resulted in a massive loss of agricultural land.[70] To varying degrees, the Assamese peasants also became a partner in these various Assamese nationalist-led political and cultural movements. Their participation contributed to the strength of these movements.

While the peasant agitations became more widespread, though often scattered, the widespread nature of these agitations considerably cemented the social base of these movements. Meanwhile, scarcity of land was quickly translated into a political slogan. That unrestricted migration from East Pakistan into Assam had contributed to this increasing land scarcity began to be discussed in the public domain. This semantic shift — identifying migration causing land scarcity — would play a critical role in slowly reshaping the agrarian question. Even the Assamese communists — sympathetic to the cause of the international proletariat — articulated their opposition to immigration as early as 1946 as a means of solving the emerging land question.[71] On the other hand, Assamese landlords increasingly engaged erstwhile East Bengali immigrants or those who had arrived recently and could work as sharecroppers.

The second half of the 1960s was also gripped by a spell of food deficit, the second one after 1950. Despite contemporary observers' understanding that Assam always remained a food-surplus province, it was not always true.[72] Since the mid-nineteenth century, the Brahmaputra valley had chiefly imported rice to feed its population.[73] A decline in the import of rice to the valley, together with a fall in the local production, led to a localized food crisis. The victims of the food crisis were not only the poor who could not afford to buy, but also the sizeable section of Assamese urban middle class. The impact was thus felt throughout Assam. Deaths due to starvation in western Assam were widely reported.[74] On its part, the government tried to ameliorate the food deficit by increasing the import of food-stuffs, procurement of paddy from individual peasants and keeping an eye on smuggling and hoarding.[75] Also, much to the dissatisfaction of peasants, the price of paddy was fixed at a low rate. Paddy procurement, at the same time, emerged as a cause of serious concern and often faced widespread resistance from the peasants.[76]

As the government failed to effectively handle the food crisis, the left parties successfully demonstrated across the state. These demonstrations demanded that the government not only ensure proper supply of food-stuffs, but also reduce the discrimination between the urban and rural population and ensure equitable distribution of land amongst the landless or those who possessed only less than one acre of land. Left parties also demanded that paddy price be increased.[77] Others, including a majority of Congressmen, highlighted the issues of food smuggling and the increasing growth of population as a result of 'infiltration' from East Pakistan as reasons for this continuous food crisis.

Opposition parties also challenged the government for its failure to effectively implement land reform programmes. Protests thus became widespread. In 3 November 1967, demonstrations led by the RCPI in Nowgaon resulted in clashes with the police and eventually the administration had to promulgate a curfew to keep the situation from going out of control.[78] Faced with strong opposition, the government admitted its failure to go ahead with land reform and even suggested how, despite limited availability of agricultural land in the state, 'the influential men of our society manage to get more land through manipulation, thereby depriving the needy'.[79]

The increasing peasant mobilization also came to be reported with some frequency in the Assamese press in the 1960s. Meetings or demonstrations were organized in different parts of the state, mostly in the countryside, by the peasant wings of the communist parties. The primary demand of these demonstrations was tenurial right for the sharecroppers or land for the landless peasantry. Most of these demonstrations, however, could not take an effective form in the early years of the 1960s, as a majority of left leaders were put behind bars on the eve of the India–China War in 1962.[80] Their release after a year and subsequent ideological split within the CPI in 1964 brought a temporary halt to rural protests. The split was largely due to ideological differences within the CPI about the political assessment of contemporary India.[81] The break-away group — now known as the Communist Party of India-Marxist (CPI-M) — thought that, unlike a positive political attitude shown by their erstwhile colleagues towards the Congress-led government, the working-class militancy and peasant radicalism still held sway. The Assam unit of CPI was also not far from this all-India split. This split, however, was to have little impact on restricting the communist mobilization of the peasantry. Rural unrest was easily translated into visible and significant political mobilization by the powerful networks of left peasant organizations. Well-attended meetings of the communist peasant organizations encouraged peasants to occupy land from tea gardens and other government-owned lands. Inspired by this renewed mobilization, in October 1967, several hundred landless people attempted to occupy land from one of the tea gardens in Lakhimpur.[82] The police arrested hundreds of them. The district administration reiterated that the unused land in tea gardens would be required for immediate expansion of this garden.

Rural protest did not go unheeded and resulted in some crucial state intervention having far-reaching ramifications in the state polity. The conservative Assamese press found these protests crucial to the political development in the state. In 1968, the Assam government reformulated its land distribution policy. The government knew well that a large number of landless people had already reclaimed land from the government-owned forests and grazing reserves. The regularization of these settlements was given priority and the government agreed to provide them with *patta*. It agreed to legalize up to a maximum of 8 bighas of such land from amongst those who had reclaimed land till January 1967. The decision to settle Assamese peasants in the grazing reserves was bound to disturb the lucrative dairy economy. But the Nepali grazers, despite a strong numerical presence but without any support from the landed Assamese gentry, could not withstand the pressures from the landless Assamese peasants.[83] This was only a temporary respite and the issue of the landless peasants really did not disappear.

Meanwhile, in March 1964, the APCC had already decided to form a committee to look into the land question of Assam.[84] The APCC also advised its own government to de-reserve grazing reserves and distribute these lands among the landless peasants.[85] In doing so, it tried to gain the electoral support of large numbers of landless Assamese and tribal peasants who were increasingly mobilized and allied with the left-wing peasant organizations. Reform measures initiated by the Congress-led government could instil temporary confidence amongst the peasantry, but the government began to lose its support amongst the nationalist Assamese landlords. It tried to expedite the land settlement process with the help of the District Land Settlement Advisory Boards. By 1967, the government had requisitioned approximately 70,000 acres of land from the tea gardens out of which an estimated 52,000 acres were distributed amongst the landless people. Few years later, in 1971, the government further claimed that it had requisitioned an estimated 1,53,000 acres of land, i.e., this was all-inclusive, out of which, it was further asserted, 73,000 acres were distributed amongst the landless people.[86]

Such claims, however, did not go unchallenged. In practice, the official claim of the number of landless people getting land came to be negated on two counts: first, the number was unusually high as this number included those who were already occupying land, and secondly, often, such promised and identified plots were more difficult to bring under cultivation than was made out to be. If the plot was difficult to bring under habitation and cultivation, the new owner would be facing the next difficult thing — lack of capital. This often resulted in the sale of such plots to absentee landowners. *Dainik Assam* published reports of discrimination in the process of land distribution. Reports also came in that often locally powerful landlords had succeeded in manipulating and convincing the bureaucracy to acquire such lands in their own name.[87] In 1971, such accusations took a more serious turn when the Assam Legislative Assembly had to admit large-scale malpractices in land allotment schemes. In May 1971, the Assembly instituted an enquiry committee to look into these allegations. The government, as per the 1958 resolution, also went ahead with the survey, selection and distribution of land from Reserved Forests, grazing reserves and other government lands. In a significant move in the hills, the North Cachar Autonomous Council — a post-Independence political and bureaucratic arrangement under the Sixth Schedule of the Indian Constitution — had even proposed to de-reserve the Reserved Forests for land reclamation by peasants and create a provision that un-classed forest areas would be brought under the conservation programme.[88]

While Assam tried to cope with the challenges of the left mobilization of the peasantry, it equally faced the wrath of the Assamese landlords. The first challenge came from the zamindars of Goalpara as their estates had been abolished. They, however, offered only a meek resistance. The strongest challenge came when the Assam government, in 1963, abolished the landlords' rights in nisf-khiraj and la-khiraj estates.[89] This fresh state intervention which eroded the traditional rights of the landed gentry was reason enough to antagonize them. And again in 1970, the government fixed the maximum limit under the Assam Ceiling Act to 75 bighas (25 acres). The Act now covered the surplus land of the tea gardens too. The upper limit of the ceiling was again brought down to 50 bighas in 1972.[90] However, the Congress was not very convinced of the upper limit of 50 acres in the Ceiling Act. It knew that such a fixation would jeopardize its hold over the landlords in Assam. This anxiety was not new. In 1964, the APCC's Land Reform Committee had even suggested a possible increase in the upper limit of this bar. The Committee had argued that allowing landlords to keep more land would lead to a stable agrarian economy.[91] The upper limit of 50 acres, it had also argued, was not at par with the practices followed in other Indian states. Despite the APCC's willingness to accord some concession to the landlords, the government refused to concede.[92]

Land acquisition through the Ceiling Act gained momentum after the 1975. After 1973 and till 1980, the Assam government claimed that an estimated half-a-million acres of land were distributed.[93] From an estimated 0.6 million acres in 1976, the area acquired reached approximately 0.23 million acres in 1980. The government continued to acquire land through the Ceiling Act till the middle of the next decade and till March 1985 an estimated total area of 0.59 million acres of land were acquired.[94] The process has never acquired any significance since then and official accounts are rather silent on any such statistics.[95] But resistance to the implementation of the provisions of the Ceiling Act was widespread. The landlords organized public meetings opposing the execution of the Act.[96] In practice, the landlords thus found several ways to retain control over their landed property. A large number of landlords could successfully evade the restrictive provisions of the Act. This was done through bifurcation of their joint families and transfer of land leases to their immediate family members and relatives. By convincing the bureaucracy, they could redistribute their landed properties among their own kinsmen and siblings. A government enquiry in 1971 found large-scale malpractices in the implementation of the Ceiling Act.[97] Rich landlords also formed fictitious co-operatives to evade the law.[98] In some places, the landlords could win the support of their tenants in defeating the cause of the Ceiling Act. Elsewhere, the benefit of ceiling surplus land went to small or landless peasants. Also, one could easily understand that good lands were retained by the landlords and only poor- and inferior-quality lands were acquired by the government. The Assamese press could understand these lapses and made sure that such malpractices were reported but mere reporting was not an effective remedy. The government admitted that a 'certain percentage of acquired land will not be readily available for distribution as these lands being either low-lying, rocky or hilly areas are not fit for immediate cultivation'.[99] Land distribution also underwent protracted bureaucratic procedures and recipients often got no more than an area of land in which they could barely build their house. The subject became more complicated in those cases where the surplus land was under the occupancy of sharecroppers or tenants. The law meant that the existing sharecroppers or tenants often would be legal owners of such land. The existing tenants were granted occupancy rights in only a small fraction of their holdings.[100] By the second half of the 1970s, it was very clear that a moderate land reform could not bring reprieve to the peasantry. Official estimates continued to give a grim picture of landownership, like a further drop in average landholding size from an estimated 3.6 acres in 1970–71 to 3.4 acres in 1976–77.[101]

Peasants Reclaimed Forest Land

In August 1971, B.K. Nehru, the Governor of Assam, passed an ordinance empowering the government to evict peasants from the Reserved Forests.[102] At the same time, the government also decided to provide tenurial security to those peasants who had occupied government-owned land till 1967.[103] Widespread reclamation of forest lands by peasants — with indirect and direct support from their political leaders — came to be seen as detrimental to the economic well-being of the forest resources in the state.[104] Subsequent to reclamation of forest lands and government's mild opposition to it, the Forest Department again asserted its claim over the forests. Various Reserved Forests across Assam again became a site of contestation between the Revenue and Forest Departments.[105] In the wake of the new attitude — due to changing understanding of forest conservation — adopted by the Forest Department, peasants inside the forest lands increasingly came to be identified as encroachers. Repeated attempts were made to evict them from inside the forests during 1973–74, but unsuccessfully. It would be a mistaken idea to suggest that the Forest Department succeeded in its struggle for rights over the forest land with the Revenue Department. On the other hand, the Assam–Nagaland boundary dispute critically helped the Forest Department to partially regain forests from the peasants.

This happened when the Assam government, by accepting the 1971 K.V.K. Sundaram Commission's — Sundaram was an advisor to the Indian home ministry — interim report on the Assam–Nagaland border dispute, had agreed to de-populate these forest tracts.[106] The Forest Department was asked to carry out partial eviction of peasants from the forested land. The most aggressive phase of eviction took place in June 1973.[107] Reaction of the peasants too was quick and widespread. Anti-eviction mobilization gained popularity and peasants were led by a combination of nationalists and communists. It was during this crucial period that, with the experiences of leading a few scattered popular civil movements, the All Assam Student Union (AASU), despite its strong nationalist leanings, made its entry into the world of rural politics. In the weeks after the eviction drive, AASU played a significant role in mobilizing the peasants. Narratives of traumas of the eviction were widely reported. Radical young intellectuals visited Nambor forests that were undergoing the eviction drive. The eviction drive also attracted the attention of others like the leaders of the ongoing communist movement in Bengal.

On the invitation of a few local youths, the communist leader Bhaskar Nandi belonging to CPI-ML faction visited the area along with the party cadres and attempted to mobilize the evicted peasants.[108] The renewed mobilization drive was grounded on the demand for tenurial security for peasants who had settled in the forests.[109] This was, however, a short-lived mobilization. Later on, Jehirul Hussain, a well-known Assamese short-story writer, recalled how a radical communist-led peasant struggle could not make any progress in Nambor as the communist leaders failed to appreciate the internal dynamics and relationship between peasants and forest lands in Doyang.[110] Hussain claimed that during this short span of time, as in other parts of the country, the communist leaders were busy in search of principal enemies of the peasants and wrongly identified the rich peasant families as their enemies. Even though the Naxalites also failed to mobilize disgruntled peasants, politicians from the CPI and the CSP filled the vacuum but occasional evictions continued. It is not difficult to presume that such eviction never actually forced the peasants to relinquish their rights over the forest lands. The reason behind this failure of the eviction drive may be found in the very character of the state political practices. The Assam government was still not in favour of a strong agenda of forest conservation as expected by the Forest Department and neither was there a mandate for this from India's national forestry programme.

Despite this, there was a general uneasiness within the Congress leadership about the increasing pressure on the forest lands. The matter became apparently clear when in 1974 the government prepared 'a detailed report of land i.e. whether wooded or cleared, fit for cultivation etc; the extent of encroachment and the area fit for constituting reserve forest'.[111] The primacy given to agriculture over forest conservation got reflected in the clearance of forests for agriculture. In fact, between 1975 and 1982, an estimated 0.29 million acres of forest land — a 0.29 per cent of the total forested area of Assam in 1981 — were converted into non-forest lands in Assam for industrial and agricultural use.[112] As forest clearance acquired a larger dimension, the government suggested that large forested tracts should be allowed for co-operative farming. At the same time, a couple of years of mobilization brought the intended result. In 1978, during Assam Legislative Assembly election, the peasants voted Soneswar Bora, a socialist leader who also led the peasants to reclaim forest land, along with other leaders with communist and socialist leanings[113] into the Assam legislature. Bora was inducted as the Agriculture Minister in the new Janata Party government.[114] Peasants considered the results of the election as a sign of success of their reclamation of forests land. They, in fact, celebrated *Doyang Bijoy Ustav* in 1978, as a mark of their rightful claim over these forests. The government awarded them with provisions of various public amenities like roads, schools, etc., but at the same time expressed its willingness to carry out eviction.

Along with the peasantization of Nambor forests, various grassroots political instruments began to operate in these areas, further helping peasantization. Members were elected from the newly settled Nambor forest area to village panchayats from 1979. In

June 1978, Golap Borbora, the state Chief Minister, agreed to open the Doyang Reserved Forest to the peasants who had already been settled there since Independence. He admitted that a process of peasantization had already taken place in parts of these Reserved Forests.[115] The short-lived Janata government, though failing to deliver any permanent tenurial rights to these peasants, nonetheless brought a sense of security to them. In July 1978, after a month of experiment with the legalization of land tenures inside the forested tracts, the government began to disallow any more forest reclamation. Despite pressure from the communist parties and communist-led peasant organizations, the Assam government declared that all encroachers would be evicted though actual eviction did not take place due to the fate of the incumbent government being uncertain.

Tenancy, Law and Making of Social Identities

> In practice, the share-croppers do not enjoy much security of tenure. They have to give up possession of land when the landlord wants it back. Regulation of rent is also ineffective and, by and large, the share cropper pays half the produce.
>
> Planning Commission of India, 1966[116]

Two decades after the enactment of the Adhiar Act, sharecropping still remained an integral part of the state's agrarian relations. Several sets of official and non-official estimates indicate the widespread practice of sharecropping and tenancy in Assam during this period. For instance, the Census of 1961 estimated that an approximately 37 per cent of cultivators were still sharecroppers in Assam. Similarly, years earlier, in 1957, the Assam government admitted that an estimated 15.6 per cent people were without land and 52.6 per cent had land below 3 acres.[117] Another estimate made by Assamese geographer M.M. Das in 1984 suggests that between 1952 and 1974, the net area sown in the province increased by 19 per cent — a comparatively higher figure than that in the previous periods. But Das also estimated that an approximately 16 per cent area, i.e., one-fifth of the total net sown area, was under tenancy, though a little less was actually under tenancy cultivation.[118] This estimate was at par with the 1951 Agricultural Census for Assam. That high incidence of tenancy continued to be prevalent in Assam came to be reflected in the Fourth Five-Year plan.[119] The government admitted that Assam, along with Andhra Pradesh, Bihar, Haryana, Punjab, West Bengal, and Tamil Nadu, still continued to hold a major portion of the total all-India share of tenants. Official statistics taken during 1970–71 indicated that one-tenth of the total peasant families were still dependent on tenancy in Assam.[120] At the same time, an estimated 40 per cent of the tenancy was based on equal crop-sharing, i.e., adhi agreement.[121] With the dissolution of zamindari estates in Goalpara — the actual process began only in 1964 — and later in Cachar, the erstwhile tenants also came to be legally categorized as sharecroppers.[122]

This statistical relook also meant that years of sharecroppers' mobilization hardly improved their condition and their relation with the landlords in Assam. In fact, the practice of sharecropping, refusing to disappear, got consolidated in different pockets. There is little doubt that in some cases, sharecroppers developed better bargaining capacity. By this time, this agrarian relation based on tenancy had acquired wider social legitimacy as well. An increasing number of absentee Assamese landlords found tenancy as the convenient method of cultivation. On the other hand, the Assamese *raiyat*'s tenurial security was partially achieved in 1958 when the Assam government slowly began to do away with the annual lease by converting them into permanent leases.[123] The annual lease system worked as an important legal restriction for the raiyats in acquiring full tenurial rights. The process of conversion from *ekchania patta* to *myadi patta* — from annual lease to permanent lease — however got entangled with bureaucratic intricacies and could never be completed. Conversion of annual patta land to permanent patta land was also a hindrance for the big landlords who found it difficult to retain control over their extended land properties.

Such a high incidence of tenancy was bound to give a fresh lease of life to tenancy politics in Assam. And it did happen so in the 1960s. The election to the Assam Legislative assembly in 1967 again reflected the increasing relevance of the tenancy question. The Congress won a majority to form the government, but the combined communist and socialist block also came back to prove their continued relevance in the political matrix of Assam.[124] Unconvinced of this electoral victory and amidst increasing popularity of communists amongst the tenants, in 1971, the Congress government decided to re-mould the Assam Tenancy Act of 1935 to grant occupancy rights to the tenants and widen the scope of the term of tenancy. To score over its political opposition, the Congress made its intention clear that it would go all the way to restrict the practice of sharecropping.[125] The need for a change in the tenancy laws had already been stated by the Assam Revenue Department as well as the Congress party in 1964.[126] This move, albeit not a difficult political move, aimed at conceding tenants in the tea gardens occupancy rights. In 1970, the APCC also re-examined the tenancy laws of the state. A majority within the Congress agreed that the best way to do this would be to repeal the Adhiar Act of 1948 and replace it with an amended tenancy law.[127] The government also opined that the Adhi Board could hardly arbiter in the disputes between landlords and tenants. On the other hand, tenants from erstwhile zamindari areas of Goalpara and Cachar also pressurized to change the Assam Tenancy Act of 1935 as this had lost its relevance. They argued that the government was also bound to amend the Assam Tenancy Act of 1935 after the abolition of zamindari system.

A draft bill to amend the Assam Tenancy Act of 1935 suggested that the occupancy right be given to the sharecroppers who had been cultivating land for two consecutive years. The provision of two years as a minimum condition for claiming occupancy rights for the tenants immediately invited the wrath of the landlords. A Congress review committee also argued that any deviation from the standard 12 years of minimum occupancy in the Indian tenancy laws would cause harm to the Assamese landlords.[128] The committee further expressed its concern that occupancy right would be a superior right, as it would allow the occupant to acquire the land by paying a stipulated fee. But it also strongly resisted the provision of bringing the annually leased land under the scope of the bill.[129] This meant that a large area would remain beyond the purview of the proposed tenancy law.

Disagreement notwithstanding, the bill was sent to a Select Committee of the Assam Assembly.[130] The Select Committee had representatives whose alliance with either landlords or tenants was well known. The Congress members were not impressed with the objective of the bill and strongly opposed it. Various reasons, viz., creation of 'another class of landlords', 'bhoodan was a better idea', 'tenants would only sell the land', 'there is not enough land' or 'small compensation',[131] were cited to justify their protest against the bill. Amidst such opposition, in June 1971, Mahendra Mohan Chaudhury, the then Chief Minister, declared the government's intention to amend the Assam Tenancy Act of 1935.[132] The government was under pressure from the more radical faction of the Congress led by Bijoy Chandra Bhagawati and also the spiralling growth of dissatisfaction among the Assamese peasantry.[133]

Admitting that no more land was available for distribution amongst the landless, the government declared that the amended Act would address the problem of both the tenants and the sharecroppers. The Chief Minister suggested that if a tenant or a sharecropper was cultivating the land of a landowner for three years consecutively, the former would be entitled to occupancy rights. The Act entitled a tenant or a sharecropper to the right of transfer or inheritance. Another provision allowed legal transfer of ownership to the tenant if the tenant paid 50 times the revenue. The Act also required that record-of-rights be prepared for all tenants. This was a dramatic shift in the political movement of the sharecroppers' movement. Also, the Assam Tenancy Act of 1935 provided that occupancy rights could be given to tenants who were cultivating a piece of land for 12 years. Not only was this Act hardly in force, but also the provision of long years of occupancy made its execution impracticable. The sharecroppers' movement of the 1940s and 1950s also rarely appropriated the provisions of the Act as grounds for mobilization. With a radical provision of only three years as a minimum period of continuous occupancy, which was normally practised in the Assamese peasant society, and also the inclusion of sharecroppers within the purview of the Assam Tenancy Act 1971, the Act came as a major boost to the sporadic but intensified peasant movement. By accepting their centrality in the agrarian relations, the Act made the sharecroppers a legal entity.

The Assam Tenancy Act came into effect in December 1971. But its actual implementation became possible only after 1973.[134] Opposition to this Act was widespread and openly articulated.[135] On the other hand, the sharecroppers and communist organizations demanded its widespread implementation.[136] Its effective implementation became crucial for the Sarat Chandra Sinha-led Congress government. In June 1973, Sinha publicly warned the landlords not to evict their sharecroppers on any pretext. He also made it clear that those who had already been evicted by their landlords would also be given occupancy rights. He warned of severe punishment to those landlords who refused to comply with the Act and assured the tenants – *ryots* – that they would remain as tenants. Sinha made it clear that the government had considered the subject very seriously.[137] The government gave the widest possible publicity to the Act. Additional initiative was taken in the districts of western Assam. Bureaucrats from the Land Records Department and Revenue Department participated in these official publicity meetings and explained the provisions of the Act.

The Assam Tenancy Act became an instrument for the Assam government to showcase its pro-peasant programme. This also coincided with the announcement of the 20-point programme of the Indian Prime Minister Indira Gandhi. Mrs Gandhi's 20-point programme laid special emphasis on tenancy reform.[138] This was largely driven by the growing peasant discontent across the country. The implementation of the 20-point programme had its repercussions in Assam too. Sinha, who had socialist leanings, spared no time in putting the Assam Tenancy Act into execution along with the the Ceiling Act which has already been discussed. Sinha was no stranger to the hardships of Assamese peasantry.[139] He was a witness to the condition of tenants in zamindari Goalpara and how their miseries were successfully capitalized on by the ever-increasing strength of communist parties. Sinha overhauled his administration for an effective implementation of the Assam Tenancy Act. The government used its tenancy reform programme to aggressively pursue its pro-peasant outlook.[140] The government became well equipped to arbiter land disputes. Over the years, as it has already been mentioned, the Assam government learnt to arbiter disputes arising out of the distribution of land. Most of these lands either belonged to tea planters or landlords.

The resistance to the Act turned out to be more than what was expected. In fact, even before the Act came into effect, large-scale eviction of tenants was completed across the valley. Large numbers of landlords cultivated their lands with the help of wage labourers. Meetings organized by the landlords opposed the implementation of the Act. Sporadic incidents of landlords attempting to evict their tenants took place as well, and such incidents were widely reported in *Dainik Assam* from the winter of 1973. Resistance also came from small and medium landlords. They demanded that the provision for transfer of permanent ownership should be withdrawn. In several places, the landlords demanded the total repeal of the Act.[141] Such dissent could hardly make the government rethink its position on the Act though the Congress even ran the risk of losing its traditional supporters.[142] A contemporary observer — defending the cause of landlords — argued that with the implementation of the Act, the 'good' relation between the landlord and tenant had come to an end.[143] The observer also claimed that the Act would permanently impair the scene of rural transformation as the fear of loss of land would never permit these landlords to take secondary occupations like petty business, jobs, etc. Admitting that the landlords refused to allow sharecroppers to cultivate their lands, the observer further showed how this practically emerged as a serious challenge to the poor peasants.

Unlike the enthusiasm of the government, the communist parties were not prepared for such a sudden turn of the situation. This resulted in the communist parties questioning the actual motive of the government behind bringing about the law. Taking a strong exception to the continued harassment of tenants by the landlords, the KS urged the government to remove the clauses of eviction from the Act.[144] Yet, public meetings organized by the communist parties demanded the immediate implementation of the Act. Despite the apprehension of communist organizations, tenants and sharecroppers, with support from their communist peasant organizations, claimed occupancy rights in several places.

The actual implementation of the law, however, unfolded a complex political journey. The upbeat tenants filed increasing numbers of civil suits claiming occupancy rights. Rent and title suits were disposed of fast. Meanwhile, the declaration of national emergency left little room for bureaucratic manipulation to deprive tenants of the benefits of the Act. Special drives were undertaken to expedite land reform and the government promised to complete land reform by mid-1976. As land reform was placed on the fast track mode between 1974 and 1976, an estimated 0.7 million acres of land — acquired through the Ceiling Act — were distributed amongst 0.2 million landless peasant families.[145] This was approximately one-tenth of the total agricultural land in Assam.[146] Most of the beneficiaries were existing sharecroppers.[147] Official estimates indicated that till 1979 an estimated 2,570,000 tenants were to be covered by the record-of-rights.[148] Unlike the case of the Adhiar Act, benefits largely went to the sharecroppers. It was at that point that the sharecroppers began to show their distinct political consciousness. Examples are not difficult to find. For instance, Muslim and Hindu sharecroppers fought protracted legal wars against their Muslim and Hindu landlords respectively.[149] At the same time, Muslim sharecroppers began to seek occupancy rights over the lands of their Hindu landlords.[150] The tenancy suits were defended by a number of lawyers who either had leftist leanings or were members of left parties.[151]

While tenancy rights were granted to all sections of tenants, the endeavour had one clear political implication: amongst those who got tenancy rights, mostly occupancy rights, a majority were East Bengali Muslim sharecroppers who used to rent in land from the Assamese absentee landlords. Its implication was clear. A good number of Assamese middle-class families, *inter alia* absentee landlords, by conceding occupancy rights to their erstwhile immigrant Muslim sharecroppers, felt deprived and considered this as loss of their resources. Discontent thus began to grow among them. The Assamese landlords or landed interests who were the traditional allies of the Congress now felt threatened. The landlords temporarily withdrew their support to the Congress and it got partially reflected in the 1978 election. In 1978, in the wake of Assam Legislative Assembly election, the Congress party, faced with a strong opposition of Assamese landlords, openly sought the support of Muslim voters. The party, however, could not win the election and a Janata-Party-led government came into power. This tussle for occupancy rights also worked as a critical ideological apparatus of the well-known anti-foreigner Assam agitation which began in 1979. Slowly, discontent of the Assamese nationalist landlords began to metamorphose to an anti-migration opposition.

To understand this, we need to go back to the 1940s again. After Partition, the Muslim sharecroppers gained importance in the valley's agrarian relations. More and more Assamese landlords came to prefer the Muslim sharecroppers to their Assamese and tribal counterparts. This shift in the choice of tenants was conditioned by a combination of factors. The Muslim peasants' skills as jute and multi-crop cultivator were well known. The high price of jute was another source of encouragement for the Assamese landlords to employ Muslim peasants. That the immigrant Muslim peasants remained outside the preview of any communist mobilization was also a matter of great relief to the Assamese landlords. Also compared to the 1940s, the East Bengali peasants were now without any political leadership which could have been a counterpoise to the Assamese landlords' nationalist views. The Assamese landlords' hunger for Muslim sharecroppers never disappeared and was sated with the continued immigration from East Pakistan. In the 1970s, a majority of the East Bengali immigrant poor peasants, who could not afford to own substantial land nor could feed their families by working as wage labour, chose to work as sharecroppers for the Assamese absentee landowners. While such an arrangement had begun in the previous decade, in the absence of any statistics on sharecropping after Independence, there, however, remains a major obstacle in getting a clear idea of the primacy and extent of such a sharecropping arrangement.

Renewed immigration from East Pakistan continued to have a rippling impact. In the 1960s, the Congress government – Mahendra Mohan Chaudhury as Chief Minister – was against any more immigration into Assam. Deportation notices were served to many of them. In 1967, the Assam government admitted that an estimated 1.7 million immigrants from East Pakistan, mostly residing in the two districts of Darrang and Nowgaon, had been served with notices of deportation.[152] Political rivals and aspiring Assamese landlords considered Chaudhury's government as a serious threat to the immigration of peasants. Till the late 1960s, increasing immigration from East Pakistan was not, however, blamed for causing scarcity of cultivable land for the Assamese peasants. This began to change in the early 1970s in the wake of the creation of Bangladesh. Immigration of East Bengali peasants into Assam suddenly acquired a larger international dimension in the aftermath of the creation of Bangladesh as an independent country.[153] Assam, as a bordering state, was a natural choice of a large number of immigrants from the densely populated northern districts of Bangladesh. The number of immigrants was variously estimated. Official estimates put it at 0.75 million. *Dainik Assam*, increasingly emerging as the mouthpiece of Assamese nationalists, claimed that the majority of immigrants were Muslim peasants.[154] The issues of immigration suddenly came to play an important role in the political debate of Assam. The immigrants were now identified as *bhaganias* – those who had fled to defend themselves. The government also put in place mechanisms to identify and recognize them largely as political refugees in the wake of political instability of the newly created Bangladesh.[155] The immigration from Bangladesh to different parts of the world gained rapid momentum till the end of the 1970s and this went into creating a huge impact on the economy of Bangladesh. The state of Assam, acting as one of the recipients of the immigrant population could accommodate them only in the most unskilled labour sector, the agrarian sector in particular.

Granting tenancy rights to the Muslim sharecroppers also meant a perceptible shift in the agrarian relations in Assam. While the relation between Hindu landlords and Muslim tenants was the dominant form of agrarian relation in pre-Partition Bengal, the Hindu Assamese landlords and Muslim tenants came to symbolize the agrarian relation in the Brahmaputra valley too. The tenancy law secured tenancy rights for the Muslim tenants of Assamese landlords. For the latter, grant of occupancy rights to their Muslim sharecroppers meant loss of their social and economic privileges. Soon, the former would be part of a larger social spectrum providing critical leadership to an Assamese nationalist mobilization around the immigration issue. As the erstwhile East Bengali Muslim sharecroppers began to get occupancy rights, many of these disputes with landlords were settled through bureaucratic interventions, and this was sure to cause further apprehension amongst the Assamese landlords. Both the Congress-led Assam government and later the Janata Dal government – which did not discontinue the tenancy reforms (1978–79) – came to be seen as a threat to the economic and social interests of landlord. This new phase of peasant mobilization, wherein immigrant tenants were at the helm of affairs, re-aligned the politics of Assam. In subsequent years, both anti-immigrant and ethnic mobilization of the tribal peasantry which rebuilt the idea of land alienation came to the forefront of Assam's political landscape.

A collective political voice, derived from the ideological strength of peasant mobilization, and of left and liberal political activity, exerted significant pressure on the political trajectory of Assam. The most significant impact of the land reform, beginning with the Assam Tenancy Act of 1971, was on the Assamese nationalist landlords. Many of them failed to maintain their socio-economic privileges derived from landed property. They began to seek their economic and social support from other alternative resources. It was at this crucial historical juncture that they came to compete with other stakeholders, including the non-Assamese traders, in the state economy. Competition over limited economic resources faced by a new Assamese middle class devoid of its landed interests turned out to be the background for the popular mobilization beginning in 1979.

One of the striking weaknesses of the immigrant Muslim peasants was their lack of organized political voice between 1947 and 1980s. Occasionally, Muslim leaders within the Congress tried to speak on behalf of the Muslim peasantry. But over the years, empowered by institutional measures initiated by the government and also by lessons learnt from their political vulnerability experienced during 1979–80, which will be discussed, the immigrant peasants looked for ways to escape from this social and economic isolation. As a result, they began to articulate their political desires more clearly. The immigrant Muslim peasants, in the meanwhile, empowered with tenurial security gained in the 1970s, introduced several changes in the agrarian economy. This had far-reaching impact on the agrarian economy of Assam. The impact manifested through the complex process of immigrant Muslim peasants raising their share of landholding in the agricultural sector and adopting the practice of multiple cropping. Deviating from their pre-Independence stance of exclusive focus on jute cultivation, Muslim peasants diversified their agrarian practices. The cultivation of rice and vegetables, and fish farming had earned them profits. The agrarian cycle they had chosen for paddy cultivation could withstand floods. Over the years, there was increased commercialization of paddy production. One primary reason for their preference to produce both paddy and jute was the fact that the net income from per hectare production of rice and jute remained approximately equivalent between 1970s and 1980s.[156]

During this period, Muslim small peasants began to accumulate land, consolidate and re-arrange their existing smaller and scattered plots. More and newly formed *char* areas were reclaimed through a complex process. In several areas, forestlands, primarily closer to riverine areas, were converted into agricultural lands. Benefits were shared by agricultural labourers along with peasants. Visible economic stratification had also taken place among the Muslim peasants depending on their ability to reclaim char land. Compared to the increasing landlessness amongst the caste-Hindu Assamese peasants, the Muslim peasants overcome the burden of landlessness through a complex process of land reclamation and land accumulation. These newly acquired lands were located mostly in the riverine areas, thus exposing the peasants both to the strengths and weaknesses of such areas. As these areas were more prone to floods, the peasants were forced to intensify, and often associated with the use of high yielding crop, their agrarian cycle. Crop diversification thus became quite a widespread practice. Credit flow into the Muslim-peasantry-dominated areas increased. Official reports suggest that there was increased per hectare use of fertilizers in the localities, largely dominated by immigrant peasants.[157] Shops dealing in manure, pesticides and seeds were more widely present in these areas compared to any other rural area.

The rapid conversion of these newly reclaimed lands was facilitated by several factors. First, these areas continued to have a presence of agricultural labourers, essentially drawn from amongst the Muslim community. Secondly, these areas retained its links with various sources of rural credit. Thirdly, the trader–creditor nexus, as in the pre-Independence era, also helped further commercialization of agrarian production. Though surplus earned from this agrarian economy was low, a process of rural capital formation was taking place simultaneously. Surplus was further invested in the process of land accumulation leading to an increase in the share of landholdings.

What was the outcome of the new agrarian economy? First, surplus from agrarian production led to capital formation amongst the Muslim peasants. Second, this agrarian capital was diverted to various mercantile activities. Unlike the previous experiences of mercantile capital — mostly of the Marwari traders, playing an ineffective role — this new phase of capital formation led to diversification of agricultural activities. Third, stratification took place within the Muslim peasants. While substantial benefits went to traders and creditors, the condition of small peasants did not change in any significant way. Influx of rural landless

Muslim peasants into the expanding urban labour market apparently increased. Often, these immigrants became victims of aggressive urban political exclusionism.

This phenomenal growth of peasant economy, over the decades, also contributed to the making of a microscopic Muslim middle class. A minuscule section of the Muslim middle class had, over the years, participated in the government employment sector or taken to various professions. What was distinctive of the social origin of this new Muslim middle class? They were markedly different from the caste-Hindu Assamese middle class or even the few Muslim middle-class families originating in the colonial era.[158] The most prominent of these differences is their relationship with the agrarian society. The Assamese nationalist middle class, after Independence, slowly distanced itself from the agrarian society.[159] This new middle class was drawn not primarily from the landed gentry. In contrast, the social and cultural ties between the Muslim peasantry and the Muslim middle class are still strong and are of paramount importance.

In the present era, the growth of a Muslim middle class has also unfolded a larger crisis. Not only does this middle class struggle to find a space within the larger cultural landscape of the Assamese nationality, but also it has to compete in a complex landscape to negotiate its' political identity.[160] In the process, they have to prove their secular credentials and their willingness to be part of the formative stages of a 'rational Assamese society'. This is done through production of a vernacular social history of Muslims in Assam. For instance, the process of syncretization between Hindu Assamese and Muslims or the contributions of the Muslim community to the Assamese literature have been repeatedly told.[161] More importantly, this middle class has been able to carve out, for itself, a limited space in the political matrix of Assam. There has been a constant attempt at forging political relationships to ensure reasonable justice to the community. Many a time, such political formations have tended to be more communitarian and stand in opposition to mainstream political formation. Stability of these political formations has remained exposed to layers of uncertainties. At the same time, vote percentage by regional political formations, strongly espousing the cause of Assamese nationalism, has significantly increased amongst the erstwhile immigrant Muslim peasants.

In 1971, the Muslim population came to constitute a fifth of the total population of Brahmaputra valley districts. The large majority of this population were poor peasants. Many of them could have dreamed of a better future during the brief period of political mobilization in the 1940s. Independence and Partition left them leaderless. Neither the Congress nor the communists were ready to defend their rights. By themselves, as far as possible, the Muslim peasants formed alliances with Hindu Assamese landlords, traders and others. They began to face new uncertainties about their citizenship of independent India. Brief respite came through the tenancy legislation of 1971 when some of the Muslim sharecroppers received tenancy rights. This inevitably invited the wrath of the Assamese landed gentry. What happened to the political aspirations of the Muslim peasantry, a subject that could not form part of this book, awaits a full-length examination.

The Agrarian Question Becomes Nationality Question

In the 1970s, as discussed earlier, the Assamese nationalist landed gentry began to face increasing opposition from the peasantry and the government. Already, they had lost their economic and social privileges partially. They were looking for an opportunity to strike back at the government and also regain their lost privileges. In May 1974, the AASU submitted a 21-point charter of demands to the government.[162] The AASU, primarily representing the interests of the Assamese nationalist landed gentry and also drawing ideological inspiration from the nationalist freedom struggle and scoring some degree of nationalist victories in the previous two decades, had gradually emerged as the platform for voicing popular political dissent.[163] Despite its nationalist bias, the AASU charter accommodated demands that held appeal for a wide cross-section of the Assamese society. Several demands had direct bearing upon the Assamese peasantry. For instance, it urged the government to end eviction in the Reserved Forests, to effectively implement the Ceiling Act and to bring to an end the continued immigration into the state. Though the nationalists generally mentioned 'outsiders', their anti-immigration rhetoric had stopped short of clearly mentioning the social identity of the immigrants.

The anti-immigration nationalist political idea acquired a new form. What was lost in the larger nationalist debate — the tone of which had increasingly sharpened — was the fact that the quantum, economic background and the nature of state support behind this immigration were different from the pre-Independence history of immigration.

The nationalist mobilization of Assamese landlords, middle class and indegenous Assamese peasants urged the Indian government to declare these immigrant peasants as illegal citizens and deport them from India. The nationalist Assamese press and Indian right-wing political groups began to give a wide negative publicity to immigration and its political and economic consequences in Assam.[164] The nationalist opposition to immigration acquired greater legitimacy when the Indian government also declared that no such illegal immigrant population would be allowed to stay in Assam.[165] Several efforts were made in the previous years to curb the flow of population from East Pakistan.[166] A popular movement, which nonetheless polarized Assamese and East Bengali Muslim peasants between 1979 and 1985, reinforced the overriding ideological supremacy of the Assamese nationalist gentry. The Assam Accord of 1985, a treaty signed between the Government of India and the Assamese nationalist agitators, broadly spelt out the legalities of immigration and citizenship.[167] The Accord declared the pre-1971 immigrants from East Pakistan as legal citizens of India. This claim over citizenship also meant regulating the Indian government's promised adoption of various institutional measures to ascertain the claim of the immigrant peasants to legal citizenship.

However, the victory of Assamese landed gentry, who supported the Assamese nationalists' entry into electoral politics, had a decisive impact on the fate of the Assam Tenancy Act. The law faced a renewed phase of hostility from the Assamese absentee landlords. Their economic and social interests were defended by the newly formed Asom Gana Parisad (AGP) which came to power in December 1985. In July 1986, Surendranath Medhi, Law Minister in the AGP ministry, determinedly criticized the Act and asked for consolidated public (read landlord) opinion favouring repeal of the Act. Defending the opposition of the Assamese landlords to the Act, Medhi suggested that the Act did not possess any virtue by which it could be called a 'social legislation'.[168] He condemned the Act for its very 'confiscatory' nature. He argued that the execution of the Act threatened the very existence of Assamese landlords.[169] Meanwhile, the new government did not fail to make promises to Assamese landless people.[170]

Inspired by this anti-tenancy stand taken by their political elites, Assam Pattadar Sangha, the collective body of the Assamese landlords, challenged the provisions of the Assam Tenancy Act in the Gauhati High Court. This body also demanded that the Assam Tenancy Act be repealed and the Assam Adhiar Protection and Regulation Act of 1948 be re-instated as an instrument of regulating relations between the landlords and their sharecroppers.[171] Unlike the Assam Tenancy Act, the latter Act would protect the Assamese landlords against any claim to tenurial right by their sharecroppers. Many landlords would join the fray in challenging the Act. Those who came to defend this intended repeal of the Assam Tenancy Act claimed that land alienation due to the Act had practically created a legal space for half-a-million illegal immigrants in Assam.[172] This view largely reflected the general worry of the Assamese landed gentry which was already translated into a larger nationalist popular movement. The attempt to repeal the Act failed as the political representatives of the Assamese landed gentry failed to muster enough numbers within the Assembly.[173] But the new political alliance between the Assamese nationalist landed gentry and their political representatives meant a partial win for the former. The Assamese nationalist gentry including the Assamese tea planters marginally improved its share of land in the 1980s.[174] The government also slowly withdrew from implementing any further tenancy reform. The agrarian question would free itself from the clutches of nationalist influences and would be ready for another round of engagement with the Assam nationalists, albeit in more complex ways, in the next couple of decades.

Conclusion

At the beginning of the twenty-first century, the rural population of Assam was estimated at 20 million, constituting approximately 88 per cent of the state's total population. The number has not changed significantly since the Census of 1901; it is a whopping 98 per cent of the total population of the province. Presently, three-fourth of the total population of Assam is primarily dependent on agriculture. This is despite a threefold increase in the population density of the Brahmaputra valley in the last 100 years. The valley, in 1901, had 5 million acres of land waiting to be reclaimed for cultivation.[1] In the following 100 years, a substantial portion of the land was reclaimed, leaving merely 0.1 million acres uncultivated.[2] Also, in 50 odd years between 1900 and 1950, the net area sown increased by 97 per cent.[3] A moderate number of peasant families — often the male members of a family — migrated to the cities in search of a better life and livelihood. In 2001, the number of rural migrants was still abysmally low, constituting only a little over 1 per cent of the total population.[4]

Assam's agrarian economy today resembles the nineteenth-century one dominated by smallholding peasant cultivation. The valley continues to be one of the highest producers of jute in India though the role of commercial agriculture is still limited.[5] At the same time, flow of capital into the peasant economy, except by way of state subsidies or government credit, is far below the national average. The peasants consider flood no more than blessings for the agrarian cycle. Irrigation hardly exists. The flagship Indian government programme of Green Revolution of the 1960s and 1970s did not cover the region. Compared to the agrarian situation of Punjab or Haryana that has improved over the decades, the rural peasant economy has worsened in Assam. Intense pressure on land could not infuse any fundamental change in the rural economy. However, the afore-cited jugglery of figures can be highly misleading if one wants to get a true picture of agrarian relations in Assam.

After decades of political mobilization around the slogan of 'land to the tiller', sharecropping is still the chief feature of the agrarian economy. Most of the sharecroppers hold only marginal plots. Official estimates are quite unanimous about their numbers. Sharecropping survives for various reasons. For one, fragmentation of landholding has increased. Absentee landownership is still a dominant form of agrarian relation as it was before. Despite the decline of the urban landed gentry, a substantial percentage of the urban population still has landed interests. Sharecroppers pay rent in varied forms similar to the way they did three decades ago. They are still without any tenurial security as before. One key difference from the situation in the mid-twentieth century is that the sharecroppers can speak to their landlords with confidence and not with deference.

From the 1960s till today, the agrarian question has come to be centred on the landless peasants. Despite the sharecroppers' integral role in spearheading the peasant mobilization, it was the landless peasants who came to the centre stage of peasant politics. Thousands of them were mobilized by the slogan of 'land to the landless'. Several acts passed by the Congress-led government acted as instruments in decisively bringing relief to the landless peasants. Nevertheless, several hundred thousand peasant families are still desperately in search of land on which they can produce crops to feed their families. They have continued to occupy government-owned lands to meet the increasing demands of agricultural land. This has invited the wrath of the state custodians of such lands.

In the second half of the twentieth century, the peasants in Assam were politically sidelined. They had been pushed to the centre stage of the political landscape in 1886 when the Assam Land Revenue Regulation was introduced, but were forced to retreat in 1986 once the Assamese nationalist landed gentry decided to repeal the Assam Tenancy Act of 1971. These 100 years of their struggle justifies the title of this book. Despite facing humiliations, the peasants initially resisted the landlords heroically, but at the end they could hardly withstand the combined pressure of the nationalist landed class and the government. Their capacity to resist was fast depleted by the political maneuverings through a series of Assamese nationalist programmes as well as ethnic mobilizations. The ideological inspirations of these new political actions are derived from the slogans of 'centre-state discrimination within the Indian federal structure', 'neo-colonialism' or even more provocative slogans of independence for Assam from India. Over the years, however, these political actions have not been able to retain their emotive appeal. Neither have they had an unrelenting impact upon the peasantry. The relationship between the Assamese nationalists and the peasantry never came to be repaired. Unlike their predominantly landed predecessors, the Assamese nationalists are now increasingly drawn from a complex combination of varied social origins. They have also appropriated the peasant heroes and metaphors in their attempts to reinforce their relationship with the peasantry.

The experience of peasant protests in the twentieth century was different from that in the nineteenth century on several counts. First, the ideological inspiration of the nineteenth-century protests was clearly drawn from the agrarian crisis and the consequent breakdown of agrarian relations. That the agrarian economy of the region had entwined itself with a series of misfortunes since the early twentieth century has already been established in the first chapter of the book. Secondly, unlike the peasant protests in the nineteenth century, those in the twentieth century identified few institutions of the Assamese agrarian society as key forces of rural exploitation. The landlords, forming a miniscule part of the agrarian society, and their tenants and sharecroppers entered into a phase of direct political hostility. Thirdly, various tribal peasant groups, till now entrenched within their traditional cultural boundaries, extended their political solidarity to other ethnic communities. Such newfound alliances were, however, short-lived. It did not take a long time for these political alliances to break down only to re-form themselves into innumerable ethnic groups which groups discarded their cultural affiliations. Fourthly, the social hegemony of the Assamese landed class began to wither away since the institutions that re-affirmed this social hegemony either disappeared or were gradually done away with. Lastly, despite these key changes, the agrarian relations continued to be still largely characterized by the features of what Assam came to see in the early twentieth century.

The beleaguered peasantry's enthusiasm for the communist political programme was short lived. There is no single explanation for this failure. But given their popularity and success, we suggest that the communists misread the complex historical evolution of the peasantry. It ignored the crucial relations between the landed Assamese nationalists and the peasantry. Not only did the communist lack charismatic leadership on whom the peasantry could fall back upon but they also could not provide any realistic remedy to the agrarian crisis. They also collaborated with the Congress-led government but could not deliver any of their promises. The landed Assamese nationalists thus easily dislodged the communists as the leaders of the peasants by the end of the century. Most legal mechanisms, meant to provide reprieve to the peasantry, were shelved by the government in collusion with the landed nationalists. The landed class exercised utmost care to appropriate these laws in retaining or restoring their privileges. Similarly, they reinstated their lost privileges partially through gains made in other arenas of social life. The landed gentry still constitutes the majority of the Assamese nationalists. Their experience of the difficult times in the mid-twentieth century continues to haunt them, and their relationship with the peasantry remains fragile. Meanwhile, sympathetic accounts of the lives and actions of the peasantry slowly found way into the Assamese nationalist literary space. The Congress, as one of the predominant political parties in the state, knew well that it could not lose its important electoral constituency, i.e., peasants, irrespective of their divergent religious and community identities. Indeed, Congress's alliance with the peasants and the nationalist landed class became the fulcrum of its political power.

Social experiments amongst the East Bengali Muslim peasantry had partially tried to adapt to the nationalist cultural and social institutions. In some ways, this is akin to what James C. Scott argues for the Zomias of South-East Asia. Scott argues that 'adaptation to the dangers or temptations of neighbouring polities is hardly a practice confined to peoples at periphery of states'.[6] The experience of the East Bengali Muslim peasantry, insofar as their attempts to be part of a newer social and political ambience — despite their not being a strong candidate for Scott's provocative formulation — are concerned, occurs in several spheres of their everyday lives such as their adherence to the norms of nationalist cultural institutions. Also, after decades of social isolation and political neglect, the erstwhile East Bengali Muslim peasants are now articulating their strong claim to being the cultural citizens of Assam. The contested but otherwise powerful nationalist narratives of migration still continue to haunt them. While their economic activities ensure the formation of rural capital, a new Muslim middle class emerging from amongst them guarantees them the much-needed political voice. This was voice distinctively lacking before the 1980s. Meanwhile, the nationalist Assamese cultural politics still tries to redefine who is an Assamese.[7] Such an effort, however, makes no attempt to address the complex economic and social transformations that have touched the lives of the East Bengali Muslim peasantry.

To turn to the tribal peasantry, their woes have become only worse over time. In the twentieth century, their agrarian practices underwent a rapid transition. The colonial rulers, despite several attempts, could not restrict the fluid nature of the tribal economy. They had inherited several virtues of the peasant society, turning from a shifting cultivator to a sedentary farmer. Slowly, the sedentary form of agrarian practice became a key feature of their economy. They too have joined the long quest of the Assamese landless peasantry for arable lands. In doing so, they face strong resistance on various fronts. A few political and legal instruments have been put in place to improve their economic and social condition, but nothing has been done to help arrest the factors which had worsened their condition. Lack of tenurial security is one among these. The tribal peasantry is now more politically self-conscious than it was in the 1950s or even earlier. Their struggle for economic justice often expresses itself in the form of forceful ethnic mobilization. As they demand more share of the state's natural resources, social stratification in their society has become visible.

The agrarian question was bound to stage a comeback to the centre stage of the political landscape. But it has, however, acquired more complexity than before. Early in the twenty-first century, a left-wing peasant organization, christened as Krishak Mukti Sangram Samiti (KMSS), temporarily mobilized these faceless peasants. Its political programme revolves around the issues of land reform, abolition of moneylending and land settlement for the landless peasants. Their leaders come from poor peasant families. Unlike like their predecessors fifty years ago, they are not conscientiously trained in the ideological programme of communism. Though they have not rejected nationalist aspirations either, they equally deny the authority of the nationalist gentry. The KMSS has brought back landlessness in the forefront of their mobilization tactics, but resolution to the problems of sharecropping and tenancy still eludes its political programme. Occasionally, anti-landlord and anti-moneylender slogans have given it a vantage point from which to bring the poor peasants and sharecroppers under its umbrella. The KMSS also defends those landless peasants who had reclaimed the government-owned forest land.[8] It is the government against which the KMSS has continued to vent its ire, thus guarding itself against any resistance from the landlords and moneylenders, whose primacy in the political fulcrum of the political life of Assam has not vanished.

This book, then, is an account of a century of political actions of the peasants centred on land, nationalist identity and resources. The book has portrayed both a picture of the difficult times of peasants and a chronicle of their never-ending struggle for rights and for undoing injustice. They have both failed and won. Their success and defeat does not necessarily lie in the heroic actions of their leaders but in a complex web of statecraft and nationalism. A compelling essence of this whole experience of peasant protests is their capability to live through much of the political turbulence. This, of course, has not helped them achieve their dreams, and they continue to remain prisoners of hope.

Notes

Introduction

1. Confidential Files, Chief Minister's Secretariat, Assam State Archives (ASA).
2. The book primarily focuses on the five erstwhile *raiyatwari*-settled districts of British Assam: Kamrup, Darrang, Nowgaon, Sibsagar, and Lakhimpur (the older spellings of the names of the districts have been used throughout). A long history of permanent land settlement oriented the rural politics in Goalpara and Cachar districts of British Assam differently from the aforementioned districts. Therefore, I have chosen not to include these two districts in the book.
3. See Udayon Misra, *The Periphery Strikes Back*, Shimla: Indian Institute of Advanced Studies (IIAS), 2000; Sanjib Baruah, *India against Itself*, New Delhi: Oxford University Press, 1999; Yasmin Saikia, *Assam and India: The Fragmented Memories*, New Delhi: Permanent Black, 2005; Girin Phukan, *Assam's Attitude to Federalism*, New Delhi: Sterling, 1984; Sanjoy Hazarika, *Strangers of the Mist: Tales of War and Peace in India's North East*, New Delhi: Penguin, 1994.
4. This book uses the term 'landlord' to identify broadly those who owned *la-khiraj* and *nisf-khiraj* estates and rented them out to tenants for cultivation. Rich peasants were called landowners. In the then popular usage, both these terms, however, overlapped.
5. I have used the term 'tribe/tribal' for those groups which are not only recognized as Scheduled Tribes by the Indian Constitution, but also maintain a relatively more distinctive economic and cultural lifestyle vis-à-vis the Assamese-speaking caste-Hindus. Distinction between the two terms, tribal and Assamese, is almost untenable now, as the identity of the present-day Assamese community is a synthesis of castes and sanskritized (as well as some not-so-sanskritized) tribes, and their boundaries are still quite vague.
6. Suryya Kumar Bhuyan, *Anglo-Assamese Relations, 1771–1826: A History of the Relations of Assam with the East India Company from 1771 to 1826, Based on Original English and Assamese Sources*, Guwahati: LBS, 1949; Nayanjot Lahiri, *Pre-Ahom Assam: Studies in the Inscriptions of Assam between the Fifth and the Thirteenth Centuries AD*, New Delhi: Munshiram Manoharlal, 1991; 'Landholding and Peasantry in the Brahmaputra Valley, c. 5th–13th Centuries AD', *Journal of the Economic and Social History of the Orient*, vol. 33, no. 2, 1990, pp. 157–68; Amalendu Guha, *Medieval and Early Colonial*

Assam: Society, Polity, Economy, Calcutta: KBS, 1991; Kanak Lal Barua, *Early History of Kamarupa from the Earliest Times to the End of the Sixteenth Century*, Shillong: Kanak Lal Barua, 1933.

7. Sanjeeb Kakoty, *Technology, Production, and Social Formation in the Evolution of the Ahom State*, New Delhi: Regency, 2003; Jahnabi Gogoi Nath, *Agrarian System of Medieval Assam*, New Delhi: Concept, 2002; Amalendu Guha, 'Medieval Economy of Assam', in Tapan Raychaudhuri and Irfan Habib (eds), *The Cambridge Economic History of India*, vol. 1 (c. 1200–c. 1750), Cambridge: Cambridge University Press, 1992, pp. 478–505; 'Ahom Migration: Its Impact on Rice Economy of Medieval Assam', *Artha Vijnana*, vol. 9, no. 2, 1967, pp. 134–57; 'The Ahom Political System: An Enquiry into State Formation in Medieval Assam: 1228–1800', in Surajit Sinha (ed.), *Tribal Polities and State Systems in Pre-Colonial Eastern and North Eastern India*, Calcutta: KPB, 1987, pp. 143–76.
8. Amalendu Guha, 'A Big Push without a Take-Off: A Case Study of Assam: 1871–1901', *Indian Economic and Social History Review (IESHR)*, vol. 5, no. 3, September 1968, pp. 199–221; Heramba Kanta Barpujari, *Assam in the Days of the Company, 1826–1858*, Guwahati: LBS, 1963.
9. Amalendu Guha, 'Agrarian Structures in the Nineteenth Century Assam', in Amalendu Guha, *Medieval and Early Colonial Assam*, pp. 219–79; Rajen Saikia, *Social and Economic History of Assam 1853–1921*, New Delhi: Manohar, 2000, pp. 81–122; Aditya Mukherjee, 'Agrarian Conditions in Assam, 1880–90: A Case Study of Five Districts of the Brahmaputra Valley', *IESHR*, vol. 16, no. 2, 1979, pp. 207–32; Shrutidev Goswami, *Aspects of Revenue Administration in Assam, 1826–1874*, New Delhi: Mittal Publications, 1987; Nandita Khadria, 'Some Aspects of the Rural Economy of Assam: A Study of the Brahmaputra Valley Districts of Assam, 1874–1914', unpublished PhD thesis, Centre for Historical Studies (CHS), Jawaharlal Nehru University (JNU), New Delhi, 1992. A new addition to this list is Ritupan Goswami, 'Rivers and History: Brahmaputra Valley in the Last Centuries', unpublished PhD dissertation, CHS, JNU, New Delhi, 2010.
10. The colonial government kept changing its policies of wasteland settlement depending on its revenue demands. Its discriminatory land settlement policy favouring the European tea planters is well known and has been widely addressed. The inherent contradictions between the colonial government's claim of implementing a liberal land settlement policy and a distinct, underlying need for revenue extraction has also been pointed out. Further, it has been argued that its attempts at land colonization were not completely successful as its land settlement policy was tilted in favour of the planters.

See Khadria, 'Some Aspects of the Rural Economy of Assam'; Rana Pratap Behal, 'Some Aspects of the Growth of the Plantation Labor Force and Labor Movements in Assam Valley districts, 1900–47', unpublished PhD thesis, CHS, JNU, New Delhi, 1983.

11. A.J.M. Mills, *Report on the Province of Assam*, Calcutta: Superintendent of Government Printing, 1854, reprint, Guwahati: Assam Publication Board, 1984; W.W. Hunter, *A Statistical Account of Assam*, 2 vols, London: Trubner, 1879.
12. Hiren Gohain, 'Assamiya Madhyabitta Sreneer Utpati Aru Bikash', in Hiren Gohain, *Sahitya Aru Chetana*, Guwahati: LBS, 1976, pp. 9–49; Prafulla Mahanta, *Asamiya Madhyabitta Srenir Itihas*, Guwahati: Purvanchal Prakash, 1991; Saikia, *Social and Economic History of Assam*; Manorama Sharma, *Social and Economic Change in Assam: Middle Class Hegemony*, New Delhi: Ajanta, 1990, reprint, 1998.
13. Most works refer to the 1861 and 1893–94 peasant uprisings. See, Amalendu Guha, *Planter Raj to Swaraj: Freedom Struggle and Electoral Politics in Assam 1826–1947*, New Delhi: PPH, 1977; Sharma, *Social and Economic Change in Assam*; Ramesh Kalita, 'Darrang Jilar Krishak Bidrohar Eti Samu Khatiyan', in Prasanna Kumar Nath (ed.), *Patharughat*, Sipajhar: Udash, 1994, pp. 76–80; Saikia, *Social and Economic History of Assam*; K.N. Dutta, *Landmarks of Freedom Movement in Assam*, Guwahati: LBS, 1957.
14. The works of colonial officials, historians and the vernacular writings of the late nineteenth century capture this history. The colonial land settlement officials were the earliest to document peasant insurgency in Assam.
15. Dutta, *Landmarks of Freedom Movement in Assam*, p. 28.
16. Representative of such scholarship is the pioneering work on the freedom movement in Assam by K.N. Dutta. Dutta studied peasant uprisings which marked the colonial role in the nineteenth century as a key element of Assam's freedom struggle. Peasants protested against the prohibition of poppy cultivation and rose against the government in 1861, when provoked by the rumours of the impending imposition of taxes on incomes and on betel nuts and pan. *Mel*s usually referred to as village councils provided leadership to these insurgencies. Dutta has also noted the participation of tribal peasants in the protests against the colonial state. See Dutta, *Landmarks of Freedom Movement in Assam*, pp. 26–27.
17. Guha, *Planter Raj to Swaraj*, pp. 6–9, 10, 50–53. Rajen Saikia also identified the three groups involved in the insurgency as the landlords (comprising the *doloi* and the *gossain*), the peasants and the colonial state. Saikia also argues that the upper strata of the peasantry took a lead owing to their own class interest. The reason behind their

participation was economic dissatisfaction. In particular, the Assam Land and Revenue Regulation of 1886 caused severe discontent among the non-cultivating rural gentry: it meant loss of both economic and social privileges. This was enough for them to instigate the peasantry against the state. The latter on their part could not ignore the command of the rural creditors and, in fact, ultimately played into their hands. He further contends that there is some historical evidence of peasants resorting to indigenous modes of protest. He has cited a reference to the Bhempuria character (a person with false arrogance) from the literary works of Lakshminath Bezbarua and the examples of peasant migration to evade paying revenue (Saikia, *Social and Economic History of Assam 1853–1921*, pp. 104–10).

18. These works arguing so show a limited understanding of the 1940s, with reference to the growth of Muslim League politics in Assam or events leading to the Partition. Immigration of peasants, primarily from East Bengal (now Bangladesh) is a matter of intense public and academic debate, as well as political rhetoric. These works tell us that as a result of this immigration, Brahmaputra valley experienced the emergence of a new socio-political order. Communalism, new economy and loss of land are thus the recurrent themes in the academic polemic. The politics of communalism evoke different responses from different scholars. In a pioneering work of its kind, Guha (*Planter Raj to Swaraj*, p. 254) discusses the issues of a pluralistic society, the Congress–Muslim League politics and the Partition problem of 1947. He discusses the background to the land settlement question that was intensely debated in the legislative arena. He further points out that communal politics and a regional Assamese Hindu chauvinism advocated by the Assamiya Samrakshini Sabha originated in this context.
19. Anil Raichaudhuri, *Asamat Bangladeshi*, Nowgaon: Jagaran Sahitya Prakasan, 2009.
20. Historical rhetoric tends to trace the growth of Muslim League and Assam Jatiya Mahasabha to the politics of land settlement in Assam with the influx of immigrant peasants. The emergence of the Sabha has been seen as a legitimate outcome of the political activities of Assam during the 1930s and 1940s. See, for instance, Nirode Kumar Barooah, *Mohini Kalar Chabi*, Guwahati: Purbanchal, 1997.
21. These works emphasized the gradual deterioration in the social relation amongst the different peasant groups and the emergence of communal politics in the Brahmaputra valley. See Amalendu Dey, 'The Muslims as a Factor in Assam Politics', *Bengal Past and Present*, vol. 96, no.2, 1977, pp. 114–17; M.N. Karna, *Agrarian Structures and Land Reform in Assam*, New Delhi: Regency, 2001.

22. Rajanikanta Bordoloi, *Dandua Droh*, Guwahati: Sahitya Prakash, 1988.
23. Birinchi Kumar Barua, *A Cultural History of Assam*, Guwahati: Bina Library, 2003.
24. Apparently, they cannot be considered as a natural partner in the affairs of politics. This partly explains why even the Assam Congress leaders did not pen down any works of their impression of the Assamese peasant society, unlike their national contemporaries. It was only inside the legislative assembly that they articulated their position on the Assamese peasant society.
25. For instance, see, Bordoloi, *Dandua Droh*.
26. Navakanta Baruah, 'Kapiliparia Sadhu', in Navakanta Baruah (ed.), *Upanyash Samagra*, Nalbari: Journal Emporium, 2002, pp.11–66; Mamoni Raisom Goswami, *Datal Hatir Uenye Khowa Howda*, Guwahati: Jyoti Prakasan, 1991; Homen Borgohain, 'Pita Putra', in Homen Borgohain, *Chairta Dasakar Fasal: Upanyash Samagra*, Guwahati: Student Stores, 1998, pp. 279–453; 'Haladhiya Charaye Baodhan Khay', in Borgohain, *Charita Dasakar Fasal*, pp. 219–77; Syed Abdul Malik, *Suruz Mukhir Swapna*, Calcutta: Bhabani Publishing Concern, 1960; Lila Gogoi, *Noi Boi Jay*, Dibrugarh: Banalata, 2004.
27. Arupjyoti Saikia, 'Oral Tradition, Nationalism and Assamese Social History: Remembering a Peasant Uprising', *IESHR*, vol. 49, no. 1, 2012, pp. 37–72.
28. Rather than making an elaborate examination of the region's agrarian history, literature in the second half of the twentieth century has been overburdened with an exclusive focus on the ideological aspects of left parties. For the post-colonial period, see Umananda Phukan, *Agricultural Development in Assam (1950–1985)*, New Delhi: Mittal Publications, 1990; P.C. Goswami, *The Economic Development of Assam*, Bombay: Asia Publishing House, 1963.
29. Since the 1980s, beginning with the subaltern studies, the study of the Indian peasant movement has seen a paradigmatic shift. In fact, peasant studies got a fresh lease of life. But, even then understanding of crucial issues of peasant politics are still beyond a general consensus. And it did not take long for the exclusion of peasant studies from general historical scholarship signalling the marginalization of the agrarian studies, the peasant movement in particular. For a comprehensive account of the Indian peasant movement of colonial and post-colonial periods, see Ghanshyam Shah, *Social Movements in India: A Review of Literature*, New Delhi: Sage, 1990.
30. Vinayak Chaturvedi, *Peasant Pasts: History and Memory in Western India*, Berkeley, CA: University of California Press, 2007.

31. Works on communist-led peasant movements in India have hardly focused their attention beyond 1947, except a few. See, for instance, Amit Kumar Gupta, *Agrarian Drama: The Leftists and the Rural Poor in India, 1934–1951*, New Delhi: Manohar, 1996. However, the study of agrarian unrest, immediately preceding Independence — and a good example is the well-known Tebhaga movement of 1946 — is confined to certain regions only and thereby hardly provides any scope beyond those areas. See, for instance, Sugata Bose, *Agrarian Bengal: Economy, Social Structure and Politics, 1919–1947*, Cambridge: Cambridge University Press, 1986. For a study of Indian electoral politics and its relation to agrarian politics, see Debal K. Singha Roy, *Peasants' Movements in Post-Colonial India*, New Delhi: Sage, 2004.
32. Ramachandra Guha, *The Unquiet Woods: Ecological Change and Peasant Resistance in the Himalaya*, New Delhi: Oxford University Press, 1989; Amita Baviskar, *In the Belly of the River: Tribal Conflicts over Development in the Narmada Valley*, New Delhi: Oxford University Press, 2004.
33. *Minutes of Evidence before the Select Committee*, 20 July 1858; *Reports from the Committees, Colonisation and Settlement in India*, vol. 8, part 2, 1857–58.
34. The adult male population of Assam was estimated to be around 25,00,000 in the mid-eighteenth century (Bhuyan, *Anglo-Assamese Relations*, p. 259).
35. Guha, 'A Big Push without a Take-Off'.
36. Arupjyoti Saikia, 'Landlords, Tenants and Agrarian Relations: Revisiting a Peasant Uprising in Colonial Assam', *Studies in History*, vol. 26, no. 2, 2010, pp. 175–209.
37. The most ardent advocate of such predominance of the peasant-cultivator and raiyatwari system was Anandaram Dhekial Phukan, an Assamese officer in the colonial administration. Phukan studied in Calcutta and extensively wrote on various affairs of the province. Regarded as the most vocal public figure of the mid-nineteenth century Assam, Phukan submitted a long petition to the Commissioner A.J.M. Mills who came to investigate the condition of Assam in 1852 (see Mills, *Report on the Province of Assam*, pp. 93–132).
38. As the area settled for special cultivation was mostly meant for tea cultivation, its distribution within Assam differed.
39. Henry Baden-Powell, *Land Systems of British India*, vol. 3, Oxford: Clarendon Press, 1892, reprint, New Delhi: Publications Division, Government of India, 1974.
40. In the pre-colonial times they had to provide physical labour to the king or his subordinates in return for his land (see, Guha, *Medieval and Early Colonial Assam*, pp. 219–52).

41. Ibid., pp. 219–44; Fatik Chandra Barua, *Report on the Survey and Settlement of the La-khiraj and Nisf-khiraj Holdings in the District of Kamrup*, Shillong: Government Press, 1884.
42. The la-khiraj estates were further divided into *brahmottor, devottar* and *dharmottar*, depending on the form of service rendered by tenants settled therein to the religious institutions. The owners of two more forms of estates known as *khat* and *chamua* grants – though such landholdings were smaller than those in the other categories – used to enjoy similar privileges as the owners of the la-khiraj estates did (Baden-Powell, *Land Systems of British India*).
43. Ibid, p. 492.
44. The all-India average was 693 while in Assam it was 766, as tabulated in the Census of India of 1911, and reproduced in *Statistical Abstract Rela-ting to British India from 1902–03 to 1912–13 and 1910–1911 to 1919–20*, vol. 55, London, Her Majesty's Stationery Office, 1922.
45. These figures are estimated from *Statistical Abstract Relating to British India*, for the respective years. Accordingly, it indicates that for 1894–95, 1903–4, 1912–13, and 1919–20, the percentage turned out to be 0.52, 0.42, 0.48, and 0.43 respectively, while the all-India average for these years remained constant at 0.18.
46. The ardent advocates of this argument were the officials of the Assam Forest Department. In 1996, many in the department began to raise doubts concerning any possible existence of good cultivable land in the forests of the central Assam districts.
47. Arupjyoti Saikia, 'State, Peasants and Land Reclamation: The Predicament of Forest Conservation in Assam, 1850s–1980s', *IESHR*, vol. 45, no. 1, 2008, pp. 77–114.
48. This categorization is inferred from an examination of the tables of landholding pattern of indigenous people provided in the *Report on the Census of Assam*, 1951, vol. 12, Shillong: Government Press, 1951. Prepared from *Census of Assam 1951*, Table 10, part 2; and *Census of Assam*, 1931, vol. 3, New Delhi: Government Press, 1932, Table 10, part 2, the following table broadly indicates the percentage of these categories between the 1931 and the 1951 censuses.

Table A: Percentage of Agricultural Categories to Total Cultivating Population

	Peasant proprietors		*Share-tenants*		*Agricultural labourers*		*Landlords*	
Districts	*1951*	*1931*	*1951*	*1931*	*1951*	*1931*	*1951*	*1931*
Kamrup	78	90	18	7	3	3	2	1
Darrang	65	92	32	6	2	1	2	0.1
Nowgaon	82	95	13	4	3	1	1	0.02
Sibsagar	75	96	22	3	1	1	1	0.08
Lakhimpur	89	97	9	3	1	1	1	0.04

49. The Census of 1951 defined landlords as those who lived only on interest from rent in land.
50. The districts of Nowgaon, Lakhimpur and Darrang had 1,645, 1,586 and 4,101 acres respectively in their share of la-khiraj land (File no. RT. 44/52, *Proceedings of the Revenue Tenancy Branch*, 1952, ASA).
51. Kamrup and Darrang had 1,46,332 and 29,068 acres of nisf-khiraj land respectively. The remaining districts, namely, Nowgaon, Sibsagar and Lakhimpur, had a low share of nisf-khiraj land, i.e, 6,118, 4,962 and 1,204 acres respectively (ibid).
52. In Kamrup, it was found that there were 20,790 persons whose livelihood was rent from land. Out of these, the total male population was 9,893 while female population was 10,957.
53. Table I-C, 'Landholdings of Indigenous Persons, Kamrup', *Report on the Census of India*, 1951, *District Census Handbook*, Kamrup, Shillong: Government Press, 1951.
54. The Census of 1951 undertook a separate enquiry for the province of Assam. Accordingly, information was collected on the pattern of landholding of different cultivating classes. The following table gives an idea of cultivators holding land as intermediaries:

Table B: Landholding of Indigenous Cultivators

Acres	*Kamrup*	*Darrang*	*Nowgaon*	*Sibsagar*	*Lakhimpur*
Below 3	2,141	557	437	416	41
3–10	1,416	535	355	405	48
More than 10	610	216	130	251	18

Source: Prepared from Table no. 1-B, 'Indigenous Persons Land-holding', *Census of Assam, 1951.*

55. Prepared from Table I-C, 'Landholdings of Indigenous Persons'. The following table gives an idea of the extent of the absentee landowners in khiraj areas:

Table C: Percentage of Absentee Landowners Owning Land

Area owned (Acres)	*Kamrup*	*Darrang*	*Nowgaon*	*Sibsagar*	*Lakhimpur*
Between 1–10	51	44	47	43	39
Between 11–30	34	39	39	35	45
31 and above	15	17	14	22	17

56. J. McSwiney, *Report on the Land Revenue Settlement of the Darrang District of Eastern Bengal and Assam Effected during the Years 1905 to 1909*, Shillong: Eastern Bengal and Assam Secretariat Press, 1906, pp. 26–27. Since the 1897 earthquake (and as a result of it),

many rivers in the Brahmaputra valley, besides Nanoi, have changed their courses.

57. *Statistical Abstract Relating to British India.*
58. An account of the early forest administration in the province of Assam can be found in Arupjyoti Saikia, *A Forests and Ecological History of Assam, 1826–2000*, New Delhi: Oxford University Press, 2011.
59. Government of Assam, *Report on the Progress of the Forest Administration of Assam, 1914–1915*, Shillong: Assam Government Press, p. 7.
60. Government of Indian, *Report on Progress of the Forest Administration of Assam, 1946–1947*, Shillong: Assam Government Press, p. 16.

Chapter 1

1. The *raiyatwari* system of land revenue settlement was introduced in the Brahmaputra valley districts of Assam, except in Goalpara, a district contiguous to Bengal, in 1866. This system allowed the ryots or peasants to receive the title to land directly from the government and pay revenue directly to the government. According to the 1901 Census of India, the flat valley covered an area of 56,000 sq. km with an estimated population of 2.6 million.
2. The figures of forest land reclamation are based on a preliminary estimate made in J.F. Richards and J. Hagen, 'A Century of Rural Expansion in Assam', *Itinerario*, vol. 11, no. 1, 1987, pp. 193–209.
3. An official report mentions that 80 per cent of the total population of Brahmaputra valley practised agriculture. This estimate has remained more or less constant since the Census of 1881 (see 'Note on the Land Revenue System in Assam', *Census of India*, 1951, vol. 12, Shillong: Government Press, 1951, Appendix II, pp. 420–31).
4. Arupjyoti Saikia, *Forests and Ecological History of Assam, 1826–2000*, New Delhi: Oxford University Press, 2011.
5. J. McSwiney, *Report on the Land Revenue Settlement of the Kamrup District of Eastern Bengal and Assam Effected during the Years 1902 to 1905*, Shillong: Eastern Bengal and Assam Secretariat Press, 1906; S.P. Desai, *Report on the Land Revenue Settlement of the Kamrup District*, Shillong: Assam Government Printing Press, 1928; J. McSwiney, *Report on the Land Revenue Settlement of the Darrang District of Eastern Bengal and Assam Effected during the Years 1905 to 1909*, Shillong: Eastern Bengal and Assam Secretariat Press, 1910; D.K. Mukherjee, *Final Report on the Land Revenue Resettlement of the Darrang District during the Years 1927–33*, Shillong: Assam Government Press, 1934; S.N. Datta, *Report on the Resettlement of the Nowgaon District during the Years 1926 (October) to 1932 (January)*, Shillong: Assam Government Press,

1933; A.R. Edwards, *Report on the Land Revenue Settlement of the Nowgaon District during the Years from 1905–1906 to 1908–1909*, Shillong: Eastern Bengal and Assam Secretariat Press, 1909; C.K. Rhodes, *Report on the Land Revenue Settlement of the Sibsagar District during the Years 1923 to 1929*, Shillong: Assam Government Press, 1929, G.S. Hart, *Report on the Land Revenue Settlement of the Sibsagar District during the Years 1902–1903 to 1905–1906*, Shillong: Eastern Bengal and Assam Secretariat Press, 1906; S.N. MacKenzie, *Final Report on the Resettlement of Land Revenue in the Lakhimpur District, Assam during the Years 1908 to 1912*, Shillong: Assam Secretariat Printing Office, 1912; C.R. Pawsey, *Report on the Resettlement of the Lakhimpur District, 1929–1935*, Shillong: Assam Government Press, 1937.

6. Desai, *Report on the Land Revenue Settlement of the Kamrup District*, p. 7.
7. Ibid., p. 31. It is also important that one carefully examines the official claim that 'practically all the available land has long been taken up' (see, 'On the Extension of Cultivation in Assam and Colonisation of Wasteland in the Province', Note by Henry Cotton, Chief Commissioner of Assam, *Assam Secretariat Proceedings* [*ASP*], Revenue-A, nos 128–38, November 1898, Assam State Archives [ASA]). Peasants were always in search of arable land, and with limited resources available, they tried to make difficult terrains arable.
8. The two tracts which had a very low incidence of sharecropping were Chapari and Khallingduar areas.
9. Mukherjee, *Final Report on the Land Revenue Resettlement of the Darrang District*, pp. 26–27.
10. More specifically, the area under sharecropping had increased from 65,823 *bighas* to 90,578 bighas (ibid., p. 30).
11. Ibid., p. 31.
12. *Report on the Census of India*, Assam, vol. 4, part 1, Calcutta: Government Press, 1901; *Report on the Census of India*, Assam, vol. 3, part 1, Shimla: Government Press, 1911; *Report on the Census of India*, Assam, vol. 3, part 1, New Delhi: Government Press, 1931; *Report on the Census of India*, Assam, vol. 12, part 1A, New Delhi: Government Press, 1951.
13. See D. Thorner and A. Thorner, *Land and Labour in India*, Bombay: Asia Publishing, 1965, for a critique of the 1951 census categories.
14. The sample survey of Sibsagar indicates that 11.2 per cent of *khiraj* land was under sub-tenancy, while for Darrang the figure was 19 per cent. After the resettlement, these districts had a much lower incidence of sharecropping.
15. Mukherjee, *Final Report on the Land Revenue Resettlement of the Darrang District*, p. 13.

16. It must be kept in mind that a few years after this resettlement exercise, the Goalpara Tenancy Act and the Assam Tenancy Act were passed in the 1930s.
17. This estimate is based on relative figures of 1900–01 and 1930–31 calculated from Appendix III of *Annual Report on the Land Revenue Administration of Assam, 1900–01*, Shillong: Government Press, 1901; *Annual Report on the Land Revenue Administration of Assam 1930–31*, Shillong: Government Press, 1931.
18. Mukherjee, *Final Report on the Land Revenue Resettlement of the Darrang District*, p. 31.
19. C.K. Rhodes, who was responsible for the resettlement exercise in Sibsagar during 1923–29, observed this development (see Rhodes, *Report on the Land Revenue Settlement of the Sibsagar District*, p. 48).
20. The number of tenants in the five districts of Brahmaputra valley, as reported in the Census of 1901, was: Kamrup 77,162; Darrang 8,314; Nowgaon 3,322; Sibsagar 9,838; and Lakhimpur 1,592. In the Census of 1951, the respective figures were recorded as 118,368; 16,468; 5,600; 21,447; and 6,094.
21. Thorner and Thorner, *Land and Labour in India*, p. 133.
22. Ibid., p. 131.
23. Amalendu Guha. *Medieval and Early Colonial Assam: Society, Polity, and Economy*, Calcutta: KBS, 1991, p. 2.
24. *ASP*, Revenue Department, Revenue-A, no. 42, 1927, ASA.
25. In Sibsagar, during the first phase of land settlement in the twentieth century, for every 5 bighas of land sublet, 2 bighas were found to have been rented out for Rs 1–8 per bigha or less; another 2 bighas for Rs 1–8 *annas* or more; and the remaining 1 bigha for Rs 2–8 annas (see Hart, *Report on the Land Revenue Settlement of the Sibsagar District*, p. 54). It was recorded that 5,600 bighas were under *chukti* rent arrangement, 4,315 bighas under *adhi* and 700 bighas rented out in lieu of mere personal services rendered by the tenants to various Vaishnava monasteries. Out of the total number of *adhiars* settled on *khiraj* area, 47.5 per cent of the adhiars paid the government-approved rent rate either in cash or kind. A very small section — less than 3 per cent — paid in kind. The next phase of settlement did not report any substantial change in the rent payment pattern (see Rhodes, *Report on the Land Revenue Settlement of the Sibsagar District*, p. 48). In 1928, in Lakhimpur district, lands were sublet at the rent rate of Rs 2–4 per bigha. In Nowgaon, khiraj landowners were reported to have realized the government rent in most of the cases. On the other hand, they rented out estates at a slightly higher rate, besides extracting small personal services (see Pawsey, *Report on the Resettlement of the Lakhimpur District*, p. 43).

26. For instance, by 1933, Darrang was found to have 82 per cent of people renting out estates on cash rent.
27. In Beltola and Ramsa *mauzas* of Kamrup, the rent per bigha varied from Rs 1 and 1 anna to Rs 1 and 8 annas, respectively. In Rani, Barduar and Chayani, the rent was Rs 2 per bigha; in Chayagaon and Barnadi, the rent varied from Rs 1 and 4 annas to Rs 1 and 12 annas per bigha (Desai, *Report on the Land Revenue Settlement of the Kamrup District*, p. 23).
28. McSwiney, *Report on the Land Revenue Settlement of the Kamrup District*, p. 33.
29. The colonial government in Assam classified the land and villages surrounding them, into three categories — first, second and third — depending on soil quality, trading facilities and population density. The first-class land yielded the highest amount of revenue.
30. Desai, *Report on the Land Revenue Settlement of the Kamrup District*, p. 24.
31. In the villages around Tezpur, landowners were found renting out at such rates in the vicinity of the town. The highest incidence of *chukti adhi* arrangement was found in Meteka–Bongaon mauza (McSwiney, *Report on the Land Revenue Settlement of the Darrang District*, pp. 26–27).
32. In Sibsagar, the urban absentee landowners received a fixed share of the crop, usually ranging from 2 to 2.5 *maunds* of paddy per bigha (*ASP*, Revenue Department, Revenue-A, no. 42, 1927, ASA).
33. In Dibrugarh, it was higher than the government-approved rate. The area that was sublet at Rs 2–8 annas formed 30, 10 and 3 per cent of the total sublet area in Dibrugarh, central Jorhat and north-western part of Sibsagar district, respectively. On the north bank of Brahmaputra in Sibsagar district, charging the government-approved rate was customary (*ASP*, Revenue Department, Revenue-A, nos 46–53, 1929, ASA).
34. *ASP*, Revenue Department, Revenue-A, no. 53–57, 1928, ASA.
35. For instance, the manager of Amchong tea estate charged Rs 5 and 5 annas per *pura* and demanded 15 days of service in the garden. The manager of Sonapur tea garden charged Rs 8 and 8 annas per pura and demanded nine days of service (ibid., p. 12).
36. In Tinsukia, the Doomdooma Tea Company owning numerous gardens charged very high rent on the land sublet. It was found that an adhiar paid rent amounting to as high as Rs 300 per bigha if he retained a bigger holding (MacKenzie, *Final Report on the Resettlement of Land Revenue in the Lakhimpur District*, p. 30).
37. Edwards, *Report on the Land Revenue Settlement of the Nowgaon District*, p. 43.
38. *ASP*, Revenue Department, Revenue-A, no. 45–51, Oriental and India Office Collection (OIOC), British Library, London, 1928.

39. Desai, *Report on the Land Revenue Settlement of the Kamrup District*, p. 12. In Tezpur, demand for land by these labourers increased the rent. In the Chaiduar area, this demand varied from Rs 2 to Rs 4 per bigha, and in some places of Naduar the annual rate was 10 or 12 annas per bigha. In the nearby Bihali, the new tenants had to pay 4–12 annas.
40. Ibid.
41. Mukherjee, *Final Report on the Land Revenue Resettlement of the Darrang District*, p. 25.
42. Ibid., p. 25
43. McSwiney, *Report on the Land Revenue Settlement of the Darrang District*, pp. 26–27.
44. Fatik Chandra Barua, *Report on the Survey and Settlement of the La-khiraj and Nisf-khiraj Holdings in the District of Kamrup*, Shillong: Assam Government Press, 1884.
45. For more details on the process of Hinduization, see Nirmal K. Bose, 'The Hindu Method of Tribal Absorption', *Science and Culture*, vol. 8, 1941, pp. 188–98.
46. For instance, *Dainik Assamiya* often reported about the condition of tribal tenants in the *la-khiraj* land of the Auniati *satra* in upper Assam.
47. The nineteenth-century trajectory of sharecropping has been dealt with extensively in Guha, *Medieval and Early Colonial Assam*, pp. 254–62.
48. 'On the Extension of Cultivation in Assam and Colonisation of Wasteland in the Province', Note by Henry Cotton.
49. Memorandum by Jagannath Baruah, President, Jorhat Sarvajanik Sabha (JSS), 12 March 1897, *ASP*, Revenue-A, nos. 128–38, November 1898, ASA.
50. Mention may be made of F.J. Monahan, Director of Land Records and Agriculture, Memorial of the Upper Assam Raiyats Association; and Memorial of Gunjanan Baruah, Secretary of Assam Association, *ASP*, Revenue-A, nos. 128–38, November 1898, ASA.
51. This development happened in places such as Guwahati and Palashbari (see *Report on the Condition of the Lower Classes of Population in India*, File no. 6, Revenue and Agricultural Department, Famine Branch, National Archives of India [NAI], nos 1–24, December 1888).
52. Ibid.
53. Note by S.P. Desai, *ASP*, Revenue Department, Settlement Branch, Revenue-A, nos 26–84, June 1939, ASA.
54. *ASP*, Revenue Department, Revenue-A, no. 65, September 1927, ASA.
55. 'On the Extension of Cultivation in Assam and Colonisation of Wasteland in the Province', Note by Henry Cotton.

56. For an account of spread and impact of kala-azar (Leishmaniasis) epidemics, see T.C. McCombie, *Kala-azar in Assam: An Account of the Preventive Operation, 1913 to 1923*, London: H.K. Lewis and Co. Ltd, 1924.
57. The figure has been computed from the census reports of 1901 and 1941 for the Brahmaputra valley, excluding Goalpara.
58. The total areas in the khiraj land in the raiyatwari districts of Assam were 1,545,382 and 3,759,002 acres for 1900–1 and 1940–41, respectively, as calculated from Appendix III of *Annual Report on the Land Revenue Administration of Assam*, Shillong: Government Press, 1942.
59. Undated petition of Dinanath Deva Goswami to Deputy Commissioner, Nowgaon, August 1946, Nowgaon District Record Room (NDRR).
60. Letter from J.F. Gruning, Deputy Commissioner, Nowgaon, to Commissioner, Assam Valley Division, 7 December 1899, *ASP*, nos 24–43, Revenue-A, June 1900, ASA.
61. There is a lack of statistics or other information to compute the distances that the migrant peasants travelled in search of land. Both tribal and caste-Hindu peasantry resorted to such *pam* cultivation (McSwiney, *Report on the Land Revenue Settlement of the Darrang District*, p. 10).
62. Atulchandra Hazarika, *Smritilekha*, Guwahati: Assam Publication Board, 1981, p. 135.
63. For an account of the typical nature of an Assamese village, see Birinchi Kumar Barua, *A Cultural History of Assam*, Guwahati: Bina Library, 2003.
64. E.C. Cotes, *The Locusts of Bengal, Madras, Assam, and Bombay, etc.*, Calcutta: Office of the Superintendent of Government Printing, 1891.
65. Reliable statistics indicating the qualitative and quantitative dimensions of land loss are not available (see Arupjyoti Saikia, 'Dancing Like Nataraj: Earthquakes and Environmental History of the Brahmaputra River Valley', paper presented at the Yale University Agrarian Studies Colloquium, 13 April 2012).
66. Rhodes, *Report on the Land Revenue Settlement of the Sibsagar District*, p. 45.
67. McSwiney, *Report on the Land Revenue Settlement of the Darrang District*, p. 13.
68. Government of Assam, *Report on the Land Revenue Settlement of the Central Group of Nowgaon*, Shillong: Government Press, 1926, ASA. Sometimes, a peasant gave out his land to another who would take half the crop and pay the land revenue (*Assam Provincial Banking Enquiry Committee Report* [*APBECR*], *1929–30*, vol. 2, Shillong: Government Press, pp. 57–60).

69. Guha, *Medieval and Early Colonial Assam*, pp. 219–79. The principal tea-growing districts of Lakhimpur, Sibsagar and Darrang had 2,47,760 permanent labourers in 1900, in addition to temporary labourers (Rana Pratap Behal, 'Forms of Labour Protest in Assam Valley Tea Plantations, 1900–1930', *Economic and Political Weekly*, vol. 20, no. 4, 1985, pp. PE19–26).
70. *Report of the Census of Assam*, 1901, vol. 4, Calcutta: Government Press, p. 163.
71. *Reassessment of North West Group of Villages in the Nowgaon District, ASP*, Revenue Department, Revenue-A nos 140–55, OIOC.
72. MacKenzie, *Final Report on the Resettlement of Land Revenue in the Lakhimpur District*, p. 30.
73. Assamese peasants were also selling annual *patta* land to the immigrants. The sale of pam land was also frequently noticed (see Letter from C.B.C. Paine, Deputy Commissioner, Nowgaon, to Deputy Secretary, Revenue Department, Memo. no. 114R, 29 March 1946, NDRR.
74. Datta, *Report on the Resettlement of the Nowgaon District*, p. 41.
75. Memo. no. 282 DO, 14 October 1947 from Sub-Deputy Collector, Nowgaon, to Deputy Commissioner, NDRR.
76. Ibid. The government was also aware of the fact that the *kamla*s came to the province only at certain times of the year for seasonal occupation and then departed (Letter from C.B.C. Paine, Deputy Commissioner, Nowgaon, to Sub-Deputy Collector, Raha, Memo. no. 3120-25R, 3 and 5 June 1943, NDRR).
77. Ibid. An estimated 2,400 such kamlas were found in the Mairabari, Lahorighat, Batradava, Dhing, and Bokani mauzas of Nowgaon.
78. Ibid. The Deputy Commissioner of Nowgaon found that out of 36,781 immigrant families, approximately 12,000 families were reportedly landless in the Juria mauza, Nowgaon.
79. A revenue official in Nowgaon noted that the majority of the landless immigrants came to work as agricultural wage labourers (Memo. no. 622 K, 20 November 1947 from Sub-Deputy Collector, Nowgaon, to Deputy Commissioner, NDRR).
80. Letter from Sub-Deputy Collector, Raha, to Deputy Commissioner, Nowgaon, 7 August 1947, NDRR.
81. Datta, *Report on the Resettlement of the Nowgaon District*, pp. 15–16.
82. *The Assam Gazette*, part 1, 18 December 1946.
83. Government of Assam, *Line System Enquiry Committee Report*, vol. 1, Shillong: Assam Government Press, 1938, p. 25.
84. Letter from W.L. Scott, Director of Land Records, Assam, to Secretary, Government of India, *ASP*, no. 136, Revenue-A, Revenue Department, 16 September 1927, ASA.

85. Guha, *Medieval and Early Colonial Assam*, pp. 219–72; Sanjib Baruah, 'Clash of Resource Use Regimes in Colonial Assam: A Nineteenth-century Puzzle Revisited', *Journal of Peasant Studies*, vol. 28, no. 3, 2001, pp. 109–24.
86. In the nineteenth century, tea plantations had already caused extraordinary land speculation and, following them, the jute-industries did so in the next century.
87. In 1930s, a revenue official was surprised to find that those *rupit* lands, which could be purchased at Rs 5 to Rs 10 per bigha earlier, could not be purchased below Rs 20 to Rs 40 per bigha.
88. In another instance, the Deputy Collector of Nowgaon reported that after selling their lands to the immigrants, some tribal peasants permanently moved out of the Dhing mauza to Mayang while others took up wastelands for cultivation in Dhing only (Letter from C.B.C. Paine, Deputy Commissioner, Nowgaon, to Deputy Secretary, Revenue Department).
89. Letter from Sub-Deputy Collector, Barpeta, to Deputy Commissioner, Kamrup, Memo. no. 1130, 31 July 1945, NDRR.
90. Report of the Sub-Deputy Collector, Sadar Sub Division, Case no. 494–534/1997, 6 November 1947, NDRR. In Nowgaon, the Lalung Hingis colony was opened as a part of the land colonization scheme. Land was given to landless peasants on annual leases. Later on, in an inquiry, the revenue administration found that land-owners employed immigrant peasants to work as adhiars. The administration maintained that the Assamese peasants were easily tempted to sell their lands to the immigrant peasants. For instance, one rich peasant, Mohendra Nath Bora, had sold 7 bighas of land to the Muslim immigrants. He had also sold some land to the Assamese peasants and the latter had employed immigrants on the adhi. Further, land belonging to 15 people was found entirely occupied by immigrant peasants. The landowners defended themselves by claiming that they were cultivating the lands by employing immigrant landowners (Speech by A.W. Botham, *Assam Legislative Council Proceedings* [*ALCP*], 3 April 1928).
91. In another instance, C.B.C. Paine, Deputy Commissioner of Nowgaon, mentioned that Lalung (Tiwa) peasants with occupancy rights over land sold their lands to immigrant peasants from another area. He cited the example of a Lalung peasant who sold his land and occupied land in a professional grazing reserve (Letter from C.B.C. Paine, Deputy Commissioner, Nowgaon, to Deputy Secretary, Revenue Department, Memo. no. 114R, 29 March 1946, NDRR).
92. A landless peasant was defined as anyone who in his own name or in the name of his family or any of its members had got less than 5 bighas of land. The deputy commissioners of various districts apprehended that the land resolutions might accelerate immigrant

peasants' occupation of the tribal peasants' land (see File no. GDA no. 3252-R, Revenue Department, 21 June 1940, ASA).

93. *Report on the Census of India*, Assam, vol. 3, 1911, p. 190.
94. Guha, *Medieval and Early Colonial Assam*, pp. 219–62.
95. Ibid.
96. The district of Sibsagar had 40,894 acres of la-khiraj land, while the districts of Nowgaon, Lakhimpur and Darrang had 1645, 1586 and 4101 acres of la-khiraj land respectively (File no. RT. 44/52, Tenancy Branch, Revenue Department, 1952, ASA).
97. Desai, *Report on the Land Revenue Settlement of the Kamrup District*, p. 9.
98. McSwiney, *Report on the Land Revenue Settlement of the Darrang District*, p. 32.
99. Ibid., p. 10. About 85 per cent of the state's half-rate paying acreage and 40 per cent of the revenue-free acreage were concentrated in Kamrup in 1895–96. Nowgaon, Sibsagar and Lakhimpur had 6,118, 4,962, and 1,204 acres of *nisf-khiraj* lands respectively.
100. MacKenzie, *Final Report on the Resettlement of Land Revenue in the Lakhimpur District*, p. 30. During 1951, a survey was conducted in the two districts of Darrang and Sibsagar. This survey also indicated higher instances of tenancy in both la-khiraj and nisf-khiraj lands of the two districts, 51 per cent and 49.47 per cent, respectively ('Sample Survey of the Agricultural Holding in Darrang and Sibsagar', Appendix VI, *Report on the Census of India*, 1951, Assam, vol. 12, part 1A).
101. Land held under la-khiraj and nisf-khiraj was quite high in the Guwahati subdivision, i.e., 25 per cent.
102. Desai, *Report on the Land Revenue Settlement of the Kamrup District*, p. 11; *Report on the Census of India*, Assam, vol. 3, 1911.
103. Such references are available in *The Assam Gazette* from the year 1874.
104. Section 72 of *Assam Land Revenue Manual* empowered the revenue administration to notify such sales (see C.S. Rodes, *Assam Land Revenue Mannual*, Shillong: Government Press, 1906, 4th edition, 1931.
105. The place was Madhupur village of the Bahjani mauza, *The Assam Gazette*, part 9, 10 July 1935.
106. Most of the large estates that were auctioned off were in the Hatichong locality of Nowgaon (see *The Assam Gazette*, part 9, 26 June 1944).
107. In 1935 , an estate of 1952 bighas in Sualkuchi village of Pub-bansar mauza was sold out. Ten caste Hindu persons including one pleader jointly owned the estate. In another instance, nisf-khiraj estates of Babu Amar Kumar Mukherjee of Bhowanipur mauza and Narayan Chandra Dev Misra of Barpeta mauza, consisting of 207 bighas and

1029 bighas respectively were auctioned for the owners' failure to pay the revenue of Rs 609 and Rs 548, respectively (*The Assam Gazette*, part 9, 10 May 1944).

108. In one such case, two persons, Suganchand, a Marwari trader, and Krishna Chandra Barua, an Assamese pleader, bought an estate in Barigaon village of Pachim-Banbhag mauza in 1931. The phenomenon of nisf-khiraj lands being sold by the original owners to different points of buyers at different time was discussed in the Legislative Council in 1933. The Council member Mahendra Lal Das said, '[T]here has been a lot of transfers of these grants from the original grantee to third persons who are utilizing the land with a lot of gain' (Speech by M.L. Das, *ALCP*, 21 March 1933).
109. Report on Assessment of the Bajali Group of Villages in the Kamrup District, *ASP*, Revenue-A, December 1927, ASA.
110. 'Sample Survey of Agricultural Holdings in Darrang and Sibsagar', in Appendix VI of *Report on the Census of India*, Assam, vol. 12, part 1, 1951, pp. 271–301.
111. In Sariahtali and Namati mauzas, nisf-khiraj estate owners Harendra Nath Chaudhury, Ramananda Chaudhury, Binduram Chaudhury, Charan Barua, and Pravat Narayan Chaudhury had rented out their lands to immigrant peasants (*The Assam Gazette*, part 9, 14 November 1951).
112. Letter from Deputy Commissioner, Darrang, to Commissioner, Assam Valley Division, Memo. no. 1436, Revenue Department, 8 July 1926, ASA. The Director of the Land Records noted that many nisf-khiraj estate owners had settled immigrant peasants on the wastelands (Letter from W.L. Scott, Director of Land Records, Assam, to Secretary, Government of India, *ASP*, no. 136 Revenue-A, Revenue Department, 16 September 1927, ASA).
113. B.B. Chaudhuri, 'Agrarian Relations: Eastern India', D. Kumar and M. Desai (eds), *The Cambridge Economic History of India*, vol. 2 (c. 1757–c. 1970), New Delhi: Orient Longman, 1982, p. 123.
114. *Report on the Census of India*, Bengal, part 1, vol. 5, New Delhi: Government Press, 1921, pp. 32–33.
115. The first jute mill was established in 1855. By the turn of the century, Calcutta jute mills were posing a stiff challenge to Dundee jute mills and by the end of the First World War completely dethroned them (T. Sethia, 'The Rise of the Jute Manufacturing Industry in Colonial India: A Global Perspective', *Journal of World History*, vol. 7, no. 1, 1996, pp. 72, 96). The pressure for bringing more land under jute cultivation can thus be gauged from this rapid growth.
116. *Statistical Abstract Relating to British India*, London: His Majesty's Stationery Office, from 1902–03 to 1912–13 and 1910–11 to 1919–20, vol. 55, 1922.

117. Sethia, 'The Rise of the Jute Manufacturing Industry in Colonial India, p. 96; Gordon Thomas Stewart, *Jute and Empire: The Calcutta Jute Wallahs and the Landscapes of Empire*, Manchester: Manchester University Press, 1998.
118. The Bengal jute industrialists explicitly pressurized the Indian government to expand jute acreage in the Brahmaputra valley (Letter from H.M. Haywood, Secretary, Indian Jute Mills Association, to Secretary to Chief Commissioner of Assam, 9 May 1912, *ASP*, nos 10–16, Agriculture A, November 1912, ASA).
119. F.J. Monahan, *Assam Jute Cultivation*, Shillong: Government Press, 1898.
120. B.C. Basu [Assistant Director to Land Records and Agriculture, Assam], 'Note on Jute Cultivation' in Monahan, *Assam Jute Cultivation*.
121. 'Report of the Address Delivered by Mr. H.J.S. Cotton, C.S.I., Chief Commissioner of Assam, on the 29th April, 1897, at a Meeting of the Members of the Bengal Chamber of Commerce', in Government of Assam, *The Colonisation of Wastelands in Assam*, Calcutta: The India Daily News Office, 1899, pp. 35–37.
122. Ibid.
123. Ibid.
124. Report of J. Sherer, Deputy Commissioner, Nowgaon, 1873, cited in Jogendranarayan Bhuyan (ed.), *Unavimsa Satikar Assam Samvada*, Dibrugarh: Dibrugarh University Press, 1990, pp. 84–94.
125. The narratives of clashes between landlords and tenants in these areas have found mention in several works (see, for instance, Sayed Abdul Maksud, *Maulana Abdul Hamid Khan Bhasani*, Dhaka: Bangla Academy, 1994, pp. 25–26).
126. The Un-classed State Forests (USF) was a category of forests as per the Assam Forest Regulation of 1891. The forested tracts which had not been surveyed and were covered with grasslands or thinly distributed and the less marketable timber were declared as USF. These areas were administered by the revenue department (see, Chapter 2, in Saikia *Forests and Ecological History of Assam*).
127. Most peasants migrated from the districts of Mymmensing and Sylhet in East Bengal. For a brief background to their economic and ecological condition, see F.A. Sachse, *Mymensingh District Gazetteer*, vol. 1, Calcutta: Bengal Secretariat Book Depot, 1917.
128. This estimate has been based on *Statistical Abstract Relating to British India*. This figure includes the acreage in Cachar.
129. Indian Central Jute Committee, *Report on the Marketing and Transport of Jute in India*, Calcutta: Indian Central Jute Committee, 1940, p. 66, Table 8. See the following table:

Table D: Estimated Area under Jute Cultivation in Assam

(,000 omitted, in acres)

Year	*Acreage*	*Year*	*Acreage*
1928–29	149	1934–35	195
1929–30	118	1935–36	157
1930–31	157	1936–37	192
1931–32	219	1937–38	99
1932–33	303	1938–39	127
1933–34	281	1939–40	157

130. Between 1903 and 1920, the growth of paddy acreage was only 12 per cent (*Statistical Abstract Relating to British India*).
131. The winter rice produced in the Brahmaputra valley excluding Lakhimpur in 1924 amounted to 1,212,600 tonnes. This figure for the year 1931 was marginally higher, i.e., 1,129,400 tonnes. Even on the eve of Independence, the amount remained static with an amount of 1,327,600 tonnes (Government of Assam, *Agricultural Statistics of Assam*, Calcutta: Government Press, 1951).
132. For a history of railways in Assam, see S. Hilaly, *The Railways in Assam: 1885–1947*, New Delhi: Pilgrims Publishing, 2007.
133. The colonization programme was first introduced in Bokani and Lahorighat mauzas in Nowgaon district.
134. *ASP*, Revenue-A, December 1930, nos 395–464, Letter no. 126, R/10.3.1930 to Secretary, Revenue Department, Government of Assam, from Commissioner, Assam Valley Division, p. 16. In most of the cases, existing professional grazing reserves were thrown open for colonization. Imposition of grazing taxes preceded this intervention on the part of the colonial state, but provoked sharp reactions from both indigenous peasants and Congress political leaders (see Amalendu Guha, *Planter Raj to Swaraj: Freedom Struggle and Electoral Politics in Assam 1826–1947*, New Delhi: PPH, 1977, pp. 94, 160, 196–97; *Annual Report on the Land Revenue Administration of Assam, 1929–30*, Shillong: Government Press, 1931, p. 7). A development officer was appointed in 1930 for Barpathar land colonization scheme and the same move was suggested for north Lakhimpur as well.
135. Various such petitions are included in the official proceedings. See for instance, Petition of Rahijuddin Mia and 8 Others for Cancellation of Grazing Reserve Called Chandmama Kheli etc., *ASP*, Revenue-A, nos 395–464, December 1930, ASA.
136. Amalendu Guha, 'East Bengal Immigrants and Maulana Abdul Hamid Khan Bhasani in Assam Politics, 1928–47', *Indian Economic and Social History Review*, vol. 13, no. 4, October 1976, p. 422.
137. *Annual Report on the Land Revenue Administration of Assam, 1928–29*, Shillong: Government Press, 1929, p. 5.

138. *Annual Report on the Land Revenue Administration of Assam, 1933–34*, Shillong: Government Press, 1935, p. 6.
139. Prepared from *Annual Report on the Land Revenue Administration of Assam, 1928–29*; *Annual Report on the Land Revenue Administration of Assam, 1934–35*.
140. A perceptive immigrant jute farmer poetically captured this nexus between jute producers and traders:

 In August–September the heart leaps with joy as jute is ready,
 Then it's stacked neatly in the Marwari's warehouse
 So much toiling and tilling all for jute
 All jute went to the Marwari's warehouse for free
 . . . In the end in the account book of the Marwari
 All jute gone but a thousand rupees debt.
 . . . You have done a great service to Assam o garland of debt
 Killed all with temptation of jute.

 (K.M. Ahmad, *Hual Goni, Pater Kabita*, Calcutta: Ahmad Ali Khandarkar, 1930, p. 13).

141. To get an all-Indian picture of the conditions of peasantry, see Sugata Bose (ed.), *Credit, Markets and the Agrarian Economy of Colonial India*, New Delhi: Oxford University Press, 1994; I.J. Catanach, *Rural Credit in Western India, 1875–1930: Rural Credit and the Co-operative Movement in the Bombay Presidency*, Berkeley, CA: University of California Press, 1970; P.J. Musgrave, 'Rural Credit and Rural Society in the United Provinces, 1860–1920', in Clive Dewey and A.G. Hopkins (eds), *The Imperial Impact: Studies in the Economic History of Africa and India*, London: The Anthem Press, 1978, pp. 216–32; Tirthankar Roy, *Economic History of India, 1857–1947*, New Delhi: Oxford University Press, 2001, pp. 76–77. For a discussion of the conditions of Bengal peasantry, see Sugata Bose, *Peasant Labour and Colonial Capital: Rural Bengal since 1770*, Cambridge: Cambridge University Press, 1993; Also, see, *Agrarian Bengal: Economy, Social Structure and Politics, 1919–1947*, Cambridge: Cambridge University Press, 1986. Also, see, Amiya Kumar Bagchi (ed.), *Money and Credit in Indian History: From Early Medieval Times*, New Delhi: Tulika Books, 2002. For an analysis of the theoretical aspects of the rate of interest in usury, see Amit Bhaduri, 'On the Formation of Usurious Interest rates in Backward Agriculture', in Amit Bhaduri, *Unconventional Economic Essays*, New Delhi: Oxford University Press, 1999, 200–41.
142. For an analysis of the nineteenth-century Assamese agrarian structure see Guha, *Medieval and Early Colonial Assam*, pp. 219–79 and Aditya Mukherjee, 'Agrarian Conditions in Assam, 1880–1890: A Case Study of Five Districts of the Brahmaputra valley', *Indian Economic and Social History Review* (*IESHR*), vol. 16, no. 2, 1979, pp. 207–32.

143. Evidence of many families quickly acquiring wealth through moneylending is not difficult to find in the Assamese literary works.
144. See Rajen Saikia, *Social and Economic History of Assam 1853–1921*, New Delhi: Manohar, 2000.
145. *Report on Census of India*, Assam, vol. 4, part 1, p. 165.
146. The high concentration of moneylenders in Kamrup could be explained by the presence of Assamese landlords and traders, along with Marwari traders in several pockets of the district.
147. *APBECR*, vol. 1, p. 25.
148. The *APBECR* is itself an important source for understanding the dynamics of credit market in the peasant economy of Assam. A series of enquiries throughout British India produced a number of reports on the practices of moneylending in the first few decades of the twentieth century. For a detailed discussion on the intellectual origin of these reports and their weakness, see M. Raghavan, 'Some Aspects of Growth and Distribution of Rice in India', *Social Scientist*, vol. 28, nos 5–6, May–June 1999, pp. 62–85.
149. For details, see Chapter 4 in this volume.
150. In Sibsagar, one in every four persons was found indebted during the third decade of the twentieth century. In Lakhimpur, a large number of peasants were found indebted (*APBECR*, vol. 1, pp. 172–83).
151. In Sisi mauza of Dibrugarh, all the 6,000 Miri peasants were found in debt (MacKenzie, *Final Report on the Resettlement of Land Revenue in the Lakhimpur District*, pp. 14–15). In Golaghat, it was noticed that out of the 44 families in Bagonjeng village, 13 families were in debt. Each family had incurred a debt of Rs 104 on an average (*APBECR*, vol. 1, p. 26).
152. *APBECR*, vol. 1, p. 26.
153. Ibid., p. 24.
154. Evidence of Kalisaran Sen, in *APBECR*, vol. 2, p. 105. Also see Gaurishankar Bhattacharjya, *Sabinaya Nibedan*, Guwahati: Sahitya Prakash, 1999.
155. *APBECR*, vol. 1, p. 156.
156. Datta, *Report on the Resettlement of the Nowgaon District*, p. 41.
157. The following table indicates a general pattern of credit flow:

Table E: Pattern of Credit Flow

District	*Sources of credit*	*Mortgage*	*Interest*	*To return after*
Darrang	mahajan and faria	Nil	Rs 18–24 per rupee	6 months
Nowgaon	mahajan	On security of ornaments, on *dadan* basis	Rs 12–1 per rupee	6 months

Source: Note by Deputy Commissioner, Nowgaon, Revenue Department, File no. /231/2, 1938, NDRR.

158. The Census of India, 1891, for the first time entered a few professional moneylenders in Kamrup.
159. Information on the life and activities of these moneylenders from Kabul, popularly called *kabuliwalas* is scant. Most of them never aspired to get hold of the land of indebted peasants. They tried their best to recover the principal and interest over a long period of time, often through coercive methods, which was in marked contrast to other moneylenders like the Marwari trader.
160. *APBECR*, vol. 1. p. 36.
161. Ibid., p. 51.
162. Evidence of Jaganth Bujar Baruah, in *APBECR*, vol. 2, p. 500.
163. During the 1905–6 resettlement in Nowgaon, all the mauzas were found having at least two shops of the *kayas* (Marwari traders-cum-moneylenders).
164. Government of India, 'Rural Credit and Indebtedness', in Government of India, *Report of the Famine Inquiry Commission, 1943*, Appendix III, New Delhi: Government Printing Press, 1945, pp. 461–62.
165. *APBECR*, vol. 2, p. 51.
166. Government of India, *Report of the Famine Inquiry Commission 1943*, Appendix III.
167. *APBECR*, vol. 2, p. 36.
168. Evidence of Jaganth Bujar Baruah, in *APBECR*, vol. 2, p. 500.
169. *APBECR*, vol. 2, p. 37.
170. Ibid., pp. 57–60.
171. Evidence of Kanak Lal Barua, in Government of India, *Royal Commission of Agriculture in India*, vol. 5, Calcutta: Central Publication Branch, 1927, pp. 1–46.
172. Evidence of Narayan Barua, in Government of India, *Royal Commission of Agriculture*, vol. 5, pp. 197–208.
173. Evidence of Kirtinath Sarma Barua, in *APBECR*, vol. 2, p. 396. The report estimated that out of the amount borrowed, the peasants spent 30 per cent on the purchase of cattle, 11 per cent on the repayment of previous debts, 11 per cent on the payment of land revenue, and an estimated 15 per cent on other transactions. The tribal, caste-Hindu and Muslim peasants — all observed the custom of paying dowry worth about Rs 80–150 on their daughters' marriages.
174. *APBECR*, vol. 2, p. 50.
175. Peasants, in order to spend on *upanayana* — initiation ceremony of an upper-caste boy — in emulation of the upper castes would be perennially indebted to moneylenders (Rhodes, *Report on the Land Revenue Settlement of the Sibsagar District*, p. 44). It was also noted that 'quite ordinary peasant will spend as much as Rs 400 on the ceremony and be in debts for years in consequence since public opinion demands that all be feasted and proper gifts bestowed' (ibid.).

176. Statements like 'generally speaking the more ignorant and helpless a borrower ... the more likely he is to be victimized' were quite often made by officials. They agreed that the Kachari peasants in the outlying parts of Mangaldai 'are most improvident and use in some places an extra-ordinary large portion of their paddy crops in brewing laopani' (*APBECR*, vol. 1, p. 29).
177. *APBECR*, vol. 2, p. 50. Also, see Datta, *Report on the Resettlement of the Nowgaon District*, p. 41.
178. Marwari moneylenders had extensive financial transactions with the tea-garden owners. Often, they acted as intermediaries between the gardens and managing houses in Calcutta. For instance, one Marwari moneylender Jodhraj Singh from whom Goswami had borrowed money had financial transactions with a tea garden in Badulipar tea estate in Sibsagar district (T.C. Deva Goswami, *Jibon Sonwaran*, Golaghat: Rangamati Gomotha Mahara Satra, 1982, pp. 9–10).
179. For a careful analysis and ethnographic study of the role played by co-operative credit societies in rural Assam in the pre-Independence period, see Kishore Bhattacharjee, 'Structure and Individual in Assamese Society: A Study of Family, Kinship, Caste and Religion', unpublished PhD thesis, Gauhati University, 1990. Bhattacharjee shows how rich peasant families, depending on their caste and other social privileges, reaped benefits like easy loans, etc., from the early co-operative societies in rural Assam. The number of such societies increased manifold in the next couple of decades.
180. *ASP*, nos 46–53, Revenue-A, Revenue Department, September, 1929, ASA.
181. Ibid.
182. 'Sample Survey of Darrang', in *Report on the Census of India*, Assam, vol. 12, part 2, 1951, pp. 251–58.
183. Letter from Settlement Officer, Kamrup, to Director of Land Records, 9 March 1928, *ASP*, Revenue Department, Revenue-A, September, 1928, ASA.
184. Mukherjee, *Final Report on the Land Revenue Resettlement of the Darrang District*, p. 18. Trade was practically in the hands of Marwari traders in Kamrup and Darrang. There were Marwari merchants in Mangaldai (Darrang) who had even established their trading firms for jute trading.
185. In Palashbari and Chayagaon, Kamrup district, the shopkeepers were most visible and well entranched in a few villages, viz., Amtola, Nahirov and Kaimari. In Sibsagar, since the early part of the twentieth century, Marwari traders had established a number of shops in almost every village and also purchased the produce from the peasants, but at a price 30 per cent lower rate than the market

price. But sometimes peasants sold their produce in the garden lines, i.e., residential quarters of tea-garden workers inside the garden rather than at the *haats* (Hart, *Report on the Land Revenue Settlement of the Sibsagar District*, p. 42).

186. Desai, *Report on the Land Revenue Settlement of the Kamrup District*, p. 13.
187. *APBECR*, vol. 1, p. 24.
188. on the south bank of Brahmaputra, Palashbari was the principal centre of trade. But, there were also markets at Chayagaon, Boko, Singra, Dhupdhara, Halim, Beltola, and Sonapur.
189. Desai, *Report on the Land Revenue Settlement of the Kamrup District*, p. 17.
190. Mukherjee, *Final Report on the Land Revenue Resettlement of the Darrang District*, p. 20.
191. Desai, *Report on the Land Revenue Settlement of the Kamrup District*, p. 12.
192. R.M. Martin, *The History, Antiquities, Topography, and Statistics of Eastern India*, vol. 3, London: W.H. Allen and Co., 1838, reprint, New Delhi: Asian Educational Service, 1988, p. 267.
193. Ibid., p. 268.
194. Between 1913 and 1920, the acreage of jute cultivation in Assam increased from 98,351 acres to 137,337 acres. This increase coincided with the early phase of immigration of East Bengali peasants (*Statistical Abstract Relating to British India*).
195. Indian Central Jute Committee, *Report on the Marketing and Transport of Jute in India*, p.15.
196. The relation between cash crop production and capital is best explained in Shahid Amin, *Sugarcane and Sugar in Gorakhpur: An Inquiry into Peasant Production for Capitalist Enterprise in Colonial India*, New Delhi: Oxford University Press, 1984.
197. *ASP*, nos 46–53, Revenue-A, Revenue Department, September, 1929, ASA.
198. Resettlement Reports of Kamrup, Darrang, Nowgaon, Sibsagar, and Lakhimpur for the 1920s and early 1930s.
199. *Annual Report on the Land Revenue Administration of Assam, 1929–30*, Shillong: Government Press, 1930. Also, see Chief Secretary's Fortnightly Report to Secretary of State (hereafter Fortnightly Report) second half of June 1929.
200. *Annual Report on the Land Revenue Administration of Assam, 1932–33*, Shillong: Government Press, 1933, p. 14.
201. *Annual Report on the Land Revenue Administration of Assam, 1933–34*, Shillong: Government Press, 1934, p. 14.
202. Ibid., p. 15.
203. The annual reports on the land revenue administration of Assam reported this phenomenon throughout the 1930s and 1940s.

204. 'Resolutions Regarding the Condition of the Raiyats', Speech by W.L. Scott, 13 March, 1936, *ALCP*. He also stated that the total number of lands auctioned during 1934–35 was 4,575 in the Assam province. However in 1920s, while giving evidence before the Royal Commission on Agriculture in India, he, as Director of Land Records of Assam, claimed that indebtedness was not as pressing a problem in Assam as in Bengal.
205. Prepared from the date of relevant years in the *Annual Report on the Land Revenue Administration of Assam.*
206. The debt-trapped peasants often mortgaged their land to the moneylenders. This credit relationship between peasants and moneylenders came to be known as *bandhak*. It is important to note here that an early Assamese dictionary *Hemkosha*, critically acclaimed for its observations on the contemporary society, did not mention this word in its first edition (*Hemkosha*, ed. P.R.T. Gourdon and Compiled by Hemchandra Barua, Shillong: Government Press, 1900). It was only in the later Assamese lexicon, *Chandra-Kanta Abhidhan*, whose social origin went back to 1920s took note of the word, since it must had been in circulation at that time (see Maheswar Neog [ed.], *Chandra Kanta Abhidhan*, Guwahati: Gauhati University Publication Division, 1987).
207. *Annual Reports on the Land Revenue Administration Assam* during 1931–1932 and 1932–1933.
208. B.B. Chaudhuri, 'Agrarian Relations: Eastern India' in D. Kumar and M. Desai (eds), *The Cambridge Economic History of India*, vol. 2, (c. 1757–c. 1970), New Delhi: Orient Longman, p. 148.
209. See A.V. Chadravarkar, 'Money and Credit' in Kumar and Desai, (eds), *The Cambridge Economic History of India*, pp. 762–803.
210. *Annual Report of the Land Revenue Administration of Assam, 1931–1932*, p. 2, para. 6.
211. Fortnightly Report, first half of August 1930
212. Fortnightly Report, first half of October 1930.
213. A copy of the text is available in the Oriental and India Office Collection (OIOC), British Library, London. For a fuller exploration of this text, see Arupjyoti Saikia, 'Pater-Kabita-Huyal Goni', *Dainik Janambhumi*, 7 November 2006.
214. *Annual Report on the Land Revenue Administration of Assam, 1942–1943*, Shillong: Government Press, 1944, p. 3.
215. Fortnightly Report, first half of June 1945.
216. Fortnightly Report, second half of November 1944. This speculation in land prices was primarily due to speculations in the jute market. It was noted that peasants 'are taking up every possible piece of land for cultivation' (Fortnightly Report, first half of November 1943).
217. Ibid., p. 17.

218. *Annual Report on the Land Revenue Administration of Assam, 1938–1939*, Shillong: Government Press, 1940, pp. 4, 17.
219. *Annual Reports on the Land Revenue Administration of Assam*, 1946, 1947, 1948, 1949, and 1950.
220. Because of the severe and rapid price rise, particularly of food items during this time, the government even provided relief by way of food items at concessional prices to the low-paid government servants in Assam (Note by Finance Department, no. 8/18 w/13, Finance Department, New Delhi, 23 July, 1943, in File no. 104/4/43-Public/1943, Government of India, Home [public], NAI).
221. Approximately, it was about 12 annas less in the case of a maund of paddy (*APBECR*, vol. 1. p. 51).
222. Edwards, *Report on the Land Revenue Settlement of the Nowgaon District*, p. 31.
223. *APBECR*, vol. 1. p. 56.
224. Ibid., p. 51.
225. Notification no. 3089R, 27 September 1919, *ASP*, Revenue Department, Revenue-A, September 1928, ASA.
226. The restriction, as it stood, was of little value to anyone in preventing land from passing from the hands of the cultivators. Also, it only made it difficult for the peasants to obtain the necessary capital to invest in agriculture (*APBECR*, vol. 2, p. 156).
227. *APBECR*, vol. 1. p. 156.
228. Ibid., p. 156.
229. Letter from H.M. Pritchard, Deputy Commissioner, Nowgaon, to Commissioner, Assam Valley Division, 16 May 1927, *ASP*, Revenue-A, September 1928, ASA.
230. *Report on the Census of India*, Assam, vol. 3, part 1, 1911, p. 151.
231. *ASP*, Revenue Department, Revenue-A, November 1919, no. 1, OIOC.
232. Government of India, *Report of the Famine Inquiry Commission*, p. 447.
233. Evidence of Settlement Officer of Darrang in *APBECR*, vol. 1, p. 156.
234. Ibid.
235. Pawsey, *Report on the Resettlement of the Lakhimpur District*, pp. 52–53; Hart, *Report on the Land Revenue Settlement of the Sibsagar District*, p. 54.
236. Ibid., p. 55. About 70 per cent of the total khiraj lands had been sublet in these areas.
237. The practice was noticed in the south-western part of the Sibsagar district between Sibsagar and Jagi, where traders and moneylenders, after obtaining the title, usually sublet it to others (*ASP*, Revenue-A, no. 212, December, 1927, ASA).
238. Prepared from Table no. 1-B titled 'Indigenous Persons Landholding', in *Report on the Census of India*, Assam, 1951, vol. 12, Shillong:

Government Press, 1951. This table illustrates the distribution of lands amongst the peasant proprietors. See the following table:

Table F: Percentage of Land Owned by Peasant Proprietors

Districts	0 bigha or landless	1–10 bighas	11–30 bighas	Above 31 bighas
Kamrup	17	38	39	7
Darrang	31	33	29	7
Nowgaon	41	25	26	8
Sibsagar	26	40	28	6
Lakhimpur	23	35	34	8

239. Refer Table 1 in Introduction.
240. Prepared from 'Indigenous Persons Land-holding', Table no. 1-D, *Report on the Census of India*, Assam, 1951. The following table indicates the size of sharecroppers' holding in different districts:

Table G: Percentage of Peasant Families Renting Land

Districts	1–10 bighas	11–30 bighas	Above 31 bighas
Kamrup	75	23	2
Darrang	67	31	2
Nowgaon	73	23	4
Sibsagar	79	19	2
Lakhimpur	76	21	3

241. *Report on the Census of India*, Assam, 1921, vol. 3, Shillong: Government, 1923.
242. This percentage was 0.84 of the total agricultural population in the valley.
243. Saikia, *Social and Economic History of Assam*, p. 110.
244. There are factors which should be taken into consideration too for understanding this problem. Legal complications concerning the annual patta lands, sale of the revenue-free and half-revenue-free lands, absence of tenancy acts, and heavy fragmentation of land were some of the important areas which need to be examined in detail. The cultural complexity, threat of wild animals and inadequate technology for land reclamation also contributed to the growing number of agricultural labourers.
245. Demi-official communication between Deputy Secretary, Tenancy Branch, Revenue (Reforms) Department, Government of Assam, and Anil Roy Chaudhury, no. RRT 34/59/139, Shillong, 20 May 1960, ASA.
246. Government of India, *District Census Report, Kamrup*, New Delhi: Government Press, 1951. According to the Census of 1951 of

the 10,761 persons practising agriculture in Beltola, there were 3,626 peasant proprietors, 3,614 sharecroppers, 439 agricultural labourers, and 50 landlords. Only a few villages like Borchapara, Hatigaon and Sarumataria had a nominal presence of rich peasants known as *matigiri*.

247. *District Census Report*, Kamrup, 1951. For example, in Betkuchi village out of the total 580 families, approximately 126 families were those of peasant proprietors and 420 families, of sharecroppers.
248. Mention may be made of villages like Jatia, Udalbakra, Bonda, Birkuchi, Borsajai, and Maidam Sarumataria.
249. Mauzas like Dharmapur and Upar Barbhag, Tihu, Rampur, Chayani, Namati, Nambharbhag, Dimaria, and Borduar had a large number of families whose only income was rent from the land.

Chapter 2

1. The social history of petitions and their importance in the making of modern politics has been superbly discussed in Lex Heerma van Voss (ed.), *Petitions in Social History*, Cambridge: Cambridge University Press, 2002.
2. For a perceptive discussion on the content and career of this memorandum, see Maheswar Neog, *Anandaram Dhekial Phukan: Plea for Assam and Assamese*, Jorhat: Assam Sahitya Sabha, 1977.
3. These petitions, numerically voluminous, hardly find space in the Assam State Archives (ASA). They are classified as records to be destroyed at frequent intervals. The district record rooms in Assam have somehow been able to retain these petitions from the early twentieth century (though not preserved and classified in a professional manner) till the present time (only fate knows when they will disappear). They are kept in gunny bags often co-habiting with snakes and heavy layers of dust. The reason for this state of neglect is understandable, as these records hardly pose any threat to the Indian state. At the same time, it is too challenging to estimate, even approximately, the total number of such petitions submitted to various agencies till the eve of independence. For the purpose of writing this book, I have largely relied on the petitions preserved in the Nowgaon District Record Room (NDRR).
4. The rate of literacy, according to the 1951 Census of India, was less than one-fifth of the total population of the state.
5. The reference is to the Sensoah-Moriabari segment of Assam Bengal railway in Nowgaon district.
6. Letter from Deputy Commissioner, Nowgaon, the Sub-deputy Collector, Kampur, Memo. no. 726/5/18, 2 April 1946, NDRR.
7. Letter from K.W.P. Marwar, Deputy Commissioner, Nowgaon, to Divisional Engineer, Assam Bengal Railway, Lumding, Memo. no. 1941R, 25 June 1935, NDRR.

8. S.B. Medhi, *Transport System and Economic Development in Assam*, Guwahati: Assam Publication Board, 1978.
9. A couple of years later, in 1929, Madhav Chandra Bezbarua, a leading Assamese nationalist, engaged in flood relief works amongst the same peasants. He could only find the railway track as the safest place to live in during a flood (see M.C. Bezbarua, 'Banpani Prapirita Thair Majat Charidin', *Abahan*, vol. 5, no. 8, 1934, pp. 953–66).
10. Petition of Villagers of Village Birah-Bebejia to Chief Commissioner, in Letter no. 653R from Deputy Commissioner, Nowgaon, to Commissioner, Assam Valley Division, 28 June 1922, NDRR.
11. Petition of Mahayan Nath and 79 Others, Reference no. RF/46/45/7, 3 October 1946, NDRR.
12. Speech by Bhimbar Deuri and by Sayidur Rahman, 3 March 1941, *Assam Legislative Council Proceedings* (*ALCP*).
13. In the neighbouring Darjeeling, the Bengal government also introduced a similar system in 1911. See K. Sivaramakrishnan, *Modern Forests: Statemaking and Environmental Change in Colonial Eastern India*, New Delhi: Oxford University Press, 1999, p. 195.
14. Homeswar Goswami, *Population Trends in the Brahmaputra Valley, 1881-1931*, New Delhi: Mittal Publications, 1985, Table 5.7, p. 106.
15. G.S. Hart, *Note on a Tour Inspection of Goalpara (Assam), Buxa, Jalpaiguri, Kalimpong, Kurseong Forest Divisions (Bengal)*, Shimla: Government Press, June 1920.
16. The figures for these three districts are: Kamrup 346,116 *bighas*; Darrang 140,875 bighas; and Nowgaon 170,769 bighas (see Speech by Bhimbar Deuri, 3 March 1941, *ALCP*).
17. Speech by Bishnuram Medhi, 9 September 1946, *Assam Legislative Assembly Proceedings* (*ALAP*).
18. Petition of Villagers of Village Birah-Bebejia to Chief Commissioner, Revenue Miscellaneous, 1944, NDRR.
19. Letter from Commissioner, Assam Valley Division, to the Deputy Commissioner of Nowgaon, Memo. no. 2113, 18 July 1922, NDRR.
20. Petition of Ghinlaga Kalita and Others; Petition of Govindaram Gaonbura; Petition of Govinda Satola; and Petition of Homeswar Bhuyan, RF/46/45/7, 3 October 1946, NDRR.
21. For a fuller treatment of the Assamese social structure and the *khel* system, see Kishore Bhattacharjee, 'Structure and Individual in Assamese Society: A Study of Family, Kinship, Caste and Religion', unpublished PhD thesis, Gauhati University, Guwahati, 1990.
22. P.S. Gupta (ed.), *Towards Freedom Movement, 1943–44*, vol. 2, New Delhi: Oxford University Press, 1997, p. 2086.
23. *Tinidiniya Assamiya* (3 May 1938) reported how a local *mauzadar* in Katani, Jorhat, attached the property of the peasants.
24. Speech by Purna Chandra Sarma, 4 December 1941, *ALAP*.

25. *Annual Report on the Police Administration of Assam*, 1945.
26. Ibid.
27. Krishna Sarma, a key Assamese congress leader and a successful organizer of Congress units across Assam, had perceptively captured how these sabhas became important institutions for Assam Congress (see, Krishna Nath Sarma, *Krishna Sarmar Dairy*, Guwahati: Assam Publication Board, 1972; Padmna Nath Barthakur, *Swadhinatar Ranor Sanswarparat*, Dibrugarh: Kaustav Prakasan, 2006).
28. Sarma, *Krishna Sarmar Dairy*, pp. 203–4.
29. Ibid., p. 250.
30. Presidential Address of Harekrisna Das, *Tinidiniya Assamiya*, 10 April 1936.
31. Ibid.
32. *Tinidiniya Assamiya*, 4 September 1936.
33. Ibid., 11 August 1936.
34. Ibid., 15 May 1936.
35. Ibid., 8 September 1936.
36. Ibid., 10 April 1936.
37. Ibid., 20 April 1940.
38. Ibid., 7 March 1936.
39. Ibid., 10 January 1936.
40. *Sadiniya Assamiya*, 11 July 1936.
41. A.J. Laine, Revenue Minister in the Assam government, admitted in the Assam Legislative Council that Tapajuli fuel reserve had been included in the Barpeta Colonization Scheme (Speech by A.J. Laine, 9 March 1931, *ALCP*, vol. 1).
42. *Tinidiniya Assamiya*, 10 April 1936. The conference was given a wide coverage: the resolutions and the presidential addresses were published in full length. It was further reported that 'it was attended by six to seven thousands people everyday and 210 delegates participated'.
43. 'Raijalai Binit Guhari: Nikhil Goalpara Krishak Sanmilan', *Tinidiniya Assamiya*, 25 February 1936.
44. *Tinidiniya Assamiya*, 10 April 1936.
45. For an insight of a contemporary Congress man into the works of ryot sabhas, see Sarma, *Krishna Sarmar Dairy*.
46. In the Jorhat subdivision of Sibsagar, there were 29 such sabhas. Every ryot sabha had to send delegates to the provincial conference ('Report of Radhanath Hazarika, Joint Secretary, Jorhat Ryot-Sabha', *Tinidiniya Assamiya*, 18 February 1936).
47. Amalendu Guha, *Planter Raj to Swaraj: Freedom Struggle and Electoral Politics in Assam, 1826–1947*, New Delhi: PPH, 1977, p. 68.
48. Jyananath Bora, *Assomot Bideshi*, ed. Prasenjit Chaudhuri, Guwahati: Barua Agency, 1925, reprint, Guwahati: Chetana Prakash, 1996.

49. Padmanath Gohain Barua, a leading Assamese nationalist, wrote in 1932 that such immigration would create crisis for the Assamese peasantry (P. Bhattacharya, 'Asomot Bideshi', *Abahan*, vol. 4, no. 5, 1932 [1858 *saka*], pp. 612–13). Madhab Chandra Bezbaroa, another influential Assamese nationalist, submitted a memorandum to Jawaharlal Nehru, the then President of Indian National Congress, on behalf of the Young Assamese Association in 1937; one of the main thrusts of the memorandum was the question of East Bengali migration was seen as a moderate threat to the Assamese cultural nationalism by Bengali-speaking Hindus who had migrated to Assam from Bengal (M. Ibrahim Ali [ed.], *Madhab Chandra Bezbaroa*, Guwahati: R.P. Bezbaroa, 2001, Appendix C).
50. Kamalakanta Bhattacharya was known for his scathing criticism of the underdevelopment of Assam in the colonial times (Prafulladutta Goswami (ed.), *Kamalakanta Bhattacharya Rachanawali*, Guwahati: Assam Publication Board, 2007, p. 22).
51. In 1938, the Assam Legislative Assembly adopted a resolution to look into the complaints received against the functioning of Line System. Members of the Line System Enquiry Committee, constituted as a result of this resolution, visited several places in western Assam and submitted a three-volume report in 1938 (Government of Assam, *Line System Enquiry Committee Report*, 3 vols, Shillong: Government Press, 1938).
52. 'Note of Dissent' by Rabi Chandra Kachari, Kameswar Das and Sarveswar Baruah, in Government of Assam, *Line System Enquiry Committee Report*, vol. 1, p. 20.
53. A *mauza* or revenue circle could range in area from a few square miles to 200 square miles. The mauzadar, one of the influential persons in a mauza, was responsible for collecting and depositing the revenue of the mauza under his jurisdiction. This revenue administration system came into being in 1870.
54. 'Bilasoni', cited in 'Editorial', *Chetana*, vol. 4, no. 10, 1922.
55. 'Asomot Orajakota', in *Chetana*, vol. 1, no. 5, cited in Suchibrata Roychaudhury (ed.), *Chetanar Chinta: Collection of the Editorial of Chetana*, Jorhat: Assam Sahitya Sabha, 1999, pp. 84–85, emphasis added.
56. Speech by Kameswar Das, 17 March 1945, *ALAP*.
57. In the budget session of the Assam Legislative Council in 1943, Karka Dalay Miri, a tribal member, claimed that Miri peasants of Ranganadi in Naoboicha mauza often got into trouble with the East Bengali peasants. Another tribal member, Rabi Chandra Kachari, narrated similar experiences from Darrang; he too claimed that the new land settlement policy had also displaced the Assamese peasants (Speech

by Rabi Chandra Kachari, Budget Session 1944, *ALAP*; Speech by Karka Dalay Miri, 27 March 1945, *ALAP*; Speech by Dhirsing Deuri, 26 February 1940, *ALAP*).
58. Speech by Lakheswar Barooah, 6 December 1941, *ALAP*.
59. Speech by Dhirsing Deuri, Budget Session 1945, *ALAP*.
60. Petition of Hira Kachari and Other Villagers of the Barpeta Gaon, Petition no. 541/1939–41 in the Court of Deputy Commissioner, File no. XVIII/28 July 1936, NDRR.
61. Petition of Hira Kachari and Other Villagers of the Barpeta Gaon, Petition no. 456/1941 in the Court of Deputy Commissioner, December 1942, NDRR.
62. From Deputy Commissioner, Darrang, to Commissioner, Assam Valley Division, no. 1436 Revenue Department, 8 July 1926, ASA.
63. Ibid.
64. Ibid.
65. Ibid.
66. Report of the Inspector General of Police, in Government of Assam, *Line System Enquiry Committee Report*, vol. 2.
67. Report of the Inspector General of Police, in Government of Assam, *Line System Enquiry Committee Report*, vol. 1.
68. Fortnightly Report, first half of May 1931.
69. Fortnightly Report, first half of June 1931.
70. This comment is based on the basis of the Fortnightly Report between 1943 and 1945.
71. Fortnightly Report, first half of November 1943.
72. Fortnightly Report, first half of March 1945.
73. Fortnightly Report, first half of March 1945.
74. In Barpeta, there were six murders in the first week of May in 1943 (Fortnightly Report, second half of May 1943).
75. Fortnightly Report, first half of May 1943; Also see Fortnightly Report, second half of August 1943.
76. Special police officers had to be appointed to help local police curb the unlawful activities of immigrant peasants in Kamrup (*Annual Report on the Police Administration of Assam*, 1939, p. 22).
77. Fortnightly Report, first half of August 1943.
78. Fortnightly Report, first and second half of May 1943.
79. Ibid.
80. Complied from *Annual Jail Administration Report of Assam*, 1934–50, Oriental and India Office Collection (OIOC), London.
81. F.A. Sachse, *Mymensingh District Gazetteer*, vol. 1, Calcutta: Bengal Secretariat Book Depot, 1917.
82. *Annual Report on the Police Administration of Assam*, 1939, p. 21.

83. F.N.A. Sachse, *Final Report on the Survey and Settlement Operations in the District of Mymensingh, 1908–1919*, Calcutta: Government Press, 1920, p. 29.
84. Hamid was a resident of Sonai Bara Pam village, Batradava, Nowgaon. Sonai Bara Pam was one of the areas freshly reclaimed by the immigrant peasants. A copy of the book is available in the vernacular tract collection of Asia and Africa Collection of the British Library. The book was printed by Sulemani Press, 155, Masjidbari Street, by Ahmed Ali Khandarkar from Sonai Bara Pam in Nowgaon. It was priced at 2 *annas*.
85. *Dainik Assamiya* (6 May 1946) reported such an incident in a grazing reserve of Barpeta. In this instance, the East Bengali peasants had occupied the Bornagar grazing reserve, which had been under the occupation of the military forces earlier, i.e., during the Second World War. Later on, the East Bengali peasants found that none of them had got any *patta* for their land that was promised by the *mattabar* during the encroachment. Subsequently, the mattabar had appropriated the patta for the land. Such cases of land being occupied by the mattabar are found in NDRR.
86. For an account of the Bengal famine of 1943, see Paul R. Greenough, *Prosperity and Misery in Modern Bengal: The Famine of 1943-1944*, New Delhi: Oxford University Press, 1982.
87. 'Starving Families Migrate to Assam: Famine in East Bengal', *Times of India*, 5 November 1943.
88. Notice by Secretary to Revenue Department, no. 4488-R, *The Assam Gazette*, 19 October 1940.
89. *Annual Report on the Annual Police Administration of Assam*, 1939, p. 23.
90. Speech by Adur Rouf, Budget Session 1945, *ALAP*.
91. W.A. Cosgrave, District Commissioner of Kamrup, felt that the local settlement officer should thoroughly go through the past history of professional grazing reserves with the help of a competent clerk ('Colonization Scheme for Barpeta Subdivision in the Kamrup', *Assam Secretariat Proceedings* [*ASP*], Revenue-A, nos 395–464, December 1930, ASA).
92. Ibid. See the petition of Chandicharan Talukdar and 10 others submitted to the Finance Minister for keeping the Mani Simla reserve free from occupation by the immigrant peasants (*ASP*, Revenue-A, nos 395–464, December 1930, ASA).
93. Mahesh Rangarajan, *Fencing the Forest*, New Delhi: Oxford University Press, 1996, p. 5.
94. See Chapter 4 in Arupjyoti Saikia, *Forests and Ecological History of Assam, 1826–2000*, New Delhi: Oxford University Press, 2011.
95. Rana Pratap Behal, 'Some Aspects of the Growth of the Plantation Labor Force and Labor Movements in Assam Valley districts,

1900–47', unpublished PhD thesis, Centre for Historical Studies (CHS), Jawaharlal Nehru University (JNU), New Delhi, 1983, p. 153.

96. 'Governor's Note', File 1-22, *ASP*, Revenue-A, September 1926, ASA. Also, see Letter of Additional Deputy Commissioner, Nowgaon, to Haldhar Bhuyan, Member of Legislative Assembly, 30 November 1946, NDRR.
97. The nationalist Assam Association resolved that such a move will be prejudicial to the interests of the Assamese peasants and would diminish the value of land. *Assamiya* published an editorial on 29 August 1919 opposing this move (*ASP*, Revenue Department, Revenue-A, nos 1–10, November 1919, OICC).
98. 'Notes on Colonization Scheme for Barpeta Subdivision in the District of Kamrup', *ASP*, Revenue-A, nos 395–465, December 1930, ASA.
99. Petition of Puran Gaonbura and Mohammad Sarafat Ali, 1934, NDRR.
100. Speech by Rohini Kumar Chaudhury, 16 November 1944, *ALAP*.
101. Ibid.
102. Speech by Kameswar Das, 29 February 1940, *ALAP*.
103. The term 'encroacher' or 'encroachment' is used to highlight the process of forcible occupation of government land. The use of the term in no way suggests an uncritical acceptance of the statist explanation of peasant land occupation.
104. In 1919 and 1920, the Indian government continuously registered a loss of Rs 57,306,135 and Rs 236,528,835, respectively. The Assam government's total land revenue collection declined from Rs 1, 351,412 in 1909–10 to Rs 6, 07,689 in 1919–20 (*Statistical Abstract Relating to British India from 1910–11 to 1919–20*, vol. 55, London: His Majesty's Stationery Office, 1922).
105. Secretary, Revenue Department to the Commissioner, Assam Valley Division, Memo. no. 4204-R, 28 December 1937, NDRR.
106. *The Assam Tribune*, 1 December 1939, cited in Guha, *Planter Raj to Swaraj*, p. 262.
107. A.G. Patton (Secretary, Revenue Department, Government of Assam), Press communiqué, 2 December 194, NDRR.
108. Letter from Secretary, Revenue Department, Government of Assam, to Commissioner, Assam Valley Division, no. 2180/14-R, 3 January 1941, NDRR.
109. See Chapter 4 in this volume.
110. *The Assam Gazette*, 25 August 1943.
111. Note by S.P. Desai to all district commissioners, October 1943, NDRR.
112. 'Return for the Acceleration of the Land Settlement Scheme for the Month of August, 1944', Speech by Munawwar Ali, 14 November 1944, *ALAP*.

113. Ibid.
114. Speech by Abdul Rouf, Budget Session, 1945, *ALAP*.
115. Speech by Abdul Hamid Khan, 17 March 1944, *ALAP*.
116. N.N. Mitra (ed.), *Indian Annual Registrar*, vol. 1, January–June 1947, Calcutta: Annual Register Office, 1947.
117. Press Statement of Mahendra Mohan Chaudhury, Secretary, Congress Parliamentary Party, in *Sadiniya Assamiya*, 15 June 1946.
118. See Chapter 4 in this volume.
119. *Dainik Assamiya*, 16 May 1947.
120. Speech by Surendranath Buragohain, Budget Session 1945, *ALAP*.
121. Letter from Sub-Deputy Collector, Mangaldai, to Commissioner, Assam Valley Division, Memo. no. 3261, 9 June 1944, NDRR.
122. The source of this information is an appeal suit of a few East Bengali peasants against Assamese tribal peasants in Nowgaon (Appeal of Lokaman Sarkar and Three Others, File no. XVIII/28 of 1936, Revenue Branch, Revenue Department, NDRR).
123. Ibid.
124. Ibid.
125. The NDRR has a large number of similar litigations. See, for instance, Packet no. 268/1936 (1937).
126. *Dainik Assamiya* (28 February 1948) complained that one Damodar Pathak sold 10 bighas of annual patta lands to an East Bengali, Tarik Ali, in spite of protest by local landless peasants.
127. Speech by Karka Dalay Miri, 7 August 1937, *ALAP*.
128. Speech by Sarveswar Barua, 24 February 1938, *ALAP*.
129. Rajendra Prasad, *Autobiography*, New Delhi: Penguin, 2010, pp. 252–53.
130. Note by A.G. Patton, Secretary, Revenue Department, Assam, RD, 68/44/52, 15 January 1945, NDRR.
131. Ibid., RD, 68/44, 13 July 1945, NDRR.
132. Ibid.
133. Speech by Mahi Chandra Bora and Munawwar Ali, 27 November 1943, *ALAP*.
134. Speech by Munawwar Ali, 18 November 1944, *ALAP*.
135. Ibid.
136. File no. 54 of 1944, Settlement Branch, Revenue Department, NDRR.
137. Speech by Beliram Das, 16 November 1944, *ALAP*. Also, see File no. 54 of 1944, Settlement Branch, Revenue Department, NDRR.
138. There was a report of encroachment upon the grazing reserves of Baghpori, Karpori, Haripori, Missamari, and Koreikhora in Mangaldai; and of Borjmari, Kumali and Siporal, and Bandia Chapari in Tezpur (Government of Assam, *Report of the Special Officer Appointed for the Examination of the Professional Grazing*

Reserves in the Assam Valley, Shillong: Assam Government Press, 1944).

139. Speech by Beliram Das, 16 November 1944, *ALAP*.
140. Resolution no. 2 of the Emergency Meeting of the Grazers Association, Tezpur, 19 January 1947, NDRR.
141. Petition of Chabilal Sarma and Others, Petition no. 2804/5/8, 4 August 1945, NDRR.
142. Chief Secretary's Fortnightly Report to Secretary of State (hereafter Fortnightly Report), first half of April 1943.
143. Speech by Beliram Das, 22 March 1945, *ALAP*.
144. Government of Assam, *Line System Enquiry Committee Report*, vol. 1, p. 5.
145. Ibid., p. 7.
146. Petition of Rahijuddin Mia and Eight Others for the cancellation of grazing reserve in Chandmama, Kheli, Khatateri, and Gerali in mauza Rupasi, Barpeta subdivision, Kamrup, *ASP*, Revenue-A, nos 395–464, December 1930, ASA; Memo. of Taimuddin Mandal and Others, *ASP*, Revenue-A, nos 395–464, December 1930, ASA.
147. In Assam, the primary livelihood of the Nepalese was cattle breeding. For a discussion on their incorporation and acculturation in the Assamese peasantry, see Jayeeta Sharma, *Empire's Garden: Assam and the Making of India*, New Delhi: Permanent Black, 2011, pp. 92–96.
148. They were primarily from places like Bhowanipur, Kharija, Bijui-Dawka, Chakabansi, Rupasi, and Khutaghat.
149. Petition of Chandicharan Talukdar and Others, *ASP*, Revenue-A, nos 395–464, December 1930, ASA.
150. Petition of Chandicharan Talukdar and Others, *ASP*, Revenue-A, no. 414, December 1930, ASA; Petition of Rahijuddin Mia and Eight Others for the cancellation of grazing reserve in Chandmama, Kheli, Khatateri, and Gerali in mauza Rupasi, Barpeta subdivision, Kamrup, *ASP*, Revenue-A, nos 395–464, December 1930, ASA; Memo. of Taimuddin Mandal and Others, *ASP*, Revenue-A, nos 395–464, December 1930, ASA.
151. Note by A.G. Patton, Secretary, Revenue Department, Assam, RD 68/44, 13 July 1945, NDRR.
152. For discussion on the Partition question in Bengal, see Joya Chatterjee, *Bengal Divided: Hindu Communalism and Partition 1932–1947*, New Delhi: Foundation Books, 1996; *The Spoils of Partition: Bengal and India, 1947–1967*, Cambridge: Cambridge University Press, 2007.
153. Abdul Hamid Khan was popularly known as Bhasani. For biographical details, see Sayed Abdul Maksud, *Maulana Abdul Hamid Khan Bhasani*, Dhaka: Bangla Academy, 1994; Arefin Badal (ed.), *Maulana Bhasani*, Dhaka: Dhansiri, 1977.

154. Group imbroligo arose out of the non-acceptance by Indian nationalists, of the British government's grouping proposal of dividing India into three groups whereby Assam was supposed to be part of Muslim-dominated Group C. For a perceptive account of the grouping controversy, see Guha, *Planter Raj to Swaraj*, Chapter 8.
155. After Partition, Bhasani moved to East Pakistan and remained instrumental in defending the cause of the poor (William van Schendel, *A History of Bangladesh*, London: Cambridge University Press, 2009; also, see M. Rashiduzzaman, 'The National Awami Party of Pakistan: Leftist Politics in Crisis', *Pacific Affairs*, vol. 43, no. 3, 1970, pp. 394–409).
156. Circular by Secretary, Revenue Department, Letter no. RL. 25/42/42, 19 September 1942, ASA.
157. Ibid.
158. Speech by Abdul Hamid Khan, 11 November 1945, *ALAP*.
159. S.P. Desai, Commissioner, Assam Valley Division to Deputy Commissioner, Nowgaon, Memo. no. RS 135/45, 4 September 1945, NDRR.
160. See Chapter 4 in this volume for a detailed discussion on the land settlement policy of Assam government. Also, see Chapter 4 in Nirode Kumar Barooah, *Gopinath Bordoloi: The Assam Problem and Nehru's Centre*, Guwahati: Bhabani Print and Publications, 2010, *Gopinath Bordoloi Aru Assam: Tetia Aru Etia*, Guwahati: B.N. Bordoloi, 2010, pp. 156–58.
161. Note by A.G. Patton, Secretary, Revenue Department, File no. RD/68/44/42 and also Press Note, *The Assam Gazette*, 8 December 1946.
162. Between 1937 and 1947, except for two short durations, it was the Muslim League which formed the government; Guha, *Planter Raj to Swaraj*, p. 358, Appendix 16.
163. *Abstract of the Assam Police Intelligence Weekly Report* (*APWR*), Assam, 24 March 1946.
164. *APWR*, Cachar, 25 March 1946.
165. The Deputy Commissioner of Kamrup demanded that 'clear instructions should be issued' (see Letter from Deputy Commissioner, Kamrup, to Commissioner, Assam Valley Division, Letter no. 2273R , 4 June 1945, File no. 10/F/1945, NDRR).
166. Ibid.
167. Ibid.
168. In April, the All India Muslim League instructed Saadulla to demand the inclusion of Assam in Pakistan from the Cabinet Mission ('Whole of Assam for Eastern Pakistan: Demand to be Made', *The Times of India*, 2 April 1946). On 5 March 1946 in a well-attended meeting of the Muslim League in Shillong, the capital city of Assam, Mohammad Ali Jinnah, President of Muslim League, reiterated that Assam must

be included in future Pakistan. The meeting was attended by both Assamese Hindus and tribal population ('Inclusion of Assam in Pakistan', *The Times of India*, 6 March 1946).

169. See, A.F.M. Abdul Hai, *Adarsha-Khetiak*, Mymensingh: Abdul Hai, 1921, p. 32. Addressing his fellow peasantry, Hai said: 'My dear unlettered peasant brothers of Bengal. Do you remember when you had sold your jute and aping the ways of the rich had covered your roofs with tin, had spent 500 rupees even after paying nazar salami to the landlord in order to dig a pond? Had not you hoped to grow more jute the next year and so borrowed money to spend on the wedding of your son, on fireworks to greet the new bride? And today most of you are on your way towards the jungle of Assam' (ibid.). Sugata Bose ('Roots of "Communal Violence" in Rural Bengal', *Modern Asian Studies*, vol. 16, no. 3, 1982, pp. 469–71, n. 32–34) also refers to such folk poems written by East Bengali peasants.
170. Maksud, *Maulana Abdul Hamid Khan Bhasani*, p. 51.
171. During the height of political mobilization of Muslim immigrant peasants, Bhasani wrote in the most poignant way:

    Pakistan is our only demand
    History justifies it,
    Numbers confirm it,
    Justice claims it,
    Destiny demands it,
    Posterity awaits it,
    Plebiscite verdicts it.
    (Maksud, *Maulana Abdul Hamid Khan Bhasani*, p. 51).

172. File no. RD, 56/1946, Revenue Department, Tenancy Branch, ASA; Maksud, *Maulana Abdul Hamid Khan Bhasani*, pp. 51–52.
173. *APWR*, Darrang, 25 August 1946.
174. Ibid. Also, see Maksud, *Maulana Abdul Hamid Khan Bhasani*, *p*. 50
175. Ibid.
176. Ibid.
177. *APWR*, Goalpara, 21 September 1946, emphasis added.
178. *APWR*, Kamrup, 30 March 1946.
179. *APWR*, Goalpara, 21 September 1946.
180. *APWR*, Goalpara, 18 October 1946 and 25 October 1946.
181. Ibid.
182. *The Times of India*, 21 December 1946.
183. N.N. Mitra (ed.), *Indian Annual Register*, vol. 1, January–June 1947, Calcutta: Annual Register Office, 1947.
184. Ibid.
185. *APWR*, Assam, 22 March 1947.

186. *APWR*, Kamrup, 22 March 1947.
187. Fortnightly Report, first half of July 1946.
188. File no. 19/46–47, *Political History of Assam* (*PHA*) files; *APWR*, April 1947. *Dainik Assamiya* (26 March 1947) reported the 'presence of 8000 East Bengals armed with arrow, spear, and bow'. Also, see Fortnightly Report, second half of March 1947.
189. Fortnightly Report, second half of March 1947.
190. Fortnightly Report, first half of March 1947.
191. *The Times of India*, 12 June 1947.
192. For the intensified propaganda of Assom Jatiya Mahasabha during this period, see Guha, *Planter Raj to Swaraj*, pp. 202–303.
193. *Dainik Assamiya*, 1 April 1947.
194. Ibid.
195. *Dainik Assamiya*, 26 March 1947.
196. *Dainik Assamiya*, 31 March 1945.
197. Petition of Beliram Das at the Deputy Commissioner's Court, Kamrup, 20 November 1946, File no. 97/46, *PHA* Files, ASA.
198. File no. 97/1946, *PHA* Files, ASA.
199. Ibid.
200. For more on the Noakhali violence, see Rakesh Batabyal, *Communalism in Bengal: From Famine to Noakhali, 1943–47*, New Delhi: Sage, 2005.
201. Representation of Nandalal Chaudhury and Others, File no. 97/46, *PHA* files, ASA.
202. In their representation to the District Commissioner of Kamrup, the Assamese peasants claimed: '[T]he number of men has been increasing day by day and it is known that they have been taking training with dangerous weapons from some twelve pathans for some time and this evening some twenty-five pathans have left for that place. The people of North Guwahati who live near about are apprehending danger even this night. We therefore pray that you would very kindly send a batch of armed police to Rajaduar of North Guwahati' (Representation of Ananda Prasad Seal and Four Others, File no. 97/1947, *PHA* files, ASA; also, see Report of the Police Investigation Officer, File no. 97/46, *PHA* files, ASA.
203. Fortnightly Report, second half of April 1947.
204. *Dainik Assamiya*, 25 April 1947.
205. Letter from Deputy Commissioner, Nowgaon, to Sub-Deputy Collector, Kamrup, Memo. no. 726/5/18, 2 April 1946, NDRR.
206. *APWR*, Assam, 17 May 1947.
207. Letter from Pitambor Deva Goswami to Shri Jawaharlal Nehru, Prime Minister of India, 26 January 1962, cited in D. Nath, *The Majuli Island: Society, Economy and Culture*, New Delhi: Anshah Publishing House, 2009, Appendix XIV, pp. 361–65.

208. *The Times of India*, 22 March 1948.
209. *The Assam Gazette*, part 4, 29 July 1950.
210. 'Demand for Firm Action against Assam Immigrants', *The Times of India*, 14 February 1950. Revenue Minister Bishnuram Medhi put the figure at 400,000. Demographers have not scrutinized these figures. Another study, based on Indian census figures, estimated that 0.8 million people migrated to Assam (see Anil Saikia, Homeswar Goswami and Atul Goswami [eds], *Population Growth in Assam: 1951–1991*, New Delhi: Akansha, 2003, p. 114).
211. 'Refugee Problem in Assam', *The Times of India*, 16 May 1949.
212. Letter from Bishnuram Medhi to Secretary, Revenue Department, Camp Nowgaon, 4 December 1949, NDRR.
213. CID Report (1 February 1950) on the Deputy Commissioner's Memo. no. 6877/5/62R, 31 December 1949, NDRR.
214. Ibid.
215. A similar resolution was passed in a public meeting at Nellie on 30 October 1949, 'praying for permission to utilize 1000 bighas of land of Bamungaon professional grazing reserve for collective cultivation' (Letter from Omeo Kumar Das to Deputy Commissioner, Nowgaon, File no. 3901, 10 November 1949, NDRR).

Chapter 3

1. Gautam Bhadra, *Iman O Nishan*, Calcutta: Subarnarekha, 1994.
2. For a full account of the history of tenant–zamindar conflicts, see Santo Barman, *Zamindari System in Assam during British Rule: A Case Study of Goalpara District*, Guwahati: Spectrum, 1994, pp. 142–57. Also, see A.J. Laine, *Account of the Land Tenure System of Goalpara*, Shillong: Government Press, 1917.
3. Gunabhiram Barua, *Ram Nabami*, ed. Prasenjit Chaudhury, Guwahati: Chetana Prakash, 1991, p. 48.
4. For a brief overview of these legal battles, see Arupjyoti Saikia, 'Landl-ords, Tenants and Agrarian Relations: Revisiting a Peasant Uprising in Colonial Assam', *Studies in History*, vol. 26, no. 2, 2010, pp. 175–209.
5. The estates were distributed in the villages of Borbangsar and Borbamkhata in Uttar-Bajali *mauza* of the Barpeta subdivision of Kamrup district.
6. An official survey of 1883 estimated that both Parbatia Goswami and Madhav Devalay, another such estate owner, had an estimated 1,000 tenants under them. Goswami alone had 41,000 acres of land spread in 31 mauzas (see Fatik Chandra Barua, *Report on the Survey and Settlement of the La-khiraj and Nisf-khiraj Holdings in the District of Kamrup*, Shillong: Government Press, 1884).

7. Petition of Hareswar Chaudhury and Others, no. 16–21, File no. S-212R/1918, *Assam Secretariat Proceedings* (*ASP*), Revenue-A, Revenue Department, February 1919, Oriental and India Office Collection (OIOC), London.
8. Letter from B. Duara, Sub-Divsional Officer (SDO), Barpeta, to Deputy Commissioner, Kamrup, 15 July 1918 (no. 20), no. 16–21, File no. S-212R/1918, *ASP*, Revenue-A, Revenue Depart-ment, February 1919, OIOC.
9. Ibid.
10. P.R.T. Gordon, Commissioner, Assam Valley Divisions, opined: 'in the absence of a tenancy law in the Kamrup ... no other course seems to be open than on a breach of ... nisf-khiraj lease, being proved that the nisf-khiraj holder should be called upon by the DC to show cause why his ... lease should not be cancelled by the government' (Letter from P.R.T. Gordon, Commissioner, Assam Valley Divisions, to Chief Secretary, to Chief Commissioner of Assam, File no. S-212R/1918, *ASP*, Revenue-A, no. 16–21, Revenue Department, 14 November 1918, OIOC).
11. Letter from Deputy Commissioner to Commissioner, Assam Valley Divisions, File no. S-212R/1918, *ASP*, Revenue-A, no. 16–21, Revenue Department, 1 August 1918, OIOC.
12. The number of sub-tenants in the *nisf-khiraj* estates of Kamrup was estimated at 15,200 (ibid.).
13. Letter from Deputy Commissioner to Commissioner, Assam Valley Divisions, File no. S-212R/1918, *ASP*, Revenue-A, no. 16–21, Revenue Department, 1 August 1918, OIOC.
14. Memo. from Deputy Commissioner, Nowgaon, to Commissioner, Assam Valley Divisions, File no. AVD. no. 2971, 29 August 1933, Assam Valley Division, Nowgaon District Record Room (NDRR).
15. Heramba Kanta Barpujari, *Political History of Assam*, vol. 2, Guwahati: Government of Assam, 1978, p. 189.
16. Speech by Rohini Kumar Chaudhury, 21 March 1933, *Assam Legislative Council Proceedings* (*ALCP*).
17. Ibid.
18. Ibid.
19. 'Flood Havoc in Assam: Official Statement', *The Times of India*, 24 July 1934; 'Flood Havoc in Assam', *The Times of India*, 10 June 1936.
20. Memo. from Deputy Commissioner, Nowgaon, to Commissioner, Assam Valley Divisions, File no. AVD. 3110R, 3 September 1938, NDRR.
21. For instance, *Tinidiniya Assamiya* during 1934–39 widely reported about the Act.

22. Memo. from Deputy Commissioner, Nowgaon, to Commissioner, Assam Valley Divisions, File no. AVD. 3110R, 3 September 1938, NDRR.
23. Petition of Haladhar Bhuyan to Deputy Commissioner, Nowgaon, File no. DRT, 12 February 1939, NDRR.
24. *The Assam Gazette*, part 2, 10 October 1940.
25. Section 79 of the Assam Tenancy Act 1935.
26. The government had claimed in 1949 that there was no demand from the tenants of the other parts for preparation of record-of-rights (Speech by Bishnuram Medhi, 13 September 1949, *Assam Legislative Assembly Proceedings* [*ALAP*]).
27. Amalendu Guha, *Planter Raj to Swaraj: Freedom Struggle and Electoral Politics in Assam* 1826–1947, New Delhi: PPH, 1977, p. 147. The government continued with this policy of land revenue remission till 1941–42.
28. Memo. from Deputy Commissioner, Nowgaon, to Commissioner, Assam Valley Divisions, File no. AVD. 3110R, 3 September 1938, NDRR.
29. Ibid.
30. 'Assam Praja Sanmilan', *Tinidiniya Assamiya*, 7 April 1936. It is to be noted that *Tinidiniya Assamiya* reported the meeting as a 'Praja Sanmilan'. In the public language too, the words, 'ryot' and 'people', were used synonymously.
31. The report mentioned that landlords coerced two low-caste *adhiars* — Boloram Keot and Ganai Keot — to pay *adhi*.
32. 'Resolution no. 1 of the Assam Praja Sanmilani', *Tinidiniya Assamiya*, 7 April 1936.
33. Letter from Deputy Commissioner, Nowgaon, to Commissioner, Assam Valley Divisions, File no. DRT 1390, 12 February 1939, NDRR.
34. This section is based on a number of books on the history of Assamese literary criticism. For instance, see Homen Borgohain (ed.), *Asamiya Sahityar Buranji*, vol. 6, Guwahati: ABILAC, 1993.
35. The finest example of this new and radical literary tradition was *Abahan*. Edited by Dinanath Sarma (1896–1978), *Abahan* was first published in 1929 and continued to be published till 1947.
36. Chandraprasad Saikia, *Asamar Batori Kakat Alocanir Dersa Basharia Itihash*, Guwahati: Profulla Chandra Borua, 1998.
37. Uma Sarma, *Bat Buli Buli Bhagari Parile*, Guwahati: Natun Sahitya Parisad, 1989.
38. For biographical details of Tagore, see Manjula Basu, *Saumendranath Tagore: Karme O Manane*, Kolkata: Tagore Research Institute, 2007.
39. Following is an account of the ideological position of the Revolutionary Communist Party of India (RCPI) in the language of the government: 'It is a fact that the Communist League of India [was]

formed by Saumendranath Tagore in March 1938 which changed its name to RCPI in April-May of 1943 . . . [I]t does not see eye to eye with the extremist parties or owe any allegiance to any ex-India body. It is opposed to the CPI and has shown traces of Trotskyite influence . . . Despite minor ideological and factional differences all Trotskyite groups in India have preached an almost identical doctrine. The violent overthrow of recognized authority is the primary objective; other objectives include utopian labor conditions, the expropriation of capitalist and landlords, the liquidation of agricultural debts and the abolition of the Indian state' (Intelligence Bureau on RCPI, File no. 7/7/47, Home [political-I], National Archives of India [hereafter, NAI]). For Trotskyite political ideology, see Baruch Kuei-paz, *The Social and Political Thought of Leon Trotsky*, Oxford: Oxford University Press, 1978.

40. Anon., *Historical Development of Communist Movement in India* gives a full-length account of the growth of RCPI and its ideological moorings (File no. 1942/30A, P.C. Joshi Memorial Archives, Jawaharlal Nehru University [JNU], New Delhi).
41. Ibid.
42. *Tinidiniya Assamiya*, 8 November 1938. The meeting was chaired by P.C. Ray, a prominent teacher of the college.
43. Haridas Deka, *Jivan Aru Sangram,* Guwahati: LBS, 1992, p. 26.
44. Among those who joined the Communist League were Haren Kalita, Haridas Deka, Tarunsen Deka, Upen Sarma, Ananda Chandra Das, Taracharan Majumadar, Gokul Medhi, Arabinda Ghosh, Loknath Barua, Umakanta Sarma, Bhupen Mahanta, N. Buragohain, Khagendranath Barbarua, Uma Sarma, and Kamini Goswami (see Deka, *Jivan Aru Sangram*, p. 29).
45. Guha, *Planter Raj to Swaraj*, pp. 285–87.
46. The evidence of an anti-grouping popular protest can be found in Assam Provincial Congress Committee papers (APCC), especially files related to the grouping question, in Nehru Memorial Museum and Library (NMML).
47. The conference was held on 5 and 6 June 1946. Before the conference, Assam Provincial Student Federation (APSF) President Upen Das gave a press statement in *Dainik Assamiya* on the subjects to be discussed in the conference. He said, '[T]he meeting would protest against the proposed plan of the cabinet mission to include Assam in group C and thereby to nullify the identity of Assam . . . which is a national problem of Assam' (*Dainik Assamiya*, 2 June 1946).
48. *Dainik Assamiya*, 11 June 1946. Khagendranath Barbarua, Haren Kalita, and Upen Sarma also attended the conference.
49. *Dainik Assamiya*, 15 February 1947. The conference held in Nakulgaon near Rangia, Kamrup.
50. *Dainik Assamiya*, 9 February 1947.
51. Ibid.

52. *The Assam Tribune*, 13 June 1947.
53. Deka, *Jivan Aru Sangram*, p. 33. A number of big boats were used to ferry both goods and people.
54. R.J. Alexander, *International Trotskyism, 1929–1985: A Documented Analysis of the Movement*, Duke: Duke University Press, 1991, pp. 529–30.
55. Ibid.; Tarunsen Deka, *Mukti Sangramar Adharat Jiban Katha*, Guwahati: R.D. Printers and Publishers, 1993.
56. Pranesh Chandra Biswas, 'Peasant Struggles and Growth of the Kishan Sabha in Assam', in Amalendu Guha, *Zamindarkalin Goalpara Zillar Artha Samajik Abastha: Eti Oitihasik Dristipat*, Guwahati: Natun Sahitya Parisad, 2000, p. 89.
57. William R. Pinch, *Peasants and Monks in British India*, New Delhi: Oxford University Press, 1996, pp. 5–7.
58. Dadhi Mahanta, *Assamat Communist Andolanor Janma Aru Bikashar Sambandhe*, Guwahati: Communist Party Prakasani, 1993, p. 50. Also, see File no. 183-C.50, 1947, Confidential Files, Governor's Secretariat, ASA.
59. Two other units, Mauza Krishak Panchayat and Jila Krishak Panchayat, along with Gaon Krishak Panchatyat, constituted the total number of units at the district level and all such units came under the Krishak Banua Panchayat (KBP).
60. KBP, *Sambidhan: Krishak Banua Panchayat* (*Constitution of the Assam Krishak Banua Panchayat*), Guwahati: KBP, 1948. This was adopted at the second general conference in 1948.
61. Ibid. Also, see Deka, *Jivan Aru Sangram*, pp. 74–75.
62. Sriman P. Goswami, 'Comrade Dhiren Duttar Smritit', in Chidananda Saikia (ed.), *Dhiren Datta Smriti Grantha*, Golaghat: Dhiren Datta Smritirakha Samiti, 1974, p. 7; Guha, *Planter Raj to Swaraj*, p. 250. Several prominent members of the Indian communist movement, namely, Somnath Lahiri, Biswanath Mukherji, and Amiya Dasgupta, attended the meeting held in Missamara.
63. *Tinidiniya Assamiya*, 17 November 1940.
64. Dadhi Mahanta, 'Jatitya Mukti Aru Samajtantrar Sangramat Comrade Dhiren Duutor Abadan', in Saikia, *Dhiren Datta Smriti Grantha*, p. 132; Biswas, 'Peasant Struggles and Growth of the Kishan Sabha in Assam', p. 89.
65. Dadhi Mahanta, 'Asamat Communist Andolonar Bikash', in Saikia, *Dhiren Datta Smriti Grantha*, p. 130.
66. G.D. Overstreet and M. Windmiller, *Communism in India*, Berkeley, CA: University of California Press, 1959, pp. 179–80.
67. This account is based on Mahanta, *Assamat Communist Andolanor Janma Aru Bikashar Sambandhe*, pp. 79–91.
68. Gaurishankar Bhattacharjya, who later became a member of the Assam Legislative Assembly, was the first General Secretary of All India Student Federation (AISF).

69. Guha, *Planter Raj to Swaraj*, pp. 192–95.
70. Ibid., p. 187. Probably, Jaganath Bhattacharya participated in the conference 'not as delegate or representative of Kishan Sabha' (Biswas, 'Peasant Struggles and Growth of the Kishan Sabha in Assam', p. 88).
71. At the same time, the numbers of the primary members in the Surma valley was reported to be 11,520. In Golaghat, a local pleader, Khageswar Tamuly, was the official contact person of the All India Kisan Sabha (AIKS). The AIKS membership from Assam increased in the next 10 years, and in 1954 it was estimated to be 15,764 (S. Gopal, *Jawaharlal Nehru: A Biography, 1889–1947*, vol. 1, New Delhi: Oxford University Press, 1981, p. 188; Overstreet and Windmiller, *Communism in India*, p. 387). For further details, see F.T. Jannuzi, *India's Persistent Dilemma: The Political Economy of Agrarian Reform*, New Delhi: Orient Blackswan, 1996, pp. 31–33.
72. 'Indulal Yagnik Papers', in P.S. Gupta (ed.), *Towards Freedom, 1943–44*, vol. 2, New Delhi: Oxford University Press, 1997, p. 2086.
73. In 1945, the primary membership of AIKS in the valley increased to 7,900 (*People's War*, 25 March 1945; 'Indulal Yagnik Papers', p. 2086).
74. The police mentioned the peasant organizations of Communist Party of India (CPI) and Congress Socialist Party (CSP) as 'Krishak Sabhas' (KSs). Often, the CPI and the CSP also issued their respective pamphlets in the name of Krishak Sabhas. However, it was also found that the KS was the peasant front of CPI, and the Hind Kishan Panchayat that of CSP.
75. Maheswar Neog, *Anandaram Dhekial Phukan: Plea for Assam and Assamese*, Jorhat: Assam Sahitya Sabha, 1977, p. 97.
76. 'Note by Gunabhiram Sarma Borua', in Lord Dufferin, *Report on the Condition of the Lower Classes of Population in Bengal*, Calcutta: Government Press, 1888, p. 31.
77. Arvind N. Das, *Agrarian Movements in India: Studies on 20th Century Bihar*, London: Routledge, 1982.
78. Kedarnath Goswami, *Krishakar Mukti*, Guwahati: Pragati Prakash Bhavan, 1944. Also, see Haridas Deka, *Biplabi Khetiak*, Guwahati: Pragati Prakash Bhavan, 1944. The latter was a small booklet authored by Deka, Secretary of the Radical Institute, a study circle of the RCPI.
79. It was kept in the British Library and then transferred to the NAI, New Delhi, as a proscribed text (proscribed material 1884–85/pp Ass-b: 1 PIB/202/2, NAI). This was the time when the Communist League, and later on the RCPI, published several tracts on Marxian politics (see Deka, *Jivan Aru Sangram*, p. 58).
80. Bhupen Mahanta, *Biplabi Khetiak*, Guwahati: Radical Institute, n.d ., in proscribed material 1884–85/pp Ass-b: 1 PIB/202/2, NAI.
81. Ibid., p. 16.

82. The RCPI perceived the Assamese peasant society as consisting of *bhumihin* (landless), *garib khetaiak* (poor peasants) and *gaon-majur* (village labourer) (see KBP, 'Bikhyat Khetiak Neta Gobinda Kalita Greptar: Congress Sarkarar Fascist Daman Neetir Aru Ek Adhya'['Arrest of Govinda Kalita: Chapter in the Fascist Policy of the Congress Government'], a pamphlet issued in the name of Haren Kalita, Bishnu Rabha, Nabin Medhi, Loknath Baruah, and Aniram Basumatari, Assam Police Intelligence Record Room [hereafter APIRR], September 1949; 'November Divas Saptah Palan Karak', a pamphlet by the RCPI, 29 October 1949, APIRR).
83. Interview with Ambu Bora, erstwhile RCPI leader, Guwahati, 8 and 14 June 1996; Interview with Prafulla Mishra, erstwhile editor of *Shillong Observer* who interacted with the leading CPI leader Humayun Kabir and was himself a key communist sympathizer, Guwahati, October 1996.
84. Such absentee landholders included Bishnuram Medhi owning 200 *bighas*; Umesh Chandra Medhi (pleader), owning 1,000 bighas; Kaliprasad Baruah, owning 700 bighas; Tarun Phukan's family, owning 1,500 bighas; Kali Charan Sen, owning 1,000 bighas; and Pampu Ingti, owning 600 bighas. Also included in the list were the names of Jogendra Nath Baruah, Omkar Mal, Kamakhya Baruah (pleader), Ikram Rasul, and Kunja Thakur.
85. KBP, 'Bikhyat Khetiak Neta Gobinda Kalita Greptar', p. 2.
86. The work was written by a party activist, Gokul Pathak, with an introductory note by Mahendranath Das, Secretary of the CSP unit of Barpeta mauza. The page in which the price of the booklet was printed is not available. It was claimed in the preface that 'it contained only few of the grievances of the peasants though they have lot of other problems as well'.
87. CSP, *Agrarian Programme of Socialist Party*, 1948, File no. I/C-6/14-C 49/50, APIRR.
88. See Chapter 6 in this volume for an elaborate discussion on the issue of price rise.
89. The CSP specified that land, thus, distributed should be within the minimum and maximum limits of 12 and 30 acres respectively, of average productivity per family so that a family earned not less than Rs 100 and not more than Rs 300 per month.
90. The CPI's stand on the peasant question is detailed in a 1949 pamphlet 'Nowgaon Zillah Krishak Sabhar Ahban' issued by its Nowgaon district unit, and preserved in the APIRR.
91. Speech by Gaurishankar Bhattacharjya, December 1948, *Proceedings of the Assam Provincial Organization of CPI*, File no. A-3(6)1947, APIRR.
92. 'Resolution on Land Settlement and Eviction in Assam', in CPI, *Assam Fights for Freedom and Democracy: Draft Resolutions of Assam Communists*, Guwahati, 1948, File no. A-3(6)1947, APIRR.

93. Ibid.
94. Ibid.
95. During 1947–48, the RCPI proposed to start the Dashchhay movement — demanding 10 parts of the produce to the producer and six to the owner — in the 24 Paragana district of Bengal too (*Extract from Secret Information of 5 February 1948*, File no. A-3[6]48, APIRR).
96. *Report of the Proceedings of the Open Meeting of the First Session of the Assam Provincial Communist Party Held at Guwahati on 13 February 1948*, File no. A-3(6)48, APIRR.
97. Memo. from Ministry of Home, Government of India, to K.R. Chaudhuri, Deputy Inspector General, Assam Police, 25 February 1948, File no. A-3(6)48, APIRR.
98. For details on the Tebhaga movement in Bengal, see Adrienne Cooper, *Sharecropping and Share Croppers' Struggles in Bengal 1930–1950*, Calcutta: KPB, 1988.
99. Memo. from Ministry of Home, Government of India to K.R. Chaudhuri.
100. Ibid.
101. Assam Provincial Organizing Committee (APOC), 'Resolution on the Main Structure of the Future Constitution of Assam', 19–24 August 1947, File no. I/A-3 (6)/II, 1947, APIRR.
102. Most of the works of Bishnu Prasad Rabha are available in edited volumes that also represent competing claims of Assamese political history. See, for instance, Jogesh Das and Sarveswar Barua (eds), *Bishnuprasad Rabha Rachana Samahar*, 2 vols, Tezpur: Rabha Rachanawali Prakasan Sangha, 1989, reprint 2008, and 1997; Bishnu Rabha Sowarani Gabesana Samiti (ed.), *Bishnu Rabha Rachanawali*, vol. 1, Guwahati: Journal Emporium, 1982; Hiren Gohain (ed.), *Sainik Silpi Bishnu Rabha*, Guwahati: Journal Emporium, 1982, reprint 2002. A biographical sketch of Rabha can be found in Sivanath Barman, *Assamiya Jivani Abhidhan*, Guwahati: Banalata, 1993; Parama Majumdar, *Satirthar Dristit Bishnu Rabha*, Nalbari: Journal Emporium, 1992. The important works of Rabha that are relevant for understanding his perspective on the peasant question are *Mukti Deol* and *Sonamua Gaon* and the preface to the work *Sonpahi*.
103. 'Statement of Bishnu Prasad Rabha', Memo. no. PF/B-21/8874-76/SD, Dhubri, 27 August 1952, APIRR.
104. Rabha partially translated the American author and journalist Jack Belden's works on the Chinese revolution and published it as *Sonpahi* (see Das and Barua [eds], *Bishnuprasad Rabha Rachana Samahar*, vol. 1, pp. 571–89; also, see Jack Belden, *China Shakes the World*, London: Harper, 1949).

105. Chief Secretary's Fortnightly Report to the Secretary of State (hereafter, Fortnightly Report), first half of January 1943.
106. Prepared from Table 1-B titled 'Indegenous Persons Land-holding', in *Census of Assam*, 1951, vol. 2, part 3.
107. Interview with Govinda Kalita, Guwahati, 18 June 1995.
108. *Abstract of the Assam Police Intelligence Weekly Report* (*APWR*), Kamrup, 12 December 1941.
109. Interview with Govinda Kalita; *APWR*, Kamrup, 12 December 1941. The *Annual Report on the Land Revenue Administration of Assam* and vernacular newspapers carried reports on frequent land erosion in these areas.
110. The KBP pamphlet, 'Bikhyat Khetiak Neta Govinda Kalita Greptar', claimed that the peasants had gheraoed the Deputy Commissioner and also the house of the Congress leader Muhammad Taybulla for several hours.
111. 'Bikhyat Khetiak Neta Govinda Kalita Greptar'.
112. Interview with Govinda Kalita.
113. An account of this can be found in Deka, *Mukti Sangramar Adharat Jiban Katha*, pp. 46–47 and Deka, *Jivan Aru Sangram*, p. 41.
114. Amongst the landowners who were the first to accept the demands of KBP was the grandfather of Haridas Deka. He had a landholding on the outskirts of Guwahati and was compelled by the KBP workers to agree to their demands (Deka, *Jivan Aru Sangram*, p. 42).
115. A comprehensive account of the KBP's version of the growth of peasant movement in southern Kamrup is found in 'Bikhyat Krishak Neta Govinda Kalita Greptar'.
116. Interview with Ambu Bora.
117. Memo. from Ministry of Home to K.R. Chaudhuri.
118. *APWR*, Kamrup, 21 July 1945.
119. Ibid.
120. *Dainik Assamiya*, 28 July 1945.
121. In May 1943, an approximately 86,718 *maunds* of smuggled paddy and rice were seized in Goalpara (Fortnightly Report, first half of May 1943).
122. Fortnightly Report, first half of January 1943.
123. Ibid.; Fortnightly Report, second half of May 1943.
124. Deka, *Mukti Sangramar Adharat Jiban Katha*, pp. 46–47.
125. *APWR*, Kamrup, 12 July 1944. Also, see RCPI, 'Communist Parteer Istahar', pamphlet, 1944, APIRR.
126. *APWR*, Kamrup, 12 July 1944.
127. Fortnightly Report, first half of June 1945.
128. Deka, *Jivan Aru Sangram*, p. 54; *APWR*, Kamrup, 30 November 1945.
129. Ibid.

130. A.R. Desai, *Rural Sociology in India*, Bombay: Popular Prakashan, 1977, pp. 418–20.
131. Ibid., p. 418.
132. Deka, *Jivan Aru Sangram*, p. 62.
133. Kedarnath Goswami, a charismatic intellectual of the KBP, travelled widely and attended a meeting of 200 peasants held in Borbil, Dibrugarh. Subsequently, Goswami was able to form KBP units in Borbil, Muliabari and Golabasti (*APWR*, Lakhimpur, 8 March 1947). Kanuram Datta, Syed Taibul Hussain and Durgeswar Das; and Kartik Deka, Rajen Ray and Padmadhar Sonwal became the presidents and secretaries of the Borbil, Muliabari and Gola basti KBP units, respectively.
134. Interview with Govinda Kalita.
135. Biswas, 'Peasant Struggles and Growth of the Kishan Sabha in Assam', pp. 101–2.
136. *APWR*, Goalpara, 28 December 1946.
137. The resolutions asked for Rs 7, Rs 30 and Rs 25 per maund of paddy, jute and mustard respectively.
138. *APWR*, Goalpara, 28 December 1946. It also sought the abolition of the restriction on the sale of cotton yarn by the government after the Second World War.
139. *APWR*, Goalpara, 11 January 1947.
140. Biswas, 'Peasant Struggles and Growth of the Kishan Sabha in Assam', p. 101.
141. Gaurishankar Bhattacharjya, *Sabinaya Nibedan*, Guwahati: Sahitya Prakash, 1999, p. 636. Young communist leader Dhireswar Kalita, along with local tribal peasant leaders, played an important role in mobilizing the sharecroppers.
142. The conference also adopted a resolution asking both Mahatma Gandhi and Muhammad Ali Jinnah to come to terms with the Cabinet Mission proposals. The police opined that the conference could not suggest any agreeable political solution other than a mere patchwork. It also focused on the growing demand for Pakistan and the grim future of the political and cultural status of Assamese in Pakistan, if Assam were to be merged with it.
143. CPI, *Assam Fights for Freedom and Democracy*.
144. P.C. Joshi, 'On Immediate Solidarity Campaign with the Tebhaga Struggle', Political Circular no. 1/47, File no. I/A-3(6)47/9, January 1947, APIRR.
145. *Detailed Note on Communist Activity*, by Deputy Inspector General of Assam Police and Intelligence, 23 January 1947, p. 2, APIRR.
146. Ibid.
147. The success of this mobilization became clear with the holding of several conferences. For instance, Bilashipara Krishak Sanmilan,

presided over by Gaurishankar Bhattacharjya, discussed the problems created by the fluctuating jute prices and addressed the landlord–adhiar conflict. Another conference held after the one in Bilashipara was Futukibari Krishak Sanmilan. Narendra Brahma, an adhiar from Futukibari, took a leading part in organizing it (Guha, *Zamindarkalin Goalpara Zillar Artha Samajik Abastha*, p. 101).

148. *Dainik Assamiya*, 30 January 1948. The second conference of the Assam Talatiya Ryot Sangha was held in Titabor in early 1948. The CSP leaders Nilamoni Phukan, Harinarayan Barua, Sankar Chandra Barua and Chakreswar Saikia attended it. Harinarayan Barua stressed the fact that the landless should get land (*Dainik Assamiya*, 8 February 1948; *Socialist Party Activity*, File no. 1, 7 March 1948, APIRR).
149. It was decided that the adhiar would give 30 puras of paddy for one pura of first-class land and 25 puras for one pura of second-class land. Those who had more than 12 puras of land should get the government rent along with additional 8 *annas* (*Socialist Party Activity*).
150. Ibid.
151. Memo., 'On Communist Agitation', by Harold Dennehy, Chief Secretary to Government of Assam, to Commissioner, Assam Valley Division, 14 February,1947, File no.I/A-5(6)-F/47, APIRR.
152. Ibid.
153. Fortnightly Report, first half of February 1947.
154. Ibid.
155. Ibid.
156. 'Note on Communism', File no. I/A-3(6)/48/X, APIRR.
157. Ibid.
158. Ibid.
159. *APWR*, Assam, 25 June 1947.
160. Fortnightly Report, first half of January 1947.
161. Various KS meetings decided to allow peasants to encroach upon the forest reserves. One such encroachment occurred in the Kaki forest reserve. The government admitted the probable involvement of a communist organization in this encroachment (Fortnightly Report, first half of March 1947 and first half of April 1947).
162. They had some success in organizing strikes among the sweepers of Dibrugarh and Jorhat municipalities (Fortnightly Report, first half of March 1947; interview with Gopal Das, erstwhile RCPI activist, Guwahati, 7 March 1995; interview with Mohanlal Mukherjee, erstwhile RCPI leader, Guwahati, 12 and 14 June 1996).
163. Saumendranath Tagore, in one meeting, dwelt pointedly on the right of the peasants to resort to violence in course of self-defence when his liberty or interests were challenged.
164. Benjamin Zacariah, *Nehru*, London: Routledge, 2004, p. 231.

165. In its thinly attended political rallies, the RCPI continued to remind people of this 'false independence' gained by the country. A representative example of such dismissal of the independence by the RCPI was a public meeting held in Sorbhog, where the RCPI leader Upen Sarma claimed that the 'present independence is not real independence'. He reminded his audience that even after the country got independence all the people would not get proper food and clothing. He exhorted the labourers and peasants to form a Labour Panchayat to be able to solve their grievances (*APWR*, Kamrup, 21 August 1947).
166. The KBP organized numerous meetings wherein the plight of the sharecroppers occupied the centre stage. Though these meetings emphasized the state of agrarian relations, they became a larger platform for the propagation of the RCPI's political manifesto. On 21 December 1947, the Palashbari unit of KBP organized a meeting which had a considerable presence of peasants. Local pleader Habiram Deka chaired the meeting. The police noted that a meeting in Bangsar condemned the repressive measures of the Bengal govern-ment against peasants and labour organizations such as arrests and detentions of their leaders without trial, and passed resolutions demanding free and compulsory education, provisions for medical aid in villages, and certain improvements in land tenure (*APWR*, Kamrup, 13 December 1947).
167. In one such meeting of tribal peasants held on 1 December 1947 in Tiniali, which was at a little distance from Guwahati, Aniram Basumatari of Goalpara, who chaired the meeting, spoke on the problem of sharecropping in Assam. He stressed that it had become a common factor all over Assam (*APWR*, Assam, 6 December 1947).
168. *APWR*, Kamrup, 18 March 1948.
169. *APWR*, Kamrup, 17 January 1948. In another meeting, attended by about 150 villagers, and presided over by Golok Chandra Barua of Guwahati, the RCPI leader Nabin Medhi asked the sharecroppers not to pay rent in cash or kind. Other speakers, including the president, also exhorted them to stop paying rent to the landlords and start a propaganda against the ruling Congress government (*APWR*, Kamrup, 24 January 1948).
170. *APWR*, Kamrup, 17 January 1948.
171. *A Short Note on CPI Activities in Kamrup between 1948–49*, File no. A-3 (6) M/47, APIRR.
172. Ibid.
173. *Dainik Assamiya*, 12 January 1948.
174. The sharecroppers started agitating to pay land revenue in coins. On the basis of adult suffrage, a Panchayat was formed in villages.

The middle peasants agreed to accept 10 puras of paddy (presumably per pura of land) as land revenue from the poor sharecroppers cultivating their land. They also agreed to participate in the struggle proposed to be launched by the poor peasants against the landowners (ibid.).

175. *A Short Note on the CPI Activities in Nowgaon*, 1948, File no. I/A-3(6)-J/47, APIRR.
176. Ibid.
177. The KS branches were formed in Khetri and Rampur villages of Beltola.
178. *A Short Note on CPI Activities in Kamrup between 1948–49.*
179. Chief Secretary's Fortnightly Report to Secretary of State (hereafter, Fortnightly Report), first half of March 1947.
180. Memo. from Central Intelligence Officer to Deputy Inspector General of Police, Memo. no. SA14/105-6, 20 January 1948, File no. A-3(6)48, APIRR.
181. *APWR*, Kamrup, 6 March 1948.
182. *APWR*, Assam, 20 March 1948.
183. *Dainik Assamiya*, 24 March 1948 and 2 September 1948.
184. Ibid.
185. *Dainik Assamiya*, 24 March 1948.
186. *Dainik Assamiya* reported how the Jokai Tea Company had been granted 1,500 acres of land in Tinsukia by the Assam government. As the land had been lying vacant for a long time, landless peasants from the nearby villages occupied it. As they began cultivation, the company sold the land to local businessman Nandeswsar Chakravarty. The new owner complained to the police about the 'illegal' encroachments upon his land by the landless peasants.
187. 'Matihin Rayatar Oparat Soshan', *Dainik Assamiya*, 28 October 1947. Similar anonymous letters appeared in the Assamese press.
188. Ibid.
189. *Dainik Assamiya*, 27 January 1948. A committee consisting of a sub-deputy collector and *mandals* conducted the census.
190. *Dainik Assamiya*, 29 November 1947.
191. Ibid.
192. *APWR*, Kamrup, 10 January 1948.
193. *Dainik Assamiya*, 26 February 1948.
194. Speech by Harinarayan Barua, 28 March 1948, *ALAP*.
195. Speech by Beliram Das, 28 March 1948, *ALAP*.
196. Ibid.
197. Speech by Binode J. Sarwan, 3 April 1948, *ALAP*.
198. Speech by Muhammad Saadulla, 12 March 1948, *ALAP*.
199. Saadulla told that 'adhiars had stopped giving rent to Guwahati-based Hindu and Muslim landowners, even the *pandas* of the Kamakhya temple causing severe economic hardship' (ibid.).

200. Speech by Beliram Das, 28 March 1948, *ALAP*.
201. *APWR*, Kamrup, 30 December 1947.
202. *APWR*, Kamrup, 3 January 1948.
203. Fortnightly Report, second half of January 1947.
204. Fortnightly Report, first half of February 1947.
205. Ibid.
206. Letter from Harold Dennehy, Chief Secretary to Government of Assam, to Commissioner, Assam Valley Division, 14 February 1947, File no. I/A-5(S) F/47, APIRR.
207. Speech by Beliram Das, 28 March 1948, *ALAP*.
208. In March 1947, police reported that both Haren Hazra, the CPI leader from Jorhat, and Upen Das, the RCPI leader, were addressing the tea garden labourers, sweepers and match factory workers (*APWR*, Sibsagar, 8 March 1947).
209. Guha, *Planter Raj to Swaraj*, p. 305.
210. The subject is discussed in detail in Chapter 4.
211. Aniram Basumatari was the president of the Assam Kachari Sanmilan. He also worked with the police department as a sub–inspector (*CID Report*, Shillong, 27 September 1948, File no. IA-3(6) 48, XI, APIRR).
212. Memo. from Central Intelligence Officer to Deputy Inspector General of Police, Memo no. SA 14/105-6, 20 January 1948, File no. A-3(6)48, APIRR.
213. The CPI activists asked the peasants 'to occupy all the surplus land in Assam if necessary by applying force' ('Note on Communist Activities', File no. A-3(6) 48, 30 January 1948, APIRR). Peasants from Howaipur, Kaki, Kharikhana, Chitolmari, Bhalukmari, and Odali villages in Nowgaon participated in these meetings. The Muslim League leaders who attended it as well included Dr Monohar Ali.
214. The police reported that in a meeting held on 26 December 1947, at the house of Fayen Akanda of Akandapara in Darrang district, local schoolteachers and communist leaders actively participated. Pranesh Biswas, the leading communist leader, too spoke in the meeting. Later, a Krishak Sabha was also formed. Raisuddin of Moamari, another schoolteacher, was made the president of the peasant organization with 15 other immigrant peasants as members (*APWR*, Darrang, 10 January 1948).
215. This change in the political orientation came after the adoption of the Birbhum thesis of the RCPI and the Ranadive line of the CPI. The RCPI's new political programme was adopted in May 1948 (*Draft Political Thesis Second Congress of CPI*, December 1947, Packet no. 1948/3Q-G, P.C. Joshi Archives). The programme is discussed in detail in Chapter 5 of this volume.

Chapter 4

1. *Assam Secretariat Proceedings (ASP)*, Revenue Department, Revenue-A, nos 128–38, Oriental and India Office Collection (OIOC), British Library, London, 1898.
2. Speech by Rohini Kumar Chaudhuri, 21 March 1933, *Assam Legislative Council Proceedings* (*ALCP*); also, B.H. Baden-Powell, *The Land Systems of British India*, vol. 3, Oxford: Clarendon Press 1892, reprint, New Delhi: Publications Division, Government of India, 1974, p. 416. The Act provided occupancy rights to tenants.
3. Ibid.
4. Speech by A.J. Laine, 21 March 1933, *ALCP*.
5. *ASP*, Revenue Department, Revenue-A, nos 128–38, 1898, OIOC.
6. Petition of Jorhat Sarvajanik Sabha, 12 March 1897, *ASP*, Revenue Department, Revenue-A, nos 128–38, 1898, OIOC.
7. Ibid.
8. Petition of The Upper Assam Ryots' Association, 11 March 1897, *ASP*, Revenue Department, Revenue-A, nos 128–38, 1898, OIOC.
9. Ibid.
10. Ibid.
11. Ibid.
12. Memo. by J. Buckinghum, 2 March 1897, *ASP*, Revenue Department, Revenue-A, nos 128–38, 1898, OIOC.
13. Speech by A.J. Laine, 21 March 1933.
14. Ibid.
15. This has been discussed in Chapter 3 of this volume.
16. Speech by Rohini Kumar Chaudhury, 21 March 1933.
17. Ibid.
18. *Tinidiniya Assamiya*, 24 November 1932 and 5, 12 and 23 February 1933, quoted in speech by Rohini Kumar Chaudhury, 21 March 1933.
19. Among the members were Kashinath Saikia of Jorhat, Brindaban Saikia of Nowgaon and Nilambar Datta of Lakhimpur.
20. The motion was originally in the name of Rai Bahadur Nilambar Datta. It stated, '[T]his council recommends to the governor of Assam that they introduce at an early date a special Tenancy Act' (Speech by Rohini Kumar Chaudhury, 21 March 1933).
21. The Goalpara Tenancy Act granted occupancy rights to sub-tenants and under-tenants and protection to tenants against eviction and indiscriminate imposition of rent in the zamindari areas of Goalpara.
22. Speech by A.J. Laine, 21 March 1933.
23. Speech by A.J. Laine, 7 March 1935, *ALCP*.
24. The bill makes it clear that the government did not want to encroach upon the 'just rights of the landlords' ('Assam Tenancy Bill', in *The Assam Gazette*, part 5, 12 September 1934).

25. Brindaban Goswami asserted that he belonged to neither the landlord group nor the tenant group (Speech by Brindaban Goswami, 7 June 1935, *ALCP*).
26. These amendments were proposed by Khan Bahadur Maulavi Nuriddin Ahmed, Khan Bahadur Maulavi Keramat Ali, Babu Hirendra Chandra Chakravarti, and Haji Idris Ali Barlaskar, all from Surma valley.
27. Speech by Nuruddin Ahmed, 5 June 1935, *ALCP*.
28. The Act was published in *The Assam Gazette*, part 4, 2 October 1935. The Act received the consent of the governor on 31 July 1935 and that of the viceroy on 18 September 1935. It came to be known as the Assam Act III of 1935.
29. The Act granted occupancy rights to tenants over land under continuous cultivation by them for a period of 12 years or more. It also provided that in no case should the rent be enhanced by more than three *anna*s per rupee at one time.
30. For a brief introduction of the *satras*' relation with the Congress and anti-British nationalist mobilization, see Chapter 17 of Tirthanath Sarma, *Auniati Satrar Buranji*, Calcutta: Auniati Satra, 1975, reprint, 2004.
31. 'Statement and Objects and Reasons to the Assam Tenancy (Amendment) Bill, 1940', *The Assam Gazette*, part 5, 14 February 1940.
32. *Assam Provincial Banking Enquiry Committee Report* (*APBECR*), *1929–30*, vol. 1, Shillong: Government Press, 1930, p. 21.
33. Speech by Munawwar Ali, 2 March 1923, *ALCP*.
34. Speech by Munawwar Ali, 10 April 1928, *ALCP*.
35. *APBECR*, vol. 1, p. 2.
36. For details on the conflict between Hindu creditors and Muslim debtors in rural Bengal, see J.H. Broomfield, *Elite Conflict in a Plural Society: Twentieth-Century Bengal*, Berkeley, CA: University of California Press, 1968, p. 287.
37. Speech by Maulavi Khalique Chaudhury, 21 March 1933, *ALCP*.
38. Speech by Sarveswar Barua, 21 March 1933, *ALCP*.
39. B.B. Chaudhuri, *Peasant History of Late Pre-Colonial and Colonial India*, New Delhi: Pearson, 2008, p. 563.
40. 'Inquiry to Agricultural Indebtedness in India: Non-official Motion Carried Complexity of Problem', *The Times of India*, 25 September 1936.
41. 'Notification no. 5748 GT', 20 December 1934, *The Assam Gazette*, 26 December 1934.
42. The bill was published on 27 September 1933 (*The Assam Gazette*, part 5, 27 September 1933; 'Report of the Select Committee on the Assam Moneylenders Bill, 1933', *The Assam Gazette*, part 5, 21 March 1934). The Select Committee consisted of 17 members, all with landed interests. Of them, Kasinath Saikia, Brindaban Chandra Goswami,

Rohini Kumar Chaudhury, Sarveswar Barua and Muhammad Saadulla rep-resented the Brahmaputra valley as non-official members.

43. 'The Assam Money Lenders Act', *The Assam Gazette,* 26 December 1934.
44. Amalendu Guha, *Planter Raj to Swaraj: Freedom Struggle and Electoral Politics in Assam, 1826-1947*, New Delhi: PPH, 1977, p. 205.
45. *Annual Report on the Land Revenue Administration of Assam, 1939–1940*, Shillong: Government Press, 1940, p. 14. The South Kamrup Debt Conciliation Board, in the first year, dealt with 258 cases. The total amount involved was Rs 101,193. The Guwahati Board dealt with 886 cases in 1940–41. But the moneylenders used to file most of the cases. Between 1945 and 1946, all these boards were closed down (*Annual Report on the Land Revenue Administration Report of Assam, 1945–1946*, Shillong: Government Press, 1946, p. 14).
46. *Annual Report on the Assam Land Revenue Administration Report of Assam, 1945–1946*, p. 14.
47. *The Times of India*, 23 August 1975.
48. *Dainik Assamiya*, 9 March 1948.
49. Government Letter to Commissioner of Divisions, Memo. no. 23.46.21, 5 March 1947, Clause (6) of Section 13, Nowgaon District Record Room (NDRR).
50. Memo. from Deputy Commissioner, Nowgaon, to Secretary, Revenue Department, Memo. no. 2796/5/9R, 14 October 1947, NDRR.
51. Evidence of Dhaniram Talukdar, in Government of Assam, *Line System Enquiry Committee Report*, vol. 2, Shillong: Assam Government Press, 1938, p. 1.
52. Prabhat Narayan Chaudhury, Secretary of the North Kamrup Krishak Sanmilani, represented the Nalbari landlords.
53. Evidence of Jadav Chandra Das, Pleader, Secretary (Bar Association, Barpeta), in Government of Assam, *Line System Enquiry Committee Report*, vol. 2, p. 3.
54. Evidence of Sayed Akbar Ali of Mursa, Dost Mohammad Khan of Rangia and Bahudhan Gaonbura of Khalmari, in Government of Assam, *Line System Enquiry Committee Report*, vol. 2, pp. 8–9.
55. Evidence of Bahudhan Gaonbura of Khalmari, in Government of India, *Line System Enquiry Committee Report*, vol. 2, pp. 8–9.
56. Ibid.
57. Ibid.
58. Speech by Bishnuram Medhi, 12 March 1948, *Assam Legislative Assembly Proceedings* (*ALAP*).
59. He made it amply clear that 'the pressures from the adhiars led to the introduction of the bill' (ibid.).
60. Ibid.
61. Ibid.
62. Speech by Emrain Hussain Chaudhury, 13 March 1948, *ALAP*.

63. Speech by Muhammad Saadulla, 12 March 1948, *ALAP*.
64. Speech by Harinarayan Barua, 13 March 1948, *ALAP*. He was a Congress member of the Legislative Assembly from Sibsagar district.
65. Speech by Dharanidhar Basumatary, 13 March 1948, *ALAP*.
66. Harinarayan Barua informed the house about the Secretary of the Congress Legislative Party writing to the district congress committees, bar library, etc., inviting their opinion on the bill (Speech by Harinarayan Barua, 13 March 1948).
67. *Dainik Assamiya*, 13 January 1948. The committee collected evidence from five select centres.
68. Speech by Harinarayan Barua, 13 March 1948.
69. *Dainik Assamiya*, 13 January 1948.
70. Ibid.
71. For Bishuram Medhi, 'the main idea is to give protection to the tenants ... on enquiry we have found that exorbitant rate of rent in kind is realized from the tenant and on refusal they are evicted and great hardship is caused' (Speech by Bishnuram Medhi, 12 March 1948).
72. *Abstract of the Assam Police Intelligence Weekly Report* (*APWR*), Kamrup, 5 April 1948.
73. At a meeting of the Revolutionary Communist Party (RCPI) held in Azra, Guwahati, Upen Sarma, one of the leaders, criticized the bill. There was a small procession of 200 sharecroppers against the bill in Guwahati. At a conference of railway workers in Guwahati, Bishnu Prasad Rabha also criticized the bill by arguing that it would be beneficial only to the landlords. An estimated 3,000 sharecroppers from the south bank of Brahmaputra in Kamrup district staged a demonstration, demanding inclusion in the bill of provisions for sufficient protection against eviction by landlords (see *APWR*, Kamrup, 5 April 1948). The CSP too organized a number of meetings, mostly in Golaghat and Darrang, to discuss the bill (see *Dainik Assamiya*, 19 March 1948). One such meeting was held in Borhola village of Amguri *mauza* on 11 January 1948. The meeting was mostly attended by sharecroppers (*Dainik Assamiya*, 30 January 1948).
74. Speech by Muhammad Saadulla, 12 March 1948.
75. Ibid.
76. Ibid.
77. Ibid.
78. Ibid.
79. Ibid.
80. Speech by Emrain Hussain Chaudhury, 13 March 1948, *ALAP*.
81. The two members were Binode J. Sarwan and P.M. Sarwan, who were elected to the Assembly from the plantation sector.
82. Speech by Binode J. Sarwan, 18 March 1948, *ALAP*.
83. Speech by Binode J. Sarwan, 13 March 1948, *ALAP*.

84. Speech by Beliram Das, 2 April 1948, *ALAP*.
85. Ibid.
86. Speech by Harinarayan Barua, 13 March 1948.
87. Speech by Muhammad Saadulla, 13 March 1948, *ALAP*.
88. Speech by Dandeswar Hazarika, 13 March 1948, *ALAP*.
89. Ibid.
90. Speech by Harinarayan Barua, 13 March 1948.
91. A total of 33 amendments were tabled and few of them were withdrawn before discussion under the government's pressure (Speech by Speaker, 2 April 1948, *ALAP*).
92. Speech by Beliram Das, 2 April 1948.
93. Speech by Maulavi Muhammad Abdul Kashem, 3 April 1948, *ALAP*.
94. Speech by P.M. Sarwan, 2 April 1948, *ALAP*.
95. These amendment were moved by Gaurikanta Talukdar (Speech by Gaurikanta Talukdar, 3 April 1948, *ALAP*).
96. Speech by Lakshmidhar Bora, 3 April 1948, *ALAP*. For political views of Bora, see Lakshmidhar Bora, *Muktijujar Sonwaranat*, Guwahati: Assam Publication Board, 1984.
97. It was clear from the discussions that the members had in mind those absentee landowners, viz., pleaders, clerks, petty businessmen, professional and teachers who owned 20–40 bighas of land and rented out their land under the *adhi* system.
98. Speech by Bishnuram Medhi, 2 April 1948, *ALAP*.
99. *The Assam Gazette*, 16 June 1948.
100. Ibid.
101. Speech by Maulavi Muhammad Abdul Kashem, 2 April 1948, *ALAP*.
102. Speech by Dandeswar Hazarika, 13 March 1948, *ALAP*.
103. Speech by Bishnuram Medhi, 3 April 1948, *ALAP*.
104. Section 6A and 6B of the Act provided for this type of rent arrangement.
105. The discussion of Muslim League politics in the province of Assam is based on a reading of the Legislative Assembly debates and Guha, *Planter Raj to Swaraj: Freedom Struggle and Electoral Politics in Assam, 1826–1947*, New Delhi, PPH, 1977, pp. 243–49.
106. Various aspects of the ryot sabha movement have been discussed in Chapter 3 of this volume.
107. The discussion of the early days of Tribal League is based on Indivar Deuri, 'Bodo Janagosthir Antardwanda: Eti Artha Samajik Distipat', in Indivar Deuri (ed.), *Janagosthiya Samasya: Ateet Bartaman Bhabishyat*, Guwahati: Journal Emporium, 2001, pp. 97–109.
108. *Appeal of Nowgaon District Krishak Sabha*, pamphlet, Assam Police Intelligence Record Room (APIRR).

109. Interview with Dhireswar Kalita, Guwahati, 20 December 1996. He said that the CPI opposed the Act on the ground that the Act will lead to a nexus between revenue officers and landlords depriving the sharecroppers of their rights.
110. Amalendu Guha, *Zamindarkalin Goalpara Zillar Artha Samajik Abastha: Ekti Oitihasik Dristipat*, Guwahati: Natun Sahitya Parisad, 2000, p. 103.
111. Tarunsen Deka, *Mukti Sangramar Adharat Jiban Katha*, Guwahati: R.D. Printers and Publishers, 1993, p. 123.
112. *Panchayat*, 24 April 1948. The Assam police seized a few copies of *Panchayat*, which are available in the APIRR, Kahilipara, Guwahati.
113. Ibid.
114. In June 1948, a demonstration was held in Guwahati, which was joined by the *adhiars* and landless peasants of Palashbari, Rangia, Rani, and Beltola (Memo. from S.M. Dutta, Chief Intelligence Officer, Shillong, to Deputy Inspector General of Assam Police, Memo. no. SA/14/823 dated 22 June 1948, File no. I/A-3(6) 48/VII, APIRR).
115. Haridas Deka, *Jivan Aru Sangram*, Guwahati: LBS, 1992, p. 84.
116. *Sadiniya Assamiya*, 25 June 1948; Interview with Birendra Kumar Bhattacharya, former Congress Socialist Party (CSP) leader and a leading literary figure, New Delhi, January 1995.
117. *Resolution of the Third Party Conference of the Congress Socialist Party*, October 1948, APIRR.
118. Editorial, *Dainik Assamiya*, 14 March 1948.
119. Ibid.
120. *The Assam Tribune*, 20 March 1948.
121. Editorial, *Natun Assamiya*, 26 March 1948.
122. The meeting was chaired by Dharanidhar Das, a Congress leader and a landlord (*Dainik Assamiya*, 3 March 1948).
123. *The Resolution of the Pattadar Sangha*, June 1948, File no. I/A-9/S, APIRR.
124. *The Assam Tribune*, 1 December 1939, cited in Guha, *Planter Raj to Swaraj, p.* 262.
125. Guha, *Planter Raj to Swaraj,* p. 262.
126. Ibid., p. 281.
127. *The Assam Gazette*, 25 August 1943.
128. Memo. from S.P. Desai, Secretary, Revenue Department, Assam, to all district commissioners, October 1943, NDRR.
129. 'Return for the Acceleration of the Land Settlement Scheme for the Month of August, 1944', Speech by Munawar Ali, 14 November 1944, *ALAP*.
130. Ibid.

131. N.N. Mitra (ed.), *Indian Annual Registrar*, vol. 1, January–June 1947, Calcutta: Annual Register Office, 1947.
132. Press Statement of Mahendra Mohan Chaudhury, Secretary, Congress Parliamentary Party, *Sadiniya Assamiya*, 15 June 1946.
133. This has been discussed in a separate section of this chapter.
134. Speech by Abdul Rouf, Budget Session, 18 March 1945, *ALAP*.
135. Speech by Abdul Hamid Khan, 17 March 1944, *ALAP*.
136. *Dainik Assamiya*, 16 May 1947.
137. Speech by Surendranath Buragohain, Budget Session, 20 March 1945, *ALAP*.
138. Ibid.
139. See Chapter 6 in this volume for further discussion.
140. *Dainik Assamiya*, 11 August 1945. Similar letters appeared quite frequently during 1950–52 in the Assamese newspapers.
141. Editorial, *Sadiniya Assamiya*, 24 June 1950.
142. Assam Provincial Congress Committee Papers, Holding no. R 3099, Nehru Memorial Museum and Library (NMML). The committee members included M.M. Tayebulla, Khagen Nath, Haren Chandra Phukan, Harinarayan Barua, Raichandra Nath, Digendra Nath, Rashbihari Sarma, Robin Kakati, and Sriman Prafulla Goswami.
143. Ibid.
144. *Natun Assamiya*, 7 December 1950.
145. Assam Provincial Congress Committee Papers, Holding no. R 3099, NMML. Bijoy Chandra Bhagwati and Robin Kakati moved a resolution admitting the prevalence of landlessness in Assam.
146. For a brief review of the protests against the Zamindari Abolition Act in northern India, see Arvind N. Das, *Agrarian Movements in India: Studies on 20th Century Bihar*, London: Routledge, 1982.
147. The religious practice 'Brahma' is named so after Kalicharan Brahma (1862–1938), the founder-leader of the movement. The liberal religious and social ideas of Brahma became popular amongst the Bodos in the 1920s. His popularity also came from his anti-zamindari stand. Often, he negotiated with zamindars to grant tax concession to traders and timber merchants. For details, see Jayeeta Sharma, *Empire's Garden: Assam and the Making of India*, New Delhi: Permanent Black, 2011; M.C. Paul, 'Reform Movements among the Boro-Kachari', *The Eastern Anthropologist*, vol. 20, no. 1, 1991, pp. 57–68.
148. Examples of such political platforms include All Assam Tribal League, All Assam Ahom Sabha and All Assam Chutia Sanmilan. Of these, the All Assam Tribal League claimed wider representation of different ethnic groups. For details on All Assam Ahom Sabha, see Padmanath Gohain Barua, 'Presidential Address of All Assam Ahom Sabha', in Padmanath Gohain Barua, *Padmanath Gohain*

Barua Rachanavali, Guwahati: Assam Publication Board, 1987, pp. 933–45; for details of All Assam Tribal League, see Deuri, 'Bodo Janagoshir Antardanda'; Memorandum submitted by All Assam Chutia Sanmilan to the Government of India, 1929, Assam State Archives (ASA).

149. See Chapter 1 for a detailed discussion of the process of land transfer from the peasants to the traders.
150. *Presidential Address of the Kamrup District Tribal Conference*, First Conference, 23 December 1938, Boroma, Kamrup, ASA.
151. *Bulletin no. 2*, Assam Tribal League, Resolution of the Third Conference, 1939, Dharamtul, Nowgaon, ASA.
152. *The Assam Tribune*, 28 June 1940.
153. Speech by Bhimbar Deuri, 4 March 1941, *ALCP*.
154. The convention was held from 21 to 23 March 1945 at Khasi National Durbar Hall, Shillong. MacDanald Konger proposed this resolution which was seconded by Dhanbor Pator and supported by Haricharan Brahma. Another resolution urged the government to take steps to stop further immigration into the zamindari estates of Goalpara and the *la-khiraj* and *nisf-khiraj* lands of Kamrup and other districts and pass a legislation to this effect.
155. The documents containing Ahom Sabha's discourse on the peasant question include *Presidential Address of Sadau Assam Ahom Sanmilan*, 20–21 April 1935, Dibrugarh, ASA; *Resolution passed at the Golden Jubilee Conference of Ahom Sabha, Sibsagar*, 12–13 February 1944, File no. 358, 1948, *Political History of Assam* (*PHA*) Files ASA; *Ahom Raijalai Jaruri Janani*, 25 July 1947 and 26 June 1948, ASA; *Bulletin of the Sadau Assam Ahom Sanmilan*, no. 2, 1945, ASA; and Memorandum on the Ahoms as Minority by Ahom Minority Rights Sub-Committee, ASA.
156. *Presidential Address of Sadau Assam Ahom Sanmilan.*
157. *Resolution passed at the Golden Jubilee Conference of Ahom Sabha.*
158. *Resolution of All Assam Ahom Sabha*, 12–13 January 1944, File no. 231, *PHA* Files, ASA.
159. *Resolutions of Assamiya Samrakshini Sabha*, 1926, File no. 59, 1926, *PHA* Files, ASA.
160. Ibid.
161. *Tinidiniya Assamiya*, 12 September 1935.
162. Ibid.
163. Jyananath Bora, *Assomot Bideshi*, ed. Prasenjit Chaudhuri, Guwahati: Barua Agency, 1925, reprint, Guwahati: Chetana Prakash, 1996.
164. In 1943, Karka Dalay Miri complained in the Assembly that Miri peasants of Ranganadi areas in Lakhimpur had often faced trouble from the East Bengali immigrant peasants. He told that in 1941 the

Miri peasants had make a representation before the local authorities, for the reservation of some portions of land, but eventually they were settled with the immigrant peasants only (Speech by Karka Dalay Miri, 27 March 1943, *ALAP*). On the other hand, Rabi Chandra Kachari also alleged that the Kachari peasants had to face trouble in Mangaldai in Darrang district. He gave long narratives of how Mymmensingia peasants in thousands had chased away the local Kachari tribal peasants and occupied the professional grazing reserves (Speech by Rabi Chandra Kachari, 27 March 1944, *ALAP*). Another Tribal League member, Dhirsing Deuri, complained that large numbers of immigrant peasants had forcibly encroached upon the areas of Mikir peasants. He referred to the Lahorighat reserve in Nowgaon district, reserved for the tribal peasants, where the land speculators had managed to get a periodic *patta* and sold it to the immigrant peasants (Speech by Dhirsing Deuri, 27 March 1944, *ALAP*). All these tribal legislators narrated how land speculators were making profit by selling lands to the immigrant peasants.

165. Tour Diary of district collectors of Nowgaon and Darrang, April 1943, NDRR.
166. *ASP*, Revenue-A, Revenue Department, nos 39–52, June 1928, OIOC.
167. In 1926, the area of such land that had been transferred to the immigrant peasants was 10,266, 834, 1403, and 4507 bighas in the districts of Goalpara, Kamrup, Darrang, and Nowgaon, respectively. In Nowgaon, the largest area was transferred in Samaguri, which was 1816 bighas (Letter from J. Hezlett, Commissioner, Assam Valley Division, to Second Secretary, Government of India, 18 July 1926, *ASP*, Revenue-A, Revenue Department, nos 94–130, OIOC).
168. Rai Bahadur Krishnachandra Chowdhury of Uzanbazar and Rai Bahadur Mahidhar Bhuyan were a few among those who supported the move for the legislative amendment to the manual (*ASP*, Revenue-A, Revenue Department, nos 39–52, June 1928, OIOC).
169. Note by S.P. Desai, Settlement Officer, Kamrup, to Commissioner, Assam Valley Division, 24 January 1928. Ibid.
170. Guha, *Planter Raj to Swaraj*, p. 184.
171. Speech by Bishnuram Medhi, 1 September 1947, *ALAP*.
172. To remove the fear of other non-tribal communities, Bishnuram Medhi made it clear that the government could exercise the right to specify the communities' entitlement for protection under this land settlement policy.
173. Bishnuram Medhi, who led the official debate, reminded his opposition colleagues that an all party meeting had already endorsed the initiative (Speech by Bishnuram Medhi, 1 September 1947).

174. The bill mentioned that under the new land settlement policy within tribal belts and blocks 'preference will be given to persons whose religion, mode of life, agricultural customs and habits are the more akin to those of the classes for whose protection the belt and block was constituted'. The amended Act retained this provision ('Assam Act XV of 1947', in *The Assam Gazette*, 22 October 1947).
175. Speech by Dandeswar Hazarika, 1 September 1947, *ALAP*.
176. *The Assam Gazette*, 22 October 1947. The approximate total area under the tribal belt and block was 6,200 square miles in 1947. The total geographical area in the Brahmaputra valley is 22,000 square miles. The primary concentration of the belt and blocks was in Nowgaon. For details see, B.N. Bordoloi, *Transfer and Alienation of Tribal Lands in Assam*, Guwahati: B.N. Bordoloi, 1991, pp. 82–87.
177. Bordoloi, *Transfer and Alienation of Tribal Lands in Assam*, pp. 263–74. Also, see Jogendra Kumar Basumatory, *Bhaiamor Janajatir Bhumi Samachya*, memorandum submitted by Assam Tribal League to the Assam Chief Minister, Dhubri, 1966, ASA.

Chapter 5

1. In the 1946 Indian provincial assembly election, the Communist Party of India (CPI) contested for eight seats in Bombay, Bengal, Orissa, and Madras and got a little less than 3 per cent of the total votes polled. The election was held under limited franchise and hence the results do not portray the actual popular support for the party (see G.D. Overstreet and M. Windmiller, *Communism in India,* Berkeley, CA: University of California Press, 1959, pp. 236–37; Joya Chatterjee, *The Spoils of Partition: Bengal and India, 1947–1967,* Cambridge: Cambridge University Press, 2007, p. 212; Mridula Mukherjee, *Peasants in India's Non-Violent Revolution: Practice and Theory*, New Delhi: Sage, 2004, p. 225; Sekhar Bandyopadhyaya, *From Plassey to Partition: A History of Modern India,* New Delhi: Orient Blackswan, 2004, p. 448).
2. *Second Congress of the CPI: Opening Report by Comrade B.T. Ranadive on the Draft Political Thesis*, CP Publication, 1948, P.C. Joshi Archives, Jawaharlal Nehru University (JNU), New Delhi.
3. Ibid.
4. Ibid.
5. Ibid.
6. The second conference of the CPI, held in December 1947 in Calcutta, adopted a political thesis, which declared: '[T]he agrarian areas of India have become a huge volcano, which has started erupting every now and then. The desperation of the peasants is seen in the great Tebhaga struggle of Bengal, the Telengana struggle of the Nizam's domain, the struggle of the aboriginal Worlies in Bombay, the great

struggles of the peasants of Bihar for the Baksat land. Out of the several un-coordinated struggles is coming forth the single demand – 'Abolition of Landlordism: Land to the Tiller' (*Draft Political Thesis of the Second Congress of the CPI*, December 1947, Packet no. 1948/3Q-G, P.C. Joshi Archives; also, see Amit Kumar Gupta, *Agrarian Drama: The Leftists and the Rural Poor in India, 1934–1951*, New Delhi: Manohar, 1996).

7. In the latter half of 1949, the CPI Central Politburo dissolved the Assam Provincial Organizing Committee (APOC) for supporting P.C. Joshi and also for advocating a different path for the future (*Note on the Assam Provincial Communist Party*, File no. 55/1949, *PB Resolution on Assam PC*, 1949, File no. 53/1949, P.C. Joshi Archives).
8. The mainstream position of the Revolutionary Communist Party of India (RCPI) has been elaborated in 'The Present Situation and the Task of the Party', a resolution adopted in the 4th conference of the party held in May 1948, P.C. Joshi Archives, pp. 18–19.
9. Ibid.
10. Ibid.
11. Pannalal argued that gaining control over small localities and then making further advances would be the most appropriate path towards achieving revolutionary gains, as India did not have the objective social conditions of Russian and it must adopt a path of guerrilla warfare to achieve this end (Pannalal Dasgupta, *Samajtantrabad Aji Kena*, Calcutta, n.d.).
12. Manjula Basu, *Saumendranath Thakur: Karme O Manane*, Kolkata: Tagore Research Institute, 2007, pp. 150–55.
13. Haridas Deka, *Jivan Aru Sangram*, Guwahati: LBS, 1992, p. 84.
14. Chatterjee, *The Spoils of Partition*, p. 227.
15. Ibid.
16. Extract from Government of India letter no. 15, 'Daily Summary of Information', 13 May 1948, File no. A-3(50)48, Assam Police Intelligence Record Room (APIRR).
17. Karl Hack, *Defence and Decolonisation in Southeast Asia: Britain, Malaya and Singapore*, London: Routledge, 2000, p. 68.
18. Deka, *Jivan Aru Sangram*, p. 75.
19. Ibid., p. 85.
20. In some places, the RCPI could assert temporary control over local natural resources or methods of their extraction. Haridas Deka proudly remembered how contractors of the Forest Department were working in the hill forests after taking permission of the Krishak Banua Panchayats (KBPs) (Deka, *Jivan Aru Sangram*, p. 93).
21. Speech by Beliram Das, 25 March 1949, *Assam Legislative Assembly Proceedings* (*ALAP*).

22. Government Notification no. RT/1/48/103 (part) by S.J. Duncan, Secretary, Finance and Revenue Department, 25 June 1948, File no. RT 42/52, *Proceedings of Revenue Tenancy Department*, Assam State Archives (ASA). The southern Kamrup comprised two large *mauzas* of Palashbari and Beltola. According to the Census of 1951, Beltola mauza was predominantly characterized by the presence of sharecroppers and small peasants.
23. Tarunsen Deka, *Mukti Sangramar Adharat Jiban Katha*, Guwahati: R.D. Printers and Publishers, 1993, p. 186.
24. Interview with Govinda Kalita, erstwhile KBP leader, Guwahati, 18 June 1995; interview with Ambu Bora, erstwile RCPI leader and also involved in the peasant movement as a student, Guwahati, 8 and 14 June 1996.
25. Interview with Bhaghi Majhi, sharecropper from Beltola, Guwahati, 31 December 1995; interviews with Ambu Bora and Govinda Kalita.
26. Interviews with Ambu Bora and Bhaghi Majhi; interview with Kamala Majumdar, an erstwhile important RCPI leader who took a leading part in the armed struggle of sharecroppers, Guwahati, 19 June 1995.
27. Speech by Bishnuram Medhi, 13 March, 1949, *ALAP*; Government Notification no. RT/1/48/103, part 1. Also, see speech by Beliram Das, 25 March 1949, *ALAP*.
28. *Abstract of the Assam Police Intelligence Weekly Report* (*APWR*), Kamrup, 26 June 1948.
29. *APWR*, Kamrup, 10 July 1948.
30. Ibid.
31. *APWR*, Kamrup, 15 May 1948.
32. Prafulladatta Goswami, *Kencha Patar Kanpani*, Guwahati: LBS, 1952, reprint 1991. For a critical review of this work, see Hiren Gohain, 'Asomiya Upanyasar Esha Bachar', in Sonit Bijoy Das and Munin Bayan (eds), *Hiren Gohain Rachanawali*, vol. 1, Guwahati: Katha Publication, 2009, p. 496; Govindaprasad Sarma, 'Asamiya Upanyasor Dhara 1939–89', in Homen Borgohain (ed.), *Asamiya Sahityar Buranji*, vol. 6, Guwahati: ABILAC, pp. 122–23.
33. For instance, a local *mahajan* in Rani mauza, who had a small grocery shop and rented out 15 *bighas* of land to an *adhiar* from the same village agreed to take one-third of the produce. The sharecroppers did not demand any printed receipt of rent paid (interview with Dhireswar Kalita, Guwahati, 20 December 1996).
34. Speech by Beliram Das, 2 April 1949, *ALAP*; interview with Dhireswar Kalita; Deka, *Mukti Sangramar Adharat Jiban Katha*, p. 123.
35. The police admitted that only in one instance it was able to seize paddy from the houses of sharecroppers 'in peaceful way', but not before actually being challenged by them (*APWR*, Kamrup, 5 June 1948).

36. *APWR*, Kamrup, 5 June 1948.
37. *Dainik Assamiya* (12 June 1949) reported that landlords agreed to take 10–15 puras of paddy from their sharecroppers. However, the KBP, in a conference held in Bongra, Kamrup, asked the sharecroppers to pay rent at the rate of 8–10 puras of paddy.
38. Beliram Das and Lakhidhar Bora, both members of the Assam Legislative Assembly had landed interests and often acted as representatives of landlords. See File no. I/A-36(6)48/vvii, APIRR; Memo. by Deputy Inspector General of Police (DIG), Memo. no. I/C-b(12D) 48/130, 1 July 1948, APIRR.
39. *APWR*, Kamrup, 15 May 1948.
40. Ibid.; Memo. from S.M. Dutta, CID officer, Shillong, to DIG of Assam Police, Memo. no. S.A/14/823, 22 June 1948, APIRR.
41. Interview with Dhireswar Kalita; interview with Kamini Sarma, an erstwhile RCPI leader who later joined the CPI, Rangia, Kamrup, 21 June 1995.
42. *APWR*, Kamrup, 15 May 1948.
43. Ibid.
44. In one of the instances of sharecroppers resorting to violence, the police received a report from the manager of Amchong tea estate on 4 June 1948. In his letter, the manager reported his apprehension about a probable attack on the estate by the Karbi sharecroppers of the neighbouring Sonapur. In fact, a large number of sharecroppers subsequently came to the tea estate, attacked the manager's bungalow, kept the manager in confinement and set fire to the bungalow. The police later reported how these sharecroppers were under the influence of liquor and armed with bamboo sticks and other weapons. The police admitted that it had to face a good deal of trouble to bring the situation under control. It also admitted that the principal cause of this violence was an incident which took place in the evening of 3 June 1948, when *sardar* of the garden went to demand rent from a Karbi adhiar of the garden, and the latter refused to pay rent, as a result of which, the sardar assaulted him, thereby provoking the sharecroppers to attack the garden (*APWR*, Kamrup, 5 July 1948).
45. In one such instance, the police reported how 'the pro-communist tenants of Sib Barua, Girdhari Mandal, Lalit Sarma and Guluk Barua of Sapekhati are delaying payment of their rent to the landlords, though they do not openly say that they will withhold payments' (*APWR*, Assam, 12 January 1949). There are also instances of sharecroppers retaining their land despite being evicted by their landlords and cultivating it in the next harvesting session. The police, thus, reported how the 'lands of Giridhar Sarma, Lalit Bhattacharya and Golak Chandra Barua of Sapekhati have been ploughed by the old

tenants without the consent of the owners', despite their being evicted in the previous year (*APWR*, Assam, 29 June 1949; interview with Jogen Hazarika, erstwhile CPI leader, New Delhi, 2000; interview with Dhireswar Kalita).

46. *APWR*, Kamrup, 5 June 1948.
47. On 3 June 1948, a landowner Bhabadhar Chaudhuri from Mailata village in Palashbari took possession of his land from his sharecroppers, thereby angering them. They, with the help of the KBP cadres, mobilized other villagers, along with those from neighbouring villages. An estimated 1,000 villagers, comprising sharecroppers and small peasants, dared Chaudhuri to evict them and ploughed the land. Chaudhury could re-assert his claim only with the support of police (*APWR*, Kamrup, 5 June 1948).
48. *Review of Communism in Assam*, February 1949, File no. I/A-3(8) H-47, APIRR.
49. Ibid.
50. For instance, one landowner, Kanak Barua, owned lands in several villages of Kamrup. When he was refused his *adhi*, he, accompanied by an immigrant Muslim adhiar, Hussain Ali, went to collect it from these villages. This provoked the sharecroppers who set the house of Hussain Ali on fire (*APWR*, Kamrup, 26 February 1949).
51. When Harekrishna Das sent his *mohori*, Sarat Chandra Sharma, to collect adhi from Saokuchi village where he had his land, the sharecroppers assaulted him (*APWR*, Kamrup, 8 January 1949).
52. For instance, in February 1949, a few hundred tribal sharecroppers set fire to a house of Harokabadur Chetri, an agricultural labourer of landowner Karuna Barua of Guwahati, in Dhalbama village. They were armed with weapons and physically injured Prem Bahadur Chetri and Dhanmaya Chetri, two other agricultural labourers of Karuna Barua, who had gone there to collect Barua's share of paddy (*APWR*, Kamrup, 26 February 1949).
53. For instance, on 18 February 1949, several tribal sharecroppers burnt down the house of one Matiraj, a village headman of Udalbakra village in Beltola, as the latter had paid adhi to his landlord. In another instance, a Nepali sharecropper and his wife were physically assaulted and his house in Dhalbama village in Beltola burnt down on the night of 19 February as he too had paid adhi. In yet another instance, in Beltola on February 1949, when Hiren Phukan, a Guwahati-based landowner went to collect his adhi from his sharecropper Pati Mikir, he decided to keep his adhi in Pati Mikir's house, but several other sharecroppers, led by KBP leaders Dhambarudar Injal, Kukur Kachari of Kotalabari and Tota Mikir of Saokuchi, refused to give him the adhi and returned the empty bags to Phukan. On the next day, a similar fate awaited another landlord Rajachandra Bharali of Kumarpara,

Guwahati. He collected some paddy from his sharecroppers in Moinakhurung and kept it in the house of one of his sharecroppers. On the same night, several tribal sharecroppers seized the paddy and burnt the gunny bags (*APWR*, Kamrup, 19 February 1949).

54. *APWR*, Kamrup, 26 February 1949.
55. *APWR*, Kamrup, 8, 15 and 22 January 1949; *APWR*, Sibsagar, 29 January, 5 and 19 February 1949; *APWR*, Lakhimpur, 12 and 26 February, 5 March 1949; *APWR*, Darrang, 18, 19 and 26 March, 2 April 1949.
56. In one such instance on 1 January 1949, a landowner Padmadhar Bora went to Kalitakuchi village, with his servants, to collect adhi from his sharecropper Bihram Mikir. He collected his adhi though Bihram Mikir refused to be present when the landowner came to his house. On his way back, several KBP cadres attacked him and his retinue, snatched away Padmadhar's bicycle and threw the adhi from his cart (*APWR*, Kamrup, 8 January 1949).
57. *Review of Communism in Assam*, February 1949.
58. *APWR*, Darrang, 29 January 1949.
59. In Tengakhat area of Dibrugarh, there was a conflict between the sharecroppers and the landowners. As many as 15 sharecroppers were taken into custody. In Jalanigrant, the KS came in conflict with the landowners and four peasants were arrested. See *APWR*, Lakhimpur, 5 June 1948.
60. As reported in *APWR*, Assam, 31 December 1949, '[a]bout 2 or 3 of the peasants of the Hatichong Jojori, Deobali and Singia areas in Nowgaon have joined the Communist sponsored Kisan organization and stopped payment of rent in cash or kind ... New Communist workers have been drafted to Titabor, Sibsagar to keep the winter campaign going'.
61. *APWR*, Nowgaon, 17 December 1948.
62. *APWR*, Nowgaon, 10 December 1949.
63. *Review of Communism in Assam*, March 1949, File no. I-A-3(5)H-47, APIRR.
64. For instance, Mahendra Saikia, a landlord from Titabor, accepted one-fourth of the produce (ibid.).
65. In June 1948, the CPI's APOC decided to strengthen its base among the peasantry. Peasant panchayats were formed in different localities, the sharecroppers in the new areas were organized, asked not to pay half of the produce as rent and to refuse paying rent in kind (*Kishan Fronts in Sibsagar District*, pamphlet issued by APOC, File no. I/A-3 (8) H-47, APIRR; Suren Hazarika, *Samajbadar Sandhanat*, Jorhat: Suren Hazarika, 1993, p. 19).
66. Memo. no. 10370/c, 16 December 1949, File no. 3/6-48 XI, APIRR.
67. *APWR*, Kamrup, 12 February 1949.

68. A few activists of the peasant organizations in Beltola mauza threatened the new sharecroppers not to plough the land of the landlords and instigated the evicted sharecroppers to claim their occupancy rights (*APWR*, Kamrup, 9 July 1949).
69. According to police reports, in Paneri of Darrang district, tribal peasants 'under the instigation of underground communist Aniram Basumatari resorted to lawlessness and violent activity along with refusal to adhi'. In Sibsagar, peasants of Gadhulibazar, Dhupdhara, Athkel, Nazira, Silakhati, Abhoipur, Sapekhati, and Baruachariali stopped paying rent to their landlords. The police recorded these incidences as 'quite rampant'. See *APWR*, Kamrup, 9 July 1949; *Kishan Fronts in Sibsagar District*.
70. For instance, on 28 June 1949, some old sharecroppers continued to plough the land of landowner L.N. Thakur, which he had recently purchased from another landowner (*APWR*, Kamrup, 9 July 1949).
71. File no. I/A-5(6)/49, APIRR. Many interviewees – Gopal Das, an RCPI activist whose brother was a front-ranking KBP leader, and Govinda Kalita – also recalled 'large-scale' burning of moneylenders' documents in Sualkuchi.
72. In Dibrugarh, the RCPI organized the tribal villages in Nohajar, Maharani, Bagtoli, Burikhowang, Kolowa, and other neighbouring tribal villages of Moran (*APWR*, Lakhimpur, 10 December 1949). In Dibrugarh, the Congress Socialist Party (CSP) also mobilized the sharecroppers. The CSP leader Nagen Kakati appealed to the villagers of Jokai to forcibly seize crops from the land of Haridas Konwar. Konwar had filed a case in the civil court, complaining about his difficulty in retrieving the seized paddy. The police also reported that several CSP leaders, including Premadhar Baglari and Nagen Kakati, had been inciting the sharecroppers not to pay rent to their landholders. In November 1949, the Sibsagar district unit of CPI decided to start 'stop paddy campaign' to mobilize the sharecroppers for not parting with their produce of paddy in Titabor, Forkating, Baruabamungaon, Bhalukmara, Dhekial, Barpathar, Kakodanga, and Namti. These places were adjacent to several tea gardens, whose workers, the CPI leadership thought, would support the campaign (*APWR*, Lakhimpur, 17 December 1949).
73. *APWR*, Darrang, 7 January 1950.
74. Interview with Dhireswar Kalita.
75. *Review of Communism in Assam*, July 1949, APIRR.
76. On 1 January 1950, one such meeting took place between the landlords and their sharecroppers in Udalbakra, Beltola. The landlords were optimistic about the settlement in the near future, but failed to secure the consent of sharecroppers to pay rent.
77. *APWR*, Sibsagar, 7 January 1950.

78. For instance, landlords of Hatkhola in Tinsukia also refused to give their sharecroppers land for cultivation during the sowing season (*Natun Assamiya*, 10 October 1950).
79. *APWR*, Kamrup, 23 December 1950.
80. Ibid. A cyclostyled bulletin titled *Pran galeo adhi dhan nidiba, matir daklal ein nidiba* [*We will give our lives but not adhi and not our land*] was found in circulation in these localities.
81. For instance, in Patia village of Titabar mauza in Sibsagar district, a landowner named Rakta Jamal evicted his pre-existing sharecroppers and gave his lands to a 'few powerful [i.e., rich and under no communist influence] sharecroppers' for cultivation (*Natun Assamiya*, 15 November 1950).
82. *Natun Assamiya*, 15 November 1950.
83. *Natun Assamiya*, 5 February 1951.
84. Petition by Kamrup Devalay Ryot Sangha, 12 July 1952, File no. RT 39/52, Tenancy Branch, Revenue Department, *Proceedings of Revenue Tenancy Department*, ASA.
85. The earliest examples of such writings are the literary works of Gunabhiram Barua and Hemchandra Barua. See, for instance, Hemchandra Barua, 'Bahire Rong Song Bhitare Kuwabhaturi', in Hemchandra Barua, *Hemchandra Barua Rachanavali*, ed. Jatindranath Goswami, Guwahati: Hemkosh Prakasan, 1999, pp. 23–46. Decades later, such Assamese liberal nationalist literati were joined by more such figures including Lakshminath Bezbaroa in their opposition to the authority of gossains. See, for instance, Lakshminath Bezbaroa, 'Nomal', in Lakshminath Bezbaroa, *Lakshminath Bezbarua Granthavali*, ed. Jatindranath Goswami, vol. 2, Guwahati: Sahitya Prakash, 1988, pp. 1041–48.
86. Ananta Charan Bhagwati, a landlord and government official in Kumarpara area of Beltola mauza, evicted his tribal sharecroppers in Lakhara, which was far away from his residence. He reasoned that he had to choose the sharecroppers from his own village to allow him to monitor issues related to his land and agriculture (*Petition of Ananta Charan Bhagwati*, File no. RT 42/52, Tenancy Branch, Revenue Department, *Proceedings of Revenue Tenancy Department*, ASA).
87. This estimate is based on India Jute Mill Association, *Annual Summary of Jute and Gunny Statistics*, Calcutta: Indian Jute Mill Association, 1963. Also, see Prashant Bharadwaj and James Fenske, 'Partition, Migration, and Jute Cultivation in India', *Journal of Development Studies*, vol. 48, no. 8, 2012, pp. 1084–107; Anil Rai, 'Trends in the Jute Industry since Independence', *Social Scientist*, vol. 6, nos 6-7, 1978, pp. 83–102.
88. The police recorded that in a few places, the tribal sharecroppers even gave adhi to their landlords for the year 1948–49 (*APWR*, Kamrup, 4 April 1949, 14 May 1949, 5 June 1949).

89. In 1952, the Congress clarified that the Left parties' attempt to mobilize the sharecroppers during the election failed to elicit any sympathy from the urban middle class.
90. 'Adhiar Ain Kakatate Thakil', *Natun Assamiya*, 1 January 1952.
91. Haladhar Bhuyan, a member of Assam Legislative Assembly from Nowgaon, noted this growing fear of landlords in Nowgaon. Perhaps, the Tebhaga movement in Bengal and the subsequent talks of giving occupancy rights to sharecroppers could have caused this fear.
92. The Adhiar Act came into effect in Golaghat subdivision in August 1948 (File no. RT 42/52, Tenancy Branch, Revenue Department, *Proceedings of Revenue Tenancy Department*, ASA).
93. The Act came into effect in Darrang district on 19 October 1949. Subsequently, it was extended to other districts according to the following schedule: Sibsagar subdivision on 8 November 1951; Golaghat subdivision on 12 August 1948; Nowgaon district on 7 October 1948; and Bargoan and Naharbari mauza of Darrang district on 16 June 1949. The remaining mauzas of Tezpur subdivision came under the Act on 27 April 1950; Northern bank of Brahmaputra in Kamrup on 14 April 1954 (*The Assam Gazette*, 14 January 1954; File no. RT 42/52, Tenancy Branch, Revenue Department, *Proceedings of Revenue Tenancy Department*, ASA).
94. 'Even the landowner came to an understanding with the sharecroppers and the land was sold out to raise money for occasions like marriage[s]' (Suren Hazarika, *Samajbadar Sandhanat*, p. 70).
95. *Dainik Assamiya*, 9 June 1948. Anthropologist Audrey Cantlie, who carried out field work in this area in the 1970s, also noted this incident, which was fresh in the local people's memories (Audrey Cantlie, 'Preface' to Audrey Cantlie, *The Assamese*, London: Curzon Press, 1984). The earliest reference to a public debate among the Brahmin landlords in Jorhat on whether they should cultivate the land by themselves or not, can be traced to a pamphlet published in 1925. The pamphlet entitled *Brahmanor Bidhaba Bibah, Hala Karson Ebang Puspita Kanya Bibah* was published by Jorhat Samaj Samsakarar in 1925. The participants in the debate unanimously suggested that 'they should plough the land themselves in the context of new situation'. Though there is no mention of any conflict with tenants, it is highly probable that there was a simmering tension within the landlords regarding the rights of sharecroppers. Also, see Amalendu Guha, 'Medieval Economy of Assam', in Tapan Raychaudhuri and Irfan Habib (eds), *The Cambridge Economic History of India*, vol. 1, (c. 1200–c. 1750), Cambridge: Cambridge University Press, 1992, p. 485.
96. The number of cases filed under this Act in the *raiyatwari* districts of Assam were 220, 17 and 205, for the years 1950, 1951 and 1951 respectively. In 1952, an estimated 180 cases were filed in the two

districts of Kamrup and Sibsagar only (File no. RT 51/52,Tenancy Branch, Revenue Department, *Proceedings of Revenue Tenancy Department*, ASA).

97. Note by L.P. Goswami, General Secretary, Assam Krishak Sabha, File no. A.5(4) U.48, APIRR.
98. Provisions 4, 5, 10 of the Assam Adhiar Protection and Rights Act or Assam Act III of 1948.
99. Speech by Ranendra Mohan Das, 20 September 1952, *ALAP*.
100. *Kishan Fronts in Sibsagar District*.
101. Numerous meetings were organized protesting against the landlords who had been evicting their sharecroppers and compelling the latter to pay rent at the earlier rates. A meeting held in Titabor in early 1951 expressed resentment against the non-committal attitude of the administration towards the Act. Not all such meetings were organized under the banner of communist or socialist parties (*Resolution of Rashtriya Krishak Sangha*, File no. RT 4/51, *Proceedings of Revenue Tenancy Department*, ASA).
102. The legal and public dispute between Ramani Priya Chaudhury from Guwahati and her sharecroppers at Beltola is illustrative of this point. In 1950, the sharecroppers of Chaudhury wanted to pay her rent at a reduced rate instead of the normal rate. This prompted the latter to file a case seeking their eviction. This came as a major blow to the sharecroppers as they had limited avenues to defend themselves in the court. The court supported the landlord and this prompted the sharecroppers to negotiate with her. They could not look forward to support from their leaders either, since most were behind bars. Chaudhury was in no mood to allow the rebellious sharecroppers to continue tilling her land. Armed with a court order, Chaudhury virtually chased out her sharecroppers from the land. She even put flags on her paddy fields as a mark of her rights over the land. In April 1951, these defeated sharecroppers met the Assam Revenue Minister and recounted their plight. The sharecroppers, desperately hopeful of retaining their land, knew well that they could no more use the Adhiar Act as their defence but must bury their hatchet in a tactful way. They cited crop failure as a reason for their inability to pay rent. Moreover, they invoked provisions for the protection of permanent tenants against eviction under the Assam Tenancy Act of 1935. None of these, however, could persuade the government to defend them against their landlord (File no. RT 4/51, *Proceedings of Revenue Tenancy Department*, ASA).
103. *Dainik Assamiya*, 1 August 1948. An instance of sharecroppers approaching the court mentioned in the daily took place in Majgaon village of Amguri mauza, where the land had been cultivated by the sharecroppers for the past seven years.

104. *Dainik Assamiya* (18 August 1948) reported how on the day of one such final trial at the court of Jorhat, people came in large numbers as visitors to witness the legal proceedings.
105. A large number of sharecroppers, mostly former tea garden labourers and tribals, from Itakhola, Tengabasti and Kolabasti villages of North Jamuguri mauza, demanded that the landlords personally come and collect their adhi. The landlords, however, did not go to collect their adhi and forbade their sharecroppers to reap the standing crops. But the latter decided to reap the harvest and take their share in the presence of local village headmen. This resulted in a strong retaliation from a few landlords. In one instance, Jan Mahmod, a landowner, physically assaulted his sharecroppers when they decided to reap the crop but this could hardly stop them from doing so. The administration agreed to the sharecroppers' demand and allow them to retain their share of produce as per the Adhiar Act (*Natun Assamiya*, 2 December 1949 and 9 January 1950).
106. The Assamese Congress leader Robin Kakati was of the view that the extension of the Act would help Congress to control the landlord–sharecropper conflict (*Assam Provincial Congress Committee Papers*, 1949, Nehru Memorial Museum and Library [NMML], New Delhi). Another influential Congress leader Bijoy Chandra Bhagawati admitted that landlords from Tezpur had pressurized him to have the Act expanded in its scope (interview with Bijoy Chandra Bhagawati, New Delhi, December 1995).
107. The CSP believed that the Act, in spite of having pro-landlord provisions, would still protect the rights of sharecroppers ('Letter to the Editor' by Golok Kakaki, General Secretary, Tezpur Krisak Sabha, *Natun Assamiya*, 16 October 1949).
108. District Congress Committee of Sibsagar, *Copy of Resolution No. 2*, File no. 26/51, *Proceedings of Revenue Tenancy Department*, ASA.
109. A public meeting, held on 8 February 1951 in Abhaypur mauza and presided over by the Subdivisional Collector of Sibsagar district, demanded that the government fix the rate of rent and extend the Assam Adhiar Protection and Regulation Act of 1948, to Sibsagar subdivision. The District Congress Committee also passed a resolution in January 1951 on the enforcement of this Act in Sibsagar subdivision (Letter of Durgeswar Saikia, Secretary, Sibsagar District Congress Committee to Revenue Minister, Assam, 24 April 1951, File no. RT 26/51, *Proceedings of Revenue Tenancy Department*, ASA).
110. Ibid.
111. *Dainik Assamiya*, 5 December 1948; *Natun Assamiya*, 14 January 1949.
112. For instance, in December 1947, Krishak Sabha of Titabor mauza, in a meeting, held in Namsungi village and presided over by CSP

leader Lakshmi Prasad Goswami, passed one such resolution. The resolution claimed that 'the landless and those sharecroppers who don't have enough land for cultivation had to give too much of bribe to get land' (*Dainik Assamiya*, 5 December 1947).

113. *Kishan Fronts in Sibsagar District.*
114. Speech by Bishnuram Medhi, 29 March 1949, *ALAP.*
115. Landless peasants from Bajali also demanded the opening of government wasteland and grazing reserves. These peasants submitted a memorandum before the governor and an estimated 500 peasants staged a demonstration (*Natun Assamiya*, 16 February 1951).
116. The Indian censuses put the figures of those who emigrated from districts of western Assam during this period at 1,00,000 (*Census of India*, Assam 1951, vol.12, part I-A, pp. 32–33; *Census of India*, Assam 1961, vol.3, part III-C, Table D, pp. 218–19).
117. Notification no. EVC 51/51/14, *The Assam Gazette*, part 9, 14 November 1951.
118. For instance, in Namati village, landowner Prabhatnarayan Chaudhury had a few migrant sharecroppers and once they had emigrated from the village, he rented out the land to Assamese Hindu sharecroppers (ibid.).
119. The flood-affected people in Khuamoua mauza demanded that land from the nearby Namrup wasteland be distributed among them, as they were landless. They also demanded that they be given better land (File no. RT 6/5, Tenancy Branch, Revenue Department, *Proceedings of Revenue Tenancy Department*, ASA).
120. For example, Owguri professional grazing reserve was encroached upon by landless peasants, who had also occupied grazing reserves in Simaluguri mauza of Sibsagar. Further, a large number of landless peasants from the Ahom community occupied grazing reserves in Jhanji (Speech by Hareswar Das, 10 March 1951, *ALAP*; Speech by Harinarayan Barua, 18 March 1949; *ALAP*; *APWR*, Kamrup, 9 April 1949).
121. *Dainik Assamiya,* 10 November 1948.
122. *Natun Assamiya,* 29 September 1949.
123. For instance, we only find evidence for landless peasants forcibly occupying about 150 bighas of land owned by a police officer in Amguri-Kharikatia mauza (Hazarika, *Samajbadar Sandhanat,* p. 143).
124. *Communist Influence in Tea Gardens and Labour Organisation in Sibsagar District*, Note from Superintendent of Police, Sibsagar, to DIG, Assam Police, 22 December 1949, File no. A-3(6)(K)47, APIRR.
125. According to the police, 'tea garden labours who had rich experience of the class struggle could influence the peasants' (*Kishan Fronts in*

Sibsagar District). It further noted: 'At the same time the tea gardens had witnessed labour unrest and came into direct confrontation with the management' (ibid.). A representative example of such tension was: 'during the last 4 months of 1948 tea garden labours were restive and they had fighting attitude towards the management particularly in Mekipur and Sonali tea estates. They were conscious about the huge profit made by the proprietors ... the CPI planned to exploit it even if necessary by indenting party workers from other places' (ibid.).

126. Ibid.
127. Ibid. Also, see *Notes on CPI Activities in Sibsagar District*, File no. IA -3(6)47, APIRR.
128. The CSP district unit in Darrang called Darrang Hind Krishak Panchayat held a meeting in Mangaldai on 20 November 1949, where Sandhiram Saharia, a CSP leader, urged the peasants 'to form "land army" in every village'. He further advised that '[t]hey should continue their reclamation work as usual and start cultivation on the wastelands of Noanadee tea estates' (Letter from Special Superintendent of Assam Police to Chief Secretary of Assam, 2 December 1949, File no. c-6[14] c/50, APIRR).
129. On 28 September 1949, the Executive Committee meeting of the Darrang District Socialist party demanded that the government distribute land among the landless and flood-affected people of southern Mangaldai. It also decided that the peasants should squat in the wastelands of Noanadee (Rontholy) and Singrimari tea estates in Kalaigaon mauza (*Note on the Socialist Party of Darrang*, File no. I/A-3[10]H-47, APIRR).
130. For instance, a procession organized by the CSP in Mangaldai was attended by peasants from Sipajhar, Roinakuchi, Dahi, Rangamati, Kokrai, and Hindu-Gopa mauzas. The participants raised the slogans like *banpanit prapirata khetiakak mati diak, nagal jar mati tar* and *sram jar fasal tar* ('give land to peasants who lost land in flood and erosion', 'land to the tiller' and 'crop belongs to those who labour') (ibid.).
131. *Natun Assamiya*, 12 November 1949.
132. *Natun Assamiya*, 4 and 21 February 1950.
133. After verbal assurances from the Deputy Commissioner, the agitating peasants retreated. They assembled for a meeting at the Tezpur Town Hall, where Golok Kakoti and Amalendu Guha — the latter was then a young college teacher who later became a well-known historian — discussed the land distribution policy of the government (ibid.).
134. Prior to the occupation of the land of Diplonga tea garden, there were a number of public meetings in Satiya, Jamuguri and around Diplonga,

which were addressed by local CSP leaders like Surendranath Hazarika, Golok Kakoty and Bodhanchandra Mahanta (*Natun Assamiya,* 4 and 21 February 1950).

135. Bishanath Tea Company Limited sent a detailed account of what happened in Diplonga tea estate to the Political Secretary of the Planting and Commerce Group in the Assam Legislative Assembly (File no. RT 30/51, Tenancy Branch, Revenue Department, *Proceedings of Revenue Tenancy Department*, ASA).
136. These tea estates were East India Tea Company, Dangdhara Grant, Scottish Asom Tea Company, Deogharia Grant, Tairun Tea Company, Bibijan-Mahima Grant, and Rangdoi Grant (*Natun Assamiya,* 19 March 1950).
137. *Natun Assamiya,* 25 January 1950.
138. *Natun Assamiya*, 26 December 1950.
139. CSP, *Pamphlet on Giladhari Satyagraha*, 1 June 1950, APIRR.
140. 'Bhumihin Khetiakar Satyagraha', *Sadiniya Assamiya*, 10 June 1950.
141. *The Assam Tribune*, 15 June 1950.
142. In a meeting held in Golaghat in mid-June 1950, CSP leaders 'decided to make the Ghiladhari a success by requisitioning volunteers from other places of Assam and to observe 18 June as Giladhari day'. The meeting was attended by Bipinpal Das, Rupram Sut, Khagen Gogoi, Lakshmi Prasad Goswami, Sankar Prasad Barua, Bangsidhar Dutta, Chakradhar Saikia, Naren Sarma, and Nibaran Bora (File no. C-6[14]/e/50, APIRR).
143. CSP, *Pamphlet on Giladhari Satyagraha*, APIRR.
144. This information is from a printed pamphlet on Giladhari sataygraha authored by a young socialist Dugdhanath Saikia and published by the Young Socialist League (File no. C-6[14]e/50, APIRR).
145. *Natun Assamiya,* 2 and 12 December 1950.
146. For instance, lands of the East India Company tea garden in Amguri and Kharikatia mauzas of Titabor circle were also occupied by the landless peasants. About 100 landless peasants, led by the CSP unit in Titabor, occupied the Dhangdhara fee simple grant land (*Natun Assamiya*, 19 December 1953). In another instance, more than 300 peasants of eight villages including Panigaon, Satgaon and Kadharli, led by Lakshmi Prasad Goswami, a memorandum before the Deputy Commissioner, demanding proper redistribution of land in Moamari grazing reserve of Darrang district (*Natun Assamiya*, 5 October 1950).
147. For instance, on 5 October 1950, a meeting was held in Melamati village. It was chaired by Bipinpal Das; Hareswar Goswami, two prominent CSP leaders of Assam, delivered speeches. The meeting urged the government to distribute the fee simple grant lands of

Titabor among the local landless peasants within a stipulated time period (*Natun Assamiya*, 13 October 1950).

148. For instance, Mangaldai Krishak Sabha organized a well-attended meeting in Ghorabandha village of Sipajhar mauza, in which it was decided that 7–8,000 bighas of unutilized lands in Singamari and Nuannadi tea gardens should be occupied by the landless peasants. It also directed flood-affected peasants of southern Mangaldai to reclaim land from the aforementioned gardens 14 October 1950 onwards. Consequently, a committee was formed to supervise this land reclamation process (*Natun Assamiya,* 11 October 1950).
149. For instance, on 19 February 1950, 500 landless peasants from Satia, Jamuguri and Biswanath Chariali mauzas took out a procession in Tezpur, demanding that wastelands in Diplong tea garden be distributed among them. Both CSP and CPI activists participated in the procession (*Natun Assamiya*, 20 February 1950).
150. *Natun Assamiya,* 12 October 1949.
151. *Sadiniya Assamiya,* 27 January 1951.
152. For instance, in December 1950, in a meeting of peasants and labourers, Jogendranath Rajmedhi, General Secretary of Dumduma Central Chah Majdur Sangha, debarred the local land-less peasants from occupying lands of the Tangia tea garden. He appealed to them to follow the legal procedure of staking their claims to the land of the tea garden. He further claimed that he was already in communication with the government for the distribution of land among the landless peasants. Rajmedhi's intervention and assurance came after a decision taken by the local landless peasants to squat in almost 1,000 acres of lands (*Natun Assamiya,* 31 December 1950).
153. Letter from Tongani Tea Company Limited to Secretary, Indian Tea Association, 11 January 1951, quoted in letter from Political Secretary, Planting and Commerce Group, to Secretary, Home Department, Government of Assam, Letter no. 72, 27 January 1951, File no. RT 30/51, Tenancy Branch, Revenue Department, *Proceedings of Revenue Tenancy Department*, ASA.
154. Ibid.
155. *Natun Assamiya*, 13 February 1951.
156. Ibid.
157. Ibid.
158. Hazarika, *Samajbadar Sandhanat,* p. 54.
159. Such settlement did not ensure any tenurial security to the new settlers, but they had presumed superior occupancy rights compared to the pre-existing settlers. For details, see Arupjyoti Saikia, *Forests and Ecological History of Assam, 1826–2000*, New Delhi: Oxford University Press, 2011, pp. 322–25.
160. *Natun Assamiya*, 1 May 1951.

161. *Natun Assamiya*, 8 October 1949.
162. Dayal Chandra Das, while commenting on the discrepancies in the land distribution policy, claimed that Muslim immigrant peasants were being preferred to Assamese peasants (*Natun Assamiya*, 4 August 1949).
163. Circular no. 2-NE-1950–51, by Ashok Mehta, General Secretary, CSP, APIRR.
164. In one such instance, it was reported how several landless peasants from Naharkatiya mauza in Dibrugarh occupied the Kachumari grazing reserve and were subsequently evicted. The evicted peasants deftly used the instrument of petition to the Deputy Commissioner to delay their eviction and prolong their occupation. In most cases, the local leaders played a crucial role (Speech by P.M. Sarwan and by Hareswar Das, 4 September 1951, *ALAP*). *Natun Assamiya* (29 March 1950) reported a procession of peasants from Golaghat on 22 March 1950 demanding land. There were also reports of landless peasants from Nazira mauza under banner of the Nazira Mauza Kishan Panchayat demanding land from Liguri Phukuri, Makipur and Hatipati tea gardens (*Dainik Assamiya*, 24 May 1951).
165. *Natun Assamiya*, 11 January 1951.
166. In 1951, Rajendranath Barua, a Congress member of the Legislative Assembly from Jorhat, reported how flooding had made more than 2,000 bighas of lands unproductive, affecting more than 300 peasant families (Speech by Rajendranath Barua, 1 September 1951, *ALAP*).
167. In the winter months of February and March 1950, several public meetings were organized in Golaghat. These were addressed mostly by local Congress leaders. In one such meeting, the President, Bhandra Kanta Phukan, a Congressman, warned the landless peasants that all future land reclamation must be peaceful and legal (*Natun Assamiya*, 27 March 1950).
168. Speech by Harinarayan Barua, 1 September 1951, *ALAP*. Barua was also a member of Land Settlement Board of Sibsagar district.
169. Speech by Hareswar Das, 30 March 1951, *ALAP*.
170. Speech by Bishnuram Medhi, 8 March 1952, *ALAP*.
171. Speech by Bishnuram Medhi, 9 March 1951, *ALAP*; Speech by Hareswar Das, 10 March 1951, *ALAP*.
172. *Natun Assamiya*, 26 January 1951.
173. Speech by Hareswar Das, 20 September 1952, *ALAP*.
174. Ibid. In 1950, the Assam government opened 1,000 bighas of land from the Bamungaon grazing reserve in Raha.
175. Speech by Hareswar Das, 10 March 1951, *ALAP*.
176. *Dainik Assamiya*, 5 December 1947.

177. Interview with Suren Hazarika, erstwhile CPI leader active in upper Assam and in Golaghat subdivision of Sibsagar district, Jorhat, 28 September 1998.
178. File no. I/A 5/5(F)47, APIRR.
179. Secret letter from Gopinath Bordoloi to Jawaharlal Nehru, 12 October 1949, New Delhi, Confidential Files, Chief Minister's Secretariat, ASA.
180. Ibid.
181. The press continued to report the trouble caused by Chinese communists in border areas. *The Times of India* (28 February 1951), for instance, reported: 'Government have not yet denied a report that chieftains of the Mishimi tribe, on the Indo-Tibetan border, paid a courtesy call on the Chinese commander to whom presents were given … the Government have during the past year been endeavouring to combat the Red menace within their border areas but the communist activities have not been yet suppressed'.
182. File no. I/A-3(6)K/47, APIRR.
183. Gauhati High Court, *Nirendra Mohan Lahiri and Others versus Government of Assam*, 19 November 1948, available at http://indiankanoon.org/doc/428287/ (accessed on 11 September 2012); Gauhati High Court, *Tarunsen Deka and Others versus Government of Assam*, 3 December 1948, available at <http://indiankanoon.org/doc/1462849/> (accessed on 11 September 2012).
184. On 19 September 1949, Maulavi Muhammad Abdul Kashem moved a resolution in the Assam legislative Assembly for the formation of an advisory committee. The committee would devise ways and means to 'free the country from the grips of growing menace of communists' (Speech of Maulavi Muhammad Abdul Kashem, 19 September 1949, *ALAP*). The motion was withdrawn as the government admitted that various committees were already working to look in to the various problems of the province (Speech by Gopinath Bordoloi, 19 September 1949, *ALAP*).
185. *Natun Assamiya*, 22 September 1948.
186. The entire Beltola mauza was declared a disturbed area in April 1949 (*Annual Report on the Police Administration of Assam*, 1949, p. 11). The whole Sibsagar subdivision was also declared a disturbed area in the mid-1950 (speech by Emrain Hussain Chaudhury, 6 October 1950, *ALAP*).
187. The government increased the deployment of police forces in Panbari and Ramsarani mauzas, as well as in Khasi and Jaintia hills, and decided to monitor the 'conduct of the inhabitants' (Notification no. c. 260/49, in *The Assam Gazette*, part 2, 6 July 1949).
188. *Natun Assamiya*, 8 September 1950.

189. Notification no. c.387/50/6, in *The Assam Gazette*, 5 July 1950.
190. Speech by Bishnuram Medhi, Budget Session, 9 March 1951, *ALAP*.
191. *Annual Report on the Police Administration of Assam*, 1948, p. 11.
192. Memo. by Superintendent of Police, Lakhimpur, 25 October 1949, File no. A 3(6)M/47, APIRR.
193. The government proscribed these pamphlets under Section 19 of the Indian Press (Emergency Powers) Act of 1931. The exact number of pamphlets that were proscribed could not be ascertained, as there are no official or unofficial estimates. Following is a list of representative titles of some of these pamphlets compiled from their references in *The Assam Gazette* and *APWR*: *Congressi Sarkaror Krishak Raijor Opport Chaloa Nirlajja Domon Nitir Birudhey Dibalai Raijalai Krishak Banua Panchayatar Ahban*, 1949; *Guirella Warfare, Desh aru Khetiak Bachabar Upay, Mati Bhat Kapor Swadhinata Aru Ganatantar Karane Saktisali Krishak Gorhi tolak, Ganatantrak Hatya Karak Sharajantra Byartha Karak, Beltolat Police Raj, Beltola Khetia Raijar Oparat Chala Congress Sarkarar Daman Nitir Tandab Opharai Pelaook, Tribal Raijor Oporot Congressi Charkarar Tandab lila Pratisodhar karany Sajo Haok, Jan Goleo Dhan Nidio-Nangal Jar Mati Tar*.
194. Speech by Emrain Hussain Chaudhury, 6 October 1950, *ALAP*.
195. Speech by Bishnuram Medhi, 6 October 1950, *ALAP*.
196. Ibid.
197. *Krishak Sabhaur Abedon*, hand-written pamphlet of the Krishak Sabha, APIRR.
198. Statement of K.R. Chaudhury, DIG, Assam Police, quoted in *Natun Assamiya*, 31 January 1951.
199. Ibid.
200. Ibid.
201. *Natun Assamiya*, 24 May 1951. The most well-publicized such camp was in the southern hills of Guwahati.
202. *Natun Assamiya*, 24 June 1952.
203. *Natun Assamiya*, 6 September 1952.
204. *The Times of India*, 28 February 1951.
205. Ibid.
206. Ibid.
207. *Lal Nichan*, vol. 2, no. 1, 23 April 1952.
208. Deka, *Jivan Aru Sangram*, p. 54; Deka, *Mukti Sangramar Adharat Jiban Katha*, p. 132.
209. *Natun Assamiya*, 9 May 1951.
210. *Lal Nichan*, vol. 2, no. 1, 23 April 1952, pp. 1–2.
211. Gupta, *Agrarian Drama*, p. 213.

212. Personal reminiscences of Pranesh Biswas, quoted in Amalendu Guha, *Zamindarkalin Goalpara Zillar Artha Samajik Abastha: Eti Oitihasik Dristipat*, Guwahati: Natun Sahitya Parisad, 2000, p. 103.
213. Statement of Policy of the CPI, All India Conference, Calcutta, 1951, in CPI, *Documents of the Communist Movement in India*, vol. 6 (1949–1951), Calcutta: CPI, 1997.
214. In 1950, the Communist Information Bureau, a Russia-influenced platform of world communist organizations, condemned the CPI for its tactics and use of violence. In response to this criticism, the CPI leadership was replaced, first by way of replacing Ranadive by Rajeswar Rao from Andhra Pradesh and then Rao by Ajoy Ghosh, in quick succession. In 1951, the CPI also rejected the Chinese guerrilla model and violence in Telengana was put to stop. See Geoffrey Jukes, *The Soviet Union in Asia*, Berkeley, CA: University of California Press, 1973, p. 104. Also, see Overstreet and Windmiller, *Communism in India*, pp. 306–10.
215. The socialists and communists together got 22 per cent of the total votes polled as against the 43.48 per cent votes for the Congress. Beliram Das and Rohini Kumar Chaudhury, who had defended the landlords earlier, were voted to Lok Sabha in this election (Election Commission of India, *Statistical Report on General Election, 1951 to the Legislative Assembly of Assam*, New Delhi: Government Press, 1952).
216. *Natun Assamiya,* 1 November 1952. *Natun Assamiya* also emphasized the changing ideological stand of RCPI.
217. Lakhyadhar Chaudhury, *Manuh Bichari*, Guwahati: Assam Publication Board, 1992, p. 85.

Chapter 6

1. Gopal Das, a leader of the Revolutionary Communist Party of India (RCPI) narrated how in many places of Rani *mauza*, he took an active part in organizing the poor peasants to loot the granaries of rich peasants and landlords.
2. *Communist Situation in Assam*, 1949, File no. I/A-3(8) H-47, Assam Police Intelligence Record Room (APIRR).
3. Police Memo. no. A/I-3/49(50), APIRR. Interview with Govinda Kalita. Kalita spearheaded such a movement in south Kamrup.
4. Interview with Govinda Kalita, erstwhile Krishak Banua Panchayat (KBP) Leader, Guwahati, 18 June 1995.
5. Police Memo. no. A/I-3/49(50), APIRR.
6. Ibid.
7. Interview with Sarat Rabha, erstwhile Communist Party of India (CPI) student activist involved in the peasant movement in Goalpara, Guwahati, 22 June 1997.

8. *Review of Communism in Assam*, February 1949, File no. I/A-3(8) H-47, APIRR.
9. This anonymous letter was written in ink on a torn newspaper page (File no. A/I 3/49[50], APIRR).
10. Ibid.
11. As in the earlier instance, this poster was also written on torn news paper pages in ink (File no. A/I 3/49[50], APIRR).
12. Interview with Govinda Kalita; with Kamini Sarma, erstwhile leader of the RCPI and, later, the CPI, Rangia, Kamrup, 21 June 1995; and with Sarat Rabha.
13. Speech by Beliram Das, 3 October 1950, *Assam Legislative Assembly Proceedings* (*ALAP*). In his speech, referred to the localities of Palashbari, Boko and Chayagaon.
14. Interview with Gopal Das, erstwhile RCPI activist, Guwahati, 7 March 1995.
15. *Annual Report on the Police Administration of Assam*, 1949, p. 11.
16. Speech by Bidyapati Singh, 3 October 1950, *ALAP*.
17. File no. I-A/5-8, 1949, APIRR.
18. Interviews with Govinda Kalita and Gopal Das.
19. Speech by Bishnuram Medhi, 20 September 1952, *ALAP*. The manager of a trading firm owned by a Marwari trader was killed in this accident.
20. Ibid.
21. Telegram to Chief Minister of Rajasthan from Marwari Panchayat, File no. 10 [PS]-PA/51-1951, Ministry of States, National Archives of India (NAI).
22. In 1951, KBP cadres looted paddy from the Dighalikuchi *satra*, the granary of Dhola Koch of Deolpara of Palashbari and Mukunda Mahajan (Speech by Bishnuram Medhi, 25 March 1952, *ALAP*).
23. *Natun Assamiya,* 30 July 1950.
24. *Sadiniya Assamiya*, 10 June 1950.
25. 'Jur Julumkai Chahaki Manuhar Bharalar Dhan Adaya' ['Forcible Collection of Paddy from the Granary of Rich People'], *Sadiniya Assamiya*, 10 June 1950.
26. Letter from Government of Assam to Ministry of Home Affairs, File no. 8/51/289, 12 March 1952, NAI.
27. Such leaflets are found for the years 1949 and 1951 in the APIRR.
28. KBP, *Dakhin Kamrupat Dia-hhikha*, pamphlet, File no. 1-9/A-49, APIRR.
29. RCPI, *Durbhikha Pirita Sakalak Sahaya Karak*, a pamphlet issued in the name of Bishnu Rabha and others, File no. I/3-(5), 49, APIRR).
30. Haridas Deka, *Durbhikha Pirtok Sahay Karak*, leaflet, 1950, APIRR.
31. Ibid.

32. RCPI, *Durbhikha Protirodhar Andolon Gorhi Tolok: Bhat Kaporor Samashya Raijai Mochan Kariba Lagiba, Dhonir Sarkare Nakare, Raijok Vote Nalage, Bhate Lage.* A reference to this leaflet is also found in *The Assam Gazette*, 14 November 1951.
33. Note by Deputy Inspector General of Police, Assam, 2 August 1950, APIRR.
34. Chief Secretary's Fortnightly Report to Secretary of State (hereafter, Fortnightly Report), first half of June 1930.
35. In the November 1942 session of the Assam Legislative Assembly, the government admitted 'heavy rise in the prices of all food stuffs in India'. It further admitted that it 'is trying to get supplies and sell them to the public at reasonable rates' (Speech by Sir Muhammad Saadulla, 12 November 1942, *ALAP*).
36. A.G. Patton, Secretary, Revenue Department, Note no. 4488-R, *The Assam Gazette*, October 1939.
37. *Report of the Price of Essential Commodities*, in *The Assam Gazette*, 1938, 1944, 1946, 1948, and 1951. The market price of rice (unhusked) per *maund* was Rs 1 and 13 *anna*s in Kamrup and Rs 1 and 6 *anna*s in Nowgaon (*The Assam Gazette*, 1939; Speech by Mahendra Mohan Chaudhury, 30 August 1951, *ALAP*).
38. See *The Assam Gazette*, part 2, 7 July l944.
39. Speech by Mahendra Mohan Chaudhuri, 30 August 1951, *ALAP*.
40. Editorial, *Dainik Assamiya*, 6 February 1946.
41. *Dainik Assamiya*, 7 February 1946.
42. *The Assam Gazette*, part 9, 26 May 1948.
43. Fortnightly Report, first half of July 1943.
44. Speech by Beliram Das, 4 September 1951, *ALAP* .
45. Statement by Sriman Prafulladatta Goswami, *Sadiniya Assamiya*, 22 September 1945, Nehru Memorial Museum and Library (NMML).
46. R.C. Woodford, Director of Agriculture, 'Second Forecast of the Winter Rice Crop of Assam 1947–48' *The Assam Gazette*, 28 January 1948.
47. This observation is based on the resolution on food crisis and newspaper reports.
48. These are two contiguous mauzas of Jorhat town (speeches by P.M. Sarwan and Mahendra Mohan Chaudhury, 30 September 1951, *ALAP*).
49. Speech by Emrain Hussain Chaudhury, 30 September 1951, *ALAP*.
50. A representative resolution was passed in a peasant meeting held in Bamun Phukhuri of the Jorhat subdivision in 1951 (Speech by Harinarayan Barua, 1 September 1951, *ALAP*).
51. The prices were fixed at Rs 10 and Rs 17 for the Jorhat subdivision for rice and paddy, respectively. In other localities, prices were fixed at similar rates (*The Assam Gazette*, 24 February 1951).
52. Speech by Mahendra Mohan Chaudhury, 4 September 1951, *ALAP*.

53. Speech by Harinarayan Barua, 1 September 1951, *ALAP*.
54. 'The peasants did not fill their granary with paddy. Those one or two families who had paddy in their granary was not for personal consumption. It was meant to save the starved peasants from a famine like situation. A village having a population of 20, only 4 or 5 families might have paddy stocks while the remaining families are without any such stock ... These villagers stocked paddy to help fellow villagers during the famine like situation' (Speech by Hemchandra Hazarika, 1 September 1951, *ALAP*).
55. Speech by Mahendra Mohan Chaudhuri, Food Minister, Government of Assam, 15 September 1951, *ALAP*.
56. In the Assam Legislative Assembly, Nalini Kumar Chaudhury demanded that the prices of jute be fixed (Speech by Nalini Kumar Chaudhury, 1 September 1951, *ALAP*).
57. By the end of 1938, the price of jute per maund was Rs 5 at Nowgaon, which showed signs of increase as compared to the price in 1937, which was Rs 4 and 12 annas.
58. Declining paddy production was aggravated by the earthquake of 1950. There were communal disturbances in the preceding year as well as damage to the standing crop by pests (Governor's Speech, Budget Session 1951, *ALAP*). The government admitted that the sudden influx of 'several lakh of refugees' as fallout of Partition disturbances had also put pressure on the foodstocks. The quantum of crops damaged by insects in different districts was estimated at 18,933 tonnes by the district officers (Speech by Mahendra Mohan Chaudhury, 30 August 1951, *ALAP*).
59. Ibid. For a fuller account of the impact of the 1950 earthquake in Assam, see F. Kingdon-Ward, 'The Assam Earthquake of 1950', *The Geographical Journal,* vol. 121, no. 2, 1955, pp. 290–303.
60. 'Letter of Biswanath Barpujari', *Dainik Assamiya*, 21 February 1948.
61. 'Letter to the Editor', *Sadiniya Assamiya*, 19 September 1949.
62. 'Letter to the Editor', *Natun Assamiya*, 28 September 1949.
63. The *Dainik Assamiya* on 11 June 1948 published a report of deaths due to starvation in the flood-affected Laopara and Noapara areas of Kamrup district. The Assam government, however, asserted that the deaths occurred because of fever (*The Assam Gazette*, part 9, 7 July 1948). Deaths due to starvation were also reported from the Bordubi area in Dibrugarh in *The Statesman* (Speech by Emrain Hussain Chaudhury, 30 September 1951, *ALAP*). The government denied that any such death had occurred in the Brahmaputra valley.
64. The villages mentioned were Narara Karara, Radhakuchi, Aagadala, and Nowgaon in Karara mauza (*Sadiniya Assamiya*, 15 May 1949).
65. *Sadiniya Assamiya*, 20 March 1950. In 1951, Joychandra Chaudhury, General Secretary of Krishak Majdur Praja Party, came out with a statement recounting the severe scarcity of food grains in Nalbari (*Natun Assamiya*, 15 September 1951).

66. 'The rich peasants did not yield their surplus to the procurement department' (Speech by J.S. Hardman, 1 September 1951, *ALAP*) though the government had even offered corrugated sheets of tin in exchange of rice to the procurement department.
67. Speech by Gaurikanta Talukdar, 3 October 1950, *ALAP*.
68. In the August–September session of 1951, Emrain Hussain Chaudhury moved a similar kind of resolution. In November 1944, Abdul Ban Chaudhuri moved such a motion in the Assam Legislative Assembly.
69. 'The authorities suddenly refreshed themselves with the condition of the state of "theft dacoity" due to economic condition as the after-effects of the War' (Speech by Gopinath Bordoloi, 27 March 1950.
70. *The Assam Gazette,* 2 November 1949. Also, see *Annual Report on the Land Revenue Administration of Assam, 1947–1948*, Shillong: Government Press, 1948, p. 23.
71. Speech by Gaurikanta Talukdar, 3 October 1950, *ALAP*.
72. Ibid.
73. Speech by Motiram Bora, 3 October 1950, *ALAP*.
74. In September 1951, Chief Minister Bishnuram Medhi informed the house that during 1947–51, the number of petty crimes had increased. He ascribed this increase to political activity: '[p]robably the feeling of violence encouraged by anti-social elements and different political parties who believe in violence for achieving their political objects as they incite people to violence' (Speech by Bishnuram Medhi, 4 September 1951, *ALAP*).
75. A.C. Campbell, Deputy Commissioner of Kamrup, Note 2, in Lord Dufferin, *Report on the Condition of the Lower Classes of Population in Bengal*, Calcutta: Government Press, pp. 10–20.
76. *The Assam Gazette,* part 9, 21 April 1948. 'Cloth situation had deterio-rated since the Second World War. In some places, prices of cloth went up by 200 per cent' (Speech by Abdul Hamid Khan, 12 November 1942, *ALAP*).
77. For details, see P.C. Bansil, *India, Food Resources and Population: A Historical and Analytical Study*, Bombay: Vora Publishers, 1958, pp. 11–64.
78. 'Need for Uniform System of Food Procurement: Mr. J. Daulatram's Call to Provinces and States', *The Times of India,* 2 August 1949.
79. 'Less Food for More Mouths', *The Times of India*, 10 December 1948; 'Talk of Impending Famine Baseless: No Cause for Panic in India', *The Times of India*, 26 July 1950.
80. During 1951–52, two resolutions were discussed in the Assam Legislative Assembly about the severe food crisis in various parts of the Brahmaputra valley.
81. Speech by Emrain Hussain Chaudhury, 30 September 1951, *ALAP*.
82. Ibid.

83. Regarding the total number of such shops, no information is available. It was informed in the House that there were more than 40 such shops in the Jorhat subdivision (ibid).
84. Speech by Governor of Assam, 8 March 1951, *ALAP*.
85. For an overview of the phase of intense women's participation in the national freedom movement, see Dipti Sarma, *Assamese Women in the Freedom Struggle*, Calcutta: Punthi Pustak, 1993.
86. *Assam Police Intelligence Weekly Report* (*APWR*), Kamrup, 29 January 1949.
87. *APWR*, Kamrup, 2 April 1949.
88. *APWR*, Kamrup, 5 August 1949.
89. Interview with Dhireswar Kalita, Guwahati, 20 December 1996. It was also found that during the police operations to arrest the communist leaders, the women members were usually spared.
90. Assamese novels have narratives of this period which have mentioned how women members of the peasant families openly refused to show the customary reverence to the landlord families. In one such novel, *Kencha Patar Kanpani*, the son of a landlord and the central protagonist lamented how he failed to receive the earlier respect and reverence shown to him as the movement had spread into their area (Prafulladatta Goswami, *Kencha Patar Kanpani*, Guwahati: LBS, 1991).
91. *APWR*, Kamrup, 30 April 1949.
92. Ibid.
93. *Review of Communism in Assam*, March 1949, File no. I-A-3(S) H-47, APIRR.
94. *Natun Assamiya*, 9 November 1949.
95. In another case, on 29 October 1949, both men and women from Jajari and Kachamari joined a procession to the Nowgaon town shouting anti-government slogans. They demanded land and an urgent solution to the problem of cloth scarcity. In the next month police again reported that about 70 men and women came out in a procession from Jajori, Hatichong, Majoroti with *lathi*s bearing playcards with violent slogans and paraded on the main roads of the town and later went to jail, shouting slogans on a megaphone (*APWR*, Nowgaon, 5 November and 17 December 1949).
96. The police mentioned how two women peasants successfully escorted the peasant leader Bistu Bora to Boko (*APWR*, Kamrup, 3 July 1949).
97. During the days he stayed 'underground', he was sheltered at the house of Surma Purakayastha and Tulshi Chakrabarti of Garali in Jorhat.
98. *Natun Assamiya*, on 10 October 1950, reported how two women cadres, Anima Bora and Rohini Saikia, were arrested from a secret office of the CPI.

99. Haridas Deka, *Jivan Aru Sangram*, Guwahati: LBS, 1992, p. 83. The Congress Socialist Party (CSP) neither had any women front nor incorporated any women-oriented issues in its movement.
100. Ibid.
101. File no. S/1 183-c/50, Confidential Files, Governor's Secretariat, Assam State Archives (ASA). Sabitri Chetia, who was in the forefront of Pragati Nari Mukti Sangha (PNMS), was the younger sister of Haridas Deka.
102. Kamala Majumdar, another member of PNMS, was in charge of *Lal Nichan* and *Panchayat*, the mouthpieces of the RCPI.
103. Ibid.
104. The 'chairperson' of one such gathering was a woman as it appears from the pencil-written pages of the 'proceeding'. The meeting was held in Lakhara of southern Kamrup. It discussed various organizational issues about the ongoing peasant movement. In this meeting, an allegation was brought against one *adhiar* that he had begun paying rent to his landlord (File no. I/A-8 [6]/50, APIRR).
105. For instance, one Swarnalata Khaund held the post of Joint Secretary of Mahila Atma Rakha Samity in Sibsagar.
106. Interview with Kamala Majumdar, Guwahati, 19 June 1995. Also, see Kamala Majumdar, 'Haren Kalitar Smritit', in Hiren Medhi (ed.), *Biplabi Haren Kalita*, Guwahati: Haren Kalita Sowarani Samiti, 1994, pp. 73–77.
107. Usha Datta Verma, *Din Guli Mor*, Calcutta: Biswagyan, 1993.
108. Police prepared a list of 143 cadres that included 10 women cadres in the district of Sibsagar (*Women Fronts in Sibsagar*, File no. I/A 3-6 k-47, APIRR). In northern Kamrup, Bimalasen Deka, Kamala Medhi and Rajani Bodo; and in eastern Assam, Sabitri Chetia, Konamai Konwar, and Jogyalata Bezbarua were few amongst those.
109. *Women Fronts in Sibsagar*.
110. Ibid.
111. A pattern of incorporation of female family members in the CPI could not be noticed. Communist leaders' wives, daughters and other close family members were also prominent women members of the party. For instance, Malbhog's wife Maghuri Katani, Rushai Katani's wife Someswari Katani, Katia Tamuli's daughter Baghi Tamuli and Somnath Khaund's wife Swarnalata Khaund were active members of the CPI.
112. The district conference of the CPI's women unit was held in mid-1949. It was noted in the conference that 'in spite of police repression and protest and obstructions from the male members the *Mahila* convention was held at Furkating with 60 delegates ... The members were mainly from middle class peasants and hence there was vacillation' (*Women Fronts in Sibsagar*).
113. In Nowgaon district, several women units were formed in places like Lumding, Chakalaghat, Nowgaon town, and Dharamtul (*A Short Note on the CPI Activists in Nowgaon*, 1948, File no. I/A-3[6]-J/47, APIRR).

114. In June 1949, the CPI distributed a leaflet entitled *Call of Kamrup District Mahila Atma Raksha Sanmeelan*. It exhorted women to organize themselves in the wake of ever-increasing economic stringency through the mechanism of *Mahila Samity* (*A Short Note on the CPI Activists in Nowgaon*).
115. Ibid. In the Durang hill of Khetri, women from all peasant families belonging to Barman, Muslim and Nepali communities — amongst a total of 34 families — formed the Durang Hill Mahila Committee. In the same unit, there existed a four-member Durang Gaon Khet-Majur Committee.
116. Most of the members came from tribal villages in Ganeshpara, Dhundalpara, Datal, Manapara, Dhalbum, Mainakhurung, Ambari Katalipara, and Rampur. There was one committee at Pandu, six at Beltola with 120 members, one at Khetri, and one at Guwahati.
117. *Dainik Assamiya*, 2 October 1948. Also, see Anon., *Bolo Basumatari Smritigrantha*, Guwahati: Bolo Basumatari Sonwarni Samiti, 2000.
118. *Dainik Assamiya*, 2 October 1948.
119. *Review of Communism in Assam*, March 1949, File no. I-A-3(8) H-47 and File no. A-3(6)(J)47, APIRR.
120. Government of Assam, *Line System Enquiry Committee Report*, vol. 2, Shillong: Assam Government Press, 1938, p. 121.
121. Ibid., p. 123.
122. Maheswar Neog, *Sankardev and His Times: Early History of the Vaiṣṇava Faith and Movement in Assam*, Guwahati: Gauhati University, 1965.
123. See Chapter 1 in this volume for a detailed discussion on this rent-free and half-rent-liable estates.
124. Satyendra Nath Sarma, *The Neo-Vaishnavite Movement and Satra Institution of Assam*, Guwahati: LBS, 1999, Appendix V.
125. Suryya Kumar Bhuyan, *Anglo-Assamese Relations, 1771–1826: A History of the Relations of Assam with the East India Company from 1771 to 1826, Based on Original English and Assamese Sources*, Guwahati: LBS, 1974, p. 251.
126. For an analysis of the twentieth-century *khel* system, see Kishore Bhattacharjee, 'Structure and Individual in Assamese Society: A Study of Family, Kinship, Caste and Religion', PhD thesis, Gauhati University, Guwahati, 1990.
127. The account of Sankardeva Sangha is based on the official history of the Sangha and the interviews with those associated with it since the early years of its formation (Hema Saikia [ed.], *Itihas: Srimanta Sankardev Sangha [Pratham Khanda]*, Sibsagar: Sankardev Sangha, 1985).
128. Audrey Cantlie, *The Assamese*, London: Curzon Press, 1984, pp. 273–92.
129. For details of Assamese Vaishnava literature, see Neog, *Sankardev and His Times*.

130. Jogendranarayan Bhuyan, 'Vaishnav Sahityar Mudran-Prakasan', in Sibnath Barman (ed.), *Asamiya Sahityar Buranji*, vol. 2, Guwahati: ABILAC, 1997, pp. 647–59.
131. *Tinidiniya Assamiya*, 5 January 1935.
132. *Haldhar Bhuyan Smritigrantha*, Nowgaon, 1976; *Srimanta Sankardev Sanghar Padadhikarsakalar Abhibhasan*, Nowgaon: Srimanta Sankardev Sangha, 2005.
133. See Chapter 5 in this volume.
134. Hari Prasad Chaliha, *Ramakanta Muktiar Ata: Byakti Aru Pratibha*, Guwahati: Saundarya Prasad Chaliha, 1998.
135. Saikia (ed.), *Itihas*.
136. 'Report on the First Conference on Sangha', *Dainik Janambhumi*, 5 February 2007.
137. Cantlie, *The Assamese*, pp. 273–92.
138. Interview with Liladhar Kakoty, Nowgaon, 26 December 1997. Kakoty was associated with Srimanta Sankardeva Sangha since its early days.
139. File no. RT 31/52, Revenue Tenancy Branch, Revenue Department, ASA.
140. Ibid.
141. For an appraisal of lower-caste mobilization in Assam, see Jayeeta Sarma, *Empire's Garden:* Assam *and the Making of India*, New Delhi: Permanent Black, 2011, pp. 214–17.
142. The Census of Assam in 1881 recorded 69,404 persons engaged in fishing. This number included the persons from Sylhet as well ('Caste and Tribes', in *Report on the Census of Assam*, 1881, p. 94).
143. Gaurikanta Talukdar, *Kalitar Bratyodharar Abashyakata*, Guwahati: Sarveswar Bhattacharya, 1929.
144. During my archival work in the APIRR, Nowgaon, I came across an example of large-scale abandonement of caste-based surnames. This came to my notice during a comparison of land records of two settlements. In the pre-1921 settlement, an entire village had a surname 'Dom', while in the subsequent settlement after the Census of 1921 none retained it. For anyone without an under-standing of this caste dynamics, it would appear that an entire village population had migrated elsewhere. The villagers adopted new surnames indicating their understanding of social mobility, as well as relevance of surnames as indicative of this process.
145. See, for instance, Saneswar Dutta (ed.), *Prachin Kamrupia Kayastha Samajar Itibirta*, Guwahati: Harinarayan Dutta Barua, 1941, reprint, Guwahati: LBS, 2000.
146. Indian Statutory Commission, 'Memorandum Submitted by the Government of Assam', in *Report of the Indian Statutory Commission*, vol. 14, London: His Majesty's Stationery Office, 1930.
147. Sarma, *Empire's Garden*, p. 217.

148. See Maheswar Neog, *Guru Charit Katha*, Guwahati: LBS, 1999, pp. 32–34.
149. Memo. by S.N. Dutta, Settlement Officer, Nowgaon, to Director of Land Records, Assam, File no. 393S, Nowgaon, 31 October 1930, *Assam Secretariat Proceedings* (*ASP*), Revenue Department, Revenue A, nos 140–55, September 1931, ASA.
150. File no. CL-22 AICC papers, vol. 2, 1946–47, NMML.
151. Fortnightly Report, first half of January 1946.
152. Ibid.
153. *Tinidiniya Assamiya*, 25 January 1947.
154. *Dainik Assamiya*, 20 May 1947.
155. *Tinidiniya Assamiya*, 25 January 1947.
156. *Tinidiniya Assamiya,* 29 September 1941.
157. Suryasikha Pathak, 'Tribal Politics in the Assam: 1933–1947', *Economic and Political Weekly*, vol. 45, no. 10, 2010, pp. 61–69.
158. For an anthropological description of the khel, see Introduction in this volume.
159. In May 1948, the RCPI cadres committed a 'robbery' at the local branch of Comilla Union Bank in Guwahati (Tarunsen Deka, *Mukti Sangramar Adhartat Jiban Katha*, 1993, Guwahati: R.D. Printers and Publishers, p. 123). The police, which mentioned it as 'political dacoity' in its report claimed that Rs 197,500 was stolen from the bank. In the next year, the RCPI activists 'looted' Rs 60,000, which was the property of the railways, from a running train at Amguri in Sibsagar (*Annual Report on the Police Administration of Assam*, 1949, p. 11).
160. Statement of Superintendent of Police, Kamrup, quoted in *Natun Assamiya,* 6 September 1952. By 1952, the RCPI cadres had collected money from seven *mauzadar*s in Kamrup.
161. This term was referred to me by Bhagi Maji.
162. *Annual Report on the Police Administration of Assam*, 1948.
163. *Annual Report on the Police Administration of Assam*, 1950.
164. Deka, *Mukti Sangramar Adharat Jiban Katha,* p. 145.
165. *Annual Report on the Police Administration of Assam*, 1950, p. 11. Police cited various examples of murders by the RCPI activists.
166. *Natun Assamiya,* 11 August 1950.
167. Budget Speech of the Assam Finance Minister, 9 March 1951, *ALAP.*
168. Ibid.
169. *Annual Report on the Police Administration of Assam*, 1949, p. 45.
170. Ibid.
171. Interview with Gopal Das.
172. Deka, *Jivan Aru Sangram*, p. 63.
173. Interview with Dhireswar Kalita.
174. Confidential Note by Bimala Prasad Chaliha, Minister of Finance, Government of Assam, 8 November 1948, APIRR.
175. Ibid.

176. Deka, *Jivan Aru Sangram*, p. 54.
177. *CID Report to the Superintendent of Police of Sibsagar*, Memo. no. 164, 22 October 1949, File no. A-3/6/2(47), APIRR.
178. This part on the activities of Bishnu Rabha is based on the statement made by him in 1952 before the police after he was arrested. The long statement gives a narrative of his involvement in peasant mobilization. Also, I have relied on several collections on his life and times. (For instance, Hiren Gohain, *Sainik Silpi Bishnu Rabha;* Guwahati: Journal Emporium, 1982, reprint, 2002; Das and Barua, *Bishnuprasad Rabha Rachana Samahar*, vols 1 and 2; note 183 below.
179. 'Introduction: Sonpahi', in Das and Barua, *Bishnuprasad Rabha Rachana Samahar*, vol. 2, pp. 646–54.
180. Tilak Das, *Bishnu Rabha Etia Kiman Rati*, 1977, reprint, Guwahati: Chandra Prakash, 1992.
181. Interview with Mohanlal Mukherjee, 12 and 14 June 1996.
182. Jogesh Das and Sarveswar Barua (eds), 'Bishnuprasad Rabha', in *Bishnuprasad Rava Rachanavali*, vol. 1, Tezpur: Rava Rachanavali Prakashan Sangha, 1989, reprint 2008, pp. xxi–xxxii.
183. This comment is based on his statement made before the trial magistrate and also his preface to the drama *Sonpahi*. See Confessional Statement of Bishnuprasad Rabha before the Police, 1952, AIPRR; Superintendent of Police, Goalpara, Memo. no. P/7-B-21/8874-76/CD, Dhubri, 4 August 1952; Das and Barua (eds), *Bishnuprasad Rava Rachanavali*, vol. 1, pp. 564–70.
184. This is referred to in *Farengdao*, a biographical novel on Bishnu Rabha (Medini Chaudhury, *Farengdao*, Kokrajhar: Bairathi Publications, 1982).
185. The earliest such example of collaboration between the peasants and the communist peasant organizations was that in Palashbari and Beltola. While in Beltola a local monk himself initiated a movement for bringing the communist peasant organizations' activists to the area, in Palashbari, the KBP crept in to the already established network of local leaders. A local monk, popularly known as Ramdas Babaji, from Beltola invited Haridas Deka, as the leader of the KBP, to visit the villages of Beltola mauza. He impressed on Deka the condition of the sharecroppers in Beltola. Deka asked the monk to organize a meeting. Later on, as promised, Deka, along with Nihar Mukherjee, another young RCPI leader, went to the locality. A meeting with the local sharecroppers, who were heavily indebted to the local *mahajans*, agreed to form a local unit of the KBP and raise the standard demands of the KBP: rent receipt in return for rent payment and reduction in rent. In Palashbari, Govinda Kalita was already an influential leader among the sharecroppers and landless peasants. The KBP involved itself with him and his works. See

Deka, *Jivan Aru Sangram*, p. 62; interview with Nihar Mukherjee, Guwahati, 15 and 16 June 1996.
186. *Constitution of the KBP*, File no. A-3/6/2(47), APIRR.
187. Deka, *Jivan Aru Sangram*, p. 54.
188. Abdul Matlib, *Jana Neta Khagen Barbaruah: Karma Aru Byaktitwa*, Amguri: Khagen Barbarua Smarak Grantha Sampadana Samiti, 2001.
189. File no. A-3/6/2/(47), APIRR.
190. *Kishan Fronts in Sibsagar*, File no. I/A-3 (8)47, APIRR.
191. Deka, *Jivan Aru Sangram*, p. 81.
192. *Review of Communism in Assam*, August 1949, File no. I-3/6-50, APIRR.
193. Ibid.
194. *Dainik Assamiya*, 23 February, 1949.
195. Note by Deputy Inspector General, Assam Police, File no. I/A-5/3 K-49, APIRR.
196. 'Details about the Communist Outrage at Dibrugarh on 17 July 1949', Press Note no. 708, Shillong, 6 August 1949, APIRR. Also, see *The Times of India*, 20 July, 1949.
197. *Dainik Assamiya*, 18 July 1949.
198. The police claimed to have arrested 429 persons in this incident, popularly known as Naliapool incident ('Details about the Communist Outrage at Dibrugarh on 17 July 1949').
199. Jyotiprasad Agarwala, 'Naliapoolor Bipad Sanket', in Hiren Gohain (ed.), *Jyotiprasad Rachanavali*, Guwahati: Assam Publication Board, 2003, pp. 543–49.
200. *The Times of India*, 27 July 1949.

Chapter 7

1. See Chapter 7 in Arupjyoti Saikia, *Forests and Ecological History of Assam, 1826–2000*, New Delhi: Oxford University Press.
2. Communist Party of India (CPI), *Guidelines of the History of the Communist Party of India*, New Delhi: CPI, 1974, pp. 86–87.
3. Pannalal Dasgupta, *Revolutionary Gandhi*, trans. K.V. Subrahmonyan, Calcatta: Earthcare Books, 2011.
4. Confiscated Letter of Bishnu Rabha, File no. I-A/3(6)53, Assam Police Intelligence Record Room (AIPRR). Probably, the letter was addressed to Haridas Deka.
5. In the election to the State Assembly, the Communist Party of India (CPI) got approximately 14 per cent votes in the assemblies that they had contested. From two other leading left-wing parties, Kisan Mazdoor Praja Party and Socialist Party, also shared 32 per cent votes in the seats they had contested. The CPI leader Gaurishankar Bhattacharjya won the crucial Guwahati Assembly Constituency by defeating Rajabala Das of the Congress party.

6. An illustrative example of the unwillingness of the revenue court to implement the provisions of the Adhiar Act was from the Kamalpur *mauza* of Kamrup where the Assamese and tribal *adhiars* of the landlord, Deva Kanta Dutta, sought the help of the revenue court to allow them to pay their rent in cash rather than in kind. The court refused to interfere and asked the adhiars to pay as wished by the landlords (File no. RRT 17/60, Revenue-R, Tenancy Branch, Assam State Archives [ASA]).
7. For details on the UP Zamindari Abolition Bill, see Thomas R. Metcalf, 'Landlords Without Land: The U.P. Zamindars Today', *Pacific Affairs*, vol. 40, nos 1–2, 1967, pp. 5–18.
8. Zamindars' Association, *Notes of the Goalpara Zamindars Association on Assam State Acquisition of Zamindaries Bill*, 1948, p. 2, ASA.
9. *Raja Bhairebendra Narayan Bhup versus the State of Assam*, 1956 available at http://www.indiacourts.in/RAJA-BHAIREBENDRA-NARAYAN-BHUP-Vs.-THE-STATE-OF-ASSAM(with-connected-appeal)_9b79d311-a817-4a58-bd0f-f17671752e24 (accessed on 18 September 2012).
10. The All India Congress Commitee (AICC) was apprehensive that the powerful *zamindars*' lobby would do its best to defer or sabotage the implementation of the Abolition Bill and thus ensure that the Presidential consent through the Union Cabinet approval be made mandatory (Narendra Chandra Dutta, *Land Problems and Land Reforms in Assam*, New Delhi: S. Chand, 1968).
11. The Assam government agreed to give bonds worth Rs 50 million as compensation, but till 1964 it could give only Rs 7 million (Government of India, *Implementation of Land Reforms: A Review by the Land Reforms Implementation Committee of the National Development Council*, New Delhi: Planning Commission, 1966, pp. 35–36).
12. Economist P.C. Goswami argued that by keeping the upper limit of landholding to 150 *bighas*, the Act virtually covered less than 1 per cent of the landlord families in Assam (P.C. Goswami, 'Land Reform in Assam', *Economic and Political Weekly*, vol. 4, no. 42, 1969, pp. 1662–1664).
13. R.P. Saikia, 'Notes on the Land Reform of Assam', *APCC Papers*, 1955, Nehru Memorial Museum and Library (NMML).
14. Planning Commission of India, *Land Reform in India*, New Delhi: Government Press, 1963.
15. H.D. Malviya, *Land Reforms in India*, New Delhi: All India Congress Committee, 1954.
16. In Gohpur, the landless peasants from Niz-Gohpur, Tangana, Bilatiya, Borigaon, Dhenudhar, and Konibari demanded the distribution of government wasteland lying between Gohpur and Ghaghra tea garden. In a meeting of the Krishak Sabha (KS) in April 1954, the speakers lamented the fact that in spite of their repeated appeals,

the government had not paid any heed to it (*Sadiniya Assamiya*, 1 May 1954).

17. In August 1945, the Working Committee of the Assam Provincial Congress Commitee (APCC) set up a standing committee to study the land problems of Assam and advise the APCC on the policy to be adopted (Ruplekha Borgohain, *Politics of Land Reforms in Assam*, New Delhi: Reliance Publishing House, 1992, Chapter 1).
18. In a resolution adopted on 19 March 1950, the APCC stated: '[T]he committee considered at length the desirability of organizing, after the ideology of the Congress, the agricultural labourers in the province who are being sought to be won over by interested parties with various slogans and accordingly resolved that AICC be referred to as what should be the procedure for doing so' (*APCC Papers*, Microfilm, 19 March 1950, NMML).
19. The Committee was headed by M. Tayebulla with Khogen Nath, Haren Phukan, Harinarayan Barua, Raichand Nath, Digendra Nath Kaviraj, Rasbehari Sharma, Robin Kakati, and Prafulladatta Goswami.
20. In a resolution moved by Bijoyachandra Bhagawati and Robin Kakati, they claimed that the land question had acquired a crucial position and the matter must be taken up by the APCC urgently (*APCC Papers*, Microfilm, 19 January 1951, NMML).
21. 'Extract of the Proceedings of the State of Assam in the Revenue Settlement Department', in *Resolutions of Land Settlement Policy of Government of Assam from 1939 to 1950*, File no. RSS 5/50/9, 20 February 1950, Shillong, ASA.
22. In May 1955, APCC officially declared the need for immediate 'land reform measures' (Letter from Secretary, APCC, to Chief Minister, Government of Assam, 6 June 1955, *APCC Papers*, NMML). The sub-committee was formed to study and advice policies related to the land reform measures in Assam.
23. Note prepared by Secretary, Assam Revenue Department, to Minister, Revenue, Government of Assam, 4 June 1965, File no. RSS 152/69/5, 30 May 1969, *APCC Papers*, NMML.
24. Letter from Secretary, Revenue Department, Government of Assam, to Secretary, APCC, File no. RSS 152/69/5, 30 May 1969, *APCC Papers* (NMML).
25. The government also admitted that the displacement of the peasants was due to various kinds of industrial developments and all put together the number of such families came to 60,000. The number of people who emmigrated from East Pakistan and required land was estimated to be 150,000. At the same time, the government admitted that large patches of land recently requisitioned from tea gardens were not fit for peasant cultivation.
26. This estimate was arrived at by comparing the figures of both Census Reports of 1961 and National Sample Survey (16th Round) (Note by Revenue Department prepared for the APCC).

27. Letter from Bimala Prasad Chaliha to Minister of Revenue and Minister of Forests, Government of India, New Delhi, 17 April 1954, File no. AFR, 222/54, ASA.
28. Speech by Mahendra Mohan Chaudhury, Revenue Minister, Assam Legislative Assembly, quoted in *Dainik Assam*, 3 June 1967.
29. Arupjyoti Saikia, 'State, Peasants and Land Reclamation: The Predicament of Forest Conservation in Assam, 1850s–1980s', *Indian Economic and Social History Review* (*IESHR*), vol. 45, no. 1, 2008, pp. 77–114.
30. *Proceedings of Forest Standing Committee*, Assam Congress Parliamentary Party, 30 March 1963, File no. FA, 337/67, 1967, ASA.
31. Letter of Additional Deputy Commissioner, Jorhat, to Divisional Forest Officer, Golaghat, 31 March 1987, File no. JRS, 34/85/51, ASA.
32. The Divisional Forest Officer (DFO), in an official letter to the Conservator of Forest (Headquarter), Assam, admitted that there were a number of villages which could be defined as encroached villages inside the Nambor Reserved Forests even after 1980 (Letter from the DFO, Golaghat, to Conservator of Forests, 21 January 2004, File no. A/40/[C]-58-59). The DFO appended a list of villages which came after and before 1980.
33. Such peasants came mainly from Kamarbhandha, Forkating, Titabor, Borpathar, Sarupathar, Ghiladhari, or Khumtai which were all located close to various Reserved Forests.
34. Such cases involved peasant families which lost their lands due to the establishment of Salekati Thermal Power station in Bongaigaon in western Assam and were officially rehabilitated in Tengani.
35. This account is based on my field work in Doyang-Tegani in 2007 where I interviewed peasant families who migrated to those places after 1950.
36. 'Bhoodan and Gramdan', *Time*, 29 December 1958.
37. Mankumar Sen, *Gandhian Way and the Bhoodan Movement*, Varanasi: Sarva Seva Sangh Prakashan, 1964, pp. 40–41.
38. Often, villagers retracted from their promise to part with their land as Gramdan village when they realized that this meant actual loss of control over their own land (Petition of Kanak Chandra Gogoi and Others to Sub-Deputy Collector, North Lakhimpur, 2 March 1965, File no. RRT 17/60, Revenue-R, Tenancy Branch, ASA).
39. Petition of Landlords from North Lakhimpur to SDO, Lakhimpur, 2 March 1965, File no. RRT 17/60, Revenue-R, Tenancy Branch, ASA.
40. *Dainik Assamiya*, 23 October 1967. Chaudhury addressed a public meeting in Golaghat attended by a wide cross-section of peasants.
41. On several occasions, Chaudhury, as Revenue Minister, indicated his anti-absentee-landlord position. For instance, speaking in a public rally in Kamrup, he suggested that all intermediaries should be removed (*Dainik Assamiya*, 24 April 1967).
42. *Dainik Assamiya*, 25 November 1966.

43. Extraordinary Edition, *The Assam Gazette*, 12 April 1961.
44. Government of Assam, *Land Reform in Assam*, Guwahati: Government Press, 1973. In total, the government could take over an approximately 75,000 acres of land from various institutions by April 1970 (Budget Speech by Finance Minister, Government of Assam, 28 March 1971, *Assam Legislative Assembly Proceedings* [*ALAP*]).
45. Election Commission of India, *Statistical Report on General Election, 1957 to the Legislative Assembly of Assam*, New Delhi: Government Press, 1957. In the election, both the Communist Party of India (CPI) and Praja Socialist Party collectively scored a little more than 20 per cent of the total votes polled.
46. *Rules of the Assam Adhiar Association*, in *APCC Papers*, Packet no. 86, File no. 10, 1957, NMML.
47. Pranesh Chandra Biswas, 'Some Aspects of the Assam Government's Agrarian Reform Laws', *All India Kisan Sabha, News Bulletin*, vol. 1, no. 3, 1952.
48. Speech by Nilamoni Phukan, 6 September 1951, *ALAP*.
49. File no. RT 47/51, Revenue Tenancy Branch, Revenue Department, ASA; File no. RT 12/51(ASA); Speech by Nilamoni Phukan, 6, 18 and 19 September 1952, *ALAP*.
50. File no. RT-47/52, Tenancy Branch, Revenue Department, ASA.
51. Ibid.
52. Speech by Hareswar Das, 6 September 1952, *ALAP*.
53. Ibid.
54. Speech by Maulavi Md Umaruddin, 6 September 1952, *ALAP*.
55. Speech by Gaurishankar Bhattacharjya, 18 September 1952, *ALAP*.
56. The Congress leader Harinarayan Barua claimed that the extreme reliance of CPI and CSP on the adhiar electorate cost them dearly in the 1952 election, the benefit of which was reaped by the Congress along with the support of small and medium landowners (Speech by Harinarayan Barua, 18 September 1952, *ALAP*).
57. *The Assam Tribune*, 27 December 1953; File no. Revenue Tenancy-42/52, ASA. The sharecroppers pointed out that the Act was being rendered dead by government apathy. They also highlighted how the coming of the Zamindari Abolition Act had legally converted a large number of tenants into sharecroppers.
58. *Khetiak Raijor Najya Dabi Mani Labo Lagiba*, printed pamphlets of North Bank Krishak Sanmilan, 1953, File no. RT 42/52, ASA. These meetings were attended by sharecroppers of Silghopa mauza.
59. Resolution no. 4, Ibid.
60. These resolutions were adopted by the entire *raij* (people) on behalf of the sharecroppers which implies a strong community solidarity (*Resolution of Sanderighopa Area Committee*, Sila Area Committee, File no. RT 42/52, ASA).

61. Welcome Address by General Secretary and President of the North Kamrup Nisf-Khiraj Tenants Parisad, First Conference, April 1957, *APCC Papers*, NMML.
62. Speech by Nilamoni Borthakur, 29 July 1957, *ALAP*.
63. In several suits filed in the Gauhati High Court, the landlords were refused any permission to evict their sharecroppers.
64. Rama Datta, 'Adhiar Ainor Kerun Ache', *Dainik Assamiya*, 16 February 1973.
65. Led by their communist leaders, villagers of Chakri Charipani and Dangdhara Charali of Titabor organized a meeting in Dhangdhara Charali village on 27 November 1953. As many as 1,000 people attended the meeting. The meeting was presided over by Amulya Barua, a CPI leader. Suren Hazarika, another CPI leader, was also present in the meeting. See copy of Memo. no. C 1/53/1755, 21 December 1953, from Chief Secretary to Government of Assam, File no. RT 42/52, ASA.
66. Letter from Sarat Chandra Goswami, General Secretary, APCC, to Sidhinath Sarma, Revenue Minister, Government of Assam, 18 May 1964, *AICC Papers*, NMML.
67. Ibid.
68. In 1960, the Assam Legislative Assembly passed the the Assam Official Language Act which declared Assam as an officially unilingual state making Assamese the only official language. This resulted in strong protests from the Bengali-speaking population and riots broke out in various parts of Assam. The issue came to a temporary rest in 1961, after months of violence in rural and urban areas when the Assam government accepted Bengali as the second official language in Bengali-dominated districts. For a brief overview of the issue, see Sandhya Goswami, *Language Politics in Assam*, New Delhi: Ajanta Publications, 1997.
69. Arupjyoti Saikia, 'Imperialism, Geology and Petroleum: History of Oil in Colonial Assam', *Economic and Political Weekly*, vol. 46, no. 12, 2011, pp. 48–55.
70. Centre for Science and Environment (CSE), *Floods, Flood Plains and Environmental Myths*, New Delhi: CSE, 1991, p. 4, Table 2.
71. The Assam branch of CPI in 1946, in a political resolution, argued that migration should be stopped immediately so that an imminent land crisis could be averted. ('Resolution on Land Settlement and Eviction in Assam', in CPI, *Assam Fights for Freedom and Democracy Draft Resolutions of Assam Communists*, Guwahati, 1948, File no. A-3(6) 1947).
72. 'Temporary Food Shortages Make People Restive In Surplus State', *The Times of India*, 25 September 1965.

73. Most accounts of Assam in the late nineteenth and the early twentieth centuries suggested trend on increase of rice imports into the valley (*Report on the Administration of the Province of Assam, 1892–1893*, Shillong: Government Press, 1893, p. 51).
74. *The Times of India*, 11 May 1968.
75. *Dainik Assamiya*, 28 September 1967.
76. *Dainik Assamiya* reported how in the districts of eastern Assam, peasants publicly protested against the procurement policy of the government (*Dainik Assamiya*, 20 September 1967).
77. In the annual conference of Cachar Krishak Sabha in October 1967, CPI leaders Achintya Biswas and Biresh Misra urged the government to increase the paddy price from Rs 22 to Rs 27. In the same month, the government decided to fix the price of paddy at Rs 22, though the Congress Legislators suggested a higher price of Rs 23 (*Dainik Assam*, 3 November 1967).
78. *Dainik Assamiya*, 4 November 1967.
79. This was a statement made by the Revenue Minister of Assam in 1970 and quoted in Anon., 'Food Crisis is Back', *Economic and Political Weekly*, vol. 3, no. 24, 1968, pp. 898–99.
80. 'India Will Not Place Herself at Mercy of an Arrogant Aggressor', *The Times of India*, 23 November 1962.
81. E.M.S. Namboodiripad, *The Frontline Years: Selected Articles*, New Delhi: Left Word, 2010, pp. 104–5.
82. *Dainik Assamiya*, 27 October 1967.
83. An instance of such marginalization of grazers could be seen in Sariahtali Professional Grazing Reserves (PGR) in Nowgaon. The grazers petitioned the Revenue Minister of Assam seeking cancellation of the de-reservation proposal. But a subsequent order of Land Settlement Advisory Board categorically ordered de-reservation of the PGR.
84. *Report on the Proceedings of APCC*, 24 March 1964, *APCC Papers*, NMML. The meeting also agreed that the Standing Committee would submit its proposals early so that some concrete measures could be adopted in the same year.
85. The APCC and its district units, under the banner of Krishak Sabha, submitted memoranda to the Assam government, seeking land distribution. In 1970, Nowgaon District Congress Committee submitted a memorandum to the Revenue Minister of Assam demanding the distribution of land as identified by the Committee. The government was quick to respond and took necessary bureaucratic measures to make arrangement for land distribution.
86. *Dainik Assamiya*, 21 June 1971.
87. *Dainik Assamiya*, 28 July 1967.
88. *Dainik Assamiya*, 5 June 1967.

89. Through the Assam State Acquisition of Lands Belonging to Religious or Charitable Institutions of Public Nature Act of 1959, the government acquired approximately 3,30,000 bighas of land. These lands, the government claimed, were transferred to the tenants (Bhumidhar Barman, 'Land Reforms Secure Tenants' Interests', *The Times of India,* 22 November 1976).
90. S.K. Dutta, '50-bigha Limit in Assam Hailed', *The Times of India*, 6 November 1972.
91. 'Resolutions of the APCC Land Reform Sub-committee', File no. RSS 152/69/5 30 May 1969, in *APCC Papers*, NMML.
92. Note Prepared by Secretary, Assam Revenue Department, to Minister of Revenue, Government of Assam, 4 June 1965, File no. RSS 152/69/5, 30 May 1969, in *APCC Papers*, NMML.
93. This was in comparison to 17,000 acres brought under this Act till 1964 (Notes Prepared by the Revenue Department to Standing Committee of APCC in 1964).
94. Government of Assam, *Annual Economic Statistics*, 1984–85, Guwahati: Government Press, 1985, Chapter 4, Table 4.4.
95. Government of Assam, *Annual Economic Statistics*, 1979–80, Guwahati: Government Press, 1980, Chapter 4, Section 4.9.0.
96. In Nowgaon, a well-attended public meeting organized by these landlords under the auspices of Nowgaon Bar Association wanted the immediate repeal of this Act. The meeting was attended by several lawyers and landlords including Kushadev Goswami, Gopal Chandra Bora and Pit Singh Konwar. The meeting formed a 41-member committee to take measures to challenge the Act (*Dainik Assamiya*, 21 September 1973).
97. Government of Assam, *Enquiry Report on the Allegations Brought by Shri Govinda Kalita, M.L.A., before the House on 19th and 20th May, 1971 Regarding Settlement of Lands in and around Gauhati and Other Allied Matters*, Shillong: Assam Secretariat Press, 1971.
98. Dutta, '50-bigha Limit in Assam Hailed'.
99. Barman, 'Land Reforms Secure Tenants' Interests'.
100. In an order passed in 1970, the Revenue Department instructed that not more than 0.5 bighas of land be given to the occupying tenant (Letter from Deputy Secretary, Revenue Department, to SDO, Barpeta, File no. RRT/7/70/6, 30 January 1970, ASA).
101 Tabulated from Table 4.2 in Government of Assam, *Economic Statistics of Assam*, 1976–1977, Chapter 4.
102 'Editorial', *Dainik Assamiya*, 27 August 1971; *Dainik Assam*, 5 October 1971.
103 *Dainik Assamiya*, 21 May 1971.
104. *Dainik Assamiya* published several editorials exposing the damages caused to the forested tracts of Assam by continued peasantization

in these areas. It was since 1973 that the government had expressed its anxiety about the need for distribution of land amongst the landless as well as the growing deforestation in the state.

105. Saikia, *Forests and Ecological History of Assam*, pp. 337–38.
106. This view is echoed in Debajit Phukan, *Assam Nagaland Sima Samasya*, Golaghat: Phukan Grantha Prakash, 2001, p. 71; 'Sangsthapan Aru Simanta Rakshyar Dayitat Doyang Bananchalar Barangoni', *Dainik Assamiya*, 23 July 1973; 'Steps to Reduce Assam–Nagaland Boundary Tension', *The Times of India*, 16 March 1972; 'Assam Alleges Harassment by Nagaland', *The Times of India*, 17 February 1971; K.N. Malik, 'Centre Withheld Sundaram Report', *The Times of India*, 15 February 1979.
107. Government of Assam, *Assam Information*, vol. 24, Guwahati: Government Press, 1973, pp. 8–9.
108. Saikia, *Forests and Ecological History of Assam*, pp. 337–40.
109. Phukan, *Assam Nagaland Sima Samasya*, pp. 71–74.
110. Jehirul Hussain, 'Doyangor Andolan: Kichu Purani Katha', *Dainik Janambhumi*, 29 June 2004.
111. Minutes of Meeting held under the chairmanship of Minister, Revenue and Forest, Dispur, 1 December 1974.
112. National Remote Sensing Agency, *Mapping of Forest Cover in India from Satellite Imagery 1970–75 and 1980–82*, Summary Report, North Eastern States/Union Territories, Hyderabad: National Remote Sensing Agency, 1983.
113. Anon., 'End to Congress Monopoly: Assam', *Economic and Political Weekly*, vol. 13, no. 10, 1978, p. 481.
114. Out of the 126 seats in the Assam Legislative Assembly, candidates belonging to various communist parties won 23 seats (Election Commission of India, *Statistical Report on General Election, 1978 to the Legislative Assembly of Assam*, New Delhi: Government Press, 1978).
115. Speech by Chief Minister Golap Borbora, 17 June 1978, *ALAP*.
116. Government of India, *Implementation of Land Reforms*, p. 6.
117. Speech by Hareswar Das, Revenue Minister, Government of Assam, 4 July 1957, *ALAP*.
118. M.M. Das, *Peasant Agriculture in Assam*, New Delhi: Inter India Publications.
119. Government of India, *Fourth Five Year Plan (1969–74)*, New Delhi: Government Press, 1969, pp. 174–77.
120. Estimate based on J.N. Sarma (ed.), *World Agricultural Census, Assam, 1970–71*, Guwahati: Government of Assam, 1976, Tables 3(a), 3(b) and 3(c).
121. Table 1.2 in P.K. Kuri, *Tenancy Relations in Backward Agriculture: A Study in Rural Assam*, New Delhi: Mittal, 2004, pp. 6–7.

122. *The Times of India*, 3 January 1964.
123. 'No Proper Records of Rights: Land Reforms in Assam a Vast Task', *The Times of India*, 4 January 1958.
124. Election Commission of India, *Statistical Report on General Election, 1967 to the Legislative Assembly of Assam*, New Delhi: Government Press, 1967. The CPI, the newly formed Communist Party of India (Marxist) (CPI[M]), the Praja Socialist Party, and the Sanghata Socialist Party got respectively 30 per cent, 15 per cent, 23 per cent and 26 per cent of votes in the seats they had contested.
125. 'It is deemed expedient to prohibit sub-letting outright in future' (Assam Legislative Assembly, *Statement of Objects and Reasons, Report on the Select Committee on the Assam* ([*Temporarily Settled*]) *Tenancy Bill 1970*, Shillong, 1971).
126. *Proposal for Amendment of the Assam (Temporarily Settled Districts) Tenancy Act, 1935*, Revenue, R, Tenancy Branch, File no. RRT-66 of 1964, ASA.
127. Till 1963, the Act had undergone several amendments but did not really bring any legal benefit to the sharecroppers. Unlike the *zamindari* areas in Goalpara and Cachar, the numerical distribution of the tenants was much lower than the sharecroppers.
128. The Committee opined: 'So considering all these things it is clear that the period of 12 years has a historical background in the land system of India and it cannot be said to be unreasonable either for the landlord or tenant. We see no reason to depart from the said period for conferring right of occupancy right of occupancy on tenants' (Opinion of the Sub-committee on the Assam Tenancy Bill, *APCC Papers*, Packet no. 140, File no. 1, NMML)
129. It was argued that this would go against the very legal scope and meaning of the annual leased land.
130. Assam Legislative Assembly, *Report on the Select Committee on the Assam (Temporarily Settled) Tenancy Bill 1970*, Shillong, 1971.
131. Ibid.
132. Statement of Assam Chief Minister, *Dainik Assamiya*, 6 June 1971.
133. Anon., 'After Chaliha in Assam', *Economic and Political Weekly*, vol. 5, no. 45, 1970, pp. 1795–1796.
134. *The Assam Gazette*, Extraordinary edition, 10 December 1971.
135. 'Praja Swatva Ain Pratyaharor Dabi', *Dainik Assamiya*, 26 June 1973; 'Praja Swatva Ain Sansodhanor Dabi', *Dainik Assamiya*, 9 August 1973.
136. 'Praja Swatva Ain Kajyakori Kararor Dabi', *Dainik Assamiya*, 29 June 1973.

137. Chaudhury, in fact, made it clear that his government had no right to continue in office if his government could not implement the Act to protect the interests of the tenants and sharecroppers.
138. In several Indian states, Gandhi's populist reformist programme could moderately influence tenancy reforms (A. Kohli, *The State and Poverty in India*, Cambridge: Cambridge University Press, 1989, pp. 166–79, 214–17).
139. Sarat Chandra Sinha, *Andhar Bidara Kad*, Guwahati: Buniyad Publications, 1997.
140. Barman, 'Land Reforms Secure Tenants' Interests'.
141. The idea of the total repeal of the Act was mostly articulated in Kamrup.
142. A group of landlords, on behalf of the Assam Landlords Association, which happened to be a loosely organized platform of the landlords formed after 1948, met Sarat Chandra Sinha in Sibsagar and asked for immediate amendment of the Act. The landlords argued that implementation of the Act would be detrimental to the interests of the small and medium landlords. They also indicated that further implementation of the Act would aggravate agrarian relations in the countryside. *Dainik Assamiya*, however, reported that the Chief Minister had expressed strongly about his willingness to implement the Act (*Dainik Assamiya*, 4 June 1973).
143. Prabhat Chandra Sarma, 'Prajaswata Ain Aru Eiyar Karjyakarita', *Dainik Assamiya*, 11 June, 1973. There were others too who voiced their concern about the landed interests of Assamese middle-class families once the Act would come into effect.
144. 'Press Release of Krishak Sabha', *Dainik Assamiya*, 10 June 1973.
145. Barman, 'Land Reforms Secure Tenants' Interests'.
146. 'Landholding Pattern of Assam 1976–1977', Government of Assam, available at http://www.indiastat.com/table/agriculture/2/agriculturallandholdings/153/522927/data.aspx (accessed on 8 September 2012).
147. Of the approximately 20,000 people who acquired tenancy were the pre-existing tenants.
148. Government of Assam, *Annual Economic Statistics*, 1979–80, Chapter 4, Section 4.9.0.
149. Records in the APIRR clearly indicted such a trend.
150. I have not come across any instance of an agrarian relationship determined by Hindu sharecroppers vis-à-vis Muslim landlords in the *raiyatwari*-settled districts of Assam.
151. A number of left leaders were well-known legal practitioners. Amongst them Niren Lahiri, Gaurishankar Bhattacharjya and Tarunsen Deka had left behind illustrious legal careers.

152. Statement of Bimala Prasad Chaliha, Chief Minister, 9 November 1967, *ALAP*.
153. See William van Schendel, *A History of Bangladesh*, Cambridge: Cambridge University Press, 2009.
154. 'Press Statement', *Dainik Assamiya*, 19 September 1971.
155. 'Editorial', *Dainik Assamiya*, 14 May 1971; Partha N. Mukherji, 'The Great Migration of 1971: II', *Economic and Political Weekly*, vol. 9, no. 10, 1974, pp. 399, 401, 403 and 405–8.
156. M.V. Nadkarni and K.H. Vedini, 'Accelerating Commercialisation of Agriculture: Dynamic Agriculture and Stagnating Peasants?', *Economic and Political Weekly*, vol. 31, no. 26, 1996, pp. A63–A73.
157. Anon., *Report on Study on the Increasing Pattern of Uses of Fertilizers, Pesticides and Other Chemicals the Field of Agriculture in Darrang, Barpeta, Nagaon and Kamrup Districts of Assam*, Guwahati: NEOLAND Technologies, 2003.
158. It is logical to make a distinction between the middle class mainly formed from the immigrant Muslims and the Assamese middle class originating in the colonial set-up.
159. A partial discussion on the historiography of Assamese middle class can be found in Rajen Saikia, *Social and Economic History of Assam 1853–1921*, New Delhi: Manohar, 2000, pp. 159–92.
160. See Makhanlal Kar, *Muslims in Assam Politics*, New Delhi: Omsons, 1990.
161. For a bibliographical reference to Muslim writers writing in Assamese, see Appendix and Bibliography in Ismail Hussain, *Asamar Char-Chaporir Loka-Sahitya*, Guwahati: Banalata, 2002.
162. *The Assam Tribune*, 5 May 1974.
163. During 1954–57, nationalists in Assam won a decisive victory over the Indian federal government by changing its policy to establish a refinery in Assam (D. Barua, 'The Refinery Movement in Assam', *Economic and Political Weekly*, vol. 46, no. 1, 2011, pp. 63–69). In the early 1960s, the All Assam Student Union (AASU) also spearheaded another movement which led to the acceptance of Assamese as the only official language of Assam.
164. 'President's Rule in Assam Demanded: Jan Sangh Resolution on Checking Pak Infiltration', *The Times of India*, 12 August 1963.
165. Union Home Minister Guljarilal Nanda, speaking in a well attended public meeting of Muslim peasants in central Assam, asked the recent immigrants to leave Assam ('No Mercy Will Be Shown to Illegal Infiltrants: Nanda Says It Is Better "To Quit with Grace"', *The Times of India*, 19 March 1964). Several years before, Jawaharlal Nehru had also signaled that the refugees from East Pakistan must

leave India ('Future Migrants from East Pakistan: "Final Decision Necessary"', *The Times of India*, 14 November 1957).

166. 'Pakistan Willing for a Limited Accord: Five-hour Talks on Eviction Issue', *The Times of India*, 11 April 1964.
167. For details, see Herambakanta Barpujari, *Uttar Purbanchalar Samasya Aru Rajniti*, Guwahati: GL Publications, 1999, pp. 47–74.
168. Surendranath Medhi, 'Is the Assam Tenancy Act of 1971 a Social Legislation?', *The Assam Tribune*, 24 July 1986.
169. The suggestion put forward by the Law Minister had led to a heated debate. Sailen Medhi, an RCPI leader and lawyer, even questioned the propriety of Surendranath Medhi in openly criticiz-ing the Act in the press (Durlav Chandra Mahanta, 'Ejan Sahakarmir Dristit Shri Sailen Medhi' in Yamini Phukan [ed.], *Sailen Medhi: Byaktitwa Aru Samaj Chinta*, Guwahati: 80th Birthday Celebration Committee, 2009, pp. 36–37).
170. 'Editorial', *The Assam Tribune*, 27 July 1987.
171. The Assam Pattadar Sangha filed a suit in the Gauhati High Court challenging the provisions of eviction in the Assam Tenancy Act of 1971 (Civil Rule no. 125 of 1985, Gauhati High Court).
172. *The Assam Tribune* published several essays and letters to the editors opining against the Assam Tenancy Act. For instance, see Chandi Charan Barman, 'The Assam Tenancy Act: A Discussion', *The Assam Tribune*, 29 June 1986.
173. Durlav Chandra Mahanta, 'Ejan Sahakarmir Dristit Shri Sailen Medhi'. Communist opposition to the repeal of the Act also came to the surface. Sailen Medhi, a senior leader of the Revolutionary Communist Party of India (RCPI), wrote in *The Assam Tribune* questioning the propriety of the Law Minister for publicly opposing an Act (*The Assam Tribune*, 30 July 1986). The communists also influenced a privilege motion in the Assam Legislative Assembly against the Law Minister questioning his public stand (*The Assam Tribune*, 6 August 1986).
174. This estimate is based on figures provided by the National Sample Survey (NSS) Data, Government of India (*Some Aspects of Operational Land Holdings in India, 2002–03*, NSS Report no. 492, Chapter 3, Table 3.6).

Conclusion

1. *Census of India, Assam*, 1901, vol. 1, p. 5.
2. The figure for 2001 includes all the districts of Assam. These two figures are not comparable as both differed in the nature of the survey done and the total area covered (Government of Assam, *Statistical Survey of Assam*, Guwahati: Government Press, 2001).

3. B.B. Chaudhury, *Peasant History of Late Pre-colonial and Colonial India*, New Delhi: Pearson, 2008, p. 331.
4. *Census of India*, 2001, Migration Tables (D1 Appendix) (D2 and D3 Tables).
5. Assam follows West Bengal and Bihar as the third-highest producer of jute in the country. It has an average share of 7 per cent of the total area under jute cultivation (*Selected State-wise Area for Jute in India* [2000–2001 to 2009–2010], http://www.indiastat.com/table/agriculture/2/juteandmesta/17206/419831/data.aspx, accessed 17 March 2012).
6. James C. Scott, *The Art of Being Not Governed: An Anarchist History of Upland Southeast Asia*, New Delhi: Orient Blackswan, 2010, p. 332.
7. For a brief review of the debate on the question of who is an Assamese, see Chandan Kumar Sarma, *Assomiya Kon: Ek Samajtattvik Abalokan*, Guwahati: Span Publications, 2006.
8. In 2006 the Indian government passed the Scheduled Tribes and Other Forest Dwellers Forest Rights Act, intended to restore the rights of access to and use of forest land and produce to the 'forest dwellers' which had taken away from them while implementing the colonial forestry programme.

Bibliography

Primary Sources

Assam State Archives (ASA)

Assam Secretariat Proceedings (*ASP*), 1900–47.
Confidential Files, Chief Minister's Secretariat.
Confidential Files, Governor's Secretariat, 1947–50.
Papers of Assom Samraksini Sabha, 1929–30.
Political History of Assam (*PHA*) Files.
Proceedings of Revenue and Agricultural Department.
Proceedings of Revenue Tenancy Department, 1948–52.
Proceedings of the Forest Department.

National Archives of India (NAI)

Proceedings of the Home Political Department, 1920–47.
Proceedings of the Home Public Department.
Proceedings of the Ministry of States (including the fortnightly reports).
Proceedings of the Political Department, Ministry of States.
Proceedings of the Revenue and Agricultural Department.

Oriental and India Office Collection (OIOC), London

Annual Jail Administration Report of Assam, 1934–50.
Annual Report on the Police Administration of Assam, 1946–50.
Immigrant Department Files, 1880–99.
Revenue and Agricultural Department Files, 1874–99.

Nehru Memorial Museum and Library, New Delhi

All India Congress Committee (*AICC*) *Papers*, 1947–75.
Assam Provincial Congress Committee (*APCC*) *Papers*, 1937–53.
Bhimbar Deuri Papers, 1944–47.
S. Gopal (ed.), *Collected Works of Jawaharlal Nehru*, series 1, vols 1–14.
Gopinath Bordoloi Papers, 1947–50.
Pannalal Das Gupta (oral transcript).

Nowgaon District Record Room (NDRR)

Miscellaneous Files of Revenue and Agriculture, Forest and Revenue Tenancy Departments, 1874–1947.

Village and Mauza Notes, 1910s.

Assam Police Intelligence Record Room (APIRR), Special Branch, Kahilipara, Guwahati

'Note on Communism', File no. I/A-3(6)/48/X.
A Short Note on CPI Activities in Kamrup between 1948–49, File no. A-3(6) M/47.
A Short Note on the CPI Activities in Nowgaon, 1948, File no. I/A-3(6)-J/47.
Abstract of the Assam Police Intelligence Weekly Report (*APWR*).
APOC, *Kishan Fronts in Sibsagar District*, pamphlet, File no. I/A-3(8) H-47.
Appeal of Nowgaon District Krishak Sabha, pamphlet
Assam Provincial Organizing Committee (APOC), 'Resolution on the Main Structure of the Future Constitution of Assam', 19–24 August 1947, File no. I/A-3 (6)/II, 1947.
Bishnuram Medhi on Communism, Official Notes, 27 November 1948.
CID Report, Shillong, 27 September 1948, File no. IA-3(6) 48, XI.
CID Report to the Superintendent of Police of Sibsagar, Memo. no. 164, 22 October 1949, File no. A-3/6/2(47).
Circular no. 2-NE-1950–51, by Ashok Mehta, General Secretary, CSP.
Climate of Insurrection in Far East, Intelligence Note.
Communist Influence in Tea Gardens and Labour Organisation in Sibsagar District, Note from Superintendent Police of the Sibsagar to DIG of Assam Police, 22 December 1949, File no. A-3(6)(K)47.
Communist Movement in Barpathar Side, Dibrugarh, Intelligence Report.
Communist Situation in Assam, 1949, File no. I/A-3(8) H-47.
Confiscated Letter of Bishnu Rabha, File no. I-A/3(6)53.
CPI, *Assam Fights for Freedom and Democracy: Draft Resolutions of Assam Communists*, Guwahati, 1948, File no. A-3(6)1947.
——, *Proceedings of the Assam Provincial Organization of CPI*, File no. A-3(6), 1947.
——, 'Nowgaon Zillah Krishak Sabhar Ahban', 1949.
CPI Circular to Provincial Committee on Tebhaga Agitation.
CPI Circular, Bombay, 1947.
CSP, *Agrarian Programme of Socialist Party*, 1948, File no. I/C-6/14-C 49/50.
——, *Pamphlet on Giladhari Satyagraha*.
——, *Resolution of the Third Party Conference of the Congress Socialist Party*, October 1948.
Durbhikha Pirita Sakalak Sahaya Karak, pamphlet issued by the RCPI in the name of Bishnu Rabha and others, File no. I/3-(5), 49.
Deputy Inspectors General of Police Note on Communist (notes are found for the period 1948–51).

Detailed Note on Communist Activity, by Deputy Inspector General of Police and Intelligence, Assam, 23 January 1947.
Draft Agrarian Policy of CSP, 1949–50.
Extract from Secret Information of 5 February, 1948, File no A-3(6) 48.
Government of India letter no. 15, Daily Summary of Information, 13 May 1948, File no. A- 3(50)48.
Intercepted Letters of Bisnhu Rabha, Mohanlal Mukherjee and Nalini Misra, 1950–53.
Joshi, P.C., 'On Immediate Solidarity Campaign with the Tebhaga Struggle', Political Circular no. 1/47, File no. I/A-3(6)47/9, January 1947.
Krishak Sabha, *Krishak Sabhar Abedon*, pamphlet.
Krishak Banua Panchayat (KBP), 'Bikhyat Khetiak Neta Gobinda Kalita Greptar: Congress Sarkarar Fascist Daman Neetir Aru Ek Adhya' ('Arrest of Govinda Kalita: Another Chapter in the Fascist Policy of the Congress Government'), a pamphlet issued in the name of Haren Kalita, Bishnu Rabha, Nabin Medhi, Loknath Baruah, and Aniram Basumatari, September 1949.
——, *Constitution of the KBP*, File no. A-3/6/2(47).
——, *Dakhin Kamrupat Dia-hhikha*, pamphlet, File no. 1-9/A-49.
Labour Protest, Intelligence Report, 26 August 1948.
Letter from Harold Dennehy, Chief Secretary to Government of Assam, to Commissioner of Assam Valley Division, 14 February 1947, File no. I/A-5(S) F/47.
Memo. from Central Intelligence Officer to Deputy Inspector General of Police, Memo. no. SA 14/105-6, 20 January 1948, File no. A-3(6)48.
Memo. from Ministry of Home, Government of India, to K.R. Chaudhuri, Deputy Inspector General, Assam Police, File no. A-3(6) 48, 25 February 1948.
Memo., 'On Communist Agitation', by Harold Dennehy, Chief Secretary to Government of Assam, to Commissioner of Assam Valley Division, 14 February, 1947, File no. I/A-5(6)-F/47.
Ministry of Home Affairs Circular on Strengthening Intelligence in Rural Areas, New Delhi, 1948.
Note on Communist Activities, File no. A-3(6)48, 30 January 1948.
Note on Communist Hold among Railway Men, by Deputy Inspector General of Police and Intelligence, Assam, 1948.
Note on the Activities of School Teachers of Sibsagar District.
Note on the Communist Uprisings in Burma, 1950.
Note on the CPI, Dibrugarh District.
Note on the CPI, Kamrup district committee, 29 November 1948.
Note on the Present Situation in India with Regard to Illicit Arms, December 1948.

Note on Socialist Party Activists in Nowgaon and Darrang Districts, by Deputy Inspector General of Police and Intelligence, Assam, 1948–50.
Note on the Socialist Party of Darrang, File no. I/A-3(10)H-47.
Notes on CPI Activities in Sibsagar District, File no. IA -3(6)47.
Pamphlet of the CSP, Provincial Conference, 1950.
Pathak, Gokul, *Khetiak*, Barpeta: CSP, 1948.
Present Policy of Socialist Party, Note by Deputy Inspector General of Police and Intelligence, Assam, 1949.
Proceedings of the CSP (Assam), January 1950.
RCPI, 'November Divas Saptah Palan Karak', pamphlet, 29 October 1949.
——, 'Communist Parteer Istahar', pamphlet, 1944.
Report of the General Secretary of Assam Krishak Sabha, 1949.
Report of the Proceedings of the Open Meeting of the First Session of the Assam Provincial Communist Party Held at Guwahati on 13 February 1948, File no. A-3(6) 48.
Report on Arms Collection by CPI and RCPI, by Deputy Inspector General of Police and Intelligence, Assam, 1950.
Report on the CPI, by Deputy Inspector General of Police and Intelligence, Assam, February 1948.
Report on the First Session of CPI's Assam Unit, 1948.
Review of Communism in Assam, Notes by Assam Police Intelligence Department, 1948–50.
Secret Report by Jyotimoy Nandi, Police Intelligence Secret Report.
Socialist Party Activity, File no. 1, 7 March 1948.
Women Fronts in Sibsagar, File no. I/A 3-6 k-47.

P.C. Joshi Archives or Archives on Contemporary History, Jawaharlal Nehru University (JNU), New Delhi

All India Kishan Sabha, News Bulletin, 1952.
Draft Political Thesis of the Second Congress of the CPI, December 1947, Packet no. 1948/3Q-G.
Ist Year of Struggle CPI, 1948.
Note on the Assam Provincial Communist Party, 1949, File no. 55/1949, *PB Resolution on Assam PC*, 1949, File no. 53/1949.
RPCI, 'The Present Situation and the Task of the Party', resolution adopted at the 4th conference of the RCPI, May 1948.
Second Congress of the CPI: Opening Report by Comrade B.T. Ranadive on the Draft Political Thesis, CP Publication, 1948.
Strategy and Tactics in the Struggle for People's Democratic Revolution, 1949.

Census, Gazettes and Gazetteers

Allen, B.C., *Districts Gazetteers of Assam* (volumes on Kamrup, Darrang, Nowgaon, Sibsagar, and Lakhimpur), Shillong: Government Press, 1905.

Census of India 1951, reports on districts of Assam: Kamrup, Darrang, Nowgaon, Lakhimpur, and Sibsagar, Shillong: Government Press.

Government of India, *District Census Report*, Kamrup, New Delhi: Government Press, 1951.

O'Malley, L.S.S., *Bengal District Gazetteer, Pabna*, Calcutta: Bengal Secretariat Book Depot, 1923.

——, *Report on the Census of India*, Bengal, vol. 5, Calcutta: Bengal Secretariat Book Depot, 1911.

Report on the Census of India, Assam, 1901, vol. 4, Calcutta: Government Press, 1901.

Report on the Census of India, Assam, 1911, vol. 3, part 1, Shimla: Government Press, 1911.

Report on the Census of India, Bengal, 1921, vol. 5, part 1, New Delhi: Government Press, 1921.

Report on the Census of India, Assam, 1921, vol. 3, Shillong: Government Press, 1923.

Report on the Census of India, Assam, 1931, vol. 3, part 1, New Delhi: Government Press, 1932.

Report on the Census of India, Assam, 1941, New Delhi: Government Press, 1942.

Report on the Census of India, Assam, 1951, vol. 12, part 1A, Shillong: Government Press, 1951.

Sachse, F.A., *Mymensingh District Gazetteer*, vol. 1, Calcutta: Bengal Secretariat Book Depot, 1917.

Secretary of State for India in Council, *Imperial Gazetter of India*, vols 1–6, Oxford: Clarendon Press, 1908–9.

The Assam Gazette, Shillong: Government Press, 1874–1952.

Other Published Reports

Agricultural Labor Enquiry: Report on the Intensive Survey of Agricultural Labour, vol. 1, New Delhi: Government Press, 1953.

Anon., *Report on Study on the Increasing Pattern of Uses of Fertilizers, Pesticides and Other Chemicals the Field of Agriculture in Darrang, Barpeta, Nagaon and Kamrup Districts of Assam*, Guwahati: NEOLAND Technologies, 2013.

Annual Administrative Reports of Assam, 1874–1947.

Annual Progress Report, Forest Department, 1874–1950.

Annual Report on the Land Revenue Administration of Assam, 1874–1950.

Annual Survey and Settlement Reports, 1883–1927.
Assam Legislative Assembly Proceedings (ALAP), 1937–54, Shillong: Government Press.
Assam Legislative Council Proceedings (ALCP), 1921–45, Shillong: Government Press.
Assam Provincial Banking Enquiry Committee Report (APBECR), 1929–30, 2 vols, Shillong: Government Press, 1930.
Assam Valley Reassessment Report, Department of Land Records and Agriculture, Shillong: Government Press, 1893.
Barua, Fatik Chandra, *Report on the Survey and Settlement of the La-khiraj and Nisf-khiraj Holdings in the District of Kamrup*, Shillong: Government Press, 1884.
Darrah, H.J., *Note on the Work Done by the Land Records Department in the Assam Valley Districts*, Shillong: Government Press, 1894.
Datta, S.N., *Report on the Resettlement of the Nowgong District, during the Years 1926 (October) to 1932 (January)*, Shillong: Assam Government Press, 1933.
Desai, S.P., *Report on the Land Revenue Settlement of the Kamrup District*, Shillong: Assam Government Printing Press, 1928.
Dufferin, Lord, *Report on the Condition of the Lower Classes of Population in Bengal*, Calcutta: Government Press, 1888.
Edwards, A.R., *Report on the Land Revenue Settlement of the Nowgong District during the Years 1905–1906 to 1908–1909*, Shillong: Eastern Bengal and Assam Secretariat Press, 1909.
Election Commission of India, *Statistical Report on General Election, 1978 to the Legislative Assembly of Assam*, New Delhi: Government Press, 1978.
——, *Statistical Report on General Election, 1957 to the Legislative Assembly of Assam*, New Delhi: Government Press, 1957.
——, *Report on the First General Election of India*, vol. 2, New Delhi: Government Press, 1953.
——, *Statistical Report on General Election, 1951 to the Legislative Assembly of Assam*, New Delhi: Government Press, 1952.
Goswami, P., *A Study in Rural Change in Assam, Dispur*, Jorhat: Agro-Economic Research Center, for North East India, 1967.
Government of Assam, *Statistical Survey of Assam*, Guwahati: Government Press, 2001.
——, *Annual Economic Statistics*, 1984–85, Guwahati: Government Press, 1985.
——, *Annual Economic Statistics*, 1979–80, Guwahati: Government Press, 1980.
——, *Assam Information*, vol. 24, Guwahati: Government Press, 1973.
——, *Enquiry Report on the Allegations Brought by Shri Govinda Kalia, M.L.A., before the House on 19th and 20th May, 1971 Regarding*

Settlement of Land in and around Gauhati and Other Allied Matters, Shillong: Assam Secretariat Press, 1971.

——, *Agricultural Statistics of Assam*, Calcutta: Government Press, 1951.

——, *Report of the Special Officer Appointed for the Examination of the Professional Grazing Reserves in the Assam Valley*, Shillong: Assam Government Press, 1944.

——, *Line System Enquiry Committee Report*, 3 vols, Shillong: Assam Government Press, 1938.

——, *The Colonisation of Wastelands in Assam*, Calcutta: The India Daily News Office, 1899.

——, *Report on the Administration of the Province of Assam, 1892–93*, Shillong: Government Press, 1893.

Government of India, *Fourth Five Year Plan (1969–74)*, New Delhi: Government Press, 1969.

——, *Report of the Famine Inquiry Commission, 1943*, New Delhi: Government Printing Press, 1945.

Hart, G.S., *Note on a Tour Inspection of Goalpara (Assam), Buxa, Jalpaiguri, Kalimpong, Kurseong Forest Divisions (Bengal)*, Shimla: Government Press, 1920.

Hart, S.G., *Report on the Land Revenue Settlement of the Sibsagar District during the Years 1902–1903 to 1905–1906*, Shillong: Eastern Bengal and Assam Secretariat Press, 1906.

India Jute Mill Association, *Annual Summary of Jute and Gunny Statistics*, Calcutta: Indian Jute Mill Association, 1963.

Indian Central Jute Committee, *Report on the Marketing and Transport of Jute in India*, Calcutta: Indian Central Jute Committee, 1940.

Indian Statutory Commission, *Report on the Indian Statutory Commission*, vol. 14, London: His Majesty's Stationery Office, 1930.

Laine, A.J., *An Account of the Land Tenure System of Goalpara*, Shillong: Government Press, 1917.

MacKenzie, S.N., *Final Report on the Resettlement of Land Revenue in the Lakhimpur District, Assam during the Years 1908 to 1912*, Shillong: Assam Secretariat Printing Office, 1912.

McSwiney, J., *Report on the Land Revenue Settlement of the Darrang District of Eastern Bengal and Assam Effected during the Years 1905 to 1909*, Shillong: Eastern Bengal and Assam Secretariat Press, 1910.

——, *Report on the Land Revenue Settlement of the Kamrup District of Eastern Bengal and Assam Effected during the Years 1902 to 1905*, Shillong: Eastern Bengal and Assam Secretariat Press, 1906.

Mitra, N.N. (ed.), *Indian Annual Register*, vol. 1, January–June 1947, Calcutta: Annual Register Office, 1947.

Monahan, F.J., *Assam Jute Cultivation*, Shillong: Government Press, 1898.
Mukherjee, D.K., *Final Report on the Land Revenue Resettlement of the Darrang District during the Years 1927–33*, Shillong: Assam Government Press, 1934.
National Remote Sensing Agency, *Mapping of Forest Cover in India from Satellite Imagery 1970–75 and 1980–82*, Summary Report, North Eastern States/Union Territories, Hyderabad: National Remote Sensing Agency, 1983.
Pawsey, C.R., *Report on the Resettlement of the Lakhimpur District, 1929–1935*, Shillong: Assam Government Press, 1937.
Prance, B.C., *Final Report on the Survey and Settlement Operations in the Riparian Areas of Pabna*, Calcutta: Bengal Secretariat Book Depot, 1916.
Rhodes, C.K., *Report on the Land Revenue Settlement of the Sibsagar District during the Years 1923 to 1929*, Shillong: Assam Government Press, 1929.
Rodes, C.S., *Assam Land Revenue Manual*, Shillong: Government Press, 1906, 4th edition, 1931.
Sachse, F.A., *Final Report on the Survey and Settlement Operations in the District of Mymensingh, 1908–1919*, Calcutta: Government Press, 1920.
Sarma, J.N. (ed.), *World Agricultural Census, Assam, 1970–71*, Guwahati: Government of Assam, 1976.
Statistical Abstract Relating to British India from 1902–03 to 1912–13 and 1910–11 to 1919–20, vol. 55, London: His Majesty's Stationery Office, 1922.
The Customary Laws and Practices of the Dimacha-Kacharis of Assam, Guwahati: Law Research Institute, 1979.
The Customary Laws and Practices of the Pati Rabha of Assam, Guwahati: Law Research Institute, 1979.

Proscribed Materials

Das, Joychandra, *Bidrohi Khetiak* (Assamese).
Mahanta, Bhupen, *Biplabi Khetiak* (Assamese), Guwahati: Radical Institute, n.d., in proscribed material 1884–85/pp Ass-b: 1 PIB/202/2, NAI.
Pamphlets (8) issued by RCPI and CPI (1942–47).

Newspapers and Journals

Abahan
Chetana
Dainik Assamiya

Lal Nichan
Natun Assam
Panchayat
People's Age
People's War
Sadiniya Assamiya
Tinidiniya Assamiya
The Assam Tribune
The Times of India

Interviews

Abani Lahiri, CPI leader involved in the Tebhaga movement in districts of north Bengal districts, New Delhi, 12 November 1998.

Ambu Bora, RCPI leader involved in the peasant movement as a student, Guwahati, 8 and 14 June 1996.

Baneswar Saikia, leader and General Secretary of the RCPI, Nowgaon, 14 May 1996.

Bhaghi Majhi, sharecropper from Beltola, Guwahati, 31 December 1995.

Bhogeswar Dutta, in-charge of the peasant unit of the State CPI, and organizer of the peasant movement during 1970s, Guwahati, 29 August 1998 and 4 July 1999.

Bijoy Chandra Bhagawati, Congress leader, New Delhi, December 1995.

Birendra Kumar Bhattacharya, CSP leader and a leading literary figure, New Delhi, January, 1995.

Deba Bora, erstwhile CPI activist in Darrang and Nowgaon districts, Guwahati, 22 June 1997.

Dhireswar Kalita, CPI leader, MP from Guwahati constituency and peasant activist in southern Kamrup in the post-Independence period, Guwahati, 20 December 1996.

Gopal Das, RCPI activist, Guwahati, 7 March 1995.

Govinda Kalita, KBP leader, Guwahati, 18 June 1995.

Indivar Deuri, son of Bhimbar Deuri, the first President of Assam Tribal League, Guwahati, 22 June 1997.

Jogen Gogoi, CPI leader in Sibsagar district, Guwahati, 24 June 1997.

Jogen Hazarika, CPI leader, New Delhi, June 2000.

Kamala Majumdar, RCPI leader who took a leading part in the sharecroppers' movement of 1948–52, Guwahati, 19 June 1995.

Kamini Sarma, RCPI and, later, CPI leader, Rangia, Kamrup, 21 June 1995.

Keshav Mahanta, CPI activist in the 1950s active on the cultural front, New Delhi, 12 March 1998.

Liladhar Kakoty, an organizational committee member of All Assam Sankardeva Sangha, Nowgaon, 26 December 1997.

Mohanlal Mukherjee, RCPI activist who led the party's armed wing, Guwahati, 12 and 14 June 1996.

Nihar Mukherjee, erstwhile RCPI leader, Guwahati, 15 and 16 June 1996.

Phani Bora, CPI leader associated with the peasant mobilization during 1948–52, Guwahati, 12 and 17 June 2000.

Prafulla, Mishra, editor of *Shillong Observer*, Guwahati, October 1996.

Sandhyarani Brahma Chaudhuri, daughter of Rupnath Brahma, a tribal leader and member of the Assam Legislative Assembly in the 1940s, Guwahati, 25 June 1997.

Sarat Rabha, CPI student activist involved in the peasant movement in Goalpara, Guwahati, 22 June 1997.

Suren Hazarika, CPI leader active in upper Assam and in Golaghat subdivision of Sibsagar district, Jorhat, 28 September 1998.

Pamphlets

Beltola Khetiak Raijar Oparat Chala Congress Charkarar Daman Nitir Tandab Opharai Pelaook.

Beltolat Police Raj.

Congressi Charkaror Krishak Raijar Opparat Chaloa Nirlajja Daman Nitir Biruddhe Dibalai Raijalai Krishak Banua Panchayatar Ahban, 1949.

Desh Aru Khetiak Bachabar Upay.

Fight to Stop Attack on the Communist Party.

Ghiladhari Satyagraha, Young Socialist Leagar Ekashar.

Ganatantrak Hatya Karak Sharajantra Byartha Karak.

Guirella Warfare.

Jan Goleo Dhan Nidio-Nangal Jar Mati Tar.

Krishak Sabhar Ahban.

Mati Bhat Kapor Swadhinata Aru Ganatantar Karane Saktisali Krishak Gorhi Tolak.

Tribal Raijar Oparat Congresi Charkarar Tandab Lila Pratisodhar karaney Saju Haok.

Krishak Sabhar Abedan, 5 pamphlets, 1952.

Secondary Sources (Assamese and Bengali)

Agarwala, Jyotiprasad, 'Naliapoolor Bipad Sanket', in Hiren Gohain (ed.), *Jyotiprasad Rachanavali*, Guwahati: Assam Publication Board, 2003, pp. 543–49.

Ahmad, K.M., *Hual Goni: Pater Kabita*, Calcutta: Ahmad Ali Khandarkar, 1930.

Ali, M. Ibrahim (ed.), *Madhab Chandra Bezbaroa*, Guwahati: R.P. Bezbaroa, 2001.

Anon., *Bolo Basumatari Smritigrantha*, Guwahati: Basumatari Sonwarani Samiti, 2000.

Badal, Arefin (ed.), *Maulana Bhasani*, Dhaka: Dhansiri, 1977.

Barman, Sivanath, *Assamiya Jivani Abhidhan*, Guwahati: Banalata, 1992.

Barman, Sivanath (ed.), *Asamiya Sahityar Buranji*, vol. 2, Guwahati: ABILAC, 1997.

Barooah, Nirode Kumar, *Gopinath Bordoloi Aru Assam: Tetia Aru Etia*, Guwahati: B.N. Bordoloi, 2010.

——, *Mohini Kalar Chabi*, Guwahati: Purbanchal, 1997.

Barpujari, Herambakanta, *Uttar Purbanchalar Samasya Aru Rajniti*, Guwahati: GL Publications, 1999.

Barthakur, Padma Nath, *Swadhinatar Ranor Sanswarparat*, Dibrugarh: Kaustav Prakasan, 2006.

Barua, Gunabhiram, *Ram Nabami*, ed. Prasenjit Chaudhury, Guwahati: Chetana Prakash, 1991.

Barua, Hemchandra, 'Bahire Rong Song Bhitare Kuwabhaturi', in Hemchandra Barua, *Hemchandra Barua Rachanavali* (ed.), Jatindranath Goswami, Guwahati: Hemkosh Prakasan, 1999, pp. 23–46.

Baruah, Navakanta, 'Kapiliparia Sadhu', in Navakanta Baruah (ed.), *Upanyash Samagra*, Nalbari: Journal Emporium, 2002, pp. 11–66.

Barua, Padmanath Gohain, *Padmanath Gohain Barua Rachanavali*, Guwahati: Assam Publication Board, 1987.

Basu, Manjula, *Saumendranath Thakur: Karme O Manane*, Kolkata: Tagore Research Institute, 2007.

Bezbaroa, Lakshminath, *Lakshminath Bezbaroa Granthavali*, ed. Jatindra Nath Goswami, vol. 2, Guwahati: Sahitya Prakash, 1988.

——, 'Nomal', in Lakshminath Bezbaroa, *Lakshminath Bezbaroa Granthavali*, ed. Jatindranath Goswami, vol. 2, Guwahati: Sahitya Prakash, 1988, pp. 1041–48.

Bezbarua, M.C., 'Banpani Prapirita Thair Majat Charidin', *Abahan*, vol. 5, no. 8, 1934, pp. 953–66.

Bhadra, Gautam, *Iman O Nishan*, Calcutta: Subarnarekha, 1994.

Bhattacharjya, Gaurisankar, *Sabinay Nibedan*, Guwahati: Sahitya Prakash, 1999.

Bhattacharya, Birendra Kumar, *Dersha Bacharar Assomiya Samskrtit Ebhumuki*, Guwahati: Assam Publication Board, 1978.

Bhattacharya, Pramod Chandra, *Assamar Janajati*, Guwahati: LBS, 1984.

Bhattacharya, P., 'Asomot Bideshi', *Abahan*, vol. 4, no. 5, 1932 (1858 *saka*).

Bhuyan, Jogendranarayan, *Unavimsa Satikar Assam Samvada*, Dibrugarh: Dibrugarh University, 1990.

Bhuyan, Jogendranarayan, *Uwali Jowa Nathir Para*, Nowgaon: Jogendranarayan Bhuyan, 1991.

——, 'Vaishnav Sahityar Mudran-Prakasan', in Sivanath Barman (ed.), *Asamiya Sahityar Buranji*, vol. 2, Guwahati: ABILAC, 1997, pp. 647–59.

Bishnu Rabha Sowarani Gabesana Samiti (ed.), *Bishnu Rabha Rachanawali*, vol. 1, Guwahati: Journal Emporium, 1982.

Bora, Jnananath, *Assomot Bideshi*, ed. Prasenjit Chaudhuri, Guwahati: Barua Agency, 1925, reprint, Guwahati: Chetana Prakash, 1996.

Bora, Lakshmidhar, *Muktijujar Sonwaranat*, Guwahati: Assam Publication Board, 1984.

Bordoloi, Rajanikanta, *Dandua Droh*, Guwahati: Sahitya Prakash, 1988.

Borgohain, Homen (ed.), 'Haladhiya Charaye Baodhan Khay', in Homen Borgohain, *Chairta Dasakar Fasal: Upanyash Samagra*, Guwahati: Student Stores, 1998, pp. 219–77.

——, 'Pita Putra', in Homen Borgohain, *Charita Dasakar Fasal: Upanyash Samagra*, Guwahati: Student Stores, 1998, pp. 279–453.

——, *Asamiya Sahityar Buranji*, vol. 6, Guwahati: ABILAC, 1993.

Chaliha, Hariprasad, *Ramakanta Muktiar Ata, Byakti Aru Prativa*, Guwahati: Saundarya Prasad Chaliha, 1998.

Chandra, Amitabh, *Abibhakta Banglai Communist Andolon*, Calcutta: Pustak Bipani, 1992.

Chaudhuri, Gurupad, *Bowati Sutir Chapari*, Guwahati: Bani Mandir, 1999.

Chaudhuri, Lakhyadhar, *Manuh Bichari*, Guwahati: Assam Publication Board, 1992.

——, *Obhati Chao, Rajnitir ka, kha Sikote*, Guwahati, n.d.

Chaudhury, Medini, *Farengadao*, Kokrajhar: Bairathi Publications, 1982.

Chaudhury, Prosenjit, *Assamar Chah-Banua Aru Unaish Satikar Bidwat Samaj*, Guwahati: Student's Store, 1989.

Das, Amiya Kumar, *Jiban Smriti*, Guwahati: Assam Publication Board, 1979.

Das, Jogesh and Sarveswar Barua (eds), *Bishnuprasad Rava Rachana Samahar*, vol. 1, Tezpur: Rabha Rachanawali Prakashan Sangha, 1989, reprint, 2008.

——, *Bishnuprasad Rava Rachana Samahar*, vol. 2, Tezpur: Rabha Rachanawali Prakashan Sangha, 1997.

Das, Sonit Bijoy and Munin Bayan (eds), *Hiren Gohain Rachanawali*, vol. 1, Guwahati: Katha Publication, 2009.

Das, Tilak, *Bishnu Rabha Etia Kiman Rati*, 1977, reprint, Guwahati: Chandra Prakash, 1992.

Das, Nishis Ranjan. *Swadhinata Andolone Barak Upatakyar Obismarania Koikjan Communist Neta*, Karimganj, 1997.

Dasgupta, Mrinal Kranti, *Je Path Die Elam*, Silchar: Rafique Ahmed, 1994.
Dasgupta, Pannalal, *Samajtantrabad Aji Kena*, Calcutta, n.d.
Deka, Haridas, *Jivan Aru Sangram*, Guwahati: LBS, 1992.
——, *Biplabi Khetiak*, Guwahati: Pragati Prakash Bhavan, 1944.
Deka, Tarunsen, *Mukti Sangramar Adharat Jiban Katha*, Guwahati: R.D. Printers and Publishers, 1993.
Deuri, Bhimbar, *The Assam Tribal League* (Bulletin), n.p.: All Assam Tribal League, 1940.
Deuri, Indivar (ed.), *Janagosthiya Samasya: Ateet Bartaman Bhabishyat*, Guwahati: Journal Emporium, 2001.
Deuri, Indivar, 'Bodo Janagosthir Antardwanda: Eti Artha Samajik Distipat', in Indivar Deuri (ed.), *Janagosthiya Samasya: Ateet Bartaman Bhabishyat*, Guwahati: Journal Emporium, 2001, pp. 97–109.
Dutta, Saneswar (ed.), *Prachin Kamrupia Kayastha Samajar Itibirta*, Guwahati: Harinarayan Dutta Barua, 1941, reprint, Guwahati: Prachin Kamrup-Kayastha Samaj, 2000.
Gohain, Hiren (ed.), *Jyotiprasad Rachanavali*, Guwahati: Assam Publication Board, 2003.
——, *Sainik Silpi Bishnu Rabha*, Guwahati: Journal Emporium, 1982, reprint, 2002.
Gohain, Hiren, 'Asomiya Upanyasar Esha Bachar', in Sonit Bijoy Das and Munin Bayan (eds), *Hiren Gohain Rachanawali*, vol. 1, Guwahati: Katha Publication, 2009, pp. 492–97.
——, *Asamar Jatiya Jivanat Mahapurusia Parampara*, Guwahati: LBS, 1987, reprint 1994.
——, 'Assamiya Madhyabitta Srenir Utpati Aru Bikash', in Hiren Gohain, *Sahitya Aru Chetana*, Guwahati: LBS, 1976, pp. 9–49.
——, *Sahitya Aru Chetana*, Guwahati: LBS, 1976.
Gogoi, Lila, *Noi Boi Jay*, Dibrugarh: Banalata, 2004.
——, *Tai Samskrtir Rup Rekha*, Calcutta: Shree Bhumi, 1985, reprint, Dibrugarh: Banalata, 1994.
Goswami, K.D., *Satra Samskritir Ruprekha*, Guwahati: Bani Prakash, 1973, reprint, Dibrugarh: Banalata, 1986.
Goswami, Kedarnath, *Krishakar Mukti*, Guwahati: Pragati Prakash Bhavan, 1944.
Goswami, Mamoni Raisom, *Datal Hatir Unye Khowa Howda*, Guwahati: Jyoti Prakasan, 1991.
Goswami, Prafulladatta (ed.), *Kencha Patar Kanpani*, Guwahati: LBS, 1952, reprint 1991.
Goswami, Prafulladatta, *Kamalakanta Bhattacharya Rachanawali*, Guwahati: Assam Publication Board, 2007.

Goswami, Pratap Chandra, *Kamrupia Samaj Aru Jiban Smriti*, Guwahati.

Goswami, Sriman P., 'Comrade Dhiren Duttar Smriti', in Chidananda Saikia (ed.), *Dhiren Datta Smriti Grantha*, Golaghat: Dhiren Datta Smritirakha Samiti, 1974, pp. 5–9.

Goswami, T.C. Deva, *Jibon Sonwaran*, Golaghat: Rangamati Gomotha Mahara Satra, 1982.

Guha, Amalendu, *Zamindarkalin Goalpara Zillar Artha Samajik Abastha: Eti Oitihasik Dristipat*, Guwahati: Natun Sahitya Parisad, 2000.

Hai, A.F.M. Abdul, *Adarsha-Khetiak*, Mymensingh: Abdul Hai, 1921.

Haldhar Bhuyan Smritigrantha, Nowgaon, 1976.

Hazarika, Atulchandra, *Smritilekha*, Guwahati: Assam Publication Board, 1981.

Hazarika, Suren, *Samajbadar Sandhanat*, Jorhat: Suren Hazarika, 1993.

Hemkosha, ed. P.R.T. Gourdon and compiled by Hem Chandra Barua, Shillong: Government Press, 1900.

Hussain, Ismail, *Asamar Char-Chaporir Loka-Sahitya*, Guwahati: Banalata, 2002.

Kalita, Benudhar, *Phulagurir Dheva,* Nowgaon: L. Kalita et al., 1995.

Khaklary, Jadunath, *Kacharir Katha,* Jorhat, 1927.

Krishak Banua Panchayat (KBP), *Sambidhan: Krishak Banua Panchayat* (*Constitution of the Assam Krishak Banua Panchayat*), Guwahati: KBP, 1948.

Mahanta, Dadhi, 'Asamat Communist Andolonar Bikash', in Chidananda Saikia (ed.), *Dhiren Datta Smriti Grantha*, Golaghat: Dhiren Datta Smritirakha Samiti, 1974, pp. 129–40.

——, 'Jatitya Mukti Aru Samajtantrar Sangramat Comrade Dhiren Duttor Abadan', in Chidananda Saikia (ed.), *Dhiren Datta Smriti Grantha*, Golaghat: Dhiren Datta Smritirakha Samiti, 1974, pp. 114–45.

Mahanta, Durlav Chandra, 'Ejan Sahakarmir Dristit Shri Sailen Medhi', in Yamini Phukan (ed.), *Sailen Medhi: Byaktitwa Aru Samaj Chinta*, Guwahati: 80th Birthday Celebration Committee, 2009.

Mahanta, Prafulla, *Asamiya Madhya Srenir Itihas*, Guwahati: Purvanchal Prakash, 1991.

Majumdar, Kamala, 'Haren Kalitar Smritit', in Hiren Medhi (ed.), *Biplabi Haren Kalita*, Guwahati: Haren Kalita Sowarani Samiti, 1994, pp. 73–77.

Majumdar, Parama, *Satirthar Dristit Bishnu Rabha*, Nalbari: Journal Emporium, 1992.

Malakar, S.C., *Sangrami Sudhakkha Karmajyogi: Bhupen Chandra Mahanta*, Guwahati: Dwijen Chandra Mahanta and Chandana Mahanta, 2006.

Malik, Syed Abdul, *Suruzmukhir Swapna*, Calcutta: Bhabani Publishing Concern, 1960.
Maksud, Sayed Abdul, *Maulana Abdul Hamid Khan Bhasani*, Dhaka: Bangla Academy, 1994.
Matlib, Abdul, *Jana Neta Khagen Barbaruah: Karma Aru Byaktitwa*, Amguri: Khagen Barbarua Smarak Grantha Sampadana Samiti, 2001.
Medhi Hiren (ed.), *Biplabi Haren Kalita* (souvenir), Guwahati: Haren Kalita Sowarani Samiti, 1994.
Mukherjee, Mohanlal, *Sahakarmir Darpanat Bishnuprasad Rabha*, Guwahati: Student's Store, 1989, reprint 1992.
Neog, Maheswar, (ed.), *Chandra Kanta Abhidhan*, Guwahati: Gauhati University Publication Division, 1987.
——, *Guru Charit Katha*, Guwahati: LBS, 1999.
Phukan, Debajit, *Assam Nagaland Sima Samasya*, Golaghat: Phukan Grantha Prakash, 2001.
Phukan, Yamini (ed.), *Sailen Medhi: Byaktitwa Aru Samaj Chinta*, Guwahati: 80th Birthday Celebration Committee, 2009.
Ray Choudhury, Ambikagiri, *Mor Jivan Dhumuhar Echati*, Guwahati: Kausalya Devi Ray Chowdhury, 1973.
Rai, Dhanjay, *Bish Sataker Dinajpur: Motontor O Krishak Andolon*, Calcutta: Punascha, 1997.
Rasul, Mahmmad Abdul, *Krishak Sabhar Itihas*, Calcutta, 1990.
Roychoudhury, Anil, *Asamat Bangladeshi*, Nowgaon: Jagaran Sahitya Prakasan, 2009.
——, *Achintya Rachanavali*, Guwahati: Natun Sahitya Parisad, 1998.
——, *Namani Assomor Madhyasreni*, Guwahati: Barua Agency, 1998.
Roychaudhury, Suchibrata (ed.), *Chetanar Chinta: Collection of the Editorial of Chetana*, Jorhat: Assam Sahitya Sabha, 1999.
Saikia, Arupjyoti, 'Pater-Kabita-Huyal Goni', *Dainik Janambhumi*, 7 November 2006.
Saikia, Bhabendra Nath, *Trin-Mul Rajnitikar Tita-Mitha Kahini*, Nowgaon: Gunin Bora, 2001.
Saikia, Chandraprasad, *Asamar Batori Kakat Alocanir Dersa Basharia Itihash*, Guwahati: Profulla Chandra Borua, 1998.
Saikia, Chidananda (ed.), *Dhiren Datta Smriti Grantha*, Golaghat: Dhiren Datta Smriti Rakkha Samiti, 1974.
Saikia, Hema (ed.), *Itihas: Srimanta Sankardev Sangha (Pratham Khanda)*, Sibsagar: Sankardev Sangha, 1985.
Saikia, Rajen, 'Patharughat, Eti Anya Mat', *Sanlap*, 2001, pp. 216–26.
Sanyal, Hiteshranjan, *Swarejer Pathe*, Calcutta: Papyrus, 1994.
——, *Bangla Kirtaner Itihas*, Calcutta: KPB, 1989.

Sarma, Chandan Kumar, *Assomiya Kon: Ek Samajtattvik Abalokan*, Guwahati: Span Publications, 2006.
Sarma, Govindaprasad, 'Asamiya Upanyasar Dhara 1939–89', in Homen Borgohain (ed.), *Asamiya Sahityar Buranji*, vol. 6, Guwahati: ABILAC, 1993, pp. 120–76.
Sarma, Krishna Nath, *Krishna Sarmar Diary*, Guwahati: Assam Publication Board, 1972.
Sarma, Nabin Chandra, *Axamiya Loka Samskritir Abhas*, Guwahati: Bani Prakash, 1982.
Sarma, Tirthanath, *Auniati Satrar Buranji*, Calcutta: Auniati Satra, 1975, reprint, 2004.
Sarma, Uma, *Bat Buli Buli Bhagari Parile*, Guwahati: Natun Sahitya Parisad, 1989.
Sinha, Sarat Chandra, *Andhar Bidara Kad*, Guwahati: Buniyad Publications, 1997.
Srimanta, Sankardev Sanghar Padadhikarsakalar Abhibhasan, Nowgaon: Srimanta Sankardev Sangha, 2005.
Talukdar, Gaurikanta, *Kalitar Bratyodharar Abashyakata*, Guwahati: Sarveswar Bhattacharya, 1929.
Verma, Usha Datta, *Din Guli Mor*, Calcutta: Biswagyan, 1993.

Secondary Sources (English)

Adas, Michael, *State, Market and Peasant in Colonial South and South-East Asia*, London: Variorum, 1998.
Ahmed, A., *Anatomy of the Rural Poverty in Assam,* Guwahati: Mittal Publications, 1987.
Alexander, R.J., *International Trotskyism, 1929–1985: A Documented Analysis of the Movement*, Duke, NC: Duke University Press, 1991.
Ali, Imran, *The Punjab under Imperialism, 1885–1947*, Princeton, NJ: Princeton University Press, 1988.
Amin, Shahid, *Sugarcane and Sugar in Gorakhpur: An Inquiry into Peasant Production for Capitalist Enterprise in Colonial India*, New Delhi: Oxford University Press, 1984.
Anon., 'End to Congress Monopoly', *Economic and Political Weekly*, vol. 13, no. 10, 1978, p. 481.
——, 'After Chaliha in Assam', *Economic and Political Weekly*, vol. 5, no. 45, 1970, pp. 1795–1796.
——, 'Food Crisis is Back', *Economic and Political Weekly*, vol. 3, no. 24, 1968, pp. 898–99.
——, *History of Chutia People*, 1946.
Arnold, David, 'Famine in Peasant Consciousness and Peasant Action: Madras, 1876–8', in Ranajit Guha (ed.), *Subaltern Studies: Writings*

on South Asian History, New Delhi: Oxford University Press, 1984, pp. 62–115.

——, 'Gramsci and Peasant Subalternity in India', *Journal of Peasant Studies,* vol. 15, no. 1, 1984, pp. 155–77.

——, 'Dacoity and Rural Crime in Madras, 1860–1940', *Journal of Peasant Studies*, vol. 6, no. 2, 1978, pp. 140–67.

Baden-Powell, Henry, *The Land Systems of British India*, vol. 3, Oxford: Clarendon Press, 1892, reprint, New Delhi: Publications Division, Government of India, 1974.

Bagchi, Amiya Kumar (ed.), *Money and Credit in Indian History: From Early Medieval Times*, New Delhi: Tulika Books, 2002.

Baker, Christopher John, *An Indian Rural Economy, 1880–1955: The Tamilnad Countryside*, New Delhi: Oxford University Press, 1984.

Baker, Christopher J. and David Washbrook, *South India: Political Institutions and Political Change, 1880–1940*, New Delhi: Macmillan, 1975.

Baker, David, 'State Policy, Market Economy and Tribal Decline', *Indian Economic and Social History Review*, vol. 28, no. 4, 1991, pp. 341–70.

Bandyopadhyaya, Sekhar, *From Plassey to Partition: A History of Modern India*, New Delhi: Orient Blackswan, 2004.

Banerjee, Prathama, 'Debt, Time and Extravagance: Money and the Making of Primitives in Colonial Bengal', *Indian Economic And Social History Review*, vol. 37, no. 4, 2000, pp. 423–55.

Bansil, P.C., *India, Food Resources and Population: A Historical and Analytical Study*, Bombay: Vora Publishers, 1958.

Barman, Santo, *Zamindari System in Assam during British Rule: A Case Study of Goalpara District*, Guwahati: Spectrum, 1994.

Barooah, Nirode Kumar, *Gopinath Bordoloi: The Assam Problem and Nehru's Centre*, Guwahati: Bhabani Print and Publications, 2010.

Barpujari, Heramba Kanta, *Political History of Assam*, vol. 2, Guwahati: Government of Assam, 1978.

——, *Assam in the Days of the Company, 1826–1858*, Guwahati: LBS, 1963.

Barua, Birinchi Kumar, *A Cultural History of Assam*, Guwahati: Bina Library, 2003.

Barua, D., 'The Refinery Movement in Assam', *Economic and Political Weekly*, vol. 46, no. 1, 2011, pp. 63–69.

Barua, Kanak Lal, *Early History of Kamarupa from The Earliest Times to the End of the Sixteenth Century*, Shillong: Kanak Lal Barua, 1933.

Barua, Khanindra Chandra, *Critical days of Assam*, Guwahati: K.C. Barua, 1972.

Baruah, Sanjib, 'Clash of Resource Use Regimes in Colonial Assam: A Nineteenth-Century Puzzle Revisited', *Journal of Peasant Studies*, vol. 28, no. 3, 2001, pp. 109–24.

Baruah, Sanjib, *India against Itself*, New Delhi: Oxford University Press, 1999.
Barua, Swarnalata, *A Comprehensive History of Assam,* New Delhi: Munshiram Manoharlal, 1985.
Batabyal, Rakesh, *Communalism in Bengal: From Famine to Noakhali, 1943–47*, New Delhi: Sage, 2005.
Baviskar, Amita, *In the Belly of the River: Tribal Conflicts Over Development in the Narmada Valley*, New Delhi: Oxford University Press, 2004.
Behal, Rana Pratap, 'Forms of Labour Protest in Assam Valley Tea Plantations, 1900–1930', *Economic and Political Weekly*, vol. 20, no. 4, 1985, pp. PE19–26.
——, 'Some Aspects of the Growth of the Plantation Labor Force and Labor Movements in Assam Valley Districts, 1900–47', unpublished PhD thesis, Centre for Historical Studies (CHS), Jawaharlal Nehru University (JNU), New Delhi, 1983.
Belden, Jack, *China Shakes the World*, London: Harper, 1949.
Bhadra Ranajit K., 'Rural Class Structure in Post-Independence Assam', *Economic and Political Weekly*, vol. 14, no. 4, 1979, pp. 165–67.
Bhaduri, Amit, 'On the Formation of Usurious Interest Rates in Backward Agriculture', in Amit Bhaduri, *Unconventional Economic Essays*, New Delhi: Oxford University Press, 1999, pp. 200–41.
Bhattacharjee, Kishore, 'Structure and Individual in Assamese Society: A Study of Family, Kinship, Caste and Religion', unpublished PhD thesis, Gauhati University, Guwahati, 1990.
Bharadwaj, Prashant and James Fenske, 'Partition, Migration, and Jute Cultivation in India', *Journal of Development Studies*, vol. 48, no. 8, 2012, pp. 1084–1107.
Bhattacharya, Neeladri, 'The Logic of Tenancy Cultivation', *Indian Economic and Social History Review*, vol. 20, no. 2, 1983, pp. 121–70.
Bhattacharya, Sabyasachi, Sumit Guha, Raman Mahadevan, Sakti Padhi, D. Rajasekhar, and G.N. Rao (eds), *The South Indian Economy: Agrarian Change, Industrial Structure and State Policy, 1914–1947*, New Delhi: Oxford University Press, 1991.
Bhattacharya, Sanjoy, 'The Colonial State and the Communist Party of India, 1942–45: A Reappraisal', *South Asia Research*, vol. 15, no. 1, 1995, pp. 48–77.
Bhuyan, Suryya Kumar, *Anglo-Assamese Relations, 1771–1826: A History of the Relations of Assam with the East India Company from 1771 to 1826, Based on Original English and Assamese Sources*, Guwahati: LBS, 1974.
Biswas, Pranesh Chandra, 'Peasant Struggles and Growth of the Kishan Sabha in Assam', in Amalendu Guha (ed.), *Zamindarkalin Goalpara Zillar Artha Samajik Abastha: Eti Oitihasik Dristipat*, Guwahati: Natun Sahitya Prisad, 2000.

Biswas, Pranesh Chandra, 'Some Aspects of the Assam Government's Agrarian Reform Laws', *All India Kisan Sabha, News Bulletin*, vol. 1, no. 3, 1952, pp. 22–25.

Blyn, G., *Agricultural Trends in India, 1891–1947: Output, Availability, and Productivity*, Philadelphia: University of Pennsylvania, 1966.

Bordoloi, B.N., *Transfer and Alienation of Tribal Lands in Assam*, Guwahati: B.N. Bordoloi, 1991.

Borgohain, Rooplekha, *Politics of Land Reforms in Assam*, New Delhi: Reliance Publishing House, 1992.

Bose, Nirmal K., 'The Hindu Method of Tribal Absorption', *Science and Culture*, vol. 8, 1941, pp. 188–98.

Bose, Sugata (ed.), *Credit, Markets and the Agrarian Economy of Colonial India*, New Delhi: Oxford University Press, 1994.

Bose, Sugata, *Peasant Labour and Colonial Capital: Rural Bengal since 1770*, Cambridge: Cambridge University Press, 1993.

——, *Agrarian Bengal: Economy, Social Structure, and Politics, 1919–1947*, Cambridge: Cambridge University Press, 1986.

——, 'Roots of "Communal" Violence in Rural Bengal', *Modern Asian Studies*, vol. 16, no. 3, 1982, pp. 463–91.

Boyce, James, *Agrarian Impasse in Bengal: Institutional Constraints to Technological Change*, New York: Oxford University Press, 1987.

Brass, Tom, 'The Agrarian Myth, the New Populism and the New Right', *Journal of Peasant Studies*, vol. 24, no. 4, 1997, pp. 201–45.

——, 'Trotskyism, Hugo Blanco and the Ideology of a Peruvian Peasant Movement', *Journal of Peasant Studies*, vol. 16, no. 2, 1989, pp. 173–97.

Breman, Jan, *Of Peasants, Migrants and Paupers: Rural Labour Circulation and Capitalist Production in West India*, New Delhi: Oxford University Press, 1985.

——, *Patronage and Exploitation: Changing Agrarian Relations in South Gujarat, India*, Berkeley, CA: University of California Press, 1974.

Broomfield, J.H., *Elite Conflict in a Plural Society: Twentieth-Century Bengal*, Berkeley, CA: University of California Press, 1968.

Byres, Terence J., 'Historical Perspectives on Sharecropping', *Journal of Peasant Studies*, vol. 10, nos 2 and 3, 1983, pp. 7–40.

Cantlie, Audrey, *The Assamese*, London: Curzon Press, 1984.

Catanach, I.J., *Rural Credit in Western India, 1875–1930: Rural Credit and the Co-operative Movement in the Bombay Presidency*, Berkeley, CA: University of California Press, 1970.

Centre for Science and Environment (CSE), *Floods, Flood Plains and Environmental Myths*, New Delhi: CSE, 1991.

Chadravarkar, A.V., 'Money and Credit', in D. Kumar and M. Desai (eds), *The Cambridge Economic History of India*, vol. 2 (c. 1757–c. 1970), New Delhi: Orient Longman, 1982, pp. 762–803.

Charlesworth, Neil, *Peasants and Imperial Rule: Agriculture and Agrarian Society in the Bombay Presidency, 1850–1935*, Cambridge: Cambridge University Press, 1985.

——, *British Rule and the Indian Economy, 1800–1914*, New Delhi, 1982.

Chatterjee, Joya, *The Spoils of Partition: Bengal and India, 1947–1967*, Cambridge: Cambridge University Press, 2007.

——, *Bengal Divided: Hindu Communalism and Partition, 1932–1947*, New Delhi: Foundation Books, 1996.

Chatterjee, Partha, 'The Colonial State and Peasant Resistance in Bengal, 1920–47', *Past and Present*, no. 110, 1986, pp. 169–204.

——, *Bengal 1920–1947: The Land Question*, Calcutta: K.P. Bagchi, 1984.

——, 'Agrarian Relations and Communalism in Bengal, 1926–1935', in Ranajit Guha (ed.), *Subaltern Studies*, vol. 1, New Delhi: Oxford University Press, 1982, pp. 9–38.

Chaturvedi, Vinayak, *Peasant Pasts: History and Memory in Western India*, Berkeley, CA: University of California Press, 2007.

Chaudhuri, B.B., *Peasant History of Late Pre-Colonial and Colonial India*, New Delhi: Pearson, 2008.

——, 'Agrarian Relations: Eastern India', in D. Kumar and M. Desai (eds), *The Cambridge Economic History of India*, vol. 2 (c. 1757–c. 1970), New Delhi: Orient Longman, 1982, pp. 86–177.

——, 'Eastern India', in D. Kumar and M. Desai (eds), *The Cambridge Economic History of India*, vol. 2 (c. 1757–c. 1970), New Delhi: Orient Longman, 1982, pp. 86–177.

——, 'The Process of Depeasantization in Bengal and Bihar, 1885–1947', *Indian Historical Review*, vol. 2, no. 1, 1975, pp. 105–55.

Chaudhuri, K. N. and Clive J. Dewey (eds), *Economy and Society: Essays in Indian Economic and Social History*, New Delhi: Oxford University Press, 1979.

Communist Party of India (CPI), *Documents of the Communist Movement in India*, vol. 6 (1949–1951), Calcutta: CPI, 1997.

——, *Guidelines of the History of the Communist Party of India*, New Delhi: CPI, 1974.

Cooper, Adrienne, *Sharecropping and Sharecroppers' Struggles in Bengal 1930–1950*, Calcutta: KPB, 1988.

Cotes, E.C., *The Locusts of Bengal, Madras, Assam, and Bombay, etc.*, Calcutta: Office of the Superintendent of Government Printing, 1891.

Das, Arvind N., *Agrarian Movements in India: Studies on 20th Century Bihar*, London: Routledge, 1982.

Das, Durga (ed.), *Sardar Patel's Correspondence*, 10 vols, Ahmedabad: Navajivan Publishing House, 1971–74.

Das, M.M., *Peasant Agriculture in Assam*, New Delhi: Inter India Publications, 1984.

Dasgupta, Pannalal, *Revolutionary Gandhi*, trans. K.V. Subrahmonyan, Calcutta: Earthcare Books, 2011.

Dasgupta, Ranjit, *Economy, Society and Politics in Bengal: Jalpaiguri 1869–1947*, New Delhi: Oxford University Press, 1992.

Davidson, Alastair, "Gramsci, the Peasantry and the Popular Culture" in *Journal of Peasant Studies*, vol. 11, no. 4, 1984, pp. 139–54.

Desai, A.R. (ed.), *Peasants Struggles in India*, New Delhi: Oxford University Press, 1979.

Desai, A.R., *Rural Sociology in India*, Bombay: Popular Prakashan, 1977.

Dass, S.K., 'Immigration and Demographic Transformation of Assam 1891–1981' *Economic and Political Weekly*, vol. 15, no. 9, 1980, pp. 850–59.

Dey, Amalendu, 'The Muslims as a Factor in Assam Politics', *Bengal Past and Present,* vol. 96, no. 2, 1977, pp. 114–17.

Dewey, Clive and A.G. Hopkins (eds), *The Imperial Impact: Studies in the Economic History of Africa and India*, London: Anthem Press, 1978.

Dhanagare, D. N., *Peasant Movements in India, 1920–1950*, New Delhi: Oxford University Press, 1983.

Dirks, Nicholas. B., 'From Little King to Landlord: Property, Law and The Gift Under The Madras Permanent Settlement', *Comparative Studies in History and Society*, vol. 28, 1986, pp. 307–33.

Dutta, K.N., *Landmarks of the Freedom Struggles in Assam*, Guwahati: LBS, 1957.

Dutta, Narendra Chandra, *Land Problems and Land Reforms in Assam*, New Delhi: S. Chand, 1968.

Dyson, Tim (ed.), *India's Historical Demography: Studies in Famine, Disease, and Society*, Curzon: Westwood, 1989.

Eaton, Richard M., *The Rise of Islam and the Bengal Frontier, 1204–1760,* New Delhi: Oxford University Press, 1997.

Foster, George M., 'Peasants Society and the Image of Limited God', *American Anthropologist,* vol. 67, no. 2, 1965, pp. 293–315.

Fox, Richard, *From Zamindar to Ballot Box: Community Change in a North Indian Market Town*, Ithaca, NY: Cornell University Press, 1969.

Frankel, Francine, *India's Political Economy, 1947–1977: The Gradual Revolution*, Princeton, NJ: Princeton University Press, 1978.

Freitag, Sandria, *Collective Action and Community: Public Arenas and the Emergence of Communalism in North India*, New Delhi: Oxford University Press, 1990.

Frykenberg, Robert Eric (ed.), *Land Control and Social Structure in Indian History*, Madison: University of Wisconsin Press, 1969.

Frykenberg, Robert Eric, *Land Tenure and Peasant in South Asia*, New Delhi: Orient Longman, 1977.

——, *Guntur District, 1788–1848: A History of Local Influence and Central Authority in South India*, New Delhi: Oxford University Press, 1965.

Gait, Edward, *A History of Assam*, Culcutta: Tracker, Spink & Co., 1906.

Ghosh, Parimal, *Brave Men of the Hills: Resistance and Rebellion in Burma, 1825–1932*, London: C. Hurst, 2000.

Gopal, S., *Jawaharlal Nehru: A Biography, 1889–1947*, vol. 1, New Delhi: Oxford University Press, 1981.

Gough, Kathleen, *Rural Change in Southeast India: 1950s to 1980s*, New Delhi: Oxford University Press, 1989.

——, *Rural Society in Southeast India*, Cambridge: Cambridge University Press, 1981.

Goswami, Homeswar, *Population Trends in the Brahmaputra Valley, 1881–1931*, New Delhi: Mittal Publications, 1985.

Goswami, M.C., 'Tribe-Peasant-Caste Relation in North-East India', Presidential Address, in *Indian Science Congress Proceedings*, 1971, pp. 1–18.

Goswami, P.C., 'Land Reform in Assam', *Economic and Political Weekly*, vol. 4, no. 42, 1969, pp. 1662–1664.

——, *Economic Development of Assam*, Bombay: Asia Publishing House, 1963.

Goswami, Priyam, *Assam in the Nineteenth Century: Industrialization and Colonial Penetration*, Guwahati: Spectrum, 1999.

Goswami, Ritupan, 'Rivers and History: Brahmaputra Valley in the Last Centuries', unpublished PhD thesis, Centre for Historical Studies (CHS), Jawaharlal Nehru University (JNU), New Delhi, 2010.

Goswami, S.D., 'Agrarian Politics and Peasant Militancy in Post Mutiny Assam', *North East Quarterly*, vol. 1, no. 1, 1982, pp. 6–13.

Goswami, S.K., *A History of Revenue Administration in Assam 1228–1826 AD*, Guwahati: Spectrum, 1986.

Goswami, Sandhya, *Language Politics in Assam*, New Delhi: Ajanta Publications, 1997.

Goswami, Shrutidev, *Aspects of Revenue Administration in Assam, 1826–1874*, New Delhi: Mittal Publications, 1987.

Government of Assam, *Land Reform in Assam*, Guwahati: Government Press, 1973.

Government of India, *Implementation of Land Reforms: A Review by the Land Reforms Implementation Committee of the National Development Council*, New Delhi: Planning Commission, 1997.

——, *Royal Commission of Agriculture in India*, vol. 5, Calcutta: Government of India, 1927.

Greenough, Paul R., *Prosperity and Misery in Modern Bengal: The Famine of 1943–1944*, New Delhi: Oxford University Press, 1982.

——, 'Indian Famines and Peasant Victims: The Case of Bengal in 1943–44', *Modern Asian Studies*, vol. 14, no.2, 1980, pp. 205–35.

Guha, Amalendu, 'Medieval Economy of Assam', in Tapan Raychaudhuri and Irfan Habib (eds), *The Cambridge Economic History of India*, vol. 1 (c. 1200–c. 1750), Cambridge: Cambridge University Press, 1992, pp. 478–505.

——, *Medieval and Early Colonial Assam: Society, Polity, and Economy*, Calcutta: KBS, 1991.

——, 'The Ahom Political System: An Enquiry into State Formation in Medieval Assam: 1228–1800', in Surajit Sinha (ed.), *Tribal Polities and State Systems in Pre-Colonial Eastern and North Eastern India*, Calcutta: KPB, 1987, pp. 143–76.

——, *Planter Raj to Swaraj: Freedom Struggle and Electoral Politics in Assam, 1826–1947*, New Delhi: PPH, 1977.

——, 'East Bengal Immigrants and Maulana Abdul Hamid Khan Bhasani in Assam Politics, 1928–47', *IESHR*, vol. 13, no. 4, 1976, pp. 419–55.

——, 'A Big Push Without a Take-Off: A Case Study of Assam: 1871–1901', *Indian Economic and Social History Review (IESHR)*, vol. 5, no. 3, 1968, pp. 199–221.

——, 'Ahom Migration: Its Impact on Rice Economy of Medieval Assam', *Artha Vijnana*, vol. 9, no. 2, 1967, pp. 134–57.

Guha, Ramachandra, *The Unquiet Woods: Ecological Change and Peasant Resistance in the Himalaya*, New Delhi: Oxford University Press, 1989.

Guha, Ranajit, *Elementary Aspects of Peasant Insurgency in Colonial India*, New Delhi, 1983.

——, *A Rule of Property for Bengal*, New Delhi: Oxford University Press, 1962.

Guha, Sumit, *The Agrarian Economy of the Bombay Deccan, 1818–1941*, New Delhi: Oxford University Press, 1985.

Gupta, Amit Kumar, *Agrarian Drama: The Leftists and the Rural Poor in India 1934–1951*, New Delhi: Manohar, 1996.

Gupta, P.S. (ed.), *Towards Freedom Movement, 1943–44*, vol. 2, New Delhi: Oxford University Press, 1997.

Hack, Karl, *Defence and Decolonisation in Southeast Asia: Britain, Malaya and Singapore*, London: Routledge, 2000.

Hazarika, Sanjoy, *Strangers of the Mist: Tales of War and Peace in India's North East*, New Delhi: Penguin, 1994.

Hilaly, S., *The Railways in Assam: 1885–1947*, New Delhi: Pilgrims Publishing, 2007.

Hunter, W.W., *A Statistical Account of Assam*, 2 vols, London: Trubner, 1879.

Islam, Sirajul, *Bengal Land Tenure: The Origin and Growth of Intermediate Interests in The Nineteenth Century*, Rotterdam: Comparative Asian Studies Program, 1988.

Jannuzi, F.T., *India's Persistent Dilemma: The Political Economy of Agrarian Reform*, New Delhi: Orient Blackswan, 1996.

Jones, Gareth Stedman, *Outcast London*, London: Harmondsworth, 1992.

Jukes, Geoffrey, *The Soviet Union in Asia*, Berkeley, CA: University of California Press, 1973.

Kakoty, Sanjeeb, *Technology, Production, and Social Formation in The Evolution of the Ahom State*, New Delhi: Regency, 2003.

Kalita, Ramesh, 'Women and the Agrarian Struggles in Assam: An Empirico-Historical Approach', *Proceedings of North-East India Historical Association,* vol. 17, 1997, pp. 168–83.

——, 'Darrang Jilar Krishak Bidrohar Eti Samu Khatiyan', in Prasanna Kumar Nath (ed.), *Patharughat*, Sipajhar: Udash, 1994, pp. 76–80.

Kar, Makhanlal, *Muslims In Assam Politics*, New Delhi: Omsons, 1990.

Karna, M.N., *Agrarian Structures And Land Reform in Assam*, New Delhi: Regency, 2001.

Khadria, Nandita, 'Some Aspects of the Rural Economy of Assam: A Study of the Brahmaputra Valley Districts of Assam, 1874–1914', unpublished PhD thesis, Centre for Historical Studies (CHS), Jawaharlal Nehru University (JNU), New Delhi, 1992.

Kingdon-Ward, F., 'The Assam Earthquake of 1950', *The Geographical Journal*, vol. 121, no. 2, 1955, pp. 290–303.

Kohli, A., *The State and Poverty in India*, Cambridge: Cambridge University Press, 1989.

Kuei-paz, Baruch, *The Social and Political Thought of Leon Trotsky*, Oxford: Oxford University Press, 1978.

Kumar, D. and M. Desai (eds), *The Cambridge Economic History of India*, vol. 2 (c. 1757–c. 1970), New Delhi: Orient Longman, 1982.

Kumar, D., *Land and Caste In South India: Agricultural Labour in Madras Presidency in The Nineteenth Century*, New Delhi: Cambridge University Press, 1992.

Kuri, P.K., *Tenancy Relations in Backward Agriculture: A Study in Rural Assam*, New Delhi: Mittal Publications, 2004.

Lahiri, Nayanjot, *Pre-Ahom Assam: Studies in The Inscriptions of Assam Between the Fifth and The Thirteenth Centuries AD*, New Delhi: Munshiram Manoharlal, 1991.

——, 'Landholding and Peasantry in The Brahmaputra Valley, c. 5th–13th Centuries AD', *Journal of the Economic and Social History of the Orient*, vol. 33, no. 2, 1990, pp. 157–68.

Ludden, David, *A Peasant History of South Asia*, Oxford: Oxford University Press, 1999.

——, *Peasant History in South India*, Princeton, NJ: Princeton University Press, 1985.

Malviya, H.D., *Land Reforms in India*, New Delhi: All India Congress Committee, 1954.

Martin, R.M., *The History, Antiquities, Topography, and Statistics of Eastern India*, vol. 3, London: W.H. Allen and Co., 1838, reprint, New Delhi: Asian Educational Service, 1988.

McCombie, T.C., *Kala-azar in Assam: An Account of the Preventive Operation, 1913 to 1923*, London: H.K. Lewis and Co. Ltd, 1924.

Medhi, S.B., 'Is the Assam Tenancy Act of 1971 a Social Legislation?', *The Assam Tribune*, 24 July, 1986.

——, *Transport System and Economic Development in Assam*, Guwahati: Assam Publication Board, 1978.

Metcalf, Thomas R., 'Landlords Without Land: The U. P. Zamindars Today', *Pacific Affairs* , vol. 40, nos 1 and 2, 1967, pp. 5–18.

Mills, A.J.M., *Report on the Province of Assam*, Calcutta: Superintendent of Government Printing, 1854, reprint, Guwahati: Assam Publication Board, 1984.

Misra, Udayon, *The Periphery Strikes Back*, Shimla: Indian Institute of Advanced Studies (IIAS), 2000.

Mukherjee, Aditya, 'Agrarian Conditions in Assam, 1880–1890: A Case Study of Five Districts of the Brahmaputra Valley', *IESHR*, vol. 16, no. 2, 1979, pp. 207–32.

Mukherjee, Mridula, *Peasants in India's Non-Violent Revolution: Practice and Theory*, New Delhi: Sage, 2004.

Mukherjee, Partha N., 'The Great Migration of 1971: II', *Economic and Political Weekly*, vol. 9, no. 10, 1974, pp. 399–408.

Musgrave, P.J., 'Rural Credit and Rural Society in the United Provinces, 1860–1920', in Clive Dewey and A.G. Hopkins (eds), *The Imperial Impact: Studies in the Economic History of Africa and India*, London: Anthem Press, 1978, pp. 216–32.

Nadkarni, M.V. and K.H. Vedini, 'Accelerating Commercialisation of Agriculture: Dynamic Agriculture and Stagnating Peasants?', *Economic and Political Weekly*, vol. 31, no. 26, 1996, pp. A63–73.

Namboodiripad, E.M.S., *The Frontline Years: Selected Articles*, New Delhi: Left Word, 2010.

Nath, D., *The Majuli Island: Society, Economy and Culture*, New Delhi: Anshah Publishing House, 2009.

Nath, Jahnabi Gogoi, *Agrarian System of Medieval Assam*, New Delhi: Concept, 2002.

Neog, Maheswar, *Socio-Political Events in Assam Leading to the Militancy of the Mayamoria Vaishnavas*, Calcutta: Center for Studies of Social Systems, 1982.

Neog, Maheswar, *Anandaram Dhekial Phukan: Plea for Assam and Assamese*, Jorhat: Assam Sahitya Sabha, 1977.
——, *Sankardeva and His Times: Early History of the Vaiṣṇava Faith*, Guwahati: Gauhati University, 1965.
Neale, Walter C., *Economic Change in Rural India: Land Tenure and Reform in the United Provinces, 1800–1955*, New Haven, CT: Yale University Press, 1962.
Overstreet, G.D. and M. Windmiller, *Communism in India*, Berkeley, CA: University of California Press, 1959.
Pathak, Suryasikha, 'Tribal Politics in the Assam: 1933–1947', *Economic and Political Weekly*, vol. 45, no. 10, 2010, pp. 61–69.
Patnaik, Utsa, *Agrarian Relations and Accumulation: The `Mode of Production' Debate in India*, Bombay: Oxford University Press, 1990.
——, 'Ascertaining the Economic Characteristics of Peasant Classes-in-Themselves in Rural India: a Methodological and Empirical Exercise', *Journal of Peasant Studies*, vol. 15, no. 3, 1987–88, pp. 301–33.
——, 'Classical Theory of Rent and Its Application to India: Some Preliminary Thoughts on Sharecropping', *Journal of Peasant Studies*, vol. 10, nos 2–3, 1983, pp. 71–87.
Patnaik, Utsa and Manjari Dingwaney, *Chains of Servitude: Bondage and Slavery in India*, Madras, 1985.
Paul, M.C., 'Reform Movements among the Boro-Kachari', *The Eastern Anthropologist*, vol. 20, no. 1, 1991, pp. 57–68.
Phukan, Girin, *Assam's Attitude to Federalism*, New Delhi: Sterling, 1984.
Phukan, Umananda, *Agricultural Development in Assam (1950–1985)*, New Delhi: Mittal Publications, 1990.
Pinch, William R., *Peasants and Monks in British India*, New Delhi: Oxford University Press, 1996.
Planning Commission of India, *Land Reform in India*, New Delhi: Government Press, 1963.
Prakash, Gyan, *The World of the Rural Labourer in Colonial India*, New Delhi: Oxford University Press, 1992.
Prasad, Rajendra, *Autobiography*, New Delhi: Penguin, 2010.
Rai, Anil, 'Trends in the Jute Industry since Independence', *Social Scientist*, vol. 6, nos 6 and 7, 1978, pp. 83–102.
Raghavan, M., 'Some Aspects of Growth and Distribution of Rice in India', *Social Scientist*, vol. 28, nos 5 and 6, 1999, pp. 62–85.
Rangarajan, Mahesh, *Fencing the Forest*, New Delhi: Oxford University Press, 1996.
Rashiduzzaman, M., 'The National Awami Party of Pakistan: Leftist Politics in Crisis', *Pacific Affairs*, vol. 43, no. 3, 1970, pp. 394–409.
Ray, Ratnalekha, *Change in Bengal Agrarian Society, c. 1760–1850*, New Delhi: Manohar, 1979.

Redfield, Robert, *The Little Community and Peasant Society and Culture*, London and Chicago: University of Chicago Press, 1969.

Richards, J.F and J. Hagen, 'A Century of Rural Expansion in Assam', *Itinerario*, vol. 11, no. 1, 1987, pp. 193–209.

Robb, Peter (ed.), *Rural India: Land, Power and Society under British Rule*, New Delhi: Oxford University Press, 1992.

Rothermund, Dietmar, *An Economic History of India: From Pre-Colonial Times to 1991*, 2nd ed., New Delhi: Routledge, 1993.

——, *Government, Landlord and Peasant in India: Agrarian Relations under British Rule, 1865–1935*, Wiesbaden: Steiner, 1978.

Roy, Tirthankar, *Economic History of India, 1857–1947*, New Delhi: Oxford University Press, 2001.

Rude, George, *The Crowd in History: A Study of Popular Disturbances in France and England, 1730–1848*, London: Serif, 1995.

Sabean, David, *Power in the Blood: Popular Culture and Village Discourse in Early Modern Germany*, Cambridge: Cambridge University Press, 1984.

Saikia, Anil, Homeswar Goswami and Atul Goswami (eds), *Population Growth in Assam: 1951–1991*, New Delhi: Akansha, 2003.

Saikia, Arupjyoti, 'Dancing Like Nataraj: Earthquakes and Environmental History of the Brahmaputra River Valley', paper presented at the Yale University Agrarian Studies Colloquium, 13 April 2012.

——, 'Oral Tradition, Nationalism and Assamese Social History: Remembering a Peasant Uprising', *IESHR*, vol. 49, no. 1, 2012, pp. 37–72.

——, *Forests and Ecological History of Assam, 1826–2000*, New Delhi: Oxford University Press, 2011.

——, 'Imperialism, Geology and Petroleum: History of Oil in Colonial Assam', *Economic and Political Weekly*, vol. 46, no. 12, 2011, pp. 48–55.

——, 'Landlords, Tenants and Agrarian Relations: Revisiting a Peasant Uprising in Colonial Assam', *Studies in History*, vol. 26, no. 2, 2010, pp. 175–209.

——, 'State, Peasants and Land Reclamation: The Predica-ment of Forest Conservation in Assam, 1850s–1980s', *IESHR*, vol. 45, no. 1, 2008, pp. 77–114.

Saikia, Rajen, *Social and Economic History of Assam 1853–1921*, New Delhi, Manohar, 2000.

Saikia, Yasmin, *Assam and India: The Fragmented Memories*, New Delhi: Permanent Black, 2005.

Sarma, Dipti, *Assamese Women in the Freedom Struggle*, Calcutta: Punthi Pustak, 1993.

Sarma, S.N., *The Neo-Vaishnavite Movement and Satra Institution of Assam*, Guwahati: LBS, 1999.

——, *A Social-Economic and Cultural History of Medieval Assam 1200–1800 AD*, Guwahati: Pratima Devi, 1989.

Scott, James. C., *The Art of Being Not Governed: An Anarchist History of Upland Southeast Asia*, New Delhi: Orient Blackswan, 2010.
——, *Domination and the Arts of Resistance: Hidden Trans-cript*, New Haven, CT: Yale University Press, 1990.
——, *Weapons of the Weak: Everyday Forms of Peasant Resistance*, New Delhi: Oxford University Press, 1990.
Sen, Mankumar, *Gandhian Way and the Bhoodan Movement*, Varanasi: Sarva Seva Sangh Prakashan, 1964.
Sethia, T., 'The Rise of the Jute Manufacturing Industry in Colonial India: A Global Perspective', *Journal of World History*, vol. 7, no. 1, 1996, pp. 71–99.
Shah, Ghanshyam, *Social Movements in India: A Review of Literature*, New Delhi: Sage, 1990.
Shanin, Teodor, 'The Nature and Logic of the Peasant Economy', *Journal of Peasant Studies,* vol. 1, no. 2, 1974, pp. 63–80.
Sharma, Jayeeta, *Empire's Garden: Assam and the Making of India*, New Delhi: Permanent Black, 2011.
Sharma, Manorama, *Social and Economic Change in Assam: Middle Class Hegemony*, New Delhi: Ajanta, 1990, reprint, 1998.
Siddiqi, Majid Hayat, *Agrarian Unrest in North India: The United Provinces, 1918–1922*, New Delhi, 1978.
Singh, K. S., *Tribal Movements in India*, vol. 2, New Delhi: Manohar, 1983.
Singha Roy, Debal K., *Peasants' Movements in Post-Colonial India*, New Delhi: Sage, 2004.
Sivaramakrishnan, K., *Modern Forests: Statemaking and Environmental Change in Colonial Eastern India*, New Delhi: Oxford University Press, 1999.
Stein, Burton, *The Making of Agrarian Policy in British India, 1770–1900,* New Delhi: Oxford University Press, 1998.
Stewart, Gordon Thomas, *Jute and Empire: The Calcutta Jute Wallahs and the Landscapes of Empire*, Manchester: Manchester University Press, 1998.
Stokes, Eric, *The Peasant Armed: the Indian Rebellion of 1857*, Oxford: Oxford University Press, 1986.
——, *The Peasant and the Raj: Studies in Agrarian Society and Peasant Rebellion in Colonial India*, New Delhi: Cambridge University Press, 1978.
Stree Shakti Sanghatana, *We Were Making History: Women and the Telengana Uprising*, London: Zed, 1989.
Taxton, Ralph, *China Turned Right Side Up*, New Haven, CT: Yale University Press, 1983.
Thompson, E.P., 'Folklore, Anthropology and Social History', *Indian Historical Review*, vol. 2, no. 2, 1976, pp. 247–66.

Thorner, D. and A. Thorner, *Land and Labour in India*, Bombay: Asia Publishing, 1962.
van Schendel, William, *A History of Bangladesh*, Cambridge: Cambridge University Press, 2009.
van Voss, Lex Heerma (ed.), *Petitions in Social History*, Cambridge: Cambridge University Press, 2002.
Washbrook, David, 'Progress and Problems: South Asian Economic and Social History, c. 1720–1860', *Modern Asian Studies*, vol. 22, no. 1, 1988, pp. 57–96.
——, 'Law, State and Agrarian Society in Colonial India', *Modern Asian Studies*, vol. 15, no. 3, 1981, pp. 649–721.
——, *The Emergence of Provincial Politics: The Madras Presidency, 1870–1920*, Cambridge: Cambridge University Press, 1976.
Whitcombe, Elizabeth, *Agrarian Conditions in Northern India: The United Provinces Under British Rule, 1860–1900*, vol. 1, Berkeley, CA: University of California Press, 1972.
Yang, Anand A, *The Limited Raj: Agrarian Relations in Colonial India, Saran District, 1793–1920*, New Delhi: Oxford University Press, 1989.
Zacariah, Benjamin, *Nehru*, London: Routledge, 2004.

Web Resources

Gauhati High Court, *Haren Kalita versus Government of Assam*, 29 April 1953, available at http://indiankanoon.org/doc/135247/ (accessed on 10 August 2012).
——, *Nirendra Mohan Lahiri and Others versus Government of Assam*, 19 November 1948, available at http://indiankanoon.org/doc/428287/ (accessed on 11 September 2012).
——, *Raja Bhairebendra Narayan Bhup versus the State of Assam*, available at http://www.indiacourts.in/RAJA-BHAIREBENDRA NARAYAN-BHUP-Vs.-THE-STATE-OF-ASSAM(with-connected appeal)_9b79d311-a817-4a58-bd0f-f17671752e24 (accessed on 18 September 2012).
——, *Tarunsen Deka and Others versus Government of Assam*, 3 December 1948, available at <http://indiankanoon.org/doc/1462849/> (accessed on 11 September 2012).
Selected State-wise Area for Jute in India (2000–2001 to 2009–2010), http://www.indiastat.com/table/agriculture/2/juteandmesta/17206/419831/data.aspx (accessed on 17 March 2012).

About the Author

Arupjyoti Saikia is Associate Professor of History, Department of Humanities and Social Sciences, Indian Institute of Technology Guwahati, Assam. He received his PhD from the University of Delhi. He has authored *A Forests and Ecological History of Assam* (2011), apart from articles in edited volumes and journals such as *Indian Economic and Social History Review*, *Studies in History*, *Indian Historical Review*, and *Journal of Peasant Studies*. He was the recipient of a post-doctoral fellowship at the Agrarian Studies Program, Yale University (2011–12). He also regularly writes articles in Assamese.

Index